Encountering the Manuscripts

Encountering the Manuscripts

An Introduction to New Testament
Paleography & Textual Criticism

Philip Comfort

BROADMAN
&HOLMAN
PUBLISHERS

NASHVILLE, TENNESSEE

Published by Broadman & Holman Publishers
Nashville, Tennessee

Dewey Decimal Classification: 220.48
Subject Heading: BIBLE, GREEK VERSIONS \ BIBLE, GREEK LANGUAGE,
STYLE \ MANUSCRIPTS, GREEK

1 2 3 4 5 6 7 8 9 10 09 08 07 06 05

Contents

Abbreviations

BAGD   *Greek-English Lexicon of the New Testament and Other Early Christian Literature* (Bauer, Ardnt, Gingrich, Danker) [1958]

DJD   *Discoveries in the Judean Desert*

GLH   *Greek Literary Hands* (C. H. Roberts)

GMAW   *Greek Manuscripts of the Ancient World* (2nd ed., E. G. Turner)

H   *Catalogue des Papyrus Litteraires Juifs et Chretiens,* von Haelst

ISBE   *International Standard Bible Encyclopedia* (4 vols., Bromiley) [1979–1988]

LSJ   *A Greek-English Lexicon* (9th ed., Liddell, Scott, Jones)

MM   *The Vocabulary of the Greek New Testament* (Moulton and Milligan) [1930]

Montev   *La Papirologia* (2nd ed.), O. Montevecchi

NA^{26} *Novum Testamentum Graece* (26th ed., Nestle-Aland) [1979]

NA^{27} *Novum Testamentum Graece* (27th ed., Nestle-Aland) [1993]

NBD   *New Bible Dictionary* (2nd ed., Douglas, Hillyer) [1982]

NU   text of Nestle-Aland 26th/27th [N] and the United Bible Societies 3rd/4th [U]

TBD   *Tyndale Bible Dictionary* (Elwell, Comfort) [2001]

TCGNT *A Textual Commentary on the Greek New Testament* (2nd ed., Metzger) [1994]

TDNT   *Theological Dictionary of the New Testament* (10 vols., Kittel, Friedrich; trans. Bromiley) [1964–76]

UBS^3 United Bible Societies' *Greek New Testament* (3rd ed., Metzger et al) [1975]

UBS^4 United Bible Societies' *Greek New Testament* (4th corrected ed., Metzger et al) [1993]

The Oxyrhynchus manuscripts cited throughout this book are not given the same bibliographic treatment as the other works because the reader can easily locate the particular manuscript according to the papyrus number.

The *editio princeps* for each of the New Testament manuscripts cited throughout this book is found with each manuscript listed in chapter 2.

Preface

This volume is the product of several years of study in New Testament manuscripts. During this period I examined—many times over—every single word of every early New Testament manuscript (dated pre-AD 300), and thereby produced a volume entitled *The Text of the Earliest Greek New Testament Manuscripts* (coeditor, David Barrett). I traveled to many states and several countries (including England, France, and Switzerland) to examine actual manuscripts. I engrossed myself in the manuscripts of the earliest Christian scribes so as to comprehend their level of competency and their interaction with the text as readers. My doctoral dissertation specifically examined the reader receptions of three scribes who produced Gospels ($\mathfrak{P}^{45}$, $\mathfrak{P}^{66}$, and $\mathfrak{P}^{75}$).

During these years, I have also focused my energies on New Testament textual criticism itself, as well as on how it has impacted English translations of the New Testament. This prompted me to produce the volume *Early Manuscripts and Modern Translations of the New Testament*, followed by *New Testament Text and Translation Commentary*. As one who has worked in both New Testament textual criticism and English translation work (I had the privilege of being the New Testament translation coordinator for the New Living Translation), I have been keenly aware of how important it is to make sure that our English translations reflect the best textual evidence. Since I have made contributions in this area in the previously mentioned volumes, this book—in the main—does not focus on how textual criticism has or has not impacted English versions. However, chapter 4—on the nomina sacra—does offer some thoughts on how English translators should handle the translation of *pneuma* (whether "Spirit" or "spirit") and other divine titles.

This volume focuses on the most significant New Testament manuscripts from the perspective of paleography and textual criticism. Paleography pertains to the dating of the manuscripts, as well as to the calligraphic features of the manuscripts themselves. Each manuscript has a story to tell; each manuscript gives us a window into the transmission of the New Testament text in the earliest centuries of the church. Textual criticism pertains to critical evaluation of the trustworthiness of the text of each manuscript with respect to recovering the original wording of the Greek New Testament. This volume includes the two areas of study by looking at both paleography and textual criticism as we open the New Testament manuscripts.

In this volume I attempt (1) to explore scribal participation in the production of the earliest New Testament writings, especially by examining calligraphic and paleographic features of the earliest New Testament manuscripts; (2) to give an annotated list of all significant Greek manuscripts and early versions; (3) to assign dates for the earliest New Testament manuscripts; (4) to examine the nomina sacra in the early New Testament manuscripts; (5) to present the history of textual variation in the early centuries of the church; (6) to explore various methods of recovering the original wording of the Greek New Testament and for this goal to assess the New Testament manuscripts as to their textual groupings and their influence on New Testament textual criticism; and (7) to provide concrete examples for the praxis of textual criticism, and in so doing to identify how the papyri influenced the text of the Greek New Testament.

The overall purpose of the book is to help students interact with the New Testament text first by knowing and working with the manuscripts themselves and then by knowing and working with the tools of textual criticism.

Chapter One

The Manuscript Publications of the Greek New Testament

Before students begin their studies of New Testament manuscripts and New Testament textual criticism, they need some background on New Testament manuscript production in the early centuries of the church. This background will help students understand how the New Testament was published, transmitted, and distributed to the earliest Christians. Thus, in this chapter we will explore how the New Testament was published through manuscript production. We will examine the extant New Testament manuscripts and other manuscripts of Christian writings to gain insights about the publication of the Greek New Testament in the early centuries of the church. We will begin with the original publications, then explore the features of the earliest manuscripts in an effort to reconstruct the history of New Testament publication. Since manuscript production was critical to the dissemination of the New Testament writings, our studies must begin here. Of course, this very production created all the textual variants in successive manuscripts and created the need for textual criticism. Thus, our studies need to commence with the publishing process, then examine the manuscripts themselves (chapters 2 through 4), and then on to textual criticism (in chaps. 5 through 7).

Defining Publication

When modern readers think of publishing, they think of written material—whether it be books, magazines, or newspapers. For the ancients, publishing meant both oral and written dissemination. For something to be published, whether it be a poem or a political proclamation, meant that it was broadcast to a number of people by oral and/or written proclamation. In most instances, a written account was made to be a vehicle for oral proclamation. Seldom was the written account in and of itself the sole means of getting something "published." Many of the ancients could not read; they depended on oral delivery if they were ever to receive a publication.

Ancient poets, therefore, published their poems by proclaiming them orally. Homer published his *Iliad* and *Odyssey* orally; others, after his time, wrote these poems down. Socrates, the eminent Greek philosopher, published his ideas orally. As far as we know, he did not write them down. Others, particularly Plato, gave the world a written account of Socrates' publishing endeavors. Most Greek poets in the fifth century BC and thereafter wrote their poems and presented them orally. An eminent example of this is Pindar, who lived from 522 to 443 BC. The greatest of all lyric poets, he wrote poems to be recited for the athletic victors when they returned home from competition in Olympia, Delphi, Nemea, and Corinth.

Jesus, the mystical poet and prophet, followed the tradition of oral publishing. As far as we know, he did not write down his teachings. He published the good news via oral proclamation. Many of his teachings were presented in a poetic mode similar to the Old Testament prophecies. The poetic proclamation aided memorization. Jesus was also the master of the parable. These stories were simple, unique, and therefore very memorable. A survey of the Gospels indicates that Jesus' publishing program— via his traveling throughout Galilee and Judea and proclaiming the good news of the kingdom—was extensive and effective. Thousands and thousands of people heard the word from Jesus himself. In ancient times, the method of oral publication was far more effective than written publication. Books were expensive to make, and many people did not read. Most relied on oral proclamation and aural reception to receive messages. Indeed, most education was based upon oral delivery and aural reception/ memorization to transmit texts. Thus, Jesus taught his disciples orally, and they committed his teachings to memory. When it came time, several years later, for the disciples to put these teachings into writing, they were aided by the Holy Spirit, who would remind the disciples of all that Jesus had taught them (John 14:26). Jesus' disciples, commissioned by him, continued the same publishing work after Jesus' death and resurrection. This publishing is known as the *kerygma* (Greek for "proclamation"). The word *kerygma* is taken straight from a well-known practice in ancient times. A king publicized his decrees throughout his empire by means of a *kerux* (a town crier or herald). This person, who often served as a close confidant of the king, would travel throughout the realm, announcing to the people whatever the king wished to make known. In English, we known him as a herald. Each New Testament disciple considered himself or herself to be like the *kerux*—a herald and publisher of the Good News.

Paul called himself "a herald and an apostle" (1 Tim. 2:7; 2 Tim. 1:11), for it was his function as an apostle to be a herald. Paul and the other New Testament apostles had a common proclamation *(kerygma)* to take to the world. This proclamation was a "publishing" of the death, resurrection, and exaltation of Jesus. At first, the publishing was oral—via preaching in various cities throughout the Greco-Roman world. Eventually, the publishing was both oral and written—via the writings of the apostles, which were proclaimed in churches throughout the world. As can be gathered from the book of Acts and the writings of Paul, the basic kerygma always focused on Jesus' resurrection. This supernatural act of God in history authenticates the words and works of Jesus and constitutes the basis for the Christian hope of immortality. Without the resurrection, the church would be no more than a group of well-intentioned, religious people who had placed their faith in the superior philosophical and ethical teachings of an unusually gifted man. The resurrection is proof positive that Jesus is who he said he was. Thus, the kerygma is a declaration that Christ is risen from the dead, and by that great act God has brought salvation.

The early apostles proclaimed this kerygma to all the believers. At the same time, they rehearsed the deeds and words of Jesus. Thus, the first-century Christians initially received an oral presentation of the gospel from the apostles who had been with Jesus (see Acts 2:42) and then, written documents that preserved the oral and perpetuated the apostolic tradition (see Luke 1:1–4). The oral proclamation was considered a form of catechetical instruction (from the Greek word *katecheo*; see BAGD, 423)—a teacher rehearsing Jesus' words and deeds, with the congregation orally repeating what was taught and committing it to memory. (This was the way nearly all teaching occured in hellenistic times.) According to Galatians 6:6, the teachers in the early church were considered the catechists, the oral proclaimers of the word (see also 1 Cor. 14:19). According to the preface to his Gospel (1:1–4), Luke wanted to affirm, via the written word, what Theophilus had already been taught by catechism—i.e., oral recitation. Thus, the written word in Luke's Gospel was the inscribed replication of the oral proclamation.

After the death of the apostles and those who were their immediate associates, the written text became more important. Second-generation Christians (and later ones) probably would have received the gospel for the first time via one of the written Gospels. But even most of these believers would not have read the Gospel for themselves; rather, it would have been read to them in church meetings by those trained in oral reading (i.e., lectors). In this manner, the kerygma would have continued to be published orally with the help of written documents.

Of all the apostles, Paul was probably the most effective herald and publisher of the kerygma. His numerous apostolic journeys took him to hundreds of cities and villages, where he would proclaim the good news of Jesus' resurrection and salvation. In due course, Paul realized that his publishing efforts were limited by space and time—he could only be in one locality at one time. Thus, Paul expanded his publishing efforts by sending out coworkers with the gospel and by publishing encyclical epistles, which he sent with these coworkers (who, in turn, would read them to various churches). Papyrus and pen would become another, more expedient vehicle for publishing Paul's revelations concerning Christ and the church. (This is discussed in greater detail below.)

The apostles Peter and John also took advantage of the written medium to publish their accounts of Jesus' life and teachings, as well as their teachings about the Christian life. As with Paul, they first published the kerygma via oral proclamation. But later in life, each of these eminent apostles published written accounts of Jesus' ministry in order to preserve an accurate, apostolic presentation of the kerygma—one that would last after their deaths. According to tradition, Peter's Gospel came to us through the pen of Mark, and John himself penned a Gospel in his old age. Both of these apostles also published epistles recounting their personal encounters with Jesus Christ (see 2 Pet. 1:12–21; 1 John 1:1–4), their proclamations of apostolic truth, and their exhortations to effective Christian living.

The major point of this brief introduction to the publishing process is that the good news of the New Testament first came in the form of oral proclamation, then in written form—primarily to sustain the continuance of the oral proclamation as originally proclaimed by Jesus' handpicked apostles. Had not the apostles written down the kerygma, had it continued only as oral tradition, the gospel would have been continually changed through the ages, according to the whims of whoever proclaimed it. Eventually, the gospel would have become totally different from what it was in its beginnings. Thus, the written publications preserve the integrity of apostolic truth as expressed by the first followers of Jesus. Generation after generation of Christians have depended on the validity of these published documents for their faith and lives.

The Original Writings

In order to understand the early stages of the written text of the various books of the New Testament, I think it is helpful to employ language from the publishing world. In ancient times, as in modern, books were "published." Of course, the number of copies published in ancient times was far less than in modern times. Nonetheless, there are many parallels as to procedure.

A modern writer first composes his or her writing by using pen and paper, a typewriter, or a computer. The words put down in writing for the very first time are the "original" text or what is called the "autograph." It is possible that the writer will be completely satisfied with this text and never make any further changes. But this is rare. The more likely scenario is that the writer will make further revisions with the intent of improving the writing for potential publication. Thus, the writing will go through several drafts before being finalized. A modern author can also use the services of a professional "ghost writer" and/or a secretary (scribe) who transcribes dictated material. The author would then review and revise this draft. Once the author is satisified with his or her final draft, the text is sent off to a publisher. The publisher will then edit the text, in cooperation with the author, and then publish the first authorized text. This "authorized" text is the archetypal text, the text from which all the initial copies in the first print run are made. The author's original text, stuffed away in some desk drawer, will probably be very different from the final, archetypal published text. In any event, the final published work is credited to the author and becomes the standard text (or archetypal manuscript) from which all copies should be made in the future.

The situation for the New Testament writings has many parallels to the publishing process just described. First, an author would write a book—such as John composing his Gospel or Paul dictating an epistle. These are called the autographs. We know that several of the books of the New Testament (especially the epistles) were dictated to an amanuensis, and others were written by the author himself. The usual procedure for a dictated epistle was for the amanuensis to take down the speaker's words (often in shorthand) and then produce a transcript, which the author could then review, edit, and sign in his own handwriting. Two New Testament epistles provide the name of the amanuensis: Tertius for Romans (16:22) and Silvanus (another name for Silas) for 1 Peter (5:12). We can discern that Paul must have dictated other epistles because he specifically noted that he provided the concluding salutation in his own handwriting: 1 Corinthians (16:21), Galatians (6:11), Colossians (4:18), and 2 Thessalonians (3:17). He said that he did this at the end of all his epistles to authenticate them and guard them against forgery. The words in 2 Thessalonians 3:17 are quite interesting, for Paul signed off the epistle in his own hand, saying "this is the way I write it." As such, he authenticated his bonefida signature. This was a common practice in ancient letter writing—where the writer served as an amanuensis and the author signed off—see, for example P. Oxyrhynchus 3057 (late first/early second century), considered by some to be the earliest extant Christian letter[1] (excluding the NT epistles); and see P. London 2078 (dated AD 81–96).

Silas (otherwise known as Silvanus) helped Peter write his first epistle (5:12). This means that Silas either functioned as an amanuensis for Peter, or translated Peter's letter (from Aramaic to Greek) as Peter dictated it, or composed a letter based on Peter's thoughts. This was not an unusual practice in ancient times, nor in modern. Certain people, not gifted with writing, give that task to another, who puts down in words the thoughts of the author. (In modern times, this person is often called "the ghost writer.") This ancient practice of employing the help of others for writing documents could help us understand why there is such a discrepancy in style between Peter's two epistles (1 Peter and 2 Peter). In short, Peter used two different writers. Thus, 2 Peter contains the final thoughts of Peter, written by another (perhaps Jude, whose own epistle is so similar to 2 Peter), and perhaps published posthumously. History also tells us that Peter was the author behind Mark's Gospel.[2] In this case, it is more like shared authorship—in the sense that Peter would be credited with the Gospel history/story and Mark with the literary presentation of this Gospel story.

It is possible that Silvanus (also known as Silas) was one of the earliest Christian scribes. He was one of those who composed the letter from the Jerusalem Council to Antioch (Acts 15:22). Thereafter, he is seen as Paul's close coworker, and also as Peter's. His name appears in the prescript of both 1 and 2 Thessalonians (for he was a cowriter with Paul), and then at the end of 1 Peter (5:12). Some scholars see resemblances among 1 and 2 Thessalonians, the decree of Acts 15, and 1 Peter. Silas and/or other prominent Christian scribes may have been responsible for putting together the published version of various books of the New Testament.[3]

For some books of the New Testament, there may be little difference between the autograph and the original published text. This is especially true for the short letters written by the author himself, for there would have been little cause for editing. This is the situation for 2 John (v. 12), 3 John (v. 13), and Jude (v. 3), and probably other occasional epistles (i.e., letters written primarily to meet the need of the occasion). But other books seem to have gone through two stages: the book was first written; then it was edited for publication. The "published" works include the four Gospels (originally published separately), Acts, Romans, Ephesians, Hebrews, 1 Peter, and Revelation. Each of these books, from the onset, were intended for an audience greater than one locality. By the end of the first century, it is very likely that there were additional publications of the Gospels in one collection, as well as a collection of Pauline Epistles, each of which could be called "authorized" in that they were produced under the purview of some coworker of the apostles (such as Silvanus).

Features of the Original Writing

None of the autographs or archetypal texts of any book of the New Testament exist to this day; therefore, we do not know exactly what they looked like. However, by drawing from the known sources of extant documents of the first century and by using a little creative imagination, we could surmise that any or all of the original writings of the New Testament could have several of the following features.

Handwriting of the Autographs

The autographs themselves, as the originally written texts, could have been in any kind of handwriting. One would expect that it was not necessarily polished inasmuch as this text would or could have been subject to editing. In other words, the autograph would be similar to what we call a first draft. If we saw the first draft of an autograph, there might be editorial corrections written between the lines or in the margins, either by the author or an amanuensis, or both. In fact, the best way to spot an autograph (in its first draft) is the presence of substantive corrections written in the same hand as the main body of the text. P. Oxyrhynchus 2070, an anti-Jewish dialogue (presumably composed by a Christian), is an excellent example of an "autograph," for it has numerous corrections written in the same hand as the text. Presumably, authors such as Luke and the writer of the book of Hebrews would have corrected their own texts prior to publication. Other New Testament writers seem to have let their writings be published without thorough editing. One thinks, for example, of some of the writings of Paul, which retain anacolutha in many places—the direct indication of dictation left uncorrected (see, for example, Eph. 3:18). One also thinks of John's Apocalypse, which bears the marks of John recording his revelation, then publishing it without correcting several grammatical mistakes (see, for example, Rev. 1:4, 15; 10:7; 11:1; 14:19; 16:4).[4]

Museums and libraries around the world have hundreds (if not thousands) of manuscripts from the first century written in what would be called a "documentary" hand (described below). These manuscripts exhibit the wide variety of hands that penned letters and documents in that era. I would suggest the reader to look at a number of excellent books on the subject, which present photographs and descriptions of manuscripts of this era. For starters, I recommend these volumes: *Greek Literary Hands* (GLH), C. H. Roberts; *Greek Manuscripts of the Ancient World* (GMAW), E. G. Turner; and *La Papirologia,* Orsolina Montevecchi. To be more specific, I would suggest that the following manuscripts could give a general idea of what one of the New Testament autographs might have looked like.

P. London 2078 (AD 81–96)

P. Fayum 110 (AD 94) (see GLH 11b)

P. Oxyrhynchus 270 (AD 94)

P. Oxyrhynchus 3057, presumed to be the earliest Christian letter (late first/early second c.)

These manuscripts present a legible hand, written somewhat quickly. They are definitely not polished works—that is, they are not the kind of productions one would expect to see in the first "published" text—if the author intended to make a good impression. Another manuscript, $\mathfrak{P}^{52}$ (a papyrus manuscript of John dated ca.110) also gives an idea of what one might see in an autograph. The writing is legible, written somewhat quickly, in a casual style modeling that found in P. Fayum 110.

Different Hands in the Autographs

If we were looking for an autograph, we could also look for two different handwritings in the text—that of the amanuensis and that of the author. It was customary in hellenistic times for the author of a letter to dictate the letter or official document to his or her amanuensis and then sign off in his own handwriting—usually in cursive, so as to distinguish one's personal signature. There are countless examples of this phenomenon in the extant papyri preserving letters and documents. For good examples, I refer the reader to P. Fayum 110 (AD 110; for photo, see p. 147 in this volume); P. London II, 308 (AD 146; for photo, see Montevecci, plate 52); P. Oxyrhynchus 246 (AD 66); P. Oxyrhynchus 286 (AD 82); P. Oxyrhynchus 3057 (ca.100, perhaps the earliest Christian letter). Another noteworthy example is a letter about sending books between Alexandria and Oxyrhynchus. This original letter, known as P. Oxyrhynchus 2192, shows the main body of the letter in one handwriting, followed by three short notes in three different hands.

In three of Paul's letters, we see explicit references to the practice of the writer signing off in his own hand (1 Cor. 16:21; Col. 4:18; 2 Thess. 3:17–18). In 2 Thessalonians 3:17–18, Paul said, "I, Paul, write this greeting with my own hand, which is my signature in every letter—this is the way I write it." At this point, Paul concluded the epistle with his own signature, probably in cursive (so as to give it his personal distinctiveness). In two other letters (Gal. 6:11–18; Philem. 19–25), Paul took up the stylus and wrote in his own hand something—and then probably continued writing until the end of the letter. In Galatians 6:11, he noted how he wrote in large script—i.e., larger than the script of his amanuensis. (A textual variant in Gal. 6:11 indicates that he wrote in a "different" hand.)[5] In Philemon, he took the pen from the amanuensis, and wrote in his own hand, "I, Paul, will repay." These are the only explicit references to Paul writing in his own hand. It can be inferred, however, that all of Paul's final greetings of grace and peace would have been written in his own hand. This would include Romans 15:33 (assuming chap. 16 to be a separate attachment; see 𝔓[46]); 1 Cor. 16:21–24; 2 Cor. 13:13; Gal. 6:11–18; Eph. 6:23–24; Phil. 4:21–23; Col. 4:18; 1 Thess. 5:26–28; 2 Thess. 3:17–18; 1 Tim. 6:21b; 2 Tim. 6:22; Titus 3:15; and Philem 19–25.

By extension, the same distinction of hands would be found in the other New Testament letters. This would include the final greetings and blessings in Hebrews 13:24–25; 1 Peter 5:12–14; 2 John 13; 3 John 14; and Revelation 22:21. If the author also wrote the concluding doxologies, this would include Romans 16:25–27 (which appears at the end of chap. 14 in some manuscripts and at the end of chap. 15 in 𝔓[46]); 2 Peter 3:18; Jude 24–25—presuming, of course, these were part of the original writings. As such, only two New Testament epistles would lack any kind of special calligraphy at the end—namely, James and 1 John. I think that 2 John and 3 John were written from start to finish by the same hand—that of the author's (see 2 John 12 and 3 John 13).

It is also possible that an autograph of John's Gospel, in the second edition which includes chapter 21, would show a different hand at John 21:24b, where it says, "and we know that his testimony is true . . . ." Most likely, this is the attestation of some of John's contemporaries who knew that what John wrote was true. Some scholars think these contemporaries were the Ephesian elders. (John resided in Ephesus in his later years.) Westcott wrote, "The words were probably added by the Ephesian elders, to whom the preceding narrative had been given both orally and in writing."[6] In the autograph this would appear in a distinguished hand, one different from the rest of the text.

Endings in the Autographs Shorter Than in Later Manuscripts

The autographs (and/or archetypes) would have shorter endings than what we see in later manuscripts. If, by some good fortune, a person found the first autograph of John's Gospel, the discoverer would see that it ended with John 20:31. Clearly, the last chapter (21) was appended at some later time. It could have been added to the second draft prior to publication or appended as an epilogue to a publication in its second edition.[7]

The discoverer of the autograph of Mark's Gospel could find a manuscript that ended at Mark 16:8 (as in Sinaiticus and Vaticanus)—or more likely, in my opinion, the discoverer would see that the Gospel ended with some wording that followed *ephobounta gar* (for they were afraid), which I don't think goes with the previous words (*kai oudeni ouden eipan* [and they said nothing to anyone]) but begins a new thought, as is customary with the function of the word *gar*. Who would end a sentence, much less an entire Gospel, with that word?[8] Thus, it stands to reason that the next sentence spoke of the women's fear, which may have eventually been relieved, and of some kind of subsequent appearance of the risen Jesus. In short, I think a discoverer of the original manuscript, prior to the loss of the last sheet of Mark's codex, would see some kind of additional wording different from what is appended in the various extant endings to Mark.

It is also very likely that several of the concluding doxologies and blessings in the New Testament epistles would be absent or significantly shorter than what is displayed in later manuscripts. Textual variation in nearly all the concluding verses, as well as shorter texts in many of the earlier manuscripts, strongly suggests that the original endings to most of the epistles were short and sweet. Let us begin with the last word to show up in many manuscripts—the word *amen*. A study of the textual evidence reveals that in nearly every instance, the *amen* is a scribal addition. Only three epistles (Romans, Galatians, Jude) appear to have a genuine *amen* for the last word. Obviously, the word *amen* was added for oral, liturgical presentation. (The word *amen* was also appended in later manuscripts to the end of each Gospel and Acts.)

When we study the other features of the concluding verses—the final greetings, the blessings of grace and peace, and some doxologies—it is evident that they were expanded throughout the course of textual transmission. For example, one can look at the textual variants for verses such as Philippians 4:23; 2 Timothy 4:22; Titus 3:15; 1 Peter 5:14; 2 Peter 3:18; Jude 25 and clearly see the expansions. Two other examples are worth noting. The second-century papyrus $\mathfrak{P}^{87}$ ends Philemon with the terse "Grace be with you," as opposed to the fuller reading, "The grace of the Lord Jesus Christ be with your spirit." And the third-century papyrus $\mathfrak{P}^{72}$ ends 1 Peter with the wording, "Greet one another with the kiss of love," without then adding, "Peace be to all the ones in Christ," as is found in all other manuscripts. These two shorter endings probably reveal a more primitive, sparser text—one closer to the look of the autographs.

No Inscriptions or Subscriptions

The original writings, both as autographs and published archetypes, would not have had inscriptions (titles) or subscriptions. All of these were added later. None of the four Gospels would have been titled as "Gospel" (*euaggelion*), for that was a second-century description of these writings. It is possible that the original codex of $\mathfrak{P}^{66}$ was left untitled; the title *euaggelion kata Ioannen* (Gospel according to John) may have been added by a later hand (see comments on $\mathfrak{P}^{66}$ in chap. 3). The book of Acts would not have been titled this way by Luke, and John did not title his apocalypse as Revelation. The epistles, by character and disposition, would not have been titled. Certain epistles, which were encyclicals, such as that known as Ephesians, did not have the name of the city in the opening address. We know this because the words "in Ephesus" (in Eph. 1:1) are lacking in the three earliest manuscripts ($\mathfrak{P}^{46}$ ℵ B) and because the name of the city was filled in as the letter circulated from city to city. Thus, the autograph would have opened with the wording for the addressee as "to the faithful being in [name of city] and faithful in Christ Jesus."

The Presence of Nomina Sacra

The autographs may or may not have included the primary nomina sacra for *Kurios* (Lord), *Christos* (Christ), *Iesous* (Jesus), and *theos* (God) in their most primitive forms. Thus far, there has not been one New Testament manuscript or Christian Greek Old Testament manuscript discovered which shows these divine titles written in any way other than the nomina sacra form. These manuscripts go back to the end of the first century and the beginning of the second. As such, it stands to reason that the nomina sacra may have been included in the original writings and, if not, at least in the earliest publications. I present a full discussion of this phenomenon in chapter 3.

Handwriting of the Archetypes

The handwriting of archetypal texts is a different story than the autographs because published archetypal texts would normally have a polished look to them. As such, the script likely would have been in what is typically called "bookhand" or, at least, "reformed documentary" script (a full description of these handwriting types is found below). If the author used the services of a professional scribe to produce the archetypal text, it could have had either of these calligraphic looks. If the author did the archetype himself, then the calligraphic features would be inferior—unless, of course, the author also happened to be a trained penman.

Allowing myself some creative thinking here, I would imagine the script of several of the New Testament archetypes to have resembled the handwriting style of something like the Greek Minor Prophet Scrolls from Nahal Hever (8Hev XIIgr), which have been dated to the early first century AD—slightly earlier than the New Testament autographs. These manuscripts may have the closest correspondence to the earliest New Testament manuscripts inasmuch as Jewish scriptoral practices could have easily been carried over by Jewish-Christian scribes. I also think some of the late first-century and early second-century Greek Old Testament manuscripts produced by Christians could provide some resemblance to what we might see in mid-to-late first-century New Testament archetypes. I am thinking preeminently of Chester Beatty VI (Numbers and Deuteronomy), which displays a good Roman hand, typical of that period. I am also thinking of P. Yale 1 (Genesis), P. Baden 4.56 (Exodus and Deuteronomy), though both of these are more casual in appearance than the Beatty manuscript.

Other nonbiblical manuscripts with a similar reformed documentary look, dated to the middle of the first century (the time period for the writing of most New Testament books), are as follows:

P. Oxyrhynchus 2555 (after AD 46)

P. Oxyrhynchus 3700 (before AD 48–49)

P. Oxyrhynchus 2471 (ca.AD 50) (for photo see GMAW 64), P. Med. 70.01 (AD 55) (for photo see Montev. 42)

P. Oxyrhynchus 246 (AD 66) (for photo see GLH 10c)

The handwriting style of these manuscripts could perhaps be similar to what we would see in a first-century manuscript of a New Testament book because I would imagine that the earliest New Testament writings would have been written by those familiar with making documentary texts and then attempting to give them the best look possible. Hence, the look would be "reformed documentary" (described below). However, if the earliest publications were produced by professional scribes accustomed to producing literary texts, the look would be that of a book hand, as found in some of the following first-century manuscripts:

P. Fayum 6 (early first century)

P. Fayum 7 (early first century)

P. Oxyrhynchus 2987 (ca. AD 78–79)

In my opinion, not one of the extant New Testament manuscripts has a mid-first-century look. A few New Testament manuscripts (namely, 𝔓⁵² and 𝔓¹⁰⁴) resemble hands of the late first century or early second century. (These are discussed in detail in chap. 3.)

In the end, I must emphasize that I have allowed myself some creative reconstruction here—for the sake of giving students some idea of what the autographs and archetypes of the individual books of the New Testament may have looked like.

The Publication of the New Testament Books

Before I launch into a discussion of New Testament manuscript production, it is important to give an overview of the earliest publication process of the individual books and collections of books (such as the four Gospels and Paul's major epistles), because both are essential to understanding the early phases of the transmission of the New Testament text.

The publication of the New Testament writings came about in several stages: first, as individual writings; second, as collections (such as the four Gospels and Paul's major Epistles); third, as an entire entity, the New Testament (with all 27 books of the canon). The individual writings were published between AD 49 and 90; the Pauline collections were published by AD 100–25, and Gospel collections were published by the early second century. The entire New Testament was not published as a unit until the early fourth century—and, at that, it was included with the Greek Old Testament in one codex (as in Codex Vaticanus and Codex Sinaiticus).

In the discussion that follows, I focus primarily on the first two phases of publication. In this regard, I would not follow the pattern put forth by David Trobisch in *The First Edition of the New Testament*, who focuses his energies on what he calls a "Canonical Edition" of the New Testament (with all 27 books). He is careful not to date this edition, but it could not have come about any earlier than the third century.[9] As such, the editorial work he addresses is a much later publishing endeavor than the one I imagine. The editorial process I address pertains to the original publications with authorial superintendence (in the first stage) and the collecting together of these writings into larger volumes (in the second stage). As for Paul's major epistles, Paul himself may have made the collection—or, at least, promoted it. (This is discussed below.)

Publication of the Gospels

The Gospels are the documents of Jesus' words and deeds, written by eyewitnesses. Since he himself did not leave any written records that we know of, we must rely on the accounts of his companions for the true accounting of his life and words. By way of analogy, we could consider the writings of Plato about Socrates. As far as we know, Socrates wrote nothing. What we know about Socrates comes from two of his disciples, Plato and Xenophon. Likewise, what we know about Jesus comes from a few of his disciples. What kept these disciples—whether of Plato or of Jesus—from composing fabrications? The answer is straightforward: the living presence of the other disciples who could challenge fabricators on anything they said. One among the Twelve could have testified against any falsification. And there was also a group of seventy-two other disciples (Luke 10:1). Further, there were more witnesses than these. According to 1 Corinthians 15:6, Jesus had at least five hundred followers by the time he had finished his ministry, all of whom witnessed the risen Christ. Most of these were still alive at the time of Paul's writing. Since 1 Corinthians is usually dated around AD 56/57, Paul made this statement just a few years prior to the time the Synoptic Gospels were composed. Any of the original witnesses could have exposed false writings concerning Jesus. Of these five hundred disciples, 120 went to Jerusalem to begin the church (Acts 1:14). After the church began, the early believers relied on the words of the apostles to teach them about Jesus' life and ministry (see Acts 2:42). This oral transmission about Jesus' life and teachings, together with the Septuagint, provided the verbal sustenance for the early church.

From Oral Proclamation to Written Word.——When Luke mentioned the written accounts about Jesus' life that were current in the first century, he called them "narratives" (see Luke 1:1). The term "gospel" (*euaggelion*) was not used as a descriptor of these written accounts until the middle of the second century (see Justin Martyr,

Dialogue with Trypho 10.2; 100.1; Irenaeus, *Against Heresies* 3.1.1; Clement of Alexandria, *Stromateis* 1.21). Luke told his readers that he wrote his Gospel "narrative" to affirm what Theophilis had already been taught. The Greek expression in 1:4 is very revealing. In an expanded rendering, it could be translated "that you might know the certainty of the words you have been taught by word of mouth." Theophilus, typical of most Christians in that era, had received the "sayings" or "logia" of Jesus by oral recitation (*katechethes logon*). But Luke thought Theophilus needed a written affirmation of what he had been taught orally. It is important to note that Luke didn't say his written account would redact the oral account in any way; rather, the written would affirm or substantiate the oral message ("that you might know the certainty/veracity of the things you have been taught"). As such, the written Gospel became an accurate extension and continuation of the oral. Tradition tells us that Mark compiled a Gospel based on Peter's oral messages about Jesus' ministry. And many scholars think John first preached many of the chapters that later he composed as a Gospel narrative. Thus, the Gospel was first published in oral form, then in written form.

Eventually, these Gospels were published. Luke's two-book sequel (Luke and Acts) was very likely sponsored (i.e., funded) by Theophilus (to whom Luke dedicated the book—see Luke 1:1–2), who may have helped with funding the publication of the Gospel. As recorded by Eusebius, Irenaeus tells us that Mark and Luke "published their Gospels." Irenaeus used the Greek term *ekdosis*, the standard term for the public dissemination of any writing. Similarly, Irenaeus wrote: "John, the disciple of the Lord, he who had leaned on his breast, also published [εξεδωκε] the Gospel, while living at Ephesus in Asia" (*Against Heresies* 3.1.2). It is significant to note that this term could refer to the official publication of a work, the master copy (archetype) from which other copies would be made.[10] For Mark, Luke, or John to "publish" their Gospels meant that they each made an official publication of their work—a master copy—from which further copies would be made for distribution.

We know that Luke was motivated to write a Gospel account that would affirm what the believers had been taught orally. But what motivated the others? One answer is that the apostles, who were eyewitnesses of Jesus, were about to pass off the scene— to make their exodus from this life to the next. Therefore, they wanted to leave the church a written testimony of Jesus' words and life before they died. Two of the four Gospel writers were apostles: Matthew and John. The latter, who is one and the same as "the beloved disciple," claims eyewitness authenticity for his Gospel (see John 1:14; 19:35; 21:24). Matthew makes no such claim for himself, but the testimony of early church history affirms this repeatedly.

The Gospels as Published Memoirs and Biographies.—Papias of Hierapolis was a scholarly historian who collected oral and written traditions about Jesus. He described the Gospel of Mark as containing *apomenmoneumata* (reminiscences or memoirs) drawn from Peter's sayings (Greek, *chreiai*); (see Eusebius, *Church History* 3.39.15). Justin Martyr, a Christian philosopher by profession, also used the word *apomenmoneumata* to describe the Gospels. Significantly, the word *apomenmoneumata* was a recognized literary form. According to Aune, the *apomenmoneumata* are "expanded chreiai, i.e., sayings and/or actions of or about specific individuals, set in narrative framework and transmitted by memory (hence 'reliable')."[11] The description of the Gospels as *apomenmoneumata* would place them in the same literary category as Xenophon's *Memorabilia* (in Greek called *apomenmoneumata*).

Thus, *apomenmoneumata*—memoirs, remembrances— is an apt literary description for the Gospels. They are not full-fledged biographies, as modern readers would think. Only Luke comes closest to presenting a full life story of Jesus Christ, from birth to death. But even so, Luke was ultimately more concerned with presenting what Jesus did and said than in producing a biography. In fact, when commenting on his own Gospel, Luke told Theophilus, "In the former book I wrote about all that Jesus began *to do and teach*, until the day he was taken up to heaven" (Acts 1:1–2). The Fourth Gospel concludes with the same emphasis: "Jesus did many other signs in the presence of his disciples, which are not recorded in this book. But these are written that you keep believing that Jesus is the Christ, the Son of God" (John 20:30–31).

Even the four Gospels are not full-fledged biographies. Hellenistic readers, familiar with biographies of great men, would have likely recognized that the four Gospels, in a limited way, were somewhat like other biographies of their day. J. A. T. Robinson posited that "Xenophon's *Memorabilia* and Plato's *Dialogues* correspond, one can say very broadly, to the approaches respectively of the Synoptists and the Fourth Gospel."[12] Other biographies appeared in the Greco-Roman world that were more popular in nature, such as the *Life of Aesop*, the *Life of Homer*, the Jewish *Lives of the Prophets*, and the life of Secundus the Silent Philosopher. The four Gospels could be included in this category of "biography" on the basis of structure and style. A comparative study by Burridge also indicates that the closest ancient genre to the Gospels is ancient biography—in terms of literary and semantic evidence.[13]

The Gospels, as with the popular biographies of the day, have a fundamentally chronological framework provided by a person's life, amplified by anecdotes, maxims, speeches, and documents. Most of these biographies were didactic in that they presented the subject as a paradigm of virtue; as a result, they were encomias. For example, Plutarch's *Lives*, written at the end of the first century and very popular throughout the Greco-Roman world, is quite like the Gospels in that the general scheme was to give the birth, youth and character, achievements, and circumstances of death, interspersed with frequent ethical reflections and anecdotes. So the primary importance of the Gospels is that they are written records of Jesus' speech and actions. Of course, each Gospel is not just a chronological display of what Jesus did and said, as if it were some kind of diary. Each Gospel is a story with a crafted narrative produced to be a work of literature. Gamble elaborates: "It can be seen more clearly today than in the heyday of form criticism that the Gospels were written in a literary context with literary skills and a literary view to readership. . . . Each of these authors [Matthew, Mark, Luke, John] was self-consciously engaged in literary composition and therefore sensible not only of his own compositional techniques and theological aims, but also of the prospects for valuation, circulation, and use of his work."[14] Each of the Gospel writers used different literary techniques to give a portrayal of Jesus Christ. Matthew used prophetic fulfillment to move his narrative along; Mark used high-paced, dramatic action; Luke employed historical details to frame the narrative; and John specialized in eyewitness accounts and monologue. What made these Gospels different from any other "memoirs" or "biographies" was that they were about Jesus Christ, who was stupendously different from all other men—he claimed to be the Son of God come from heaven. And Jesus' message was radically different from other men's. For example, his beatitudes (though similar in form to the Old Testament beatitudes found in Psalms and Proverbs) promise eschatological (not temporal) benefits to those who are meek, pure, and poor. Furthermore, the story of Jesus' life is unique: he came from heaven to be born of a virgin; he proclaimed salvation and eternal life for all who believed in him as the Messiah and Son of God; he was crucified as a criminal; he was raised from the dead and appeared to his disciples; and then he ascended back to heaven. The Gospel writers were inspired by witnessing these events, and they were inspired when they wrote about them. The apostles had not forgotten or misremembered these events when they penned them. Jesus himself guarded against this; he specifically told his disciples that he would send them the Spirit to help them remember everything he had told them (John 14:26). This Spirit, the Spirit of Jesus, guided the disciples when they composed their books.

Publication of the Epistles, Revelation, and Acts

Now, let's consider the publication of the Epistles—first, Paul's epistles. Paul wrote a few personal letters (to Timothy, Titus, and Philemon) and several epistles. There is a difference between a letter and an epistle. According to Adolf Deissman, a letter is a direct personal correspondence between two people not intended to be read by others; whereas an epistle is a stylized literary form which gives the impression of being personally directed to one or more individuals but whose real intent is to address a much wider audience.[15] Such was the intent of many of Paul's epistles. Two of Paul's epistles, Romans and Ephesians, were clearly intended, from their inception, to be encyclical treatises—to be read by all the churches. Of all Paul's nonpastoral epistles, there are only three that are written exclusively by Paul—without mentioning another coauthor per se, such as Timothy or Silvanus; the three are Romans, Galatians, and Ephesians. Galatians had to be personal because it involves a personal defense; Romans and Ephesians are single-authored because each is a magnum opus. Romans is Paul's masterpiece on the Christian life, and Ephesians is Paul's masterpiece on the church. Paul's Epistle to the Ephesians was originally an encyclical epistle, published for all the churches in the Roman province of Asia Minor.

Paul was a man with a publishing plan. At first, his goal was to travel as far and wide as possible and proclaim the gospel to as many people as possible. He wanted to reach all the way to Spain, the western end of the known world (see Rom. 15:18–24). Somewhere along the way, he realized that this form of oral publication was limited— limited by his ability or inability to travel. Thus, following Jesus' pattern, Paul sent out other coworkers with the gospel. At the same time, he realized that his writings (taken to the churches by various coworkers) would further disseminate the gospel that had been revealed to him. Thus, the written word would enlarge and perpetuate his publishing plan. As time went on, Paul became known for his "epistles," which were characterized by others as being "weighty and strong" (2 Cor. 10:10). In fact, Paul's epistles were considered much better than his oral speeches. This could indicate that Paul, knowing the value of the written word, put a great deal of effort into his writings.

Paul knew the importance of authorized apostolic letters, for he saw the authority behind the letter that came from the first Jerusalem church council. The first epistle from the church leaders who had assembled at Jerusalem was the prototype for subsequent epistles (see Acts 15). It was authoritative because it was apostolic, and it was received as God's word. If an epistle came from an apostle (or apostles), it was to be received as having the imprimatur of the Lord. This is why Paul wanted the churches to receive his word as being the word of the Lord. This is made explicit in 1 Thessalonians (2:13), an epistle he insisted had to be read to all the believers in the church (5:27). In the Second Epistle to the Thessalonians, Paul indicated that his epistles carry the same authority as his preaching (see 2:15). Paul also told his audience that if they would read what he had written, they would be able to understand the mystery of Christ, which had been revealed to him (see Eph. 3:1–6). Because Paul explained the mystery in his writings (in this case, the encyclical epistle known as "Ephesians"), he urged other churches to read this encyclical (see Col. 4:16). In so doing, Paul himself encouraged the circulation of his writings. Peter and John also had publishing plans. Peter's first epistle, written to a wide audience (the Christian diaspora in Pontus, Galatia, Cappadocia, Asia, Bithynia—see 1 Pet. 1:1), was a published work, which must have been produced in several copies from the onset, to reach his larger, intended audience. John's first epistle was also published and circulated— probably to all the churches in the Roman province of Asia Minor. First John is not any kind of occasional epistle; it is more like a treatise akin to Romans and Ephesians in that it contains John's full explanation of the Christian life and doctrine as a model for all orthodox believers to emulate. The book of Revelation, which begins with seven epistles to seven churches in this same province, must have also been inititally published in seven copies, as the book circulated from one locality to the next, by the seven "messengers" (Greek *anggeloi*—not "angels" in this context). By contrast, the personal letters (Philemon, 1 and 2 Timothy, Titus, 2 John, 3 John) were not originally "published"; therefore, their circulation was small. Second Peter also had minimal circulation in the early days of the church. Because of its popularity, the book of Hebrews seemed to have enjoyed wide circulation—this was promoted by the fact that most Christians in the East thought it was the work of Paul and therefore was included in Pauline collections (see discussion below). The book of Acts was originally published by Luke as a sequel to his Gospel (see Acts 1:1–2). Unfortunately, in due course, this book got detatched from Luke when the Gospel of Luke was placed in one-volume codices along with the other Gospels.

The Production of Manuscript Copies

Once a book was published, its circulation depended on the multiplication of copies. And multiplication of copies required manual reproduction—scribes making one copy at a time. There was no quick print. The only way to speed up the process was for one master scribe to read a text slowly while several scribes copied what they heard. This was done in ancient times for the most popular books—the books in most demand—such as Homer's *Iliad* or *Odyssey*. However, most other books were produced one by one—an individual scribe using one exemplar to make one copy.

In the earliest centuries of the church, copies of New Testament books probably would have been produced one by one. Many of those who made such copies were literate and trained (in some fashion or another) in Alexandrian scribal practices and/or Jewish scriptoral practices. Of course, there were degrees of training; some scribes would have been trained to make copies for libraries and/or the book trade; others would have been trained to produce documents; and still others would have had just enough knowledge to write Greek but no real training in making books. Indeed, a manuscript exhibits what kind of scribe produced it. A specimen of calligraphic beauty and textual accuracy tells us that the scribe was earnest in making a good copy; a specimen of scrawled Greek and multiple errors left uncorrected tells us that the scribe was uneducated and generally incapable of making a good copy.

In ancient times, there were schools for the training of scribes. To master the difficult art of writing on clay or penning elegant majuscule letters probably required as much time then as it takes students now to develop the ability to read and write. Would-be scribes could either enter a regular school or work as an apprentice under a private teacher, though most of them apparently followed the latter procedure. The schools were attached to the temples or scriptoria and were widely separated. Scribes who were willing to teach could be found everywhere—even in the smaller towns. In fact, most of the scribes had at least one apprentice, who was treated like a son while learning the profession. Such students learned not only from private tutoring but also from the example of their teacher. This kind of education was sufficient to equip young scribes for the normal commercial branches of the craft. They were fully prepared to handle the necessary formulas for the various kinds of legal and business documents, and they could easily take dictation for private correspondence. There are Assyrian reliefs picturing scribes taking dictation from an Assyrian monarch.

For additional study and training, however, it was necessary to attend the regular schools. For example, only the schools adjacent to the temples had the proper facilities to teach the sciences (including mathematics) and literature, which the more advanced scribes had to master. There a budding scribe could study to become even a priest or a "scientist." In the ruins of ancient cities archaeologists have discovered "textbooks" used by the pupils. Excavators have also uncovered schoolrooms with benches on which the students sat. Some of the ancient Near Eastern texts that have been unearthed are nothing but schoolboy exercises or student copies of originals. Naturally such copies are usually not as beautiful or as legible as the originals, which were written by master scribes.

When the teacher wanted to give the students an assignment, he had available in the temple school virtually every type of text imaginable. For elementary work he could have the students practice writing a list of cuneiform signs, much like our learning the letters of the alphabet—except that there were some six hundred signs. Another simple assignment would have been to copy dictionaries containing lists of stones, cities, animals, and gods. After such preparatory work the students could then move to literary texts and, for example, accurately reproduce a portion of one of the great epics, a hymn, or a prayer. Thus, through arduous study and a lengthy program of instruction and practice, a gifted student could become qualified for scribal service in almost any field. Unfortunately, the masses did not have access to developing reading, writing, and professional ability.

In biblical times, the scribe undertook a wide range of writing tasks. Often the scribe sat at the gate of the city or in an open area undertaking numerous kinds of writing tasks for illiterate citizens, correspondence, writing of receipts, and contracts. More officially, he kept records and wrote annals. Religious scribes copied the Scriptures. Several of these men are mentioned in the Old Testament: Shebna (2 Kings 18:18, 37), Shaphan (2 Kings 22:8–12), Ezra (Ezra 7:6, 11; Neh. 8:1, 9, 13; 12:26, 36), Baruch (Jer. 36:26, 32), and Jonathan (Jer. 37:15, 20). In Jesus' day the scribes were highly trained in the art of writing and also in the Law. Jesus and the disciples had many contacts with them and their associates, the priests and Pharisees (Matt. 2:4; 5:20; 7:29; 8:19; 9:3; 12:38; Mark 1:22; 2:6, 16; 3:22; 7:1, 5; 11:18; Luke 5:21, 30; 6:7; 9:22; 11:53; Acts 4:5; 6:12, 23:9).

When many of the early New Testament papyri were first discovered (in the early 1900s), scholars did not think they were produced by scribes with professional training. Indeed, some scholars deemed them as the work of illiterate men who had little regard for making accurate copies of the New Testament. For example, Kenyon said,

"The earliest Christians, a poor, scattered, often illiterate body, looking for the return of the Lord at no distant date, were not likely to care sedulously for minute accuracy of transcription or to preserve their books religiously for the benefit of posterity."[16] Some of the early manuscripts display the kind of disregard Kenyon described. Among the early New Testament papyri, we see the hand of a schoolboy practicing his lettering using the book of Romans ($\mathfrak{P}^{10}$), the careless hand of one barely literate in Greek ($\mathfrak{P}^9$), and some scrawled amulets (such as $\mathfrak{P}^{78}$). We also see manuscripts where the scribe was prone to paraphrase (as in $\mathfrak{P}^{45}$), or where scribes were greatly influenced by the profuse "Western" expansions in the book of Acts (as in $\mathfrak{P}^{38}$, $\mathfrak{P}^{48}$, $\mathfrak{P}^{112}$), or where a scribe was extremely erratic both textually and calligraphically (as in $\mathfrak{P}^{72}$).

However, since many more papyri have been discovered after the time Kenyon made these observations, we have been able to study many more copies and to determine that not all the copies were poor reproductions. (Indeed, once Kenyon himself edited the Chester Beatty papyri, he changed his thinking.) In fact, the entire body of early New Testament papyri exhibit a wide variety of scribal workmanship. As noted by various papyrologists (such as Grenfell, Hunt, Roberts, Wilcken, Hunger, Skeat, Cavallo, Seider, and Turner), using slightly different nomenclature, it seems that the handwriting of the early New Testament manuscripts can be placed in four categories: professional (bookhand), reformed documentary, documentary, and common. (Paleographers also often describe the professional and reformed documentary hands as "formal" and the other hands as "informal.")

The professional scribe could produce a page with well-stroked letters (slowly formed), bilinearity (i.e., all letters except phi and psi are kept within imaginary upper and lower lines), with even spacing between letters in *scriptio continua* (continuous letters with no spaces between words), no ligatures, and no (or few) abbreviations of numerals. Literary hands also display punctuation and spacing at the end of sections. Turner said a bookhand is "a handwriting in capitals strictly or roughly bilinear, usually made slowly" (GMAW, 3). C. H. Roberts said that the bookhand exhibits "clarity, regularity, and impersonality" (GLH, xi). In short, the bookhand aims at being both beautiful and legible. Several other manuscripts show the workmanship of those trained at making quality documents. The handwriting of these scribes is typically called "reformed documentary" if the scribe was attempting to imitate a literary look, or simply "documentary" if a bit less polished. The documentary style reveals that the scribe was accustomed to making legal documents or writing correspondence for individuals. He or she would work more quickly—allowing for quickly stroked letters, nonbilinearity, some ligature, and abbreviations of numbers. During the first three centuries of the Christian era, professional scribes were hired to work in the scriptoria of libraries, or for dealers in the book trade, or for individuals who needed secretarial service. Often, a scribe was multifunctional; he or she could work in any or all of these capacities.[17] Thus, a manuscript displaying a reformed documentary hand could have been done by a professional, just as easily as a manuscript displaying a bookhand. Some of the New Testament manuscripts that look to be "reformed documentary" could, indeed, be the work of a professional who was simply working at a quicker pace.

Most of the early New Testament manuscripts (of the second and third centuries) display a documentary look or a reformed documentary look. And a few other manuscripts exhibit a "common" hand—that is, it looks like the work of a person just barely able to write Greek.

The Professional Bookhand.—Some of the early New Testament manuscripts were clearly produced by professionals who were able to produce literary texts. On the top of this list is the Gospel codex known as $\mathfrak{P}^{4+64+67}$ (displaying well-crafted calligraphy, paragraph markings, double-columns, and punctuation). Affirming the professional quality of this manuscript, the papyrologist C. H. Roberts indicated that the text was divided into sections according to a system also found in $\mathfrak{P}^{75}$, which also recurs in some great fourth-century manuscripts ($\aleph$ and B)—a system that clearly was not created by the scribe. Therefore, Roberts remarked, "Once again we find in a manuscript of this early period a characteristic that appears to be not specifically Egyptian but of wider application."[18]

Other professionally produced manuscripts displaying a bookhand are $\mathfrak{P}^{30}$ (with clear Biblical Uncial), $\mathfrak{P}^{39}$ (a beautiful specimen of early Biblical Uncial), $\mathfrak{P}^{46}$ (exhibiting stichoi notations, which are typical of scribes working for pay), $\mathfrak{P}^{66}$ (most likely the product of a scriptorium), $\mathfrak{P}^{75}$ (the work of an extremely well-trained scribe), $\mathfrak{P}^{77}$ + $\mathfrak{P}^{103}$ (displaying well-crafted calligraphy, standard paragraph markings, and punctuation), $\mathfrak{P}^{95}$ (showing a small portion of John), and $\mathfrak{P}^{104}$ (a gem among the early papyri). The evidence of the extant papyri dated pre-AD 300 indicates that there are, at least, nine extant professionally made manuscripts whose calligraphy is well deserving of the description "bookhand": $\mathfrak{P}^{4+64+67}$, $\mathfrak{P}^{39}$, $\mathfrak{P}^{46}$, $\mathfrak{P}^{66}$, $\mathfrak{P}^{75}$, $\mathfrak{P}^{77}$, $\mathfrak{P}^{95}$, $\mathfrak{P}^{103}$, and $\mathfrak{P}^{104}$. Each of these manuscripts is discussed in the next chapter.

Reformed Documentary.—We know that many of the early New Testament papyri were written in what is called "the reformed documentary hand" (i.e., the scribe knew he was working on a manuscript that was not just a legal document but a literary work). In *The Birth of the Codex* Roberts and Skeat wrote:

> The Christian manuscripts of the second century, although not reaching a
> high standard of calligraphy, generally exhibit a competent style of writing
> which has been called "reformed documentary" and which is likely to be the
> work of experienced scribes, whether Christian or not. . . . And it is therefore a
> reasonable assumption that the scribes of the Christian texts received pay for
> their work.[19]

According to this estimation, manuscripts exhibiting a "reformed documentary" hand could be the work of a scribe who worked for individuals in producing documents. As to their making New Testament manuscripts, they may have been employed for their services in making copies for individual Christians, or these well-trained scribes may have rendered service for a Christian congregation. Among the extant papyri that predate AD 300, we have at least fifteen "reformed documentary" New Testament manuscripts, according to my estimation. They are $\mathfrak{P}^1$, $\mathfrak{P}^{30}$, $\mathfrak{P}^{32}$, $\mathfrak{P}^{35}$, $\mathfrak{P}^{38}$, $\mathfrak{P}^{45}$, $\mathfrak{P}^{52}$, $\mathfrak{P}^{69}$, $\mathfrak{P}^{87}$, $\mathfrak{P}^{90}$, $\mathfrak{P}^{100}$, $\mathfrak{P}^{102}$, $\mathfrak{P}^{108}$, $\mathfrak{P}^{109}$, $\mathfrak{P}^{110}$. Each of these manuscripts, with its calligraphic features, is discussed in chapter 2.

Documentary.——It appears that most of the earliest manuscripts were not the product of the book trade but of communities whose members included businessmen and minor officials accustomed to writing documents. A copy displaying a "documentary" hand will not be as uniform in appearance as those done by professionals. The lettering on each line will not attempt to be bilinear (i.e., keep an even line on both the tops and bottoms of the letters across the line). The initial letter on each line will often be larger than the rest of the letters. This can be seen, for example, in a documentary text such as P. Bremer 5 (AD 117). The enlarged letter at the beginning of a line and/or new section is a feature of documentary texts, as well as Jewish Greek manuscripts, specifically those found at Nahal Hever. (This is discussed below.) In documentary texts, punctuation will be sporadic, and the text will usually display numerical abbreviations, which were commonly done by those producing documents. Two Revelation texts, $\mathfrak{P}^{47}$ and $\mathfrak{P}^{98}$, are good examples of this. Furthermore, a documentary hand will often display spaces between words or between groups of words (as was often done in legal contracts). This was not done by scribes producing literary texts.

The majority of extant, early New Testament manuscripts are documentary or reformed documentary. These were produced by churchmen or women who had been trained in writing documents and who then transferred this skill to making copies of Scripture for specific individuals who had hired their services and/or for their congregations. As pointed out by Gamble, many of these scribes were very likely the church lectors. It was their job to keep copies of Scripture, make new ones as needed, and to prepare the text for reading it to the congregation.[20] According to my study, nearly half (27) of the early New Testament papyri are "documentary." They are as follows: $\mathfrak{P}^5$, $\mathfrak{P}^{13}$, $\mathfrak{P}^{15+16}$, $\mathfrak{P}^{17}$, $\mathfrak{P}^{20}$, $\mathfrak{P}^{22}$, $\mathfrak{P}^{23}$, $\mathfrak{P}^{27}$, $\mathfrak{P}^{28}$, $\mathfrak{P}^{29}$, $\mathfrak{P}^{37}$, $\mathfrak{P}^{47}$, $\mathfrak{P}^{48}$, $\mathfrak{P}^{49+65}$, $\mathfrak{P}^{50}$, $\mathfrak{P}^{53}$, $\mathfrak{P}^{70}$, $\mathfrak{P}^{80}$, $\mathfrak{P}^{91}$, $\mathfrak{P}^{92}$, $\mathfrak{P}^{101}$, $\mathfrak{P}^{106}$, $\mathfrak{P}^{107}$, $\mathfrak{P}^{108}$, $\mathfrak{P}^{111}$, $\mathfrak{P}^{113}$, and $\mathfrak{P}^{114}$. Each of these manuscripts, with the calligraphic features, is described in the next chapter.[21]

Common.——Sometimes it is difficult to distinguish between a "documentary" hand poorly produced and a "common" hand. However, a common hand usually exhibits the work of one barely able to write Greek. $\mathfrak{P}^{10}$, mentioned above, shows the work of one learning to write Greek; it is a good example of what could be called a "common" hand. $\mathfrak{P}^9$ (having a portion of 1 John) is also undeniably "common." So is $\mathfrak{P}^{78}$, an amulet. Interestingly, many of the Revelation manuscripts exhibit a common hand. This is true for $\mathfrak{P}^{18}$ and $\mathfrak{P}^{24}$, and even more so for $\mathfrak{P}^{98}$. Other papyri containing Revelation are documentary; this is especially true for $\mathfrak{P}^{47}$. This could be a coincidence of archaeology, or it could suggest that Revelation was not being read in the churches and therefore not being copied by trained scribes.

Scriptoria and Writing Centers in the Early Christian Church

Did the early church (before the time of Constantine) have any scriptoria producing Christian writings—of the Old Testament, New Testament, and other Christian writings? If so, where? Various scholars have proposed some major cities—such as Alexandria, Caeserea, Antioch, Jerusalem, and Rome. To this list could be added the town of Oxyrhynchus, Egypt. Unfortunately, we have no direct archaeological evidence that Christian scholars were making copies of Old Testament books and New Testament books in any of these cities except Oxyrhynchus. One would hope that there would be archaeological finds from Alexandria, Egypt, especially because it was the site of the great library, scriptoria, and an early Christian intellectual center. But nothing has come from Alexandria. The reasons are straightforward: (1) the great library was destroyed twice over—the fires consuming any biblical texts, and (2) Alexandria is located on the wet Mediterranean—the dampness destroying any manuscripts. However, church history and certain manuscript discoveries from other parts in Egypt suggest that Alexandria had a Christian scriptorium or writing center.

Christianity spread to Alexandria sometime during the first century. Many Jews also lived in this city. Two centuries earlier, certain hellenistic Jews in Alexandria had produced the Septuagint (of the Pentateuch) for the great Alexandrian library. Christians adopted this text as their own and used it to prove the veracity of Jesus' claim to being the Messiah. Christian exposition of the Septuagint caused the Jews to abandon the Septuagint and make new translations of the Hebrew text. The Christians in the Alexandrian church continued to use the Septuagint as the basis of their apologetics and exposition. At the same time, they also used various New Testament books for instruction and exposition. Soon after Christianity spread to Alexandria, the Christians in that city began a catechetical school called the Didaskelion—a kind of teaching center. Eusebius (*Ecclesiastical History* 5.10.1) implies that the school began well before the time Pantaenus took charge of it (AD 160–180). Several scholars have surmised that Pantaenus began a scriptorium and may have been involved with New Testament textual criticism. However, we have no direct evidence as such. That brings us to his successor, Origen. Origen had the service of a number of secretaries and scribes, both in Alexandria and later in Caesarea. Eusebius said, "As [Origen] dictated, there were ready at hand more than seven shorthand-writers, who relieved each other at fixed intervals, and as many copyists, as well as girls trained for beautiful writing" (*Ecclesiastical History* 6.23). Origen needed these secretaries and scribes for the voluminous output of his own original writings. We do not know if he employed their services (or that of other scribes) in making copies of the New Testament. Most of Origen's other scribal labor went into his Hexpala project. According to Gamble's estimation, this large staff provided by Ambrose indicates that Ambrose was intent "not only on the rapid production of the great scholar's work but also on its wide availability to Christians of inquiring minds. . . . Here for the first time in my survey are the details of something resembling a genuine publishing operation in a Christian setting."[22]

Another city in Egypt—one which had close connections with Alexandria—which probably had a scriptorium or writing center for Christian manuscripts is Oxyrhynchus. The papyrologist C. H. Roberts believed that Oxyrhynchus was probably an intellectual center for Christianity in rural Egypt. This is suggested by the presence of an autograph manuscript of an anti-Jewish dialogue (P. Oxyrhynchus 2070), dated in the third century. This is also suggested by the number of Christian manuscripts discovered in Oxyrhynchus. Thus, Roberts posited the existence of a Christian scriptorium in Oxyrhynchus as early as the late second century.[23] But can we conclude this from the extant documents?

Of all the manuscripts discovered in Oxyrhynchus, many are nonliterary documents (i.e., letters, legal documents, business transactions); they were written by common folk—"tradesmen, farmers, minor government officials to whom knowledge of and writing in Greek was an essential skill, but who had few or no literary interests."[24] Other manuscripts were literary—such as the works of Homer, Pindar, and Philo. Copies of these literary works were often produced by professionals and/or those acquainted with professional scriptoral practices. Furthermore, Oxyrhynchus has yielded hundreds of biblical texts and Christian writings. To date, there are 116 papyrus manuscripts of the New Testament; 43 of these have come from Oxyrhynchus. (See pages 48–49 for a listing of Oxyrhynchus New Testament papyri that predate AD 300.)[25] Thus, nearly half of the extant New Testament papyrus manuscripts have come from this ancient Egyptian city. Almost all of the Oxyrhynchus manuscripts date between 200 and 400, and a few have been dated in the second century: $\mathfrak{P}^{32}$, $\mathfrak{P}^{52}$, $\mathfrak{P}^{77}$, $\mathfrak{P}^{90}$, and $\mathfrak{P}^{104}$. A few other papyri have been dated at the end of the second century (ca. 200): $\mathfrak{P}^{1}$, $\mathfrak{P}^{27}$, $\mathfrak{P}^{108}$. There is evidence that some of these manuscripts were produced by the same scribes ($\mathfrak{P}^{15}$ and $\mathfrak{P}^{16}$; $\mathfrak{P}^{20}$ and $\mathfrak{P}^{27}$; $\mathfrak{P}^{77}$ and $\mathfrak{P}^{103}$), but there are no other prominent, common textual features that would suggest that these manuscripts were produced in one local scriptorium. Rather, most of these manuscripts display that they were the work of individual scribes writing in a documentary or reformed documentary hand. At best, we can say that Oxyrhynchus may have had a writing center where one or two scribes worked on making copies of literary texts and biblical texts. Another possible scenario is that the biblical writings discovered at Oxyrhynchus were originally produced in Alexandria. We know for a fact that intellectuals at Oxyrhychus obtained most of their books from Alexandria. Indeed, Oxyrhynchus had many significant connections with Alexandria, especially with regard to scholarship and scriptoral practices. According to the paleographer E. G. Turner, a number of Alexandrians owned property in Oxyrhynchus, several of whom were professors of the famous Alexandrian Museum. Some of these professors, while living in Oxyrhynchus, corresponded with certain Alexandrians about obtaining copies of various works of literature. These copies would have been produced by the Alexandrian scriptorium and then sent to Oxyrhyhnchus.[26] Thus, certain manuscripts found in Oxyrhynchus would likely have been produced in Alexandria. However, we have no way of knowing if this included any biblical manuscripts.

There is yet one more possibility of linking some New Testament manuscripts to Alexandria. The Bodmer Gospel papyri, $\mathfrak{P}^{66}$ and $\mathfrak{P}^{75}$, came from Jabal Abu Manna and probably once belonged to a Christian monastery established by Pachomius in the early fourth century. In the 1950s several early biblical manuscripts were discovered in cliffs near this monastery. These manuscripts, technically called the Dishna Papers, are more commonly known as the Bodmer biblical papyri because they were purchased by Martin Bodmer (founder of the Bodmer Library of World Literature in Cologny, a suburb of Geneva) from a dealer in Cairo in the 1950s and 1960s. However, the dealer never revealed where the manuscripts came from. For over twenty years, scholars were guessing that the discovery of the ancient manuscripts was in the region between Panopolis (modern Akmim) and Thebes.[27] James Robinson, an expert in the Nag Hammadi manuscripts, was able to pinpoint the place of discovery while attempting to find out where the Nag Hammadi manuscripts came from. The Bodmer biblical papyri (or Dishna Papers) were discovered seven years after the Nag Hammadi codices and in close proximity (in the Dishna plain, east of the Nile River). (Dishna is midway between Panopolis and Thebes.) In 1945 the Nag Hammadi manuscripts were found in Jabal al-Tarif (just north of Chenoboskion—near Nag Hammadi, the city where the discovery was first reported). In 1952 the Bodmer papyri were found in Jabal Abu Manna, which is also located just north of the Dishna plain, twelve kilometers east of Jabal al-Tarif.[28] According to Robinson, it is quite likely that these manuscripts were part of a library of a Pachomian monastery. Within a few kilometers of Jabal Abu Manna lies the ruins of the ancient basillica of Pachomius (in Faw Qibli).[29] Pachomius (287–346) brought monasticism to this area around AD 320. By the time of his death, there were thousands of monks in eleven monasteries in a radius of sixty miles along the Nile River. A century later there were nearly fifty thousand monks in the area. As part of their daily regimen, these monks read and memorized the Scriptures—especially the New Testament and Psalms. Pachomius himself took an active role in this practice in that he read the Scriptures aloud to his first congregation (i.e., he was the lector). Since Pachomius knew both Coptic and Greek (as did other monks in his monasteries), some of the monks must have read the Scriptures in both languages. Of course, more monks read Coptic than Greek, and with the passing of time (beginning in the fifth century) almost all read only Coptic.

Because the library in the Pachomian monastery started after 320, all earlier manuscripts—especially the New Testament papyri—must have been produced in other scriptoria and given to the library. The manuscripts dated in the fourth and fifth centuries are of two types: those that were the result of poor craftmanship and those that appear to have been done professionally. It is therefore quite likely that the poor monks produced some of their own poorly made books and that they were given professionally made manuscripts from an outside scriptorium—very likely from Alexandria, inasmuch as Athanasius from Alexandria often visited Pachomius's monastery.

Even if a link between certain New Testament manuscripts and an Alexandrian scriptorium cannot be established with certainty, we are certain that various second-century New Testament manuscripts were produced by professional scribes. These scribes may have worked in a Christian scriptorium or in a secular scriptorium—and then applied their skills to making a copy of New Testament books. Or these scribes, once trained in a scriptorium, could have been working in what Gamble has called "a writing center, where texts were copied by more than a single scribe."[30]Among the several professional-looking manuscripts, two manuscripts come to mind as being the most likely candidates for having been done in a scriptorium: $\mathfrak{P}^{46}$ and $\mathfrak{P}^{66}$. The scribe who produced $\mathfrak{P}^{46}$ was a professional scribe because there are stichoi notations at the end of several books (see the conclusion of Romans, 2 Corinthians, Ephesians, Philippians). The stichoi were used by professionals to note how many lines had been copied for commensurate pay. Most likely, an employee of the scriptorium paginated the codex and indicated the stichoi. The scribe himself made a few corrections as he went, and then several other readers made corrections here and there.[31] It is also fairly certain that $\mathfrak{P}^{66}$ was the product of a scriptorium or writing center. The first copyist of this manuscript had his work thoroughly checked by a diorthotes, according to a different exemplar—just the way it would happen in a scriptorium. Of course, it can be argued that an individual who purchased the manuscript made all the corrections, which was a common practice in ancient times. But the extent of corrections in $\mathfrak{P}^{66}$ and the fact that the paginator (a different scribe) made many of the corrections speaks against this (see description of $\mathfrak{P}^{66}$ in chap. 2). It was more the exception than the rule in ancient times that a manuscript would be fully checked by a diorthotes. $\mathfrak{P}^{66}$ has other markings of being professionally produced. The extant manuscript still shows the pinpricks in the corners of each leaf of the papyri; these served as a guide for left hand justification and right hand. The manuscript also exhibits a consistent set of marginal and interlinear correction signs. Another sign of professionally produced manuscript is the use of the diple (>) in the margin, which was used to signal a correction in the text and/or the need for a correction in the text. There are very few of these in the extant New Testament manuscripts. The scribe of 𝔓⁴⁸ used a diple to note a correction in Acts 23:27. (This is not a paragraphus marker, because there are no others in the MS and because Acts 23:27 is an odd place to begin a new paragraph. This needs to be corrected in *Text of Earliest MSS*, 354.) Another early manuscript, P. Oxyrhynchus 405, has diple markings. This manuscript preserves Matthew's record of Jesus' baptism in a portion of Irenaeus's *Against Heresies* 3.9, in which Matthew 3:16–17 is quoted. The account of Jesus' baptism, as recorded in Matthew 3:16–17, is repeated in the course of Irenaeus's argument; Matthew's text is designated in a special way—with a diple (>) at the beginning of each line of the quotation. If used according to standard scriptoral practice, such signs would indicate that the wording in this quote needed fixing (or, at least, checking). Unfortunately, the text is broken in half, but a careful transcriptional reconstruction reveals that this manuscript most likely concurs with ℵ and B (in excluding αυτω and the definite articles before πνευμα and θεου in Matt. 3:16).

Shared Features of Jewish and Christian Manuscripts

Before I conclude this section on Christian scriptoria and writing centers, I would suggest that some of the earliest Christian manuscripts could reveal the influence of Jewish scriptoral practices. If this link can be substantiated, then it stands to reason that the earliest Christian writing centers may have been—to some degree—carryovers from Jewish scriptoria. When one examines the Greek Old Testament manuscripts and the Christian Old Testament (and New Testament) manuscripts, we see some common features. For starters, we see the shared appearance of an enlarged letter at the beginning of each line. This could be attributed to Jewish influence, rather than to documentary (as is often done). This observation comes from Peter Parsons, who compared some of the documentary features of the Minor Prophet Scrolls from Nahal Hever with early Christian manuscripts. Parsons made these comments:

> Most of this material [in the Greek Minor Prophets] is documentary; but the comparison is rather appropriate, since the use of enlarged initials at line beginning . . . and phrase beginning . . . and (set out in the margin) to mark a new section . . . gives this manuscript a documentary look. The fact is itself remarkable. Early Christian books show the same characteristic; copies of the Greek classics do not. It has therefore been tempting to argue that the texts of the Early Church stood closer to the world of business than to that of literature, and to draw conclusions about the social milieu in which the texts circulated or the esteem in which they were held. Now we see the same thing in a Jewish manuscript of a pre-Christian date. This may suggest that the Christians inherited the practise, rather than inventing it.[32]

C. H. Roberts was of the same opinion, saying, "Documentary practise may not have been the only influence on Christian scribes." Roberts then goes on to explain that the Minor Prophets scrolls show this "enlarged letter, preceded by a small blank space, marking the beginning of a new phrase, while verses are marked off by larger spaces."[33]

As for Christian Old Testament manuscripts, the feature of the enlarged letter at the beginning of the line can be seen in several of Chester Beatty Greek Old Testament manuscripts: V (Gen.), VI (Num.-Deut.), VII (Isa.), VIII (Jer.), X (Dan.). In my examination of early New Testament manuscripts, I have seen this feature in the following papyri: $\mathfrak{P}^{13}$ (somewhat), $\mathfrak{P}^{23}$, $\mathfrak{P}^{32}$, $\mathfrak{P}^{46}$ (somewhat), $\mathfrak{P}^{53}$, $\mathfrak{P}^{70}$, $\mathfrak{P}^{72}$, $\mathfrak{P}^{78}$, $\mathfrak{P}^{90}$, and $\mathfrak{P}^{109}$. The second physical feature of New Testament manuscripts which may have been influenced from Jewish Greek Old Testament manuscripts is the invention of the nomen sacrum for *kurios* (Lord). As I will argue in chapter 4, it seems that the best explanation for this invention came from Christians producing copies of the Septuagint who then provided an alternative way to display the sacred title, YHWH. Instead of writing the Hebrew Tetragrammaton in a Greek text, they invented a Greek nomen sacrum, $\overline{\text{KC}}$ for denoting "LORD."

The Codex

Having spoken of some similarities between Jewish Old Testament manuscripts and Christian Old Testament manuscripts, we now come to a matter of significant distinction. In the making of books, Jews used scrolls, while Christians used codices—at least, Christians from the end of the first century and thereafter. The first-generation Christians, who were mostly Jews, probably read the Old Testament from scrolls. The founder of the Christian church, Jesus, is said to have read a passage in Isaiah from "a scroll" (Luke 4:17). Saul of Tarsus, in his Jewish training, would have used scrolls; later on, he likely switched to the codex format (this is discussed below).

Only a few extant manuscripts of the New Testament were written on scrolls ($\mathfrak{P}^{13}$, $\mathfrak{P}^{18}$, $\mathfrak{P}^{98}$), but all these papyri were written on the back of other existing writings. Thus, none of these works were originally composed in the scroll format. ($\mathfrak{P}^{22}$, written on a roll, is an oddity not yet explained.) All other New Testament manuscripts were written on codices. As far as we know, late first-century Christians and those thereafter used the codex. It is very likely that Christians abandoned the scroll in favor of the codex to make a distinction between their sacred writings and those of the Jews. This practice (which began either in Rome or Antioch) was a break with Judaism and shows a kind of uniformity in the formation and dissemination of the early text. The codex book form enabled Christians to place several books together in one volume, which was an impossiblity with the scroll. For example, only one Gospel or one of Paul's larger epistles (such as Romans) could fit on a scroll. Thus, the early Christians probably adopted the codex form in order to accommodate the placing together of all four Gospels and of all Paul's major epistles. Scholars such as T. C. Skeat and

Graham Stanton have provided convincing arguments that the Christians' adoption of the codex was motivated by a desire to establish the fourfold Gospel as the authoritative norm for the church.[34] But it seems just as likely that the codex was first adopted for the sake of placing all of Paul's major epistles (Romans-2 Thessalonians) into one volume—inasmuch as this was a sought-after and recognized collection in the life of the early church. Of particular note is the indication in 2 Peter 3:16–17 that Paul's writings (as a collection) were considered "Scripture" early in the life of the church.

Prior to the first century, writers used a form of the codex known as *tabula* in Latin and *codex* in Greek. According to Roberts and Skeat, this was a group of wooden tablets tied together, each of which had a wax surface protected by a surrounding wooden frame.[35] Writers would use these codices to make notes for one of four purposes: (1) to record the thoughts of others; (2) to keep extracts from other works; (3) to make personal notes; (4) to make notes for business purposes. A tax collector such as Matthew, accustomed to using such a codex for business notes, could have used such a wooden codex for taking notes on Jesus' speech. Mark could have done the same with Peter's speech. Writers also used another kind of notebook, called *membranae* in Latin and *membranas* in Greek (a Latin loanword). The Greeks did not invent any other word to describe a codex. Thus, *membranas* was the universal Greek term for the codex. In its earliest form, the codex was a notebook with parchments which allowed for erasing (see Martial's *Epistle* 14.7.184). These were used in much the same way as the wooden tablets: for making notes or rough drafts. They were very popular among lawyers and writers. Both of these codices were precursors to the full-formed papyrus codex.

A papyrus codex was constructed by folding one or more sheets of papyrus in the middle and sewing them together at the spine. This construction was most advantageous because (1) it enabled the scribe to write on both sides (most scrolls had writing on one side only); (2) it facilitated easier access to particular passages (as opposed to a scroll, which had to be unrolled); (3) it enabled the Christians to bind together all four Gospels (or any combination thereof) or all of Paul's epistles, etc.; and (4) it made it easier for any individual or local church to make its own volumes of the New Testament or any portion thereof. In short, the codex was a very practical book. Christians adopted it, just as others did, because it provided the most economical and practical means of publishing the Christian message. To add to this practicality and economy, Christians generally used papyrus codices instead of vellum or parchment, which were more expensive. Parchment codices were made for churches during the fourth century and thereafter because churches, no longer persecuted by the Roman government, could afford both to make and to keep such documents.

From the New Testament itself, we are given a few glimpses of what kind of writing materials the first-century Christians used. We know that the apostle John used papyrus when he wrote a short letter to a sister church. This is apparent in his closing statement to 2 John, where he says, "Although I have much to write to you, I would rather not use paper and ink; rather, I hope to come to you and talk with you face to face, so that our joy may be full" (v. 12). The Greek word for "paper" is *chartou*; it was customarily used to designate a sheet of papyrus. John's small letter probably covered no more than one sheet—written on the front and back. He would have used several sheets of papyrus to write his first epistle and many more (about forty) to write his Gospel. By way of interest, John's two short epistles also note that he used "pen" and "ink." The "pen" (Greek, *kalamus*) was a reed cut to a point and split like a quill pen (3 John 13). The ink (Greek *melanos*) was usually a black carbon (charcoal) mixed with gum or oil for use on parchment or mixed with a metallic substance for papyrus (2 John 12). It was kept in an inkhorn as a dried substance on which the scribe would dip or rub his moistened pen. In Paul's final epistle (2 Timothy), he gives a directive to Timothy that gives us some insight into what kind of writing materials he was using. He told Timothy to bring to him *ta biblia malista tas membranas*. This has been interpreted in various ways, three of which are quite significant:

1. Paul was asking for "the scrolls" (presumably copies of Old Testament books) and "the parchment codices" (presumably copies of various New Testament books—perhaps of Paul's epistles or the Gospels).

2. Paul was asking for "the books" (presumably copies of Old Testament and New Testament books) *and* "the parchments" (perhaps blank writing material or notebooks containing rough drafts).

Both of these interpretations understand that Paul was asking for two different kinds of documents. But another interpretation (espoused by Skeat) posits that *malista tas membranas* is a further definition of *ta biblia* because *malista* has a particularizing function.[36] Thus, the third interpretation:

3. Paul was asking for "his books—that is, his parchment notebooks" (which were codices—note the term *membranas).*

If this third interpretation is correct, it suggests that Paul was anxious to get some of his written notes or rough drafts he had left behind when he was arrested. Since he could have secured Old Testament writings from various sources, it stands to reason that he would have been anxious to have his collection of epistles and/or his writings not yet published. Of course, this is conjectural. This much we can be sure of: Paul was using codices, whether in completed book form or in notebook form. And since Paul himself made mention of codices, it stands to reason that Paul's epistles were the first to be collected into codex form. Before I conclude this section, I should note that another New Testament passage could very likely involve a codex. In the book of Revelation, there is mention of a special book, which only Jesus, the Lamb of God, is worthy to open (5:1–9). Most scholars have thought that this book was a scroll, but it is just as likely that it was a codex—for three reasons:

1. The book is said to be located "on" (Greek, *epi*) Jesus' right hand. This suggests a codex far more than a scroll, which would be grasped "in" (Greek, *en*) one's hand.

2. The book is said to have writing on the inside and on the outside. Some scrolls did have writing on both sides; they were called opisthographs. But this was rare because the unrolling of the scroll would wear off the letters on the outside. The codex form suits writing on both sides perfectly; in fact, that is what a codex was designed for.

3. A scroll hardly suits the scenario in which one broken seal after another (up to seven seals) reveals one revelation after another, as is the case when each seal is broken in the following chapters of Revelation. If it were a scroll, it could not be opened until all the seals were removed. In a codex, however, removing each seal would enable the book to be opened sequentially—quarto by quarto (or, to use a modern publishing term, "signature by signature"—a group of twelve pages or sixteen pages).[37] I would not want to be dogmatic on this view, but at least it must be posited that the book in Revelation 5 is just as likely a codex as it is a scroll.

The Earliest Christian Codices

We can surmise that the codex was in use by the end of the first century and that it was being used by Christians before and after the turn of the first century.[38] This evaluation is based on the fact that all of the earliest extant Christian manuscripts were produced in codex form. These manuscripts include Old Testament texts (for Christian use), New Testament texts, noncanonical writings, the writings of the church fathers, and other theological pieces. As will be fully discussed in chapter 4, we can tell that a Greek Old Testament manuscript is of Christian origin, as opposed to Jewish, by the presence of nomina sacra (as opposed to the Tetragrammaton). Many of these manuscripts are listed by C. H. Roberts in his seminal work *Manuscript, Society, and Belief in Early Christian Egypt* (13–14). Others are listed in van Haelst's *Catalogue des Papyrus Litteraires Juifs et Chretiens* (noted below by H). I list them below with brief comments. A detailed discussion about the dates of all these second-century manuscripts is found in chapter 3 (with accompanying bibliography).

Christian Old Testament Codices

1. P. Yale 1, Genesis (H 12). This was dated ca. AD 80–100 by Welles, who produced the *editio princeps*. If this dating is accurate, it is the earliest copy of any Christian manuscript. Other scholars, however, date it to the second century.

2. P. Baden 4.56 (P. Heidelberg inv. 8), Exodus and Deuteronomy (H 33). The editor of the *editio princeps*, Turner, dated it to the second century; so also van Haelst.

3. P. Chester Beatty VI, Numbers and Deuteronomy (H 52). The editor of the *editio princeps*, Kenyon, dated it to ca. 150. In this dating, he was supported by H. I. Bell, Wilhelm Schubart, U. Wilcken, who dated it "second century." Seider dated it to the middle of the second century.

4. P. Antinoopolis 7, Psalms (H 179). The editor of the *editio princeps*, H. I. Bell, dated this to the second century.

5. P. Leipzig inv. 170, Psalms (H 224). This was dated by C. H. Roberts to the second century.

6. Bodleian Gr. Bib. g. 5, Psalms (H 151). The editors of the *editio princeps*, Barns and Kilpatrick, dated it to the second century.

7. P. Oxyrhynchus 656, Genesis (H 13). The editors of the *editio princeps*, Grenfell and Hunt, noted that its style completely accords with second-century manuscripts; but they dated the manuscript to the third century—on the basis that they did not think that the codex was in existence until the late second or early third century. Bell and Skeat redated P. Oxy. 656 to the late second century.

8. P. Oxyrhynchus 1074, Exodus (H 40). The editors of the *editio princeps*, Grenfell and Hunt, said, "This hand could not be referred to a time later than the reign of Diocletian, and might well be placed at the beginning of the third century or even earlier." W. Schubart dated it as "second century."

9. Chester Beatty Papyrus VIII, Jeremiah (H 304). The editor of the *editio princeps*, Kenyon, dated it "second or second/third." Roberts dated it "second century."

10. Chester Beatty Papyrus IX, Ezekiel, Daniel, Esther (H 315). The editor of the *editio princeps*, Kenyon, cited Wilcken as dating it in the second century, though Kenyon himself said "there is no reason to place it later than the first half of the third."

Early New Testament Codices

If one were to go by the Alands' dating of the New Testament manuscripts, there would be only three documents dated to the second century: $\mathfrak{P}^{52}$, $\mathfrak{P}^{90}$, and $\mathfrak{P}^{104}$. $\mathfrak{P}^{98}$ is listed in the second century but with a question mark. Three other papyri are dated as ca. 200—namely, $\mathfrak{P}^{32}$, $\mathfrak{P}^{46}$, and $\mathfrak{P}^{66}$.[39] But in the opinion of various paleographers, these dates are too conservative. In recent years, paleographic studies have placed far more papyri in the second century (a detailed discussion concerning this dating is found in chap. 2). These manuscripts are as follows:

1. $\mathfrak{P}^{4}$+$\mathfrak{P}^{64}$+$\mathfrak{P}^{67}$ (Suppl. Gr. 1120 + Gr. 17 + P. Barceloa 1), Matthew and Luke. This manuscript belongs to the third quarter of the second century, as assigned by T. C. Skeat and others.

2. $\mathfrak{P}^{32}$ (P. Rylands 5), Titus. This manuscript belongs to the second century, as assigned by T. C. Skeat and others.

3. $\mathfrak{P}^{46}$ (Chester Beatty II), Paul's major epistles (lacking Pastorals). This manuscript, usually dated ca. 200, is probably earlier, according to Wilckens, Kim, and me.

4. $\mathfrak{P}^{52}$ (P. Rylands 457), John 18. This manuscript has been hailed as the earliest extant witness of the New Testament (ca. 115–125) by a host of paleographers, such as Roberts (the editor of the *editio princeps*), Bell, Turner, Cavallo.

5. $\mathfrak{P}^{66}$ (P. Bodmer II), John. This manuscript, usually dated as ca. 200, has been dated to the mid-second century by paleographers such as Hunger, Cavallo, and Seider.

6. $\mathfrak{P}^{77}$ (P. Oxy. 2683 + P. Oxy. 4405), Matthew 23. This manuscript was dated as late second century by Roberts, the editor of the *editio princeps*.

7. $\mathfrak{P}^{90}$ (P. Oxy. 3523), John 18–19. This manuscript was dated as late second century by T. C. Skeat, the editor of the *editio princeps*.

8. $\mathfrak{P}^{98}$ (P. IFAO inv. 237b), Revelation 1. This manuscript was dated as late second century by Wagner, the editor of the *editio princeps*.

9. $\mathfrak{P}^{103}$ (P. Oxy. 4403). This manuscript was dated as late second century by Thomas, the editor of the *editio princeps*. The manuscript may be part of the same codex as $\mathfrak{P}^{77}$. If not, it certainly appears to be the work of the same scribe.

10. $\mathfrak{P}^{104}$ (P. Oxy. 4404). This manuscript was dated as late second century by Thomas, the editor of the *editio princeps*.

Other Christian Codices of the Second Century[40]

1. P. Egerton 2, Unknown Gospel. This gospel was probably composed around 120–130, yet the copy which was discovered could be not later than 150. It bears remarkable resemblance to $\mathfrak{P}^{52}$.[41]

2. P. Oxyrhynchus 1, Gospel of Thomas. Grenfell and Hunt dated it to the second or third century. H. I. Bell said that the earlier date is not at all unlikely. C. H. Roberts placed it in the second century.[42]

3. P. Geneva 253, Christian Homily. This is a late second-century Christian homily, containing portions of Matthew 10:11–13, 29–31 (or Luke 10:5–6; 12:6–7).[43]

4. P. Oxyrhynchus 406, Theological Treatise? This is a codex dated ca. 200 preserving either a portion of a theological treatise or an unknown New Testament epistle.[44]

The above lists of Christian Old Testament codices, New Testament codices, and other Christian codices help us realize that Christians were using the codex in the early second century, and very likely before. Only one Christian manuscript (P. Oxyrhynchus 405) has been found that was produced in scroll form (excluding, of course, those manuscripts that were written on the back of scrolls). This demonstrates that Christians had purposely and universally separated ties with the Jewish form of the book—the scroll. This also indicates that there was a kind of standard for Christian bookmaking, and thereby tells us that individuals were not acting independently.

The Codex and New Testament Collections

With the advent of the codex before the end of the first century, Christians had a convenient book format for producing single-book volumes or multibook volumes. Because of the fragmentary nature of many of the extant early manuscripts, it is difficult to determine if they originally came from a single-book codex or a multibook codex. However, some of the extant papyri provide enough evidence to make this determination. Extant pagination numerals, multiple folios, and/or whole codices provide the evidence.

Before we consider the various collections, it is important to know that certain manuscripts (usually listed as single entities) actually belonged to the same codex. If one looks at the list of the papyri in the appendix to NA^{27}, there are only two combinations of manuscripts cited: $\mathfrak{P}^{33+}\mathfrak{P}^{58}$ and $\mathfrak{P}^{64+}\mathfrak{P}^{67}$. This is incomplete. The list should include $\mathfrak{P}^{4+}\mathfrak{P}^{64+}\mathfrak{P}^{67}$, $\mathfrak{P}^{15+}\mathfrak{P}^{16}$, $\mathfrak{P}^{49+}\mathfrak{P}^{65}$, and probably $\mathfrak{P}^{77+}\mathfrak{P}^{103}$.[45] These book combinations add to the list of New Testament papyri that contain more than one book.

The Gospels

From the extant manuscript evidence, it can be determined that Gospel manuscripts circulated as individual Gospels. We know this because individual Gospels in codex form are preserved in several early manuscripts, as follows:

$\mathfrak{P}^{1}$ (Matthew)—pagination. The first page of this manuscript displays an alpha at the top header of the recto, signaling the first page. A beta follows on the verso. These could be the beginning pages of a single Gospel codex or the beginning of a multiple Gospel collection, with Matthew coming first.

$\mathfrak{P}^{5}$ (John)—folio format. The extant folio format makes it clear that this was a single Gospel codex. (For details, see *Text of Earliest MSS*, 73).

$\mathfrak{P}^{39}$ (John)—pagination. The pagination of this codex, oδ [= 74] on the recto of the extant sheet, and the large sumptuous calligraphy indicate that this was a single-Gospel codex of John.

$\mathfrak{P}^{66}$ (John)—extant codex. The extant manuscript was found as a single codex of John's Gospel.

$\mathfrak{P}^{106}$ (John)—pagination. The extant pagination of this manuscript, gamma [= 3] on the recto and delta [= 4] on the verso, indicates that this was probably a single codex of John's Gospel—unless, of course, other Gospels followed John.

Because the Gospels were individual publications from their inception, it took a while for a collection of these four books to be made. The collecting process was earlier for Paul's epistles (see discussion below). During the first and early second centuries, each Gospel primarily had its own independent life. But by the middle of the second century, it appears that churches or individuals began to make codex collections of the Gospels. Various church fathers, such as Justin Martyr and Irenaeus, were speaking of a fourfold Gospel collection in the second century.

Early Gospel collections are found in the following second- and third-century manuscripts:

$\mathfrak{P}^{4+}\mathfrak{P}^{64+}\mathfrak{P}^{67}$ (with Matthew and Luke—and perhaps all four originally, as argued by Skeat)[46]

$\mathfrak{P}^{75}$ (Luke, John)

0171 (Matthew and Luke).

Gospel collections (exclusive of any other books) continue in the subsequent centuries, as is evidenced by codex W (the Freer Gospels—all four, ca. 400), codex N (fifth century), codex Q (fifth century), codex T (fifth century), 042 (sixth century), 043 (sixth century), 067 (fifth century), 070 (sixth century), 078 (sixth century), 087 (6th century), and 083 (sixth-seventh century)

Gospels plus Acts collections are preserved in $\mathfrak{P}^{45}$ (all four Gospels and Acts) and $\mathfrak{P}^{53}$ (Matthew and Acts). Other extant Gospel manuscripts could have come from Gospel collections, but we have no way of knowing this—unless pagination numerals are preserved.

This documentation shows that the Gospels in the second century were being circulated as individual books and as collected books. The same pattern happened in the third century. By the time we get to the fourth century, it is likely that most church codices contained all four Gospels. Such is the case for Codex Siniaticus, Codex Vaticanus, and the Freer Gospels.

Paul's Epistles

As Paul's epistles circulated to various churches, neighboring churches began to collect copies of epistles he had written to a neighboring church. This is implicit in Colossians 4:16, wherein Paul asked the church in Colossae to exchange epistles with the neighboring Laodicean church. Most likely, the epistle "from Laodicea" mentioned in Colossians 4:16 is the epistle we call Ephesians, which was an encyclical intended for all the churches in that area, including Laodicea, Colossae, Ephesus. Paul's language indicates that this epistle would be coming *from* Laodicea to Colossae—and then probably on to Ephesus, its final destination. In any event, this exchange implies that each church made a copy of their own epistle before sending it on. Paul's epistles were originally sent to the various churches under his ministry: Rome, Corinth, Thessalonica, Philippi, churches in Galatia, and churches in Asia Minor (including Ephesus and Colossae). These churches would have kept the original manuscript, from which copies would be made for other nearby churches.

Paul himself probably kept copies of his own epistles. This was usual practice in those days. Having done a study of letter collections published in antiquity, Trobisch was able "to uncover typical patterns of how letter collections grow." He "found that almost all of them originate from the author, who would often publish more than one collection of selected letters."[47] As previously mentioned, Paul's statement to Timothy in 2 Timothy 4:13 suggests that when Paul asked Timothy to bring him his books, most especially, his parchment notebooks (which were codices), Paul was asking for copies of his epistles, not Old Testament scrolls. While in prison prior to his execution, Paul could have spent his time putting together a collection of his epistles.

Paul had always had a publishing plan. He kept track of the letters he had written to various churches (see 1 Cor. 5:7; 2 Cor. 7:8); he urged the churches to accept his writings as apostolic truth by the way he appealed to his apostolic position at the beginning of each letter (see the opening verses of all the major epistles); and he signed off his letters with his own hand to give them his personal signatorial authority (see Gal. 6:11; 2 Thess. 3:17). His epistles were his way of disseminating the revelations Christ had given him. He urged his readers to pay attention to what he wrote (Eph. 3:1–6), to accept it as the word of God (1 Thess 2:13), and to not accept anyone who taught differently (Gal 1:6–9). He also urged his younger coworkers, such as Timothy, to guard the deposit he had entrusted to them—both his life and words (2 Tim. 1:12–14). How else could these words be guarded if they were not written, published, and circulated to all the churches? Thus, it stands to reason that Paul took care to complete his collection prior to his death.

However, it is also possible that someone in Paul's circle, after Paul's death, collected his epistles into one corpus, which would include Romans, 1 and 2 Corinthians, Ephesians, Galatians, Philippians, Colossians, Philemon, 1 and 2 Thessalonians, and perhaps Hebrews (thought by many to be Pauline)—but not the Pastoral Epistles, which were intended for private use, not public. The collector or compiler could have been Luke or Timothy. Moule argued for Luke, saying "It is entirely in keeping with his historian's temperament to collect them."[48] But it is far more likely that it was Timothy. After all, he is the stated coauthor of several of the epistles: 2 Corinthians, Philippians, Colossians, 1 and 2 Thessalonians, and Philemon. This would have put him in an excellent position to be the collector of Paul's writings. Timothy was also the recipient of two epistles, 1 and 2 Timothy, and Timothy was the one whom Paul directed to get "his books, most especially the parchment codices" and bring them to Paul while he was in prison (2 Tim. 4:13). It is quite possible that Timothy did not get to Paul before his execution. This would mean that Timothy would be the keeper of Paul's books and writings. Even if he did reach Paul in time, Timothy would have been the one to keep the collection.

As was just mentioned, Paul had charged Timothy "to guard the deposit" that Paul had given to him—to pass on to the next generation of teachers the sacred trust. This "deposit" included Paul's apostolic life and words (see 2 Tim. 1:12–14). One primary way to "guard" Paul's words was to preserve his writings. Thus, Timothy may have felt obligated to collect Paul's writings so that his teaching could be passed on from generation to generation. Furthermore, Timothy had been charged by Paul to make public readings of the Scripture in the church meetings. This would have meant that

Timothy was a lector for the church, and as a lector he would have naturally kept copies of Paul's writings.

Timothy would not have included the two epistles addressed to him personally when he made the Pauline corpus because these were private letters and not intended for the general church audience. It is for this same reason that the Epistle to Titus was not included. It is quite possible, even likely, that Timothy did not even know about this private epistle. In later years it surfaced and then became part of the Pauline collection. The earliest physical evidence of Paul's Epistle to Titus is found in $\mathfrak{P}^{32}$ (dated mid to late second century). The Epistle to Philemon was included in the original Pauline corpus because it was not a private letter. This document was not just a personal note from Paul to Philemon, his friend; it was addressed to Philemon, to Apphia (presumably Philemon's wife), to Archippus, and to the congregation of believers that met in Philemon's house (vv. 1–2).

Whoever the collector of Paul's epistles was (Luke or Timothy), he also may have taken on the role of a compiling editor who arranged all of Paul's writings into one corpus. For example, this compiler could have connected Paul's third epistle to the Corinthians (2 Cor. 10–13) to the fourth (2 Cor. 1–9). But it is very unlikely that the compiler would have changed Paul's original wording because the original, individual manuscripts (or early copies thereof) still would have been in existence in various local churches; therefore, any individual who had read Paul's original work could have exposed the redacted work as fraudulent.

In any event, Paul's epistles were being collected between AD 60 and 100. The earliest date for the collection comes from the reference in 2 Peter 3:15–16, which indicates a well-known collection of Paul's writings that are categorized as "Scripture." If Peter authored 2 Peter, this had to have been written before Peter's death in AD 66/67. If 2 Peter was published posthumously, then we have a later date. Either way, the reference in 2 Peter 3:15–16 tells us that Paul's epistles were being collected and read in many churches during the second half of the first century. Zuntz was confident that there was a Pauline corpus by AD 100.[49] Gamble also argued that the Pauline collection was assembled by the end of the first century and that it was circulating among several churches in codex form before the circulation of the fourfold Gospel in codex form.[50] The earliest manuscript evidence for a Pauline collection comes from $\mathfrak{P}^{46}$. Kenyon dated it AD 200, but that is too late. Kim dated it ca. 85, but that is too early. I would date it around 150 (see comments in chap. 2). $\mathfrak{P}^{46}$ has all of Paul's church epistles and Hebrews in one volume. The extant manuscript preserves Romans 5:17 through 1 Thessalonians 5:28 (with Hebrews following Romans). The lost leaves on the front end of the codex (seven leaves = 14 pages) would have been filled by Romans 1:1–5:16. The seven leaves (= 14 pages) on the back end would have easily been filled by 2 Thessalonians and Philemon, with about nine pages left blank. This amount is too small to have accommodated all the Pastoral Epistles (1 Tim.,

2 Tim., Titus), even if the scribe attempted to fit more letters per page. Of course, the scribe could have added another two leaves (= 8 pages) at the end of the codex to accomodate all three Pastoral Epistles. Such a practice is not unheard of, but is rare. The more usual practice is to add one leaf, not two, if and when the scribe realized he was running out of room. The long and short of this is that we cannot be certain that $\mathfrak{P}^{46}$ did contain the Pastoral Epistles or did not contain them.[51] The earliest extant codex to display unquestionably all of Paul's major epistles and Hebrews, Philemon, and the Pastorals is codex I of the early fifth century.

Various second-century and third-century papyrus codices, though extant in fragmented form, indicate the early formation of a Pauline collection:

$\mathfrak{P}^{13}$ Hebrews (the pagination indicates that another epistle originally preceded it—probably Romans, as in $\mathfrak{P}^{46}$)

$\mathfrak{P}^{15+}\mathfrak{P}^{16}$ (from the same codex preserving portions of 1 Cor. and Phil.)

$\mathfrak{P}^{30}$ (preserving portions of 1 Thess. and 2 Thess.)

$\mathfrak{P}^{49+}\mathfrak{P}^{65}$ (from the same codex preserving portions of Eph. and 1 Thess.)

$\mathfrak{P}^{92}$ (preserving portions of Eph. and 2 Thess.)

The existence of second-century and third-century Pauline codices affirms the theory proposed by Zuntz that a Pauline corpus was formulated by AD 100. Thereafter, most of Paul's letters would have been copied as part of a collection, and not as individual letters. Thus, the rest of the extant Pauline manuscripts, though showing only one epistle, were probably part of a collection, but we have no way of knowing for sure unless there are clues left such as pagination and codex format. Collections of Pauline Letters, as individual volumes (exclusive of other books of the New Testament), continue to appear in the following centuries, as evidenced in codex I (5th century), 0208 (6th century), and 0209 (7th century).

Paul's epistles and the four Gospels formed the primary canon for the New Testament text read by Christians in the first two centuries of the church. This is not to say that other Christians, here and there, were not reading the other books of the New Testament—books such as Acts, the General Epistles, and Revelation. Believers were reading these books, but they were not as widely known as Paul's epistles and the four Gospels.

Collections of the Other New Testament Writings

The way was paved for a New Testament canon early in the church age by the fact that various books were being collected by congregations—especially Paul's epistles and the four Gospels. Because the Gospels were individual publications from their inception, it took a while for a collection of these four books to be made. The collecting process was quicker for Paul's epistles.

The other books took longer to make their way into the New Testament canon. This was true primarily because they were not so conveniently grouped together as were the Gospels or Paul's epistles. In time, however, collections of other books occurred.

The Book of Hebrews.——Early Christians in the East (especially in Egypt) considered the book of Hebrews to be part of the Pauline writings. So Hebrews was included in the Pauline corpus. This is evident in the second-century manuscript $\mathfrak{P}^{46}$, where Hebrews immediately follows Romans and precedes 1 Corinthians. The copyist of another papyrus manuscript, $\mathfrak{P}^{13}$, may have used an exemplar formatted like $\mathfrak{P}^{46}$, for the pagination in $\mathfrak{P}^{13}$ indicates that another book (the length of Romans) preceded Hebrews. One of the recently published papyri, $\mathfrak{P}^{114}$, may have been an individual codex of Hebrews because the extant leaf preserves what seems to have been a title page followed by the opening chapter of Hebrews. But it is also possible that $\mathfrak{P}^{114}$ could have been the first part of a Pauline codex, which placed Hebrews first.

The Book of Acts and the General Epistles (Praxapostolos).——The General Epistles were not collected in the early centuries of the church, as were the Gospels and Paul's epistles. Nonetheless, they had some individual circulation. The Epistle of James has been preserved in three third-century manuscripts: $\mathfrak{P}^{20}$, $\mathfrak{P}^{23}$, and $\mathfrak{P}^{100}$. Peter's first epistle was accepted from the onset as authentic; it was quite well preserved in its early textual transmission. This textual fidelity is manifest in one late third-century manuscript, $\mathfrak{P}^{72}$ (Papyrus Bodmer VII–VIII), and another fourth-century manuscript, $\mathfrak{P}^{81}$.

The original text of 2 Peter and Jude was not as well preserved in the early period of textual transmission because these books were not readily acknowledged as apostolic by all sectors of the early church. Manuscript evidence for these books is quite diverse and marked by independence. This is evident in the two papyri, $\mathfrak{P}^{72}$ (especially for Jude) and $\mathfrak{P}^{78}$.

Unlike John's Gospel, which was very popular throughout the early church, John's epistles were far less known and read. A portion of 1 John exists in one third-century papyrus, $\mathfrak{P}^{9}$ (a product of careless copying), and a portion of 2 John exists in one fourth-century parchment manuscript, 0232 (P. Antinoopolis 12). This manuscript is an accurate copy of 2 John. The editor, C. H. Roberts, said the manuscript could have originally contained the Johannine corpus in the following order: Gospel, Revelation, Epistles. He calculated this on the basis that the pagination of 2 John is numbered as "164" and "165" and then noted that there are "approximately 400 words to the page."[52] This is wrong! There are about 350 letters (not words!) to the page, which means that about 57,000 letters preceded 2 John. This could accommodate about 9,000 words, the length of James, 1–2 Peter, Jude, and 1 John. Probably, 3 John followed 2 John in this codex. As such, 0232 is the earliest extant witness to a collection of General Epistles, not a Johannine collection.

The book of Acts got separated from its companion volume, the Gospel of Luke, when Luke was attached to the other three Gospels. Thereafter, Acts went its separate way. There is one third-century codex ($\mathfrak{P}^{38}$), whose pagination (page "59" for Acts 19) indicates that this was a single codex of Acts. Eventually, the book of Acts and the General Epistles became companions—beginning in the fourth century. This combination, known as Praxapostolos, is displayed in the book arrangement of Codex Bezae (ca. 400), in 0166 (Acts and James, of the 5th century), in 093 (6th century), and in one important papyrus manuscript, $\mathfrak{P}^{74}$, Papyrus Bodmer XVII (from the seventh century). Codex 048 (5th century) contains the Praxapostolos and Pauline Epistles, thereby showing a bringing together of two separate collections into one codex.

Acts and the General Epistles suffered a rocky road on their way into the New Testament canon. Many Christians in the first three to four centuries did not know of these writings and/or did not use them. Thus, their textual history is spotty, and their transmission is somewhat erratic.[53]

The Book of Revelation.—The early textual history of Revelation is not very clear. It seems that many of the major churches had difficulty receiving it as a canonical work anytime before the fourth century. Nonetheless, individual Christians continued to read it and make copies of it. What is remarkable is that nearly all of our early, extant copies of Revelation were evidently not produced by highly trained writers, which strongly suggests that their copies of Revelation were not intended for church use but for private use. This is most evident in the second-century manuscript $\mathfrak{P}^{98}$, as well as in the two manuscripts of the third century, $\mathfrak{P}^{18}$ and $\mathfrak{P}^{24}$. The Chester Beatty manuscript, $\mathfrak{P}^{47}$, also shows that it was the work of one who did not normally produce literary manuscripts. The only early manuscript of Revelation to reveal that it was produced by one trained in writing documents is the recently published papyrus, $\mathfrak{P}^{115}$ (dated to the third century). I would call the hand "reformed documentary."

Book Collections and Canonization

The fact that the early Christian churches were making collections of the four Gospels—and only the four, as well as making collections of Paul's epistles (which often included Hebrews), shows that these works were considered canonized Scripture early in the history of the church. Since the collections were made for use in church meetings, these were the writings that the Christians deemed worthy of apostolic status—that is, they were the writings that formulated apostolic truth. In due course, the book of Acts and the General Epistles (the Praxapostolos) were given the same recognition. And the book of Revelation came last. Thus, the formation of the canon was a process, rather than an event, which took several hundred years to reach completion in all parts of the Roman Empire. Local canons were the basis for comparison, and out of them eventually emerged the general canon that exists in

Christendom today, although some of the Eastern churches have a New Testament that is slightly smaller than that accepted in the West. The twenty-seven books now included in the New Testament canon were first given notice (as far as we know) in what is called the *Muratorian Canon* (dated ca. 170). An eighth-century copy of this document was discovered and published in 1740 by the librarian L. A. Muratori. The manuscript is mutilated at both ends, but the remaining text names all twenty-seven books of the New Testament, while recording doubts about such books as 2 Peter, Jude, 2 and 3 John, and Revelation. Although we do not have such lists from the third century, the writings of the church fathers indicate the same inclusions and similar doubts about the same books. In the beginning of the fourth century, Eusebius was the chief proponent of establishing the four Gospels as well as other recognized books as comprising the New Testament canon. But it was not until the middle of the fourth century that the canon was established once and for all. In his *Festal Letter* for Easter (367), Athanasius of Alexandria included information designed to eliminate once and for all the use of certain apocryphal books. This letter, with its admonition, "Let no one add to these; let nothing be taken away," provides the earliest extant document which specifies the twenty-seven books without qualification. At the close of the century the Council of Carthage (397) decreed that "aside from the canonical Scriptures nothing is to be read in church under the Name of Divine Scriptures." This also lists the twenty-seven books of the New Testament as we have them today.

Significantly, from the fourth century we have codices containing all twenty-seven books of the Greek New Testament, usually bound together with the Greek Old Testament. This is evident in Codex Vaticanus, Codex Sinaiticus, Codex Ephraemi Rescriptus.[54]

The Distribution of Manuscripts

As we consider the publication and distribution of the New Testament books, it must be kept in mind that there is a great difference between the quantity of books published in ancient times as compared to the twenty-first century. In modern times, books are published in vast quantities by means of the printing press. In ancient times, most books were published by making one copy at a time. This was done manually by a scribe copying an exemplar (or what was called an *antigraph*). In some instances, a popular work—such as Homer's *Iliad* or the *Odyssey*—was "mass produced" by several scribes making one copy each, as the exemplar text was read to them by one master-reader. Later in Christian history during the Byzantine era, copies of the Bible were produced in the same manner by monks in monasteries. But in the early centuries of the church, most copies of the New Testament were produced one by one.

During the second half of the first century, copies of New Testament books were produced, distributed, and circulated (by making new copies) throughout the churches in the Roman Empire in a spontaneous manner. Various local churches were already collecting Paul's epistles written to other churches (Col. 4:16) and evidently making their own copies as early as AD 60. The four Gospels were also being collected in the beginning of the second century. Is it possible to make a reasonable guess concerning how many copies would have been produced and in circulation by the end of the third century? We may be able to do this for the Pauline Epistles and the four Gospels, but not for the other portions of the New Testament because their distribution was limited during this period.

The written publications of various New Testament books were not published and circulated as trade books would be; rather, they were published for circulation in the churches. This would mean that a number of copies of the original manuscript (the archetypal exemplar) would be made initially and then distributed to various churches. Production of New Testament manuscripts in the early centuries was somewhat slow because manuscripts were made on a one-by-one basis, as well as on a "per-need" basis. This means that when local churches needed copies, manuscripts were produced one at a time, usually by a person in the church who was a man or woman of letters—or at least, by one who knew how to write documents. Most of our manuscripts of the second and third centuries manifest this. However, there is some evidence of professionals (with "bookhands") working on manuscripts in the second century, as discussed above.

The circulation and distribution of manuscripts from one locality to the next was not necessarily a slow process, inasmuch as most of these manuscripts would have been hand-delivered, not sent via the Roman postal routes. The Roman postal system did not stress speed or regularity, and although the mail moved speedily over short distances, it could take weeks over long distances or over water. Usually the mail system of the emperors did not benefit the ordinary public; rather, it was an added tax burden. Wealthy families had their own slaves deliver mail; businesses employed letter carriers; and the poor asked traveling friends to carry messages.[55] This is how documents were circulated among the Christian churches. For example, a letter written by Christian leaders in Jerusalem to the churches of Asia Minor was hand-delivered and read by the apostles Judas Barsabbas and Silas (Acts 15:22–29). Later, Paul requested Timothy (1 Thess. 3:2), Tychicus (Col. 4:7, 9), and Epaphroditus (Phil. 2:25; 4:18) to serve as messengers for his letters. It also stands to reason that the *anggeloi* of the seven churches addressed in the book of Revelation were not divine "angels" (as so many commentators espouse), but were the seven "messengers" who took the book of Revelation to each of seven churches noted in chapters 1–3. In this way, the book of Revelation was initially distributed to seven churches in the Roman province of Asia (known as Asia Minor).

The Size of the Churches

Before we consider how many books (or collections) of the New Testament were distributed in the early centuries of the church, we need to explore just how large the church was in the first and second centuries. The church in Jerusalem, begun in AD 30, grew by leaps and bounds in its early days. Beginning with 120 faithful followers, three thousand more became believers on the day of Pentecost, two thousand more just a short while later, and then even thousands more shortly thereafter (see Acts 1:15; 2:41; 4:4; 5:14). Even though many of these believers fled Jerusalem due to persecution (Acts 8:1), there were still thousands of believers in Jerusalem in the mid-50s (see Acts 21:20). Estimates of Jerusalem's population at this time range from twenty-five thousand to eighty-five thousand. Josephus recorded that there were a total of six thousand Pharisees in Palestine. Thus, a total of five thousand Jewish Christian men (not counting women and children) was a very high percentage of the population! At the same time, there were multitudes of believers in Judea, Galilee, and Samaria—due to the diaspora created by the persecution in Jerusalem and to many new converts (see Acts 8:1; 9:31). Many who became believers on the day of Pentecost had been assembled in Jerusalem from across the Greco-Roman world. As Luke put it, there were "Parthians, Medes, Elamites, people from Mesopotamia, Judea, Cappadocia, Pontus, the province of Asia, Phrygia, Pamphylia, Egypt, and the areas of Libya toward Cyrene, visitors from Rome (both Jews and converts to Judaism), Cretans, and Arabians" (Acts 1:9–11 NLT). Some of the new believers stayed in Jerusalem, but others traveled back to their homes, undoubtedly taking the gospel with them. Evidently, this is how the church in Rome began; it was not started by any of the twelve apostles or the apostle Paul. Some individuals must have brought the gospel there, and the church started to grow. It is possible that Andronicus and Junia (or "Julia" in some manuscripts, Rom. 16:7) were the apostles who raised up the church in Rome. Paul says they became apostles before he did, which means they must have become apostles before AD 32/33. As apostles, they must have witnessed Christ's ministry and seen the risen Christ. In any event, by the year AD 49 there must have been a significant number of Jewish Christians in Rome, for the Roman historian Suetonius mentions that Claudius's edict to expel Jews from Rome was prompted by too much fervor over one called "Chrestus" (= Christ). Suetonius wrote, "Because the Jews of Rome were indulging in constant riots at the instigation of Chrestus he [Claudius] expelled them from the city" (*Claudius* 25.4). The writer could easily have been uncertain of the spelling, because "Chrestus" (meaning "kind one" or "useful one"), a common slave name, was pronounced virtually the same as "Christus." It appears that Suetonius sought to convey to his readers that Chrestus was the founder of a movement (presumably Christianity). Luke related that Aquila and Priscilla were among those who had been ordered to leave the imperial city (Acts 18:2), and they were already Christians by the time they met Paul. Therefore, it stands to reason that Jews and Jewish-Christians had been expelled from Rome.

By the time Paul wrote to Romans (AD 56/57), there is evidence of at least five meeting places or house churches in the city (see Rom. 16:5, 10–11, 14–15), which had a population of nearly one million. When the persecutions instigated by Nero broke out against the Christians in AD 64–68, historians such as Tacitus spoke of an "immense multitude" of Christians that perished in the persecution (*Annals* 15.44.2–8). Clement, refering to the same persecution, also mentions a "vast multitude of the elect" (*Epistle to the Corinthians,* chap. 6). By the end of the first century, one must figure that the Christians would have had several copies of the Pauline corpus and the four Gospels to serve the growing Christian communities.

The church in Egypt must have also been started by new believers returning from Jerusalem to Egypt after their conversion at Pentecost. The earliest reference we have to an Egyptian Christian is found in Acts 18:24–25, where we are told about Apollos, the Alexandrian, who "had been instructed in the way of the Lord [i.e., the Lord Jesus]" before coming to Ephesus. Some "Western" manuscripts (D it^{gig}) have an alternate reading: "He had been instructed in his own country in the word of the Lord." Even though this reading is not original, "the implication of the statement no doubt accords with historical fact"[56] and thereby suggests that Christianity had come to Alexandria by AD 50. The text, without the "Western" addition, also implies that Apollos must have received instruction in the way of the Lord Jesus before he came to Asia.

The church in Alexandria had a tremendous basis for growth because Alexandria had a large Jewish population with connections in Jerusalem and Palestine. The Jewish population was so large that scholars are convinced that the Jews occupied one quarter of the city. Although we have no records of the church there in the first century, the evidence of a thriving church community and Christian academy in the second century points to a previous, fertile beginning.

Ephesus (with the surrounding churches) also must have had a substantially large church. Paul had used this city to commence a significant ministry (see Acts 19:10). And according to what we can gather from 1 and 2 Timothy (Paul's letters to Timothy, who was a leader in Ephesus), the church must have been substantial. We know that the church had elders, deacons, a large group of widows (some of whom were on the waiting list to get church support), young women, older men, young men, many faithful believers, and some heretics. Interestingly, it is in connection with Ephesus and neighboring Colossae that we first hear of the churches making copies of Paul's epistles (see Col. 4:16). According to Irenaeus, the apostle John, after his exile on the island of Patmos (Rev. 1:9), returned to live in Ephesus until the time of the emperor Trajan (AD 98–117). John's epistles would have gone to this church and to the churches in the area. This is affirmed by the fact that the book of Revelation was addressed to the seven churches in that area (the Roman province of Asia), one of which was Ephesus. Antioch of Syria was also a very large, significant church. Jerusalem Christians fled to Antioch to escape persecution (Acts 11:19). The church there grew strong under the teaching of men like Barnabas and Paul. The term *Christians* was first used in Antioch (11:26)—by outsiders. Acts 13 records that the first missionaries were sent from there. The Jerusalem church council's statement on requirements for Gentile believers was in part a result of the work in Antioch among Gentiles (see Acts 15 and Gal. 2). We know from church history that Antioch continued to be a significant center in the early centuries of the church.

The growth of the churches in Rome, Alexandria, Ephesus, and Antioch was probably typical of other major areas in the Greco-Roman world. Such was the case in Bithynia (north of the Roman province of Asia, addressed in 1 Pet. 1:1) at the beginning of the second century. Pliny the Younger, the Roman governor of Bithynia, writing to Trajan around AD 112, asked Trajan for advice on how to proceed with the persecution against Christians. He wrote:

> The matter seemed to me worth deliberation, especially on account of the number of those in danger; for many of all ages and every rank, and also of both sexes are brought into present or future danger. The contagion of that superstition has penetrated not the cities only, but the villages and the country. (Ep. 96.1–9)

This letter, written by an unbeliever, indicates the tremendous spread of Christianity—even in an area that had not been visited by the apostle Paul (see Acts 16:7).

By the mid-second century, Justin Martyr said, "There is no people, Greek or barbarian, or of any other race, by whatsoever appellation or manners they may be distinguished, however ignorant of arts or agriculture, whether they dwell in tents or wander about in covered wagons—among whom prayers and thanksgivings are not offered in the name of the crucified Jesus to the Father and Creator of all things."

This statement would be considered an exaggeration if Justin was speaking of the entire globe, but hardly so if he was speaking of the Greco-Roman world. By the end of the second century, there was a church in almost every major city. We know this because we have a fairly good idea about how many churches were established in the Roman Empire in the first two centuries. The churches that were established in the first century are as follows (grouped regionally):

- Jerusalem, Joppa, Gaza, Pella, Caesarea, Capernaum, Tyre, Sidon, Ptolemais
- Alexandria, Memphis, Babylon (in Egypt), Cyrene
- Tripolis, Paphos, Salamis, Antioch, Tarsus, Edessa, Derbe, Iconium, Lystra, Antioch in Pisidia, Sardis, Philadelphia, Laodicea, Colossae, Miletus, Ephesus, Pergamum, Thyatira, Troas
- Philippi, Apollonia, Thessalonica, Berea, Athens, Corinth, Cenchrea, Cnossus, Pompeii, Puteoli, Rome

The churches that were established in the second century are as follows (grouped regionally):

- Cirta, Lambesis, Madaaurus, Hadrumetum, Uthina, Carthage, Naueratis, Oxyrhynchus
- Jamnia, Neapolis, Philadelphia (east of Jerusalem), Bostra, Betsaida, Beirut, Laodicea (Syria), Apamea, Dura-Europos
- Commagene, Samsat, Malatya, Nisibis, Beit Zabde, Caesarea Mazaca, Ancyra, Amisus, Sinope, Ionopolis, Amastris, Nicomedia, Tralles, Magnesia
- Byzantium, Debeltum, Edessa, Larissa, Same, Sparta, Gortyna, Solona, Ostia, Antium, Syracuse, Vienne, Lyons, Trier, Mainz, Cologne, London, Leon, Astorga, Saragossa, Merida, Corduba, Hispalis

There were, of course, other churches in villages and the countryside. But these city churches totaled forty-three in the first century and another fifty-four in the second. Roughly, one hundred local churches were in existence by the year 200. It is not unreasonable to imagine that each church had one copy of the Pauline epistles by AD 80–100, as well as one copy of the four Gospels soon thereafter (at least by 120–150). The question is, How frequently would new copies of church manuscripts have been made? Normally, paleographers figure a period of twenty-five to fifty years when dating a literary text (written on the recto) given over to documentary use (on the verso). In other words, if the documentary text happens to supply a date of AD 175, paleographers figure that the literary text must be dated AD 125–150, inasmuch as the owner would not have surrendered a literary text to documentary use until the literary text had been well used. But copies of New Testament writings would have been used far more frequently, it would seem, than a literary text owned by an individual. Thus, I conjecture that new copies needed to be produced at least every twenty to twenty-five years, if not earlier. This would mean that the manuscript would have been used about a thousand times (52 times a year—on Sundays—for 20+ years) and become worn through use. Of course, a codex could have worn out earlier or later. This is a rough estimate.

Given a twenty-five year lifespan for a church codex, whether of Paul's epistles or of the four Gospels, it could be guessed that there would be about two hundred copies by the beginning of the second century. There would be an additional 250–300 church copies by the end of second century.

As was discussed before, the four Gospels were read in the churches by the end of the first century and beginning of the second. Individual Gospels were read during the 50s, 60s, 70s, and 80s. As such, a succession of manuscript copies for individual Gospels can begin with the 50s-60s, whereas the dating for a fourfold Gospel codex cannot begin before the 80s or 90s. Therefore, a succession of manuscript copies being produced every twenty years or so would have produced about 275 copies by the beginning of the second century. There would have been an additional 300 copies by the end of the second century. Again, this number is minimal, especially when it is understood that this number does not include personal copies or copies of individual Gospels. Taking these into consideration would probably double the number to 600 copies by the end of the second century. We have far more manuscripts from the third century, because far more new churches were born in the third century. But the numbers for the beginning of the second century and late second century are telling. The number of churches doubled in the third and fourth centuries. This means that there could have been over a thousand Gospel codices and a thousand Pauline epistle codices by the year 300.

Thus far, I have been speaking of copies made only for church use. We need also to consider that many copies were made for private use. Though many Christians in the early centuries depended on the oral reading of Scriptures to know what the New Testament says, there were many males, as well as a few females, who had been educated to the extent that they could both read and write. It is true that a number of excavated documents signed with an "X" indicate that there were many illiterates who depended upon scribes, but other documents show that there were many people trained to read and write for themselves.[57]

Some Christians, as literates, could read the Scriptures for themselves. They were educated, and they could afford copies of the Scriptures; so they also read the Scriptures in private. Some of the more wealthy Christians had Bibles copied at their own expense and then gave them to poorer brothers and sisters. For example, Pamphilus had Bibles copied to keep in stock for distribution to those in need (Jerome, *Against Rufinus* 1.9). And some of the writings of several early church fathers indicate Christians were encouraged to read the Scriptures in private. For example, Irenaeus encouraged the unrestricted use of Scripture (*Against Heresies* 5.20.2). Clement of Alexandria exhorted married couples to read the Scriptures together (*Paedagogus* 2.10.96), promoted personal study of Scripture (*Paedagogus* 3.12.87), and said that such reading should be done before the chief meal of the day (*Stromata* 7.7.49). Origen, who believed the Scriptures were accesible to all, spoke frequently of individuals reading Scriptures at home, as well as at church (*Homily on Genesis* 2.8), and recommended that Christians read the Old Testament Apocrypha, Psalms, Gospels, and Epistles (*Homily on Numbers* 27.10). Since many private copies of the New Testament or portions thereof were being made in the early centuries of the church, we cannot estimate the total number of copies in circulation. What we do know is that by the time we get to the Diocletian persecution, Roman authorities were well aware that there were many copies of New Testament Scriptures throughout the empire. Thus, Diocletian attempted to rid his empire of Christian sacred books and thereby rid the empire of Christianity. Diocletian believed the old Roman religion would help to reinforce imperial unity. His policy formed the background to the persecution against the Christians. An edict issued at Nicodemia on February 23, 303, enjoined the demolition of churches and the burning of Christian books. This was the first Roman persecution that was designed not only to destroy Christians but to eradicate their sacred text, the New Testament.

Eusebius, the first church historian, witnessed the persecution and wrote of the many atrocities committed by the Romans against Christians. He wrote, "All this [persecution] has been fulfilled in our day, when we saw with our own eyes, our houses of worship thrown down from their elevation, [and] the sacred Scriptures of inspiration committed to the flames in the midst of the markets" (*Ecclesiastical History* 8.2.1).

Those who were the most severely persecuted were the Christians living in Palestine, Egypt, and North Africa. Throughout the third century, Christians had secured permission from the government to purchase property and erect church buildings. These buildings were now demolished, and the property was confiscated. The church historian W. H. C. Frend wrote:

> No one in an official position in any part of the empire is recorded to have failed to carry out the emperor's orders. . . . All over the empire the authorities set about burning down Christian churches and collecting copies of Scriptures. In proconsular Africa, for which there is good documentation, the first thing people knew of the emperor's orders was the sight of churches going up in flames.[58]

Many Christians complied with the orders and handed over their copies of the Scriptures. However, some Christians kept their copies of the Scriptures from being destroyed. Leaders such as Felix, bishop of Thibiuca, refused to hand over the Scriptures and suffered martyrdom as a consequence. Other Christian leaders fooled the authorities by handing over heretical works or medical books. Others hid their texts.

In Africa, Alexandria was hit first and hardest. Bishop Peter fled from Alexandria to Oxyrhynchus. But the persecution followed him into rural Egypt. By the end of the third century we know that there were at least two Christian churches in Oxyrhynchus, Egypt—one in the north and and one in the south. These churches were probably destroyed in the persecution under Diocletian.[59] Hearing of the persecution in Alexandria and beyond, various Christians in rural Egypt would have done their best to get the New Testament manuscripts and other Christian writings out of their churches and hide them in their homes, in caves, or wherever else they could keep them from being confiscated by the authorities.

One Christian living in Coptos, Egypt, hid two treatises of Philo of Alexandria in a jar inside a hollow wall of his home. The codex had been stuffed with papyri fragments from Matthew and Luke. Very likely, the owner of this manuscript "concealed it with the intention of removing it from its hiding place when danger had passed, either when Coptos was beseiged and sacked by Diocletian in AD 292 or later in his reign during the last and severest of the persecutions."[60]

In the North African city of Cirta (capital of Numidia), the mayor attempted to confiscate all the Scriptures from Bishop Paul. After searching the home in which the Christians used to meet and finding only one copy of the Christian Scriptures, Paul was called upon to tell the mayor where he had hid other copies. Paul had been wise; the other copies had been taken to the homes of all the readers (or *lectors*—those who read the Scriptures in church meetings) in that church. The wife of one of the readers handed over the books, and the house was searched to make sure there were no others.[61] In Abitina (in North Africa) the bishop handed over the Scriptures on demand. But his congregation disowned his act and carried on the church meeting in the home of the reader, Emeritus. When the interrogators asked Emeritus to hand over his copies, he refused, saying he had "the Scriptures engraved on his heart." Others from Carthage shared the same sentiments. They all were imprisoned but would never recant. Their attitude about the Bible (both testaments) was steadfast: to alter a single letter of Scripture was sacreligious and an insult to their author, and it followed that to destroy the testaments and divine commands of Almighty God and the Lord Jesus Christ by handing them over to be burned merited lasting damnation in unextinguishable fire.[62]

Sadly, many copies of the New Testament perished in the flames of the Diocletian persecution. But not all. Several second-century and third-century New Testament manuscripts have been discovered in Oxyrhynchus, all of which survived this persecution. Entire (or nearly entire) Christian libraries escaped the Diocletian persecution. Two collections of biblical manuscripts known as the Beatty papyri and Bodmer papyri were also preserved from the flames.[63]

There is no question that Oxyrhynchus has provided the greatest yield of biblical writings. The total number of extant Christian writings—whether from the Old Testament, New Testament, or extrabiblical literature—reveals that many people in this community were actively engaged in reading Christian literature. A study of the Oxyrhynchus Christian writings also reveals that there were a number of manuscripts prepared for individual readers, as well as a number of manuscripts prepared for churches.

In total, forty-six papyrus manuscripts containing portions of the New Testament have been discovered at Oxyrhynchus. Almost all of these manuscripts date between 200 and 400, and a few have been dated in the second century: $\mathfrak{P}^{32}$, $\mathfrak{P}^{52}$, $\mathfrak{P}^{77}$, $\mathfrak{P}^{90}$, $\mathfrak{P}^{103}$, $\mathfrak{P}^{104}$. Twenty-one of these papyri were published in *The Oxyrhynchus Papyri* by 1922: $\mathfrak{P}^{1}$, $\mathfrak{P}^{5}$, $\mathfrak{P}^{9}$, $\mathfrak{P}^{10}$, $\mathfrak{P}^{13}$, $\mathfrak{P}^{15}$, $\mathfrak{P}^{16}$, $\mathfrak{P}^{17}$, $\mathfrak{P}^{18}$, $\mathfrak{P}^{19}$, $\mathfrak{P}^{20}$, $\mathfrak{P}^{21}$, $\mathfrak{P}^{22}$, $\mathfrak{P}^{23}$, $\mathfrak{P}^{24}$, $\mathfrak{P}^{26}$, $\mathfrak{P}^{27}$, $\mathfrak{P}^{28}$, $\mathfrak{P}^{29}$, $\mathfrak{P}^{30}$, and $\mathfrak{P}^{39}$; one papyrus published in 1941 ($\mathfrak{P}^{51}$); three more were published in 1957 ($\mathfrak{P}^{69}$, $\mathfrak{P}^{70}$, and $\mathfrak{P}^{71}$); two more in 1968 ($\mathfrak{P}^{77}$ and $\mathfrak{P}^{78}$); one more in 1983 ($\mathfrak{P}^{90}$), and seventeen more in 1996–1997 ($\mathfrak{P}^{100}$-$\mathfrak{P}^{116}$). Three more New Testament papyri were published in *Papiri greci e latini della Societa Italiana*: $\mathfrak{P}^{35}$, $\mathfrak{P}^{36}$, and $\mathfrak{P}^{48}$. A few other papyri are thought to have come from Oxyrhynchus: $\mathfrak{P}^{32}$, $\mathfrak{P}^{52}$,

$\mathfrak{P}^{82}$, and $\mathfrak{P}^{85}$.[64] And one Princeton Papyrus manuscript (P. 15) came from Oxyrhynchus: $\mathfrak{P}^{54}$. In addition to the papyrus manuscripts, several vellum New Testament manuscripts were discovered at Oxyrhynchus. Those published in *The Oxyrhynchus Papyri* are 069, 071, 0162, 0163, 0169, and 0206. Three other vellum manuscripts were published in *Papiri greci e latini della Societa Italiana*: 0172, 0173, 0176.

Some of the manuscripts from this collection are noteworthy in that they all appear to have been made for church reading. This is evident in the bookhand, the large type, and overall attractive appearance. Among the earliest New Testament manuscripts, I have in mind $\mathfrak{P}^{30}$, $\mathfrak{P}^{39}$, and $\mathfrak{P}^{104}$. Other early Oxyrhynchus manuscripts display a hand just short of these others, but the calligraphy and size of letters strongly suggests that they were prepared for church reading. This is evident in $\mathfrak{P}^{1}$, $\mathfrak{P}^{5}$, $\mathfrak{P}^{15+}\mathfrak{P}^{16}$, $\mathfrak{P}^{23}$, $\mathfrak{P}^{48}$, $\mathfrak{P}^{77}$ + $\mathfrak{P}^{103}$, $\mathfrak{P}^{90}$, $\mathfrak{P}^{95}$, $\mathfrak{P}^{108}$, and $\mathfrak{P}^{109}$. As for the other Oxyrhynchus New Testament manuscripts, one could argue that several must have been made for public dissemination. Others, however, were probably produced by individuals for private use. Among the early papyri in this category would be $\mathfrak{P}^{9}$, $\mathfrak{P}^{17}$, $\mathfrak{P}^{18}$, $\mathfrak{P}^{24}$, $\mathfrak{P}^{106}$, and $\mathfrak{P}^{107}$.

This quick survey suggests that Oxyrhynchus had Christians reading the New Testament privately and Christian communities hearing the reading of Scriptures while congregated. We know this because some manuscripts were prepared for church use; others for private use. If Oxyrhynchus was like other Christian communities in the second and third centuries, it is representative of a normal situation in the local churches. Manuscripts were steadily being produced for private and public use.

After the Diocletian persecution and Constantine's decision to make Christianity a "legal" religion, the number of copies of Scriptures would have dramatically increased. The new acceptance of Christianity allowed for both the open publication and distribution of New Testament manuscripts. In AD 331 Constantine asked Eusebius to prepare fifty copies of entire Bible codices for distribution to the churches he wanted to build in Constantinople (*Life of Constantine* 4.36); this tells us that the time had come for Bible production and distribution. If Constantine wanted fifty copies for just Constantinople, how many more copies were being produced for the other churches? Since the church had just suffered the Diocletian persecution, wherein many copies of the New Testament were destroyed, the time had come for extensive reproduction and distribution. In the following decades, as the church grew, so did the production and distribution of Bibles. We do not know how many were produced. J. Duplacy estimated that the total number of manuscripts of the Greek New Testament produced in the fourth century was between fifteen hundred and two thousand. This allows for about four or five copies produced by each church (or diocese) during this century. There were about four hundred dioceses towards AD 400.[65]

One event around AD 420 gives information about the number of copies of the fourfold Gospels codices circulating at the time. In his *Treatise on Heresies* (1.20), Theodoret, bishop of Cyprus on the Euphrates in upper Syria in AD 423, discovered that orthodox Christians in that region were in danger of being corrupted by using Tatian's Diatessaron (a work that wove together the narrative of the four Gospels into one and thereby presented a harmony). So Theodoret destroyed all the copies of the Diatessaron he could find (about 200) and put in their place the separate Gospels of the four evangelists. This is a significant number: two hundred copies of the four Gospels in the early fifth century in just one region!

The Final Step in the Publishing Process: Reading the New Testament Books to the Members of the Church

The first step in the publishing process was to get the book written; the second, to get it distributed and circulated; the third, to get it out to the members of congregations by oral reading. This brings us back to the very beginning of this chapter, where we saw that publication via oral proclamation was the prime form of publication in the early days of the church. The written word served to augment this mode of publication and to keep it consistent and therefore authoritative.

According to the custom of the day, the amanuensis or secretary of official documents was often the same person who carried the document to its destination and read it aloud to its intended audience. Since this person had been present at the time of writing, he could explain to the hearers anything that needed explaining. Since most people were not literate (on average, only 10 percent of the population in hellenistic times could read), they depended on oral reading for communication. Thus, for example, some of the epistles written by Paul could have been delivered by his amanuensis, who would then read the letter to the church and explain anything that needed explaining. In this light, it is possible that Tychicus was Paul's amanuensis for Ephesians (see Eph. 6:21–22) and Colossians (see Col. 4:7–8). He wrote down the epistles for Paul, as Paul dictated, and then delivered them to the Ephesians and Colossians. Most likely, the letter to the Ephesians is the encyclical epistle that traveled with Tychicus to Ephesus, Laodicea (see Col. 4:16), and other churches in the Roman province of Asia Minor. (See commentary on Eph. 1:1 in chap. 7.)

We must also realize that during the era of the early church, few individuals had their own copies of New Testament books. Separate copies of New Testament books were generally not distributed to church members. In church meetings, the usual practice was that one reader (or lector) would read the Scriptures aloud to the rest of the congregation. According to Burtchaell, Christians adopted many of the Jewish synagogal practices in their church meetings.[66] This was only natural because many of the early Christians were Jews. In the early Christian meetings, Christians read the Septuagint, as well as various books of the New Testament. In the church meetings, the Scriptures were read aloud to the congregation by the lector or reader. "Public recitation of scripture which was part of Temple worship became the essential feature of synagogal worship in pre-Christian times and appears in the New Testament as a well-established custom."[67]

Jesus himself was a model for this pattern. The Gospel of Luke tells us that it was Jesus' custom to go to the synagogue in Nazareth (his hometown) on the sabbath and read from the Scriptures. On a particular sabbath just after his baptism, Jesus stood up to read; the attendants handed to him the scroll of Isaiah. He unrolled it and read from Isaiah 61:1–2, and then proclaimed that this Scripture had just been fulfilled—meaning, he was the One anointed by the Lord with the Spirit to proclaim the gospel, release the captives, give sight to the blind, liberate the oppressed, and proclaim the year of the Lord's favor. If Jesus was reading from the Hebrew text (and it is likely that he was), it would have been customary for him to substitute the name Adonai (LORD) in place of YHWH, which appears in both verses. As a practiced reader, he would have known how to decipher the Tetragrammaton.[68]

In church meetings, Christians were encouraged to recite the Scriptures to one another and sing the psalms (1 Cor. 14:26; Eph. 5:18–19; Col. 3:16). Church leaders were exhorted to read the Scriptures aloud to their congregation (see 1 Tim. 4:13). Whereas the Jews would read the Law and then the Prophets, the Christians would read the Prophets (with special emphasis on messianic fulfillment) and the Gospels. After the first century, the written Gospels were regularly read in church meetings. Writing around AD 155, Justin Martyr indicated that when all the believers would assemble on the Lord's Day for worship and communion, "the memoirs of the apostles or the writings of the Prophets are read as long as time permits" (*Apology* 1.67).

Gamble reasoned that the practice of the liturgical reading of Scripture began in the first century and was an established custom of the churches by the early second century.[69] As such, each church community would have had a collection of Old Testament and New Testament books with a number of readers. These readers would have kept various books in their possession because public reading would have required study of the texts in advance.

As in the synagogue, so in the church: one person was usually assigned to be the reader. There are allusions and clear references to this "reader" in the New Testament itself. This "reader" may be alluded to in Matthew 24:15 and Mark 13:14 by way of a parenthetical expression: "let the reader understand." (The use of the singular in Greek points to one reader—the one who read the Gospel to the congregation.) Other passages clearly point to the one who reads the Scriptures aloud to an assembly of believers. In 1 Timothy 4:13, Paul urged Timothy to "give attention to the reading." Significantly, Paul didn't even need to provide a direct object to the expression "give attention to the reading," for the expression seems to have become an idiom for the public oral reading of Scripture. Revelation 1:3 promises a blessing "to the one who reads the prophecy of this book"—speaking specifically of each of the readers who would read aloud the book of Revelation to each of the seven churches addressed in the book. It is very likely that each reader for each of the seven churches was also a scribe who made a copy of the entire book of Revelation before it was sent on to the next church. This is a far more likely scenario than that John made seven copies at Patmos. Furthermore, it concurs with the way official encyclicals were distributed throughout the Roman world.

As with the synagogues, so in the churches, it is possible that the readers were also the scribes. If not, the readers relied upon the work of the scribes to produce the manuscripts for oral reading. These Christian scribes would often have the same training as the Jewish *sopherim*—in reading, copying, translating, and interpreting, or they could have been former *sopherim* who converted to Christianity. Or, if these scribes did not have a Jewish background, they would have been trained in Alexandrian scriptorial practices or, at least, educated enough to produce documents. Either way, they would have been among the most educated in the Christian congregations and therefore the most qualified not only to produce written copies of Scripture but also to read them and interpret them. Even if they weren't the lectors, they had significant input in shaping or reshaping a text according to their reception of it. The congregation, for the most part, would depend on them for the oral dissemination (publication) of Scripture.

An interesting insight concerning the relationship between scribes and readers is found in the subscription to 1 Peter and to 2 Peter in $\mathfrak{P}^{72}$, where in both places it says, "Peace to the one having written [i.e., the scribe] and to the one having read [i.e., the lector]." As such, the scribe of $\mathfrak{P}^{72}$ was asking for a blessing of God's peace on the scribe [presumably himself] and on the lector. As such, the scribe knew that the publication of 1 Peter and 2 Peter was dependent on the twofold process—the copying of the text and the oral reading of it.

The lectors were trained to read the texts in Greek and to perhaps provide interpretations. In the early days of the church, the reader was simply a member of the church who knew Greek well enough to read it (as well as to write it). In the third century, lectors were appointed to this function but not ordained. *The Apostolic Tradition* (1.12) says, "The reader is appointed by the bishop's handing to him the book, for he does not have hands laid upon him." One such reader was Procopius (martyred in AD 303 during Diocletian's persecution). Eusebius said he had rendered a great service to the church both as reader and as translator from Greek into Aramaic (*Martyrs of Palestine* 1.1). Other lectors were Pachomius and his companion Theodore, who both read the Scriptures to their fellow monks. After the fourth century, the lector was generally a minor church office. According to the *Apostolic Church Order,* the reader must also be able to instruct and to narrate. And according to Basil, in the fourth century, lectors read from the Law, the Prophets, the Epistles, Acts, and the Gospels (*Apostolic Constitutions* 8.5.5).

The Evidence of the Early Papyri

All the early Greek New Testament manuscripts, as with all Greek literature, were written in what is called *scriptora continua*, which means there was no spacing between words. Thus, a reader had to have some training for individualizing words as he or she read a text aloud. However, many manuscripts had certain lectoral markings which aided the reader. These are present in documents preserving Greek literature, as well as in the Greek Bible. The first form of lectoral markings was punctuation. There is a common myth perpetuated about the ancient Greek New Testament that the early manuscripts had no punctuation. This is far from the truth. Nearly every manuscript has punctuation marks, such as the midpoint, the highpoint, and even an occasional period. These were placed by various scribes to indicate thought separations. Scribes also used a colon to indicate semantic units. This was especially popular in poetry. Interestingly, three papyri ($\mathfrak{P}^{13}$, $\mathfrak{P}^{17}$, $\mathfrak{P}^{46}$) have these colons in the book of Hebrews, one of the most poetic books in all of the New Testament. The colon was used also by the scribe of $\mathfrak{P}^{49\,+}$ $\mathfrak{P}^{65}$.

The second form of lectoral markings has to do with markings of new paragraphs and/or sections. Scribes often left spaces between words to signal a new paragraph. Or they outdented (called ekdesis) a new line by one or two spaces to indicate a new paragraph or section. (In English, we do the opposite; we indent to indicate a new paragraph.) This system of outdenting is found in the professionally produced papyri, $\mathfrak{P}^{4+64+67}$, $\mathfrak{P}^{75}$, and $\mathfrak{P}^{77}$. The same kind of system appears later in Codex Vaticanus (B). Scribes also used lines (or dashes) extending from the margin into the text above a line of words to indicate the beginning of a new section. This system is also found in the aforementioned papyri, $\mathfrak{P}^{4+64+67}$, $\mathfrak{P}^{75}$, and $\mathfrak{P}^{77}$.[70] The third form of lectoral markings found in the early New Testament manuscripts is that of the slash mark, designating thought pauses. When one looks at the early manuscripts, it is evident that these were not placed there by the original scribe but by a lector who placed the slash marks in preparation for oral reading. This is very evident, for example, in $\mathfrak{P}^{46}$, where only the books of Romans and Hebrews display these secondary slash marks. Evidently, the other books were not read aloud or, at least, were not marked as such for reading. We see the same phenomenon in $\mathfrak{P}^{66}$, where only certain chapters are marked with secondary slash marks. (I refer the reader to *The Text of the Earliest New Testament Greek Manuscripts* for a typescript that shows these markings, as well as the punctuation marks and spacing mentioned above.) Significantly, many of the early papyri display these lectoral markings; this is especially true in P. Baden 456 (Exod.; Deut.), $\mathfrak{P}^{45}$, $\mathfrak{P}^{46}$, $\mathfrak{P}^{47}$, $\mathfrak{P}^{50}$, $\mathfrak{P}^{66}$, and P. Michigan 130 (Shepherd of Hermas). As such, we know that these documents were read aloud in church meetings. There is another physical feature that distinguishes private copies and church copies. Church copies usually have large print (for ecclesiastical oration) on larger sheets and a good quality handwriting. Prime examples of church manuscripts can be seen in $\mathfrak{P}^{4+64+67}$, $\mathfrak{P}^{39}$, $\mathfrak{P}^{66}$, and $\mathfrak{P}^{75}$. In studying both

Christian and non-Christian codices, E. G. Turner came to the same conclusion—namely, that there was a tendency in early Christian manuscripts for scribes to write fewer lines to the page and fewer letters to the line than was usual. This was not accidental. These copies were made to facilitate public reading.[71] Indeed it can be observed in several Christian manuscripts that the scribe, writing with practiced hand, wrote his letters larger than usual. Such examples can be seen in P. Chester Beatty VI (Num., Deut.), VIII (Jer.), IX-X (Dan., Ezek.), XI (Ecclesiasticus), P. Michigan 130 (Shepherd of Hermas), P. Yale 1 (Gen.), P. Egerton 2 (Unknown Gospel), $\mathfrak{P}^1$ (Matt,), $\mathfrak{P}^5$ (John), $\mathfrak{P}^{66}$ (John), and $\mathfrak{P}^{75}$ (Luke, John).

Finally, it should be noted that the evidence of the extant manuscripts could give us some idea about which books of the New Testament were being read by the early Christians. For example, the sampling of extant New Testament papyri allows us to see what books were popular and what weren't in Egypt prior to AD 300.[72] Among the Gospels, Matthew and John were extremely popular (represented by 12 and 15 manuscripts, respectively). Luke, far less so (in 4 manuscripts), while Mark is found in only one manuscript, $\mathfrak{P}^{45}$. There are 5 manuscripts of Acts, and 5 of Paul's major epistles. There is one copy each of Philemon and Titus. Only 1 and 2 Timothy are absent. Egyptian Christians were also reading Hebrews (5 copies), James (3 copies), 1 and 2 Peter (1 copy), Jude (2 copies), 1 John (1 copy) and Revelation (4 copies). We should be careful about drawing absolute conclusions from this sampling because it is, after all, nothing more than that; other books must have been present that did not survive the weather or the worm. Nevertheless, the extant papyri give us an idea of what books were the most popular.

Chapter Two

Significant Manuscripts and Printed Editions

The student's first step in learning the science of New Testament textual criticism is to become familiar with the most important manuscripts of the New Testament. The best way to become familiar with these manuscripts is to see them in museums and/or examine them in rare book rooms in libraries. Often I have made travel plans for the sole purpose of examining manuscripts. And wherever I have traveled, I have made it a point to see as many actual manuscripts as possible. There is nothing more exciting and rewarding than spending time with the earliest copies of the New Testament. For this reason, I have provided the housing location for each manuscript in the list below. The second best way to know these manuscripts is to look at photographs, which are published in the standard works of New Testament manuscripts and New Testament textual criticism. I would recommend the following volumes: *The Text of the New Testament*, Kurt and Barbara Aland; *Manuscripts of the Ancient World*, Metzger; *Principal Uncial Manuscripts*, Hatch; *The Text of the Earliest New Testament Greek Manuscripts*, Comfort and Barrett. Each of these has some excellent photographs. Photographs also appear in chapter 3 of this volume.

The third way to become familiar with the significant manuscripts is to begin reading them. The student can do this with good photographs. At first, you will need the help of transcriptions printed in the *editio princeps* (listed with each manuscript below) and/or a printed edition of the Greek New Testament. Then you will become accustomed to the *scriptura continuum* (all the words running together), the uncial letters, and the sporadic punctuation. The student will also encounter the nomina sacra—special written forms of the divine names. I have devoted an entire chapter to the nomina sacra because these are not replicated in printed editions and because they are an essential feature of the early text (see chap. 4).

Students also need to become familiar with the significant printed editions of the Greek New Testament. They should purchase some of these, begin to read them, and get accustomed to the critical apparatus in each one; for it is the critical apparatus which displays textual variants, together with the listing of manuscripts noted in the first part of this chapter. These variants provide the raw material by which we practice textual criticism. A student should study the manuscript, learn its individual features and textual character, and memorize its siglum—i.e., ℵ stands for codex Siniaticus, B stands for codex Vaticanus, $\mathfrak{P}^{52}$ for papyrus 52, etc.

Before the fifteenth century, when Johannes Gutenberg invented movable type for the printing press, all copies of any work of literature were made by hand (hence, the name "manuscript"). To date, there are 116 New Testament papyrus manuscripts, about 300 uncial manuscripts (listed with an 0 first, as in 0162 and 0171), and about 2,800 minuscule manuscripts (listed with numbers from 1 to 2829). The reader should see the Alands' listings in *The Text of the New Testament* (96–101, 105, 128) and see appendix 1, "Codices Graeci et Latini" in *Novum Testamentum Graece* (27th ed.). For more recent papyri, see *The Text of the Earliest New Testament Greek Manuscripts* (Comfort and Barrett, 2001). Metzger adds 2,209 Greek lectionaries to this list.[1] Therefore, we have over 5,500 manuscript copies of the Greek New Testament or portions thereof. No other work of Greek literature can boast of such numbers. Homer's *Iliad*, the greatest of all Greek classical works, is extant in about 650 manuscripts; and Euripides' tragedies exist in about 330 manuscripts. The numbers on all the other works of Greek literature are far less.

Furthermore, it must be said that the period of time between the original composition and the next surviving manuscript is much shorter for the New Testament than for any other work in Greek literature. The lapse for most classical Greek works is about eight hundred to a thousand years, whereas the lapse for many books in the New Testament is around one hundred years. Because of the abundant wealth of manuscripts and because several of the manuscripts are dated in the early centuries of the church, New Testament textual scholars have a great advantage over classical textual scholars.

Complete lists with short descriptions of all the manuscripts are provided by the Alands in *The Text of the New Testament* (section three, "The Manuscripts of the Greek New Testament"). Metzger, in *The Text of the New Testament* (1968; 7th printing, 1980), has also supplied lists and descriptions of the New Testament manuscripts. References to Aland and Metzger in the following description come from these two sources. A fuller discussion of the early papyrus manuscripts (with bibliography) can be found in *The Text of the Earliest New Testament Greek Manuscripts* (Comfort and Barrett, eds.), abbreviated as *Text of Earliest MSS*.

The bibliography provided for each of the following manuscripts is usually the primary edition of the transcription (the *editio princeps*) of the text and/or facsimile edition. A complete bibliography for these manuscripts (and many more) can be found in J. K. Elliott's work, *A Bibliography of Greek New Testament Manuscripts* (Cambridge University Press, 1989). The manuscripts listed below are among the most important witnesses to the text of the New Testament. All the papyri and other manuscripts dated before AD 300 also are listed.

The Papyri

Generally speaking, the papyrus manuscripts are among the most important witnesses for reconstructing the original text of the New Testament. It is not the material they are written on (papyrus) that makes them so valuable but rather the date when they were written. Several of the most significant papyri are dated from the second century to the early third. These manuscripts, therefore, provide the earliest direct witness to the autographs. The papyri can be placed in four large categories: (1) the Oxyrhynchus papyri, (2) the Beatty papyri, (3) the Bodmer papyri, and (4) other significant papyri.

The Oxyrhynchus Papyri

Beginning in 1898 Grenfell and Hunt discovered thousands of papyrus fragments in the ancient rubbish heaps of Oxyrhynchus, Egypt. This site yielded volumes of papyrus fragments containing all sorts of written material (literature, business and legal contracts, letters, etc.), together with biblical manuscripts. Nearly half of the 115 New Testament papyri have come from Oxyrhynchus. The Oxyrhynchus papyri were discovered between 1898 and 1907 by Grenfell and Hunt and then by the Italian exploration society from 1910 to 1913 and 1927 to 1934. Of the fifty Oxyrhynchus papyri, about half were published between 1898 and the 1930s. These include $\mathfrak{P}^1$, $\mathfrak{P}^5$, $\mathfrak{P}^{9-10}$, $\mathfrak{P}^{13}$, $\mathfrak{P}^{15-18}$, $\mathfrak{P}^{20-24}$, $\mathfrak{P}^{27-30}$, $\mathfrak{P}^{35-36}$, $\mathfrak{P}^{39}$, $\mathfrak{P}^{48}$. In addition to the twenty-five New Testament papyri they published in the early part of this century, they have given us another twenty-five in the second part of the century— (as numbered by Aland): $\mathfrak{P}^{51}$, $\mathfrak{P}^{65}$, $\mathfrak{P}^{69}$, $\mathfrak{P}^{70}$, $\mathfrak{P}^{71}$, $\mathfrak{P}^{77}$, $\mathfrak{P}^{78}$, $\mathfrak{P}^{90}$, $\mathfrak{P}^{100}$ through $\mathfrak{P}^{116}$; these last seventeen have come out in the late 1990s.

The following are some of the most significant Oxyrhynchus papyri: $\mathfrak{P}^1$ (Matt. 1), $\mathfrak{P}^5$ (John 1, 16), $\mathfrak{P}^{13}$ (Heb. 2–5, 10–12), $\mathfrak{P}^{22}$ (John 15–16), $\mathfrak{P}^{77}$ (Matt. 23), $\mathfrak{P}^{90}$ (John 18), $\mathfrak{P}^{104}$ (Matt. 21), $\mathfrak{P}^{115}$ (Rev. 3–12).

The Chester Beatty Papyri

The Beatty papyri were purchased from a dealer in Egypt during the 1930s by Chester Beatty and by the University of Michigan. Quite possibly the manuscripts came from the ruins of the library belonging to a church, a Christian scholar, or a monastery—perhaps in the Fayum or the east bank of the Nile about Atfih, the ancient Aphroditopolis, from which Antony, the founder of Egyptian monasticism, came. Among the New Testament manuscripts are $\mathfrak{P}^{45}$ (Gospels and Acts, ca. 200), $\mathfrak{P}^{46}$ (Paul's epistles, ca. 150–200), and $\mathfrak{P}^{47}$ (Revelation, late third). The substantial content of these papyri and their early dates made them immediately significant, so much so that the translators of the RSV claimed that their revision of the ERV was prompted by these manuscripts (see Introduction to the RSV). And, for the first time, these papyri (and those published earlier) were cited in the Nestle text in significant fashion (see 16th edition, 1936). Detailed studies of these papyri followed in suit by scholars such as Kenyon, Zuntz, Schofield, Schmid, Aland, Colwell, and Royse.

The Bodmer Papyri

The Bodmer papyri (named after the owner, M. Martin Bodmer) were purchased from a dealer in Egypt during the 1950s and 1960s. The Bodmer biblical papyri (or Dishna Papers) were discovered seven years after the Nag Hammadi codices in close proximity (in the Dishna plain, east of the Nile River). (Dishna is midway between Panopolis and Thebes.) In 1945 the Nag Hammadi manuscripts were found in Jabal al-Tarif (just north of Chenoboskion, near the city of Nag Hammadi, where the discovery was first reported). In 1952 the Bodmer papyri were found in Jabal Abu Manna, which is also located just north of the Dishna plain, twelve kilometers east of Jabal al-Tarif. It is quite likely that all these manuscripts were part of a library of a Pachomian monastery. Within a few kilometers of Jabal Abu Manna lie the ruins of the ancient basillica of Pachomius (in Faw Qibli). The New Testament papyri in this collection are as follows: $\mathfrak{P}^{66}$ (ca. 150, containing almost all of John), $\mathfrak{P}^{72}$ (third c., having all of 1 and 2 Peter and Jude), and $\mathfrak{P}^{73}$ (Matthew, seventh c.), $\mathfrak{P}^{74}$ (Acts, General Epistles, seventh c.), and $\mathfrak{P}^{75}$ (Luke and John, ca. 175–200). These manuscripts were studied extensively by scholars such as Colwell, Fee, Kubo, Aland, Porter, and Royse. I also did an extensive study of $\mathfrak{P}^{66}$ and $\mathfrak{P}^{75}$ for a doctoral dissertation (see bibliography: Comfort 1997).

Other Significant Papyri

A few significant New Testament papyri were also published early in the twentieth century. One notable manuscript is $\mathfrak{P}^{4}$, which has portions of Luke 1–6. It was later realized that this manuscript is part of the same codex as $\mathfrak{P}^{64}+\mathfrak{P}^{67}$. Another is $\mathfrak{P}^{32}$ (dated late second c. by Roberts and Skeat); it contains a portion of Titus 1–2. Another small but significant papyrus, known as $\mathfrak{P}^{52}$, was published in 1935, when Colin Roberts announced that he had found a small codex fragment of John 18, which he dated to ca. 125 (a date that was confirmed by other eminent papyrologists such as Kenyon, Bell, and Deissman). As the earliest extant New Testament papyri, this manuscript challenged theories about the Fourth Gospel being composed in the early second century. It also opened the way for dating New Testament papyri earlier than they had been up until then because it was now clear to paleographers that the Christian codex must have existed in the first century. A few other significant, early papyri are $\mathfrak{P}^{87}$, an early copy of Philemon; $\mathfrak{P}^{91}$, a third-century fragment of Acts 2; $\mathfrak{P}^{92}$, a third-century codex of Ephesians and 1 Thessalonians; and $\mathfrak{P}^{98}$, a late-second century fragment of Revelation 1.

Finally, it should be mentioned that new fragments of already-published manuscripts and fresh reconstructions of previously published manuscripts have gone to press in recent years. Kurt Aland identified new fragments of $\mathfrak{P}^{66}$ and $\mathfrak{P}^{75}$. Two additional leaves of $\mathfrak{P}^{45}$ were published—one by Zuntz and another by Skeat and McGing. Three small fragments of $\mathfrak{P}^{4}$, one new fragment of $\mathfrak{P}^{30}$, two new fragments of $\mathfrak{P}^{40}$, and several new fragments of $\mathfrak{P}^{66}$ were published for the first time in a work I edited (with Barrett), *The Text of the Earliest New Testament Manuscripts*. This work also includes several new reconstructions, especially of $\mathfrak{P}^{46}$ and $\mathfrak{P}^{66}$. Some of the same reconstructions of $\mathfrak{P}^{46}$ appear in volumes 2 and 3 of the Aland's *Das Neue Testament auf Papyrus*.

For each manuscript listed below, the siglum is listed first, followed by bibliography for the *editio principes* (publication of the first transcription), housing location of the manuscript, date of manuscript (the date for each manuscript before AD 300 is fully discussed in chap. 3), and comments concerning the textual character of the manuscript.

$\mathfrak{P}^1$ (P. Oxy. 2)
- Grenfell and Hunt, *Oxyrhynchus Papyri* I (1898), no. 2, 4–7.
- Matthew 1:1–9, 12, 14–20
- Philadelphia, Pennsylvania: University Museum, University of Pennsylvania (E 2746)
- Early third century
- The copyist of $\mathfrak{P}^1$ seems to have faithfully followed a very reliable exemplar. Where there are major variants, $\mathfrak{P}^1$ agrees with the best Alexandrian witnesses, especially B, from which it rarely varies.

$\mathfrak{P}^{4+64+67}$ (fragments of same codex)
- $\mathfrak{P}^4$ (P. Paris Bibl. Nat. Suppl. Gr. 1120) contains portions of Luke 1–6. Parts of this were originally published by Vincent Scheil, "Archeologie, Varia," *Revue Biblique* 1 (1892): 113–15. A more complete transcription was provided by J. Merell, "Nouveaux fragments papyrus IV," in *Revue Biblique* 47 (1938): 5–22. $\mathfrak{P}^{64}$ (P. Magdalene 18) and $\mathfrak{P}^{67}$ (P. Barcelona Inv. 1) contain portions of Matthew 3, 5, and 26. $\mathfrak{P}^{64}$ was first published by Colin Roberts in "An Early Papyrus of the First Gospel" (*Harvard Theological Review* 46 (1953): 233–37. $\mathfrak{P}^{67}$ was first published by P. Roca-Puig in a booklet called *Un Papiro Griego del Evangelio de San Mateo* (Barcelona, 1957). After Colin Roberts realized that $\mathfrak{P}^{64}$ and $\mathfrak{P}^{67}$ were two parts of the same manuscript and then confirmed this with Roca-Puig, the latter published another article entitled, "Nueva publicacion del papiro numero uno de Barcelona" in *Helmantica* 37 (1961): 5–20, in which Roca-Puig gives a full presentation of the entire manuscript. Colin Roberts appended a note to this article explaining how he had discovered that $\mathfrak{P}^{64}$ and $\mathfrak{P}^{67}$ were part of the same manuscript. I have presented a full argument for the common identity of $\mathfrak{P}^{4+64+67}$.[2] T. C. Skeat has also argued that these three manuscripts belong to the same codex.[3] As such, $\mathfrak{P}^{4+64+67}$, as part of the same

codex, should be assigned the same date. (Fuller bibliography is found in *Text of Earliest MSS*, 43–45.)

- $\mathfrak{P}^4$: Paris, France: Bibliotheque Nationale (Suppl. Gr. 1120)
- $\mathfrak{P}^{64}$: Oxford, England: Oxford University, Magdalen College Library (Gr. 17)
- $\mathfrak{P}^{67}$: Barcelona, Spain: Fundacion San Lucas Evangelista (P. Barc. 1)
- Middle to late second century
- The text of $\mathfrak{P}^{4+64+67}$ is extremely good, showing remarkable agreement with $\mathfrak{P}^{75}$ (in Luke), as well as with $\aleph$ and B.

$\mathfrak{P}^5$ (P. Oxy. 208)

- Two separate portions were unearthed from Oxyrhynchus by Grenfell and Hunt, both from the same papyrus manuscript. The first portion contains John 1:23–31, 33–40 on one fragment and John 20:11–17 on another— probably on the first and last quires of a manuscript containing only the Gospel of John. This portion was published in volume II of *Oxyrhynchus Papyri* in 1899 (no. 208); the second portion—containing John 16:14–30—was not published until 1922 in volume 15 of *Oxyrhynchus Papyri*.
- John 1:23–31, 33–40; 16:14–30; 20:11–17, 19–20, 22–25
- London, England: British Museum (Inv. nos. 782, 2484)
- Early third century
- After examining the first portion, Grenfell and Hunt said, "The text is a good one, and appears to have affinities with that of Codex Sinaiticus, with which the papyrus agrees in several readings not found elsewhere." The agreement of $\mathfrak{P}^5$ with $\aleph$ against B is evident in critical passages (John 1:34; 16:22, 27, 28). This impression, however, was slightly modified after their inspection of the second portion. The affinity between $\mathfrak{P}^5$ and $\aleph$ is still there, but it is less pronounced. The papyrus, written in a documentary hand, is marked for its brevity.

$\mathfrak{P}^9$ (P. Oxy. 402)

- Grenfell and Hunt, *Oxyrhynchus Papyri* III (1903): no. 402, 2–3.
- 1 John 4:11–12, 15–17
- Cambridge, Massachusetts: Harvard University, Semitic Museum (no. 3736)
- Third century
- The manuscript was written very carelessly in a common hand. The handwriting is crude and irregular, and the copy contains some unintelligible spellings.

$\mathfrak{P}^{12}$ (Amherst Papyri 3b)
- Grenfell and Hunt, *The Amherst Papyri* vol. 1; London, 1900:28–31.
- Hebrews 1:1
- New York: Pierpont Morgan Library (no. Gr. 3)
- ca. 285
- It may have been a writing exercise or an amulet.

$\mathfrak{P}^{13}$ (P. Oxy. 657 and PSI 1292)
- Grenfell and Hunt, *Oxyrhynchus Papyri* 4 (1904): no. 657, 36–48; Vittorio Bartolletti and M. Norsi, *Papiri greci e latini della Societa Italiana* (1951), PSI 1292, 209–210.
- Hebrews 2:14–5:5; 10:8–22; 10:29–11:13; 11:28–12:7; it contains 12 columns from a roll—with pagination from 47–50, 61–65, 67–69; 23–27 lines per column. (The pagination reveals that another epistle may have preceded this one—perhaps Romans, as in $\mathfrak{P}^{46}$.)
- London, England: British Library (Inv. no. 1532v); Florence, Italy: Biblioteca Laurenziana (no. 1292)
- Early third century
- $\mathfrak{P}^{13}$ very often agrees with B, and it supplements B where it is lacking—namely, from Hebrews 9:14 to the end of Hebrews. $\mathfrak{P}^{13}$ and $\mathfrak{P}^{46}$ display nearly the same text. Out of a total of eighty-eight variation-units, there are seventy-one agreements and only seventeen disagreements. (The copyists of $\mathfrak{P}^{13}$ and $\mathfrak{P}^{46}$ made similar use of double points for punctuation.)

$\mathfrak{P}^{15} + \mathfrak{P}^{16}$

Grenfell and Hunt conjectured that $\mathfrak{P}^{15}$ and $\mathfrak{P}^{16}$ might have been parts of the same manuscript, written in a documentary hand. Both manuscripts have the same formation of letters, line space, and punctuation (indicated by spacing). The only notable difference is the color of ink on both manuscripts. However, this distinction could indicate that the same scribe switched to a different ink sometime after making 1 Corinthians and before copying Philippians. $\mathfrak{P}^{15}$ displays a black ink (the more expensive type—a carbon-based ink), whereas $\mathfrak{P}^{16}$ displays a brownish ink (the less expensive type—blended with iron sulfate and gum arabic). Since these manuscripts are probably from the same codex, it only stands to reason that they were originally a part of a Pauline corpus. Furthermore, the two must have the same date (late third century), not third century for $\mathfrak{P}^{15}$ and third/fourth century for $\mathfrak{P}^{16}$ (as listed in appendix 1 of NA[27]).

$\mathfrak{P}^{15}$ (P. Oxy. 1008)
- Grenfell and Hunt, *Oxyrhynchus Papyri* VII (1910), no. 1008, 4–8.
- 1 Corinthians 7:18–8:4
- Cairo, Egypt: Egyptian Museum of Antiquities (JE 47423)
- Late third century
- This manuscript was part of the same codex to which $\mathfrak{P}^{16}$ belonged. The manuscript is proto-Alexandrian, showing the greatest agreement with B.

$\mathfrak{P}^{16}$ (P. Oxy. 1009)
- Grenfell and Hunt, *Oxyrhynchus Papyri* VII (1910), no. 1009, 8–11.
- Philippians 3:10–17; 4:2–8
- Cairo, Egypt: Egyptian Museum of Antiquities (JE 47424)
- Late third century
- This manuscript was part of the same codex to which $\mathfrak{P}^{15}$ belonged. The manuscript is proto-Alexandrian, showing the greatest agreement with ℵ and then B.

$\mathfrak{P}^{18}$ (P. Oxy. 1079)
- Grenfell and Hunt, *Oxyrhynchus Papyri* VIII (1911), 13–14.
- Revelation 1:4–7
- London, England: British Library (inv. no. 2053v)
- Third century
- A miniature codex, this manuscript shows the greatest agreement with C.

$\mathfrak{P}^{20}$ (P. Oxy. 1171)
- Grenfell and Hunt, *Oxyrhynchus Papyri* IX, no. 1171, 9–11.
- James 2:19–3:9
- Princeton, New Jersey: University Libraries (AM 4117)
- Early third century
- The manuscript is a fairly reliable copy; the text is clearly proto-Alexandrian, showing the greatest agreement with ℵ and B.

$\mathfrak{P}^{22}$ (P. Oxy. 1228)
- Grenfell and Hunt, *Oxyrhynchus Papyri* X (1914), no. 1228, 14–16.
- John 15:25–16:2, 21–32 (two consecutive columns of a roll; the reverse side is blank)
- Glasgow, Scotland: University Library (Ms. 2-X, 1)
- Third century
- $\mathfrak{P}^{22}$ displays an independent text.

$\mathfrak{P}^{23}$ (P. Oxy. 1229)
- Grenfell and Hunt, *Oxyrhynchus Papyri* X, no. 1229, 16–18.
- James 1:10–12, 15–18
- Urbana, Illinois: University of Illinois (G. P. 1229)
- ca. 200
- The manuscript is an accurate copy; the text is clearly proto-Alexandrian, showing the greatest agreement with ℵ A C (which represent the best text of the General Epistles).

$\mathfrak{P}^{24}$ (P. Oxy. 1230)
- Grenfell and Hunt, *Oxyrhynchus Papyri* X (1914), no. 1230, 18–19.
- Revelation 5:5–8; 6:5–8
- Newton Centre, Massachusetts: Andover Newton Theological School, Franklin Trask Library (O.P. 1230).
- Third century (earliest extant manuscript of Revelation 5–6)
- $\mathfrak{P}^{24}$ shows textual agreement with A, but it is too small to determine its overall textual affinities.

$\mathfrak{P}^{27}$ (P. Oxy. 1355)
- Grenfell and Hunt, *Oxyrhynchus Papyri* XI, no. 1355, 9–12.
- Romans 8:12–22, 24–27; 8:33–9:3, 5–9
- Cambridge, England: Cambridge University Library (Add. Mss. 7211)
- Early third century
- The scribe of $\mathfrak{P}^{27}$ may have also written $\mathfrak{P}^{20}$ (an early copy of James). His work is reliable; it shows general agreement with ℵ B and other Alexandrian witnesses.

$\mathfrak{P}^{28}$ (P. Oxy. 1596)
- Grenfell and Hunt, *Oxyrhynchus Papyri* XIII (1919), no. 1596, 8–10.
- John 6:8–12, 17–22
- Berkeley, California: Pacific School of Religion, Palestine Institute Museum (Pap. 2)
- Late third century
- $\mathfrak{P}^{28}$ is proto-Alexandrian, showing more agreement with $\mathfrak{P}^{75}$ than any other manuscript.

$\mathfrak{P}^{29}$ (P. Oxy. 1597)
- Grenfell and Hunt, *Oxyrhynchus Papyri* Vol. XIII (1919), nos. 1597, 10–12.
- Acts 26:7–8, 20
- Oxford, England: Bodleian Library (Gr. bibl. g. 4 [P])

- Early third century
- $\mathfrak{P}^{29}$ might be related to the D-type text, but the fragment is too small to be certain of its textual character.

$\mathfrak{P}^{30}$ (P. Oxy. 1598)

- Grenfell and Hunt, *Oxyrhynchus Papyri* XIII, no. 1598, 12–14. A new portion in 2 Thessalonians 2 was identified by Comfort and Barrett (*Text of Earliest MSS*, 128–33).
- 1 Thessalonians 4:12–13, 16–17; 5:3, 8–10, 12–18, 25–28; 2 Thessalonians 1:1–2; 2:1, 9–11
- Ghent, Belgium: Rijksuninersiteit, Univ. Bibliotheek (inv. 61)
- Early third century
- $\mathfrak{P}^{30}$, a carefully executed manuscript, exhibits the greatest agreement with ℵ and then with B.

$\mathfrak{P}^{32}$ (P. Rylands 5)

- A. S. Hunt, *Catalogue of the Greek Papyri in the John Rylands Library* I (Manchester, 1911), 10–11 (Papyrus Ryland 5).
- Titus 1:11–15; 2:3–8
- Manchester, England: John Rylands University Library (Gr. P. 5)
- Middle to late second century
- $\mathfrak{P}^{32}$, a reliable manuscript, shows agreement with ℵ and with F G. Since F and G (nearly identical manuscripts) go back to the same archetype, it is possible that $\mathfrak{P}^{32}$ could be traced to the same source.

$\mathfrak{P}^{37}$ (Michigan Papyrus 1570)

- Henry A. Sanders, "An Early Papyrus Fragment of the Gospel of Matthew in the Michigan Collection" in *Harvard Theological Review* 19 (1926): 215–26.
- Matthew 26:19–52
- Ann Arbor, Michigan: University of Michigan (Inv. no. 1570)
- Third century
- $\mathfrak{P}^{37}$ has an independent text, showing some affinities with $\mathfrak{P}^{45}$.

$\mathfrak{P}^{38}$ (Michigan Papyrus 1571)

- Henry A. Sanders, "A Papyrus Fragment of Acts in the Michigan Collection" in *Harvard Theological Review* 20 (1927): 1–19.
- Acts 18:27–19:6, 12–16
- Ann Arbor, Michigan: University of Michigan Library (Inv. no. 1571)

- Early third century
- $\mathfrak{P}^{38}$, having a D-text, is a representative of the "Western" form of Acts.

$\mathfrak{P}^{39}$ (P. Oxy. 1780)

- Grenfell and Hunt, *Oxyrhynchus Papyri* XV (1922), no. 1780, 7–8.
- John 8:14–22
- Rochester, New York: Ambrose Swabey Library (Inv. no. 8864)
- Early third century
- $\mathfrak{P}^{39}$ is proto-Alexandrian, agreeing with $\mathfrak{P}^{75}$ and B.

$\mathfrak{P}^{40}$ (P. Heidelberg 645)

- Friedrich Bilabel, "Romerbrieffragmente" in *Veroffentilichungen aus den Badischen Papyrussammlungen* IV (1924), 28–31, 124–27 (P. Baden 57).
- Romans 1:24–27, 31–2:3; 3:21–4:8; 6:2–5, 15–16; 9:16–17, 27 [fragment a + d (Rom. 1:24–27, 31–2:3); fragment b (3:21–4:8); fragment c (Rom. 6:4b–5, 16); fragment e (Rom. 9:16–17, 27); with two previously unidentified fragments, one of which has been newly identified by Comfort and Barrett as Romans 6:2–4a and 6:15 (this could called fragment f)—see *Text of Earliest MSS*, 150–54).
- Heidelberg, Germany: Papyrussammlung der Universität (Inv. no. 645)
- Third century
- Although the scribe was occasionally careless in his work, the text manifests a proto-Alexandrian exemplar, agreeing mostly with ℵ and then A B.

$\mathfrak{P}^{45}$ (Chester Beatty Papyrus I)

- Frederic G. Kenyon, *Chester Beatty Biblical Papyri* II/1: *The Gospels and Acts, Text* (London, 1933); II/2: *The Gospels and Acts, Plates* (London, 1934); Gunther Zuntz, "Reconstruction of One Leaf of the Chester Beatty Papyrus of the Gospels and Acts (Mt 25:41–26:39)," *Chronique d'Egypte* 26 (1951): 191–211; T. C. Skeat and B. C. McGing, "Notes on Chester Beatty Papyrus I (Gospels and Acts)," pp. 21–25 in *Hermathena* 150 (1991). (This provides a reconstruction of John 4:51–5:2, 21–25.)
- Matthew 20:24–32; 21:13–19; 25:41–26:39; Mark 4:36–9:31; 11:27–12:28; Luke 6:31–7:7; 9:26–14:33; John 4:51–5:2, 21–25; 10:7–25; 10:30–11:10, 18–36, 42–57; Acts 4:27–17:17 (with many lacunae). According to Kenyon, the order of books in the original intact manuscript was probably as follows: Matthew, John, Luke, Mark, Acts (the so-called Western order).
- Dublin, Ireland: Chester Beatty Collection (I)
- Early third century (ca. 200)

- The text of $\mathfrak{P}^{45}$ varies. According to a study done by Colwell, the scribe of $\mathfrak{P}^{45}$ worked "without any intention of exactly reproducing his source." He wrote with a great amount of freedom—"harmonizing, smoothing out, substituting almost whimsically." In short, "the scribe does not actually copy words. He sees through the language to its idea-content, and copies that—often in words of his own choosing, or in words rearranged as to order."[4]

  It was apparent to Colwell that the scribe of $\mathfrak{P}^{45}$ copied his exemplar phrase by phrase and clause by clause (as opposed to more careful copyists who transcribe the text word by word as in $\mathfrak{P}^{75}$). While copying phrases and clauses, he worked at reproducing what he imagined to be the thought of each phrase. Thus, he transposed and omitted many words and deleted several phrases. Colwell said, "The most striking aspect of his style is its conciseness. The dispensable word is dispensed with. He omits adverbs, adjectives, nouns, participles, verbs, personal pronouns—without any compensating habit of addition."[5]

  Another study on $\mathfrak{P}^{45}$ done by Royse affirms Colwell's observations about the scribe's penchant for brevity. Royse comments, "The scribe has a marked tendency to omit portions of text, often (as it seems) accidentally but perhaps also by deliberate pruning."[6] The result of this pruning is that the scribe produced a very readable text, with very little need of correction.

  Further study of the manuscript shows that the omissions were not simply the result of scribal excision for the sake of trimming. In Mark 6:40 the scribe of $\mathfrak{P}^{45}$ made a deletion to bring Mark's account into harmony with Matthew's (see 14:19) or John's (see 6:10). In John 11:25 the scribe of $\mathfrak{P}^{45}$ thought it tautological to add "and the life" to "I am the resurrection" because the latter is Jesus' poignant rejoinder to Martha, who believed in the final resurrection as being nothing more than an event. And in John 11:49 the change reveals the scribe's knowledge of history and his sensitivity to the accurateness of the historicity of the text.[7]

  The text of $\mathfrak{P}^{45}$ varies with each book. According to Kenyon, $\mathfrak{P}^{45}$ in Mark shows a strong affinity with those manuscripts which used to be called Caesarean (i.e., W f[1] f[13] 565 700). In Matthew, Luke, and John, $\mathfrak{P}^{45}$ stands midway between the Alexandrian manuscripts and so-called Western manuscripts. In Acts, $\mathfrak{P}^{45}$ shows the greatest affinity with the Alexandrian uncials (ℵ A B C)—as over against the manuscripts with a D-text.

$\mathfrak{P}^{46}$ (Chester Beatty Papyrus II)

- Frederic G. Kenyon, *The Chester Beatty Biblical Papyri III/1: Pauline Epistles and Revelation, Text* (London, 1934); *III/3* (Supplement): *Pauline Epistles, Text* (London, 1936); *III/4: Pauline Epistles, Plates* (London, 1937); Henry A.

Sanders, *A Third-century Papyrus Codex of the Epistles of Paul* (Ann Arbor: University of Michigan Press, 1935).

- The papyrus has most of Paul's epistles (excluding the Pastorals) in this order: Romans 5:17–6:14; 8:15–15:9; 15:11–16:27; Hebrews 1:1–13:25; 1 Corinthians 1:1–16:22; 2 Corinthians 1:1–13:13; Ephesians 1:1–6:24; Galatians 1:1–6:18; Philippians 1:1–4:23; Colossians 1:1–4:18; 1 Thessalonians 1:1; 1:9–2:3; 5:5–9, 23–28 (with minor lacunae in each of the books).

- The University of Michigan library has thirty leaves containing the following portions: Romans 11:35–14:8; Romans 15:11–Hebrews 8:8; Hebrews 9:10–26; 1 Corinthians 2:3–3:5; 2 Corinthians 9:7–13:14; Ephesians; Galatians 1:1–6:10. The Chester Beatty Collection has fifty-six leaves containing Romans 5:17–6:14; 8:15–11:35; 14:19–15:11; Hebrews 8:9–9:10; Hebrews 9:26–1 Corinthians 2:3; 1 Corinthians 3:6–2 Corinthians 9:7; Galatians 6:10–18; Philippians; Colossians; 1 Thessalonians 1:1–2:3; 5:5–28.

- Middle second century

- On the whole, the text of $\mathfrak{P}^{46}$ is fairly reliable. The scribe who produced this manuscript used an early, excellent exemplar. He was a professional scribe, for there are stichoi notations at the end of several books (see the conclusion of Romans, 2 Corinthians, Ephesians, Philippians). The stichoi were used by professionals to note how many lines had been copied for commensurate pay. Most likely, an official of a scriptorium (perhaps connected wth a church library) paginated the codex and indicated the stichoi. The scribe himself made a few corrections as he went, and then several other readers made corrections here and there. Thus, the manuscript was very well used—probably by various members of the church.

  The text of $\mathfrak{P}^{46}$ shows a strong affinity with B (especially in Ephesians, Colossians, and Hebrews) and next with Å. $\mathfrak{P}^{46}$ agrees much less with the later representatives of the Alexandrian text (namely, A C P 33). In short, $\mathfrak{P}^{46}$ is proto-Alexandrian. In Hebrews, $\mathfrak{P}^{46}$ and $\mathfrak{P}^{13}$ display nearly the same text. Out of a total of eighty-eight variation-units, there are seventy-one agreements and only seventeen disagreements.

$\mathfrak{P}^{47}$ (Chester Beatty Papyrus III)

- Frederic G. Kenyon, *Chester Beatty Biblical Papyri III/1: Pauline Epistles and Revelation, Text* (London: 1934); III/2: *Revelation, Plates* (London: 1936)
- Revelation 9:10–17:2
- Dublin, Ireland: Chester Beatty collection (III)

- Third century
- The manuscript is closest in its textual character to ℵ. $\mathfrak{P}^{47}$ and ℵ form one early textual alliance for Revelation; their testimony is generally considered to be somewhat inferior to that found in $\mathfrak{P}^{115}$ A C.

$\mathfrak{P}^{48}$ (PSI 1165)

- G. Vitelli and S. G. Mercati, *Pubblicazioni della Societa Italiana, Papiri Greci e Latini* 10 (1932): 112–18.
- Acts 23:11–17, 23–29
- Florence, Italy: Biblioteca Laurenziana (no. 1165)
- Third century
- $\mathfrak{P}^{48}$, displaying a D-text, is a representative of the "Western" form of the book of Acts.

$\mathfrak{P}^{49}+^{65}$ (Yale Papyrus 415 + PSI 1373)

- W. H. P. Hatch and C. B. Wells, "A Hitherto Unpublished Fragment of the Epistle to the Ephesians" in *Harvard Theological Review* 51 (1958): 33–37; John F. Oates, Alan E. Samuel, C. Bradford Welles, *Yale Papyri in the Beinecke Rare Book and Manuscript Library* (New Haven: American Society of Papyrologists, 1967), 9–13; Vittorio Bartoletti, *Pubblicazioni della Societa Italiana, Papiri Greci e Latini* 14 (1957): 5–7. Two further publications of the Yale manuscript, $\mathfrak{P}^{49}$, offer further revisions: (1) Susan Stephens, *Yale Papyri in the Beinecke Rare Book and Manuscript Library* II, 1–2 (1985); (2) Stephen Emmel, "Biblical Papyri in the Beinecke Library," *Zeitschrift für Papyrologie und Epigraphik* 112 (1986): 291–94.
- $\mathfrak{P}^{49}$ is in New Haven, Connecticut: Yale University Library (inv. 415 + 531); $\mathfrak{P}^{65}$ is in Florence, Italy: Istituto di Papirologia G. Vitelli (PSI 1373)
- Ephesians 4:16–29; 4:31–5:13; 1 Thessalonians 1:3–10; 2:1, 6–13
- Third century
- $\mathfrak{P}^{49}$ (Ephesians) and $\mathfrak{P}^{65}$ (1 Thessalonians). $\mathfrak{P}^{49}$ was first published in 1948 by Hatch and Welles. $\mathfrak{P}^{65}$ was published in 1957 by Bartoletti, who indicated that he thought $\mathfrak{P}^{49}$ and $\mathfrak{P}^{65}$ were produced by the same scribe. $\mathfrak{P}^{49}$ (which is Yale Papyrus 415 + 531) was republished in a superior transcription by Oates and Welles in the Yale Papyri series. These editors then affirmed that the two manuscripts came from the same hand. Both manifest a very idiosyncratic formation of certain letters, such as the tilted lambda, tilted sigma, doubled curved and extended iota, and long-tailed upsilon. Welles remarked that "there is not a single case of difference in the letter shapes in the two papyri." And in both manuscripts the nomina sacra are written with a crossbar extending to the right (the width of one letter).

I have presented the case for the two manuscripts coming from the same codex.[8] Textually speaking, $\mathfrak{P}^{49}+{}^{65}$ show strong agreement with ℵ and B.

$\mathfrak{P}^{50}$ (P. Yale 1543)
- Oates, Samuel, Welles, *Yale Papyri in the Beinecke Rare Book and Manuscript Library* (New Haven, 1967), 15–21.
- Acts 8:26–32; 10:26–31
- Late third/early fourth century.
- New Haven, Connecticut: Yale University Library (P. 1543)
- The text generally concurs with B and ℵ.

$\mathfrak{P}^{52}$ (P. Rylands 457)
- C. H. Roberts, *An Unpublished Fragment of the Fourth Gospel in the John Rylands Library* (Manchester: 1935). This was republished with a few alterations in the *Bulletin of the John Rylands Library* XX (1936): 45–55; and then again in the *Catalogue of the Greek and Latin Papyri in the John Rylands Library* iii (Manchester: 1938), 1–3. The last publication contains critical notes and bibliography of scholarly reviews.
- John 18:31–34, 37–38
- Manchester, England: John Rylands Library (Gr. P. 457)
- ca. 110–125
- Though the amount of text in $\mathfrak{P}^{52}$ is hardly enough to make a positive judgment about its textual character, the text seems to be "Alexandrian." Its greatest value is its early date, for it testifies to the fact that the autograph of John's Gospel must have been written before the close of the first century.

$\mathfrak{P}^{53}$ (Michigan Papyrus 6652)
- Henry A. Sanders, "A Third Century Papyrus of Matthew and Acts" in *Quantulacumque: Studies Presented to Kirsopp Lake*, editors R. Casey, S. Lake, A. K. Lake (London: 1937), 151–61.
- Matthew 26:29–40; Acts 9:33–10:1 (Sanders said the two fragments are probably part of the same manuscript. This was confirmed by H. I. Bell. The two fragments were found together; they were part of a codex containing the four Gospels and Acts or just Matthew and Acts.)
- Ann Arbor, Michigan: University of Michigan Library (inv. no. 6652)
- Middle third century
- $\mathfrak{P}^{53}$ is proto-Alexandrian.

$\mathfrak{P}^{66}$ (Papyrus Bodmer II)
- Victor Martin, *Papyrus Bodmer II: Evangile de Jean, 1–14* (Cologny/Geneva, 1956); *Papyrus Bodmer II: Supplement, Evangile de Jean, 14–21*

(Cologny/Geneva, 1958); Victor Martin and J. W. B. Barns, *Papyrus Bodmer II: Supplement, Evangile de Jean, 14–21* (Cologny/Geneva, 1962); Kurt Aland, "Neue neutestamentliche Papyri III," in *New Testament Studies* 20 (1974): 357–81 (a publication containing previously unidentified fragments belonging to the same manuscript); M. Gronewald, "Christliche Texts, 214 Johannes Evangelium: Kap 19:8–11, 13–15, 18–20, 23–24," pp. 73–76 in *Kolner Papyri Band 5* (a publication containing previously unidentified fragments belonging to the same manuscript). New portions are also reconstructed in *Text of Earliest MSS* (see citation on p. 388).

- John 1:1–6:11; 6:35–14:26, 29–30; 15:2–26; 16:2–4, 6–7; 16:10–20:20, 22–23; 20:25–21:9
- Geneva/Cologny, Switzerland: Bibliotheca Bodmeriana; one leaf in Institut für Altertumskunde Papyrologie/Epigraphik
- Middle second century
- A full description of the work of the scribe and the correctors is found in *Text of Earliest MSS*, 381–88. The original scribe was quite free in his interaction with the text; he produced several singular readings that reveal his independent interpretation of the text. While the numerous scribal mistakes would seem to indicate that the scribe was inattentive, many of the singular readings—prior to correction—reveal that he was not detached from the narrative of the text. Rather, he became so absorbed in his reading that he often forgot the exact words he was copying. His task as a copyist was to duplicate the exemplar word for word, but this was frustrated by the fact that he was reading the text in logical semantic chunks and often became a coproducer of a new text. As a result, he continually had to stop his reading and make many in-process corrections. But he left several places uncorrected, which were later corrected by the *diorthotes*. A paleographic study of the second corrector's handwriting reveals that the first paginator is the same as the second corrector because the hands line up exactly. As noted by Fee, many of these corrections bring the manuscript into line with an Alexandrian-type text.[9] This corrector could have been an official proofreader in the scriptorium who used a different exemplar to make his emendations.

Fee's studies on $\mathfrak{P}^{66c}$ and $\mathfrak{P}^{75}$ in John 1–9 show that $\mathfrak{P}^{66c}$ demonstrates more agreement with $\mathfrak{P}^{75}$ than does $\mathfrak{P}^{66*}$. This means that $\mathfrak{P}^{66}$ was often corrected in the direction of $\mathfrak{P}^{75}$ in John 1–9. When we add John 10–21 to the equation and track $\mathfrak{P}^{66}$ corrected's relationship to $\mathfrak{P}^{75}$ in John 10:1–15:8 and then to B in 15:9–21:22, where $\mathfrak{P}^{75}$ is not extant (presuming B to be the closest textual extension of $\mathfrak{P}^{75}$), then the percentage of agreement goes up significantly. Of the 450 corrections in $\mathfrak{P}^{66}$, about 50 are of nonsense readings. Of the remaining 400, 284 made the text of $\mathfrak{P}^{66}$ normative (i.e., in agreement with a text supported by all witnesses). Of the remaining 116 corrections, 88 brought the text into conformity with $\mathfrak{P}^{75}$ in John 1:1–13:10 and 14:8–15:10; and with B in the remaining sections of John. This means that 75 percent of the substantive changes conformed $\mathfrak{P}^{66}$ to a $\mathfrak{P}^{75}$/B type text. (A further, detailed discussion of the scribal habits of $\mathfrak{P}^{66}$ is found in chap. 6.)

$\mathfrak{P}^{69}$ (P. Oxy. 2383)
- Lobel, Roberts, Turner, Barns, *Oxyrhynchus Papyri* XXIV (London, 1957), no. 2383, 1–4.
- Luke 22:41, 45–48, 58–61. The manuscript does not include Luke 22:41–44. The editors were fairly confident that the only reason to account for this large lacuna would be that the copyist's exemplar did not contain Luke 22:43–44.
- Oxford, England: Ashmolean Museum
- Middle third century
- $\mathfrak{P}^{69}$ displays an independent text.

$\mathfrak{P}^{70}$ (P. Oxy. 2384)
- Lobel, Roberts, Turner, Barns, *Oxyrhynchus Papyri* XXIV (London, 1957), no. 2384, 4–5. M. Naldini, "Nuovi frammenti del vangelo di Matteo," *Prometheus* 1 (1975): 195–200. (After the Istituto di Papirologia realized that they possessed another part of the same manuscript previously published in *Oxyrhynchus Papyri*, Naldini made this publication.)
- Matthew 2:13–16; 2:22–3:1; 11:26–27; 12:4–5; 24:3–6, 12–15
- Oxford, England: Ashmolean Museum—portion with Matthew 11 and 12; Florence, Italy: Istituto di Papirologia, G. Vitelli (CNR 419–20)—portion with Matthew 2–3, 24
- Late third century
- $\mathfrak{P}^{70}$ has a fairly reliable text, though somewhat carelessly written.

$\mathfrak{P}^{72}$ (Papyrus Bodmer VII-VIII)
- Michael Testuz, *Papyrus Bodmer VII-IX: L'Epitre de Jude, Les deux Epitres de Pierre, Les Psaumes 33 et 34* (Cologny/Geneva, 1959); Carlo M. Martini, *Beati Petri Apostoli Epistulae, Ex Papyro Bodmeriano VIII* (Milan, 1968); Sakae Kubo, $\mathfrak{P}^{72}$ *and the Codex Vaticanus* in *Studies and Documents* 27 (University of Utah Press, 1965).
- 1 Peter 1:1–5:14; 2 Peter 1:1–3:18; Jude 1–25 (in the same document as the Nativity of Mary, the apocryphal correspondence of Paul to the

Corinthians, the eleventh ode of Solomon, Melito's Homily on the Passover,
a fragment of a hymn, the Apology of Phileas, and Psalms 33 and 34)
- Geneva/Cologny, Switzerland: Bibliotheca Bodmeriana (1 and 2 Peter now
  in Biblioteca Vaticana)
- Late third/early fourth century (ca. 300)
- $\mathfrak{P}^{72}$ is a small codex made for private use and not for church meetings.
  Scholars think that four scribes took part in producing the entire manuscript (for contents, see above). First Peter has clear Alexandrian affinities—especially with B and then with A. Second Peter and (especially) Jude
  display more of an uncontrolled-type text (usually associated with the
  Western text), with several independent readings.

$\mathfrak{P}^{74}$ (Papyrus Bodmer XVII)

- Rudolf Kasser, *Papyrus Bodmer XV II: Actes de Apotres, Epitres de Jacques, Pierre,
  Jean et Jude* (Cologny/Geneva, 1961).
- Acts and General Epistles (with lacunae)
- Geneva/Cologny, Switzerland: Bibliotheca Bodmeriana
- Seventh century
- Despite the late date, this manuscript is important because it presents an
  Alexandrian text and is an excellent witness for the book of Acts.

$\mathfrak{P}^{75}$ (Papyrus Bodmer XIV-XV)

- Rudolf Kasser and Victor Martin, *Papyrus Bodmer XIV-XV*, I: *XIV: Luc chap
  3–24*; II:xV: *Jean chap. 1–15* (Cologny/Geneva, 1961); Kurt Aland, "Neue
  neutestamentliche Papyri III," *New Testament Studies* 22 (1976): 375–96
  (a publication containing previously unidentified fragments of the same
  manuscript).
- Luke 3:18–4:2; 4:34–5:10; 5:37–18:18; 22:4–24:53; John 1:1–11:45,
  48–57; 12:3–13:1, 8–9; 14:8–30; 15:7–8
- Geneva/Cologny, Switzerland: Bibliotheca Bodmeriana
- Late second century
- The copyist of $\mathfrak{P}^{75}$ was a professional Christian scribe. The professionalism
  shows through in his tight calligraphy and controlled copying. The large
  typeface indicates that the manuscript was composed to be read aloud to a
  Christian congregation. The scribe even added a system of sectional divisions to aid any would-be lector. As to the scribe's scriptoral acumen, he is
  probably the best of all the early Christian scribes. Concerning the scribe
  who made this excellent copy, Colwell said, "His impulse to improve style
  is for the most part defeated by the obligation to make an exact copy."[10]
  And concerning his work Colwell commented: "In $\mathfrak{P}^{75}$ the text that is produced can be explained in all its variants as the result of a single force,

namely the disciplined scribe who writes with the intention of being careful and accurate. There is no evidence of revision of his work by anyone else, or in fact of any real revision, or check. . . . The control had been drilled into the scribe before he started writing."[11] Calvin Porter clearly established the fact that $\mathfrak{P}^{75}$ displays the kind of text that was used in making Codex Vaticanus. Porter demonstrated 87 percent agreement between $\mathfrak{P}^{75}$ and B. In general, textual scholars have a high regard for the textual fidelity of $\mathfrak{P}^{75}$.[12]

$\mathfrak{P}^{77}$ (P. Oxy. 2683 + P. Oxy. 4405) + $\mathfrak{P}^{103}$ (P. Oxy. 4403)?

- The first portion of $\mathfrak{P}^{77}$ was edited by Ingrams, Kingston, Parsons, Rea in *Oxyrhynchus Papyri*, XXXIV (London: 1968), no. 2683, 1–3. The second portion was edited by J. David Thomas, *Oxyrhynchus Papyri*, LXIV (London: 1997), no. 4405, 8–9. $\mathfrak{P}^{103}$ probably belongs to the same codex (see discussion in *Text of Earliest MSS*, 609).
- Matthew 23:30–39; with Matthew 13:55–56; 14:3–5 (from P. Oxy. 4403)
- Oxford, England: Ashmolean Museum
- Middle to late second century
- The manuscript is clearly a literary production. According to Roberts, $\mathfrak{P}^{77}$ was written "in an elegant hand [and] has what was or became a standard system of chapter division, as well as punctuation and breathings."[13] $\mathfrak{P}^{77}$ has the closest affinity with $\aleph$.

$\mathfrak{P}^{78}$ (P. Oxy. 2684)

- Ingrams, Kingston, Parsons, Rea, *Oxyrhynchus Papyri*, vol. 34 (1968): 4–6
- Jude 4–5, 7–8
- Oxford, England: Ashmolean Museum
- Third/fourth century
- $\mathfrak{P}^{78}$ displays a free text.

$\mathfrak{P}^{80}$ (P. Barcelona 83)

- R. Roca-Puig, "Papiro del evangelio de San Juan con 'Hermeneia,'in *Atti dell' XI Congresso Internazionale di Papirologia* (Milan, 1966), 226–36.
- John 3:34 (with hermeneia)
- Barcelona, Spain: Fundacion San Lucas Evangelista (inv. no. 83)
- Third century
- $\mathfrak{P}^{80}$ is too fragmentary to determine its textual character.

$\mathfrak{P}^{87}$ (Inv. Nr. 12)

- Kramer, Romer, Hagedorn, *Kolner Papyri 4: Papyrologica Coloniensa* Vol. VII (1982): 28–31

- Philemon 13–15, 24–25
- Cologne: Institut für Alterumskunde, P. Col theol. 12
- Late second century
- $\mathfrak{P}^{87}$ is probably proto-Alexandrian.

$\mathfrak{P}^{90}$ (P. Oxy. 3523)

- Theodore A. Skeat, *Oxyrhynchus Papyri* L (1983): no. 3523, 3–8.
- John 18:36–19:7
- Oxford, England: Ashmolean Museum
- Late second century
- $\mathfrak{P}^{90}$ has more textual affinity with $\mathfrak{P}^{66}$ than with any other single manuscript, though it does not concur with $\mathfrak{P}^{66}$ in its entirety. Otherwise, it shows some affinity with $\aleph$.

$\mathfrak{P}^{91}$ (P. Macquarie Inv. 360 + P. Mil. Vogl. Inv. 1224)

- Claudio Gallazzi, "P. Mil. Vogl. Inv. 1224: *Novum Testamentum,* Act. 2,30–37 E 2, 46–3,2" in *Bulletin of American Society of Papyrologists* 19 (1982): 39–45; S. R. Pickering, "The Macquarie Papyrus of the Acts of the Apostles," a preliminary report (Aug. 30, 1984); S. R. Pickering, "P. Macquarie Inv. 360 (+ P. Mil. Vogl. Inv. 1224): Acta Apostolorum 2.30–37, 2.46–3.2," in *Zeitschrift für Papyrologie und Epigraphik* 65 (1986): 76–79. In this publication, the transcription for both portions of the manuscript is given.
- Acts 2:30–37, 46–3:2. One portion (the larger one): Milan, Italy: Istituto di Papirologia, Universita Degli Studi di Milano (P. Mil. Vogl. Inv. 1224); the other portion (the smaller one): North Ryde, Australia: Ancient History Documentary Research Centre at Macquarie University (P. Macquarie inv. 360)
- Middle third century
- $\mathfrak{P}^{91}$ is proto-Alexandrian, though the extant portion is too fragmentary to be sure.

$\mathfrak{P}^{92}$ (P. Narmuthis inv. 69.39a and 69.229a)

- Claudio Gallazzi, "Frammenti di un Codice con le Epistole di Paolo," in *Zeitschrift für Papyrologie und Epigraphik* 46 (1982): 117–22.
- Ephesians 1:11–13, 19–21; 2 Thessalonians 1:4–5, 11–12
- Cairo, Egypt: Museo Egizio del Cairo (P. Narmuthis inv. 69.39a and 69.229a)
- Late third/early fourth century—ca. 300 (contains the earliest extant portion of 2 Thessalonians)
- $\mathfrak{P}^{92}$ shows strong affinity with $\mathfrak{P}^{46}$, $\aleph$, and B.

$\mathfrak{P}^{95}$ (Firenze PL II/31)
- Jean Lenaerts, "Un papyrus l'Evangile de Jean: PL II/31," in *Chronique d'Egypte* 60 (1985): 117–20.
- John 5:26–29, 36–38
- Early third century
- Firenze: Biblioteca Medicea Laurenziana (PL II/31)
- $\mathfrak{P}^{95}$ is proto-Alexandrian, though it is too fragmentary to be certain.

$\mathfrak{P}^{98}$ (P. IFAO inv. 237b+a)
- D. Hagedorn "P.IFAO II 31: Johannesapokalypse 1,13–20," *Zeitschrift für Papyrologie und Epigraphik* 92 (1992): 243–47, pl. IX.
- Revelation 1:13–2:1
- Cairo, Egypt: Institut Français d'Archéologie Orientale (P. IFAO inv. 237b [+a])
- Late second century
- The text shows several differences from that printed in NA[27].

$\mathfrak{P}^{100}$ (P. Oxy. 4449)
- R. Hubner, *Oxyrhynchus Papyri* LXV (1998) no. 4449, 24–29.
- James 3:13–4:4, 9–5:1
- Oxford, England: Ashmolean Museum
- Late third/early fourth century
- $\mathfrak{P}^{100}$ generally concurs with the Alexandrian witnesses, $\mathfrak{P}^{74}$ ℵ A B.

$\mathfrak{P}^{104}$ (P. Oxy. 4404)
- J. David Thomas, *Oxyrhynchus Papyri* LXIV (100): no. 4404, 6–7
- Matthew 21:34–37, 43, 45(?).
- Oxford, England: Ashmolean Museum
- Early second century
- Because it is a small fragment, its textual character cannot be determined. However, it should be noted that it does not include Matthew 21:44 (contra ℵ. B C L W Z).

$\mathfrak{P}^{106}$ (P. Oxy. 4445)
- W. E. H. Cockle, *Oxyrhynchus Papyri* LXV (1998), no. 4445, 13–17
- John 1:29–35, 40–46
- Oxford, England: Ashmolean Museum
- Early third century
- The text of $\mathfrak{P}^{106}$ is proto-Alexandrian, aligning with $\mathfrak{P}^{66}$ $\mathfrak{P}^{75}$ ℵ B.

𝔓¹⁰⁷ (P. Oxy. 4446)
- W. E. H. Cockle, *Oxyrhynchus Papyri* LXV (1998), no. 4446, 17–19.
- John 17:1–2, 11
- Oxford, England: Ashmolean Museum
- Late second/early third century
- 𝔓¹⁰⁷ has an independent text, showing more agreement with W than any other manuscript

𝔓¹⁰⁸ (P. Oxy. 4447)
- W. E. H. Cockle, *Oxyrhynchus Papyri* LXV (1999), no. 4447, 20–22.
- John 17:23–24; 18:1–5
- Oxford, England: Ashmolean Museum
- Late second/early third century (ca. 200)
- The manuscript, though small, concurs with ℵ.

𝔓¹⁰⁹ (P. Oxy. 4448)
- W. E. H. Cockle, *Oxyrhynchus Papyri* LXV (1999), no. 4448, 22–24.
- John 21:18–20, 23–25
- Oxford, England: Ashmolean Museum
- Middle to late second century
- The text is too small to determine its textual character.

𝔓¹¹⁰ (P. Oxy. 4494)
- W. E. H. Cockle, *Oxyrhynchus Papyri* LXVI (1999), no. 4494, 1–4.
- Matthew 10:13–15, 25–27
- Oxford, England: Ashmolean Museum
- Middle to late third century
- 𝔓¹¹⁰ displays an independent text.

𝔓¹¹¹ (P. Oxy. 4495)
- W. E. H. Cockle, *Oxyrhynchus Papyri*, LXVI (1999), no. 4495, 4–6.
- Luke 17:11–13, 22–23
- Oxford, England: Ashmolean Museum
- First half of the third century
- 𝔓¹¹¹ concurs with 𝔓⁷⁵ almost completely.

𝔓¹¹³ (P. Oxy. 4497)
- W. E. H. Cockle, *Oxyrhynchus Papyri*, LXVI (1999), no. 4497, 8–9.
- Romans 2:12–13, 29
- Oxford, England: Ashmolean Museum

- Third century
- $\mathfrak{P}^{113}$ is too small to determine its textual character.

$\mathfrak{P}^{114}$ (P. Oxy. 4498)
- W. E. H. Cockle, *Oxyrhynchus Papyri* LXVI (1999), no. 4498, 10–11.
- Hebrews 1:7–12
- Oxford, England: Ashmolean Museum
- Third century
- $\mathfrak{P}^{114}$ is too small to determine its textual character.

$\mathfrak{P}^{115}$ (P. Oxy. 4499)
- Juan Chapa, *Oxyrhynchus Papyri* LXVI (1999), no. 4499, 11–39.
- Revelation 2:1–3, 13–15, 27–29; 3:10–12; 5:8–9; 6:5–6; 8:3–8, 11–9:5, 7–16, 18–10:4, 8–11:5, 8–15, 18–12:5, 8–10, 12–17; 13:1–3, 6–16, 18–14:3, 5–7, 10–11, 14–15, 18–15:1, 4–7
- Oxford, England: Ashmolean Museum
- Middle third century
- $\mathfrak{P}^{115}$ aligns with A and C in its textual witness, which are generally regarded as providing the best testimony to the original text of Revelation. Thus, $\mathfrak{P}^{115}$ has superior testimony to that of $\mathfrak{P}^{47}$, which aligns with codex Sinaiticus and together form the second-best witness to the text of Revelation.

Significant Uncial Manuscripts

The manuscripts typically classified as uncials are so designated to differentiate them from papyrus manuscripts. In a sense, this is a misnomer because the real difference has to do with the material they are written on—vellum (treated animal hide) as against papyrus—not the kind of letters used. Indeed, the papyri are also written in uncials (capital letters), but the term *uncial* typically describes the majuscule lettering that was prominent in fourth-century biblical texts, such as in ℵ and B.

ℵ (Codex Sinaiticus)
- This codex was discovered by Constantin von Tischendorf in St. Catherine's Monastery (situated at the foot of Mount Sinai). Tischendorf greatly used the textual evidence of Codex Sinaiticus in preparing his critical editions of the Greek New Testament. Tischendorf issued an edition of Codex Sinaiticus printed in facsimile type in 1862: *Codex Sinaiticus Petropolitanus* (Leipzig). See also Kirsopp Lake's *Codex Sinaiticus Petropolitanus*. Oxford University Press: 1911 (a photographic reproduction), and two works by Milne and Skeat: *The Scribes and Correctors of the Codex Sinaiticus* (Oxford:

Oxford University Press, 1938) and *The Codex Sinaiticus and the Codex Alexandrinus* (London, 1951 and 1963).

- Entire Old Testament, and New Testament in this order: Four Gospels, Pauline Epistles (including Hebrews), Acts, General Epistles, Revelation. It also includes the Epistle of Barnabas and the Shepherd of Hermes. (The manuscript contains 346 leaves of fine parchment, written in four columns.)
- London, British Museum
- ca. 350–375. The codex cannot be earlier than 340 (the year Eusebius died) because the Eusebian sections of the text are indicated in the margins of the Gospels by a contemporary hand (Thompson 1912:200).
- Tischendorf thought four scribes had originally produced the codex, whom he named Scribes A, B, C, D. After reinvestigation, Milne and Skeat identified only three scribes: A (who wrote the historical and poetical books of the Old Testament, as well as most of the New Testament), B (who wrote the Prophets and the Shepherd of Hermas), and D (who wrote some Psalms, Tobit, Judith, 4 Maccabees, and redid small sections of the New Testament). Milne and Skeat demonstrated that Scribe A of Codex Vaticanus was likely the same scribe as Scribe D of Codex Sinaiticus.[14] If this is true, then ℵ is contemporary with B—perhaps produced in the same scriptorium in Alexandria.

Some scholars have detected nine correctors at work on this manuscript. Only two are typically noted, as follows:

ℵ[1] designates the corrector who worked in the scriptorium on the manuscript before it left the scriptorium.

ℵ[2] designates a group of correctors working in Caesarea in the sixth or seventh century who corrected the text by "bringing it into general conformity with the Byzantine texts."[15]

Codex Sinaiticus provides a fairly reliable witness to the New Testament; however, the scribe was not as careful as the scribe of B. He was more prone to error and to creative emendation. Hort's comparison between B and ℵ affirms this: "Turning from B to ℵ, we find ourselves dealing with the handiwork of a scribe of a different character. The omissions and repetitions of small groups of letters are rarely to be seen; but on the other hand all the ordinary laspses due to rapid and careless transcription are more numerous, including substitutions of one word for another. . . . The singular readings are very numerous, especially in the Apocalypse, and scarcely ever commend themselves on internal grounds. It can hardly be doubted that many of them are individualisms of the scribe himself."[16]

The scribe of א displayed his creativity not only in Revelation but also in John, especially in the first eight chapters. In an extensive study, Fee demonstrated that א is clearly a "Western" text in John 1:1–8:38.[17]

A (Codex Alexandrinus)

- *Facsimile of the Codex Alexandrinus*; ed. E. M. Thompson. London, 1879–1883; H. J. M. Milne and T. C. Skeat, *The Codex Sinaiticus and the Codex Alexandrinus*. London, 1951 and 1963.

- Only 773 of the original 820 or so pages still exist. The rest were lost as the book was passed down through the centuries. The surviving parts of Alexandrinus contain a Greek translation of the whole Old Testament, the Apocrypha (including four books of Maccabees and Psalm 151), most of the New Testament, and some early Christian writings (of which the *First and Second Epistles of Clement to the Corinthians* are the most important). Missing sections of the New Testament are Matthew 1:1–25:6; John 6:50–8:52; and 1 Corinthians 4:13–12:6.

- London: British Museum

- Early fifth century

- Kenyon thought the codex was the work of five scribes, to each of whom he designated a Roman numeral. According to Kenyon, scribes I and II copied the Old Testament; scribe III did Matthew, Mark, 1 Corinthians 10:8–Philemon 25; scribe IV did Luke-Acts, General Epistles, Romans 1:1–1, Corinthians 10:8; and scribe V did Revelation.[18] But Milne and Skeat argued that the whole codex was the work of two copyists (I and II).[19]

Evidently, the scribe(s) of this codex used exemplars of varying quality for various sections of the New Testament. Compared to the General Epistles and Revelation (where Alexandrinus presents a reliable witness), the exemplar used for the Gospels was of poor quality, reflecting a Byzantine text type. Furthermore, the scribe of A infused his own readings into the text. Hort said, "In the New Testament an appreciable number of the singular readings of A consist in the permutation of synonyms, and it can hardly be doubted that these readings are true individualisms."[20]

Codex Alexandrinus is a witness to the Byzantine text type in the Gospels. Its testimony in the Epistles is much better, and in Revelation it provides the best witness to the original text.

B (Codex Vaticanus)

- A photographic edition was published by the Vatican Library authorities: *Bibliorum SS. Graecorum Codex Vaticanus 1209,* Milan: Vatican Library, 1904–1907.

- Originally it must have had about 820 leaves (1,640 pages), but now it has 759—617 in the Old Testament and 142 in the New. The major gaps of the

manuscript are Genesis 1:1–46:28; 2 Samuel 2:5–7, 10–13; Psalms 106:27–138:6, Hebrews 9:14–13:25; the Pastoral Epistles; and Revelation.
- Rome: Vatican Library
- ca. 350
- This codex, generally recognized as one of the most trustworthy witnesses to the New Testament text, is the work of two scribes, who are known as A (for the Old Testament) and B (for the New Testament). According to the studies of Milne and Skeat, two correctors worked on the New Testament: designated B^1 (a corrector nearly contemporary with the scribe) and B^2 (a tenth- or eleventh-century corrector, who retouched the writing and added accents and marks of punctuation).[21]

Codex Vaticanus is generally recognized as an eminent witness—especially in the Gospels. (Its "Western" tendencies in the Epistles have lessened its value for those books.) The scribe of B did his task with rote fidelity. This is underscored by Hort's comments about this scribe's copying habits: "The final impression produced by a review of all the trustworthy signs is of patient and rather dull or mechanical type of transcription, subject now and then to the ordinary lapses which come from flagging watchfulness, but happily guiltless of ingenuity or other untimely activity of brain, and indeed unaffected by mental influences except of the most limited and unconscious kind."[22]

C (Codex Ephraemi Rescriptus)
- Constantin von Tischendorf, *Codex Ephraemi Syri rescriptus sive Fragmenta Novi Testamenti,* Leipzig, 1843 (with plates); Robert W. Lyon, "A Re-examination of Codex Ephraemi Rescriptus" in *New Testament Studies* 5 (1958–1959): 260–72. This article provides a list of corrections to Tischendorf's work.
- The codex originally contained the entire Bible but now has only parts of six Old Testament books and portions of all New Testament books except 2 Thessalonians and 2 John. The single-column Bible text, written in the fifth century AD was erased in the twelfth century and replaced by a two-column text of a Greek translation of sermons or treatises by a certain Ephraem, a fourth-century Syrian church leader.
- Paris: Bibliothèque Nationale (Codex Gr. 9)
- Early fifth century
- According to Metzger, the text of C "seems to be compounded from all the major text types, agreeing frequently with the later Koine of Byzantine type, which most scholars regard as the least valuable type of New Testament text."[23] Scholars have been able to detect various correctors, designated as follows:

C^1 original corrector

C^2 corrector of the sixth century (probably in Palestine)

C^3 corrector of the ninth century (probably in Constantinople) who added accents and breathing marks

D (Codex Bezae)

- The first edited transcription was published by F. H. Scrivener: *Bezae Codex Cantabrigiensis*, Cambridge, 1864. The facsimile edition of *Codex Bezae Cantabrigiensis* was published by Cambridge University Press in 1899.
- Greek-Latin diglot containing Matthew–Acts, 3 John, with lacunae. According to the Alands, the codex was produced either in Egypt or North Africa by a scribe whose mother tongue was Latin.[24] Parker argues that it was copied in Beirut, a center of Latin legal studies during the fifth century, where both Latin and Greek were used.[25]
- Early fifth century
- According to Parker, it was produced by a scribe who knew Latin better than Greek, and then was corrected by several scribes.[26] According to the Alands, this codex is the most controversial of the New Testament uncials because of its marked independence. Its many additions, omissions, and alterations (especially in Luke and Acts) are the work of a significant theologian.[27] A few earlier manuscripts ($\mathfrak{P}^{29?}$, $\mathfrak{P}^{38}$, $\mathfrak{P}^{48}$, and 0171) appear to be precursors to the type of text found in D, which is considered the principal witness of the Western text-type. Thus, Codex Bezae could be a copy of an earlier revised edition. This reviser must have been a scholar with a propensity for adding historical, biographical, and geographical details. More than anything, he was intent on filling in gaps in the narrative by adding circumstantial details.

D (Codex Claromontanus)—also designated D^P

- Constantin von Tischendorf, *Codex Claromontanus,* Leipzig, 1852.
- Greek-Latin diglot containing Pauline epistles including Hebrews. Two of the pages had been used before, containing faintly visible lines from Euripides' *Phaethon*. The Pauline letters are complete except for a few verses from Romans missing from both the Greek and the Latin, and a few Latin verses from 1 Corinthians.
- Paris: Bibliothèque Nationale (Codex Gr. 107, 107AB)
- Sixth century
- The Latin text is not a translation of the Greek text it parallels but an independent text copied alongside, perhaps to serve a community where Latin was understood better than Greek. Between the sixth and ninth centuries

corrections were made to the manuscript by about nine different people. The manuscript is usually described as being "Western" because its geographical origin seemed to be the western areas of the Mediterranean. However, it should be noted that "the Western readings in the Epistles are not so striking as those in the Gospels and Acts."[28]

E (Codex Laudianus 35)—also designated E[a]
- Constantin von Tischendorf, *Codex Laudianus Mon sac IX,* Leipzig, 1870.
- Acts (in Latin and Greek)
- Oxford: Bodleian Library (Gr. 35)
- Sixth century
- The text is mixed, sometimes agreeing with D, more often Byzantine. It is the earliest extant manuscript to have Acts 8:37, the Ethiopian's confession of faith.

F (Codex Augiensis)—also designated F[p]
- F. H. A. Scrivener, *An Exact Transcript of Codex Augiensis [with] a Full Collation of Fifty Manuscripts,* Cambridge, 1859.
- Pauline epistles (in Greek and Latin), with Hebrews in Latin only
- Cambridge: Trinity College (B.XVII.1)
- Ninth century
- The text of F is Western.

G (Codex Boernerianus)—also designated G[p]
- A photographic reproduction with introduction was made by A. Reichardt: *Der Codex Boernerianus*, Leipzig, 1909.
- Pauline epistles (Greek with Latin interlinear; contains superscript after Philemon for an Epistle to the Laodiceans but no text follows.)
- Dresden: Sachsische Landesbibliothek (A 145b)
- Ninth century
- The manuscript probably had the same archetype as F (F[p]), both of which resemble the manuscript 037 from St. Gall.

H (Codex Coislinianus)—also designated H[p]
- Kirsopp Lake, *Facsimiles of the Athos Fragments of the Codex H of the Pauline Epistles*, Oxford, 1905.
- Pauline epistles (parts of 1 and 2 Cor., Gal., Col., 1 Thess., Heb., 1 and 2 Tim., Titus—arranged according to the colometric edition of the Epistles prepared by Euthalius)
- Paris (22); Athos, Great Lavra (8); Kiev (3); Leningrad (3); Moscow (3); Turin (2)

- Sixth century
- The manuscript is later Alexandrian.

I (Codex Freerianus or the Washington Codex)
- Henry A. Sanders, *The New Testament Manuscripts in the Freer Collection: Part IV, The Washington Manuscript of the Fourth Gospel,* New York: Macmillan, 1914.
- Pauline epistles (1 Corinthians–Hebrews)
- Washington, D.C.: Freer Gallery of Art (06.275)
- Fifth century
- According to Sanders, this manuscript has an Egyptian text, showing more agreement with ℵ and A than with B.

L (Codex Regius)
- Constantin von Tischendorf, *Codex Regius Mon sac*, Leipzig, 1846.
- Four Gospels (nearly complete)
- Paris: Bibliothèque Nationale (Gr. 62)
- Eighth century
- Though it contains several scribal errors, the basic text is still good, generally agreeing with B. It contains two endings to the Gospel of Mark (see comments on Mark 16:9–20 in chap. 7).

P (Codex Porphyrianus)
- Constantin von Tischendorf, *Codex Porphyrianus Mon sac VI,* Leipzig, 1860.
- Acts–Revelation, a palimpset with commentary of Euthalius on Acts and Pauline epistles written (in 1301) over the biblical text
- Leningrad: Public Library (Gr. 225)
- Ninth century
- The text is Byzantine and Alexandrian—related to the Andreas type of text in Revelation.

Q (Codex Guelferbytanus B)
- Constantin von Tischendorf, *Codex Guelferbytanus Mon sac III,* Leipzig.
- Luke–John, a palimpset with Latin text of Isidore of Seville's *Origins* and *Letters* written over biblical text
- Wolfenbüttel: Herzog August Biliothek. Weissenburg 64.
- Fifth century
- The manuscript is Byzantine.

T (Codex Borgianus)
- A. A. Giorgi, *Fragmentum Evangelii S. Johannis Graecum Copto-Sahidicum,* Rome, 1789.

- Portions of Luke (6; 18–24) and John (1; 3; 4–8)—a Coptic Sahidic-Greek diglot
- Rome: Collegium de Propoganda Fide
- Fifth century
- Because it is a Coptic Sahidic-Greek diglot, there is no question that it was produced in Egypt. Codex T is one of the fifth-century manuscripts that perpetutated the kind of Alexandrian scholarship that produced Codex B. Indeed, the text of T "is very close to that represented by codex Vaticanus."[29]

W (Codex Washingtonianus or Freer Gospels—named after its owner, Charles Freer)
- Henry Sanders, *The New Testament Manuscripts in the Freer Collection: Part I, The Washington Manuscript of the Fourth Gospel,* New York: Macmillan, 1912; Henry Sanders, *Facsimile of the Washington Manuscript of the Four Gospels in the Freer Collection,* Ann Arbor, 1912.
- Matthew–Acts
- Washington, D.C.: Freer Gallery of Art (06.274)
- ca. 400
- According to Sanders, Codex W was copied from a parent manuscript (exemplar) that had been pieced together from several different manuscripts. This is obvious because the textual presentation of W is noticeably variegated and even the stratification of the text is matched by similar variations in paragraphing. Sanders suggested that the parent manuscript was probably put together shortly after the Diocletian persecution, when manuscripts of the New Testament were scarce: "The patchwork character of the parent manuscript plainly indicates origin in a time when Biblical manuscripts came near extinction in certain regions at least. As the last great persecution, in which we are expressly told that the sacred books were ordered destroyed, was begun by Diocletian in 303, we are probably justified in dating the parent of W soon after that." The scribe who collated the parent manuscript drew upon various sources to put together his Gospel codex. Based on the textual evidence, Sanders conjectured that the scribe of the parent manuscript used a text that came from North Africa (the "Western" text) for the first part of Mark, and the scribe of W used manuscripts from Antioch for Matthew and the second part of Luke "to fill the gaps in the more ancient manuscript, which he was copying" (139). Detailed textual analysis reveals the variegated textual stratifications of W, as follows: in Matthew the text is Byzantine; in Mark the text is first Western (1:1–5:30), then Caesarean in Mark 5:31–16:20 (akin to $\mathfrak{P}^{45}$); in Luke the text is first Alexandrian (1:1–8:12) then Byzantine. John is more

complicated because the first part of John (1:1–5:11), which fills a quire, was the work of a seventh-century scribe who must have replaced a damaged quire. (W^s designates the work of this scribe.) This first section has a mixture of Alexandrian and Western readings, as does the rest of John. The siglum W^s designates the work of this seventh-century scribe.

The extreme textual variation in this manuscript reveals the tremendous liberties the scribes (of the parent manuscript of W and W itself) exerted in producing a codex. They not only selected various exemplars of various portions of each Gospel (at least as many as seven different exemplars), they also harmonized and filled textual gaps. Codex W is a prime example of what happened to many New Testament manuscripts after the major shift occurred. Each Gospel as an individual literary work was used and thereby changed in order to make a fourfold Gospel codex.

Z (Codex Dublinensis)

- John Barrett, *Evangelium secundum Matthaeum ex codice rescripto in bibliotheca collegii sae Trinitatis iuxta Dublinum,* Dublin, 1801; Samuel P. Tregelles, *The Dublin Codex Rescriptus: A Supplement*, London, 1863.
- Matthew, a palimpset with patristic writings written over biblical text
- Dublin: Trinity College (K 3.4)
- Sixth century
- The text of Z is Alexandrian, agreeing with ℵ.

Δ = 037 Codex Sangallensis

- H. C. M. Rettig, *Antiquissimus quatuor evangeliorum canonicorum Codex Sangallensis Graeco-Latinus interlinearis*, Zurich, 1836.
- Four Gospels—Greek-Latin diglot, with Latin interlinear
- Gallen: Stiftbibliothek (48)
- Ninth century
- The text is Byzantine generally; later Alexandrian in Mark (similar to L).

Θ = 038 Codex Koridethi

- A transcription of the entire text was produced by Gustav Beermann and Caspar R. Gregory: *Die Koridethi Evangelien Θ 038*, Leipzig, 1913.
- Four Gospels
- Tiflis, Georgia: Manuscript Institute (Gr. 28)
- Ninth century
- The scribe was probably a Georgian who did not know Greek. He drew his letters rather than wrote them. In Matthew, Luke, and John the text is Byzantine. In Mark it is Caesarean in the sense that it agrees with the type of text that "Origen and Eusebius used in the third and fourth centuries at

Caesarea."[30] This manuscript, often associated with 565 and 700, is considered by many to be the chief representative of the Caesarean text.[31]

Ξ = 040 Codex Zacynthius
- Samuel P. Tregelles, *Codex Zacynthius,* London, 1861.
- Luke 1:1–11:33 (with lacunae)—a palimpset with a twelfth-century Gospel lectionary written over original text that is itself surrounded by commentary
- London: British and Foreign Bible Society (24)
- Sixth century
- The text is later Alexandrian; it agrees with B and contains the same system of chapter divisions as B (as well as 579).

Φ = 043 Codex Beratinus
- P. Batiffol, "Les Manuscits grecs de Berat d'Albanie et le codex purpureus **Φ**" in *Archives des missions scientifiques et litteraires*, third series, vol. 13, Paris, 1887.
- Matthew and Mark—written with silver ink on purple parchment
- Tirané: National Archives (1)
- Sixth century
- The text is Byzantine; the manuscript contains a noteworthy long addition after Matthew 20:28.

Ψ = 044 Codex Athous Laurae
- Kirsopp Lake, "Texts from Mount Athos," in *Studia Biblica et Ecclesiastica* 5:89–185, Oxford, 1903.
- Mark 9–Acts, General Epistles, Pauline epistles, Hebrews
- Monastery of the Laura, Mount Athos: Lavra (B′ 52)
- Eighth or ninth century
- The text is generally Byzantine, with Western and Alexandrian affinities in Mark, where it has two endings (as in L).

0162 (P. Oxy. 847)
- Grenfell and Hunt, *Oxyrhynchus Papyri* vol. 5 (1909): 4–5.
- John 2:11–22
- New York: Metropolitan Museum of Art (09.182.43)
- Early fourth century
- 0162 shows great affinity with $\mathfrak{P}^{66}$ and $\mathfrak{P}^{75}$, as well as with B.

0171 (PSI 2.124)
- *Pubblicazioni della Societa Italina, Papiri Greci e Latini,* vol. 1 (1912): 2–4; vol. 2 (1913): 22–25.

- A transcription of the text is printed in *New Documents Illustrating Early Christianity,* vol. 2, editor G. H. R. Horsley (1982); J. Neville Birdsall, "A fresh examination of the fragments of the gospel of St. Luke in ms. 0171 and an attempted reconstruction with special reference to the recto," pp. 212–27 in *Philologia Sacra*; editor Roger Gryson. Verlag Herder Freiburg, 1993.
- Matthew 10:17–23, 25–32; Luke 22:44–56, 61–64
- Florence: Bibliotheca Laurenziana (PSI 2.124)
- ca. 300
- 0171 is related to the D-text in Acts.

0189 (Papyrus Berlin 11765)
- A. H. Salonius., "Die griechischen Handschriftenfragmente des Neuen Testaments in den Staatlichen Museen zu Berlin," *Zeitschrift für die Neutestamentliche Wissenschaft* 26 (1927): 115–19.
- Acts 5:3–21
- Berlin, Germany: Staatliche Museen (P. 11765)
- Late second or early third century (the earliest parchment manuscript of the New Testament)
- The text nearly always agrees with the Alexandrian witnesses.

0220 (MS 113)
- W. H. P. Hatch, *Harvard Theological Review* 45 (1952): 81–85.
- Romans 4:23–5:3, 8–13
- Oslo/London: Schoyen Collection
- Third century
- 0220 agrees with B everywhere except in Romans 5:1.

Minuscules

The minuscules are manuscripts written in cursive-letter form rather than in separate-letter uncial form. The minuscules came later than the uncials—at a time when the Byzantines were mass-producing copies of the Bible via oral dictation. Since speed of copying was an issue, scribes used a cursive form rather than an uncial form.

f^1 designates a family of manuscripts including 1, 118, 131, 209
- Kirsopp Lake, *Texts and Studies* 7, Cambridge, 1902.
- Four Gospels
- Minuscule 1 is at Basel: Universitätsbibliothek (A. N. IV, 2)

- Twelfth-fourteenth century
- The text type of f[1] has been traced to a third- or fourth-century "Caesarean" archetype; the text agrees with Codex Koridethi in Mark.

f[13] designates a family of manuscripts including 13, 69, 124, 174, 230, 346, 543, 788, 826, 828, 983, 1689, 1709 (known as the Ferrar group)
- Kirsopp and Silva Lake, *Family 13 (The Ferrar Group)*, in *Studies and Documents* 11 (London and Philadelphia, 1941).
- Four Gospels
- Minuscule 13 is at Paris: Bibliothèque Nationale (Gr. 50).
- Eleventh-fifteenth century
- The text type of f[13], which has affinities with the so-called Caesarean text type, has been traced to an archetype from Calabria in southern Italy or Sicily. In these manuscripts Luke 22:43–44 follows after Matthew 26:39, and the pericope adulteress (John 7:53–8:11) appears after Luke 21:38, not after John 7:52.

Codex 33
- This manuscript was collated by S. P. Tregelles and used in his edition of the *Greek New Testament* (1857–1879).
- All of New Testament except Revelation
- Paris: Bibliothèque Nationale (Gr. 14)
- Ninth century
- This manuscript, often called "the Queen of the Cursives," is a prime example of a late manuscript that retained (for the most part) the Alexandrian text type.

Codex 81
- F. H. Scrivener, *An Exact Transcript of Codex Augiensis [with] a Full Collation of Fifty Manuscripts,* Cambridge, 1859.
- Acts, Paul's Epistles, General Epistles
- Alexandria: Greek Patriarchate 59 (255 folios); London: British Library Add. 20003 (57 folios)
- 1044 (the manuscript has a specific date)
- The text is Alexandrian.

Codex 565
- Johannes Belsheim, *Christiana Videnskabs-Selskabs Forhandlinger*, 1885 (no. 9)—text of Mark and collation of other three Gospels. Corrections were published by H. S. Cronin in *Texts and Studies* V (4); Cambridge, 1899.
- Gospels (gold letters on purple vellum)

- Leningrad: Public Library (Gr. 53)
- Ninth century
- In Mark, this manuscript is closely aligned to Codex Koridethi, a Caesarean text.

Codex 700

- H. C. Hoskier, *A Full Account and Collation of the Greek Cursive Codex Evangelium 604*; London, 1890.
- Gospels
- London: British Library (Egerton 2610)
- Eleventh century
- This manuscript greatly differs from the Textus Receptus (nearly 2,750 times) and has many singular readings. One of its most striking readings includes a variation of the Lord's Prayer (see comments on Luke 11:2).

Codex 1424 (or Family 1424)

- Gospels, Acts, General Epistles, Revelation, Paul's Epistles
- Maywood, Illinois: Jesuit-Krauss-McCormick Library (Gruber Ms. 152)
- Ninth or tenth century
- Several other manuscripts share essentially the same text as 1424 and therefore comprise a family of manuscripts: M, 7, 27, 71, 115, 160, 179, 185, 267, 349, 517, 659, 692, 827, 945, 954, 990, 1010, 1082, 1188, 1194, 1207, 1223, 1293, 1391, 1402, 1606, 1675, 2191.

Codex 1739

- A collation of the manuscript was made by Morton S. Enslin in *Six Collations of New Testament Manuscripts*, eds. Kirsopp Lake and Silva New, in *Harvard Theological Studies* 17; Cambridge, Mass., 1932.
- Acts and Epistles
- Athos: Lavra (B^42)
- Tenth century
- For the Pauline epistles, Zuntz demonstrated the textual affinities of $\mathfrak{P}^{46}$, B, 1739, Coptic Sahidic, Coptic Boharic, Clement, and Origen. The relationship between $\mathfrak{P}^{46}$ B and 1739 is remarkable because 1739 is a tenth-century manuscript that was copied from a fourth-century manuscript of excellent quality. According to a colophon, the scribe of 1739 for the Pauline epistles followed a manuscript which came from Caesarea in the library of Pamphilus and which contained an Origenian text. The three manuscripts, $\mathfrak{P}^{46}$ B and 1739, form a clear textual line: from $\mathfrak{P}^{46}$ (second century) to B (early fourth century) to 1739 (tenth century based on fourth century). Zuntz said, "Within the wider affinities of the

'Alexandrian' tradition, the Vaticanus is now seen to stand out as a member of a group with 𝔓⁴⁶ and the preancestor of 1739. The early date of the text-form which this group preserves is fixed by its oldest member, and its high quality is borne out by many striking instances. B is in fact a witness for a text, not of ca. AD 360, but of ca. AD 200."[32]

Codex 2053

- Josef Schmid, *Studien zur Geschichte des griechischen Apokalypse-Textes,* vol. 2; Munich, 1955.
- Revelation (with Oecumenius's commentary on it)
- Messian: Biblioteca Universitario (99)
- Thirteenth century
- According to Schmid, this manuscript—with A C 2344—is one of the best authorities for the book of Revelation.

Codex 2344

- Josef Schmid, *Studien zur Geschichte des griechischen Apokalypse-Textes,* vol. 2; Munich, 1955.
- Acts, General Epistles, Paul's Epistles, Revelation
- Paris: Bibliothèque Nationale (Coislin Gr. 18)
- Eleventh century
- According to Schmid, this manuscript—with A C 2053—is one of the best authorities for the book of Revelation.

The majority of minuscules are noted in NA[27] as 𝔐; in this book, as Maj. Quite often, but not always, the reading of Maj concurs with the Textus Receptus (TR). For the book of Revelation, M^A designates a number of manuscripts that follow the text of Andreas of Caesarea's commentary on Revelation, and M^K designates the great number of manuscripts that display a Koine (or Byzantine) text type.

Uncial Manuscripts from St. Catherine's Monastery

A number of uncial New Testament manuscripts were discovered at St. Catherine's Monastery in the 1970s. None of these have been published as individual texts with transcriptions. However, the Alands were permitted access to the manuscripts and have incorporated their evidence into the textual apparatus of *Novum Testamentum Graece*. These are listed with the other uncial manuscripts in appendix 1 in the 27th edition (pp. 703–4), as follows:

0278 (Paul's Epistles) ninth century
0279 (Luke 8; 22) eighth/ninth century
0281 (Matt. 6–21) seventh/eighth century
0282 (Phil. 2–3) sixth century
0285 (Rom.–2 Cor.; Eph.; 1 Tim.; Heb.; 1 Pet.) sixth century

0289 (Rom.; 1 Cor.) seventh/eighth century
0291 (Luke 8–9) seventh/eighth century
0292 (Mark 6–7) sixth century
0293 (Matt. 21; 26) sixth century
0294 (Acts 14–15) sixth/seventh century
0296 (2 Cor. 7; 1 John 5) sixth century

Ancient Versions

As the gospel spread in the early centuries of the Christian era, Christians in various countries wanted to read the Bible in their own language. As a result, many translations were made—as early as the second century. For example, there were translations in Coptic for the Egyptians, in Syriac for those whose language was Aramaic, in Gothic for the Germanic people called the Goths, and in Old Latin for the Romans and Carthagenians.

Among the ancient versions that are used for establishing the original text are the following: Old Latin, Coptic, Syriac, Gothic, Ethiopic, Armenian, and Georgian. However, readers should be aware that ancient translators, as well as modern, took liberties in the interest of style when they rendered the Greek text. In other words, there is no such thing as a literal, word-for-word rendering in any translation. Therefore, the witness of the various ancient versions is significant only when it pertains to significant verbal omissions and/or additions, as well as significant semantic differences. One should not look to the testimony of any ancient version for conclusive evidence concerning word transpositions, verb changes, articles, or other normal stylistic variations involving noun insertions, conjunction additions, and slight changes in prepositions. The citation of such versions for these kinds of variant readings in the apparatuses of critical editions of the Greek New Testament can be quite misleading. Among the more important versions are the following:

Syriac (syr)

syr^c (Syriac Curetonian)

- William Cureton, *Remains of a Very Ancient Recension of the Four Gospels in Syriac,* London, 1858. Francis Crawford Burkitt, *Evangelion da-mepharreshe: The Curetonian Version of the Four Gospels, with the Readings of the Sinai Palimpset* (vol. 1 *Text*; vol. 2 *Introduction and Notes*), Cambridge, 1904.
- Gospels
- London: British Museum
- Fifth century
- Scholars had thought that the form of the text reflected in this manuscript and the Syriac Sinaiticus (see below) came from the late second century because of their perceived association with the Diatessaron. But

this association has not been proven. Therefore, it is safer to say that Old Syriac translations began to be made in the early fourth century. The Syriac Sinaiticus represents an early stage in this process, and the Syriac Curetonian probably represents the next stage—i.e., it is a revision. Both manuscripts are generally regarded as Western.

syr[s] (Syriac Sinaiticus)

- Agnes S. Lewis, *The Old Syriac Gospels or Evangelion da-mepharreshe; being the Text of the Sinai or Syro-Antiochene Palimpset, including the latest additions and emendations, with the variants of the Curetonian Syriac,* London, 1910.
- Gospels (a palimpset)
- Fourth Century
- This manuscript is the earliest extant document of the Old Syriac translation. Together with the Syriac Curetonian, it displays an indepedent text type (see discussion above).

Old Latin

Like the Aramaic targums of Jewish worshippers, the Old Latin Bible had an informal beginning. In the early days of the Roman Empire and of the church, Greek was the language of Christians. Even the first bishops of Rome wrote and preached in Greek. As empire and church aged, Latin began to win out, especially in the West. It was natural that priests and bishops began informally to translate the Greek New Testament and Septuagint into Latin. The initial Latin version is called the Old Latin Bible. No complete manuscript of it survives. Much of the Old Testament and most of the New, however, can be reconstructed from quotations in the early church fathers. Scholars believe that an Old Latin Bible was in circulation in Carthage in North Africa as early as AD 250. From the surviving fragments and quotations there seem to have been two types of Old Latin text, the African and the European. The European existed in an Italian revision also. In textual studies the major importance of the Old Latin is in comparative study of the Septuagint because the Old Latin was translated from the Septuagint before Origen made his *Hexapla*.

Among the many extant manuscripts of the Latin New Testament, five are worthy of mention:

it[a] (Codex Vercellenis)

- Gospels (in the Western order: Matthew, John, Luke, Mark)
- Vercelli: Biblioteca Capitolare
- Fourth century
- The manuscript displays a Western text.

it[b] (Codex Veronensis)
- Gospels (in the Western order: Matthew, John, Luke, Mark)
- Verona: Biblioteca Capitolare
- Fifth century
- This text, which is Western, represents the kind Jerome used in making the Latin Vulgate.

it[d] (Codex Cantabrigiensis)
- Gospels (Western order), Acts, 3 John—the Latin text of Codex Bezae (a Greek-Latin diglot)
- Cambridge: Cambridge University Library
- Fifth century
- The Latin translation, as with the Greek text of this manuscript, displays an independent text, quite unlike other early Latin versions.

it[e] (Codex Palantinus)
- Gospels (written with silver ink on purple parchment)
- Trent: Museo Nazionale
- Fifth century
- The text is of the North African variety (as opposed to the European in it[a] and it[b]), though it is less pure than it[k].

it[k] (Codex Bobiensis)
- Matthew 1–15; Mark 8–16 (with lacunae)
- Turin: Biblioteca Universitaria Nazionale (G. VII.15)
- ca. 400
- This manuscript is the earliest and purest form of the North African variety. It is the only manuscript to display just the short ending after Mark 16:8.

Other Versions
These versions are ocassionally cited in this commentary.

Armenian (arm).——Christians from Syria carried their faith to their Armenian neighbors in eastern Asia Minor. As early as the third century, with the conversion of Tiridates III (who reigned 259–314), Armenia became a Christian kingdom—the first such in history. Sometime during the fifth century an Armenian alphabet was created so that the Bible could be translated into the language of these new believers. The Armenian translation is considered one of the most beautiful and accurate of the ancient versions of the Greek, even though textual evidence indicates it may have been done from the Syriac first and then modified according to the Greek. (The Armenian language is allied closely with the Greek in grammar, syntax, and idiom.) An old tradition says that the New Testament was the work of Mesrop (a bishop in Armenia, 390–439) who is credited with inventing both the Armenian and Georgian alphabets.

The first translations of the New Testament into Armenian were probably based on Old Syriac versions. Later translations, which have the reputation for being quite accurate, were based on Greek manuscripts of the Byzantine text type but also show affinity with Caesarean manuscripts.

Coptic (cop).——Coptic was the last stage of the Egyptian language and thus the language of the native populations who lived along the length of the Nile River. It was never supplanted by the Greek of Alexander and his generals or even threatened by the Latin of the Caesars. Its script is composed of twenty-five Greek uncials and seven cursives taken over from Egyptian writing to express sounds not in the Greek.

Through the centuries it developed at least five main dialects: Achmimic, sub-Achmimic (Memphitic), Sahidic, Fayumic, and Bohairic. Fragments of biblical material have been found in all five dialects. They gradually faded out of use until—by the eleventh century—only Bohairic, the language of the Delta, and Sahidic, the language of Upper Egypt, remained. They too, however, had become strictly religious languages used only in Coptic churches by the seventeenth century because of the long dominance of Arabic that began with the Islamic conquest of Egypt in 641.

The earliest translation was in Sahidic in Upper Egypt, where Greek was less universally understood. The Sahidic Old and New Testaments were probably completed by around AD 200. Greek was so much more dominant in the Delta that the translation of the Scriptures into Bohairic probably was not completed until somewhat later. Since Bohairic was the language of the Delta, however, it was also the language of the Coptic patriarch in Alexandria. When the patriarchate moved from Alexandria to Cairo in the eleventh century, the Bohairic texts went along. Bohairic gradually became the major religious language of the Coptic church. The Copts had separated from the Roman Catholic church over doctrinal issues after the Council of Chalcedon in 451 and had then been isolated from Western Christendom by centuries of Islamic rule.

There were several dialects of Coptic, the three most prominent being Boharic (designated cop^{bo}) in north Egypt, Fayyumic (cop^{fay}) in central Egypt, and Sahidic (designated cop^{sa}) in southern Egypt. We have several extant translations of the New Testament into Coptic, some dated as early as the fourth century.

Ethiopic (eth).——By the middle of the fifth century a Christian king ruled in Ethiopia (Abyssinia), and until the Islamic conquests close ties were maintained with Egyptian Christianity. The Old Testament was probably translated into Old Ethiopic (called Ge'ez) by the fourth century. The Old Ethiopic version of the Old Testament contains several books not in the Hebrew Apocrypha. Most interesting of these is the book of Enoch, which is quoted in Jude 14 and was unknown to Bible scholars until James Bruce brought a copy to Europe in 1773.

The New Testament was translated into Old Ethiopic somewhat later than the Old Testament and contains a collection of writings mentioned by Clement of Alexandria, including the Apocalypse of Peter. Both Testaments are extant in Ethiopic manuscripts. None, however, is earlier than the thirteenth century, and these manuscripts seem to rest rather heavily on the Coptic and the Arabic. Nothing survived the total chaos that reigned in Ethiopia from the seventh to the thirteenth centuries. In Paul's Epistles, the Ethiopic version frequently agrees with $\mathfrak{P}^{46}$ (and B), with little or no support from other manuscripts.[33]

Frankish.—The New Testament was translated into the ancient language of the Western European Germanic Franks, about AD 500–800. Only fragments of the Gospel of Matthew remain from an eighth-century manuscript.

Georgian (geo).—The same tradition that credits Mesrop with translating the Bible into Armenian also credits an Armenian slave woman with being the missionary through whom Georgian-speaking people became Christian. The earliest manuscripts for the Georgian Scriptures go back only to the eighth century, but behind them is a Georgian translation with Syriac and Armenian traces. Evidently the Gospels first came in the form of the Diatessaron; therefore, Georgian fragments are important in the study of that text. There is a whole manuscript copy of the Georgian Bible in two volumes in the Iberian Monastery on Mount Athos. The earliest extant manuscript is called the Adysh manuscript of 897 (designated geo[1]); two other manuscripts of the tenth century are designated geo[2].

Gothic (goth).—In the middle of the fourth century, Ulfilas translated the Bible from Greek into Gothic (for which he created the Gothic alphabet). His translation, as reflected in later editions, appears to be quite literal and dependent on the early Byzantine text.

Ulfilas may have been captured by Gothic raiders as a youth. Yet his residence by early adulthood was Constantinople, the Roman Empire's eastern capital. Here undoubtedly he received his education and began his life of service to the church. In 341 Eusebius of Nicomedia, bishop of Constantinople, consecrated Ulfilas as bishop. Soon afterward the young bishop proceeded to Dacia (north of the Danube River), and for his remaining years he served as the church's principal missionary to the western Goths in this region. The many converts indicate that Ulfilas's efforts to spread the gospel had extensive results. After several years, persecution forced Ulfilas out of Dacia, and his work thereafter originated from a residence in Moesia (south of the Danube), an area within the empire's borders.

Ulfilas's removal to Moesia also saw the beginnings of the project for which he is best remembered. This was his translation of the Old and New Testaments into the Goths' vernacular language. Toward this end, Ulfilas first had to reduce Gothic speech to writing, a task involving the invention of an alphabet based on Greek. Surviving remnants of this translation, as copied in the early Middle Ages, are the earliest extant examples of Gothic literature. Ulfilas appears to have translated the whole New Testament and also the Old Testament except for the Books of Kings (1 and 2 Samuel, 1 and 2 Kings). It is supposed that the missing Old Testament sections were omitted purposely because of Ulfilas's fear that they would only encourage the aggressive Goths.

Among Ulfilas's known writings, the only modern survivals are the Bible translation and possibly a creedal statement. The sermons and interpretive writings are no longer extant. Portions of a beautiful copy of the Gothic Bible have been preserved at the University of Uppsala, Sweden. Early sources of information about Ulfilas exist mainly in works by fifth-century church historians, primarily Philostorgius, Socrates, and Sozomen. Scattered fragments of his Old Testament translation survive, and only about half of the Gospels are preserved in the Codex Argenteus, a manuscript of Bohemian origin of the fifth or sixth century now at Uppsala in Sweden.

Diatessaron.——In the middle of the second century, Tatian, a Syrian from Mesopotamia, produced a harmony of the Gospels by weaving together the four narratives into one (hence the name Diatessaron, meaning "through the four"). This is not the same as harmonization of one Gospel account to another, wherein each Gospel is left intact but emended to appear like the others. The Diatessaron is a "cut-and-paste job." Because of this, the citation of the Diatessaron in the critical apparatus of Greek New Testaments can be misleading in that the entire text of the Diatessaron is an adaptation of the four Gospels into one new work. For example, to cite the Diatessaron as including the verse Matthew 17:21 (which is not present in codices Vaticanus and Sinaiticus) is misleading because Tatian could have simply been using Mark 9:29 at this point in his composition. The same is true for its presumed witness to the inclusion of Matthew 18:11 (which Tatian could have taken from Luke 19:10), and for the additions in Luke 11:2–4 (all of which could have been taken from Matt. 6:9–13).

In any event, the Diatessaron had a tremendous effect in Syria and in the East. Christians in Syria from the third to the fifth century generally read the Diatessaron as their Gospel text. (Ephraem's commentary in Syriac has been preserved, in part, in a fifth-century manuscript of the Chester Beatty collection, 709). As late as AD 423, Theodoret (a bishop in Syria) found that many copies of the Diatessaron were being used in his diocese. Because Tatian had become heretical later in life and because Theodoret believed his congregations were in danger of being corrupted by Tatian's work, he destroyed all the copies he could find (about two hundred of them) and replaced them with copies of the four separate Gospels. "As a result of the zeal of Bishop Theodoret, and doubtless of others like him, no complete copy of Tatian's Diatessaron is extant today."[34] Only one small fragment discovered from Dura-Europas has been unearthed—namely, 0220.

It is difficult to determine how much influence the Diatessaron had on the transmission of the text of the separate Gospels. The scholarly consensus is that some "instances of harmonization of the text of the Gospels in certain witnesses (notably the Western witnesses) are to be described to Tatian's influence."[35] These influences are not at all apparent in Egyptian manuscripts; thus, it is unlikely that the Diatessaron had much affect on Egyptian scribes either before the fourth century or thereafter.

Significant Editions of the Greek New Testament

The purpose of this section is to provide the student with a brief introduction to the significant editions of the Greek New Testament. This introduction, for the most part, will move chronologically—from the earliest editions to the most recent. The view of most textual critics is that the editions have become progressively better in the sense that the wording selected for the text more closely represents the wording of the original writings. This assessment, of course, is for each student to discover via the process of learning the science and art of New Testament textual criticism.

Textus Receptus

Although the first printed edition of the Greek New Testament was the Complutensian Polyglot (published in Spain in 1514), the printed edition of the Greek New Testament (later known as the Textus Receptus) in 1515 has achieved a lasting legacy. In the years 1514 and 1515, the well-known scholar Desiderius Erasmus was approached by a publisher, Johann Froben, to produce a manuscript of the Greek New Testament for the purpose of making a printed text. When Erasmus compiled this text, he used five or six very late Byzantine manuscripts dating from the tenth to the thirteenth century—notably, minuscule 1 and minuscule 2, both of the twelfth century.

Thus, Erasmus's text was a printed version of a Byzantine text. Many scholars consider that the Byzantine text goes back to the recensional work of Lucian of Antioch. According to Jerome (see his introduction to his Latin translation of the Gospels—see *Patrologia Latina* 29, col. 527), Lucian of Antioch was reponsible for producing a major recension of the New Testament. Another name that has been ascribed to this text is "Syrian," because of its association with Antioch in Syria. This text was a definite recension (i.e., a purposely created edition), which displays a popular text, characterized by smoothness of language, harmonization, and conflation of variant readings.

Lucian's text was produced before the Diocletian persecution (ca. 303), when many copies of the New Testament were confiscated and destroyed. Not long after this period of devastation, Constantine came to power and then recognized Christianity as a legal religion. There was, of course, a great need for copies of the New Testament to be made and distributed to churches throughout the Mediterranean world. At this time Lucian's text began to be propagated by bishops going out from the Antiochan school to churches throughout the East, taking the text with them. Lucian's text soon became the standard text of the Eastern church and formed the basis for the Byzantine text. Century after century—from the sixth to the fourteenth—the great majority of New Testament manuscripts were produced in Byzantium, all bearing the same kind of text.

Erasmus's edition, with various alterations, was published again and again by different printers. This text then went through a few more revisions by Robert Stephanus and then by Theodore Beza. Beza's text was then published by the Elzevir brothers in 1624, with a second edition in 1633. In this edition they announced that their edition contained "the text which is now *received by all,* in which we give nothing changed or corrupted." As such, the name "textus receptus" became a descriptor of this form of the Greek New Testament text. This edition became the standard Greek New Testament for several centuries until it was superceded by superior editions of the Greek New Testament, compiled from superior manuscript evidence. Both editions—that of Stephanus (1550) and the Elzevirs' text (1624)—are known as the Textus Receptus.

The Textus Receptus and the Majority Text

In recent years, a few scholars have attempted to defend the validity of what they would call the Majority Text. But the Majority Text is nearly the same as the Textus Receptus in that the TR was composed from manuscripts belonging to the Majority Text. The two terms are not completely synonymous because the TR does not consistently display a Majority Text type throughout. The Majority Text is nearly synonymous with the Byzantine Text because it was in Byzantium (and surrounds) that the Lucian text was copied again and again until it was standardized in thousands of manuscripts.

Modern advocates of the superiority of the TR over other text types are Hodges and Farstad, who produced *The Greek New Testament According to the Majority Text.* Their arguments are more theological than textual. They reason that God would not have allowed a corrupt or inferior text to be found in the majority of manuscripts, while permitting a superior text to be hidden away in a few early manuscripts somewhere in the sands of Egypt. Further, they argue that the church's adoption of the Majority Text was a vindication of its correctness, while the obscurity of the Egyptian text was a sign of its rejection. In all of this reasoning, they miss the whole idea that God may have superintended the recovery of earlier and superior manuscripts during the past few centuries. This recovery has enabled biblical scholars to use earlier and superior manuscripts in the task of recovering the original wording of the Greek New Testament.

Most contemporary scholars contend that a minority of manuscripts—primarily the earliest ones—preserve the earliest, most authentic wording of the text. Those who defend the TR (and KJV) would have to prove that these earlier manuscripts, usually having a slimmer text than what appears in later manuscripts, were purposefully trimmed at any early stage in the textual transmission. In other words, they would have to come up with good arguments as to why scribes (in the early centuries) would have purposely excised the following passages: Matthew 5:44b; 6:13b; 16:2b–3; 17:21; 18:11; 20:16b; 20:22–23; 23:14; 27:35b; Mark 7:16; 9:44, 46; 11:26; 15:28; 16:8–20; Luke 4:4b; 9:54c–56; 11:2; 17:36; 22:43–44; 23:17, 34; John 5:3b–4; 7:53–8:11; Acts 8:37; 15:34; 24:6b–8a; 28:16b, 29; Romans 16:24; 1 John 5:6b–8a. However, had these portions originally been in the text, there are no good reasons to explain why they would have been eliminated. Rather, the opposite is true: there are several good reasons to explain why they were added—such as, Gospel harmonization, the insertion of oral traditions, and theological enhancements. It is true that some of the earliest scribes were prone to shorten their texts in the interest of readability, but these deletions usually involved only a few words. Thus, most scholars see the TR as being the culmination of textual accretions.

The Texts of Bengel, Lachman, Tregelles, Tischendorf, and Alford

After the publications of the various editions of the Textus Receptus, various manuscripts were discovered and made public. This prompted certain scholars to compile a Greek text that would more closely represent the original text than did the Textus Receptus. Around 1700 John Mill produced an improved Textus Receptus, and in the 1730s Johannes Albert Bengel (known as the father of modern textual and philological studies in the New Testament) published a text that deviated from the Textus Receptus according to the evidence of earlier manuscripts.

In the 1800s certain scholars began to abandon the Textus Receptus. Karl Lachman, a classical philologist, produced a fresh text (in 1831) that represented the fourth-century manuscripts. Samuel Tregelles (self-taught in Latin, Hebrew, and Greek), devoted his entire life's work to publishing one Greek text (which came out in six parts, from 1857 to 1872).[36] As is stated in the introduction to this work, Tregelles's goal was "to exhibit the text of the New Testament in the very words in which it has been transmitted on the evidence of ancient authority."[37] During this same era, Tischendorf was devoting a lifetime of labor to discovering manuscripts and producing accurate editions of the Greek New Testament. In a letter to his fiancée he wrote, "I am confronted with a sacred task, the struggle to regain the original form of the New Testament." In fulfillment of his desire, he discovered Codex Sinaiticus, deciphered the palimpsest (meaning the text was erased and written over) Codex Ephraemi Rescriptus (C),[38] collated countless manuscripts, and produced several editions of the Greek New Testament (the eighth edition is the best). His edition, entitled *Editio octava critica maior* (1869–1872), has a critical apparatus still used by some modern textual critics.

Henry Alford also compiled a Greek text based upon the best and earliest manuscripts. In his preface to *The Greek New Testament*, a multivolume commentary on the Greek New Testament (which is his own critical edition) published in 1849, Alford said he labored for the "demolition of the unworthy and pedantic reverence for the received text, which stood in the way of all chance of discovering the genuine word of God."[39]

Westcott and Hort's *The New Testament in the Original Greek*

Aided by the work of scholars such as Tregelles and Tischendorf, two British scholars, Brooke Westcott and Fenton Hort, worked together for twenty-eight years to produce a volume entitled *The New Testament in the Original Greek* (1881). Along with this publication, they made known their theory (which was chiefly Hort's) that Codex Vaticanus and Codex Sinaiticus (along with a few other early manuscripts) represented a text that most closely replicated the original writing. They called this text the Neutral Text. (According to their studies, the Neutral Text described certain manuscripts that had the least amount of textual corruption.) This is the text that Westcott and Hort sought to reproduce in their edition called *The New Testament in the Original Greek*. Their work is historically significant in that it dethroned reliance on the Textus Receptus.

In my opinion, the text produced by Westcott and Hort (*The New Testament in the Original Greek*) is still to this day, even with so many more manuscript discoveries, a very close reproduction of the primitive text of the New Testament. Of course, I think they gave too much weight to Codex Vaticanus alone, and this needs to be tempered. This criticism aside, the Westcott and Hort text is extremely reliable. I came to this conclusion after doing my own textual studies. In many instances where I would disagree with the wording in the Nestle/UBS text in favor of a particular variant reading, I would later check with the Westcott and Hort text and realize that they had often come to the same decision. This revealed to me that I was working on the same methodological basis as they. Of course, the manuscript discoveries of the past one hundred years have changed things, but it is remarkable how often they have affirmed the decisions of Westcott and Hort.

Since their era, hundreds of other manuscripts have been discovered, especially the New Testament papyri. Had Westcott and Hort been alive today, they would have been pleased to see that several of the early papyri affirm their view that Codex Vaticanus and Codex Sinaiticus are reliable witnesses of a very primitive form of the Greek New Testament text. They would have undoubtedly altered some of their textual choices based on the evidence of the papyri. For example, the testimony of $\mathfrak{P}^{75}$ (with א and B) in several Lukan passages clearly indicates that Westcott and Hort were wrong to have excluded several passages in Luke 22–24 based on their theory of "Western noninterpolations."

Nestle's Text: (*Novum Testamentum Graece*) and UBS Text

At the beginning of the twentieth century, Eberhard Nestle used the best editions of the Greek New Testament produced in the nineteenth century to compile a text that represented the majority consensus. Kenyon describes Nestle's work as follows:

His text (in its original form) is based upon the texts of Tischendorf and Westcott-Hort, and upon that produced by Mr. F. R. Weymouth (*The Resultant Greek Testament*, 1886), which is itself the result of the comparison of the texts of Stephanus, Lachmann, Tregelles, Tischendorf, Lightfoot, Ellicott, Alford, Weiss, the Basel edition of 1880, Westcott and Hort, and the Revised Version. In later editions (1901, etc.) Weiss has been substituted for Weymouth. Of these three editions, Dr. Nestle follows the verdict of the majority, placing the reading of the minority in the margin.[40]

The work of making new editions was carried on by Eberhard Nestle's son for several years, and then came under the care of Kurt Aland. The latest edition (the 27th) of Nestle-Aland's *Novum Testamentum Graece* appeared in 1993. The same Greek text appears in another popular volume published by the United Bible Societies, called the *Greek New Testament* (fourth edition). Aland has argued that the Nestle-Aland text, 27th edition (NA[27]), comes closer to the original text of the New Testament than did Tischendorf or Westcott and Hort. Though some scholars disagree with Aland, most consider the twenty-seventh edition of the Nestle-Aland text to represent the latest and best in textual scholarship.

Nestle-Aland's *Novum Testamentum Graece* (26th and 27th editions) and the United Bible Societies' *Greek New Testament* (3rd and 4th corrected editions)—abbreviated as NA[26] and NA[27]; UBS[3] and UBS[4]

After the United Bible Societies had published two editions of the *Greek New Testament,* they decided to unite with the work being done on a new edition (the 26th) of the Nestle-Aland text—and so produce two editions containing the same text.[41] Thus, the United Bible Societies' third edition of the *Greek New Testament* and the Nestle-Aland twenty-sixth edition of *Novum Testamentum Graece* have the same text. Each, however, has different punctuation and a different critical apparatus. The United Bible Societies' text has a plenary listing of witnesses for select variation units; the Nestle-Aland text has a condensed listing of the manuscript evidence for almost all the variation units. Both editions have since gone into another edition (the fourth and twenty-seventh respectively), manifesting a multitude of corrections to the critical apparatus but not to the wording of the text itself.

In their book *The Text of the New Testament,* Kurt and Barbara Aland argue for the position that the Nestle-Aland text "comes closer to the original text of the New Testament than did Tischendorf or Westcott and Hort, not to mention von Soden."[42] And in several other passages they intimate that this text may very well be the original text. This is evident in Kurt Aland's defense of NA[26] as the new "standard text":

The new "standard text" has passed the test of the early papyri and uncials. It corresponds, in fact, to the text of the early time. . . . At no place and at no time do we find readings here [in the earliest manuscripts] that require a change in the "standard text." If the investigation conducted here in all its brevity and compactness could be presented fully, the detailed apparatus accompanying each variant would convince the last doubter. A hundred years after Westcott-Hort, the goal of an edition of the New Testament "in the original Greek" seems to have been reached. . . . The desired goal appears now to have been attained, to offer the writings of the New Testament in the form of the text that comes nearest to that which, from the hand of their authors or redactors, they set out on their journey in the church of the first and second centuries.[43]

Though the Alands should be commended for their work toward recovering the *original* text, it remains to be seen whether the Nestle-Aland text is the best replication of the original text. Nonetheless, the Nestle-Aland Greek text—the NA^{27}/UBS^4 or simply, NU)—is now generally recognized as the standard text—i.e., it is the text accepted by most of the academic community as representing the best attempt at reconstructing the original text of the Greek New Testament. This text, however, is by no means "inspired" or infallible—as many scholars will readily attest. In fact, no one in ancient times read the Greek text that is presented in NU in its totality—or in any other critical edition of the Greek New Testament, for that matter—because modern critical editions are compilations drawn from multiple manuscripts on a variation-unit by variation-unit basis.

The editors of the Nestle-Aland 26th edition and United Bible Societies' third edition (the NU text); took into consideration the newly discovered documents, as they sought to produce a more accurate text. And they did seek to produce a more accurate text than did Westcott and Hort, and in many places they have done so. However, their strong reliance on the eclectic method meant that they produced an uneven documentary text. (This is explained in chap. 6.) Therefore, even though the Nestle-Aland text advances beyond Westcott and Hort, it also presents a divergence, in my opinion. Other scholars may or may not agree.

In any event, most students and scholars today rely primarily upon the critical apparatuses of UBS^3 (corrected edition), UBS^4, NA^{26}, and NA^{27} for citations of manuscripts. The careful reader will realize that both UBS^3 and NA^{26} were thoroughly revised with respect to their critical apparatuses, especially the UBS text, which was listed as the "third, corrected edition" and then as "the fourth revised edition." But the Nestle-Aland 26th edition also needed significant revision. For example, in my article on the papyri in the Gospel of John, I noted several such errors.[44] Most of these were subsequently corrected. In another work I have written, *New Testament Text and Translation Commentary*, I note several other places where the critical apparatus of UBS^3 and UBS^4, as well as where NA^{26} and NA^{27}, can be improved.

Chapter Three

The Earliest New Testament Manuscripts

Now that we have looked at the most significant manuscripts, it is only fitting that we examine the issue of the dates for the earliest New Testament manuscripts. This is exceedingly important because the earliest manuscripts (if they are accurate) should provide the earliest and perhaps best witnesses to the wording of the autographs. Most students are simply told that such-and-such a manuscript is dated "third century" or "second century" without being told why. Students need to understand how a manuscript is dated, then they will be able to appreciate what paleographers and papyrologists have contributed to the field of New Testament textual studies.

Since there are no autographs of any New Testament book, textual critics rely upon copies to recover the original wording of the Greek New Testament. Most scholars recognize that the earlier the copy the closer it is to the original wording. Of course, an early copy could be textually aberrant if it was not produced with care. Thus, what textual critics are really looking for are manuscripts with an early date and with textual integrity. In this chapter, my goal is to establish which manuscripts are the earliest. In the following chapters, I hope to determine which manuscripts are the most reliable from a textual perspective.

Dating Manuscripts

From the onset, I need to say that I think several of the earliest New Testament manuscripts have been dated either too late and/or not precisely enough. Since the date for many of these manuscripts was already assigned when the *editio princeps* was published, it has been and will continue to be an uphill battle to get a change of date. Or if a certain date is listed for a particular manuscript in the appendix of *Novum Testamentum Graece* or the United Bible Societies' *Greek New Testament*, readers take that as the fixed, authoritative date. But I think, as do several other scholars (cited throughout), that several of the dates are not early enough. Or, at least, they do not allow for an early date. Let me give an example. $\mathfrak{P}^4$ is listed as "third century" in NA[27] and UBS[4] when almost all recent scholarship on this manuscript concurs with "late second century." At the very least, $\mathfrak{P}^4$ should be listed as "second/third century." At best, $\mathfrak{P}^4$ should be listed as "late second century." In my opinion, a new date needs to be set for about another thirty manuscripts. This is explained throughout the course of this chapter.

Another matter needs to be addressed up front. Paleographers often assigned a date to a New Testament manuscript without citing any other manuscripts displaying comparable paleographical features. This was often the case with the work of Grenfell and Hunt, who, as pioneers in papyrology, did not have enough manuscripts to draw comparisons with. Thus, their assigned dates were their best guesses. But accumulative discoveries of documents have now put us in the position of making more accurate assignments. Kenyon also did not cite any comparable manuscripts when he assigned dates for $\mathfrak{P}^{45}$, $\mathfrak{P}^{46}$, and $\mathfrak{P}^{47}$. Thus, this work must be done to determine if he was correct or not.

As the first order of business, I will discuss the various styles of handwriting in use during the Christian era (Roman Uncial, Biblical Unical, Decorated Rounded, Severe), and I will provide several examples of dated manuscripts for each. This is necessary to do first because many New Testament manuscripts have been and can be dated by comparison to manuscripts displaying these styles. Then I will discuss the dating of several Greek Old Testament and noncanonical Christian manuscripts whose calligraphy is helpful in dating New Testament manuscripts. Finally, I will discuss the dates of all New Testament manuscripts prior to AD 300, offering the studied opinions of several paleographers throughout, as well as some of my own observations.

The *editio princeps* for each of the New Testament manuscripts cited in this chapter is found in the previous chapter.

Criteria Used for Dating Manuscripts

Before I identify what I think are the earliest New Testament manuscripts, I need to stipulate the criteria I have used for dating manuscripts. These criteria are as follows: archaeological evidence, codicology, comparative palaeography, and the evolution of the nomina sacra. The third area, comparative paleography, is the most complex and therefore requires the most discussion. In this area, I will first look at the issue of determining dates for literary texts based on dated documentary manuscripts, and then I will examine comparative morphology (a study of comparable handwriting styles).

Archaeological Evidence

The first means used in dating a manuscript is to look at archaeological evidence. External and circumstantial factors can help scholars date manuscripts. For example, the *terminus ante quem* (latest possible date) for the Herculanuem manuscripts is AD 79, the date of the eruption of Mount Vesuvius, and for the Dead Sea Scrolls is AD 70, the date the Qumran caves were abandoned. Scanlin writes, "Around AD 70 Qumran was destroyed during the Jewish war and Roman invasion. Thus, assuming that the Dead Sea Scrolls found near the Qumran settlement were the product of that community, then the latest date for the manuscripts hidden in nearby caves is AD 70."[1] Of course, not all the Dead Sea Scroll manuscripts may have come from the Qumran community. The caves could have been used by other Jews hiding manuscripts at some other time.

Nonetheless, very few scholars would date any of the Dead Sea Scrolls after the middle of the first century AD (both on archaeological grounds and paleographical).

The New Testament papyrus manuscript $\mathfrak{P}^4 + \mathfrak{P}^{64} + \mathfrak{P}^{67}$ cannot be dated later than AD 200 because it was placed in strips (perhaps as binding) for a third-century codex of Philo. Some length of time must be allowed for a well-written codex to have been used to such an extent that it was torn up and used as binding.[2] The Gospel harmony manuscript 0212 cannot be dated later than AD 256 and is likely to be dated ca. 230 because the manuscript was discovered in the filling of an embankment erected in AD 256. A Christian house (in existence from 222 to 235) nearby the site of discovery was destroyed when the embankment was built.

Unfortunately, most manuscripts cannot be dated according to archaeological evidence because the attending circumstances are vague or ambiguous. Thus, for the dating of most biblical manuscripts, paleographers use the following criteria: codicology and comparative paleography, which also includes comparative stylistics and morphology.

Codicology

As was discussed in a previous chapter, the codex was in use prior to the end of the first century AD. It was the book form used exclusively by Christians for making copies of biblical writings. Therefore, any New Testament codex manuscript could be as early as the late first century. Knowledge concerning this dating of the codex increased with precision during the second half of the twentieth century, as more and more of the papyri were published. Paleographers living at the beginning of the twentieth century considered the codex to be a late second-century or early third-century invention and therefore would hardly date a Christian manuscript prior to the third century. Such was the case with Grenfell and Hunt, who assigned many third-century and fourth-century dates to Christian Old Testament manuscripts and New Testament manuscripts, when the handwriting clearly belonged to an earlier century.[3] Increased knowledge about the creation of the codex has prompted paleographers to redate many of these manuscripts to an earlier period. This redating is addressed manuscript by manuscript in the following discussion.

Comparative Paleography

Biblical manuscripts are literary manuscripts. Dates were rarely if ever written on literary manuscripts. By comparison, documentary texts (i.e., manuscripts having documentary information) often provide exact dates if not explicitly so, at least implicitly by something written in the document. These documents provide the only paleographic means for dating manuscripts.

If a literary text has been written on the recto (the best and therefore the primary side of a papyrus or parchment leaf) and a dated documentary work has been written on the verso, the date of the documentary text provides the *terminus ante quem* (latest possible date) because the documentary text will be later. For example, a literary text on the recto, having a documentary text dated AD 150 on the verso, indicates that the literary text must be dated earlier than AD 150. We cannot be sure how much earlier, but the length of time could be quite substantial, perhaps as long as fifty to one hundred years because a literary text would normally have been used (or shelved) for a long period prior to being relegated to documentary use.[4] As will be discussed below, one sumptuous literary text in the Heroninos collection, P. Rylands 16 (an unknown Comedy), was not relegated to documentary use (on the verso) for well over fifty to seventy-five, perhaps even one hundred years.

Fortunately, several manuscripts have been discovered that have a literary text on the recto and a dated documentary text on the verso. These manuscripts have enabled paleographers to establish the *terminus ante quem* (latest possible date) for the literary texts. As a rule of thumb, paleographers will usually subtract twenty-five to fifty years from the *terminus ante quem* when dating the literary text, for it is conjectured that the literary text (on the recto) must have been well used and well worn before being relegated to documentary use. Such literary texts with relatively certain dates provide models for comparative paleography.

If a literary text has been written on the verso of a documentary text (such as a letter or an official edict), which provides a date, then the documentary text provides the *terminus post quem* (the earliest possible date) for the literary text. For example, a date of AD 150 for a documentary text on the recto, with a literary text on the verso, means that the literary text cannot be dated earlier than AD 150. The length of time between the reuse of a documentary text for literary purposes would normally be shorter, probably around five to fifteen years at most inasmuch as the user would not have valued the document highly if he or she quickly put it to literary use. Let us take, for example, the Christian Psalms fragment, PSI 921 (Psalm 77:1–18). This is a fragment of Psalms written on the verso of a roll containing a bank register (on the recto) dated in AD 143/144. As such, it is quite likely that the Psalms portion should be dated anywhere between AD 155 and 170 (see comments below on this specific manuscript). Another example is P. Michigan 130, the Shepherd of Hermas. This manuscript, containing "The Mandates" of *The Shepherd*, was written on the verso of a scroll; the recto contains a document that can be dated to the reign of Marcus Aurelius (AD 161–180). Thus, it stands to reason that P. Michigan 130 could be dated AD 180–200.

The primary means of dating a New Testament manuscript, as an undated literary text, is by doing a comparative analysis with the handwriting of other dated documentary texts. The second method is to do a comparative analysis with literary manuscripts having a date based on the association with a documentary text on the recto or verso. Since several of the New Testament papyrus manuscripts exhibit a documentary hand, it is possible to find comparable dated documentary manuscripts. Fortunately, there are several documentary manuscripts that belong to the Heroninos correspondence (all dated around 260 and part of the Florentine Papyri) which have helped scholars to date several New Testament manuscripts (with a "documentary" hand), with corresponding handwriting, to the mid-third century. This pertains to $\mathfrak{P}^{17}$, $\mathfrak{P}^{37}$, $\mathfrak{P}^{53}$, $\mathfrak{P}^{80}$, and $\mathfrak{P}^{86}$. A few literary texts, each dated ca. 200 (or a little earlier in the case of P. Rylands 16), reused for documentary purposes in the Heroninos collection, can help in the dating of New Testament manuscripts such as $\mathfrak{P}^{39}$, $\mathfrak{P}^{45}$, $\mathfrak{P}^{91}$, $\mathfrak{P}^{110}$, and $\mathfrak{P}^{115}$.

Another two hundred Greek documentary papyri, dated AD 113–120, have come from the archive of Apollonios, a strategos of Hermopolis.[5] A thorough study of these manuscripts prompted the papyrologist Ulrich Wilcken to date $\mathfrak{P}^{52}$ to the same era, on the basis of comparable paleography (see discussion on $\mathfrak{P}^{52}$ below).

In the following pages, various dated documentary manuscripts and literary texts with certain dates will be cited as supporting a date I propose for the earliest New Testament manuscripts. Admittedly, dating a literary text by comparing it with other literary texts involves some subjectivity, because it is as much an art as it is a science. Dating a manuscript is usually done by the person who produces the *editio princeps* of the manuscript. Sometimes this date is accepted by other paleographers; often it is challenged. As would be expected, paleographers do not agree on dates because of the subjectivity involved in the comparative analysis. Furthermore, it must be remembered that a manuscript could have been produced by an old scribe using a style he learned as a young man, or a manuscript could have been written by a young scribe just when a certain style was nascent. These factors could add or subtract twenty-five to fifty years to or from the date of any manuscript. All things considered, it is safest to date manuscripts within a range of fifty years. This allows for an early date and a later one for each manuscript. Usually both dates are defensible because we can see a complementary style in other manuscripts at both ends.

As paleographers seek to assign a date to a manuscript, they employ comparative morphology, which is a comparative study of letter forms. Paleographers in the past (such as Kenyon) used to look for a match of certain individual letter forms. This practice called the "test-letter" theory[6] is no longer fully endorsed. Rather, paleographers look at the letters in relation to the entire piece of writing; in other words, it is the overall likeness that constitutes a morphological match. Of course, this doesn't exclude matching letters, but the match must be more than just in a few letters.

Comparative Stylistics

Another way that paleographers date manuscripts is to determine its handwriting style and thereby place it in a time period where that style was prominent. Often, a paleographer can also determine if the manuscript shows early or late features of that period by comparative analysis with other manuscripts that have firm dates. In the following discussion, I will speak of four specific styles: Roman Uncial, Biblical Uncial,

Decorated Rounded, and Severe (Slanting) Style. Several Christian manuscripts both of the Old Testament and New Testament display one of these styles.

Various papyrologists, such as Roberts[7] and Turner,[8] note scribal tendencies of the first three centuries AD. Roberts and Turner both indicate that there was a strong tendency for scribes in the first and second centuries to keep all their letters at an imaginary top line. Most bookhands display bilinearity, which is an attempt to keep all letters at an imaginary top and bottom line. Slanting handwriting begins in the second century. (Prior to that, letters were written upright.) Other second-century features are (1) the final nu on a line replaced with an extending overbar over the last letter (mid-second century), (2) a small omicron in documentary hands, which becomes prominent in third-century literary hands, and (3) angular letters (e.g., $\mathfrak{P}^{45}$, $\mathfrak{P}^{75}$) also in the late second and early third. In documentary and Greek biblical manuscripts, beginning in the first century AD and onwards, there was a strong tendency for documentary scribes to enlarge the first letter of each line and/or of each new section.

Other Features Used in Dating Manuscripts

Some paleographers take note of the ink color as an aid to making an estimation about a manuscript's date. For example, lustrous black ink (also known as carbon ink) is earlier than brown. Brown ink has probably been mixed from an iron salt or other chemical compound and therefore generally points to a date after AD 300. The issue of black ink and brown ink is significant to the dating of $\mathfrak{P}^{15}$ and $\mathfrak{P}^{16}$ (see discussion below). Metallic ink usually points to a later date. However, P. Oxyrhynchus 2269, written in metallic ink, is dated AD 269.

Turner indicates that another feature began in the early third century, namely, the use of a separating apostrophe between double consonants.[9] Some paleographers of late seem to have adopted this observation as "fact" and thereby date manuscripts having this feature as post AD 200. Some paleographers would even redate manuscripts displaying this feature. For example, Schmidt redates $\mathfrak{P}^{52}$ to ca. 200 based on the fact that its hand parallels that of the Egerton Gospel, which is now thought by some to date closer to ca. 200 based on this feature appearing in a newly published portion of the Egerton Gospel.[10] However, I would argue that the previously assigned date of such manuscripts was given by many scholars according to their observations of several paleographic features. Thus, the presence of this particular feature (the hook or apostrophe between double consonants) determines an earlier date for its emergence, not the other way around. Thus, the Egerton Gospel, dated by many to ca. 150, should still stand, and so should the date for $\mathfrak{P}^{52}$ (as early second century). Another way to come at this is to look at $\mathfrak{P}^{66}$, dated by several scholars to ca. 150 (see discussion below). Turner, however, would date $\mathfrak{P}^{66}$ later (early third) largely because of the presence of the hook between double consonants. What I would say is that the predominant dating of $\mathfrak{P}^{66}$ (i.e., the dating assigned by most scholars) predetermines the date for this particular feature. Furthermore, there are other manuscripts dated prior to AD 200 that exhibit the apostrophe or hook between double consonants:

1. BGU iii 715.5 (AD 101)

αγˀχωριμφιs

2. P. Petaus 86 (= P. Michigan 6871) (AD 185)

αγˀγων

3. SPP xxii 3.22 (second century)

απυγˀχεωs

4. P. Berol. 9570 + P. Rylands 60 (dated by the editors of the *editio princeps* to ca. 200, dated by Cavallo to ca. 50)

φαλαγˀγαs

Handwriting Styles

Four handwriting styles of the early period of Christianity are worthy of our attention for New Testament paleography. The first is called the Roman Uncial, the second is called the Biblical Uncial, the third is named the Decorated Rounded Uncial, and the fourth is the Severe (or Slanted) style. It must be said that all four styles are not always clearly distinct, nor can one exactly pinpoint the birth of one style, for there was a great deal of crossbreeding and mingling in the process. Nonetheless, there are some common features to each style, and there is a chronology for the emergence, popularity, and disappearance of each style.

The Roman Uncial

Paleographers date the emergence of the Roman Uncial as coming on the heels of the Ptolemaic period, which ended in 30 BC. Thus, early Roman Uncial begins around 30 BC, and the Roman Uncial hand can be seen throughout the first two to three centuries of the Christian era. The Roman Uncial script, generally speaking, shares the characteristics of literary manuscripts in the Roman period (as distinct from the Ptolemaic period) in that these manuscripts show a greater roundness and smoothness in the forms of letters and are somewhat larger than what was penned in the Ptolemaic period. Furthermore, the Roman Uncial typically displays decorative serifs in several letters, but not all. (By contrast, the Decorated Rounded style aims at making the decorations rounded and replete.)

Generally speaking, the Roman Uncial was a precursor to the Biblical Uncial—the one style emerging into the next. As such, it can be seen that certain paleographers interchange the two terms. However, the true Biblical Uncial differs from the Roman Uncial in that the Biblical Uncial typically displays no or little decoration and has noticeable shading, i.e., "the deliberate alternation of thick and thin pen-strokes, related to the angle at which the pen meets the paper."[11] In Kenyon's estimation, a good New Testament example of a Roman Uncial is found in the manuscript $\mathfrak{P}^{46}$.

Concerning $\mathfrak{P}^{46}$, the editor of the *editio princeps*, Kenyon said, "The letters are rather early in style and of good formation of the Roman period."[12] (See the discussion below on $\mathfrak{P}^{46}$.)

The Biblical Uncial

Another name for the Biblical Uncial is the Biblical Majuscule; this refers to large uncial letters, each stroked separately so as not to connect with other letters (as occurs with a running hand producing cursives or what is called ligatures). The term Biblical Uncial does not apply only to biblical texts; it was a term first coined by Grenfell and Hunt to describe the handwriting of certain biblical texts and then was extended to any kind of manuscript displaying that kind of handwriting, whether biblical or not. The Biblical Uncial is noted for retaining a bilinear appearance—that is, there is a conscious effort to keep a line of text within an imaginary upper and lower line. In this style, all letters except iota, rho, phi, psi, omega fit into squares of equal size, and all letters except gamma, rho, phi, psi have the same vertical extension (bilinearity). In Biblical Uncial there is a deliberate alternation of thick vertical strokes and thin horizontal strokes, with sloping strokes coming in between. In this style, rectangular strokes display right-angled shapes, and circular letters are truly circular, not oval. There are no ligatures (connecting letters) and no ornamentation at the end of strokes (such as serifs and blobs).

This style began to emerge in the first century AD. A few paleographers have recognized that a particular Herculaneum manuscript, P. Herculaneum 1457 (dated pre-AD 79), shows an early form of the Biblical Uncial. This was first recognized by Domenico Bassi in *Papiri Ercolanesi* (Tomo 1; Milan 1914 with 7 plates). W. Schubart affirmed this in his volume, *Griechische Paleographie*, 111–12, as did G. Cavallo in *Libri scritture scribi a Ercolano*, who (after referring to Bassi's work) says, "P. Herc. 1457 *tra gli esempi pui antichi di onciale biblica.*" (Cavallo considered P. Herculaneum 1457 to be an example anticipating the Biblical Uncial.) When Kim spoke of the Biblical Majuscule hand (in his article on $\mathfrak{P}^{46}$ discussed at length below) and its early type, he referred to P. Herculaneum 1457. In dating $\mathfrak{P}^{64+67}$ to the late first century, Thiede also drew attention to the Herculaneum Papyri (referring to Schubart and an article by Cavallo, see discussion below), though he did not explicitly mention P. Herc. 1457.

An early form of the Biblical Uncial style can also be seen in P. London II 141, a document dated to AD 88 (for photo, see GLH 12a). The editors of this text wrote: "This document has a special value, being written in uncials of a type more nearly approaching the uncial writing of early vellum MSS than is to be found in any other extant document which can be attributed to so early a period. Moreover, it bears an actual date, and thus affords a standard of early uncial writing." [13]

Roberts said this manuscript "is an early and dated example of the large rounded hand which is fully developed in the second century in Hawara Homer (NPS I.126) and P. Tebtunis II 265."[14] In other words, P. London II 141 is an early form of what came to be known as the Biblical Uncial.

As was just alluded to by Roberts, three noteworthy examples of Roman Uncial manuscripts showing features of the Biblical Uncial are (1) P. Hawara 24–28 (Homer's *Iliad*), dated by most paleographers to the second century (for photo, see Cavallo, pl. 2; Montev. pl. 63); (2) P. Tebtunis II 265 (for photo, see *Tebtunis Papyri*, vol. 2); and (3) P. Oxyrhynchus 20 (for photo, see Cavallo, pl. 3), dated second century. The last two mentioned papyri are very similar in appearance. In fact, the editors of *Tebtunis II 265* (Grenfell, Hunt, Goodspeed) dated it to the second century on the basis of its likeness to P. Oxyrhynchus 20.

P. Oxyrhynchus 20 has a firm date: second century. The recto contains Homer's *Iliad* (II. 730–828), written in a large upright calligraphic uncial. On the verso are some accounts in a cursive hand of the late second or early third century. The sumptuous Homer had to have been in use for quite some time before it was relegated to documentary use. Hence, I would judge that it was composed in the first half of the second century.

G. Cavallo, in his majesterial work, *Richerche sulla Maiuscola Biblica*, makes a strong case for the style known as Biblical Uncial taking definitive shape in the middle to late second century AD.[15] In order to justify this dating, he drew upon a few significant manuscripts whose dates are fairly well established. Cavallo pays special attention to P. Oxyrhynchus 661 (for photo, see Cavallo pl. 16; GLH 16a), as one of the earliest examples. This manuscript is dated with great certainty to the second half of the second century. Grenfell and Hunt said that on the verso of P. Oxyrhynchus 661 is a cursive hand "which is not later than the third century, and quite likely to fall within the second. The text of recto [P. Oxy. 661], then, can be assigned with little chance of error to the second half of the second century." C. H. Roberts, dating P. Oxyrhynchus 661 to the latter part of the second century, says it "may also rank as the earliest datable example of the Biblical Uncial style" (GLH 16a).

Cavallo cites many other manuscripts belonging to the same era (the latter part of the second century) as also displaying the Biblical Uncial. Some of the more significant ones are as follows:

1. P. Oxyrhynchus 678, late second century (Cavallo, pl. 13a). Grenfell and Hunt wrote: "It is an upright and rather heavy calligraphic hand similar to [P. Oxy.] 661, and probably, like that papyrus, of the latter part of the second century."

2. P. Oxyrhynchus 2356, dated ca. 175 (Cavallo, pl. 12). The editors wrote: "The text is written in a square upright uncial of a common type, of which it is only a moderately well made example, comparable with P. Ryl. 547 and attributable to the late second century."

3. P. Oxyrhynchus 2364, second half of second century (Cavallo, pl. 13b). The editors wrote: "The hand is a good upright uncial of the so-called biblical type very like

that of P. Berol. 13411 (which likewise contains choral lyric), [P. Oxy.] 661 (assigned to the second half of the second century), BM Inv. no. 2560."

According to Cavallo, P. Oxy. 678, 2356, 2364 should be dated "intorno all fine del terzo venticinquennio del II secolo" ("around the end of the third quarter of the second century"—175). [16]

4. P. Rylands 16, latter part of the second century (for photo, see GLH 22b). Cavallo points to P. Rylands 16 as one of the earliest examples of the Biblical Uncial. The dating of this manuscript is fairly certain because this literary text contains a documentary text on the verso (namely, a letter dated AD 255/256). The editor of P. Rylands 16, A. S. Hunt, remarked:

> The hand of [P. Rylands 16] is extremely similar to that of P. Oxyrhynchus 661 (IV, Plate V), and like it can fortunately be dated with some accuracy, since the verso is inscribed with a letter to Heroninos (cf. e.g. P. Flor. 9, intro.), written in the third year of (of Gallienus), i.e., AD 255–256. A manuscript so elaborate would probably not be quickly destroyed, and hence the text on the recto can hardly be later than about the year 215 and may well belong, as there was reason to suppose that P. Oxyrhynchus 661 belonged, to the latter part of the second century. [17]

Cavallo, more conservatively, dates P. Rylands 16 to 220–225, allowing for only thirty years before such a sumptuous manuscript was put to documentary use. C. H. Roberts (GLH 22b) would date it ca. 200. And E. G. Turner, who is usually very conservative in his dating, dated P. Rylands 16 to the second century. He posited this date because he observed that some of the documents in the Heroninos archive were already a century old before they were reused for writing letters. [18] Taking all things into consideration, it is probably best to date P. Rylands 16 to the latter part of the second century.

5. P. Berol. 7499, ca. 200 (Schubart's *Greek Pal.*, pl. 93; Cavallo, pl. 19a). Schubart dated it to the beginning of the fourth; Cavallo would date it to the end of the second century/beginning of the third.

6. P. Oxyrhynchus 2395, end of the second century (Cavallo, pl. 15b). The editors wrote: "The script is a conventional upright uncial of the 'biblical' type much like [P. Oxy.] 1179, which is assigned to the early part of the third century." But P. Oxy. 1179 could have also been written at the end of the second century.

7. P. Lit. London 78, late second century (Cavallo, pl. 14). This manuscript is a "round medium-sized rather heavy uncial hand of biblical type." [19]

8. PSI 1377 (*Illiad* IX) + P. Rylands 542 (*Illiad* V), end of second/beginning of third, ca. 200 (Cavallo, pl. 20a, b). These two manuscripts are part of the same work. Bartoletti, editor of the *editio princeps*, dated PSI 1377 "avanza l'ipotesi del II secolo: sarei invece del parere di assegnal III (inizio)" (i.e., possibly second century, more likely beginning of the third).

9. P. Oxyrhynchus 2334, later second century (Cavallo, pl. 29). The editor said it displays "a rounded, heavy hand, the precursor of the so-called 'Biblical Uncial' (cf. P. Rylands iii 547, [P. Oxy.] 2169, and 661."

10. P. Vindob. 29784, end of the second century (Cavallo, pl. 15a).

11. P. Vindob. 29768, ca. 175 (Cavallo, pl. 12a), The two P. Vindob. manuscripts are discussed below in connection with the New Testament manuscript $\mathfrak{P}^{4+64+67}$.

12. P. Oxyrhynchus 224+P. Rylands 547, later second century (Cavallo, pl. 6). These two manuscripts are part of the same text. P. Oxyrhynchus 224 was originally dated to the third century and then redated to the later second century, with the attachment of P. Rylands 547 (as part of the same manuscript), due to the influence of the dating of P. Oxyrhynchus 661, a manuscript sharing many features with P. Oxyrhynchus 224+P. Rylands 547. (P. Oxyrhynchus 224+P. Rylands 547 is discussed below in connection with the dating of $\mathfrak{P}^{4+64+67}$.)

13. P. Oxyrhynchus 2750, latter part of the second century. The editor wrote: "The hand is another example of the early Biblical uncial style similiar to [P. Oxyrhynchus] 661. . . and may be dated around the later part of the second century AD."

14. P. Oxyrhynchus 1179 (for photo, see Cavallo, pl. 28b), ca. 200. The editor wrote: "This small fragment offers another example of the 'biblical' type of uncials on papyrus. The hand closely resembles those of [P. Oxyrhynchus] 664 and P. Rylands 16, and may be assigned with some confidence to the earlier decades of the third century, if not to the end of the second."

The early New Testament manuscripts written in Biblical Uncial are as follows: $\mathfrak{P}^{4+64+67}$, $\mathfrak{P}^{30}$, $\mathfrak{P}^{35}$, $\mathfrak{P}^{39}$, $\mathfrak{P}^{40}$, $\mathfrak{P}^{70}$, $\mathfrak{P}^{95}$, 0162, and 0189. Each is discussed below.

Decorated Rounded Uncial

Another style of handwriting was prominent during the early period of the church; it is called the Decorated Rounded Uncial. In this style, every vertical stroke finishes with a serif or decorated roundel. Schubart (naming this style *Zierstil)* thought this style existed from the last century of the Ptolemaic period (first century BC) to the end of the first century AD.[20] Other scholars, such as Turner, see it as extending to the end of the second century (and perhaps even into the early third). He said, "The classification 'Formal round' is attained by far fewer hands. They are almost instantly recognizable, if only from the generous size of their letters." He sees this as a single feature of several styles that existed from the second century BC to the second century AD.[21] Concurring with Turner, Parsons writes: "Turner rightly insists that Schubart's 'decorated style' . . . is not really a style but a single feature of several styles spread over a period of four centuries from ii BC."[22]

Whether it is a single style or a single feature of several styles, manuscripts with the Decorated Rounded type of handwriting are conspicuous. There are several extant examples of dated manuscripts (i.e., manuscripts with certain dates) exhibiting this style that fall within the period of 100 BC to AD 150. Here is a representative list, cited in chronological order. (Some of the following manuscripts are also noted by Parsons, and other by Welles.)[23] Some of these manuscripts display what could be called a Formal Round and others an Informal Round. The documentary manuscripts tend to be more informal than the literary, but they often provide good comparisons for the particular biblical manuscripts written in reformed documentary and documentary hands, while the more formal often provide good comparisons for biblical manuscripts displaying a bookhand.

1. P. Rylands 586+P. Oxyrhynchus 802 (Deed of Loan, 99 BC; for photo, see GLH 8a) (later Ptolemaic decorated style)

2. P. Fouad 266 (Septuagint) (mid first century BC, a cursive note on this papyrus is unmistakably Ptolemaic; for photo, see GMAW 56)

3. Greek Minor Scroll Prophets from Nahal Hever, 8HevXIIgr (50 BC to AD 50).

4. 7Q1 (Exodus) (100 BC)

This style is clearly *Zierstil* (Decorated Rounded), according to the *editio princeps.* in DJD IV, Grote 7, Fragments of Papyrus.

5. 7Q5 (50 BC to 50 AD)

This manuscript, whose identification has been highly debated (see discussion below), clearly displays a *Zierstil* (decorated rounded style), according to the *editio princeps* in DJD IV, Grote 7, Fragments of Papyrus.

6. Several manuscripts from Herculaneum (first century BC). Many of the manuscripts from Herculaneum display a Decorated Rounded style. These manuscripts must be dated pre-AD 79, when the town was buried. However, since many of the manuscripts came from Philodemus's library or were his personal works, they probably should be dated pre-40 BC, the presumed date of Philodemus's death. Some of the more noteworthy manuscripts are P. Herc. 1005 (for photo, see Cavallo's *Ercolano*, pl. 22) ; P. Herc. 1423 (for photo, see Cavallo's *Ercolano*, pl. 50); and P. Herc. 697 (for photo, see Cavallo's *Ercolano*, pl. 32).

7. P. Murabba'at 108, dated "moitie du 1er siecle apres J.-C." (beginning of the first century AD). The hand is clearly *Zierstil*, with affinities to manuscripts like P. Berolinses 6926 and P. Oxyrhynchus 246 (see below).

We know that the caves of Murabba'at had been inhabited repeatedly from 4000 BC to the Arabian period. A great number of documents including two letters from Simon ben Koshiba (Bar Kochba) show that the caves were a refuge during the second Jewish revolt (AD 132–135).

8. P. Oxyrhynchus 1453 (Oath of Temple Lamplighters, 30–29 BC; for photo, see GLH 8b).

9. P. London II.354 (Petition to Caius Turranius, 7–4 BC; for photo, see GLH 9a) (informal round, slightly decorated).

10. P. Oxyrhynchus 2555 (after AD 46). This should be dated mid to late first century inasmuch as the document mentions a horoscope dated AD May 13, 46.

11. P. Oxyrhynchus 3700 (ca. AD 50). P. Oxyrhynchus 3700 "is given a reasonably secure *terminus ante* by the writing on the back: several sets of documentary phrases, doodling or draft, among them a date clause of AD 48–9."

12. P. Oxyrhynchus 2471 (Cancellation of a Loan, ca. AD 50; for photo, see GMAW 64).

13. P. Oxyrhynchus 246 (Return of Sheep, AD 66; for photo, see GLH 10c).

14. P. Oxyrhynchus 2987 (Petition to Gaius Aeturnius Fronto, AD 78–79).

15. P. Berol. 6926 (Romance of Ninus, Prince of Assyria; second half of first century AD; for photo, see GLH 11a). The *terminus ante quem* (latest possible date) is supplied by the verso on which are some accounts of the reign of Trajan, referring to AD 100–101. Roberts said, "Compared with the first century hands already illustrated this hand is more rounded and uniform and displays a greater tendency to equality in the size of letters; in this it anticipates the hands of the second century" (GLH 11a).

16. P. London II 141 (AD 88; for photo, see GLH 12a). Roberts said, "It is a large, rounded bookhand which is fully developed in the second century" (GLH 12a).

17. P. Lit. London 6 (first century AD; for photo, see *New Paleographic Society II*, pl. 53), a further fragment of which has been published as P. Rylands 540. This is a manuscript of the *Iliad* of which on the verso is a document dated AD 88/89.

18. P. London 130 (*Greek Papyri in the British Museum* 1.132ff; for photo, see Schubart's *Paleography* 81). This manuscript mentions a horoscope dated April 1, AD 81. Therefore, it is not likely to be later than the early part of the second century.

19. P. Oxyrhynchus 270 (AD 94).

20. P. Fayum 110 (Letter of Lucius Bellenus Gemellus to Epagathus, AD 96; for photo, see GLH 11b). Roberts said, "This is written in a rounded, regular hand . . . This hand is perhaps closer than that of any other dated document to those of the earliest Christian papyri, P. Rylands III 457 (= $\mathfrak{P}^{52}$) and P. London Christ. 1 (= Egerton Gospel)" (GLH 11b).

21. P. Berolinses 6845 (Homer's *Iliad*), dated by Schubart first/second century (for photo, see *P. Berol.*, pl. 19c).

22. P. Yale 1273 (Hesiod's *Catalogue of Women*), ca. AD 100 (for photo, see *Yale Literary Papyri*, pl. ii).

23. P. Berolinses 6854, dated to the reign of Trajan (AD 98–117; for photo, see Schubart's *Greek Pal.* 34). C. H. Roberts points to this manuscript in determining his date for Chester Beatty VI (Num.-Deut.), as being slightly later than P. Berolinses 6854. (See comments on Beatty VI below.)

24. P. Berolinses 6855, dated by Schubart as AD 135? (for photo, see *P. Berol*, pl. 22b).

25. P. Oxyrhynchus 454 + PSI 119 (Plato's *Gorgias* 507–508; second quarter of the second century, AD 125–150; for photo, see GMAW 62). The date of this manuscript is quite solid inasmuch as it was written on the verso of a roll of military accounts providing a date of sometime after AD 111. Given the rule of thumb that a literary text written on the verso of a documentary text could have occurred in a short timespan (five to twenty-five years), the Plato text could be dated anywhere between AD 115 and 140. According to Turner (in GMAW 62), the hand is a "medium-sized, upright, rounded, 'decorated,' capital . . . The hand is of the professional type, but makes an impression of informality."

26. P. Oxyrhynchus 1083 (second century; for photo see Oxy. vol. and Schubart's *Greek Pal.*, 74). Concerning the dating of this, the editors wrote: "The following fragments of a Satyric drama are written in upright uncials which are slightly above the medium size and of rather heavy and ungraceful appearance. They may be assigned to the second century, a date to which the cursive notes . . . would also seem to point."

All these aforementioned documents, nearly all of which have solid dating, provide evidence for the existence of the decorated rounded hand during a certain timeframe. Significantly, there are hardly any dated documents beyond AD 150 that provide evidence of this style. In this regard, Welles is generally correct (as was Schubart): the greatest concentration of dated manuscripts displaying the Decorated Rounded is found between the period 100 BC to AD 100 (op. cit.). The evidence indicates that this should be extended to AD 150 but not much further.

E. G. Turner disagrees. He points out that P. Oxyrhynchus 3093 (dated AD 217) displays the serifs featured in the Decorated Rounded hand (GMAW, second ed., p. 21). However, this hand is clearly not a bookhand, but a cursive with thickenings at the tops and feet of verticals and occasional serifs. Turner says, "If these 'decorations' are regarded as a legacy of Schubart's 'decorated style' (*Zierstil*), the lower terminus of that style must be extended into the third century" (Turner, as cited in P. Oxy. 3093). And in GMAW 87, he calls our attention to P. Oxyrhynchus 3030 (Official Letter of a Royal Scribe; 31 March 207 [or 211]) as providing another late example. P. J. Parsons, the editor of P. Oxyrhynchus 3030, said, "The letters are thickly ornamented with serifs and back-hooks. The general effect is much like that of [P. Oxy.] 2555, of the late first century. It is salutary to have, precisely dated, so late an example of this fragile decorated style."

Turner admits that P. Oxyrhynchus 3030 is "late survivor" of this style (see GMAW 87). As such, an early third century date is not the norm for Decorated Rounded hands, nor is the late second century, for which we do not have any comparable dated documentary manuscripts. Rather, the highest concentration would be between 100 BC and AD 125/150. Interestingly, many Christian Greek Old Testament manuscripts, displaying the Decorated Rounded hand, have accordingly been dated to the late first century or second century, while scholars have usually been reluctant to do the same for New Testament manuscripts. Nonetheless, there are a few New Testament manuscripts displaying the Decorated Rounded style which belong in the period prior to AD 150, specifically, $\mathfrak{P}^{32}$, $\mathfrak{P}^{66}$, $\mathfrak{P}^{90}$, and $\mathfrak{P}^{104}$. (Each of these is discussed below.)

Severe Style

For the most part, formal Greek handwriting remained upright during the Ptolemaic and Roman periods. In due course, however, writers began to slant their letters to the right. When handwriting is upright, the angles will be right angles and the curves will be more rounded. When handwriting slopes, the angularity of the broad letters will be emphasized and the curves look like ellipses. This kind of hand also displays a mixture of narrow letters and broad letters. Turner, therefore, calls it Formal Mixed, while Schubart names it *Strenge Stil* (Severe style). Turner was of the opinion that there was no effort in documents to make a contrast between broad and narrow letters before the age of Hadrian (117–138). (See Turner's discussion in GMAW, pp. 26–27.) This is countered by G. Cavallo in his work, *Libri scritture scribi a Ercolano*, who makes it quite clear that documents displaying wide and narrow letters appeared in Herculaneum prior to the second century.

Some second-century, third-century, and early fourth-century manuscripts, with firm dates, displaying this style are as follows:

1. P. Giss. 3, AD 117 (for photo, see GLH 15a). The date is certain; it is a libretto in celebration of the accession of Hadrian (reigned 117–138). The hand is one of the earliest examples of the broad, slanting style, which became quite popular later.

2. P. Michigan 3, second half of second century (for photo, see GLH 15c). This is dated solidly to the second half of the second century, inasmuch as a documentary text on the verso has a date of AD 190 (the *terminus ante*) written in a cursive hand.

3. P. Oxyrhynchus 2341, AD 202 (for photo, see GLH 19c). The date is certain; it is the record of a legal proceeding.

4. P. Florentine II. 108, ca. 200 (for photo, see GLH 22a). This papyri came from the Heroninos archive, a collection of papers and official documents found at Theadelphia in the Fayum. All the documents date around AD 260. The literary texts written on the rectos of many of these documents would date about fifty years earlier. Hence, this manuscript (Homer's *Iliad* III) is ca. 200.

5. P. Rylands I. 57, ca. 200 (for photo, see GLH 22c). As with the above manuscript, this is a literary piece (Demosthenes, *De Corona*) on the recto of a document in the Heroninos archive. Its date must then be ca. 200.

6. P. Florentine II. 259, ca. 260 (for photo, see GLH 22d). This is a letter in the Heroninos archive written in a professional hand that resembles the common literary hand of the day.

7. P. Oxyrhynchus 2098, first half of third century (for photo, see GLH 19b). The recto has a portion of Herodotus, book 7; on the verso is a land survey dated to the reign of Gallienus (253–268). As such, the recto should be about fifty years earlier, ca. 200–225.

8. P. Oxyrhynchus 1016, early to middle third century (for photo, see GLH 20a; GMAW 84). The dating on this is difficult because the literary text (Phaedres) is written on the verso of a document, which is a land register (published as P. Oxyrhynchus 1044), mentioning the thirteenth year of a particular unnamed Roman emperor. The date could be 173/174 (Severus) or 195/196, according to C. H. Roberts, or 204/205 (Sept. Severus), according to Hunt, or 233/234 (Severus Alexander) according to E. G. Turner (see GMAW 84 for Turner's arguments). At the latest, then, the literary text would have been written no later than ca. 240–250.

9. P. Oxyrhynchus 223, early third century (for photo, see GLH 21a). The Homer text (*Iliad* V = P. Oxyrhynchus 223) was written on the verso of Oxyrhynchite provenance dated AD 186 (= P. Oxyrhynchus 237). Thus, P. Oxyrhynchus 223 must be dated early third century.

10. P. Herm. Rees 5, ca. AD 325 (for photo, see GMAW 70). The person to whom this letter is addressed is known from the John Rylands archives as a scholasticus (government official) in the 20s of the fourth century.

The early New Testament manuscripts displaying this Severe (slanted) style are as follows: $\mathfrak{P}^{13}$, $\mathfrak{P}^{45}$, $\mathfrak{P}^{48}$, $\mathfrak{P}^{49}$, $\mathfrak{P}^{110}$, and $\mathfrak{P}^{115}$. Each is discussed below.

Dating New Testament Manuscripts According to the Evolution of the Nomina Sacra

As is fully discussed in the next chapter, it is evident that the nomina sacra went through an evolutionary process. The initial repertoire of nomina sacra included special written significations for the divine names *kurios* (Lord), *Iesous* (Jesus), *Christos* (Christ), and *theos* (God). As will be argued in the next chapter, the divine title *pneuma* (Spirit) appears in the earliest stages of textual transmission and is nearly as ancient as the other four. Another early nomen sacrum was used for the words *stauros* (cross) and *stauromai* (crucify). In due course, other nomina sacra were added for *huios* (Son) and *pater* (Father), as well as for words such as *anthropos* (man), *Israel* (Israel), *Ierosalem* (Jerusalem), and *ouranos* (heaven).

Given this evolutionary process, one would think that the fewer the nomen sacrum, the earlier the manuscript. T. C. Skeat, for example, pointed this out when he dated $\mathfrak{P}^{4+64+67}$ to the second century.[24] (This manuscript displays only the basic five nomina sacra.) However, another second-century manuscript, $\mathfrak{P}^{66}$, has far more nomina sacra. In fact, its repertoire of nomina sacra is nearly identical to that found in Chester Beatty VI (of the early to middle second century). Hunger, who dated $\mathfrak{P}^{66}$ to the first half of the second century, pointed out this concurrence of nomina sacra as one of his arguments for giving $\mathfrak{P}^{66}$ a second-century date.[25]

The problem in using the nomina sacra for dating New Testament manuscripts is that their evolution began in the first century (perhaps at the time many of the New Testament books were first written) and was well underway in the second century. Thus, by the time we get to the mid-second century, many of the divine names are displayed as nomina sacra. Some of these names are always written as such; others such as Son and Father are sometimes written as nomina sacra and sometimes not in the very same manuscript. This inconsistency in displaying the nomina sacra form, as opposed to the full (*plene*), written-out form, shows that a particular nomen sacrum was in an evolutionary process. For example, it can be observed that the titles Son and Father were evolving in the second and early third centuries and became more or less fixed nomina sacra in the third century and thereafter. For example, in the second-century manuscript $\mathfrak{P}^{4+64+67}$ Son and Father are not written as nomina sacra. In other prominent second-century manuscripts, $\mathfrak{P}^{46}$, $\mathfrak{P}^{66}$, and $\mathfrak{P}^{75}$, "Son" and "Father" are sometimes written as nomina sacra and just as often are not. In most third-century manuscripts, these two titles are consistently treated as nomina sacra; see, for example, $\mathfrak{P}^{1}$, $\mathfrak{P}^{9}$, $\mathfrak{P}^{13}$, $\mathfrak{P}^{16}$, $\mathfrak{P}^{22}$, $\mathfrak{P}^{27}$, $\mathfrak{P}^{28}$, $\mathfrak{P}^{39}$, $\mathfrak{P}^{40}$ (in part), $\mathfrak{P}^{49}$, $\mathfrak{P}^{53}$, $\mathfrak{P}^{70}$, $\mathfrak{P}^{72}$, $\mathfrak{P}^{91}$, $\mathfrak{P}^{107}$, 0162.[26] This evidence suggests that a manuscript not exhibiting nomina sacra for Father and Son or exhibiting them both in nomina sacra form and in *plene* form should be considered for a second-century date. Such is the case for $\mathfrak{P}^{45}$, which is usually dated to the third century (see discussion below).

Another example of a manuscript displaying both the nomina sacra and the full, written-out (*plene*) forms for all the names of the Trinity (Father, Son, and Spirit) is $\mathfrak{P}^{46}$. What is most significant is that the scribe did not always write the nomen sacrum for *pneuma* (Spirit) where one would expect the scribe to have done so (see discussion in next chapter). This could very well tell us that this title was not yet fixed as a nomen sacrum when the scribe of $\mathfrak{P}^{46}$ did his work; in other words, it was still developing. Since all the other second-century manuscripts consistently display *pneuma* as a nomen sacrum (when refering to the divine Spirit), this phenomenon in $\mathfrak{P}^{46}$ could indicate an early date for this manuscript.

Another issue pertains to the presence of the suspended form and short contracted form as preceding the longer contracted form (or what some call the combination form, which I think is a misnomer). As will be discussed in the next chapter, it is possible that the short contracted form (for example, $\overline{\text{IC}}$ for IHCOYC) was the first form used in the earliest Christian writings. A variation of this would be a fuller contracted form, such as $\overline{\text{IHC}}$. The question is: Is the fuller form a later evolutionary development? If so, then a manuscript with the fuller contracted form could be dated later than one with the shorter form. But it is just as likely that both forms developed concurrently or nearly concurrently. Some scholars think the suspended form of

IHCOYC (Jesus), $\overline{\text{IH}}$, was the earliest. But I have my doubts, all of which are expressed in the next chapter.

The upshot of this is that it is difficult to use the forms of the nomina sacra to date manuscripts. What can be used is the presence and/or absence of certain nomina sacra with respect to the full repertoire, as well as fluctuation in use in a particular manuscript (as in $\mathfrak{P}^{46}$).

The Earliest Christian Old Testament Manuscripts

Before we examine the earliest New Testament manuscripts, we need to identify the earliest Christian Old Testament manuscripts inasmuch as several of these manuscripts aid paleographers in dating New Testament manuscripts. We know that these manuscripts were produced by Christians because they are codices and/or contain nomina sacra. Jewish copies of the Old Testament were done on scrolls and lack nomina sacra.

Here is a listing of the earliest (pre-AD 200) Christian, Greek Old Testament manuscripts:

1. P. Yale 1, Genesis. This was dated ca. AD 90 by Oates, Samuel, and Welles, who produced the *editio princeps*. The date of the manuscript was assigned by placing it within an evolution of handwriting styles. The explanation is as follows:

> In contrast with the ever more cursive hands of the late Ptolemaic period
> [50–30 BC], it is a kind of print, wherein the letters occupy separate and
> roughly even spaces as if placed in ruled squares. Except for the iota, which was
> an obvious exception, the letters tend to be as wide as they are high and most
> observe a rule of isocephaly, terminal hastae dropping below the line to some
> extent but letters rarely rising above it. At its best, this style achieved a certain
> elegance approaching that of the uncials of a later date; so the Oxyrhynchus
> Homer dated to the first half of the second century. Properly, however, the style
> aimed at easy legibility rather than beauty. The earliest examples have something
> of a childish appearance, are rough and labored, the curves jerky rather than
> flowing. As better effect was sought with time, it took the form of attaching ser-
> ifs to all terminal lines, and these characterize the style from the middle of the
> first to the middle of the second centuries. Gradually, too, cursive features
> appear. Letters tend to be connected without lifting the pen. Curves and loops
> are employed wherever possible, and letters tend to be oval rather than round,
> sloping rather than upright, varied in height rather than even, with long and
> dashing initial and terminal strokes. Within this process it is possible to date a
> given hand typologically with some confidence, although given scribes may be
> ahead of or behind the general development.
>
> Within this sequence, the Yale Genesis stands rather early. . . . [several
> details of lettering follows]. One would not hesitate to date such a hand to the

mid-first century or even earlier. It seems quite impossible that it could be as late as AD 100.[27]

Significantly, correspondence in the Beinecke Library's "Papyrology File" has notes from C. H. Roberts, E. G. Turner, and T. C. Skeat, each initially dating the manuscript to the late first or early second century. All three of these papyrologists later changed their thinking and dated the Yale Genesis to the mid-second century.[28] In his published writings, C. H. Roberts disagreed with Welles's dating, saying that it was not backed up by any detailed study of the writing and has not found acceptance. Roberts himself dated it to the mid-second century, but he himself didn't provide a detailed analysis.[29]

2. P. Baden 4.56 (P. Heidelberg inv. 8), Exodus and Deuteronomy. The editor, Bilabel, dated it to the second century; so also H. I. Bell.[30]

3. P. Chester Beatty VI, Numbers and Deuteronomy. The editor, Kenyon, first dated it the end of the first century, saying, "It is definitely a Roman type of hand, with affinities to the great Hyperides MS. and Herodas MS., which are of the latter part of the first century. It is the work of a good professional scribe." Kenyon, then, became more specific in his dating, saying, "It is akin to, but probably later than, the long Hyperides papyrus in the British Museum, which is assigned on fairly good evidence to the end of the first century after Christ. It does not seem possible to date it [P. Beatty VI] later than the second century, or even in my opinion, after the middle of that century."[31] Kenyon notes that his dating was supported by H. I. Bell and Wilhelm Schubart, as well as by U. Wilcken, who dated it "second century," perhaps in the reign of Hadrian (117–138).[32] It should be noted that Kenyon dated P. Beatty VI by comparing it to P. Lit. London 132 (Hyperides), which he dated to the latter part of the first century, but which others would date to the first half of the second century AD, a date based on the evidence of cursive titles and subscriptions. (For Kenyon's discussion on his dating of P. Lit. London 132, which is quite thorough and solid, see his *Paleography of Greek Papyri*, 85–88.)

R. Seider dates C. Beatty VI to the middle of the second century.[33] Bell and Skeat also argued for a second-century date.[34] Montevecci dates it to the beginning of the second century (for photo, see pl. 49).[35] As is typical, Turner argues for a later date, i.e., in the third century.[36] C. H. Roberts counters Turner's dating with a lengthy argument, wherein he sees P. Chester Beatty VI as being placed firmly in the second century. In Roberts's article, he said this of Chester Beatty VI:

> This rounded Roman hand is familiar enough . . . and its origins can be traced in texts of the early second and or even late first century, and it persists into the second half of the third. . . . The problem is to decide to which stage in the development of the hand this papyrus is to be assigned.
>
> The origin of the style may be seen in the well-known letter of Gemellus of AD 94 (GLH 11b), while again among documents early examples of it are

GLH 13a of AD 125 [= P. Phil. 1] . . . and Schubart Abb. 34 [= P. Berol. 6854], a document of Trajan's reign [98–117]. On any assessment, I should place these documents earlier than P. Chester Beatty vi.[37]

The similarities between P. Chester Beatty VI and P. Philadelphia 1 are remarkable. P. Phil. 1 is a Dossier of Official Papers concerning Liturgies (for photo, see GLH 13a). Jean Scherer, the editor of this manuscript, dated it AD 103–124.[38] Roberts dates it AD 120–124, saying, "The latest of the surviving papers in this file is dated AD 120–124; all are written in the same hand and the copy of the dossier may be presumed to have been shortly after this date. The writer employs a careful and rounded hand of some elegance" (GLH 13a). Whether it is dated AD 103–124 or 120–124 is a matter of debate. Nonetheless, it belongs to the first quarter of the second century. Its comparability to the Beatty manuscript suggests the same date for both.

4. P. Antinoopolis 7, Psalms. The editor of the *editio princeps*, C. H. Roberts, dated this to the middle of the second century. He wrote, "The codex [is] written in a delicate and rounded literary hand. There are some traces of cursive influence and occasional ligatures; the script has an air of calculated irregularity found in certain styles of the first two centuries AD."[39] And then Roberts refers the reader to Schubart's *Papyrus Berolinses*: Tafeln 19a (= P. Berol. 9739); 19c (= P. Berol. 6845); 29b (= P. Berol. 9810). These manuscripts, providing legitimate parallels, are significant for the dating of P. Antinoopolis 7, inasmuch as P. Berol. 9739 is dated first/second century; P. Berol. 6845 is dated the same. P. Berol. 9810 is dated second century. Added to this, we must take note that Roberts says that the Psalms fragment resembles manuscripts of the first two centuries AD. Thus, this manuscript could (and should) be dated anywhere from the end of the first century to the end of the second century, as is the Bodleain Psalms fragment (see comments below).

5. P. Leipzig inv. 170, Psalms (118:27–64). This codex was dated by Roberts and Skeat to the second century.[40]

6. Bodleian Gr. Bib. g. 5, Psalms. The editors, Barns and Kilpatrick, dated it to the second century, noting its similarities especially with P. Antinoopolis 7 (see comments above), and also with P. Oxyrhynchus 656 and P. Oxyrhynchus 1074. Here are their comments in full: "The rounded, delicate writing of our text . . . resembles the Antinoopolis text not a little; forms of letters (e.g. H and M) which cannot be paralleled there may be found in earlier papyri: for instance P. Rylands 457 (John, first half of the second century) and the dated document P Fayum 110 (AD 94). The hand of our text has also, it is true, some resemblance to P. Oxyrhynchus 656 [which, in a footnote, Barns and Kilpatrick affirm as being second century] and 1074, both of which the first editors dated in the third century; in neither case, however, did they rule out the possibility of a second century date. If these indications can be trusted, the [Bodleian] papyrus may belong anywhere from the end of the first century to the end of the second."[41]

7. P. Oxyrhynchus 656, Genesis. The editors, Grenfell and Hunt, dated this manuscript to the third century when they should have dated it to the second century. Their reasoning was as follows: "The MS. was carefully written in round upright uncials of good size and decidedly early appearance, having in some respects more affinity with types of the second century than of the third. To the latter, however, the hand is in all probability to be assigned, though we should be inclined to place it in the earlier rather than the later part of the century." This illogical dating was probably influenced by Grenfell and Hunt thinking that the codex did not come into existence until the late second or early third century and/or that Christianity had not penetrated Middle Egypt and Upper Egypt before the third century. Bell and Skeat correctly redated P. Oxyrhynchus 656 to the latter second century.[42] And T. C. Skeat made some pertinent comments about this when he dated $\mathfrak{P}^{90}$ (a manuscript displaying a similar handwriting style) to the second century (see comments below on $\mathfrak{P}^{90}$).

As will be seen later, P. Oxyrhynchus 656 is important for the dating of $\mathfrak{P}^{32}$ and $\mathfrak{P}^{90}$. Thus, its date needs to be established by comparable documentary manuscripts. There are a few that I can confidently cite: P. London 130 (post AD 81 perhaps AD 100), P. Fayum 110 (AD 96), and P. Berol. 6854 (AD 98–117). These three appear to be slightly earlier than P. Oxyrhynchus 656. A more comparable example is P. Oxyrhynchus 454 + PSI 119 (dated 125–150). Each of these is discussed above in the section under Decorated Rounded.

8. P. Oxyrhynchus 1074, Exodus. The editors, Grenfell and Hunt, said, "This hand could not be referred to a time later than the reign of Diocletian, and might well be placed at the beginning of the third century or even earlier" (see *editio princeps*). See comments above by Barns and Kilpatrick about Bodleian Gr. Bib. g. 5, Psalms, who compare this manuscript to P. Oxyrhynchus 1074 and date both in the second century. W. Schubart dates P. Oxyrhynchus 1074 as "second century."[43] As has been pointed out, Grenfell and Hunt were too conservative in their dating. P. Oxyrhynchus 1074 is undoubtedly a second-century manuscript.

9. Chester Beatty Papyrus VIII, Jeremiah. The editor, Kenyon, dates it "second or second/third."[44] Roberts first dated it "second century" and then later as "ca. 200."[45] H. I. Bell also dates it ca. 200.[46]

10. Chester Beatty Papyrus IX, Ezekiel, Daniel, Esther. The manuscript is the work of two scribes, one for Daniel and Esther (with the best calligraphy), and another for Ezekiel. The editor, Kenyon, cited Wilcken as dating it in the second century on the basis of the work of the scribe of Daniel and Esther.[47] (Of course, the other scribe had to have been a contemporary.) Kenyon himself said, "There is no reason to place it later than the first half of the third."[48] Roberts first dated it "second century" and then later as "ca. 200."[49] H. I. Bell also dates it ca. 200.[50]

11. PSI 921 (Psalm 77:1–18). This is a fragment of a Psalter (now at Florence) written on the verso of a roll containing a bank register (on the recto) dated in

AD 143/144.[51] Bell said, "It is most unusual in a roll used again in this way to find a longer interval between recto and verso than about fifty years. The original editors dated it before rather than after AD 200."[52] This is far too conservative. Normally, reuse of a documentary text (on the recto) for literary purposes (on the verso) would not exceed ten to fifteen years. I would date PSI 921 to ca. AD 160. This Psalms fragment is clearly Christian inasmuch as it contains nomina sacra for "Lord," "God," and "Spirit."

12. P. Antinoopolis 8, Proverbs and Ecclesiastes. The editor, C. H. Roberts, says it has a hand that resembles $\mathfrak{P}^{46}$ (though a little later).[53] It should be dated early third century.

Early Christian Noncanonical Writings

A few other manuscripts need to be noted before we examine the earliest New Testament manuscripts. These are extant, second-century manuscripts of noncanonical Christian writings. These manuscripts are also helpful in dating New Testament manuscripts.

1. P. Egerton 2, Unknown Gospel. According to the editors, H. I. Bell and T. C. Skeat, this gospel was probably composed in the early part of the second century, and the copy which was discovered could be no later than 150.[54] The paleographic dating came about by a morphological comparison with the following manuscripts: $\mathfrak{P}^{52}$ (dated early second century) with which it bears unmistakable likeness; P. Berol. 6854 (a document dated in the reign of Trajan, who died in AD 117; for photo, see Schubart's *Greek Pal., 34;* GLH 12a); P. London 130 (a horoscope calculated from AD April 1, 81 and therefore not likely to be later than the early years of the second century; for photo see Schubart's Greek Pal., 81); and P. Oxyrhynchus 656 (Genesis, mid to late second century, see discussion above). Clearly, all these comparable manuscripts are dated within the period of late first century to second century, and most of them have solid documentary dating. Being somewhat conservative, Bell and Skeat then dated P. Egerton 2 to a date "later than the middle of the second century." In a subsequent article, Bell wrote, "This papyrus almost certainly falls within the period AD 120–170, and it is on the whole likely to date from the first rather than the second half of that period." [55] (It should be noted that P. London 130 bears significant resemblance to $\mathfrak{P}^{32}$; see comments there.)

A new fragment of the Egerton Gospel was published several years later as P. Köln 255.[56] This manuscript shows the word *aneneg'kon* with a hook between the consonants gamma and kappa. Because Turner argued that this was a feature prominent in the third century, the date of the Egerton Gospel is now being questioned. Indeed, the editors of P. Koln 255 cited the date as "ca. 150 (?)." Hence, the editors of this Köln fragment of the Unknown Gospel wonder if it should be ca. 200, in accordance with Turner's dating of P. Bodmer II ($\mathfrak{P}^{66}$), which he dates to ca. 200 on the basis of the presence of the hook between consonants.

However, I would argue (as I did above) that Turner's dating needs to be revised not vice versa. The dating of the Egerton Gospel to the mid-second century should still stand because of its overall morphological likeness to so many manuscripts of the early to middle second century.

2. P. Michigan 130, Shepherd of Hermas. This manuscript, containing "The Mandates" of *The Shepherd*, was written on the verso of a scroll; the recto contains a document that can be dated to the reign of Marcus Aurelius (AD 161–180). The editor, C. Bonner, dated the Hermas text to ca. 200, saying, "It is nearer to the style of the second century than to that of the third. It is a pleasure to find that Professor Hunt concurs in this opinion. I think that the verso writing may be assigned to about 200 AD."[57] The rule of thumb is that if the recto has been used for a document and the verso for a literary text, then the date of the literary text does not follow far behind that of the recto (i.e., no more than ten to twenty years). Thus, it stands to reason that P. Michigan 130 could be dated AD 180–200, making it the earliest extant manuscript of the Shepherd of Hermas. C. H. Roberts and T. C. Skeat think this manuscript belongs to the second century.[58]

3. P. Oxyrhynchus 1, Gospel of Thomas. Grenfell and Hunt dated it to the second or third century, anywhere between 150 and 300. They were vague about the date because at the time of publication (1897), there was a paucity of manuscripts from that early time period. H. I. Bell said that the earlier date is not at all unlikely.[59] C. H. Roberts and T. C. Skeat place it in the second century.[60]

4. P. Oxyrhynchus 405, Irenaeus's *Against Heresies*. This is a late second-century Oxyrhynchus fragment having part of Irenaeus's *Against Heresies*, which itself was written in AD 180. As C. H. Roberts said, "The ink was hardly dry before a copy of Irenaeus's famous work reached Oxyrhynchus!"[61]

5. P. Geneva 253, Christian Homily. This is a late second-century Christian homily, containing portions of Matthew 10:11–13, 29–31 (or Luke 10:5–6; 12:6–7). The editor of this manuscript, Jean Rudhardt, recognized the morphological similarity of the hand of P. Geneva 253 (an upright informal rounded uncial) to a number of manuscripts dated between late first century and early third, manuscripts such as G. Berol. 6890 (= BGU I 140; dated AD 119?; for photo see Schubart's *Greek Berol.* 22a; the hand is earlier than P. Geneva 253); P. Chester Beatty VI (Num.–Deut., early second century; for photo, see Montev., pl. 49); P. Oxyrhynchus 2076 (late first/early second century; for photo, see GMAW 18); P. Oxyrhynchus 2441 (middle of the second century; for photo, see GMAW 22); and P. Oxyrhynchus 654 (Gospel of Thomas; early third century).[62] Of all the manuscripts, the two second-century manuscripts, P. Chester Beatty VI and P. Oxyrhynchus 2441, have the greatest similarity. I would add that P. Geneva 253 is also very similar to $\mathfrak{P}^{20}$, and a little less so to $\mathfrak{P}^{90}$ (P. Oxyrhynchus 3523; see comments there). I would date the manuscript as second century because it could have been produced anytime in that century.

6. P. Oxyrhynchus 406. This is a portion from a codex preserving a theological treatise or an unknown Christian work containing a quotation of Isaiah 6:10 in its New Testament form (as in Matt. 13:15 and Acts 28:27)—omitting *autēn* (their) after "ears"—the pronoun is found in the LXX. The manuscript contains numerous nomina sacra (for "God," "Christ," and "crucify"). Grenfell and Hunt dated it to the third century, comparing the hand (a large upright uncial) to P. Oxyrhynchus 25 and 224. H. I. Bell dates it to ca. 200.[63]

The Earliest New Testament Manuscripts

Now we come to the actual New Testament manuscripts themselves and begin our exploration of dating the earliest New Testament manuscripts (that is, those that were most likely produced before the beginning of the fourth century). The discussion will proceed chronologically: first century (?), second century, ca. 200, and third century.

New Testament Manuscripts of the First Century?

Any New Testament scholar would wish for a first-century New Testament manuscript. But are there any? Some have argued so, specifically for the following manuscripts: 7Q4, 7Q5, $\mathfrak{P}^{46}$, $\mathfrak{P}^{52}$, and $\mathfrak{P}^{64+67}$.

The Qumran manuscripts 7Q4 and 7Q5 are unquestionably from the first century, but their identity as New Testament manuscripts is still under debate. This debate is threefold. First and foremost, the debate centers on the identification of the manuscripts. O'Callgahan (and others such as Thiede) argue for New Testament identification. Neve, Muro, and others argue for 1 Enoch 103 identification for 7Q4. (No one has yet posited a plausible Old Testament identification for 7Q5.) The second area of debate concerns the dating of the manuscripts, which must be pre-AD 68 (by universal agreement). Those scholars who have the view that many of the New Testament writings were composed prior to the fall of Jerusalem (AD 68–70) cannot say that there could be no New Testament manuscript copies prior to AD 68. Those who hold the view that many of the New Testament writings were composed in the later part of the first century have a real problem with thinking a New Testament manuscript could exist prior to AD 70. The third area of debate has to do with how New Testament manuscripts could be among the Dead Sea Scrolls. Most scholars hold the view that all the manuscripts found at Qumran were composed by the Jews in the scriptorium there. However, a few scholars think that some of the manuscripts were taken there from Jerusalem by various Jewish groups at the onset of the Jewish revolt (around AD 66–67). When one considers that all the manuscripts in Cave 7 were written in Greek, it is not farfetched to think that some Greek-speaking Jewish Christians deposited some manuscripts, both from the Old Testament and the New Testament in this cave.[64] But in the end, it is the identification of the manuscripts themselves that will solve the debate concerning the second and third issues. If the manuscripts are from the New Testament, then it stands to reason that they are very early copies that were taken by Jewish Christians to the Dead Sea caves prior to AD 68–70. If not, the other arguments are moot.

As to the other manuscripts thought by some to belong to the first century (namely, $𝔓^{46}$, $𝔓^{52}$, $𝔓^{64+67}$), I offer a thorough argument below. In brief, I think it is possible that $𝔓^{52}$ could have been written at the end of the first century, but it most likely belongs to the beginning of the second. I think $𝔓^{46}$ is mid-second century; and I think $𝔓^{64+67}$ (actually $𝔓^{4+64+67}$) is mid to late second century. I would add another manuscript that could be late first century or early second century, namely $𝔓^{104}$.

New Testament Manuscripts of the Second Century

According to the First Appendix to the Nestle-Aland text (27th edition), there are only four New Testament papyri listed as being second century: $𝔓^{52}$, $𝔓^{90}$, $𝔓^{98}$ (?), and $𝔓^{104}$. A few others are listed as "ca. 200," namely, $𝔓^{32}$, $𝔓^{46}$, $𝔓^{64}$, $𝔓^{66}$, $𝔓^{67}$, $𝔓^{98}$(?), and $𝔓^{104}$.[65] This is far too conservative, in my opinion and in the opinion of many paleographers and papyrologists. There are, at least, twelve manuscripts that should be dated to the second century, namely, $𝔓^{4+64+67}$, $𝔓^{32}$, $𝔓^{46}$, $𝔓^{52}$, $𝔓^{66}$, $𝔓^{75}$, $𝔓^{77}$ (and $𝔓^{103}$), $𝔓^{87}$, $𝔓^{98}$, $𝔓^{104}$, and $𝔓^{109}$. There are another fifteen manuscripts that could be dated to ca. 200 or early third century, namely, $𝔓^{1}$, $𝔓^{5}$, $𝔓^{13}$, $𝔓^{20}$, $𝔓^{23}$, $𝔓^{27}$, $𝔓^{29}$, $𝔓^{30}$, $𝔓^{38}$, $𝔓^{45}$, $𝔓^{48}$, $𝔓^{106}$, $𝔓^{107}$, $𝔓^{108}$, $𝔓^{109}$, 0189. These are discussed in the next section.

$𝔓^{4+64+67}$ **(portions of the same codex), middle to late second century.**— This codex, the work of a professional scribe, is an excellent example of early Biblical Uncial. The manuscript is well-stroked, with no ligatures and complete bilinearity. The manuscript displays well-crafted calligraphy, paragraph markings, punctuation, and double-columns. $𝔓^{4+64+67}$ is the only extant early New Testament manuscript to be written in double columns per page. ($𝔓^{50}$ is also double column, but it is dated ca. 300 at the very earliest.) Double-column manuscripts were standard fare for scrolls, but not for codices. As Turner said, "Scribes who copied on a codex of papyrus in single column were aware that they were writing a second-class book."[66] The implication is that the scribe of $𝔓^{4+64+67}$, who must have been accustomed to producing literary writings in double columns on scrolls, upgraded this papyrus codex by producing it in double columns.

The manuscript contains portions of Luke ($𝔓^{4}$) and Matthew ($𝔓^{64}$ and $𝔓^{67}$).

$𝔓^{4}$ (P. Paris Bibl. Nat. Suppl. Gr. 1120) contains portions of Luke 1–6. Parts of this were originally published by Vincent Scheil, "Archeologie, Varia," *Revue Biblique* 1 (1892): 113–15. A more complete transcription was provided by J. Merell, "Nouveaux fragments papyrus IV," in *Revue Biblique* 47 (1938): 5–22. A full text, with a few new additions, is found in Comfort and Barrett's *Text of the Earliest New Testament Greek Manuscripts* (43–67).

𝔓⁶⁴ (P. Magdalene 18) and 𝔓⁶⁷ (P. Barcelona Inv. 1) contain portions of Matthew 3, 5, and 26. 𝔓⁶⁴ was first published by Colin Roberts in "An Early Papyrus of the First Gospel," *Harvard Theological Review*: 46 (1953): 233–37. 𝔓⁶⁷ was first published by P. Roca-Puig in a booklet called *Un Papiro Griego del Evangelio de San Mateo* (Barcelona, 1957). After Colin Roberts realized that 𝔓⁶⁴ and 𝔓⁶⁷ were two parts of the same manuscript and then confirmed this with Roca-Puig, the latter published another article entitled "Nueva publicacion del papiro numero uno de Barcelona" in *Helmantica* 37 (1961): 5–20, in which Roca gives a full presentation of the entire manuscript. Colin Roberts appended a note to this article explaining how he had discovered that 𝔓⁶⁴ and 𝔓⁶⁷ were part of the same manuscript.

I have presented a full argument for 𝔓⁴⁺⁶⁴⁺⁶⁷ being parts of one codex.[67] Skeat has also argued that these three manuscripts have come from the same codex.[68] As such, 𝔓⁴⁺⁶⁴⁺⁶⁷, as part of the same codex, should be assigned the same date. This counters the listing in Appendix I in *Novum Testamentum* (NA²⁷), which lists 𝔓⁴ as "third century" and 𝔓⁶⁴+𝔓⁶⁷ as "ca. 200." I will begin with the dating of 𝔓⁶⁴ (the Magdalen fragment of Matthew) because its dating has been the subject of controversy in recent years. Then I will discuss 𝔓⁶⁷, its undisputed companion; and then 𝔓⁴.

The Dating of 𝔓⁶⁴.—Thiede has posited a first-century date based primarily on his observation that some of the lettering in 𝔓⁶⁴ is distinctly similar to that found in the Greek Minor Prophets Scroll 8HevXIIgr (from Nahal Hever), which has been dated by various scholars between 50 BC and AD 50. He observed that several of the letters (alpha, epsilon, iota, omicron, rho) are identical or nearly identical, whereas others are distinctly dissimilar (eta). However, the letters in 8HevXIIgr often have small serifs, whereas there are none in 𝔓⁶⁴. In fact, 8HevXIIgg is closer in style to what might be called the Decorated Rounded (discussed above), whereas the lettering in 𝔓⁶⁴ is far more identical to that of those manuscripts that are called Biblical Uncial.

Thiede also draws upon similarities with the papyri in the script of Herculaneum (dated no later than AD 79) and Greek Qumran fragments of Leviticus: pap⁴QLevLXXLeviticusᵃ and pap⁴QLevLXXLeviticusᵇ, which have been dated between the first century BC and the middle of the first century AD. Because several of the letters in these manuscripts (as well as 8HevXIIgr) are comparable to those in 𝔓⁶⁴, Thiede suggests comparable dating: "The prevailing tendency to date material of a nature comparable to Magdalen Gr. 17 to a period even preceding the earliest possible date of Matthew's Gospel suggests, with all due caution, the possibility of redating the fragments from Oxford and Barcelona (which are, after all, definitely Matthean) to a period somewhat earlier than the late second century previously assigned to them. Certainty will remain elusive, of course."[69]

In a subsequent publication, Thiede posits that the earlier date could be as early as the middle of the first century, even a date of pre-66 AD.[70] But he offers no new or compelling paleographic evidence for this dating.

My position is that $\mathfrak{P}^{64}$ (as part of $\mathfrak{P}^4$ and $\mathfrak{P}^{67}$) manifests a style (the Biblical Uncial) that did not emerge until the middle of the second century. This is explained at length below. But, first, let's review how others have dated this manuscript.

$\mathfrak{P}^{64}$ was originally dated third century by Mr. Hurleatt, the man who donated the manuscript to the Magdalen College. The papyrologist A. S. Hunt took a look at the fragments and dated to the early fourth century. In reaction to this late dating, Colin Roberts made a publication of the manuscript, dating it to ca. 200.[71] Hunt was too conservative in his dating, as was typical for much of his dating of the New Testament papyri. His fourth-century date needed adjustment, and this was done quite thoroughly by Colin Roberts, who noted that the handwriting of $\mathfrak{P}^{64}$ is a precursor to the Biblical Uncial of the third and fourth centuries. According to Roberts, the lettering in $\mathfrak{P}^{64}$ corresponds most closely with that found in P. Oxyrhynchus 843, dated by Grenfell and Hunt as ca. 200. The handwriting on this manuscript is clearly Biblical Uncial. According to Roberts, other similar hands to $\mathfrak{P}^{64}$ are exhibited in P. Oxyrhynchus 405 (ca. 200), P. Oxyrhynchus 1620 (second/third century), and P. Oxyrhynchus 1819 (second century). Thus, Roberts dated the manuscript to ca. 200, and this date was confirmed by three eminent papyrologists: Harold Bell, T. C. Skeat, and E. G. Turner.[72] T. C. Skeat later modified his dating to ca. 175 (see discussion below). Indeed, the date should be earlier because $\mathfrak{P}^{64}$ (as part of $\mathfrak{P}^4$ and $\mathfrak{P}^{67}$) is more comparable with manuscripts displaying the earliest form of the Biblical Uncial, as the following discussion will reveal.

The Dating of $\mathfrak{P}^{67}$.—The corresponding fragment, $\mathfrak{P}^{67}$, was dated by Roca-Puig to the latter part of the second century. He noted great similarities between $\mathfrak{P}^{67}$ and P. Oxyrhynchus 661, which is dated to the second half of the second century and is one of the earliest examples of the Biblical Uncial (see discussion above). A comparison of the two manuscripts affirms the remarkable similarity of handwriting. P. Roca-Puig also thinks $\mathfrak{P}^{67}$ is like P. Oxyrhynchus 224+P. Rylands 547 (late second century); for photos, see Cavallo, pl. 6, 7a). He is convinced that the number of examples of the further development of this type of hand in the third century is a sure indication that $\mathfrak{P}^{67}$ could not be later than AD 200. Roca-Puig also recognizes that scholars have been too conservative in their dating.[73] The final conclusion is that he is firm in this dating of $\mathfrak{P}^{67}$ to the late second century.

The Dating of $\mathfrak{P}^4$.—$\mathfrak{P}^4$, as part of $\mathfrak{P}^{64+67}$, figures significantly in the dating process because we know about its provenance. It had been placed in the back of a codex of Philo's treatises, which was hidden in a house in Coptos, presumably to avoid being confiscated during the persecution of AD 292 or 303, when Coptos was besieged and sacked by Diocletian.[74] The Philo Codex is itself a third-century manuscript, which could easily be dated twenty-five to fifty years prior to the time it was put in hiding. Thus, the Philo Codex can, at least, be dated to ca. 250. The Gospel fragments would have come from an old codex, which must have been well-used and well-worn long before it was placed in the Philo Codex.[75] In fact, it must have been a discarded copy replaced by another codex. Thus, it is not unlikely that $\mathfrak{P}^4$, once a handsome codex, was made as early as seventy-five to one hundred years prior to the Philo Codex. As such, we are fairly certain of a late second-century date. This does not preclude an even earlier date because the codex, a beautiful one, may have been in use more than a hundred years before it was discarded.[76]

As previously noted, T. C. Skeat makes a strong case for assigning $\mathfrak{P}^4$ and $\mathfrak{P}^{64}$ and $\mathfrak{P}^{67}$ to the same codex. In the same article he makes a good case for dating this codex ($\mathfrak{P}^{4+64+67}$) to ca. 175.[77] Skeat says that two manuscripts are very similar to $\mathfrak{P}^{4+64+67}$, namely P. Vindob. G. 29784 (for photo, see p. 135) and P. Vindob. G. 29768 (for photo, see Cavallo pl. 12a), especially the former, which is dated late second century by Cavallo in *Richerche sulla Maiuscola Biblica*. In a letter to me, Skeat said he thought the dating of P. Vindob. G. 29784 was "particularly valuable because the text of the fragment is not Christian and Cavallo was not under any pressure to date it as early as possible but could assess it on purely morphological and stylistic grounds." Another papyrologist I consulted, who wishes to remain anonymous, said he thought $\mathfrak{P}^{4+64+67}$ belonged to the reign of Marcus Aurelius (AD 161–180).

In conclusion, $\mathfrak{P}^4+\mathfrak{P}^{64}+\mathfrak{P}^{67}$ is a second-century manuscript, exhibiting an early form of the Biblical Uncial hand, and thus should be dated to the late second century (ca. 175). The handwriting style lines up remarkably well with P. Oxyrhynchus 2404 (second century), P. Oxyrhynchus 661 (ca. 150), and P. Vindob. G. 29784 (late second century). It also exhibits morphological similarities with P. Oxyrhynchus 224 + P. Rylands 547 (late second century),[78] P. Oxyrhynchus 2750 (later second century),[79] P. Oxyrhynchus 2334 (later second century),[80] P. Oxyrhynchus 2498 (late second century), and P. Rylands 16 (late second century). P. Oxyrhynchus 661 provides a solid date (see discussion above) for which the other manuscripts listed here owe their dating (by comparative morphology) to the second half of the second century. Another manuscript with a solid date is P. Rylands 16 (Comedy) because this manuscript contains a documentary text on the verso. It can be dated quite confidently to the latter part of the second century (see discussion above). Peter Head sees P. Oxyrhychus 2498 (dated by its editor, Lobel, to the late second century) as possessing significant comparison to $\mathfrak{P}^{64+67}$. He notes both the general appearance (closely written, bilinear, with slight variation between wide and narrow strokes) and the letter forms.[81] (See photos of $\mathfrak{P}^4$, $\mathfrak{P}^{64}$, and $\mathfrak{P}^{67}$ facing P. Oxy. 2404 and P. Vindob. G. 29784 on pp. 132–33.)

$\mathfrak{P}^{32}$ **(P. Rylands 5), second century.**—The manuscript, containing Titus 1:11–15; 2:3–8, displays an informal Decorated Rounded hand. It was originally dated by Hunt to the third century, as having handwriting comparable to P. Oxyrhynchus 656 (Genesis), which was also dated by Hunt to the early third century.[82] Concerning P. Oxyrhynchus 656, Grenfell and Hunt said it had more affinities with late second-century manuscripts than with third-century manuscripts, but then they illogically assigned it to the early third century (see comments above). P. Oxyrhynchus 656 is certainly a second-century manuscript. As discussed above, documentary evidence places P. Oxyrhynchus 656 in the second century, and very likely in the first half of the second century. Bell and Skeat provide an argument for a revised date for P. Oxyrhynchus 656 to the second century.[83] In this article, they indicate that Kenyon concurred with this redating. In a separate article, Bell affirmed that $\mathfrak{P}^{32}$ definitely belongs to the second century.[84] C. H. Roberts and T. C. Skeat concur with this second-century dating.[85]

There are two other second-century Greek Old Testament manuscripts with comparative styles, namely, two Psalms fragments: P. Antinoopolis 7 and Bodleian G. bib. g. 5. As noted above, both of these manuscripts can be dated from the end of the first century to the end of the second. Furthermore, $\mathfrak{P}^{32}$ must share the same date as $\mathfrak{P}^{90}$ inasmuch as both exhibit morphological likeness to P. Oxyrhynchus 656, as well as to each other. Each of these manuscripts displays the Decorated Rounded style prevalent in the second century. The date assigned to $\mathfrak{P}^{32}$, therefore, rests upon the fact that this style was not prominent after the end of the second century.

Among documentary manuscripts, P. London 130 bears remarkable similarity to $\mathfrak{P}^{32}$. When dating the Egerton Gospel, Bell and Skeat cited P. London 130 as showing comparable features.[86] P. London 130 mentions a horoscope of AD April 1, 81; as such, it can be dated safely to the early second century and more likely to AD 100. The overall appearance and lettering of this manuscript are quite comparable to what we see in $\mathfrak{P}^{32}$, far more so than with the Egerton Gospel, in my estimation. The unique likenesses can be seen in the formation of two kinds of alpha (one somewhat regular and another with an oval and swerve coming off the top and joining with the next letter), the bell-shaped delta, theta (allowing for ligature), the swooping zeta, the chi, rho, upsilon, and phi. One significant difference is that P. London 130 has the open kappa, a prominent feature of the first century, whereas $\mathfrak{P}^{32}$ has a closed kappa. In any event, $\mathfrak{P}^{32}$ seems to be a slightly later version of the kind of hand we see in P. London 130.

In the final analysis, $\mathfrak{P}^{32}$ belongs to the second century and could have been produced any time in that century. Not only is this one of the earliest New Testament manuscripts, it is the earliest of the Pastoral Epistles. No other extant manuscript of the second or third centuries preserves any portion of a Pastoral Epistle. The next earliest manuscript to contain the Pastoral Episles is Codex Sinaiticus, of the late fourth century (ca. 375). (See photo of $\mathfrak{P}^{32}$ next to P. London 130 on p. 135.)

$\mathfrak{P}^{46}$ **(Chester Beatty Papyrus II; P. Michigan inv. 6238), middle to late second century (ca. 150–175).**—This manuscript is the work of a professional

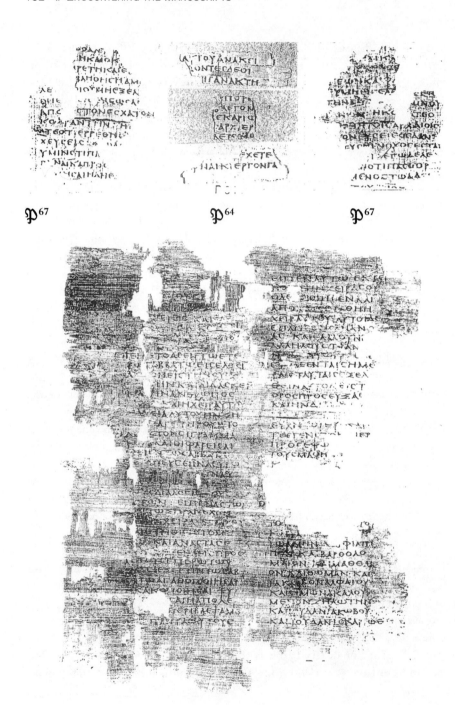

P. Oxyrhynchus 2404

P. Vindob. G. 29784

scribe, writing with a well-formed Roman Uncial. It contains almost all of Paul's major epistles (excluding the Pastorals).

Two editors worked separately on preparing editions of these manuscripts, inasmuch as part of the leaves are part of the University of Michigan collection and part of the leaves belong to the Chester Beatty collection. Sanders, working with the Michigan portions, published his *editio princeps*, while Kenyon published the entire manuscript in a complete *editio princeps*.

Sanders dated the manuscript to the third century, almost exclusively based on archaeological surmisings, and to the exclusion of any detailed paleography. Since the details of the finding are unknown, his method of dating is suspect and extremely hypothetical, as he himself admits.[87]

Kenyon's dating of $\mathfrak{P}^{46}$ to the third century is based on certain paleographic comparisons. In his first publication concerning the twelve biblical manuscripts in the Beatty collection, Kenyon made a significant comparison between $\mathfrak{P}^{46}$ (Beatty II) and the Numbers/Deuteronomy manuscript (Beatty VI): "Calligraphically the finest is also the earliest, the MS. of Numbers and Deuteronomy (no. VI). This is written in a small, square, upright hand, with light, flowing strokes and well-rounded curves. It is a definitely Roman type of hand, with affinities to the great Hyperides MS. and the Herodas MS., which are of the latter part of the first century. It is the work of a good professional scribe. Next to it come the Pauline Epistles (no. II), the Isaiah (no. VII), and the Jeremiah fragment (no. VIII)."[88]

Significantly, Kenyon placed Beatty VI in the late first century (and no later than the early second, see discussion above), with Beatty II ($\mathfrak{P}^{46}$) coming next in terms of calligraphy and paleography. But, curiously, he then placed $\mathfrak{P}^{46}$ in the third century. Why not in the second century, if it is next in line after Beatty VI? In his next publication, Kenyon continued to affirm that the letters in $\mathfrak{P}^{46}$ "are rather early in style and of good Roman formation."[89] Kenyon became a bit more definitive about his dating in that he placed $\mathfrak{P}^{46}$ in the first half of the third century. Kenyon's dating was largely influenced by the handwriting of the stichometrical notes at the end of several of the epistles, which he dated to the early part of the third century. At the same time, he noted that the papyrologist Wilcken "considers that it [$\mathfrak{P}^{46}$] may even belong to the second century, and that at any rate 'about 200 AD' would be a safe dating."[90] The date given by Ulrich Wilcken, generally recognized as one of the most eminent papyrologists (who was founder of *Archiv für Papyrusforschung*), was also influenced by his thinking that the stichometrical notes were more or less contemporary with the main hand.[91] (In due course, I will address the issue of the stichometrical notes.)

What is apparent is that Kenyon did not base his dating of $\mathfrak{P}^{46}$ on any paleographical comparisons with other manuscripts of the third century, or even the second century. This prompted Young-Kyu Kim to do such a comparison, the results of which he published in *Biblica* (1988). In a very a thorough article (which I have read and

$\mathfrak{P}^{32}$ P. London 130

reread countless times), he makes a case for dating $\mathfrak{P}^{46}$ to the reign of Domitian (AD 81–96)! He bases his dating on six criteria: (1) All literary papyri similar to $\mathfrak{P}^{46}$ in its exact style have been assigned dates between the first century BC and the early second century. (2) Comparable documentary papyri are dated early. (3) The hand-writing of $\mathfrak{P}^{46}$ is an upright informal uncial of the early type. It is a bookhand, mani-festing at times a running hand, giving way here and there to ligatures, while still trying to keep the upper line. Such a style is very rare after the first century. (4) The finials at the feet of the letters are seen in other manuscripts dated from the last quar-ter of the third century BC to the third quarter of the first century AD. (5) The hand of a certain corrector (no. 11, writing *kai*) appears in manuscripts from the second century BC to the early second century AD. (6) $\mathfrak{P}^{46}$ retains the early form *eg* instead of the later form *ek* before compounds with beta, delta, and lambda.[92]

Various notes in Kim's article indicate that he interacted with the papyrologists R. Coles, P. Parsons, and O. Montevecchi, none of whom (Kim told me in a letter) agree with his dating. However, Kim did indicate that O'Callaghan was sympathetic with his views.[93] Nonetheless, if Kim's dating is right, it greatly affects our understanding of the transmission of the New Testament text. For starters, we must consider that there was an intact Pauline corpus *before* the last two decades of the first century, which had reached the interior of Egypt prior to AD 80. And we would have to realize that professional scribes were producing such Pauline codices in the same era, because $\mathfrak{P}^{46}$ was the work of a professional. Furthermore, we would have to believe that a well-developed system of nomina sacra was in place prior to AD 80, for $\mathfrak{P}^{46}$ displays a plethora of nomina sacra. T. C. Skeat rejected Kim's dating, as did Metzger, who quotes Skeat's comments in a letter: "We would have to accept that it is, by a very wide margin, the oldest surviving Christian manuscript and the oldest surviving example of a papyrus codex. Moreover, $\mathfrak{P}^{46}$ uses an extensive and well-developed system of nomina sacra, which is difficult to believe can have existed, not merely in AD 80, but presumably in one of its ancestors. I find it therefore impossible to accept Kim's thesis."[94]

Theoretically, not one of these objections is insurmountable. A Pauline corpus of his major epistles (less the Pastorals) could have been intact by the end of the 70s or 80s (see discussion in chap. 1). This corpus could have been taken to Egypt in a few short weeks, travel was frequent and faster than is normally supposed (also see discussion in chap. 1). A system of nomina sacra could have been developed by AD 70; Skeat himself was one of the first to propose this.[95] However, it must be kept in mind that Skeat would consider that the fuller system in $\mathfrak{P}^{46}$ would have taken more years to develop. My impression of the nomina sacra in $\mathfrak{P}^{46}$ is that we see a fluid (and not yet fully developed) presentation of nomina sacra. The only fixed nomina sacra are for "Lord," "Jesus," "Christ," "God," and "cross/crucify." These are the most primitive forms. The other divine names are not written consistently as nomina sacra. Thus, "Father," "Son," and "Spirit" are sometimes written as nomen sacrum and sometimes written in full (*plene*). Other sacred words, treated by later scribes as nomina sacra, are not treated as such in $\mathfrak{P}^{46}$, namely, "Israel," "Jerusalem," and "heaven." Besides, $\mathfrak{P}^{46}$ has a less complete system of nomina sacra than does $\mathfrak{P}^{66}$, which has a parallel system to Cheater Beatty VI. And both $\mathfrak{P}^{66}$ and Chester Beatty VI are dated middle second century. Thus, the nomina sacra in $\mathfrak{P}^{46}$, being less developed, *could* indicate an even earlier date. This impression, it seems to me, is reinforced by the fact that $\mathfrak{P}^{46}$ is the only second-century manuscript to show the nomen sacrum, *pneuma*, in flux (usually written as a nomen sacrum, occasionally written in *plene*, even when denoting the divine Spirit).

Thus far, what is lacking in the rebuttals to Kim's dating of $\mathfrak{P}^{46}$ is a detailed analysis of the handwriting of the papyrus itself, which he compared to hundreds of other manuscripts. I would welcome review from expert paleographers. In the meanwhile, I offer my modest opinion.

In my estimation, most of the manuscripts from the first century that Kim sees as displaying a comparable hand to $\mathfrak{P}^{46}$ show some similarities in individual letters, but they do not do so in overall appearance and therefore do not belong to the same time period as $\mathfrak{P}^{46}$. Kim himself recognizes that several of these manuscripts display an early form of what we see later in $\mathfrak{P}^{46}$, especially with respect to the serifs at the bottom and top of letters. Very few, if any, of the documentary manuscripts (cited by Kim) evidencing a semiliterary hand dated in the same era where Kim placed $\mathfrak{P}^{46}$ (namely AD 81–96) are unquestionably comparable to the style found in $\mathfrak{P}^{46}$. The photographs and/or actual manuscripts I have examined show that the following manuscripts have an earlier form of what is later evident in $\mathfrak{P}^{46}$. These include P. Oxyrhynchus 2987 (AD 78–79); P. Oxyrhynchus 3051 (AD 89); P. Oxyrhynchus 3051 (AD 89); P. Rylands II 107 (AD 90); P. Oxyrhynchus 270 (AD 94); P. Fayum 110 (AD 94; for photo, see GLH 11b).

Among other manuscripts assigned by editors to the same era, which Kim used for comparison to $\mathfrak{P}^{46}$, are P. Oxyrhynchus 3695 (late first century); P. Gr. Berol. 6845 (last decade of first century; for photo, see Schubart's *Greek Berol.* 19c); P. Berol. 6926+P. Gen. 100 (second half of first century; for photo, see GLH 11a and Seider II 27); P. Oxyrhynchus 8 (late first/early second); P. Oxyrhynchus 2337 (later first century); P. Oxyrhynchus 211 (from the reigns of Vespasian, Domitian, Trajan, i.e., 69–117).[96] My examination of these manuscripts gave me the impression that I was looking at an earlier form of what we later see in $\mathfrak{P}^{46}$. The only exception is P. Oxyrhynchus 2337, which has many similarities with $\mathfrak{P}^{46}$. The editor of P. Oxyrhynchus 2337 said it "is a small rounded hand with occasional serifs of the same type as the elegant hand of Schubart Tafeln 19c [= P. Gr. Berol. 6845; see above]." Of all the first-century manuscripts noted by Kim, this one bears the closest resemblance to $\mathfrak{P}^{46}$, in my estimation. I would also add that another manuscript (not noted by Kim), namely P. Murabba'at 108, dated to first century AD, also has clear paleographic affinities with $\mathfrak{P}^{46}$, though the Murabba'at philosophical piece seems earlier.

My overall impression is that $\mathfrak{P}^{46}$ belongs among second-century manuscripts. As far as I can tell, it bears significant resemblance to these second-century manuscripts:

1. P. Oxyrhynchus 841 (second hand; cannot be dated later than AD 125–150; for photo, see GLH 14). This manuscript can be dated with a high degree of accuracy. The rolls on which Pindar's Paeans were written were first used for two different documents; the first contained a list of persons. According to Grenfell and Hunt, it was "written after the reign of Titus, probably in that of Domitian [81–96]" (see their comments on P. Oxyrhynchus 984).

C. H. Roberts said, "We are thus given an approximate terminus post; an approximate terminus ante is provided by the cursive scholai which are not later than the second century. The documents are themselves of Oxyrhynchite provenance; we need not assume that they were quickly re-used. The Pindar was probably written towards the middle of the century and earlier rather than later" (GLH, 14). This means that Pindar's Paeans were penned before AD 150 and probably earlier. Thus, a date of 125–150 is very reasonable. The Paeans were written by two scribes, the second of which resembles P. Oxyrhynchus 1622 (see discussion below) and $\mathfrak{P}^{46}$.

2. P. Oxyrhynchus 1622 (AD 117–138). This manuscript contains parts of Thucydides on the recto. Its importance is paleographical because, as the editor indicates, "On the verso is a contract for a loan dated in Mechier of the 11th year of Antonius Pius (AD 148), so that the recto must have been written before 148, probably in the reign of Hadrian [117–138], and is an unusually well dated specimen of second-century uncial writing."

3. P. Oxyrhynchus 3721 (which is dated to the second half of the second century, but Kim would date it earlier). The editor of P. Oxyrhynchus 3721 said it is "written in a formal round and upright hand with some decoration, comparable e.g. with XLIV 3156 only rather more normal: XXVI 2450 is an earlier example of the same style. The manuscript may be assigned to the second half of the second century." I examined P. Oxyrhynchus 3721 at the Ashmolean Museum and immediately recognized its likeness to $\mathfrak{P}^{46}$; it is one of the closest matches I have seen. (By the way, I also agree with the editor's assessments about the relationship between P. Oxyrhynchus 3721 and P. Oxyrhynchus 2450; 3156.)

4. P. Greek Berolinses 9810 [for photo, see Schubart's *Greek Berol.* 29b] (first half of second century). This manuscript is a very good comparison to $\mathfrak{P}^{46}$.

5. P. Rylands III 550 (early second century). The editor of this manuscript, C. H. Roberts, dated it to the early second century, saying it is "a good book-hand of the second century, and early rather than late in the century." This manuscript is an excellent match to $\mathfrak{P}^{46}$, thereby placing $\mathfrak{P}^{46}$ in the earlier part of the second century.

6. Commentary on the Theatetus of Plato (second century). This is a second-century manuscript noted by Thompson in *Introduction to Greek and Latin Paleography* (facsimile 13).

In the final analysis, I think $\mathfrak{P}^{46}$ belongs to the second century, and probably belongs to the middle of that century (at the latest, ca. 175), especially when we consider that it displays morphological likeness with P. Oxyrhynchus 841, second hand (ca. 125–150); P. Oxyrhynchus 2337 (late first century); and more so P. Oxyrhynchus 3721 (which is dated to the second half of the second century); P. Greek Berol. 9810 [plate 29b, Schubart] (first half of second century); and P. Rylands III 550 (early second century). By the way, this also suggests that $\mathfrak{P}^{46}$ and $\mathfrak{P}^{66}$ must be in the same era because $\mathfrak{P}^{46}$ shows great similarities with P. Oxyrhynchus 841 (second scribe) and $\mathfrak{P}^{66}$ shows notable similarities with P. Oxyrhynchus 841 (first scribe), who were contemporaries. In the final analysis, I would not date $\mathfrak{P}^{46}$ (which is Chester Beatty II) earlier than Chester Beatty VI, Numbers-Deuteronomy (see discussion above), but it is not much later. This dating allows for the formation of the Pauline corpus to have occurred and for an archetypal collection to have been produced, as well as circulate in Egypt.

Before we conclude the issue of dating $\mathfrak{P}^{46}$, we should return to the issue of the stichometric notes (i.e., notes indicating numbers of stichoi), which were key for Kenyon's dating. What should be noted is that the same hand who produced the stichometrical notes also produced the pagination and made some substantial corrections. These three features give the paleographer a good sampling of his hand. In his studies of $\mathfrak{P}^{46}$, Zuntz carefully distinguished the different hands in the manuscript (the original and two correctors). He noticed that the same hand who added the page numbers also wrote the number of stichoi under most of the epistles. He identified this hand as an official at the scriptorium who added these features and who made some corrections.[97] It stands to reason, then, that this official worked at the same time as the primary scribe; therefore, the dating of the main text must coincide with the dating of the hand who made the stichometrical notes, pagination, and some corrections. Zuntz points to several corrections in this hand throughout the book of Hebrews. Four of the corrections noted by Zuntz are quite easy to spot because they were made superlinearly: Hebrews 5:6 (*iereus*); 11:21 (*Iōsēph*); 12:25 (*pantōn*). I would add another one—an interlinear insertion at Hebrews 13:24 (*kai pantas tous agious*). The hand that produced these corrections undeniably wrote in Biblical Uncial style. This is easier to see in the corrections than in the paginations and stichoi markings. Thus, the second hand seen in $\mathfrak{P}^{46}$—that which produced the pagination, stichoi, and several corrections—is one who wrote in this Biblical Uncial style.

Young-Kyu Kim affirms that the "stichometrical notes and pagination are no doubt additions from a so-called "Biblical Majuscule hand." But he affirms the earliness of this hand with this remark: "Concerning its early type, cf. P. Herculaneum 1457 (D. Bassi, *Papiri Ercolanesi*; Tomo 1 [Milan 1914], 7 plates)." Thus, Kim maintains an early date for $\mathfrak{P}^{46}$ based on his view that the so-called Biblical Majuscule hand can be dated to pre-AD 79, as displayed in a Herculaneum manuscript. However, most paleographers do not think the Biblical Majuscule (Biblical Uncial) hand emerged until the middle of the second century (as discussed in detail above). Thus, I would argue that a date of the middle second century (up to ca. 175) covers both the hand of the main text and that of the first corrector. (See discussion on $\mathfrak{P}^{66}$, where the same issue concerning a corrector is involved.) (See photos of $\mathfrak{P}^{46}$ next to P. Rylands 550 and P. Oxy. 3721 on pp. 140–41.)

$\mathfrak{P}^{52}$ (P. Rylands 457), first quarter of the second century (100–125).— This manuscript preserves only a few verses of John's Gospel (18:31–33, 37–38). This hand, casual and rounded, clearly belongs to the early part of the second century. C. H. Roberts dated this manuscript to the first half of the second century. He noted that paleographers such as Kenyon, H. I. Bell, Deissmann, and W. H. P. Hatch

ϲαγ

ΔΙΑΚΟΝΙΑϲΤΗϹΕΙϹΤΟΥϹΑΓΙΟΥϹΚΑΙ
ΟΥΚΑΘΩϹΗΛΠΙϹΑΜΕΝΑΛΛΑΕΑΥΤΟΥϹ
ΕΔΩΚΑΝΕΝΠΡΩΤΟΝΤΩΚΩ ΚΑΙΗΜΕΙ
ΔΙΑΘΕΛΗΜΑΤΟϹ ΘΥ ΕΙϹΤΟΠΑΡΑΚΑΛΕ
ϹΑΙΗΜΑϹΤΙΤΟΝΙΝΑΚΑΘΩϹΠΡΟΕΝΗΡ
ΞΑΤΟΟΥΤΩϹΚΑΙΕΠΙΤΕΛΕϹΗΕΙϹΥΜΑϹ
ΚΑΙΤΗΝΧΑΡΙΝΤΑΥΤΗΝΑΛΛΩϹΠΕΡ
ΠΕΡΙϹϹΕΥΕΤΕΕΝΠΑΝΤΙΠΙϹΤΕΙΚΑΙΛΟΓΩ
ΚΑΙΓΝΩϹΕΙΚΑΙΠΑϹΗϹΠΟΥΔΗΚΑΙΤΗ
ΕΞΗΜΩΝΕΝΥΜΕΙΝΑΓΑΠΗΙΝΑΚΑΙ
ΕΝΤΑΥΤΗΤΗΧΑΡΙΤΙΠΕΡΙϹϹΕΥΗΤΕ
ΟΥΚΑΤΕΠΙΤΑΓΗΝΛΕΓΩΑΛΛΑΔΙΑΤΗϹ
ΕΤΕΡΩΝϹΠΟΥΔΗϹΚΑΙΤΟΤΗϹΗΜΕ
ΤΕΡΑϹΑΓΑΠΗϹΓΝΗϹΙΟΝΔΟΚΙΜΑΖΩΝ
ΓΕΙΝΩϹΚΕΤΕΓΑΡΤΗΝΧΑΡΙΝΤΟΥΚΥ
ΗΜΩΝΙΗΥΧΡΥΟΤΙΔΙΥΜΑϹΕΠΤΩ
ΧΕΥϹΕΝΠΛΟΥϹΙΟϹΩΝΙΝΑΥΜΕΙϹ
ΤΗΕΚΕΙΝΟΥΠΤΩΧΕΙΑΠΛΟΥΤΗϹΗΤΕ
ΚΑΙΓΝΩΜΗΝΕΝΤΟΥΤΩΔΙΔΩΜΙΤΟΥ
ΤΟΓΑΡΥΜΕΙΝϹΥΜΦΕΡΕΙΟΙΤΙΝΕϹϹΥΜΟ
ϹΤΟΤΕΠΟΙΗϹΑΙΑΛΛΑΚΑΙΤΟΘΕΛΕΙΝΠΡΟ
... ΕΘϹΑΠΟΠΕΡΥϹΙΝΥΝΙΔΕ
... ΡΟϹΕΠΙΤΕΛΕϹΑΤΕΟΠΩϹΚΑ
... ΓΥΜΙϹΤΟΥ ... ΕΛΕΙΝΟΥΤΩϹ
... ΔΕΕΚΤΟΥΕΧΕΙΝΕΙΓΑΡ

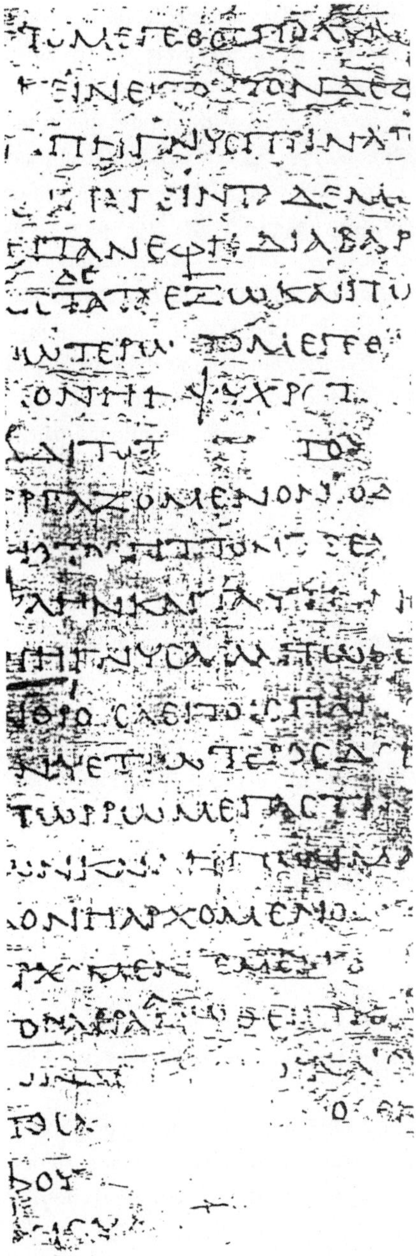

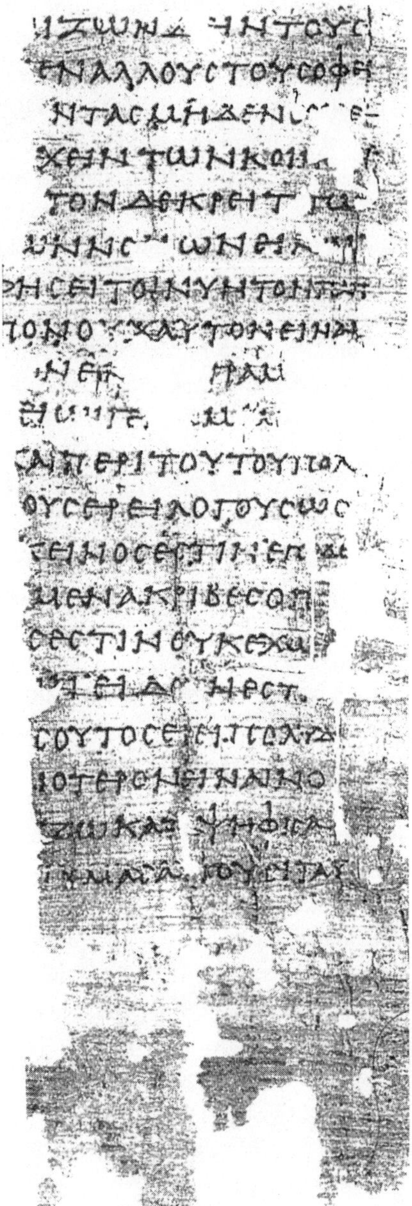

P. Oxyrhynchus 3721 **Rylands 550**

confirmed this dating.[98] Deissmann was convinced that $\mathfrak{P}^{52}$ was written at least during the reign of Hadrian (117–138) and perhaps even during the reign of Trajan
(98–117).[99] The eminent papyrologist Ulrich Wilcken indicated that, as far as
the paleography was concerned, $\mathfrak{P}^{52}$ could be contemporary with manuscripts in the
Apollonios Archives, dated AD 117–120 (the Bremer Papyri). This is quite a significant
observation inasmuch as Wilcken had just completed a publication of the Bremer
Papyri (which includes the Apollonios Archives) when he made this observation about
$\mathfrak{P}^{52}$. Therefore, he was drawing upon his keen observation of several manuscripts
dated between AD 117 and 120.[100] Though I have seen only a few manuscripts of this
archive, I can see the affinity, for example, between $\mathfrak{P}^{52}$ and Bremer Papyri 5, reproduced in Wilcken's work (note especially the similar formation of the alpha, delta, and
epsilon). My comparative study is limited; Wilcken had far more manuscripts in making his estimation. Kurt Aland has followed the lead of the aforementioned paleographers and dated $\mathfrak{P}^{52}$ "near the beginning of the second century."[101] As such, in
Aland's estimation, it is the earliest New Testament papyrus manuscript. (Of course,
manuscripts such as $\mathfrak{P}^{104}$, discussed later, were not available to Aland.)

    C. H. Roberts's dating of $\mathfrak{P}^{52}$ was derived from a comparative analysis of $\mathfrak{P}^{52}$ to
documentary manuscripts such as P. Fayum 110 (AD 94; for photo, see GLH 11b;
Montev., pl. 44), P. London 2078 (a private letter written during the reign of Domitian;
AD 81–96),[102] P. Oslo 22 (a petition dated in AD 127—note particularly the similar
formation of the eta, mu, and iota), P. Berol. 6845 (late first century; for photo, see
Greek Berol. 19c), P. Berol. 6854 (a document written before the death of Trajan in
AD 117; for photo, see Schubart's *Greek Paleography*, pl. 34), and P. Egerton 2, the
Egerton Gospel (dated ca. 150).

    I have looked at photographs of all these manuscripts and would concur with
Roberts's estimations of comparability to $\mathfrak{P}^{52}$. I would especially note P. Oslo 22. Yet
there is another manuscript that appears to be the very likeness of $\mathfrak{P}^{52}$; it is
P. Oxyrhynchus 2533. I examined the manuscript P. Oxyrhynchus 2533 at the
Ashmolean Museum and was immediately impressed by its likenesss to $\mathfrak{P}^{52}$. The edi-
tors of P. Oxyrhynchus 2533 said the handwriting could be parallel with first-century
documents, but has the appearance of being second century (to which they dated it).
I quote their comments in full:

> The text of the recto of this papyrus is a document, written in a practiced
> upright business hand, neat but employing cursive forms of varying sizes, all of
> which could be paralleled in first-century documents; the general impression,
> however, suggests the second century. On the verso is written a passage of New
> Comedy in a semi-literate hand, upright, rounded and clear; the letters are
> somewhat variable in size, and several (notably epsilon and kappa) show cursive
> forms; ligature is common. The appearance of the recto and verso texts is

superficially dissimilar, but examination of the letters shows so many identical forms that it seems likely that the writer is the same.

This indicates that the New Comedy should be dated to the early second century, for the literary piece would not have been written long after the documentary work. The strong similarity between this manuscript and $\mathfrak{P}^{52}$ helps to establish the date of $\mathfrak{P}^{52}$ as being very early in the second century.

I would also point to P. Murabba'at 113, a document dated to pre-AD 132. Its overall likeness to $\mathfrak{P}^{52}$ is immediately apparent; one can also note the epsilon-iota combination, the alpha, and delta in both manuscripts. Both manuscripts share affinities with P. London 130 (dated early second century; for photo, see Schubart's *Greek Pal..* 81) and P. Berol. 6854 (dated AD 135?; for photo, see *Greek Berol.* 22b).

The dating of $\mathfrak{P}^{52}$ to the first quarter of the second century is remarkable, especially if we accept the consensus dating for the composition of the Fourth Gospel: 80–85. This means that $\mathfrak{P}^{52}$ is probably only twenty years away from the original.

A. Schmidt has challenged the earlier dating of $\mathfrak{P}^{52}$. He has placed it near the end of the second century, close to ca. 200.[103] This redating has appealed to some scholars, but most hold with the earlier dating and still affirm that $\mathfrak{P}^{52}$ is probably the earliest New Testament manuscript. (See photos of $\mathfrak{P}^{52}$ next to P. Oxy. 2533, P. Egerton 2, and P. Fayum 110 on pp. 144–45.)

$\mathfrak{P}^{66}$ **(Papyrus Bodmer II), middle of the second century.**—This manuscript, containing most of the Gospel of John, displays a "medium-sized, rounded, 'decorated' capital, slowly written."[104] In short, $\mathfrak{P}^{66}$ displays a Decorated Rounded hand. The editor of the *editio princeps*, Victor Martin, similarly saw the hand as very stylistic and deserving of the "literary" epithet. Martin dated $\mathfrak{P}^{66}$ to ca. 200, saying it is very much like P. Oxyrhynchus 1074 (Exodus),[105] concerning which the editors said that it might well be placed at the beginning of the third century or even earlier. I have examined a good photograph of Oxyrhynchus 1074 and would agree that the hand resembles $\mathfrak{P}^{66}$, although P. Oxyrhynchus 1074 is more informal. I would place P. Oxyrhynchus 1074 in the second century (as comparable to Bodleian Gr. Bib. g. 5, Psalms), as does Schubart (see comments above). By comparison with P. Oxyrhynchus 1074, $\mathfrak{P}^{66}$ also belongs in the second century.

Herbert Hunger, founder of the Vienna Institute of Papyrology, redated $\mathfrak{P}^{66}$ to the first half of the second century.[106] Hunger contends that $\mathfrak{P}^{66}$ must be dated in the same period as $\mathfrak{P}^{52}$ (ca. 125) and P. Egerton 2 (ca. 150). If so, this means that $\mathfrak{P}^{66}$ should not be dated later than 150, and could be as early as 125. Hunger made this readjustment on the basis that $\mathfrak{P}^{66}$ has many similarities with other hands of the late first and early second century usually classified as "informal round bookhands," that is, the lettering is designed to look informal. $\mathfrak{P}^{66}$ could also be called an Informal Round, especially in exhibiting ligatures (connecting letters). Another appeal that Hunger makes for the early second-century dating of $\mathfrak{P}^{66}$ is that it shares the same system of nomina

P. Oxyrhynchus 2533

𝔓⁵²

P. Egerton 2

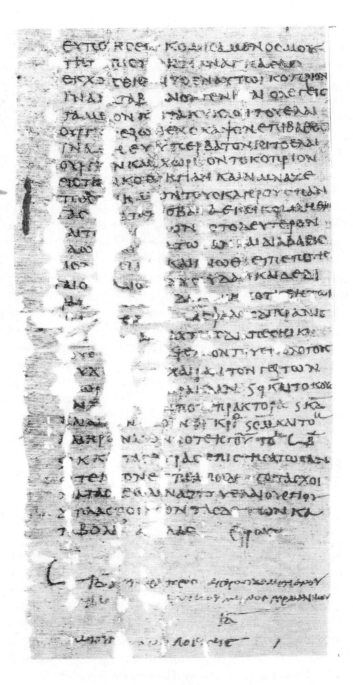

P. Fayum 110

sacra as does Chester Beatty VI (dated early to middle second century—see discussion above).

In his article, Hunger cites many manuscripts in making this assessment; these manuscripts range in date from AD 80 to AD 150. Among those that predate 100 AD, I did not see any comparable hands. Many show an earlier form of a style later exhibited in $\mathfrak{P}^{66}$. This was my observation concerning manuscripts such as P. Oxyrhynchus 286 (= P London 797, AD 82); P. Oxyrhynchus 270 (AD 94); London II 141 (AD 88), which Roberts described as "a large, rounded bookhand which is fully developed in the second century" (GLH 12a; and see photo).

However, the picture changes when we move into the second century. Several of the manuscripts noted by Hunger bear morphological resemblance to $\mathfrak{P}^{66}$. This can be seen in the following manuscripts noted by Hunger (see his article for details of morphological comparison):

1. P. Oxyrhynchus 1434 (a document dated AD 107/108)

2. P. Oxyrhynchus 2436 (a Monody with musical notations dated end of first century/early second century)

3. P. Oxyrhynchus 220 (end of first, more likely beginning of second century AD)

The editors, Grenfell and Hunt, wrote: "The hand on the recto is a round well-formed upright uncial of good size, which may be assigned to the end of the first or (more probably) the early part of the second century. Some additions and corrections in the MS. have been made in a different second century hand."

4. P. Oxyrhynchus 841, first hand (ca. 125–150; photo and comments in GLH 14)

5. P. Oxyrhynchus 2161+2162+PSI 1208–1210 (second century, all the work of the same scribe)

6. P. Berol. 9782 (second century; for photo, see Schubart's *Greek Berol.*, 31)

7. P. Lit. London 132 (dated with confidence to the first half of the second century; photo and comments in GLH 13b; and see comments above)

These last two manuscripts bear the closest resemblance to $\mathfrak{P}^{66}$, both in overall appearance and individual formation of letters. To the above mentioned manuscripts noted by Hunger, I would add the following:

1. P. Oxyrhynchus 1241 (a list of famous men; first half of second century; for photo, see Italo Gallo, pl. 8)

2. P. Oxyrhynchus 2891 (early second century). Concerning this manuscript, the editor wrote: "The writing is a fair-sized book-hand of a common type, comparable with [P. Oxy.] 220, and I suppose, to be placed early in the second century."

3. Bodleian Gr. Bib. g. 5, Psalms (middle second century—see comments above)

4. P. Oxyrhynchus 656, Genesis (second century—see comments above)

5. P. Antinoopolis 7 (middle second century—see comments above). I should also note that the handwriting of the second corrector of $\mathfrak{P}^{66}$ is remarkably similar to that found in $\mathfrak{P}^{4+64+67}$. Namely, it appears to be an early form of Biblical Uncial and very

likely belongs to the middle part of the second century.[107] Furthermore, it must be noted that the original codex may have been untitled and that a later hand added the title "Gospel according to John" (this was Turner's view; see GMAW, p. 16). An untitled Gospel codex suggests an early date for the manuscript.

In conclusion, comparative paleography strongly suggests a second-century date for $\mathfrak{P}^{66}$, and probably in the middle of that century. Quite significantly, two renowned papyrologists also place $\mathfrak{P}^{66}$ in the middle of the second century. Seider dates $\mathfrak{P}^{66}$ to the middle of the second century.[108] And Cavallo also dates $\mathfrak{P}^{66}$ to the middle of the second century.[109]

Turner does not agree with this dating. He places $\mathfrak{P}^{66}$ in the earlier third century. First of all, he allows for this dating because he sees the Decorated Rounded style as extending to the third century. However, other paleographers think the style hardly extends beyond AD 150, there being only a few exceptions that go into the third (see discussion above). Turner dates $\mathfrak{P}^{66}$ to the third century (200–250) on the basis that the broad delta, broad theta, narrow alpha (stroked in one sequence), finial end on the crossbar of epsilon, and apostrophe between double consonants are characteristics of third-century manuscripts.[110] With all due respect to Turner, I disagree. The delta is unusually wide in $\mathfrak{P}^{66}$, but there are examples of this in second-century manuscripts (see P. London 110 and P. Berol. 9782), and even in the first (P. Berol. 6926b). The body of the theta is not that broad—only the cross-through line makes it wide; even so, there are examples of this in the second century (see P. Oxyrhynchus 2161, 2213, and even P. Oxyrhynchus 216, dated late first century). The crossbar on the epsilon only rarely displays a finial—and this seems to be the result of a stop, creating a slight blob. This is very common in both the second and third centuries—as is the formation of the alpha in $\mathfrak{P}^{66}$. Furthermore, some manuscripts of the second century display the apostrophe or hook between double consonants (see previous discussion). This is also evident in one word in $\mathfrak{P}^{46}$ (*krit'tonos*) used in Hebrews, which is dated in the second century. It is also evident in the newly published portion of the Egerton Gospel (see discussion above). Thus, as I argued above, the feature of the hook between double consonants must be dated earlier inasmuch as second-century manuscripts exhibit this feature.

What must be kept in mind with Turner's dating is that he was reacting to the revised datings in the 1950s and 1960s, wherein many of the codices were given earlier dates than had been ascribed to them because paleographers began to realize that the codex began to be used by Christians in the late first century. Turner thought the revision went too far in the direction of earlier dating and therefore has posited a later date for nearly all of the New Testament manuscripts.[111] (See pp. 148–49 for photos of $\mathfrak{P}^{66}$ next to P. Oxy. 1074; P. Berol. 9782; and P. Lit. London 132.)

$\mathfrak{P}^{66}$

P. Oxyrhynchus 1074

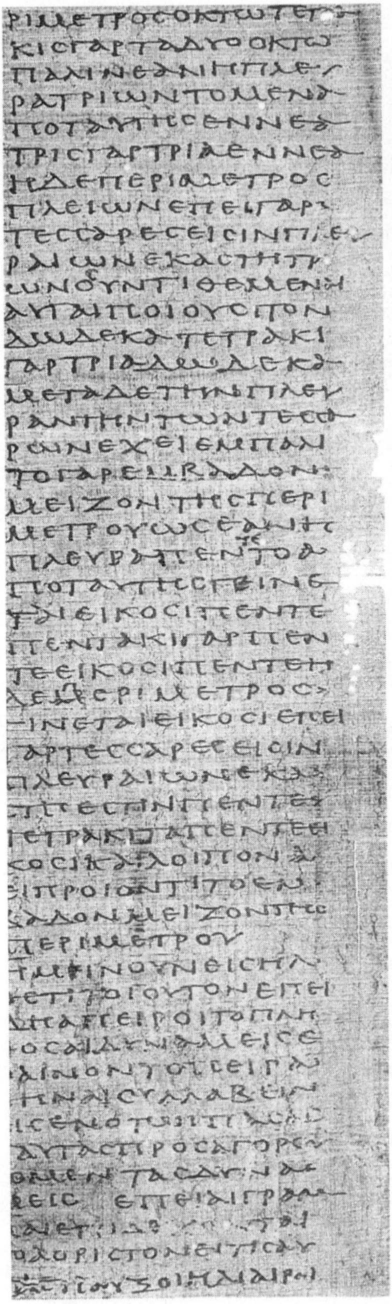

P. Berol. 9782

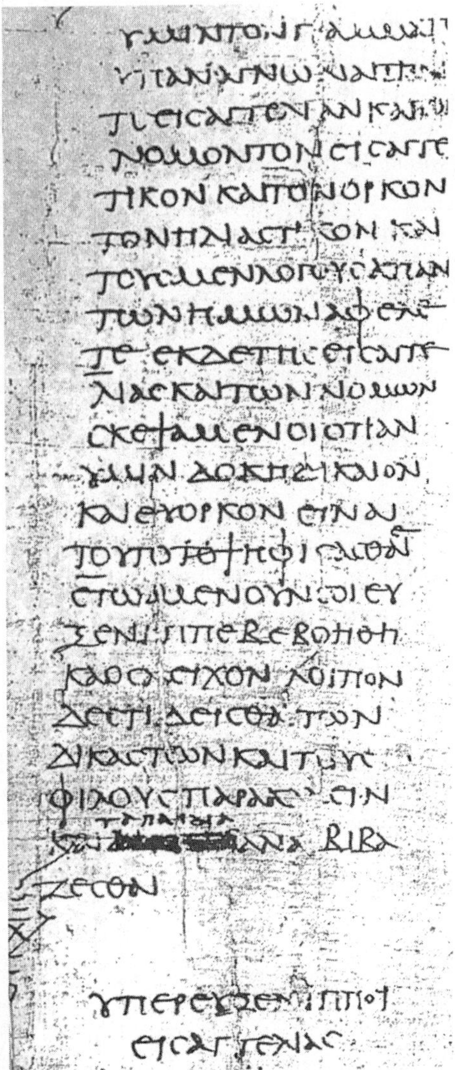

P. Lit. London 132

𝔓⁷⁵ **(Papyrus Bodmer XIV-XV), late second century.**—𝔓⁷⁵, containing most of Luke 3–24 and John 1–15, is one of the premier New Testament papyrus manuscripts. Kasser and Martin, the editors of the *editio princeps*, were correct in saying that the hand of 𝔓⁷⁵ is "a lovely vertical uncial, elegant and careful," which they dated within the period 175–225. They assigned this dating based on the comparability of 𝔓⁷⁵ with manuscripts such as P. Oxyrhynchus 2293, 2322, 2362, 2363, 2370. They said that these manuscripts, as with 𝔓⁷⁵, all display the defined angular hand of the early third century.[112] However, it should be noted that the Oxyrhynchus editors said the date should be late second or *possibly* early third for three of these manuscripts: P. Oxyrhynchus 2293, 2363, 2370.[113] Of these three, P. Oxyrhynchus 2293 (second century) is the most similar, even though 𝔓⁷⁵ is even more finely executed.

All the Oxyrhynchus papyri noted above have "assigned" dates based on comparative paleography, not documetary evidence. Thus, we need to seek a more solid date for 𝔓⁷⁵ based on comparable manuscripts with dates derived from documentary evidence. In this light, it is significant that the editors of 𝔓⁷⁵ also noted that the handwriting of 𝔓⁷⁵ is like that found in P. Fuad Univ. XIX papyrus, a documentary text about the sale of land dated specifically to AD 145–146 (for photo, see GLH 15b).

There is another group of Oxyrhynchus papyri, all belonging to the second half of the second century, that are morphologically comparable to 𝔓⁷⁵. These are P. Oxyrhynchus 1174, 1175, 2077, 2180, PSI 1302, and P. Oxyrhynchus 2452 (for photo see page 155). P. Oxyrhynchus 1174 and 1175 are parts of the same manuscript. The editor of this manuscript commented: "It may, I think, be assigned with probability to the closing decades of the second century, a date suggested as well by the character of the uncial script as by the occasional cursive marginalia."

P. Oxyrhynchus 2452 (also designated as British Museum Pap. 3036) is very similar to 𝔓⁷⁵. Concerning this manuscript the editor said, "The hand is a bold, slightly sloping, yet also squarish capital of fair size." The resemblance with 𝔓⁷⁵ is unmistakable. Note especially the formation of the angular alpha, epsilon, small omicron, rho, tau, upsilon (all with left curved descenders), and squat omega (see comments by Turner in GMAW, 27, concerning P. Oxy. 2452).

The papyrologist R. Seider dated 𝔓⁷⁵ as "2nd/3rd,"[114] which could be interpreted to mean that 𝔓⁷⁵ could be a second- or third-century manuscript, or "175–225" per the *editio princeps*. Since the majority of comparable manuscripts come from the second century, I would be inclined to date 𝔓⁷⁵ to the late second century, between 175 and 200. (See photos displaying 𝔓⁷⁵ next to P. Oxy. 2452 on pages 152–53.)

𝔓⁷⁷ **(P. Oxyrhynchus 2683 + P. Oxyrhynchus 4405) + 𝔓¹⁰³ (P. Oxyrhynchus 4403), late second century.**—This manuscript, displaying the well-crafted calligraphy of a professional scribe, contains portions of Matthew (𝔓⁷⁷ = 23:30–39; 𝔓¹⁰³ = 13:55–57; 14:3–5). When the first portion of 𝔓⁷⁷ (P. Oxyrhynchus

2683) was published, the editor (Parsons) dated it to the later second century. He said, "The writing, delicately executed with a fine pen, belongs to the same style as [P. Oxyrhynchus] 1082: epsilon, theta, omicron, sigma are generally tall, narrow and angular; hypsilon appears four times as a shaft topped with a sweeping shallow curve (as in P. Ant[inoopolis] 26, an extreme example of the manner). Hands of this type are normally assigned to the later second century AD: see [P. Oxyrhynchus] 2663 introduction. [P. Oxyrhynchus] 2683 therefore belongs among the oldest New Testament texts."

When the second portion of this manuscript (P. Oxyrhynchus 4405, having more text of Matt. 23:30–39) was published, the editor (Thomas) dated the manuscript to the late second century, but said it could also be early third.[115] I disagree, as does Parsons (see previous comments) and Roberts and Skeat, who place $\mathfrak{P}^{77}$ in the second century.[116] As noted by Parsons, the handwriting shows similarities with P. Oxyrhynchus 1082 and P. Oxyrhynchus 2663, both of the second century. It also shows some likeness to P. Oxyrhynchus 1622, a manuscript that must be dated pre-AD 148 (per the documentary text on the other side of Thucydides).

I think there is a third portion to this same manuscript, which is P. Oxyrhynchus 4403 (which has been assigned the number $\mathfrak{P}^{103}$), preserving Matthew 13:55–56; 14:3–5. If it does not belong to the same codex, at least it can be said that it was produced by the same scribe. The formation of the letters is remarkably similar (see especially the kappa, phi, and upsilon, which takes several shapes, one of which is a long shaft with a shallow bowl on top, just as in $\mathfrak{P}^{77}$). The only noticeable difference is in the formation of ksi. The average number of letters per line (25–27) is identical, as is the calculation that there would have originally been twenty lines per page. Other identical features are punctuation (a midpoint between phrases and verses) and breathing marks (diaresis). The only difference in physical appearance is that P. Oxyrhynchus 4403 is not as bilinear as $\mathfrak{P}^{77}$, but this difference is very slight. Thomas, noting all these similarities, suggests that P. Oxyrhynchus 4403 belongs to the same codex as $\mathfrak{P}^{77}$ (P. Oxyrhynchus 2683) + P. Oxyrhynchus 4405, but cannot be certain.[117] My opinion is that it is far more likely than not that all three belong to the same codex.[118] In any event, $\mathfrak{P}^{103}$ shares the same date as $\mathfrak{P}^{77}$, namely, late second century. (See the photo display of $\mathfrak{P}^{77}$ next to P. Oxy. 1082, 1622, and 2663 on pages 154–55.)

$\mathfrak{P}^{87}$ (P. Koln 4), early to middle second century.—This small manuscript, containing a portion of Philemon, exhibits a good Roman Uncial hand. The editors (Kramer, Romer, Hagedorn) of the *editio princeps* dated $\mathfrak{P}^{87}$ "early third century" because the handwriting is nearly identical to that found in $\mathfrak{P}^{46}$ and because $\mathfrak{P}^{46}$ has traditionally been dated to the beginning of the third century.[119] But if the dating of $\mathfrak{P}^{46}$ should be changed, so must the dating of $\mathfrak{P}^{87}$. In fact, $\mathfrak{P}^{87}$ appears to be even earlier than $\mathfrak{P}^{46}$ in that $\mathfrak{P}^{87}$ is more comparable to P. Oxyrhynchus 841, second hand

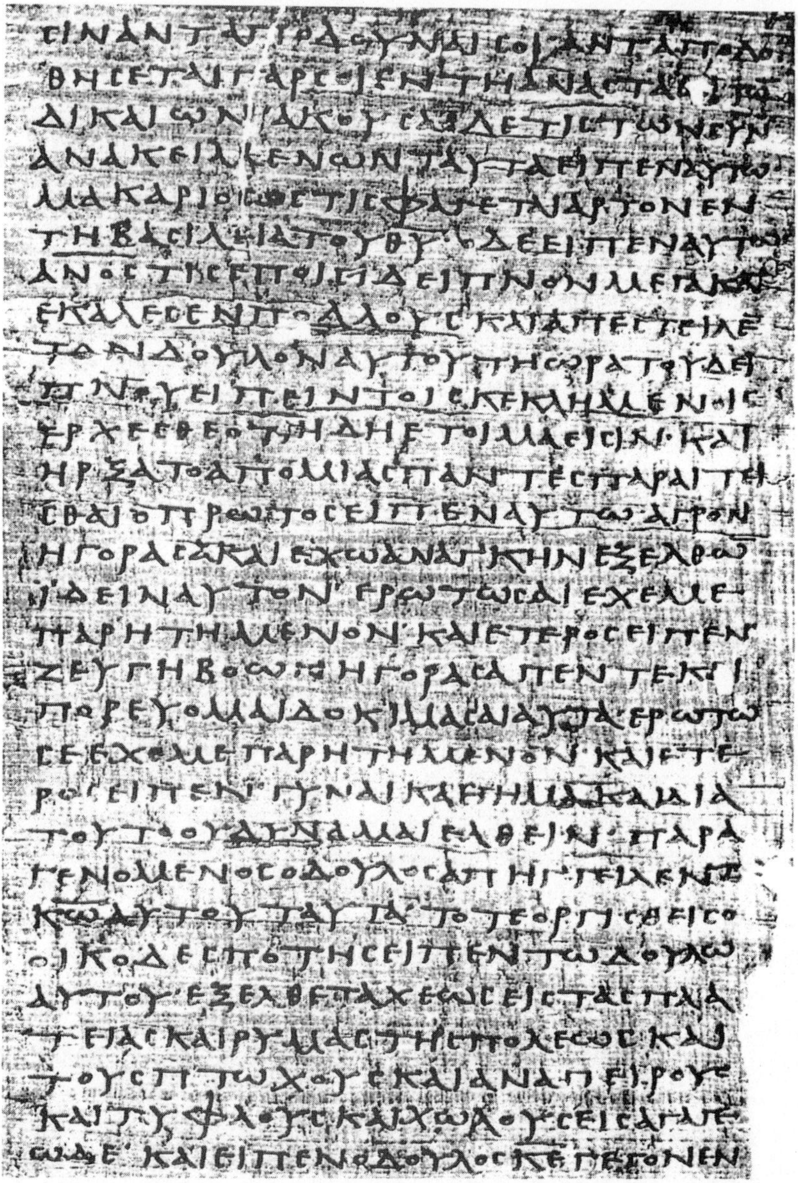

𝔓75

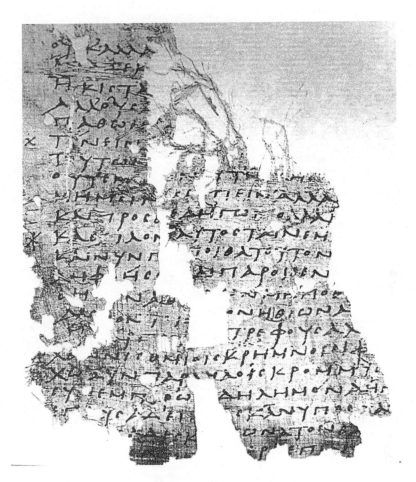

P. Oxyrhynchus 2452

(dated AD 120–30; see discussion on page 138), than is $\mathfrak{P}^{46}$. (See photos on pages 156–57 for $\mathfrak{P}^{87}$ next to P. Oxy. 841.)

$\mathfrak{P}^{90}$ **(P. Oxyrhynchus 3523), second half of second century.**—This manuscript, containing a portion of John (18:36–19:7), displays a Decorated Rounded hand. The editor of the *editio princeps*, T. C. Skeat, dated this manuscript to the late second century. He noted the similarities between $\mathfrak{P}^{90}$ and the P. Egerton 2, the Egerton Gospel (dated ca. 150), as well as between $\mathfrak{P}^{90}$ and P. Oxyrhynchus 656 (later second century).[120] While visiting the Ashmolean Museum, I observed that $\mathfrak{P}^{90}$ is indeed very similar to P. Oxyrhynchus 656.

$\mathfrak{P}^{77}$

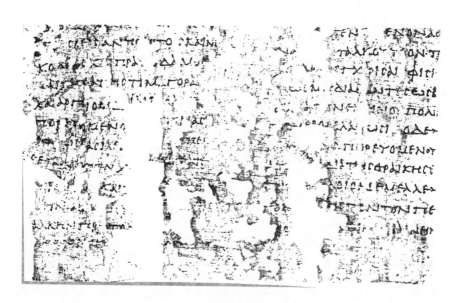

P. Oxyrhynchus 1622

P. Oxyrhynchus 2663

P. Oxyrhynchus 1082

$\mathfrak{P}^{87}$ **Recto** $\mathfrak{P}^{87}$ **Verso**

Another manuscript bearing morphological resemblance to $\mathfrak{P}^{90}$ is P. Oxyrhynchus 4022 (Menander), dated to the second century. Concerning P. Oxyrhynchus 4022, the editor remarked "the graceless and informal script, ornamented with occasional serifs, could be compared with the hands of P Oxy 841 (GLH 14)." Another manuscript is P. Yale 1273 (Hesiod's *Catalogue of Women*, ca. AD 100; for photo see *Literary Papyri*, vol. 2, pl. 17), whose lettering and overall appearance resembles $\mathfrak{P}^{90}$, though earlier. Another manuscript bearing resemblance, in my opinion, is P. Geneva 253, dated second century (see discussion above). In the end, I would think that $\mathfrak{P}^{90}$ belongs to the second century and could have been written in the middle of that century or later. (See the photo display on pages 158–59 placing $\mathfrak{P}^{90}$ and P. Oxy. 656 side by side.)

$\mathfrak{P}^{98}$ **(P. IFAO inv. 237b), middle second century.**—In the first publication of this manuscript, the editor (Wagner) dated this manuscript (thought to be a letter with a list of objects) to the second century, without knowing that it was a biblical text. The reason for this dating is that the document on the recto side of the roll was dated to the late first or early second century.[121] Later, it was discovered by Hagedorn that what was thought to be a list of objects was actually a part of the text of Revelation 1:13–20. Hagedorn reedited the text, accepting the date of second century as most likely. An English translation of his comments are as follows:

P. Oxyrhynchus 841

The dating of the fragment by palaeographic criteria is, considering its small content, not without problems. In the first edition, the 2nd century AD has been given, a dating I would principally agree with, but I don't want to exclude the third century AD. However, I don't see any elements which would recommend a later date. Another reason for the date gives the writing of the Recto which Wagner calls "end of 1st/2nd century AD." I would follow this dating according to the impression I have by the Xerox copy. By this, too, follows that the second century seems reasonable for the writing of the text of the Verso.[122]

𝔓⁹⁰

P. Oxyrhynchus 656

These comments by Hagedorn indicate that he would concur with a second-century date for the Revelation text (on the verso), but would not rule out a third-century date. He also agrees with Wagner on his dating of the recto to "end of 1st/2nd century AD." Since the general rule of thumb is to add about ten to twenty years to a literary text written on the verso of a document written on the recto, it clearly stands to reason that the date of the Revelation text is middle second century.

The hand of the Revelation text is difficult to date because it is a documentary hand, at best, and more closely resembles a common hand. (The stylus used must have been unsharpened.) Nonetheless, a fair comparison can be seen in P. Berol. 6849 (= BGU I 300; for photo, see Schubart's *Greek Berol.* 24), a documentary manuscript dated to AD 148 (note the formation of the upsilon, nu, pi, phi, psi, etc.). Another general comparison can be seen in P. Yale 171 (for photo, see *Yale Literary Papyri* I, plate v), dated ca. 150. These affirm a date of mid-second century for $\mathfrak{P}^{98}$. As such, it is the earliest fragment of Revelation.

$\mathfrak{P}^{104}$ **(P. Oxyrhynchus 4404), early second century.**—Allow me to begin by saying that I think $\mathfrak{P}^{104}$ is very possibly the earliest extant New Testament manuscript. When I first looked at this manuscript, I was immediately struck by its early style. Further comparative study with manuscripts of the late first century and early second century has reinforced my initial impression and has led me to think that $\mathfrak{P}^{104}$ should be dated anywhere from ca. 100 to 150.

The editor of the *editio princeps*, J. D. Thomas, dated this manuscript of Matthew (21:34–37, 43, 45) to the late second century. His specific comments then placed it in the second half of the second century:

> The hand is clearly "early," before ca. 250. It is very carefully written, with extensive use of serifs. It could well be considered an example of the "decorated" style or *Zierstil*, on which see GMAW, p. 21, where it is stressed that this so-called style, often found in the Ptolemaic period, is attested as late as texts from the first few years of the third century AD. . . . I should assign [P. Oxyrhynchus] 4404 with some confidence to the second half of the second century, while not wishing to exclude altogether a slightly earlier or a slightly later date. It must rank . . . as one of the earliest surviving texts of Matthew.[123]

I think $\mathfrak{P}^{104}$ is unquestionably the earliest surviving text of Matthew (earlier than $\mathfrak{P}^{64+67}$) and could not be dated later than ca. 150. My arguments are as follows. First, the handwriting is carefully executed in what could be called the Decorated Rounded or *Zierstil* style. In this style, there is a conscious effort to round letters and to finish every vertical stroke with a serif or decorated roundel. As was discussed above, Schubart (naming this style *Zierstil*) thought this style existed from the last century of the Ptolemaic period (first century BC) to the end of the first century AD. Welles was of the same opinion (see discussion above on Yale Genesis). My presentation above (under Decorated Rounded) of nearly thirty manuscripts with solid dating strongly suggests that the time frame for this style was from 100 BC to AD 150 at the latest. Turner, who has a proclivity for dating manuscripts later than most paleographers have done, sees the style as extending to the end of the second century and even into the early third. Turner cited P. Oxyrhynchus 3030 (AD 207) as an example of this style, but P. Oxyrhynchus 3030 has a mixture of *Zierstil* and other forms; it is not a good comparison, in my opinion. Turner's views seem to have influenced Thomas in his dating of $\mathfrak{P}^{104}$.

Thomas makes some comparisons between P. Oxyrhynchus 4004 ($\mathfrak{P}^{104}$) and P. Oxyrhynchus 3523 (= $\mathfrak{P}^{90}$, John), but the Matthew fragment is more elegant and earlier, in my view. The scribe of $\mathfrak{P}^{104}$ observed strict bilinearity, whereas the scribe of $\mathfrak{P}^{90}$ did not. The scribe of $\mathfrak{P}^{104}$ also avoided ligature, whereas the scribe of $\mathfrak{P}^{90}$ did not. In $\mathfrak{P}^{104}$, each letter occupies its own square, if you will. It reveals that the scribe was copying letter by letter.

In the same way, I would say that $\mathfrak{P}^{104}$ is also earlier than most other second-century biblical manuscripts displaying a decorated style; namely, it is earlier than P. Antinoopolis 7 (Psalms), P. Gr Bib g. 5 (a Bodleain manuscript of Psalms), P. Oxyrhynchus 656 (Genesis), P. Oxyrhynchus 1074 (Exodus), and more especially $\mathfrak{P}^{32}$ (Titus). (Each of these is discussed above.) These biblical manuscripts of the second century are more informal (especially allowing for ligature) than $\mathfrak{P}^{104}$, which is more rigid and ornate, and thereby reflects an earlier style.

When I study the Greek Minor Prophet Scrolls from Nahal Hever and the Greek manuscripts from Cave 7 at Qumran, it is apparent that many of the Jewish scribes used a Decorated Rounded style, which most scholars date to the period 50 BC to AD 50. Clearly, $\mathfrak{P}^{104}$ is later, but it bears the same kind of hand, perhaps coming out of the same kind of tradition, though it is more relaxed, as is evidenced in the rounded alpha. This relaxation is characteristic of the late first and early second century in other Decorated Rounded hands.

To what manuscripts, then, can we look for providing a more suitable date for $\mathfrak{P}^{104}$? Preferably, we need to find manuscripts with secure dating. The Herculaneum papyri (dated pre-AD 79) provide some good comparisons, especially since several of the manuscripts display a bilinear decorated style as found in $\mathfrak{P}^{104}$. For example, one can especially see the similarities with P. Herc. 208 (for photo, see Cavallo's *Ercolano*, pl. 56b), and even more so with P. Herc. 697 (for photo, see Cavallo's *Ercolano*, pl. 32).

Another manuscript, also with firm dating, bears clear resemblance to $\mathfrak{P}^{104}$, namely P. Oxyrhynchus 454 + PSI 119 (for photo, see GMAW 62). The date of this manuscript (mid-second century) is quite solid inasmuch as it was written on the verso of a documentary text (with military accounts) dated AD 111. The manuscript is written in a medium-sized, upright, Decorated Rounded uncial. Though similar, $\mathfrak{P}^{104}$ is more rigid and consistently decorated.

We now turn to other comparable manuscripts with assigned dates, that is, dates assigned by editors on the basis of morphological analysis, not on the basis of documentary dates. Another manuscript with similar lettering to $\mathfrak{P}^{104}$ is P. Oxyrhynchus 2743, of which the editors say it exhibits "an upright rounded book-hand of a common type to be dated in the second century. In some places the uprights have separately added serifs at the foot, in others the serifs are replaced by a hook or may be omitted." But, again, $\mathfrak{P}^{104}$ appears to be earlier in that the decoration is replete and spacing between letters exact.

Another Oxyrhynchus manuscript of the second century bearing some morphological resemblance to $\mathfrak{P}^{104}$ is P. Oxyrhynchus 3009, concerning which the editor says, "The hand is a heavy four-square one, ornamented with oblique and horizontal serifs—alpha has horizontal crossbar, beta comes well below the line, phi is very large. The general appearance recalls, e.g., PSI 1213 and . . . other examples of the Roman Uncial discussed by Cavallo. A date in the second century seems likely." 𝔓¹⁰⁴, however, does not have the same alpha, beta, or phi.

𝔓¹⁰⁴ bears more likeness to the next Oxyrhynchus papyrus, P. Oxyrhynchus 3010, which is also generally compared to PSI 1213 (for photo, see Cavallo, pl. 1). Concerning P. Oxyrhynchus 3010, the editors say, "The writing is a careful round book-hand, of the type of the great London Hyperides [P. Lit. London 132] (Roberts GLH 13b) but plentifully ornamented with horizontal serifs. Compare e.g. 2441, 2469, and introduction. It is likely to belong to the earlier second century." Nearly every letter of P. Oxyrhynchus 3010 is shaped similarly to 𝔓¹⁰⁴; note especially the letter combinations mu-epsilon-nu, and pi-rho-omicron-sigma. The comparison of P. Oxyrhynchus 3010 is justifiable, so also to 𝔓¹⁰⁴. As Decorated Rounded uncials, both 𝔓¹⁰⁴ and P. Oxyrhynchus 2441 (for photo, see GMAW 22) share several common features—note especially the formation and decoration of the alpha, iota, gamma, pi, nu. The scribe of P. Oxyrhynchus 2441 (a Pindar piece) allowed for some ligature, whereas the scribe of 𝔓¹⁰⁴ kept each letter in its own sphere, with measured distance between each letter. Of P. Oxyrhynchus 2441, the editor wrote, "The hand is a medium-sized upright rounded uncial comparable with that of [P. Oxy. 2159. 2164] but more ornamented, many of the letters being serifed, in which respect it resembles P. Ryl. 19. It may be dated about the middle of the second century."

Of P. Oxyrhynchus 2469, the editor wrote: "Though this is a distinctive hand[,] the type is found often and over a long period and the artificial style makes it more difficult to date than a script that shows cursive influences." I should put it in the second century AD. and compare [P. Oxy.] 1810, which the editors assign to the late first or early second century. Other examples of the type are [P. Oxy.] 1249 and Schubart, *Papyri Graece Berolinenses*, No. 19c.

And now we come to PSI 1213 (just mentioned) and P. Oxyrhynchus 4301 (which is very likely the work of the same scribe as PSI 1213). The editor of P. Oxyrhynchus 4301 strongly suggests that the same scribe produced both PSI 1213 and P. Oxyrhynchus 4301, and that both are probably part of the same codex preserving a portion of an Old Comedy. Of all the manuscripts discussed in connection with 𝔓¹⁰⁴, PSI 1213 and P. Oxyrhynchus 4301 (dated late first/earlier second century), written in an elegant, decorated hand of the Roman Uncial type, are the most comparable to 𝔓¹⁰⁴. One should especially note the formation of the gamma, iota, lambda, mu, pi, rho, tau; the spacing between letters; and the relationship of each letter to the binary lines.

Another comparable manuscript I have found is P. Berol. 6845 (for photo, see page 166 and Schubart's *Greek Berol.*, 19c), which Schubart dates "first/second century." The morphological likeness between P. Berol. 6845 and 𝔓¹⁰⁴ is clear. Note especially the formation of the alpha, kappa, mu, pi, rho, upsilon (as well as some letter combinations, such as alpha-rho), and the rough breathing mark. However, the lettering in P. Berol. 6845 is tighter, allowing for some ligature. And it is slightly more decorated, especially in the finials.

In the final analysis, $\mathfrak{P}^{104}$ clearly belongs in the second century, and most likely belongs to the early part. It could even be as early as ca. 100. What eludes a more definitive dating is that I have yet to find a comparable manuscript with solid documentary dating. (See photos of $\mathfrak{P}^{104}$ with P. Berol. 6845 and PSI 1213 on pages 164–65.)

$\mathfrak{P}^{109}$ (P. Oxyrhynchus 4448), late second century.—This manuscript preserves a small portion of John 21 (verses 18–20, 23–25). The editor, Cockle, noted that the handwriting of the manuscript resembles $\mathfrak{P}^{66}$, while conceding that the limited number of extant letters in $\mathfrak{P}^{109}$ prohibits a full-scale comparison with $\mathfrak{P}^{66}$. In any event, he dated $\mathfrak{P}^{109}$ as "third century" because of its comparability to $\mathfrak{P}^{66}$, which Cockle says "is usually assigned to the first part of the third century." However, several paleographers have assigned $\mathfrak{P}^{66}$ to the middle of the second century (Hunger, Seider, Cavallo), and I have argued for the same date. It would stand to reason, then, that $\mathfrak{P}^{109}$ should be dated accordingly. However, the extant letters of $\mathfrak{P}^{109}$, though rounded, do not bear any sign of decoration (as in $\mathfrak{P}^{66}$). As such, I would place the manuscript in the late second century.

Manuscripts Dated to the First Half of the Third Century

There are several New Testament manuscripts which could be dated to ca. 200; others to the beginning of the third; and still others to the first half of the third century. These manuscripts include $\mathfrak{P}^{1}$, $\mathfrak{P}^{5}$, $\mathfrak{P}^{13}$, $\mathfrak{P}^{20}$, $\mathfrak{P}^{23}$, $\mathfrak{P}^{27}$, $\mathfrak{P}^{29}$, $\mathfrak{P}^{30}$, $\mathfrak{P}^{38}$, $\mathfrak{P}^{45}$, $\mathfrak{P}^{48}$, $\mathfrak{P}^{49+65}$, $\mathfrak{P}^{69}$, $\mathfrak{P}^{107}$, $\mathfrak{P}^{108}$, $\mathfrak{P}^{111}$, $\mathfrak{P}^{115}$, 0189. The justification for the dating of each manuscript is given below.

$\mathfrak{P}^{1}$ (P. Oxyrhynchus 2), early third century.—The manuscript, containing most of Matthew 1, was originally dated by Grenfell and Hunt to the third century, which is the earliest date they gave to any New Testament manuscript. No comparable manuscripts were cited by Grenfell and Hunt. In $\mathfrak{P}^{1}$, there are no serifs; most letters are formed with straight lines and with equal space between letters, as if each letter was occupying its own square, and the scribe retains bilinearity. In short, $\mathfrak{P}^{1}$ looks like a stiff reformed documentary hand trying to look like a bookhand of the second century.

One manuscript bearing resemblance to $\mathfrak{P}^{1}$ is P. Marmarica (see GLH 18b portion, which is upright). Even though the lettering is tighter in Marmarica than in $\mathfrak{P}^{1}$, the calligraphy is similar. P. Marmarica has a certain date because it is a literary text on whose verso are land registers whose date (between 191 and 215) means that the literary text must be ca. 200.

In Kim's article about the dating of $\mathfrak{P}^{46}$, he notes that certain Christian papyri exhibit a later development of $\mathfrak{P}^{46}$'s style; namely, he sees $\mathfrak{P}^{87}$, $\mathfrak{P}^{52}$, $\mathfrak{P}^{32}$, P. Oxyrhynchus 656 (Genesis), $\mathfrak{P}^{90}$, and $\mathfrak{P}^{1}$ as being spread across the second century

𝔓104

P. Berol. 6845

PSI 1213

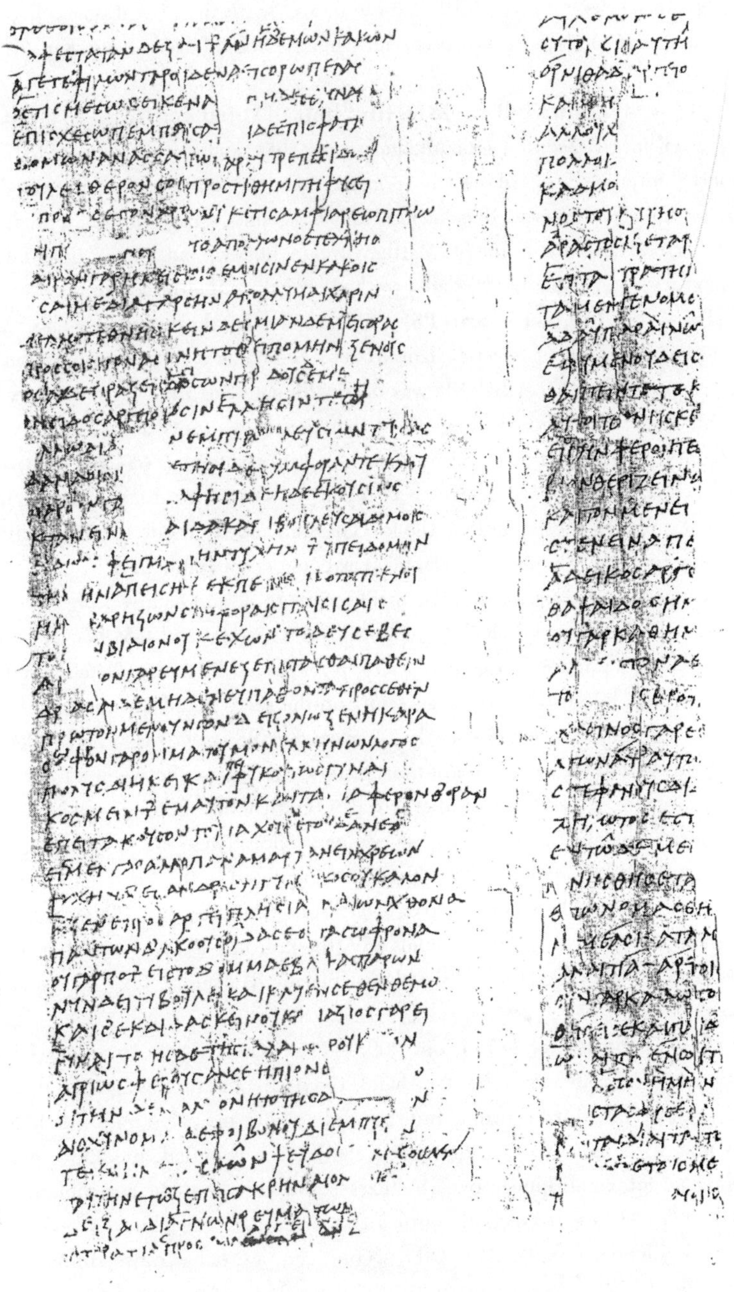

P. Oxyrhynchus 852

(according to the order noted).[124] All of these papyri, with the exception of $\mathfrak{P}^1$, are included above as second-century manuscripts. In a personal letter to me, Kim dated $\mathfrak{P}^1$ as "ca. 200."

$\mathfrak{P}^5$ **(P. Oxyrhynchus 208 + 1781), first half of third century.**—This manuscript, written in a Reformed Documentary hand, has portions of John 1; 16; 20. Grenfell and Hunt, the editors of the *editio princeps*, dated $\mathfrak{P}^5$ to the period between 200 and 300. Grenfell and Hunt said, "The handwriting is a round, upright uncial of medium size, better formed than that of the St. Matthew fragment [$\mathfrak{P}^1$], but, like it, of an informal, semiliterary type." It should be dated to the first half of the third century.

$\mathfrak{P}^{13}$ **(P. Oxyrhynchus 657 and PSI 1292), early third century.**—This manuscript, displaying a kind of Severe (slanted) style, contains a substantial portion of Hebrews (chapters 2–5; 10–12).[125] It was originally dated to the fourth century by Grenfell and Hunt, even though they stated that the manuscripts it was found with were predominantly of the third century—such as P. Oxyrhynchus 654 (ca. 250) and one third-century libelli.[126] There was even a second-century manuscript, P. Oxyrhynchus 656 (Genesis), among the lot. Grenfell and Hunt cite the handwriting of P. Oxyrhynchus 404 (Shepherd of Hermes) as being comparable to $\mathfrak{P}^{13}$.

According to my estimation, similar manuscripts to $\mathfrak{P}^{13}$ in handwriting style are as follows: (1) P. Oxyrhynchus 852 (for photo, see page 169 and GMAW 31). This manuscript (having a portion of Euripides' *Hypsipyle*) has a solid date of "late second or early third century" because there are accounts on the recto dated to the second half of the second century (for which, see P. Oxyrhynchus 985). $\mathfrak{P}^{13}$ is very similar to P. Oxyrhynchus 852 in the formation of most letters, the ligature between letters, and overall appearance. $\mathfrak{P}^{13}$ is also similar to P. Oxyrhynchus 2635 (no later than ca. 200)—note especially the long-tailed swooping upsilon. These manuscripts suggest a date of ca. 200 for $\mathfrak{P}^{13}$, which is also a date Kim suggested for $\mathfrak{P}^{13}$ in a personal letter to me. But it is probably necessary to date $\mathfrak{P}^{13}$ sometime after ca. 200 because $\mathfrak{P}^{13}$ was written on the verso of P. Oxyrhynchus 657 (the Epitome of Livy), which is dated to ca. 200, according to Cavallo.[127] (See photos placing $\mathfrak{P}^{13}$ and P. Oxy. 852 side by side on pages 166–67.)

$\mathfrak{P}^{20}$ **(P. Oxyrhynchus 1171), ca. 200.**—This manuscript, containing James 2:19–3:9, was written in a documentary hand. Grenfell and Hunt assigned a date to this manuscript of "late third century," but they did not cite any paleographic evidence for this dating. $\mathfrak{P}^{20}$, like $\mathfrak{P}^{27}$ (see discussion there), is a rounded, medium upright capital with an informal appearance. It bears some paleographic resemblance to P. Oxyrhynchus 1230 of the second century (for discussion and photo, see GMAW 17) and P. Oxyrhynchus 3830, also of the second century. It has more similarity to P. Oxyrhynchus 1075, and especially with P. Geneva 253 (a Christian homily) dated second century (see discussion above). The same scribe may have produced $\mathfrak{P}^{20}$ and

𝔓²⁷ (see discussion there). (See photos placing 𝔓²⁰ and P. Geneva 253 side by side on pages 170–71.)

𝔓²² (P. Oxyrhynchus 1228), middle of the third century.—Grenfell and Hunt noted that there is general similarity between the script in 𝔓²² and that found in P. Oxyrhynchus 654 (Logia), which can be dated confidently to the mid-third century. The hand of 𝔓²², though a bit heavier, should be dated to the same period.

𝔓²³ (P. Oxyrhynchus 1229), ca. 200 (or late second century).—This manuscript, written in a documentary hand, contains James 1:10–12, 15–18. It was originally dated fourth century by Grenfell and Hunt. Aland redated it to the third century. Neither give evidence from other manuscripts. A similar style can be seen in the first hand of P. Beatty IX (Ezekiel), which should be dated to ca. 200 (see discussion above). The appearance of 𝔓²³ seems earlier in that it exhibits small serifs in many letters (alpha, iota, lambda, mu, nu) and no small omicrons—all characteristics of the second century. Ulrich Wilcken dates it in the second century.[128] 𝔓²³ bears unmistakeable likeness to 𝔓¹⁰⁸. (See photos placing 𝔓²³ and P. Beatty IX [Ezekiel] side by side on pages 172–73.)

𝔓²⁷ (P. Oxyrhynchus 1355), ca. 200.—Grenfell and Hunt assigned a date to this manuscript of the third century, but they did not cite any paleographic evidence to support this dating. Grenfell and Hunt identified the handwriting as being similar to that of 𝔓²⁰, though smaller (see comments above). Indeed, a study of the two hands reveal that the same scribe probably produced both manuscripts. The following letters are formed identically: alpha, beta, delta, epsilon, kappa, iota, omicron, pi, rho, sigma, phi, upsilon, psi, omega. However, the eta, mu, and nu are dissimiliar enough to caution against a 100 percent positive identification. In any event, 𝔓²⁷ should be dated the same as 𝔓²⁰, to ca. 200.

𝔓²⁹ (P. Oxyrhynchus 1597), ca. 200.—Grenfell and Hunt dated this "late third, early fourth" but did not cite any paleographical support. I think this manuscript (having a small portion of Acts 26) belongs to the same era as 𝔓⁴⁵, probably ca. 200. Both manuscripts manifest some unusual, nearly identically shaped letters: a triangular theta, a squarish pi, and squarish episilon with lower inward hook. 𝔓²⁹ also has several similarities to P. Oxyrhynchus 2949 (an apocryphal Gospel), dated late second or early third.

𝔓³⁰ (P. Oxyrhynchus 1598), first half of the third century.—This manuscript, containing 1 Thess. 4–5 and 2 Thes. 1, is written in a relaxed Biblical Uncial script. Grenfell and Hunt dated the manuscript to the late third or fourth century. They said 𝔓³⁰ had some similartities with P. Oxyrhynchus 1166 but wasn't as calligraphic and formal; rather, they thought 𝔓³⁰ was more like P. Oxyrhynchus 406, which they dated to the latter part of the third century. P. Oxyrhynchus 406, however, is more likely an early-third-century manuscript. And a study of other comparable manuscripts such as P. Dura-Europos 2 (which must be dated pre-AD 255/6, the time this area fell to the Persians), P. Oxyrhynchus 867 (dated to the early third century—

$\mathfrak{P}^{20}$

slightly later than P. Oxyrhynchus 661; for photo of P. Oxy. 867, see Cavallo 21a), and P. Oxyrhynchus 1398 suggests that the date of $\mathfrak{P}^{30}$ should be early third century. The hand is also similar to $\mathfrak{P}^{70}$ (which I would redate to the third century—see comments below). In conclusion, I would think $\mathfrak{P}^{30}$ belongs to the first half of the third century.

$\mathfrak{P}^{38}$ (P. Michigan inv. 1571), ca. 200.—This manuscript, written in a Reformed Documentary hand, has portions of Acts 18–19. Sanders says that an early, comparable form of $\mathfrak{P}^{38}$ is apparent in P. Oxyrhynchus 843 (late second c.). Sanders also cites P. Oxyrhynchus 1607 (late second to early third). P. Oxyrhynchus 26 (second c.) displays an earlier stage of this hand, and P. Oxyrhynchus 849 (Acts of Peter) a later form. Other comparable examples of this kind of handwriting can be seen in P. Oxyrhynchus 37 (ca. 200), P. Oxyrhynchus 405 (ca. 200), and P. Oxyrhynchus 406 (early third century).

P. Geneva 253

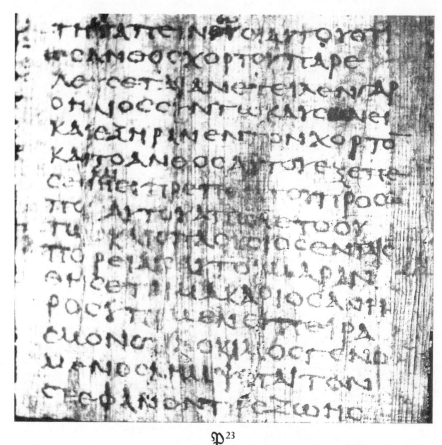

$\mathfrak{P}^{23}$

$\mathfrak{P}^{39}$ **(P. Oxyrhynchus 1780), early third century.**—This manuscript displays the work of a professional scribe who wrote in an early form of the Biblical Uncial script. This form does not appear to be as early as that found in $\mathfrak{P}^{4+64+67}$ (see discussion above and note comparable dated manuscripts). However, $\mathfrak{P}^{39}$ lines up remarkably well with P. Rylands 16, dated quite confidently to the late second/early third century (see extensive discussion above), and with P. Oxyrhynchus 25, dated early third. I would not hesitate to date $\mathfrak{P}^{39}$ as ca. 200. C. H. Roberts and T. C. Skeat assigned it to the first half of the third century.[129] (See photos on pages 174–75 for $\mathfrak{P}^{39}$ side by side with P. Rylands 16 and P. Oxyrhynchus 25.)

$\mathfrak{P}^{45}$ **(P. Chester Beatty I), ca. 200.**—This manuscript contains sizeable portions of all four Gospels and Acts. According to Kenyon, the editor of the *editio princeps*, the manuscript displays individual forms that are early in that they show the simplicity characteristic of the Roman period.[130] The curves of the epsilon and sigma and lack of exaggeration in the upsilon and phi are also signs of an early date. But the

P. Beatty IX, Ezekiel

general appearance—especially its sloping appearance (sometimes called Severe) and small omicron—has caused paleographers such as Kenyon, Hunt, Schubart, and Bell to place it in the third century.

I think 𝔓⁴⁵ could be dated ca. 200 because there are several manuscripts in this time period displaying comparable calligraphy. These are as follows:

P. Michigan 3 (for photo, see page 181 and GLH 15c) is dated solidly to the second half of the second century, inasmuch as a documentary text on the verso has a date of AD 190 (the terminus ante) written in a cursive hand.

P. Egerton 3, concerning which the editors dated the manuscript to early third on the basis of its comparability with P. Oxyrhyncus 2082 (late second) and P. Rylands 57 (ca. 200; for photo, see GLH 22c).

$\mathfrak{P}^{39}$

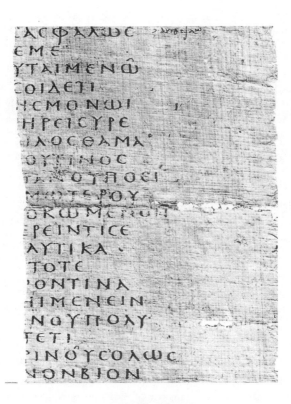

P. Rylands 16

P. Oxyrhynchus 25

P. Oxyrhynchus 2082 (Phlegon's History), dated late second century, is a very good match for $\mathfrak{P}^{45}$.

P. Oxyrhynchus 1016 (for photo, see GLH 20a; GMAW 84) has a date of early to middle third century. The dating of this is difficult because the literary text (Phaedres) is written on the verso of a document, which is a land register (published as P. Oxyrhynchus 1044), mentioning the thirteenth year of a particular unnamed Roman emperor. The date could be 173/174 (Severus) or 195/196, according to C. H. Roberts, or 204/205 (Sept. Severus), according to Hunt, or 233/234 (Severus Alexander) according to E. G. Turner (see GMAW 84 for Turner's arguments). At the latest, then, the literary text would have been written no later than ca. 240–250.

P. Oxyrhynchus 232 (Demosthenes) has a fairly firm date because of the writing on the verso. Concerning this, the editors Grenfell and Hunt said, "The verso of the papyrus is covered with parts of two columns of cursive writing (perhaps a letter) of the end of the second century or (more probably) of the first half of the third century. The Demosthenes on the recto, therefore, cannot have been written later than the early part of the third century, and may well be as old as the latter half of the second century."

P. Rylands 57 (Demosthenes) (for photo, see page 181 and GLH 22c) is dated ca. 200. The dating of this literary manuscript is quite certain inasmuch as it came from the Heroninos Archives. As such, it must predate AD 260. And since it was a literary text (on the recto), which was eventually put to use as a letter (on the verso), it is likely that the literary text is dated ca. 200. In fact, this is the date C. H. Roberts gives P. Rylands 57 (GLH 22c). (See photos of $\mathfrak{P}^{45}$ side by side with P. Mich. 3 and P. Rylands 57 side by side on pages 178–79.)

$\mathfrak{P}^{47}$ **(P. Chester Beatty III), middle third century.**—Kenyon dated this manuscript of Revelation (chaps. 9–17), written in a documentary hand, to the second half of the third century on the basis of the formation of its letters (particularly alpha, beta, epsilon, mu, sigma, and omega). In short, Kenyon dated the manuscript according to his "test-letter" methodology, which is no longer used per se by paleographers. Kenyon did not pinpoint any particular manuscripts with parallel handwriting to affirm this date.

Two other paleographers, Bell and Wilcken, had a different impression of $\mathfrak{P}^{47}$, each of whom would date $\mathfrak{P}^{47}$ to the middle or early third century. Bell describes the hand in $\mathfrak{P}^{47}$ as less formal than the others in the Beatty collection (particulary $\mathfrak{P}^{45}$ and $\mathfrak{P}^{46}$), "approximating to the cursive of documentary papyri." Bell then goes on to say that in contrast to Kenyon, who dated it in the end of the third century, "Wilcken considers the middle or even the beginning of the century possible. The question is of some importance, and it is unfortunate that the evidence of the script is so ambiguous. My own feeling, though I do not attach too much weight to these subjective impressions, is in favour of an earlier rather than a later date in the century."[131]

When I looked for manuscripts bearing comparable features, the closest parallel I can find is P. Tebtunis 268. This manuscript has a portion of a literary text (Dictys Cretensis, *Bellum Troianum*) written on the verso. On the recto are a series of revenue returns (P. Tebtunis 340) which are dated in the year 206. Given the normal time span of adding ten to fifteen years to a literary text written on the verso of a document, P. Tebtunis 268 can be dated. ca. 220.[132] The two hands (that of $\mathfrak{P}^{47}$ and P. Tebtunis 268) have an overall similar look with respect to formation of letters (short shallow strokes) and placement of letters on a line (both in spacing and informal bilinearity). P. Tebtunis 268 and $\mathfrak{P}^{69}$ (see comments below) are also similar. This places $\mathfrak{P}^{47}$ in the same general era of early to middle third century. (See photos of $\mathfrak{P}^{47}$ next to P. Tebtunis 268 on pages 182–83.)

$\mathfrak{P}^{48}$ **(PSI 1165), early third century.**—This manuscript, containing portions of Acts 23, displays the slanted, Severe style that was prevalent in the third century. The style of hand in $\mathfrak{P}^{48}$ can be seen in the following, comparable manuscripts:

P. Oxyrhynchus 223 (for photo, see GLH 21a).

The Homer text *(Iliad* V = P. Oxyrhynchus 223) was written on the verso of Oxyrhynchite provenance dated AD 186. Thus, P. Oxyrhynchus 223 must be dated early third century.

P. Oxyrhynchus 852 (175–225; for photo, see GMAW 31 and see discussion above under $\mathfrak{P}^{13}$), which is very similar to $\mathfrak{P}^{48}$ (as well as to $\mathfrak{P}^{13}$).

P. Oxyrhynchus 2341 (for photo, see GLH 19c), which is a document (Record of Legal Proceedings before the Prefect of Egypt) dated precisely to AD 202 (in cursive hand).

P. Oxyrhynchus 2635 (no later than ca. 200), which has many similarities, especially the long-tailed swooping upsilon.

These comparisons suggest that $\mathfrak{P}^{48}$ belongs to the early third century. (See photos displaying $\mathfrak{P}^{48}$ and P. Oxy. 2341 side by side on page 181.)

$\mathfrak{P}^{49}$ + $\mathfrak{P}^{65}$ **(P. Yale 415 + PSI 1373), middle of the third century.**—$\mathfrak{P}^{49}$ (Ephesians) and $\mathfrak{P}^{65}$ (1 Thessalonians) were produced by the same scribe. This was noted by Bartoletti (the editor of the PSI fragment) and can be seen in the comparison of the two manuscripts both written in a documentary hand. Both manifest a very idiosyncratic formation of certain letters, such as the tilted lambda, tilted sigma, doubled curved and extended iota, and long-tailed upsilon. Welles (the editor of the Yale fragment) remarks that "there is not a single case of difference in the letter shapes in the two papyri." And in both manuscripts the nomina sacra are written with an overbar extending to the right (the width of one letter). Elsewhere, I have a presented a case for both manuscripts being part of the same codex.[133]

Bartolleti dated $\mathfrak{P}^{65}$ to the third century but provided no paleographic description for having done so. Welles dated $\mathfrak{P}^{49}$ to the early third century and provided sufficient detail about dating it so, as follows:

𝔓⁴⁵

The script belongs to a type which shows affinities with Schubart's "stenger stil," in that letters tend to be narrow and lean to the right, but which is also under the influence of cursive hands and connects letters when this is convenient. The singular alpha and two-stroke upsilon are of the second-century type, but the delta (left open at the right to be closed by the following letter) and especially the two-stroke epsilon belong to the period of Caracalla [AD 211–217]. Of biblical papyri, Beatty I [𝔓⁴⁵] and II [𝔓⁴⁶] are similar: the latter has a very similar xi and also on occasion, places a small omicron under the horizontal of a gamma. Beatty IX X [Ezekiel, Daniel, Esther] may be a little earlier. P. Bodmer VII [𝔓⁷²] must be closely contemporary. P. Bodmer XIV XV [𝔓⁷⁵] and P. Rylands 5 [𝔓³²] belong to the same school of writing, but are better written. P. Oxy. 1171 [𝔓²⁰] and 1355 [𝔓²⁷] may well be a little later. For the second-century alpha and upsilon, one may compare Schubart, Greek Pal. Figs. 87 [= P. Oxy. 852] and 89 [P. Berol. 11628], and for the early third-century letters, PGB [= P. Greek Berol.] 19b (ca. 200), 32a (219/20), 40 (early III), and especially the edicts of Caracalla, P. Giss. 40 (Gr. Pal., Fig 47). P. Yale 2 [𝔓⁴⁹] is not as well written as these, however, and cannot be from a handsome codex.[134] [Bracketed information provided.]

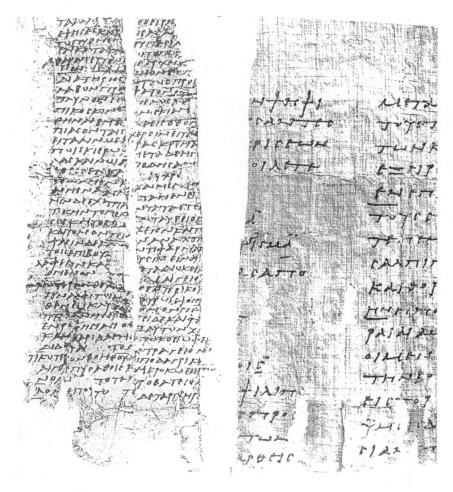

P. Mich. 3   P. Rylands 57

All the biblical manuscripts so cited for comparative purposes range from the middle of the second century to the end of the third. Welles sees 𝔓⁴⁹ as being comparable mostly to P. Bodmer VII (𝔓⁷²). Though the style is similar, 𝔓⁴⁹ appears to be earlier—on the basis of the morphological analysis Welles provided. The one documentary text resembling 𝔓⁴⁹ (+𝔓⁶⁵) is P. Giss. 40 (the edicts of the Emperor Caracalla, AD 212–215). However, P. Giss. 40, though quite similar to 𝔓⁴⁹⁺⁶⁵, more closely resembles 𝔓¹¹¹, in my opinion (see discussion there). (See photos of 𝔓⁴⁹⁺⁶⁵ on page 180.)

𝔓⁶⁹ (P. Oxyrhynchus 2383), first half of third century.—This manuscript contains a small portion of Luke 22 written in a Reformed Documentary hand. The editor of this manuscript, E. G. Turner, placed 𝔓⁶⁹ in the middle of the third century,

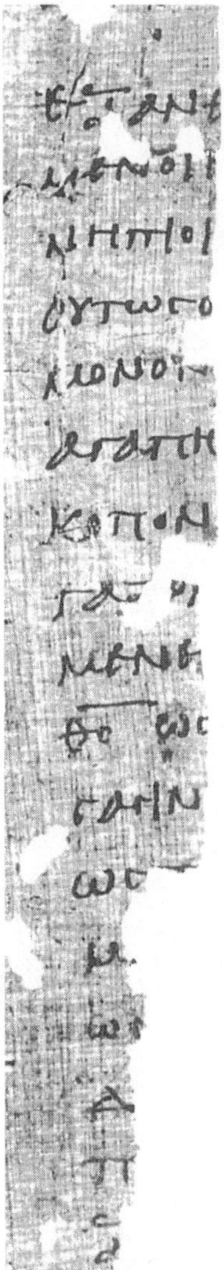

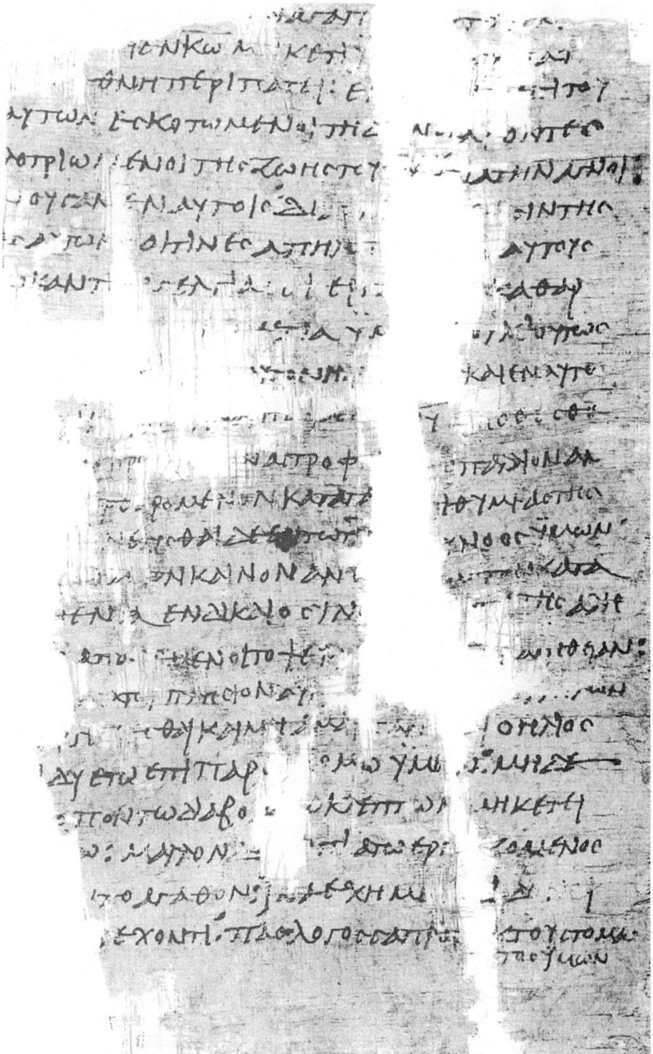

𝔓[65]

𝔓[49]

$\mathfrak{P}^{48}$

P. Oxyrhynchus 2341

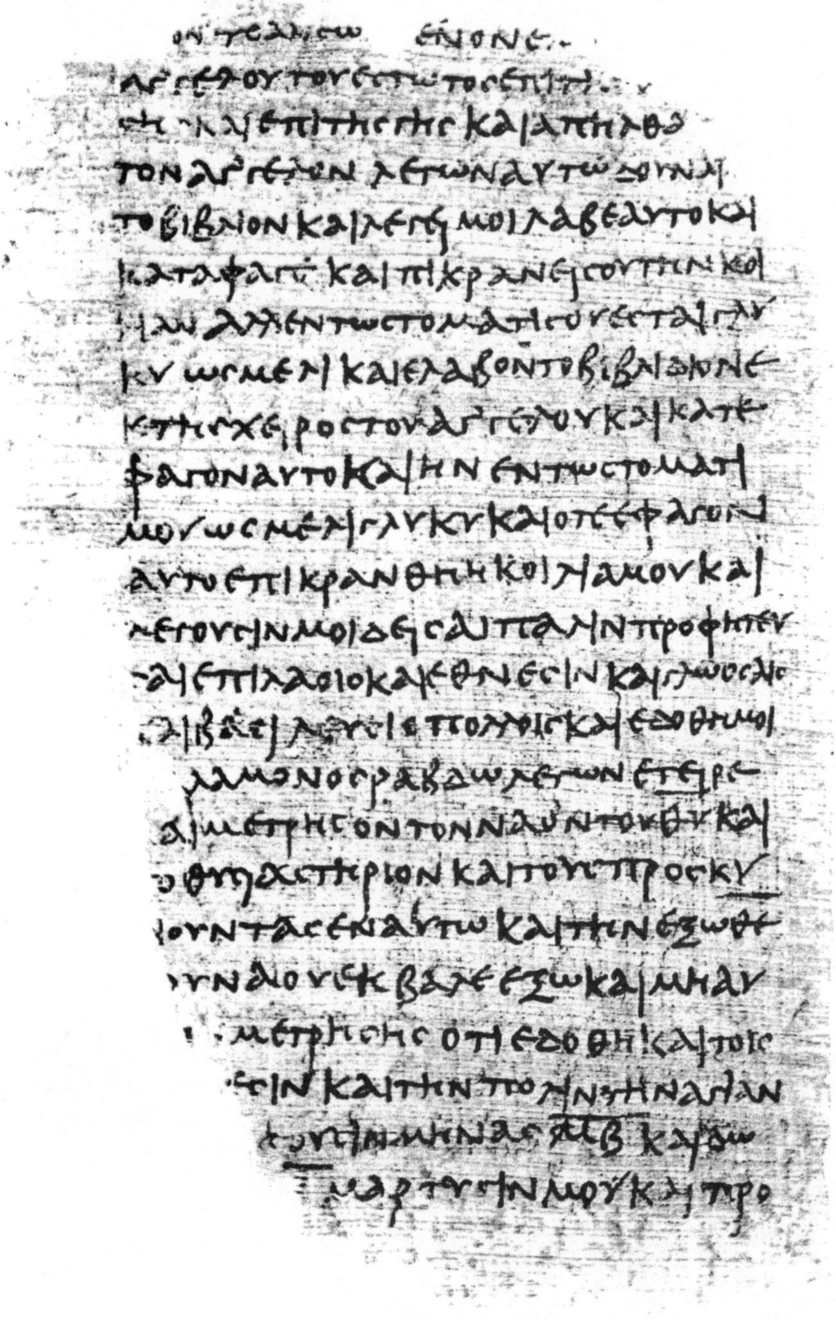

𝔓47

P. Tebtunis
268

indicating that it is more formal than P. Tebtunis 268 (for photo, see vol. 2 of *Tebtunis Papyri*) and P. London 2565 (JEA 21 [1935], plate opp. p. 224) and less formal than P. Oxyrhynchus 412 (for photo, see GLH 23a), all of which Turner said are "dated more or less securely to the middle of the third century." P. Oxyrhynchus 412 must be dated prior to the year 275/276 since the verso contains a document dated in the reign of the Emperor Tacitus (275–276). This would put P. Oxyrhynchus 412 (containing the *kestoi* of Julius Africanus) about ca. 250.

𝔓⁶⁹ appears to be most similar to P. Tebtunis 268 (note the formation of the eta, kappa, nu, sigma, etc.), in my estimation. Fortunately, P. Tebtunis 268 can be dated

𝔓⁹⁵

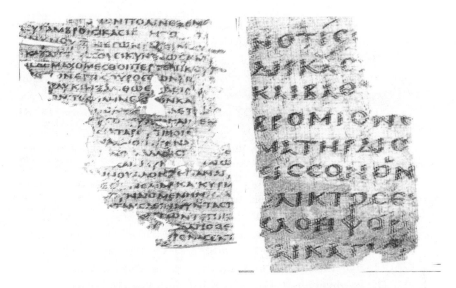

P. Rylands 542   **P. Rylands 547**

with near precision to the early part of the third century. This manuscript, preserving part of the *Trojan War* by Dictys Cretensis, was written on the back of a series of revenue returns (P. Tebtunis 380), which are dated in the year AD 206. The editors of the Tebtunis Papyri (Grenfell, Hunt, and Goodspeed), therefore, were certain that the literary text P. Tebtunis 268 belonged to the first half of the third century. "*A priori* considerations and paleographical evidence combine in favour of the view that the literary text on the verso is not appreciably later in date, and it may accordingly be assigned with confidence to the first half of the third century."[135] I would, likewise, assign $\mathfrak{P}^{69}$ to the first half of the third century, not just to the middle of the third century. (See photos displaying $\mathfrak{P}^{47}$ and P. Tebtunis 268 side by side on pages 184–85.)

$\mathfrak{P}^{95}$ **(PL II/31), ca. 200.**—This manuscript contains a small portion of John 5 (26–29, 36–38). Lenaerts, editor of the *editio princeps*, said, "L'onciale de PL II/31 se rattache indubitablement a la grande famille de la majuscule biblique et me parait pouvoir etre situee au debut du IIIe siecle: je lui comparerais notamment le P. Rylands 3, 542 du chant V de l'Iliade." The hand of $\mathfrak{P}^{95}$ is clearly Biblical Uncial. As indicated by Lenaerts, it does bear resemblance to P. Rylands 542, which was dated by Roberts (original editor) to the third century (saying, it is a "good book-hand of the best Roman style . . . small, firm and regular, and closely packed"). It must be noted that P. Rylands 542 comes from the same manuscript as PSI 1377, which was dated by Bartoletti as being anywhere from the second half of the second century to the beginning of the third—a date affirmed by Cavallo (see discussion above).

$\mathfrak{P}^{95}$ displays a larger script than P. Rylands 542 and is more relaxed. In my opinion its calligraphy and overall appearance bear notable similarities with P. Oxyrhynchus 224+P. Rylands 547 of the later second century (Cavallo, pl. 6; see discussion above), as well as with P. Oxyrhynchus 406 (dated ca. 200, which is similar to P. Oxyrhynchus 224; see discussion above). For these reasons, I would place $\mathfrak{P}^{95}$ "ca. 200." (See photos displaying $\mathfrak{P}^{95}$ on page 184 and P. Rylands 542 and 547 on page 185.)

$\mathfrak{P}^{100}$ **(P. Oxyrhynchus 4449), middle third century.**—This manuscript, written with a reformed documentary hand, contains portions of James 3–5. The editor, R. Hubner, dates the manuscript to the third or fourth century. He indicates, correctly so, that the handwriting is similar to that in $\mathfrak{P}^{106}$, dated to the third century (see discussion below) but has features found in the early fourth particularly an extended kappa. But Hubner does not cite any comparable manuscripts. The one documentary manuscript with the greatest resemblance to $\mathfrak{P}^{100}$ is P. Oxyrhynchus 1100 (dated AD 206; see GLH 20b). Thus, $\mathfrak{P}^{100}$ belongs, at least, to the middle of the third century.

$\mathfrak{P}^{106}$ **(P. Oxyrhynchus 4445), early third century.**—This manuscript contains a small portion of John 1 (29–35, 40–46), written in a documentary hand. The manuscript bears notable resemblance to P. Rylands 463 (Gospel of Mary), assigned a date by C. H. Roberts (original editor) to the early third century (for discussion and photo, see GLH 20c), and to P. Oxyrhynchus 1100 (a documentary text dated AD 206; for discussion and photo, see GLH 20b), as well as to P. Oxyrhynchus 2539 (assigned a date of second/third century).[136] $\mathfrak{P}^{106}$ bears similar likenesses to the same manuscripts and should be dated early third century.

$\mathfrak{P}^{107}$ **(P. Oxyrhynchus 4446), early third century.**—This manuscript contains a small portion of John (17:1–2, 11). The editor (Cockle) indicates that the text is "written in carbon ink in a semicursive script, which is largely bilinear. It has a slight tendency to slope to the right. It was written without excessive speed and very clearly. . . . The script bears some similarity to the hand of [P. Oxy.] XXXIII 2659, which its editor (Rea) assigned to the second century; but 4446 has differences in some letters, notably epsilon and kappa, which together with the slope mentioned above, suggest that it not be dated earlier than the third century."[137]

$\mathfrak{P}^{108}$ **(P. Oxyrhynchus 4447), ca. 200.**—This manuscript contains a small portion of John 17, written in a reformed documentary hand. This hand bears remarkable resemblance to P. Chester Beatty IX (Ezekiel), which is dated ca. 200 (see discussion above). $\mathfrak{P}^{108}$ should be dated accordingly, as also $\mathfrak{P}^{23}$ (see discussion).

$\mathfrak{P}^{111}$ **(P. Oxyrhynchus 4495), first half of the third century.**—This manuscript, having a portion of Luke 17, is written in a documentary hand. The manuscript was dated by its editor to the first half of the third century inasmuch as it bears morphological resemblance to P. Giss. 40 (a documentary text dated AD 212–15, an Edict of Caracalla). I can add three other documentary texts to support this dating: (1) P. London II. 35 (a documentary text dated AD 222; for photo, see Montev. pl. 74); (2) P. Berol 6972 (= BGU I 296, a libellus dated 219/220); (3) P. Oxyrhynchus 1480 (a documentary text about a trial between the eighteenth and twenty-third years of Caracalla = AD 210–214). (See photos of $\mathfrak{P}^{111}$ and P. Giss. 40 side by side on pages 188–89.)

$\mathfrak{P}^{115}$ **(P. Oxyrhynchus 4499), middle third century.**—This manuscript contains portions of Revelation 2–3, 5–6, 8–15, written in a reformed documentary hand, displaying a modified slanted (Severe) calligraphy, much as in $\mathfrak{P}^{45}$. The editor of this manuscript, Juan Chapa, dates the manuscript to the late third/early fourth century. He cites a few manuscripts with firm dating for justifying this date: (1) P. Florentine 108 (end of second/beginning of third; for photo, see GLH 22a); it is a literary text (*Iliad*) written on the recto later used on the verso for correspondence in the Heroninos Archives (ca. 260); (2) P. Florentine 259 from the Heroninos correspondence (ca. 260; for photo, see GLH 22b); (3) P. Oxyrhynchus 1016, dated middle of third century (for photo, see GMAW 84 and see discussion under $\mathfrak{P}^{45}$); (4) P. Hermes 4, from the Archive of Theophanes (ca. AD 315–325; for photo see Montev., pl. 87).

Of the four manuscripts, $\mathfrak{P}^{115}$ most resembles P. Florentine 108 and P. Oxyrhynchus 1016. As such, $\mathfrak{P}^{115}$ belongs in the middle of the third century. (See photos displaying $\mathfrak{P}^{115}$ side by side with P. Flor. 108, P. Flor. 259, and P. Oxy. 1016 on pages 190–91.)

0189 (P. Berlin 11765), ca. 200.—This parchment manuscript, containing Acts 5:3–21, displays a form of the Biblical Uncial hand. The editor (Salonius) of this manuscript dated it to the fourth century.[138] C. H. Roberts redated it to the second or third century; Aland accepted this date.[139] Indeed, the handwriting is much earlier than the fourth century. The finely executed handwriting is clearly Biblical Uncial and bears resemblance to late second-century manuscripts such as $\mathfrak{P}^{4+}\mathfrak{P}^{64+67}$, P. Oxyrhynchus 661, and P. Oxyrhynchus 2404, but 0189 is later in overall appearance—especially the small omicron.

Manuscripts Dated to the Second Half of the Third Century

There are several New Testament manuscripts that can be dated confidently to the second half of the third century (250–300). Several of these manuscripts are so dated by having morphological correspondence to documentary manuscripts in the Heroninos correspondence, all dated ca. 255–260. This pertains to $\mathfrak{P}^{17}$, $\mathfrak{P}^{18}$, $\mathfrak{P}^{24}$, $\mathfrak{P}^{37}$, $\mathfrak{P}^{53}$, $\mathfrak{P}^{80}$, $\mathfrak{P}^{86}$, and $\mathfrak{P}^{91}$. Other New Testament manuscripts can be placed in the second half of the third century based on other morphological features.

$\mathfrak{P}^{9}$ **(P. Oxyrhynchus 402), late third century.**—This manuscript has a small portion of 1 John 4 written in a common hand, originally dated by Grenfell and Hunt to the fourth or fifth century. However, Aland dates it to the third century.[140]

𝔓¹¹¹ Recto   𝔓¹¹¹ Verso

𝔓¹² **(Amherst Papyri 3b), AD 285–300.**—The first verse of Hebrews was penned in the upper margin of a letter written between the years 264/265 and 281/282. The marginal addition (written in a different hand) was probably added not long after the composition of the letter. (On the verso of the manuscript, another writer penned Genesis 1:1–5 LXX.)

𝔓¹⁵ + 𝔓¹⁶ **(P. Oxyrhynchus 1008 + 1009), late third century.**—These are two manuscripts; one contains portions of 1 Corinthians 7–8 and another of Philippians 3–4. Both manuscripts may or may not have been part of the same codex. The editors' (Grenfell and Hunt) comments are as follows:

> Probably this fragment [1009], containing parts of some verses from the Epistle to the Philippians, belonged to the same codex as 1008, with which it was found. At first sight it does not appear to do so, for the writing is rather smaller and the ink, instead of being black, is of a brown colour; but the formation of the letters is closely similar, the height and breadth of the column would be approximately the same, and the punctuation is effected, as in 1008, by means of blank spaces, not stops.

Grenfell and Hunt dated both manuscripts to the fourth century. This dating was influenced by the fact that the manuscripts with which 𝔓¹⁵ and 𝔓¹⁶ were discovered were fourth-century manuscripts. More precisely, the calligraphy of the manuscripts suggests a date of ca. 300. Cavallo calls the style "ogivale inclinato" (rounded, slanted uncial), which is very typical of third-century manuscripts. Aland must not think 𝔓¹⁵ and 𝔓¹⁶ belong to the same codex, because he dates them differently: 𝔓¹⁵ to the third century and 𝔓¹⁶ to "III/IV."[141] Perhaps his dating is influenced by the fact that 𝔓¹⁵ was written in black ink, and 𝔓¹⁶ in brown ink (which suggests a later date). If this is the case, then it is quite possible that the same scribe produced both at different times in his life. Or it is just as likely, as this is my view, that the same scribe used two different ink colors for the same codex. When he ran out of black, he used brown.

P. Giss. 40

P. Flor. 108

𝔓 115

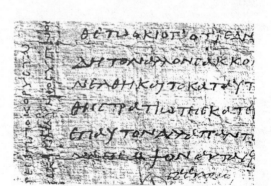

P. Flor. 259

P. Oxyrhynchus 1016

$\mathfrak{P}^{17}$ **(P. Oxyrhynchus 1078), second half of the third century.**—This manuscript has a small portion of Hebrews (9:12–19), written in a documentary hand. Grenfell and Hunt assigned it a date of "fourth century." But this conservative dating was typical of their treatment of biblical codices. The handwriting exhibits many similarities with $\mathfrak{P}^{80}$ (see comments there) and $\mathfrak{P}^{86}$, both of which have morphological similarities to manuscripts in the Heroninos correspondence (dated ca. 260).

$\mathfrak{P}^{18}$ **(P. Oxyrhynchus 1079), second half of the third century.**—The text of Revelation (1:4–6) was written on the verso of Exodus (P. Oxyrhynchus 1075), which was dated by its editors (Grenfell and Hunt) to the third century, though it looks earlier (late second/early third). The writing of Revelation travels in the opposite direction of that of Exodus—the end of one work (Exod. 40) coinciding with the beginning of the other (Rev. 1). A different scribe (untrained in writing books) used the Exodus scroll at some later date to copy the book of Revelation. A fairly good match of a documentary text is P. Florentine 194 of the Heroninos correspondence, dated ca. 260.

$\mathfrak{P}^{24}$ **(P. Oxyrhynchus 1230), second half of the third century.**—This manuscript contains a portion of Revelation 5–6, written in a common hand. Grenfell and Hunt dated the manuscript to the earlier part of the fourth century. But this dating is a bit too conservative. The handwriting exhibits affinities with $\mathfrak{P}^{18}$ and P. Florentine 194 (see discussion under $\mathfrak{P}^{18}$).

$\mathfrak{P}^{28}$ **(P. Oxyrhynchus 1596), late third century.**—This manuscript contains a portion of John 6, written in a documentary hand. Grenfell and Hunt said this manuscript was "found together with third-fourth century documents, and probably belongs to the early or middle part of the fourth century, the script being a medium-sized uncial." Grenfell and Hunt, again, were too conservative in their dating, and offered no comparative paleography. $\mathfrak{P}^{28}$ is almost certainly a third-century manuscript. The handwriting is similar to P. Oxyrhynchus 1358 (Hesiod's *Catalogue*), which must be dated in the late third century because it has a third-century document on the recto as is stated in the following: "1358 consists of two good-sized pieces, apparently having no direct connexion with each other. Their recto is inscribed with third-century official documents. . . . The literary text [Hesiod] on the verso may be referred with probability to the latter part of the same century."

$\mathfrak{P}^{35}$ **(PSI 1), third century/fourth century.**—This manuscript contains a portion of Matthew 25, written in a Biblical Uncial hand. The dating of this manuscript has been extremely varied. It was originally dated by its editor, E. Pistelli, to the seventh century (see PSI 1). Aland redated it to the fourth century. But Roberts and Skeat assigned it a date of the third century.[142] In my opinion, this is where it belongs. The handwriting is similar to that found in $\mathfrak{P}^{40}$, which was also originally dated late (sixth century) and then revised to the third century. Both these manuscripts are examples of the Biblical Uncial that postdates the manuscripts of the late second century and predates the more developed hand of the fourth century (as is found in Codices Vaticanus and Sinaiticus).

$\mathfrak{P}^{37}$ **(P. Michigan 1570), ca. 260.**—This manuscript contains a portion of Matthew 26, written in a documentary hand. The best parallels to this documentary hand are found in the correspondence of Heroninos (dated shortly before or after AD 260), especially a letter by Kopres (P. Florentine 208), dated AD 256. Other comparable manuscripts are P. Amherst 72, P. Cornell 52, and $\mathfrak{P}^{53}$ (see comments there).

$\mathfrak{P}^{40}$ **(P. Heidelberg 645), second half of the third century.**—This manuscript contains portions of Romans (1–4; 6; 9), some of which I have newly reconstructed,[143] written in a Biblical Uncial hand. The original editor, Bilabel, dated the manuscript as fifth-sixth century. However, this manuscript is quite similar to $\mathfrak{P}^{35}$ and should be dated accordingly, most likely to the second half of the third century (see comments on $\mathfrak{P}^{35}$).

$\mathfrak{P}^{50}$ **(P. Yale 1543), late third century/early fourth (ca. 300).**—This manuscript contains portions of Acts 8 and 10, written in a documentary hand. The dating of this manuscript has varied. The editor of the *editio princeps*, Kraeling, dated it to the middle of the fourth century. Aland dated it to the fourth/fifth century (with notes indicating that Roberts and Skeat date it to the fifth century, and Hunger to the fourth).[144] But Kraeling argued quite persuasively for a dating to the reign of Diocletian (284–305). Among his many arguments, he affirms that the formation of various letters (such as alpha, eta, upsilon) are early in form, as well as the use of the diaresis, which is hardly used after the third century. It is my opinion that a comparison of $\mathfrak{P}^{50}$ with $\mathfrak{P}^{72}$ reveals that both belong to the same era.

$\mathfrak{P}^{53}$ **(P. Michigan 6652), ca. 260.**—This manuscript contains portions of Matthew 26 and Acts 9–10 written in a documentary hand. Sanders dated this manuscript to ca. 260 on the basis of its general correspondence with the documentary papyri in the Heroninos collection, all dated shortly before or after AD 260. P. Florentine 189 is a fairly good match. $\mathfrak{P}^{53}$ bears resemblance to $\mathfrak{P}^{37}$, which also has correspondence in the Heroninos archives (see above).

$\mathfrak{P}^{70}$ **(P. Oxyrhynchus 2384 + PSI inv. CNR 419, 420), late third century.**—This manuscript, containing portions of Matthew 2–3; 11–12; 24, is written in a Biblical Uncial hand. E. G. Turner, the editor of the Oxyrhynchus portion of this manuscript, compares the hand of $\mathfrak{P}^{70}$ to P. Oxyrhynchus 847 (= 0162) and P. Oxyrhynchus 1224 (an uncanonical Gospel), and then dates $\mathfrak{P}^{70}$ to the late third or early fourth century. Bartoletti, the editor of the PSI portion, compares the hand to P. Oxyrhynchus 1780 (= $\mathfrak{P}^{39}$) and P. Lit. London 33 (for photos, see Cavallo, pls. 27 and 30), which are both examples of the Biblical Uncial hand. Bartoletti also gives the range of date from the late third to early fourth century. The best comparison among all these manuscripts is seen in P. Oxyrhynchus 847 (= 0162), in that both share features of the Biblical Uncial with variations, i.e., neither have strict bilinearity and both display the small omicron and slight slope to the right (see comments below on 0162).

$\mathfrak{P}^{72}$ (P. Bodmer VII/VIII), late third/early fourth (ca. 300).—This manuscript contains 1–2 Peter, Jude, written in a documentary hand that is somewhat hard to date. This hand resembles $\mathfrak{P}^{50}$, dated to the same era.

$\mathfrak{P}^{78}$ (P. Oxyrhynchus 2684), late third/early fourth (ca. 300).—This manuscript contains a small portion of Jude (vv. 4–5, 7–8), written in a documentary hand. The editor, P. Parsons, dates this to the third century or early fourth, saying, "The hand is a leisurely half-cursive, which I would assign to the third or early fourth century." Parsons provides no parallel examples from documentary papyri.

$\mathfrak{P}^{80}$ (P. Barcelona 83), ca. 260.—This manuscript contains one verse of John (3:34), written in a documentary hand. Roca-Puig indicates that $\mathfrak{P}^{80}$ has a distinct third-century look, especially evidenced by the tilt of the handwriting to the right. Furthermore, $\mathfrak{P}^{80}$ greatly resembles P. Florentine II 148 in the Heroninos correspondence (dated ca. 260). Roca-Puig also notes that several letters in $\mathfrak{P}^{80}$ look like letters in P. Florentine 108, a literary text of earlier date. But the handwriting of $\mathfrak{P}^{80}$ more closely corresponds with that found in the documentary text, P. Florentine II 148. An even better match, in my estimation, is P. Florentine 118, also from the Heroninos correspondence (ca. 260).

$\mathfrak{P}^{86}$ (P. Col. theol. 5516), late third century/early fourth (ca. 300).— This manuscript contains a portion of Matthew 5, written in a documentary hand. The editors (Charalambakis, D. Hagedorn, D. Kaimakis, L. Thungen) date this to the beginning of the fourth century, citing P. Colon. inv. 1697 (for photo, see ZPE 10, 1973, tafel 4) as illustrative. P. Colon. inv. 1697 is a dated document (AD 329). From my estimation, it bears some resemblance to $\mathfrak{P}^{86}$, but does not provide the best comparison. Manuscripts from the Heroninos correspondence show just as much comparability with $\mathfrak{P}^{86}$—manuscripts such as P. Florentine 108, 166, and especially 238 (all dated with certainty to ca. 260). For this reason, I would place $\mathfrak{P}^{86}$ somewhere between AD 329 and AD 260, or late third century/early fourth.

$\mathfrak{P}^{91}$ (P. Mil. Vogl. Inv. 1224 + P. Macquarie Inv. 360), second half of the third century.—This manuscript contains a portion of Acts 2–3, written in a documentary hand. The editors said it bears a handwriting style comparable to P. Oxyrhynchus 654 (ca. 250) and P. Florentine 120 (ca. 260) of the Heroninos correspondence. Indeed, the latter is a good match.

$\mathfrak{P}^{92}$ (P. Narmuthis 69.39a/229a), late third/early fourth century (ca. 300).—This manuscript contains a portion of Ephesians 1 and 2 Thessalonians 1, written in a documentary hand. The editor of the *editio princeps* of $\mathfrak{P}^{92}$, Claudio Gallazi, dates $\mathfrak{P}^{92}$ to the late third or early fourth century on the basis that the handwriting is quite similar to other manuscripts in the same era: P. Bodmer IX, P. Cairo Isid. 2, and P. Rylands III 489.

Of the manuscripts listed by the editor, P. Rylands 489 bears the best resemblance. The Rylands manuscript is actually part of another manuscript known as P. London 2852 (from Oxyrhynchus). Milne, the editor of the London portion, assigned the script a date to the early fourth century. However, Hunt (the editor of the Rylands fragment), was inclined to date it to the latter part of the third century, saying, "A certain freedom and absence of the rigid formality common in fourth-century MSS of this type suggests to me that a date in the later third century should not be excluded." I would say that the same applies to $\mathfrak{P}^{92}$, especially with regard to the lack of rigidity. By contrast, P. Bodmer IX, dated to the early fourth, is stiffer. (See photos displaying $\mathfrak{P}^{92}$ and P. Rylands 489 on pages 196–97.)

$\mathfrak{P}^{101}$ **(P. Oxyrhynchus 4401), third century.**—The handwriting is quite similar to that found in P. IFAO inv. 89+P. Koln VII 282, a papyrus of Menander assigned to the third century. (For photos, see ZPE 6 [1970] tafel 1a and ZPE 8 [1971] tafel 3.)

$\mathfrak{P}^{102}$ **(P. Oxyrhynchus 4402), late third century/early fourth (ca. 300).**—This manuscript contains a small portion of Matthew 4, written in a reformed documentary hand. The editor, J. David Thomas, dated the manuscript to the period from the middle of the third century to the early years of the fourth. He says there are some similarities with P. Hermes 5 (dated with certainty to ca. 315–325; for description and photo, see GMAW 70), some similarity with P. Hermes 4 (also dated with certainty to 315–325; for photo, see Montev., pl. 87), and with P. Oxyrhynchus 2601. However, $\mathfrak{P}^{102}$ seems slightly earlier than these manuscripts in that the script is upright rather than sloping to the right.

$\mathfrak{P}^{110}$ **(P. Oxyrhynchus 4494) second half of the third century.**—This small fragment, showing Matthew 10:13–15, 25–27, belongs to the late third century. It clearly displays the slanted (Severe) style prominent in the third century. The editor, Cockle, noted the similarities with $\mathfrak{P}^{45}$ and P. Florentine II 108 (of the Heroninos archive, dated ca. 260). However, Cockle thinks the exaggerated width and knotted top of the phi and alpha in $\mathfrak{P}^{110}$ suggest a later date, as is found in P. Oxyrhynchus 1778 (assigned to the fourth century). On balance, I would place it in the second half of the third century.

$\mathfrak{P}^{113}$ **(P. Oxyrhynchus 4497).**—This tiny fragment, showing only a few words in Romans 2:12–13, 19, clearly belongs in the third century, as is evident by the right angle slope of the hand, the small omicron, and formation of the letters. It bears resemblance to P. Oxyrhynchus 2619 (third century) and, to a lesser extent, to P. Oxyrhynchus 4041 (third century).

$\mathfrak{P}^{114}$ **(P. Oxyrhynchus 4498) middle to late third century.**—This manuscript, showing only Hebrews 1:7–12 on the recto (the verso is blank), has handwriting that resembles P. Oxyrhynchus 23. This Oxyrhynchus manuscript (showing a portion of Plato's *Laws* IX on the recto) has solid dating because the verso has a few scribbled lines which indicate the date of AD 295. As such, the literary text on the

$\mathfrak{P}^{92}$

verso is probably middle to late third century. Another manuscript resembling $\mathfrak{P}^{114}$ is P. Oxyrhynchus 2700 (an example of a hand common in the third century), as well as to P. Oxyrhynchus 2098, a manuscript dated with confidence to AD 200–250 (see GLH 19b and discussion above).

0162 (P. Oxyrhynchus 847) late third/early fourth century (ca. 300).— This is a parchment manuscript containing John 2:11–22, displaying a form of Biblical Uncial hand. Grenfell and Hunt noted that the large, sloping oval script is more like that found in third and fourth centuries than that of the square, heavier type which became prominent for biblical texts. The small omicron, shallow omega, and use of the diaresis make it likely that this manuscript belongs to the third rather than the fourth century. Aland dates it third/fourth century.[145]

0171 (PSI 124 + P. Berlin 11863), late third/early fourth century (ca. 300).—This manuscript contains two portions, one of Matthew 10 and another of Luke 22, displaying a form of Biblical Uncial hand. The editor of the PSI fragment (Luke 22) dated it in the beginning of the fourth century. As comparable manuscripts, he cites the following: Schubart's *Greek Berol.*, pl. 31 = P. Berol. 9782 (dated second

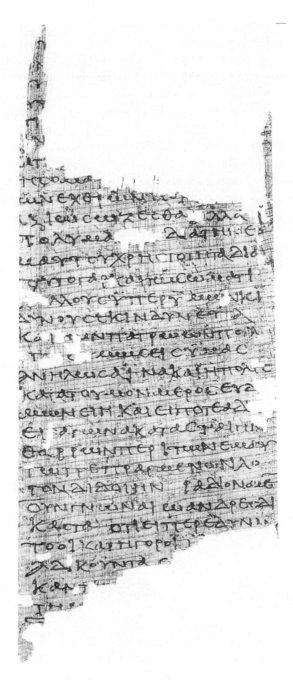

P. Rylands 489

century) and Schubart's *Greek Berol.*, pl. 43b (Hermopolis unnumbered). In my opinion, Schubart pl. 31 is too early and Schubart pl. 43b is a bit too late. The editor of the Matthew portion (P. Berlin 11863), Kurt Treu, redated it to ca. 300.[146] As with 0162, the handwriting stands midway between third-century Biblical Uncials and those more fully developed in the fourth century (such as in Codex Vaticanus and Codex Sinaiticus).

0220 (Schoyen Collection, MS 113), late third century.—This parchment manuscript, containing portions of Romans 4–5, displays handwriting that is midway between third-century Biblical Uncials and those more fully developed in the fourth century. This hand (as well as 0171) attempts to imitate the well-formed professional hands displaying the Biblical Uncial but lacks the precision. The editor of the *editio princeps*, W. H. P. Hatch, dates it to the latter part of the third century, noting that the hand is earlier than that found in codices Vaticanus and Siniaticus (both of the fourth century). Hatch does not cite any comparable manuscripts. Aland dates it third century.[147]

Chapter Four

The Nomina Sacra
in New Testament Manuscripts

A phenomenon occurred when the books of the New Testament were written, published, and distributed in the first century. Either the writers themselves or the very
earliest copyists used a special written form for the divine names. Instead of writing
out in full (in *plene*) the Greek words *kurios* (Lord), *Iēsous* (Jesus), *Christos* (Christ), *theos*
(God), and *pneuma* (Spirit), the writers and/or scribes wrote these words in special
abbreviated (or contracted) forms. Today very few know about this, even those who
read the Greek New Testament, because the nomina sacra (sacred names) are not replicated in any fashion in printed editions of the Greek New Testament. If a student is
going to know the manuscripts of the Greek New Testament, the student should be
able to recognize the nomina sacra and appreciate their significance.

Furthermore, this chapter will demonstrate how some scribes exercised a certain
amount of exegetical freedom in determining whether or not to write a word as a
nomen sacrum (singular for nomina sacra). This serves as an excellent entrée into
the next chapters, where we will explore scribal interaction with the text in light of
the creation of textual variants.

The Nomina Sacra

Anyone who reads the ancient manuscripts of the Greek New Testament is struck
by the phenomenon: the names *kurios* (Lord), *Iēsous* (Jesus), *Christos* (Christ), and *theos*
(God) are written in this unique fashion. These four titles are the primary and most
primitive divine names to be written in a special way; they can be seen in all the earliest Greek manuscripts.[1] Another early divine name written in a special way is *pneuma*
(Spirit); it may be as early as the other four or it could have been developed slightly
later. These specially written names are called nomina sacra, meaning "sacred names"
(the singular is nomen sacrum). The inventor of the term nomina sacra was L. Traube.
After his study on the nomina sacra, the most thorough study was done by
A. H. R. E. Paap.[2]

Scattered across the pages of nearly every extant Greek New Testament manuscript can be seen the following nomina sacra:

$\overline{\text{KC}}$ for κυριος (Kurios) = Lord
$\overline{\text{IH}}$ or $\overline{\text{IHC}}$ for ιησους (Iēsous) = Jesus
$\overline{\text{XP}}$ or $\overline{\text{XC}}$ or $\overline{\text{XPC}}$ for χριστος (Christos) = Christ

$\overline{\Theta C}$ for θεοs (theos) = God

$\overline{\Pi N A}$ for πνευμα (pneuma) = Spirit

By way of example, the reader can look at photos of $\mathfrak{P}^{46}$ and $\mathfrak{P}^{66}$ (on pages 140 and 148) where all five of these sacred names are written in special form.

The earliest Christian writers wrote the nomina sacra in three ways. The first way is called suspension; that is, the first two letters of the name are written and the rest are suspended. This is illustrated by $\overline{IH}$, the first two letters of IHCOYC (Jesus). The second way is called contraction, that is, the first and last letters are written with the in-between letters omitted. This is illustrated by $\overline{IC}$, the first and last letters of ιησουs (Iēsous). The third way is a longer form of contraction, as in $\overline{IHC}$, the first two letters and the last letter of IHCOYC (Iēsous).

After the scribe wrote the suspended or contracted form, he would place an over-bar over the entire name, as in $\overline{IC}$. It is quite likely that the placing of the overbar was a carryover from the way scribes wrote documents; scribes everywhere had a habit of using the overbar to signal an abbreviation. This was especially common for the use of numerals, which would be written as $\overline{IA}$ for eleven, $\overline{IB}$ for twelve, etc. The over-bar stroked above the word was a signal to the reader that the word could not be pro-nounced as written. The reader would have to know what the coded form signified in order to read it correctly.[3] Placing an overbar over the contracted or suspended nomen sacrum also helped the oral reader in working his or her way through *scriptura continuum* (words running into one another, as was common in ancient Greek texts).

The nomina sacra for Lord, Jesus, Christ, God, and Spirit are present in all extant second-century New Testament manuscripts where one or more of these nomina sacra are extant. The following second-century manuscripts that clearly show these nomina sacra are as follows:

$\mathfrak{P}^4+\mathfrak{P}^{64}+\mathfrak{P}^{67}$—Matthew, Luke

$\mathfrak{P}^{32}$—Titus

$\mathfrak{P}^{46}$—Paul's Epistles

$\mathfrak{P}^{66}$—John

$\mathfrak{P}^{75}$—Luke, John

$\mathfrak{P}^{90}$—John[4]

The nomina sacra for Lord, Jesus, God, Christ, and Spirit are also present in all the third-century New Testament manuscripts (where one or more of these names is preserved in the extant text):

$\mathfrak{P}^1$—Matthew

$\mathfrak{P}^5$—John

$\mathfrak{P}^9$—1 John

$\mathfrak{P}^{12}$—Hebrews

$\mathfrak{P}^{13}$—Hebrews

$\mathfrak{P}^{15}+\mathfrak{P}^{16}$—1 Corinthians, Philippians

𝔓¹⁷—Hebrews

𝔓¹⁸—Revelation

𝔓²⁰—James

𝔓²¹—Matthew

𝔓²²—John

𝔓²³(*vid*)—James

𝔓²⁴—Revelation

𝔓²⁷—Romans

𝔓²⁹—John

𝔓²⁹—Acts

𝔓³⁰—1 Thessalonians

𝔓³⁵—Matthew

𝔓³⁷—Matthew

𝔓³⁸—Acts

𝔓³⁹—John

𝔓⁴⁰—Romans

𝔓⁴⁵—Gospels, Acts

𝔓⁴⁷—Revelation

𝔓⁴⁸—Acts

𝔓⁴⁹+𝔓⁶⁵—Ephesians, 1 Thessalonians

𝔓⁵⁰—Acts

𝔓⁵³—Matthew

𝔓⁶⁹—Luke

𝔓⁷⁰(*vid*)—Matthew

𝔓⁷⁸—Jude

𝔓⁸⁰(*vid*)—John

𝔓⁸⁶—Matthew

𝔓⁹¹—Acts

𝔓⁹²—1 and 2 Thessalonians

𝔓¹⁰⁰—James

𝔓¹⁰¹—Matthew

𝔓¹⁰⁶—John

𝔓¹⁰⁸—John

𝔓¹¹⁰—Matthew

𝔓¹¹¹—Luke

𝔓¹¹³—Romans

𝔓¹¹⁴—Hebrews

𝔓¹¹⁵—Revelation

0162—John

0171—Matthew, Luke

0189—Acts

0220—Romans[5]

The nomina sacra are also present in Greek Old Testament manuscripts and other Christian writings produced by Christians. This includes several second-century manuscripts noted below:

P. Chester Beatty VI, Numbers, Deuteronomy

P. Baden 4.56 (P. Heidelberg inv. 8), Exodus and Deuteronomy

P. Antinoopolis 7, Psalms

PSI 921, Psalms

P. Oxyrhynchus 1074, Exodus

P. Chester Beatty Papyrus VIII, Jeremiah

P. Chester Beatty Papyrus IX, Ezekiel, Daniel, Esther[6]

Other Christian writings also use nomina sacra:

P. Geneva 253, Christian homily

P. Egerton 2, Unknown Gospel

P. Oxyrhynchus 405, fragment of Irenaeus

P. Oxyrhynchus 406, Christian homily

One of the main reasons we know that the Old Testament manuscripts are Christian manuscripts and not Jewish is the presence of nomina sacra in the text. Significantly, not one copy of the Greek Old Testament found at Qumran has these nomina sacra because this was a Jewish, not a Christian community. Jews never wrote nomina sacra the way Christians did; the Jews did things differently for one divine name and one divine name only: Yahweh. Jewish scribes would frequently write this in its Hebrew contracted form (even in paleo-Hebrew letters) and then continue on with the Greek text. Christians used KYPIOC (*kurios* = Lord) in place of Yahweh (YHWH) and wrote it in nomen sacrum form. Many Greek Old Testament manuscripts produced by Christians display this nomen sacrum. This can be seen in all six second-century Greek Old Testament manuscripts noted above. (This phenomenon is discussed at length below.)

The earliest copies of the New Testament writings (perhaps some of the autographs themselves) included these specially inscribed forms for the sacred names. These writings made the rounds from church to church and thereby influenced the scribes in each church to write certain divine titles as nomina sacra. Since there was no official rulebook as to the exact form in which the nomina sacra were to be written, there were some slight variations in form. As noted above, some writers and/or scribes used the first letter and last letter of the name; others used the first two letters and the last letter. Thus, for example, XPICTOC (Christ) was written either as $\overline{\text{XP}}$ (a very rare form), $\overline{\text{XPC}}$, or $\overline{\text{XC}}$ (the most common form). In whatever form, XPICTOC (Christ) was always written as a nomen sacrum.

The nomina sacra for Lord, Jesus, Christ, God, and Spirit must have been created in the first century (a phenomenon discussed below at length). As I will argue below, the earliest form seems to have been a contraction of Lord (KΥPIOC, *kurios*), written as $\overline{KC}$. The next name to have been written as a nomen sacrum was Jesus (IHCOΥC, *Iēsous*), written as $\overline{IH}$ or $\overline{IC}$ or $\overline{IHC}$. The contracted form for Christ (XPICTOC) was early (probably the earliest); it was maintained in most manuscripts in the form $\overline{XC}$. A longer form of contraction was also used: $\overline{XPC}$. Only two manuscripts display the suspended form, $\overline{XP}$—$\mathfrak{P}^{18}$ (Rev. 1:5) and $\mathfrak{P}^{45}$ (one time; Acts 16:18). The title "God" was contracted as $\overline{\ThetaC}$ from earliest times and remained constant thereafter.

It is difficult to say whether the nomina sacra were first written with the suspended form and then later with the contracted form, or vice versa. In arguing for the suspended form, it could be said that several early manuscripts show the suspended form. However, one of the earliest Christian manuscripts, P. Chester Beatty VI, shows the contracted form, as do several other early Christian manuscripts. The suspended form of abbreviation was very common in both documentary and literary works from the first century BC on into the second century AD. McNamee wrote, "Methods of abbreviation throughout [this] period covered are the same in literary as in documentary papyri. The most common means was suspension, in which one or more letters were omitted from the end of a word."[7]

If the prevailing practice of suspended abbreviations in the papyri was a primary influence on the formation of the Christian nomina sacra, then the suspended forms came first. If so, it is possible that scribes found these to be impracticable from a grammatical perspective inasmuch as the suspensed form could not denote grammatical function. As such, the suspended form $\overline{IH}$ may have been elongated to $\overline{IHC}$ (nominative), $\overline{IHΥ}$ (genitive), and $\overline{IHN}$ (accusative), thereby creating a contracted form. However, this phenomenon can be argued only for "Jesus." None of the other divine names went in this direction orthographically.

It could be argued that the contracted form (which allows for grammatical denotation from the onset) was primary—written either in short form (using the first letter and last) or longer form (using the first two letters and last). The contracted form was also used for abbreviations in the hellenistic writings of the first century AD, though not as extensively as the suspended form. Certain Christian scribes could have emulated this practice from the contemporary literature. Or, more likely, the contracted form could have been modeled after the Hebrew Tetragrammaton, YHWH. Since the contracted form is the prevailing form for all the primary nomina sacra (only "Jesus" and "Christ" appear in suspended form), it stands to reason that this form was primary and the suspended secondary. But I cannot be dogmatic about this.

A few other terms may have been written as nomina sacra in the original writings or, at least, in the very earliest copies the Greek words for "cross" (*stauros*) and "crucify" (*stauromai*) were written as nomina sacra. I say this because these words were written as nomina sacra in the earliest New Testament manuscripts ($\mathfrak{P}^{45}$, $\mathfrak{P}^{46}$, $\mathfrak{P}^{47}$, $\mathfrak{P}^{66}$, $\mathfrak{P}^{75}$). In due course two other divine names began to appear as nomina sacra: Father and Son. "Father" was contracted by using the first letter and last letter of ΠΑΤΗΡ as $\overline{\text{ΠΡ}}$, and Son (ΥΙΟC) was contracted as $\overline{\text{ΥC}}$. These two divine names were sometimes written out in full (*plene*) and sometimes written as nomina sacra in the early manuscripts. And sometimes there was discrepancy within the same manuscript. Thus, we can tell that these two titles were probably not written as nomina sacra in the original manuscripts but were a later development. Beginning in the second and third centuries some other titles were treated as nomina sacra—namely, "Son of Man," "Israel," "Jerusalem," and "Christian." In the fourth century, a few manuscripts (such as the well-known Codex Sinaiticus) display "mother," "David," and "Savior" as nomina sacra. Most of these will be discussed later.

As noted before, it is easy to spot any of the nomina sacra on the page of a Greek New Testament manuscript (see on pages 140 and 148) or a Christian Greek Old Testament manuscript (see photo of Ezekiel on p. 173) by looking for the overbars. The special written forms of the nomina sacra would not be enigmatic to Christian readers; they could easily decipher them. In fact, these forms would heighten their importance in the text and prompt the readers (lectors) to give them special attention when reading the text aloud to the congregation.

Making a name a nomen sacrum desecularized the term, lifting it to sacred status. For example, scribes could differentiate between "the Lord" and "lord"/"sir"/"master" by writing $\overline{\text{KC}}$ or ΚΥΡΙΟC (*plene*), and they could distinguish between "Spirit" (the divine Spirit) and "spirit" (the human spirit) by writing the first as a nomen sacrum and any other kind of spirit as *pneuma* (in *plene*). The term *pneuma* in ordinary, secular Greek meant "wind," "breath," or "spirit." Writing it as a nomen sacrum signaled that this was the divine Spirit. Scribes also uplifted the ordinary terms "cross" and "crucify" by making them nomina sacra. In this written form, they signaled Jesus' cross and crucifixion, the means by which all Christians are saved from sin.

The early Christian writers (and/or compilers of the first authoritative copies of the Scriptures) chose not to use a nomen sacrum for "Savior" in New Testament texts. This is puzzling, especially since the Greek term for "Savior" (*sōtēr*) was used for military heroes and Caesars. *The Greek-English Lexicon of the New Testament* (BAGD, 801) says that the term was "applied to personalities who [were] active in the world's affairs, in order to remove them from the ranks of ordinary humankind and place them in a significantly higher position. So it is when Epicurus is called *sōtēr* by his followers. . . . Of much greater import is the designation of the (deified) ruler as *sōtēr* (such as Ptolemy) and often in later times of the Roman emperors as well." I would think that Christians would have wanted to make *sōtēr* a nomen sacrum so as to differentiate Jesus the Savior from these glorified mortals. However, not one of the earliest New

Testament manuscripts (second and third century) show the title written as a nomen sacrum; it is always written out in *plene*. (This shows, by the way, that the nomina sacra were not created by the whims and vagaries of individual scribes.) Sometime in the first century, someone (or some group) created a system that was followed thereafter.

Two early Christian writings may have a nomen sacrum for "Savior." The first is P. Geneva 253, a theological homily dated to the end of the second century. The editor of this papyrus, Jean Rudhardt, reconstructed the manuscript to show *sōtēros* (the genitive of *sōtēr*) written twice as a nomen sacrum in the form $\overline{CC}$. My own examination of the photographs gives me pause about these two identifications. The first occurrence of the nomen sacrum is broken for the first letter and could just as likely be a nomen sacrum for *theos* or even *kurios*. As for the second occurrence, the first letter looks much closer to being a theta than a sigma; if so, the nomen sacrum is for *theos*. Another noncanonical manuscript, P. Oxyrhynchus 840 (fourth century), unquestionably has a nomen sacrum for "Savior."

I would conjecture that *sōtēr* was not made a nomen sacrum in New Testament manuscripts because it could be confused with *stauros* (cross) in various grammatical, written forms, when written as a nomen sacrum. To be specific, the genitive form of *sōtēr*, *sōtēros* could be written as $\overline{CTPC}$ in shortened form. But this could be mixed up with the nominative form of *stauros* (cross), which is also written the same. (See 1 Cor. 1:17 in $\mathfrak{P}^{46}$ for the nominative form of *stauros* written as $\overline{CTPC}$.) Since *stauros* was one of the principal nomen sacrum for Christians, it took precedence over *sōtēr*. Thus, not one extant canonical New Testament manuscript has a nomen sacrum for "Savior."

One other significant title was excluded from the canon of nomina sacra— namely, "King." In not one canonical New Testament manuscript is "King" (*basileūs*) ever written as a nomen sacrum. The noncanonical Gospel fragment, P. Egerton 2, has one instance of "King" written as a nomen sacrum, and so does, perhaps, one fourth-century liturgical work (P. Oxyrhynchus 2068).

The inclusion of certain titles and exclusion of others is significant, for it shows that there was some kind of universal recognition among Christian scribes as to which terms were to be written as a nomen sacrum and which ones were not. This points to an early standard or what could be called an early canon for acceptable and non-acceptable nomina sacra.

When one studies the extant Christian manuscripts, a general chronological evolution of which names were written as nomina sacra and which were not emerges. First, the name *Kurios* (Lord) was chosen and/or *Iēsous* (Jesus). These two were soon followed by *Christos* (Christ), *theos* (God), and *pneuma* (Spirit). These five were primary nomina sacra by the beginning of the second century. The noun for "cross" and the verb for "crucify" were also dignified as nomina sacra by the beginning of the second century. From the beginning of the second century and into the third, other names were experimented with: *anthropos* (man), *Patēr* (Father), *Huios* (Son),

Ierousalem (Jerusalem), *Israēl* (Israel), and *ouranos* (heaven). Some scribes treated them as a nomen sacrum; others did not. Some scribes in the same manuscript treated them both as nomina sacra and not as such. By the time we get to the fourth century, some experimentation is still going on (as in Codex Sinaiticus), but—for the most part—there seems to be a conscious effort to limit the nomina sacra to Lord, Jesus, Christ, and God, as in Codex Vaticanus.

The Origin of the Nomina Sacra

Thus far, we have been exploring the earliest names that Christians chose to designate as nomina sacra. We have also been looking at the various forms in which they were written, as well as the various manuscripts in which they appear. Throughout the course of this discussion, one could not help asking how the nomina sacra were created—why and when? The answers are close within grasp but still evanescent. We have several clues, but definitive proof eludes us. Nonetheless, the origin of the New Testament nomina sacra is well worth exploring.

In my estimation, the nomina sacra originated for one of two reasons: (1) a scribe or scribes (whether Jewish Christian or Gentile Christian) created a nomen sacrum form for *kurios* (Lord), reflecting knowledge of and purposeful distinction from the Hebrew Tetragrammaton, YHWH; or (2) a scribe or scribes (whether Jewish Christian or Gentile Christian) created a nomen sacrum form for *kurios* (Lord), reflecting knowledge of and purposeful distinction from the presence of *kurios* in hellenistic literature as describing a particular god or Ceasar. In the second option, the creation of the nomen sacrum could have also been for *theos* for the same reasons. Let's explore both options.

Kurios ($\overline{KC}$) in Relation to the Hebrew Tetragrammaton, YHWH

The Scriptures make clear that the name and person of God are inseparably related, in keeping with the biblical concept of what a name signifies. In the Hebrew language, the term for "name" most probably meant "sign" or "distinctive mark." In the Greek language, "name" (*onoma*) is derived from a verb that means "to know." A name, therefore, indicates that by which a person or thing is known. In biblical times, names were given in order to express something about a person or to express something through him, and not simply to hang a convenient label around his or her neck. Names were given to reveal the nature of the person, his function, or some other significant thing about him. A prime example of this is the name Jesus (Matt. 1:21), meaning "Yahweh the Savior" or "Yahweh saves," for his mission was to save the world from sin.

The Jews have always had great respect for the name of God, and so have Christians. Both revere the same God, but they know him by different names; this means they recognize different revelations of his person. The Jews call God by the names *El, Elohim, and Adonai*. And above all, they recognize God as Yahweh, the I AM

WHO I AM, but they dare not utter this name or even write it in full. The Christians recognize God as Creator, Lord, and Father. And above all, they recognize God as Jesus. This is where Jews and Christians divide. The Jews believe that Yahweh has always been the eternal, divine, transcendent God. Christians believe that Yahweh became incarnate; he is Jesus (Yahweh the Savior), the Christ, the Son of God, even God himself. The same reverential respect that Jews give to Yahweh, Christians give to Jesus. Christians, however, take great delight in uttering his name. Just read the New Testament, and you will see how often the early Christians called upon the name of Jesus.

The early Christians proclaimed Jesus' name, preached his name, and healed the sick by the power of his name (see Acts 4:7–18; 8:12; 9:28). They were willing to suffer for his name (see Acts 5:28, 40; 15:26) and even die for his name (see Acts 21:13). Often the New Testament writers didn't even need to identify his name. Rather, they would simply say "the Name," and every Christian reader would know whose name they meant—the name, Jesus Christ (see Acts 5:31; Heb. 1:4; 6:10; 13:15; James 2:7; 1 John 2:12; 3 John 7).

To the Jews, one name and one name only was sacred: Yahweh. This name was so sacred to them that they refused to utter it or even spell it out in full when they made copies of Scripture. So, they wrote it in a special way—as the Tetragrammaton, YHWH in archaic Hebrew script. To the Christians, the primary names and titles of Jesus were sacred. This included his personal name, "Jesus"; his primary title, "the Christ"; his sovereign identity, "the Lord"; and his divine identity, "God." The earliest believers also considered another title to be sacred, "the Spirit," because this Spirit was none other than the Spirit of Jesus Christ. Unlike the Jews, the earliest Christians did not refrain from uttering these names. However, like the Jews, they chose to write them in a very special way when these names were used in Scriptures. It is quite likely that the Christian use of the nomina sacra was directly related to the Jews' creation of the Tetragrammaton, YHWH, for Yahweh; and in this regard, it is very likely that the first of the nomina sacra was $\overline{\text{KC}}$ for *kurios* (Lord).

In the Hebrew language, four consonants יהוה—YHWH, pronounced "Yahweh," represent what the Bible identifies as the essential name of God. These four consonants of God's name are called the Tetragrammaton or Tetragram (from the Greek *tetra*, "four," and *gramma*, "a letter of the alphabet"). These letters are the Hebrew equivalents of English Y (or J), H, W, and H. The most widely accepted meaning of the name is "the one who is, that is, the absolute and unchangeable one."[8] By this name God made himself known to Moses at the burning bush (Exod. 3:14). Unlike the general Old Testament word for God (*elohim*), this essential name conveys a dynamic personality. In Exodus 3:14 God tells Moses, "I am who I am." This is not merely the equivalent of the English "I am he who is." Rather, the words denote one whose absolute uniqueness requires his defining himself by himself. The expression conveys the sense of a vitally real being, as if God had said to Moses, "I really am!"

Another meaning of the name is that of a creative, redeeming Savior. The Hebrew verb "to be" does not simply speak of static existence; rather, it shows a personal presence involved with a people's need for deliverance. The God of Israel saw his people's afflictions and acted on their behalf to give them freedom. The verbs used in conjunction with the Tetragrammaton are dynamic, never static. In the encounter at the bush, Moses learned that his God was really present to help. Some have therefore suggested that Exodus 3:14 be translated, "I-Am-Present is what I am."[9] This name—the name YHWH—appears in the Ten Commandments. The Jews were explicitly commanded not to take this name in vain (Exod. 20:2, 7). There is also a stern prohibition in Leviticus 24:16, "He that names the name of Yahweh shall surely be put to death." This warning against a vain or blasphemous use of the name was taken in an absolute sense, especially after Israel's deportation to Babylon—a punishment for their idolatry (Amos 6:10). Consequently, when reading the Old Testament, the Jews substituted Adonai ("Lord") for Yahweh. Thus, the Jews completely avoided uttering his name by always saying Adonai in place of the Tetragrammaton, YHWH.

In the written Hebrew text, however, the name remained written as YHWH. Jewish scribes, from ancient times, took great care in writing this sacred name in just this way. Generation after generation of Jewish scribes even formed the letters exactly the same—in paleo-Hebrew script—even when the rest of Hebrew handwriting changed throughout the ages. They believed that the ancient formation of the letters dated to the time when Moses himself first wrote them. Several of the Dead Sea Scroll manuscripts (produced between the first century BC and the first century AD) show the paleo-Hebrew script for the Tetragrammaton. For example, this ancient form can be seen in the manuscript 1QpHabakkuk.

When the Jews started to translate the Hebrew Scriptures into Greek, they persisted in using the Hebrew Tetragrammaton wherever the name Yahweh appeared. This means that the Jewish scribe switched from Greek to Hebrew whenever he came to the sacred name, and then he would write it in an allotted space from right to left (as is done in writing Hebrew). This can be seen, for example, in P. Oxyrhynchus 3522 (first century AD), which preserves a portion of Job (42:11–12). The scribe wrote first in Greek, then in Hebrew, when he copied the divine name. In the space alloted, he wrote from right to left, fitting in the Tetragrammaton (in paleo-Hebrew script) between the Greek words. It can also be seen in the Habakkuk manuscript from Kirbet Mird, as well as in the Greek Minor Prophets Scroll from Nahal Hever (8HevXIIgr). Scribes purposely left a space open for the Tetragrammaton and then filled it in with the Tetragrammaton in paleo-Hebrew letters. In Papyrus Fouad 266 (Deuteronomy, first century BC), the Greek scribe left open large spaces for the Tetragrammaton, each of which is indicated by a raised dot on each side of the space. The Tetragrammaton YHWH was added later (perhaps by a different scribe).

According to Origen (in his commentary *On Psalms*, 2:2), the Tetragrammaton was still written in paleo-Hebrew letters in Aquila's Greek translation of the Old Testament, produced in the first or second century AD. It is also likely that the original translators of the Septuagint used the Hebrew Tetragrammaton for YHWH, although later copies of the Septuagint show that scribes started to use *kurios* (Lord) as a surrogate. We know that Jews substituted Adonai (meaning "Lord") for YHWH when they read the Tetragrammaton in the Hebrew text. It is also likely that they substituted *kurios* (the Greek form for "Lord"—*kurios*) when they were reading the Greek text to a Greek-speaking audience. Origen (in his commentary on *Psalms* 2:2) tells us of both practices. Examples of *kurios* used for Yahweh can be found in the writings of Philo and in the Wisdom of Solomon (see 1:1, 7, 9; 2:13). Josephus remarked that the early Jews refused to call the emperor *kurios* because they regarded it as a name reserved for God (*Jewish War* 7.10.1).

In short, Greek-speaking Jews both wrote and spoke *kurios* in place of YHWH. As such, the written name *kurios* took on a whole new aura of significance. When Jews became Christians, they heard and/or read *kurios* in Old Testament texts, knowing that it was a substitute for YHWH, a special graphic form for the divine name. Knowing this, it could have dawned on some early Jewish-Christian scribe and/or a Gentile Christian scribe familiar with the special orthography, while making a copy of an Old Testament Greek text or putting together several Old Testament messianic proof texts (called "testimonia"), to come up with a special way of writing the divine name *kurios* in Greek. The result was $\overline{KC}$, a contracted form, using the first and last letters of *kurios*.

Interestingly, a transitional stage—between writing YHWH and $\overline{KC}$—can be witnessed in P. Oxyrhynchus 656 (Genesis). (Though this codex is dated to the second century AD, it probably reflects earlier practice.) In any event, the original scribe left a four-letter space open in four occurrences where the name "Lord" would appear, presumably for someone else to fill in the Tetragrammaton in Hebrew. But it was not filled in with the Tetragrammaton. Instead, the divine name was squeezed in by another scribe with the name $K\Upsilon PIOC$. Evidently, there was no one qualified to fill in the space with the archaic-Hebrew form, so it was filled in with the Greek surrogate.

The question remains: who produced this manuscript? A Jew or a Christian? If this manuscript had been produced by a Christian, we would expect to see a nomen sacrum here—namely, $\overline{KC}$. But if the manuscript was produced by a Jew, we would expect to see it in scroll form, not codex.[10] Either way, the manuscript could give us a glimpse as to how the nomen sacrum for *kurios* may have been originally created—even a century earlier.

One probable scenario is as follows: A certain Greek-speaking Christian (perhaps formerly a Jew) copied a Greek Old Testament text and left open four letter spaces, where appropriate, for someone else (presumably knowledgeable in Hebrew) to fill it in with the well-established Hebrew Tetragrammaton. Another Greek-speaking Christian came along and decided to use a different form for this name—one distinct from the Hebrew Tetragrammaton—when he filled in the name for the Lord. Instead of using YHWH, or even squeezing in KΥΡΙΟϹ (as did the second scribe for P. Oxyrhynchus 656), he wrote the nomen sacrum: K̄C̄.

Harry Gamble, following G. Howard, reconstructed a similar scenario for the creation of the nomina sacra:

> The ability to set off the divine name in Christian manuscripts of Septuagintal texts, not by continuing to write it in Hebrew as Jews did but in some other way, must have occurred early to Greek-speaking Christian scribes copying Jewish manuscripts. The contracted forms of *theos* and *kyrios* probably derive, as G. Howard supposes, from Gentile Christians who, lacking the support of the Jewish tradition for retaining the Tetragram in (Greek) Christian copies of Jewish texts, adopted instead clearly designated contractions of Greek equivalents "out of deference to the Jewish Christians, to mark the sacredness of the divine name which stood behind these surrogates." The principle, used at first with respect to texts of Jewish scripture, would have been extended under christological warrants to the further names, Jesus and Christ, in Christian documents.[11]

It must be kept in mind that Christians (whether Jews or Gentiles) would have first used the nomina sacra in Greek Old Testament texts, and then transferred this practice to New Testament manuscripts. These Old Testament writings could have been books of the Old Testament with continuous text (i.e., all of Exodus or all of the Psalms). It is also possible that these Old Testament writings were collections of testimonia—i.e., excerpts of Old Testament passages (with commentary) that Christians compiled as proof texts for Christian claims and that the early Christian writers used for providing quotations in their writings, such as we see in Matthew's Gospel.

We know that the Jews at Qumran assembled collections of texts with messianic implications. This can be seen in 4QTestimonia (a compilation of five scriptural texts with messianic significance—namely, Deut. 5:28; 18:18–19; Num. 24:15–17; Deut. 33:8–11; Josh. 6:26) and perhaps 4QFlorilegium (having three texts concerning eschatological figures—as found in 2 Sam. 7:10–14; Psalm 1:1; Psalm 2). As to collections produced by Christians, one clear example is P. Rylands Greek 460, which C. H. Roberts (the editor of the *editio principes*) regarded as preserving portions of a Christian book of testimonia—namely, Isaiah 42:3–4; 66:18–19; 52:15; 53:1–3, 6–7, 11–12 (an unknown verse); Genesis 26:13–14; 2 Chronicles 1:12; Deuteronomy 29:8–11.[12]

It is very likely that these kinds of testimonia books, existing in the very earliest years of the Christian church, aided the believers by providing a collection of Old Testament prophecies that were used to prove Jesus was the Messiah. These would have been the earliest written documents that the church would use both in preaching the gospel and in writing the New Testament Scriptures. As such, if the nomina sacra for "Lord" (and perhaps "God") were introduced in this early stage of Christian writings (that is, in the Old Testament quotations, $\overline{KC}$ would replace YHWH), then it would stand to reason that it would be carried over into the Gospel texts by the original writers. As for now, the earliest extant testimony for the nomina sacra does not come from the Testimonia but from continuous Old Testament texts—namely P. Chester Beatty VI (dated 100–120) and P. Baden IV. 56 (early second century)—and from the earliest New Testament manuscripts—such as $\mathfrak{P}^{4+64+67}$ (150–175) and $\mathfrak{P}^{66}$ (mid-second century, which happens to share most of the same nomina sacra forms as Chester Beatty VI).[13]

Regardless of whether the nomina sacra were invented in the testimonia stage or in early Christian Greek Old Testament manuscripts (i.e., first century), the significance is that they may have existed in written form before the Gospels and Epistles were written. As such, some of the New Testament writers themselves could have adopted these forms when they wrote their books. The presence of the nomina sacra in all the earliest extant Christian manuscripts (both of the Old Testament and the New), dating from the early second century, necessitates that it was a widespread practice established much earlier. If we can place the origin of that practice to the autographs and/or early publications of the New Testament writings, it explains the universal proliferation thereafter.

In conclusion, it must be noted that though inspired by the Tetragrammaton, the written form of the Christian nomen sacrum for "Lord" was a unique creation. Nowhere did the Jews use an overbar for the sacred name.[14] And in no way did the Christian writers simply imitate the consonantal form of YHWH; otherwise, they would have written $\overline{KPC}$. However, not one early Greek Christian manuscript has the name written in this way; all manuscripts exhibit the two-letter $\overline{KC}$ (see discussion below under "Lord").

Reaction to the Hellenistic Deification of the Caesars

We should consider one more possibility for the creation of the nomina sacra for *kurios* (Lord) and/or *theos* (God). It is possible that Gentile Christians and/or Jewish Christians wanted to distinguish the "Lord" Jesus from "Lord" Caesar or from the various gods known as "Lord," and therefore invented a nomen sacrum for *kurios*. The same can be said for *theos* (God). Pagan deities were also called "Lord" (such as "Lord Osiris" and "Lord Sarapis"). Thus, a good way to distinguish Jesus from these pagan lords was to write *kurios* as a nomen sacrum.

Even more so, "Lord" and "God" were titles claimed by the Caesars. Roman generals and emperors assumed godhood as soon as they penetrated Asia Minor, especially after Augustus Caesar came to full power (27 BC). Augustus saw his reign as the inauguration of a new age of peace for Rome and the world. The Romans acclaimed him as "savior." In Antioch, coins depicted Augustus as the incarnate Zeus or "worship-worthy Son of God," and altars were erected in his honor. After his death, temples were built in his honor, and the symbols of divinity were transferred to succeeding emperors.

Gaius Caesar, nicknamed Caligula (AD 37–41), was the first emperor to be wor-shipped in Rome during his own lifetime. On hearing of a dispute between Jews and Gentiles over worshipping him in Jamnia, he ordered a statue of himself placed in the temple in Jerusalem. His plan, which would have caused a major revolt among the Jews, was averted only by the intercession of Herod Agrippa I. Under the succeeding emperors, Claudius (AD 41–54) and Nero (AD 54–68), the cult reached ridiculous extremes. Domitian (AD 81–96) also decreed that he should be worshipped as "our Lord and God" (*Dominus et deus noster*).

The divine titles, as associated with the caesars, fill the pages of ancient docu-ments. The papyri of the first and second centuries, for example, attribute the titles *kurios* (Lord) and *theos* (God/god) to the various caesars. It could have occurred to some scribe (or group of scribes) familiar with these writings that these titles, when ascribed to God the Father and God the Son, should be written in a way that distin-guishes them from common use, so that the true God and Lord would be distinguished from the caesars. Hence, the invention of the nomen sacrum for *kurios* and *theos*, which was then extended to *Iēsous* and *Christos*.

Other Views

Before we conclude this section on the origin of the nomina sacra, we need to consider the views of the eminent papyrologist, C. H. Roberts. He believed the nom-ina sacra were created before AD 70 and could even be concurrent with the apostolic writings themselves. More specifically, he conjectured that the nomina sacra were the creation of an influential church center in the first century. This church center would have introduced the primary nomina sacra into various New Testament books soon after they were written and early in the publishing/distribution process. In *Manuscript, Society and Belief in Early Christian Egypt*, Roberts made an argument for that church to be Jerusalem. I quote him at length:

> The system of nomina sacra presupposes a degree of control and organiza-tion; the Jewish tradition of the synagogue lector, the great care taken in writing and preserving the rolls of the Law, the institution of the Geniza, if carried over in a modified form to Jewish Christianity, would explain much about our earli-est Christian manuscripts from Egypt.
>
> Seen in this perspective the nomina sacra may be plausibly viewed as the creation of the primitive Christian community, representing what might be regarded as the embryonic creed of the first Church; the four primary terms [Jesus, Christ, Lord, God] . . . together with *patēr*, *stauros*, and *pneuma* represent

the beliefs common to all Christians, some of the others [Israel, Jerusalem] the particular Jewish strain in the Jerusalem church.

That the nomina sacra are found in our earliest papyri suggests that the form of belief they enshrine, contrasting in some respects with Pauline Christianity, persisted in Alexandria well after AD 70. They would thus belong to the oldest stratum of the Christian faith and may well be contemporary with the first authorized or authoritative Christian writing. The establishment of the practice would not have been left to the whims of a single community, still less to that of an individual scribe. Everything would fall into place were we to assume that the guidelines for the treatment of the sacred names had been laid down by the Church at Jerusalem, probably before AD 70; they would carry the authority of the leaders of the Church as the first Gospels must have done. The system was too complex for the ordinary scribe to operate without either rules or an authoritative exemplar; otherwise the difficulty of figuring which was secular, which a sacred usage would have been considerable even in a small community.[15]

Historically, the church in Jerusalem, with its Jewish orientation, is known to have been enthralled with the name of Jesus—perhaps as a surrogate for the divine name, Yahweh. Furthermore, it is very likely that the Christian gospel was first taken to Alexandria by Jewish Christians from Palestine. This could help explain why the nomina sacra appear in all the early New Testament papyri discovered in Egypt. But the church center responsible for creating the nomina sacra could just as likely have been Antioch, which had become the center of Christianity for the Greek-speaking population. This is the position stated more recently by C. H. Roberts and by another eminent papyrologist, T. C. Skeat, in *The Birth of the Codex* (published in 1987).[16] However, one need not strenuously argue for Jerusalem over against Antioch or vice versa. Both were in close contact in the first century of the church, and many Jewish Christians fled to Antioch during the fall of Jerusalem in AD 66–70. In any event, Antioch would have been the most likely church center to have produced manuscript copies of both Paul's Epistles and the Gospels for distribution to the other churches. Perhaps influenced by those from the church in Jerusalem, these copies went out (after AD 70) with nomina sacra. This could explain their universal presence in all second-century manuscripts.

At the same time that Jewish Christians fled to Antioch, we can presume that many fled to Alexandria, where there was a large population of Jews. Jewish-Christian scriptoral practices begun in Jerusalem would have carried over to Alexandria, which already had an established reputation for producing manuscripts. Thus, both Antioch and Alexandria were producing New Testament manuscripts with the nomina sacra. Antioch's manuscripts (both of the Greek Old Testament and New Testament) would have naturally traveled to the west—to those churches raised up by the missionary activities having begun in Antioch—as far as to Rome and beyond. Alexandria's output would have gone to the other churches in Egypt, probably North Africa, and to the east. Whatever textual differences eventually developed between the eastern and western texts, the nomina sacra remained fairly constant.

Another explanation is that a group of Christian scribes in Alexandria invented the nomina sacra, first in producing Christian Old Testament manuscripts and in prodicing New Testament manuscripts. Alexandria is known for its production of Greek Old Testament manuscripts, as well as for its universal influence on scribal practices throughout the Greco-Roman world. Christian scribes throughout this world—both in the east and the west—soon saw what the Alexandrians were doing in their Christian manuscripts and then emulated their example.

Of course, all of this is creative reconstructing. None of it can be proven. Nonetheless, we can't let one astounding fact escape our notice: the nomina sacra for "Lord," "Jesus," "Christ," "God," and "Spirit" are present in *all* the earliest copies of the New Testament (and Christian Old Testament), beginning in the second century, thereby pointing to a first-century creation date. This indicates that the New Testament text in its early stages was being copied according to some kind of universal standard. As Roberts said, "The remarkably uniform system of nomina sacra . . . suggests that at an early date there were standard copies of the Christian scriptures."[17]

The Use and Significance of Each Nomen Sacrum

In the rest of this chapter we will look at the nomina sacra individually, noting the written forms of each nomen sacrum, as well as observing how scribes chose, in various instances, whether to use a nomen sacrum form. In other words, scribes sometimes exercised discernment in writing a particular word as a sacred title by making it a nomen sacrum or as a nonsacred (secular) title by not making it a nomen sacrum. In English, translators do the same thing by the use of capitalization or noncapitalization; they can write "Lord" or "lord," "God" or "god," "Spirit" or "spirit."

Lord (KΥPIOC) $\overline{\text{KC}}$

The form of the nomen sacrum for *kurios* (Lord) is consistently written in short contracted form ($\overline{\text{KC}}$) throughout the second and third centuries, as evidenced by the following second-century and third-century New Testament manuscripts: $\mathfrak{P}^1$, $\mathfrak{P}^{4+64+67}$, $\mathfrak{P}^5$, $\mathfrak{P}^9$, $\mathfrak{P}^{13}$, $\mathfrak{P}^{20}$, $\mathfrak{P}^{27}$, $\mathfrak{P}^{30}$, $\mathfrak{P}^{35}$, $\mathfrak{P}^{37}$, $\mathfrak{P}^{38}$, $\mathfrak{P}^{45}$, $\mathfrak{P}^{46}$, $\mathfrak{P}^{47}$, $\mathfrak{P}^{49+65}$, $\mathfrak{P}^{53}$, $\mathfrak{P}^{66}$, $\mathfrak{P}^{72}$, $\mathfrak{P}^{75}$, $\mathfrak{P}^{78}$, $\mathfrak{P}^{91}$, $\mathfrak{P}^{92}$, $\mathfrak{P}^{100}$, 0171, 0189. This is also the case with several Christian Old Testament Greek manuscripts—noting just the second-century documents: P. Chester Beatty VI, Numbers and Deuteronomy; P. Chester Beatty VII, Isaiah; P. Chester Beatty VIII, Jeremiah; P. Baden (4.56), Exodus, Deuteronomy; P. Antinoopolis 1.7: Psalms. And this is also the case with other Christian writings—noting also just the second-century documents: P Geneva 253 (Christian homily), P. Egerton 2 (unknown Gospel).

To name Jesus as "Lord" was no small matter to a Jewish Christian, who would have understood clearly that Yahweh has the same title. Indeed, the title *kurios* appears nearly six thousand times in the Septuagint as a translation of YHWH. The presence of the nomen sacrum $\overline{KC}$ in New Testament writings was a way for Christians to show that the title *kurios*, assigned to Yahweh in the Old Testament, was now ascribed to Jesus. In other words, the nomen sacrum $\overline{KC}$ would signal that Jesus was worthy of as much sacred reverence as was given to Yahweh.

Furthermore, the nomen sacrum for *kurios* (Lord) was created in an era when each caesar was considered to be "Lord." Christians stood alone in calling a man from Nazareth their "Lord." It must have had special significance for readers of the New Testament text; to see $\overline{KC}$ in a line of text was to see a symbol that represented Jesus as Lord. Only those who knew the special written form would know this. Outsiders, picking up a New Testament book, would not immediately understand that $\overline{KC}$ = *kurios*. And even if they eventually figured this out, they would not have appreciated what it meant that "the Lord" = Jesus. I am not saying that the nomina sacra were created to conceal Jesus' identity from outsiders, as if the Christians were trying to hide their beliefs behind some indecipherable code. What I am saying is that the nomina sacra were intended to be understood only by the initiates—i.e., those trained to read and decode the New Testament writings for their congregations.

In writing *kurios* as $\overline{KC}$, the New Testament writers and scribes were signaling that Jesus was the divine Lord, superior to Caesar and any god. Furthermore, the nomen sacrum indicated a distinction between Jesus' lordship and that of others who were masters and landowners, for which the term *kurios* (written in *plene*) was also used. The term *kurie* ("Lord" in the vocative) was also used as a term of respect, much in the same way as we would say "sir." In the Greek language, Jesus was addressed by many people as *kurie*. In some of these instances, we could assume that the speaker was simply being respectful and calling him "sir." For example, when the Samaritan woman addressed Jesus when he was sitting by the well, it is likely that her word *kurie* meant nothing more than "sir" (see John 4:11, 15, 19). In other instances, it is likely that the speaker was thinking that Jesus was "the Lord"—the divine one. This is characteristic of requests made to Jesus for healing, where the speaker addressed him as *kurie*.

With respect to the term *kurios*, various New Testament scribes exercised some discernment in distinguishing a divine title from that which is human. Take, for example, Paul's statement in Romans 14:4, quoted here from the NEB: "Who are you to pass judgement on someone else's servant? Whether he stands or falls is his own Master's business; and stand he will, because his Master has power to enable him to stand." In this version, both occurrences of *kurios* (master/lord) are taken to be divine. However, according to other translations (see NIV, NRSV, NJB), the first *kurios* is taken to denote a human master, and the second to denote the Lord—as in the NIV ("To his own master he stands or falls. And he will stand, for the Lord is able to make him stand"). The difference in interpretation has to do with whether one sees Paul addressing slaves in this portion of Romans or simply Christians in general. Interestingly, the scribe of $\mathfrak{P}^{46}$ made both occurrences of *kurios* nomina sacra, thereby indicating his interpretation that the passage speaks about every Christian's relationship to their Lord.

In other contexts, we get to see the written-out *kurios* (or *kurioi*—the plural) side by side with $\overline{KC}$, the nomen sacrum for "Lord." This occurs in Ephesians 6:4–5, where the Lord Jesus is set in contrast to the many masters or lords (*kurioi*) who own slaves. The same appears in the parallel passage, Colossians 3:24–26. In both passages, the "Lord" is contracted as $\overline{KC}$, whereas the "lords" are written out in full (*plene*) as *kurioi* in $\mathfrak{P}^{46}$. In another instance, the scribe of $\mathfrak{P}^{46}$ distinguished the "lords" from the "Lord" Jesus. In the statement about the many "lords" being superceded by the one Lord, Jesus Christ (1 Cor. 8:5–6), the scribe of $\mathfrak{P}^{46}$ wrote out the word *kurioi* (lords) to indicate these beings were not divine, whereas he wrote the word for "Lord" as $\overline{KC}$ to indicate that this is a divine title of Jesus.

The term *kurios* is used generically in Jesus' statement to his disciples, "a servant is not greater than his lord." In other words, he was speaking of that which characterizes lords or masters; he was not directly referring to himself, though it can be read that way. The scribe of $\mathfrak{P}^{93}$ read it as a generic reference to lordship and therefore did not write *kurios* as a nomen sacrum. The scribe of $\mathfrak{P}^{75}$ exercised some discernment between writing out *kurios* (in *plene*) or making it a sacred title. In the parable of the unjust steward, this man calls his master "lord" (Luke 16:3). The scribe chose to write out the word *kurios* (in *plene*) so as not to denote a divine title. The same thing appears in Luke 16:13, with respect to the statement "no one can serve two lords."

In Acts 25:25–26, Festus speaks of the caesar as "Lord" *(kurios)*. Significantly, in this passage the scribe of Codex Sinaiticus wrote out the name for *kurios* (in *plene*) to distinguish this "lord" from the Lord Jesus, who when he is referred to as "Lord" in 26:15 is designated with the nomen sacrum (as elsewhere throughout Codex Sinaiticus).

Jesus (IHCOYC) $\overline{IH}$, $\overline{IHC}$

As was noted above, the nomen sacrum for *Iēsous* (Jesus) appears in three forms: (1) a suspended form (the first two letters); (2) a short contracted form (the first and last letters); (3) a long contracted form (the first two letters and the last). C. H. Roberts considered that the contracted form and suspended form were both early developments. He said, "It seems that there were two lines of development, the one [the suspended form] owing to something of number symbolism, the other [the contracted form] with perhaps allusion to Alpha and Omega, taking the first and last letters."[18] (The number symbolism is explained below.)

The evidence for the suspended form ($\overline{IH}$) comes from the following manuscripts:

$\mathfrak{P}^{18}$, Revelation (third century)

$\mathfrak{P}^{45}$, Gospels and Acts (early third century) (except in two occurrences)

P. Egerton 2, an unknown Gospel (ca. 150)

0212, Diatessaron (third century)

P. Oxyrhynchus 1224, an unknown Gospel (late third century)

P. Oxyrhynchus 2070, anti-Jewish dialogue (third century)

The earliest witness for the suspended form comes from P. Egerton 2, which H. I. Bell, the well-known paleographer and editor of the *editio princeps*, dated to ca. 150 (a date confirmed by many other paleographers—see discussion in chap. 3). An additional, recently published fragment of this manuscript (P. Köln 255) displays a hook-shaped mark between a double consonant in the word *aneneg'kon*, and this is thought by Turner to be a practice that developed at the end of the second century. Hence, the date has been pushed back by some to ca. 200.[19] However, as I argued before in the previous chapter, the presence of a hook between double consonants does not mean that the date of the Egerton Gospel must now be ca. 200, but that Turner was incorrect in saying that the double hook did not appear until the beginning of the third century. Turner's theory needs to be revised, not the date of the Egerton Gospel.

The short contracted form of the name "Jesus" ($\overline{\text{IC}}$) is present in the following early manuscripts:

$\mathfrak{P}^1$, Matthew (early third)

$\mathfrak{P}^{4+64+67}$, Luke and Matthew (middle to late second)

$\mathfrak{P}^5$, John (third)

$\mathfrak{P}^{13}$, Hebrews (early third)

$\mathfrak{P}^{15} + \mathfrak{P}^{16}$, 1 Corinthians and Philippians (late third)

$\mathfrak{P}^{29}$, John (early third)

$\mathfrak{P}^{47}$, Revelation (third)

$\mathfrak{P}^{49+65}$, Ephesians and Thessalonians (third)

$\mathfrak{P}^{66}$, John (middle to late second)

$\mathfrak{P}^{75}$, Luke and John (late second)—primarily the short contracted form, occasionally the long contracted form (described below)

0220, Romans (late third)

P. Chester Beatty VI, Numbers and Deuteronomy (early second century)—primarily the short contracted form, occasionally the long contracted form (described below)

P. Egerton 3, Gospel Commentary (early third)

P. Rylands III 469, Christian Treatise (third)

P. Oxyrhynchus 5, Shepherd of Hermas (late third)

P. Geneva 253, Christian homily (late second)

Five of these manuscripts date from the second century and several from the early third. Thus, in its earliest form, it is possible that Jesus' name was written in contracted form—as $\overline{\text{IC}}$. This parallels the contracted form for *kurios*, $\overline{\text{KC}}$—most likely the earliest of the nomina sacra and the one name that is never written in any other form. If the contracted form came first, this undermines the theory that the suspended form has priority.

The theory of the priority of the suspended form developed because several scholars think that one Christian in the early second century was aware of the nomen sacrum for Jesus in the form $\overline{IH}$. That Christian was the writer of the so-called *Epistle of Barnabas*, which is actually an anonymous writing composed around AD 120–130.[20] This writer must have known of the nomen sacrum for "Jesus" because he interpreted the 318 servants of Abraham (Gen. 14:14) as pointing to Jesus' death on the cross (see 9:7–8). The only way he could have arrived at this remarkable interpretation is by knowing that the nomina sacra for "Jesus" is $\overline{IH}$. The number 300 is the numerical value of the Greek letter *T*, which is cross-shaped, and 18 is the value of the first two letters of the Greek word for Jesus = $\overline{IH}$. But I think it is unlikely that the writer was clever enough to think that the abstract number "318" symbolized the "cross of Jesus." He was probably prompted by the visual cue of $\overline{TIH}$ in the Greek text of Genesis 14:14. Seeing this, he made an immediate connection to the nomen sacrum for "Jesus," $\overline{IH}$, preceded by the tau, which is in the shape of the cross. This indicates that $\overline{IH}$ must have been a siglum well known to the early Christian community. This is affirmed by the fact that Clement of Alexandria, writing at the end of the second century, also noted the numerical significance of $\overline{IH}$ in the Genesis 14:14 passage (see *Stromata* 6.278–280).[21]

The long contracted form of Jesus' name ($\overline{IHC}$) is found in the following manuscripts:

𝔓[30]*(vid)*, 1 and 2 Thessalonians (third)

𝔓[37], Matthew (third)—with $\overline{IHC\Upsilon}$ once

𝔓[38], Acts (third)

𝔓[39], John (third)

𝔓[45], Gospels and Acts (early third) in two occurrences only

𝔓[46], Paul's Epistles (mid to late second)

𝔓[53], Matthew (third)

𝔓[69], Luke (third)

𝔓[72], 1 and Peter, Jude (late third)

𝔓[75], Luke and John (late second)—occasionally

𝔓[78], Jude (third)

𝔓[90], John (late second)[22]

𝔓[106], John (third)

𝔓[108], John (ca. 200)

𝔓[111], Luke (early third)

0162, John (ca. 300)

0171, Matthew and Luke (ca. 300)

P. Chester Beatty VI, (Num. and Deut., early second)—occasionally

P. Oxyrhynchus 405, Irenaeus's *Against Heresies* (ca. 200)

The long contracted form is found in five manuscripts from the second century and several in the third century. It is possible that this form developed very early, perhaps contemporaneously with the short form or even earlier. The evidence does not clearly indicate which form is earlier. In fact, we see both forms being used in the manuscripts 𝔓⁷⁵ and P. Chester Beatty VI.

I must note that there is no extant evidence that the name "Jesus," when referring to Jesus of Nazareth, was ever written in full (in *plene*) in any New Testament manuscript. C. H. Roberts filled in the lacuna in 𝔓⁵² with the name *Iēsous* (written in *plene*) in John 18:32 and 18:34,[23] but there is no justification from the line lengths of the extant papyrus to fill out the line as such. In fact, a nomen sacrum for "Jesus" is far more suitable for accommodating the line length of 18:32. (John 18:34 cannot be determined inasmuch as it is the last extant line of the papyrus). The editors of 𝔓⁷⁵, Martin and Kasser, reconstructed a line in John 6:11, wherein they wrote out the name *Iēsous* (Jesus) in full. However, a better reconstruction of the lines shows that it should be *artous ho* $\overline{\text{IC}}$.[24]

This foregoing discussion points to one fact: the name "Jesus" was treated as a nomen sacrum very early in the written tradition of the Christian church. Very likely it was the second nomina sacra to be created—following right behind "Lord" (if not concurrent with it). This should not surprise us, because the Messiah's personal name had divine significance from his very inception, and it only grew in significance throughout the course of Jesus' ministry and thereafter in the church. To this day, one need only hear the name "Jesus," and the identity is known. Who else in history is so well known by a single name?

Before the incarnation, Joseph was told by an angel that he should name his son "Jesus" because "he will save his people from their sins" (see Matt. 1:21). This name signifies two important aspects about the Savior: first, it means that he is Yahweh; second, it means that he is the Savior. This is his first name. It is his primary name. He is Jesus; he is Yahweh the Savior.

During his days on earth, Jesus was known by his contemporaries as Jesus of Nazareth. This created problems for Jesus because it was expected that the Messiah should come from Bethlehem, the city of David. Shortly after Jesus began his ministry, a man named Philip told his friend Nathaniel that he had found the Messiah predicted by Moses and the prophets. But when Philip named him "Jesus of Nazareth," Nathaniel retorted, "Can anything good come from Nazareth?" (see John 1:45–46). Moses had written about him in the law (Deut. 18:15–18), and the prophets had foretold his coming. The prophets, however, never said that he would come from Nazareth. The Messiah was to be born in Bethlehem (Micah 5:2). Jesus was, in fact, born in Bethlehem (Matt. 2:1), but his parents had to flee to Egypt and later return to Galilee, where Jesus was raised in the obscure town of Nazareth (Matt. 2:13–23). This gave Jesus the reputation of being a Galilean, specifically a Nazarene from the hill country of Nazareth. This was a cause of stumbling for many Jews, because they could not accept a Messiah who had not come from Bethlehem. And since Jesus never told them this, they continued to believe that he was reared from birth as a Galilean, as a Nazarene.

Throughout his ministry the Jewish leaders refused to believe that Jesus was the Messiah because he was called Jesus of Nazareth. He suffered the opproborium of being known as a Galilean and a Nazarene, not a Judean or a Bethlehemite. One of his greatest sufferings was to be misunderstood as to his true identity. However, Jesus never once discussed his Bethlehemic birth; rather, he always pointed to his divine, heavenly origin. If a person knew the One he came from, he would know that Jesus was the Christ. When Nicodemus tried to defend Jesus before the Sanhedrin, they retorted sarcastically, "Are you from Galilee, too? Look into it, and you will find that a prophet does not come out of Galilee" (John 7:52 NIV). This is as much to say, "If not even a prophet is mentioned in the Scriptures to come from Galilee, how much less the Christ?" So the Pharisees and religious rulers were confident that they could reject Jesus as having any claim to messiahship because of his Galilean origin. But they were wrong on two counts: (1) Jesus had been born in Bethlehem, the city of David (Luke 2:4–11), and therefore had legal claim to the messiahship (Micah 5:2); (2) the Scriptures do speak of the Messiah as a "great light" arising in Galilee (see Isa. 9:1–7; Matt. 4:13–16).

Nevertheless, the stigma "of Nazareth" stuck with Jesus throughout his ministry and throughout the earliest days of the church. The earliest believers had an uphill battle to fight when they began to proclaim their faith in Jesus of Nazareth. They could not tell people to "believe in Jesus"; they had to specify which Jesus they should believe in so as to distinguish him from other people with the same name. In the very first sermon preached by Peter to a multitude of Jews in Jerusalem, Peter told them about Jesus of Nazareth:

> Jesus of Nazareth, a man attested to you by God with deeds of power, wonders, and signs that God did through him among you, as you yourselves know— this man, handed over to you according to the definite plan and foreknowledge of God, you crucified and killed by the hands of those outside the law. . . . This Jesus God raised up, and of that all of us are witnesses . . . Therefore let the entire house of Israel know with certainty that God has made him both Lord and Messiah, this Jesus whom you crucified (Acts 2:22–23, 32, 36 NRSV).

When the apostles preached and performed miracles in Jerusalem, they continued to identify Jesus as "Jesus of Nazareth" (Acts 3:6, 13; 4:10; 6:14). They proclaimed that it was "this Jesus"—this Jesus of Nazareth—who was the Messiah (Acts 5:42). The distinction "of Nazareth" was important because there were many other Jews with the name "Jesus" inasmuch as Jesus was the Greek form of "Joshua"—and Joshua was a very popular name.

The New Testament mentions four other men with that name. The first is Joshua (son of Nun), whose name in Greek is *Iēsous*—the same spelling for "Jesus." He is mentioned in Luke 3:29; Acts 7:45; Hebrews 4:8; Jude 5. The second is Bar-Jesus. He was a Jewish sorcerer, a false prophet who worked with the governor of Paphos on the island of Cyprus (Acts 13:6). Bar-Jesus was also called Elymas, which was his Greek name (Acts 13:8). It was a common practice for Jews with contacts in both cultures to adopt a Greek name. (Elymas is based on an Aramaic word for "strong" and an Arabic word for "wise," which actually means "magician.") The third was a Jewish Christian. He was called "Jesus, named Justus" to distinguish him from Jesus of Nazareth. He sent his greetings to the believers at Colossae in the salutation of Paul's letter to the Colossians (4:11). The fourth is found in certain manuscripts (Codex Koridethi f¹ 700*) of Matthew 27:16–17, where the criminal who was released instead of Jesus is called "Jesus Barabbas." Origen knew of this reading, so it must have been early.[25]

After the years of Jesus' ministry and the early years of the church, there was hardly any more mention of "Jesus of Nazareth" because there was no need to distinguish the Nazarene Jesus from others with that name. For example, in all the New Testament Epistles he is known simply as "Jesus" or "Jesus Christ" or "the Lord Jesus." All the readers, being Christians, knew who was being talked about. By contrast, in the Gospels and Acts it was important to distinguish Jesus of Nazareth, the Messiah, from all others with that name. One clear-cut way to do that was to make "Jesus" a nomen sacrum. This would immediately demarcate and denote "Jesus the Savior." Furthermore, the writing of this name as a nomen sacrum uplifted the name to divine status. He was not just any Jesus; he was Jesus—Yahweh the Savior, God come to earth to save his people from their sins.

Various scribes were careful to distinguish the Lord Jesus from others with that name. For example, the scribe of 𝔓⁴ (ca. 150–175) wrote out (in *plene*) the name for *Iesou* in Luke 3:29 to thereby signify "Joshua," while writing the name of "Jesus" as a nomen sacrum ($\overline{IC}$) in nearby verses (3:21; 4:1). The scribe of 𝔓⁴⁵ (early third century) did not abbreviate "Bar-Jesus" in Acts 13:6, in contrast to his writing a nomen sacrum for "Jesus" in Acts 13:33 (the nearest extant portion in 𝔓⁴⁵ containing the name "Jesus"). The scribes of Codex Sinaiticus and Vaticanus wrote out the name "Jesus" instead of making it a nomen sacrum when transcribing the name "Jesus called Justus" in Colossians 4:11.

In our modern English Bibles, Hebrews 4:8 reads, "If Joshua had given them [Israel] rest, God would not have spoken later about another day." In the Greek text, the word for "Joshua" is exactly the same word as for "Jesus" (*Iēsous*). But scribes had a way of distinguishing "Joshua" from "Jesus" by writing out the first name in full and writing the second name as a nomen sacrum. Interestingly, the early scribes wrote the nomen sacrum for "Jesus" in Hebrews 4:8. This is the case in $\mathfrak{P}^{13}$, $\mathfrak{P}^{46}$, Codex Sinaiticus, and Codex Vaticanus. Why would they do this?

There are two explanations. One, they had become so accustomed to making *Iēsous* a nomen sacrum that they did so automatically in Hebrews 4:8, without thinking to distinguish the Old Testament Joshua from Jesus. The evidence of a Greek Old Testament manuscript from the early second century supports this. The scribe of Chester-Beatty VI (Num.–Deut., dated early second century) used the nomen sacrum form for "Joshua" because, as a Christian scribe, he had become accustomed to writing *Iēsous* (the Greek form for either Joshua or Jesus) as a nomen sacrum. Quite significantly, this shows that the habit of making the name "Jesus" a nomen sacrum must have been in full force before the beginning of the second century.

The other explanation is that some scribes may have considered that "Jesus" (not Joshua) was the subject of the sentence in Hebrews 4:8: "For if Jesus had given them [Israel] rest, God would not have spoken later about another day." We must remember that some of the New Testament writers thought that Jesus Christ (in his preincarnate form) accompanied the children of Israel in their exodus from Egypt to the good land of Canaan. Paul said that "Christ" was the Rock that accompanied the Israelites in their desert journeys (1 Cor. 10:4) and that "Christ" was the one the Israelites constantly "tested" during these times (1 Cor. 10:9, according to the testimony of $\mathfrak{P}^{46}$ D F G 1739 1881 Maj. Old Latin Syriac Coptic). Jude also indicated that it was "Jesus" who saved the people out of the land of Egypt (Jude 5, according to the superior testimony of A B 33 1739 Origen). Thus, the writer of Hebrews may have actually had "Jesus" in mind when he spoke of the One who did not bring the Israelites into their true rest. But it is just as likely that the first option was operative here: the habit of turning every occurrence of *Iēsous* into a nomen sacrum.

Christ (XPICTOC) X̄C̄, X̄P̄C̄, X̄P̄

The divine title *Christos* (Christ) is the Greek translation of the Hebrew *Messiah* (see John 1:41). Both terms come from verbs meaning "to anoint with sacred oil." As titles, they mean "the anointed one." The early Christians wanted to show their reverence for Christ by making this name a nomen sacrum. Thus, this name was written as X̄C̄ (a short contracted form), X̄P̄C̄ (a long contracted form), or X̄P̄ (a rare, suspended form).

The suspended form (X̄P̄) is found in the following early manuscripts:

$\mathfrak{P}^{18}$, Revelation (late third) (also has suspended form for *Iēsous*)

$\mathfrak{P}^{45}$, Gospels and Acts (early third) (also has suspended form for *Iēsous*)

The short contracted form (X̄C̄) is found in the following early manuscripts:

$\mathfrak{P}^{1}$, Matthew (early third)

$\mathfrak{P}^{13}$, Hebrews (third)

$\mathfrak{P}^{15}$+$\mathfrak{P}^{16}$, 1 Corinthians and Philippians (third)

$\mathfrak{P}^{40}$, Romans (third)

$\mathfrak{P}^{46}$, Paul's Epistles (middle to late second), about one-fourth of all occurrences

$\mathfrak{P}^{47}$, Revelation (late third), in some occurrences

$\mathfrak{P}^{49}$+$\mathfrak{P}^{65}$, Ephesians and 1 Thessalonians (both portions of the manuscript show the contracted form)

$\mathfrak{P}^{66}$, John (mid-second)

$\mathfrak{P}^{75}$, Luke and John (late second)

0220, Romans (late third)

P. Oxyrhynchus 405, Irenaeus's *Against Heresies* (ca. 200)

The longer contracted form ($\overline{\text{XPC}}$) is found in the following early manuscripts:

$\mathfrak{P}^{38}$, Acts (third century)

$\mathfrak{P}^{46}$, Paul's Epistles (middle to late second century), about three-fourths of all occurrences

$\mathfrak{P}^{47}$, Revelation (late third), in most occurrences

$\mathfrak{P}^{72}$, 1 and 2 Peter and Jude (ca. 300)

$\mathfrak{P}^{78}$, Jude (ca. 300)

$\mathfrak{P}^{91}$, Acts (third)

$\mathfrak{P}^{92}$, Ephesians and 2 Thessalonians (third)

$\mathfrak{P}^{106}$, John (ca. 200)

What is interesting to note about the nomen sacrum forms for Christ is that scribes would use the same form (whether suspended, contracted, or combined) they used for Jesus. Thus, we see that the scribes of $\mathfrak{P}^{18}$ and $\mathfrak{P}^{45}$ (respectively) used the suspended form for both Jesus and Christ, while the scribes of $\mathfrak{P}^{1}$, $\mathfrak{P}^{13}$, $\mathfrak{P}^{15}$+$\mathfrak{P}^{16}$, $\mathfrak{P}^{49}$+$\mathfrak{P}^{65}$, $\mathfrak{P}^{66}$, and $\mathfrak{P}^{75}$ (primarily) used the short contracted form for both Jesus and Christ, and the scribes of $\mathfrak{P}^{38}$, $\mathfrak{P}^{46}$ (primarily), $\mathfrak{P}^{72}$, $\mathfrak{P}^{78}$, and $\mathfrak{P}^{106}$ used the long contracted form for both Jesus and Christ." (This takes into account all the early manuscripts where both Jesus and Christ are extant.) Significantly, there are no exceptions to this. Even $\mathfrak{P}^{46}$ and $\mathfrak{P}^{75}$ fit the primary pattern. The nomen sacrum form for Jesus used by the scribe of $\mathfrak{P}^{46}$ is the long contracted form, $\overline{\text{IHC}}$; thus, the complimentary form for Christ in $\mathfrak{P}^{46}$ is most often the long contracted form, $\overline{\text{XPC}}$ (in 196 occurrences out of 242, the other 46 occurrences being the short contracted form). The most-used form for Jesus by the scribe of $\mathfrak{P}^{75}$ is the short contracted form, $\overline{\text{IC}}$; thus, the complimentary form for Christ in $\mathfrak{P}^{75}$ is the short contracted form, $\overline{\text{XC}}$.

As noted already, in the New Testament the title Christ is often used in combination with the name Jesus, as Jesus Christ (Matt. 1:1; Mark 1:1; Rom 1:4) and Christ Jesus (Rom. 1:1; 1 Cor. 1:1). It is also used alone as the one favored title for Jesus: the Christ (John 20:31; Rom. 15:3; Heb. 3:6; 5:5; 1 Pet. 1:11, 19). The Gospels portray Jesus as accepting the title and role of the Christ at the time of his anointing, which occurred at his baptism. At this time, he was anointed into the threefold office of prophet, priest, and king. At his baptism by John, Jesus received the outpouring of the Spirit and thereafter was directed by the Spirit throughout his ministry (Matt. 3:16–4:17).

The confession of the disciples voiced by Peter and approved by Jesus is: "You are the Christ, the Son of the living God" (Matt. 16:16). The earliest Christians proclaimed that Jesus was and is the Christ (Acts 2:36; 3:18–20; 9:22; 28:23, 31). This is the earliest (Matt. 16:16) and most basic article of the Christian confession (1 Cor. 1:23; 1 John 5:1); it affirms that Jesus perfectly fulfilled the role of anointed prophet, priest, and king as the servant of God for his people (Luke 7:16, 1 Cor. 15:25; Heb. 7:22–28; Rev. 19:16). The title Christ occurs about 530 times in the New Testament; Paul used the title more than any other writer (about 380 times). Since Paul used this title so profusely in his epistles, which are all dated between AD 49 and 65, it stands to reason that Christ was a very popular title for Jesus in the early years of the church.

Jews were very familiar with the term *Messiah* because of its use in the Old Testament with respect to the anointing of prophets, priests, and kings. And even more so, most Jews were looking for the coming of a specially anointed One, from the line of David, to be their king. But for Gentiles, the term *Messiah* meant little. This was translated into Greek as "the Christ." For example, John in his Gospel gave the Greek translation (Christ) of the Hebrew (Messiah) for the sake of his Gentile readers. When Andrew found Peter his brother, he said, "We have found the Messiah (which is translated Christ)" (1:41).

Many Romans didn't understand what the word *Christ* meant. They thought Jesus was called Chrestus (meaning "useful one"). Chrestus was a common Greek name, especially for slaves, who were "useful" to their owners (see, for example, Suetonius's *Claudius* 25.4). Chrestus also meant "kind one." It could be that this is what the Roman historian Tacitus thought when he called Jesus "Chrestus" in his record of how Nero blamed the Christians for the great fire of Rome in AD 64 and how he persecuted them:

> All human efforts, all the lavish gifts of the emperor, and the propitiations of the gods, did not banish the sinister belief [among the Romans] that the fire was the result of an order [from Nero]. Consequently, to get rid of the report, Nero fastened the guilt and inflicted the most exquisite tortures on a class hated for their abominations (*flagitia*), called Christians by the populace. Chrestus [Christ], from whom the name had its origin, suffered the extreme penalty [crucifixion] during the reign of Tiberius at the hands of one of our procurators, Pontius Pilate, and a deadly superstition, thus checked for the moment, again broke out not only in Judea, the source of the evil, but also in Rome, where all things hideous and shameful from every part of the world meet and become popular. Accordingly, an arrest was first made of all who confessed; then, upon their information, an immense multitude was convicted, not so much of the crime of

arson, as of hatred of the human race. Mockery of every sort was added to their deaths. Covered with the skins of beasts, they were torn by dogs and perished, or nailed to crosses, or were doomed to the flames. These served to illuminate the night when the daylight failed. Nero had thrown open his gardens for the spectacle, and was exhibiting a show in the circus, while he mingled with the people in the dress of a charioteer or drove about in a chariot. Hence, even for criminals who deserved extreme and exemplary punishment, there arose a feeling of compassion; for it was not, as it seemed, for the public good, but to glut one man's cruelty, that they were being destroyed. (*Annals* 15.44.2–8)

Significantly, this misunderstanding of the name carried over to the Christians, as being called by some *Chrestianous* instead of *Christianous*. In fact, *Chrestianous* was written in place of *Christianous* in all three of its occurrences (Acts 11:26; 26:28; 1 Pet. 4:16) in the first hand of Codex Sinaiticus, which were then corrected. (Codex 81 also has the spelling *Chrestianous* in Acts 11:26.)

Of all the titles ascribed to Jesus, the title "Christ" was the least troublesome to the Romans. They were deeply concerned that Jesus was hailed by some to be a new King (see Matt. 2:1–3; Acts 17:6–7). They were also troubled that he was called Lord, the Son of God, and even God, for these were titles given to the caesars. But they didn't care so much that he was the Christ, for that meant nothing to them.

To the Jews, however, this was probably the most significant title. Anyone who claimed to be "the Messiah" really had to be so; and only one person was truly qualified for that position: Jesus. This is the primary message of his allegory in John 10. Jesus said that the doorkeeper (i.e., God) would open the door to only the legitimate Shepherd (i.e., the Messiah). All others were thieves and robbers because they had to enter some other way. The thieves in Jesus' allegory are probably false messiahs. The Greek word for thieves (*lestes*) was used of revolutionaries in Jesus' day. The Messiah was supposed to be a revolutionary leader, according to popular opinion. Many such revolutionaries came on the scene, pretending (or hoping) to be Israel's Messiah (see John 10:7). But all who came as such were pretenders; the sheep (i.e., the true believers) never followed them. Jesus warned his disciples and others against false messiahs; he said that they would come "in my name, saying, 'I am the Messiah' (Matt. 24:5). In other words, they would come pretending to be the Messiah. But only one person was worthy of the name, "Messiah" or Christ"—Jesus of Nazareth.

In connection with making the name Christ a sacred title, the name Christian was also written as a nomen sacrum. In the New Testament, the word *Christian* is found in only three places (Acts 11:26; 26:28; 1 Pet 4:16). In Antioch, where many Gentiles were converted and where missionary work beyond the Jewish community began in earnest, the believers were no longer considered a Jewish sect, so their Gentile neighbors began calling them by a new name, "Christian." The Christians themselves apparently did not appreciate the name, but, like many other nicknames, "Christian" stuck. Interestingly, the scribe of $\mathfrak{P}^{45}$ used a nomen sacrum form, $\overline{\text{XPANOC}}$, for **XPICTIANOYC** (Χηριστιανους) in Acts 11:26. (By contrast, the scribe of $\mathfrak{P}^{72}$ in 1 Pet. 4:16 did not do so; he wrote out the word in full.)

God (ΘEOC) $\overline{\text{ΘC}}$

The fourth title inscripted as a nomen sacrum is *theos*. In all the earliest manuscripts of the Greek New Testament, the word *theos* is written as a nomen sacrum when the reference is to "God." There is not one New Testament manuscript that I know of where *theos* is written out in full when it designates "God." By contrast, in secular Greek literature, the word *theos* is written out in full; it is not written as a nomen sacrum.[26]

The New Testament writers and scribes distinguished their writings from secular writings and from the Jewish writings by making *theos* a nomen sacrum. All Greek texts of the Old Testament prepared by Jews have the word *theos* written out in full (in *plene*). Papyrus Fouad 266, mentioned before, is a good example. While Yahweh is written as a Tetragrammaton in paleo-Hebrew script, the word for "God" (*theos*) is not contracted.

There is another significant feature worth noting: the nomen sacrum for *theos* was used by all the Christian scribes when the term applied to God the Father *and* when it applied to God the Son. There was no distinction. And why should there be? The New Testament writers unquestionably considered Jesus, the Son of God, to be God. This is explicitly asserted in several passages, many of which are found in John's writings. It is John who tells us that "the Word was God." Not only was the Word with God from eternity, he was himself God from eternity (John 1:1). This is asserted at the beginning of the prologue to John's Gospel and at the end of the prologue (1:18), where the Son is again called the "only God" (*monogenes theos*).[27] In the Gospel narrative, Jesus declares that he existed before Abraham even came into being (8:58), and he asserts that he and the Father are one (10:30)—an assertion that the Jewish leaders undeniably understood as a claim to deity (10:31–33), for they attempted to stone him for blasphemy. At the end of the narrative, Thomas sees the risen Christ, believes in him, and proclaims, "My Lord and my God" (20:28). At the end of John's first epistle, he says that Jesus is "the true God and eternal life."[28]

Paul and Peter also affirm the deity of Jesus, each of them calling him "God." In the book of Romans, Paul praises Jesus Christ, saying, "Christ himself was a Jew as far as human nature is concerned. And he is God, who rules over everything and is worthy of eternal praise! Amen" (9:5 NLT).[29] In Philippians 2:6, Paul says that Jesus Christ was in the very form (or substance) of "God," and in Colossians 1:19 and 2:9 he says that "all God's fullness dwells in him [Christ] bodily." In Titus 2:13, he identifies Jesus as "our God and Savior."[30] Peter also named Jesus as "God and Savior" in 2 Peter 1:1. And in the next verse, he says Jesus is "our God and Lord."[31] In all of the passages just mentioned, the Christian scribes always used the nomen sacrum form for the term "God."

The Jewish leaders of Jerusalem considered it blasphemous for Jesus to claim equality with God. On more than one occasion, they wanted to stone him for his claims. Jesus told the Jewish leaders, "I and the Father are one" (John 10:30). These leaders immediately understood that he was claiming deity for himself; they wanted to stone him for his blasphemy. How could he, a mere man, make himself God? Jesus argued that it was not blasphemous to call himself the Son of God when, in fact, he was the One whom the Father consecrated and sent into the world. Furthermore, was it not true that other men had been called "gods" in the Scripture? On occasion, God had called the judges of Israel "gods," inasmuch as they were his representatives. In Psalm 82 the supreme God is said to rise in judgment against those whom he calls "gods" (Hebrew, *elohim*), because they had failed to show justice to the helpless and oppressed. These "gods" were those who were the official representatives and com-missioned agents of God. If God called them "gods," why was it blasphemous for Jesus, the One consecrated by the Father and sent into the world, to say, "I am God's Son." The Jews could not argue against this because it stands written in the irrefragable Scriptures (i.e., the Scriptures are an entire entity from which no one can remove any portion). But Jesus was greater than those men who received messages from God, for he himself was the very message from God to men. And whereas they were earthly men selected by God to represent him, the Son of God came from heaven as the con-secrated one, dedicated to do God's will on earth. Jesus was therefore justified in call-ing himself the Son of God, equal with the Father—even though the Jewish leaders considered this blasphemy.

These affirmations of Jesus' deity clearly speak against the modern notion that Jesus never claimed to be God, or even the Son of God. Many moderns say that such acclamations came only from the lips of others, not from Jesus himself. First of all, Jesus did claim to be the I AM. His audience, devout Jews, clearly understood this as a claim to deity because they wanted to stone him, the punishment for blasphemy (see John 8:54–58). Second, he claimed that he was the one who came from heaven and was going back to heaven (see John 3:13; 6:33). Third, he asserted, "I and the Father are one," an assertion his Jewish audience understood to be a claim to deity (see discussion above on John 10). Fourth, the Father himself declared that Jesus was the Son of God (see Matt. 3:17; 17:5—and parallel passages). There is no more profound, authoritative voice than the Father's! Fifth, Jesus never denounced or corrected others who called him the Son of God—or even God himself!

With respect to the use of the nomen sacrum for *theos*, not one of the early Christian manuscripts (second to fourth century) makes a written distinction between the Father being called "God" and the Son being called "God." In other words, in all instances where *theos* is used of deity, whether referring to the Father or to the Son, it is written as a nomen sacrum. This also applies to those passages where exegetes have typically made arguments about articular *theos* meaning "the God" or "God himself," in contrast to anarthrous *theos* meaning "deity" or "divinity." The usual understanding about the use of the article before *theos* is that it designates individuality and divine personality—i.e., it denotes the personhood of God, making it titular. By contrast, the absense of the article before *theos* is supposed to signal divine essence.[32] These distinctions, however, may not have been recognized by the earliest scribes if the writing of the nomen sacrum for God always designated a title, regardless of whether or not it had an article. In other words, it is well worth asking if the nomen sacrum form in and of itself communicated so powerful a signal that the distinctions between anathrous *theos* and arthrous *theos* were subsequently blurred.

Let us take, for example, John 1:1. In the clause "the Word was with God," there is an article before "God" (*ton theon*). Most exegetes understand this as pointing to God the Father. In the next clause, "the Word was God," there is no article before "God." The distinction, though a fine one, is understood by most exegetes to be intended. In the first clause, John could be indicating that the Word (the Son) was with God, the Father; in the second clause, John could be indicating that the Word (the Son) was also deity but not *the* God (i.e., God the Father). Some translators have attempted to bring out these distinctions by rendering the last clause as follows: "The Word dwelt with God, and what God was the Word was" (NEB) or "he was with God, and he was the same as God" (TEV). These renderings show equality of nature, but not equality of person. This is made even more explicit in Moffat's version: "The Logos was with God, the Logos was divine."

I must question if ancient readers interpreted the verse this way, especially when they saw the appearance of the nomen sacrum in both clauses. With or without an article, wouldn't this siglum preeminently signal a personal divine title—just by the way it was written? Wouldn't it signal that the verse is saying that the Word was with THEOS and the Word was THEOS? This is not to say that we should discount the use of the article for exegesis, but it does cause me to wonder if ancient readers of the New Testament text would have made this distinction when they saw a nomen sacrum.

In any event, the New Testament writers and/or earliest scribes made it clear that Jesus was God by self-proclamation and by the proclamation of others. This, of course, greatly agitated the Jewish leaders, who wanted to kill Jesus for blasphemy. The Roman authorities were also disturbed that Jesus was claiming to be the Son of God. The first glimpse we get of this is in Jesus' trial before Pilate, who got extremely agitated when he heard from the Jewish leaders that Jesus claimed to be "the Son of God" (see John 19:7–9). Why was he agitated? Because Romans believed that gods could visit the human race in human form. Pilate did not want to be responsible for convicting and crucifying a god! Amazingly, the Roman centurion in charge of Jesus' crucifixion saw the way Jesus died and then proclaimed, "Truly this man was God's

Son" (Mark 15:39 NRSV). After Jesus' death and resurrection, Jesus' followers had all the reason in the world to proclaim that he was God—who else but God could conquer death? Thus, they attributed to Jesus divine status. When Thomas saw the risen Jesus, he called him "my Lord and my God!" (John 20:19). Such proclamations were at odds with the Greco-Roman world that gave this status to the deities.

At least three Greco-Roman deities are mentioned in the New Testament: the Greek goddess Artemis (Acts 19:24–28, 34–35), known as Diana by the Romans, and the Greek gods Zeus and Hermes (Acts 14:12–13), known as Jupiter and Mercury (respectively) by the Romans. Diana was worshipped intensely by the Ephesians, who had built a temple in her honor. This temple was one of the wonders of the ancient world. The Ephesians made and sold small wooden images of the goddess Artemis (Diana). Like other famous idols, it was believed to have fallen from heaven (Acts 19:35). Paul's proclamation of the truth—that "gods made with hands are not gods" (Acts 19:26)—agitated the pagan worshippers of Artemis to fever pitch. For two straight hours they chanted, "Great is Artemis of the Ephesians!" (Acts 19:28, 34). Jesus' deity challenged Artemis' deity; the sale of images was declining in proportion to the apostles' proclamation of the gospel. Consequently, the Ephesian pagans strongly opposed the gospel.

In the Greek language the term for "a god" and "God" is the same: *theos*. In English we differentiate between the two by using a small *g* or a capital *G*. Christian scribes could differentiate between the two by writing out the first term for "god" (or "gods" plural) and by always writing the second term as a nomen sacrum. New Testament writers did not use the nomen sacrum for the term *theoi* (gods) because this term usually denoted idols or Greek deities (see Acts 7:40; 14:11; 19:26; 1 Cor. 8:4–6; Gal. 4:8). On one occasion, Jesus used the term in arguing for his own right to be called the Son of God. In John 10:34–35, he argued that other men had been called "gods" in the Scripture. God had called the judges of Israel "gods," inasmuch as they were his representatives. The New Testament scribes retained this distinction in John 10:33–35. When the Jews said to Jesus, "You make yourself God," the term *theos* is written as a nomen sacrum in New Tesament manuscripts. When Jesus spoke of the judges of Israel being "gods," the term *theoi* is not written as a nomen sacrum in the New Testament manuscripts.

The written distinction was clearly made in the New Testament manuscripts with respect to the terms "God" and "gods" (plural). But was the distinction made between "God" and "god" (singular)? There are five verses in the New Testament—Acts 12:22; 17:23; 19:37; 28:6; 2 Corinthians 4:4—where English translators have typically made a distinction by writing "god" (or "goddess") in lower case so as to designate a deity other than the Lord God. Let us look, for example, at the NRSV:

1. The people kept shouting, "The voice of a god, and not of a mortal!" (Acts 12:22).

2. For as I [Paul] went through the city and looked carefully at objects of your worship, I found among them an altar with the inscription, "To an unknown god" (Acts 17:23).

3. You have brought these men here who are neither temple robbers nor blasphemers of our goddess (Acts 19:37).

4. They [the islanders on Malta] were expecting him [Paul] to swell up or drop dead, but after they had waited a long time and saw that nothing unusual had happened to him, they changed their minds and began to say that he was a god (Acts 28:6).

5. The god of this world has blinded the minds of the unbelievers (2 Cor. 4:4).

Unfortunately, not one of the earliest manuscripts (second and third century) preserves any of these verses. The next earliest manuscripts, codices Vaticanus and Sinaiticus, display the nomen sacrum in four of these verses, all except Acts 19:37. There are two ways to look at this. (1) These scribes had become so accustomed to writing *theos* as a nomen sacrum that they automatically did so in these verses, regardless of the interpretation so presented. (2) These scribes did not see a distinction between "God" and "god," as modern interpreters do. To them, *theos* signals deity. Thus, in each of these verses the sense would be as follows, according to Vaticanus and Sinaiticus:

The people kept shouting, "The voice of deity, and not of man!" (Acts 12:22).

For as I [Paul] went through the city and looked carefully at your objects of worship, I found among them an altar with the inscription, "To an unknown deity" [or, "to an unknown God"]. (Acts 17:23)

They [the islanders on Malta] were expecting him [Paul] to swell up or drop dead, but after they had waited a long time and saw that nothing unusual had happened to him, they changed their minds and began to say that he was divine [or, deity]. (Acts 28:6)

The deity [or, God] of this age has blinded the minds of unbelievers. (2 Cor. 4:4)

Since we do not have any early manuscripts for these verses, we cannot be sure if some earlier scribes chose to write out *theos* so as to designate a distinction. What we do know is that two fourth-century scribes used the nomen sacrum. They can be justified for doing so if we understand that this was a common way to designate deity, not just *the* deity—the Lord God himself.

As to Acts 19:37, the scribes of codices Vaticanus and Sinaiticus wrote the word out in full (*theon*) in order to show that it is not a divine title. The feminine article *tēn* before *theon* probably prompted their decision not to make *theon* a nomen sacrum, as did the context, which points to the term "goddess" as an apt description of Artemis.

Spirit (ΠΝΕΥΜΑ) Π̄Ν̄Ᾱ

If one reads the literature on nomina sacra, it is clear that most scholars think that the four divine titles discussed above ("Lord," "Jesus," "Christ," and "God") were the primary titles to be written as nomina sacra and that all other titles were developed later. But the evidence of the extant manuscripts strongly suggests that the "Spirit" was also written as a nomen sacrum very early in the transmission of the text, if not from the beginning. If *pneuma* was not among the earliest nomina sacra, then scribes, beginning in the early second century, began to make exegetical decisions as to whether it should be written as a nomen sacrum, representing the divine Spirit, or written out in full (in *plene*), so as to designate another aspect of the *pneuma*, such as the human spirit, evil spirit, or a spiritual condition.

When we look at all the manuscripts of the second and third centuries, where the title *pneuma* (Spirit) occurs, it is written as a nomen sacrum. This is evident in the following second-century Christian Old Testament and New Testament manuscripts:

P. Chester Beatty VI, Numbers-Deuteronomy

P. Chester Beatty VII, Isaiah

P. Chester Beatty VIII, Jeremiah

P. Chester Beatty IX-X, Ezekiel, Daniel, Esther

PSI VIII.921, Psalms

𝔓⁴+𝔓⁶⁴+𝔓⁶⁷, Matthew and Luke

𝔓⁴⁶, Paul's Epistles (in nearly all occasions, discussed below)

𝔓⁶⁶, John (in all cases except one, discussed below)

𝔓⁷⁵, Luke and John

In the other second-century New Testament manuscripts, the word *pneuma* (spirit) is not extant. The evidence of the third-century manuscripts is as follows:

Freer Manuscripts, Minor Prophets

𝔓⁵, John

𝔓¹⁵+𝔓¹⁶, 1 Corinthians and Philippians

𝔓¹⁷, Hebrews

𝔓²⁰, James

𝔓²⁴, Revelation

𝔓²⁷, Romans

𝔓³⁰, 1 and 2 Thessalonians

𝔓³⁸, Acts

𝔓⁴⁵, Gospels and Acts

𝔓⁴⁷, Revelation

𝔓⁵⁰, Acts

𝔓⁷², 1 and 2 Peter, Jude

𝔓¹⁰¹, Matthew

𝔓¹⁰⁶, John

$\mathfrak{P}^{113}$, Romans

$\mathfrak{P}^{115}$, Revelation

0171, Matthew and Luke

0189, Acts

The early scribes consistently used the nomen sacrum form for *pneuma* when designating the divine Spirit. (The word *pneuma* was written out only when designating some other kind of spirit, such as evil spirits.) The only exception to this is that the scribe of $\mathfrak{P}^{46}$, in about ten occurrences, did not write *pneuma* as a nomen sacrum where one would expect the word to denote the divine Spirit. (This is discussed at length below.) What this could indicate is that $\mathfrak{P}^{46}$ is, in fact, a very early manuscript, which shows the formation of the nomen sacrum for *pneuma* in early transition—most times being written as a divine title, sometimes being written out in full (in *plene*). If this is the case, then there is evidence to suggest that the nomen sacrum for "Spirit" was developed after the nomina sacra for "Lord," "Jesus," "Christ," and "God."

Aside from the phenomenon of $\mathfrak{P}^{46}$, all the other manuscripts indicate that the title "Spirit" was treated as a sacred name as early as were the names "Lord," "Jesus," "Christ," and "God." There is good reason for this. The Spirit was extremely important to the early believers because they considered the Spirit to be the Spirit of the risen Christ—the Spirit of Jesus making himself real to the believers in his spiritual form. From the writings of the New Testament (which are explained below), we gather that the early Christians considered Jesus to be present with them and in them via his Spirit. Thus, they honored the title "Spirit" by writing it as a nomen sacrum.

When Jesus arose from the dead, three significant things happened to him. He was glorified and transfigured, and he became spirit. All three happened simultaneously. When he was resurrected, he was glorified (see Luke 24:26). At the same time, his body was transfigured into a glorious one (Phil. 3:21). Equally so—and quite mysteriously—he became life-giving spirit (1 Cor. 15:45). Paul did not say Jesus became "the Spirit"—as if the second person of the Trinity became the third, but that Jesus became spirit in the sense that his mortal existence and form were metamorphosed into a spiritual existence and form. Jesus' person was not changed through the resurrection, only his form. Christ, via resurrection, appropriated a new, spiritual form (while still retaining a body—a glorified one) that enabled him to commence a new spiritual existence. First Peter 3:18 says that Jesus was "put to death in the flesh, quickened in the spirit."

With this new spiritual existence, Christ, as spirit and through the Holy Spirit, could indwell millions of believers simultaneously. Before the resurrection, Jesus was limited by his mortal body; after his resurrection, Jesus could be experienced illimitably by all his believers. Before his resurrection, Christ could dwell only among his believers; after his resurrection, he could dwell in his believers. Because Christ became spirit through resurrection, he can be experienced by those he indwells. Prior to the resurrection the disciples could not experience Christ indwelling them because he was still a man limited by his human body. But after the resurrection there was a great change: Jesus' form changed so that he could then (and now) indwell the believers.

The Lord Jesus entered into a new kind of existence when he was raised from the dead because he was glorified and simultaneously became spirit—or, to coin a word, he was "pneumafied" (from the Greek word for "spirit," *pneuma*). It appears that when he arose, the indwelling Spirit penetrated and saturated his body so as to constitute his entire being with spirit. This is not my teaching alone; several noted Christian authors have advanced the same description of the Lord's resurrection. In fact, a great deal of study in the area of pneumatology (the study of the Spirit) points out that the risen Christ and the Spirit were united via Christ's resurrection.

In his classic, *The Resurrection of Our Lord,* William Milligan argued that the risen Christ is spirit in these words:

> The condition of our Lord after His Resurrection was viewed by the sacred writers as essentially a state of *pneuma* (spirit). Not indeed that our Lord had then no body, for it is the constant lesson of Scripture that a body was possessed by him; but that the deepest, the fundamental characteristic of His state, inter-penetrating even the body, and moulding it into a complete adaptation to and harmony with His spirit, was *pneuma*. In other words, it is proposed to inquire whether the word *pneuma* in the New Testament is not used as a short description of what our Lord was after His Resurrection, in contrast with what He was during the days of His humiliation upon earth.[33]

Milligan went on to show that several Scriptures affirm that the resurrected Christ is spirit. He cited 1 Corinthians 6:17 to show that the believer who is joined with the risen Lord must be joined to him as spirit because he who is joined to the Lord is said to be "one spirit" with him. He used 2 Corinthians 3:17–18 to demonstrate that the Lord who is the Spirit is none other than the risen Christ. He also employed 1 Timothy 3:16; Romans 1:3–4; and Hebrews 9:14 to show that the risen Lord is spirit (see pp. 248–56). In these pages Milligan cites Franz Delitzsch, who said that the divine personality in Christ "at the Resurrection interpenetrated, and as it were, absorbed the flesh so that He is now altogether spirit." Richard Gaffins, a modern writer, had this to say about Christ's resurrection:

> Christ (as incarnate) experiences a spiritual qualification and transformation so thorough, and endowment with the Spirit so complete that as a result they can now be equated. This unprecedented possession of the Spirit and the accompanying change in Christ result in a unity so close that not only can it be said simply that the Spirit makes alive, but also that Christ as Spirit makes alive.[34]

This is why Paul often speaks of the Spirit and Christ synonymously. This is evident in Romans 8:9–10. The terms "Spirit of God," "Spirit of Christ," and "Christ" are all used interchangeably. The Spirit of God is the Spirit of Christ, and the Spirit of Christ is Christ. David Somerville said,

> Being "in Christ" and being "in the Spirit" are the same thing; and in the thought of the apostle, "Christ," "the Spirit of Christ," and "the Spirit of God" are practically synonymous. At the resurrection Christ became a Life-giving Spirit to mankind.[35]

In these verses it is evident that Paul identifies the Spirit with Christ because in Christian experience they are absolutely identical. There is no such thing as an experience of Christ apart from the Spirit. Only the inexperienced would say or think that the two can be separated. The separation and/or distinction does exist in Trinitarian theology—and for very good reasons, but the separation is nearly nonexistent in actual experience. Ever since the beginning of the Christian church, the believers have experienced Christ through his Spirit—the Spirit of Christ. It is in this light that Paul can say, "Now the Lord is the Spirit . . . and we are being transformed into the [Lord's] image by the Lord, who is the Spirit" (2 Cor. 3:17–18).

All this discussion about Christ being experienced in, by, and as the Spirit affirms why the earliest scribes decided to dignify and even deify the term *pneuma* by writing it as a nomen sacrum. To the early Christians, the "Spirit" was identified with Christ and vice versa. Therefore, just as "Christ" was worthy of a divine title, so was the "Spirit." The early believers signaled the Spirit's deity by writing *pneuma* as a nomen sacrum. They distinguished the divine spirit from any other spirit—the human spirit, evil spirits, or even the wind—by not writing these as nomen sacrum. The best English equivalent to this is the way in which capital letter *S* is used by Bible translators for God's Spirit and small letter *s* is used for the human spirit or some other kind of spirit.

Translators and interpreters have been perplexed about how to render the word *pneuma* in certain verses in the New Testament. Does the particular passage indicate the divine Spirit, the human spirit, or another spirit? In several such places the translator has the option of capitalizing it or not; either rendering requires an interpretation. Thus, a translator may have wished that the original writers had made the distinction. Interestingly, it is possible that they *did* make the orthographic distinction by writing the divine spirit as nomen sacrum and by writing out any other spirit as *pneuma*. Since we do not have the autographs, we are not certain if this distinction came from the New Testament authors themselves or if it was the invention of the earliest scribes. What we do know is that the distinction shows up in the earliest New Testament manuscripts, many of which date in the second century. To be specific, the distinction between the divine Spirit written as a nomen sacrum and the human spirit written in full appears in several of the earliest New Testament manuscripts: $\mathfrak{P}^{45}$, $\mathfrak{P}^{46}$, $\mathfrak{P}^{66}$, $\mathfrak{P}^{75}$.

In four early manuscripts that have both the nomen sacrum form and the plene form, in two distinct written forms, it appears that the copyists did not act arbitrarily but rather intentionally—or perhaps even faithfully to what was in the exemplar (or, even to the original text). The verses in which the copyists of $\mathfrak{P}^{46}$, $\mathfrak{P}^{66}$, and $\mathfrak{P}^{75}$ have written out *pneuma* (in *plene*) are as follows: Luke 10:20 ($\mathfrak{P}^{75}$); John 3:6 ($\mathfrak{P}^{66}$); 3:8 ($\mathfrak{P}^{66}$*); 6:63 ($\mathfrak{P}^{66}$*); Romans 8:15, 23; 11:8; 15:13, 15 ($\mathfrak{P}^{46}$); 1 Corinthians 2:10 ($\mathfrak{P}^{46}$ twice); 2:11 ($\mathfrak{P}^{46}$); 6:17 ($\mathfrak{P}^{46}$); 14:12, 14, 32 ($\mathfrak{P}^{46}$); 2 Corinthians 3:6; 7:13; 11:4 ($\mathfrak{P}^{46}$); Philippians 3:3 ($\mathfrak{P}^{46}$, variant reading); Hebrews 9:14 ($\mathfrak{P}^{46}$); 12:9 ($\mathfrak{P}^{46}$). In most cases, the scribe wrote out the word *pneuma* in order to indicate the human spirit, that which is characteristically spirit, or an evil spirit. Let us take a brief look at these verses—first in the Gospels, and then in the Epistles.

In Luke 10:20, the scribe of $\mathfrak{P}^{75}$ wrote out the word *pneuma* in full (in *plene*) so as to designate an evil spirit. This is significant because in all other instances in both Luke and John, the scribe of $\mathfrak{P}^{75}$ wrote *pneuma* as a nomen sacrum.

In John 3:6, the copyist of $\mathfrak{P}^{66}$ distinguished the divine Spirit from the human spirit by making the first word a nomen sacrum and by writing out (in *plene*) the second (*pneuma*)—thereby indicating that the divine Spirit is that which generates and the human spirit is that which is generated; or his interpretation could be that "the Spirit begets spirit"—that is, like begets like: Spirit begets spirit. Most modern translators have a similar exegesis: "that which is born of the Spirit is spirit." The scribe of $\mathfrak{P}^{75}$ has both words for *pneuma* written as nomina sacra, but he could have been trying to demonstrate the same idea: whatever is born of the divine Spirit is also divine Spirit.

In John 3:8, there is a metaphor which is purposefully polyvalent, in that Jesus was speaking of wind, spirit, and breath at the same time (inasmuch as *pneuma* can mean all three): "The wind/spirit blows/breathes/spirits where it wills." The scribe of $\mathfrak{P}^{66}$ first started to write out the word for "wind," writing the first four letters for *pneuma* and immediately corrected it to $\overline{\Pi N A}$, the siglum for the nomen sacrum, "the Spirit." This probably shows that the scribe of $\mathfrak{P}^{66}$ recognized that *pneuma* required a different orthography for a different sense in this context but then succumbed to the standard formula for designating nomina sacra. The scribe of $\mathfrak{P}^{75}$ also wrote *pneuma* as a nomen sacrum, and even abbreviated the verbal action of the word *pnei* (literally "act as spirit" or "blow as wind") as $\overline{\Pi N E I}$. The interpretive and/or translation issue here is over the primacy of image: is it the Spirit breathing/spiriting, or is it the wind blowing? Most commentators (such as Westcott and Carson) see the wind imagery as primary, especially pointing to the words *pnei* and *phōnē*. Others (such as Barrett) say that both images are intended. Both scribes made the spiritual meaning primary.[36]

John 6:63 has two parts that involve an interpretation of the Spirit: (1) "it is the Spirit/spirit that makes alive" and (2) "the words I have spoken to you are spirit and life." As for the first part, the scribe of $\mathfrak{P}^{66}$ first wrote it in full as *pneuma*, then changed it to $\overline{\Pi N A}$. This change may indicate that the scribe had second thoughts about how this should be interpreted. In the end, his change indicates that it is the divine Spirit that gives life. In line with this understanding, most commentators and translators understand the first *pneuma* here as the Spirit of God. However, a few commentators (such as Westcott) understand it as referring to the spirit of Jesus' message just given[37]—that is, he was not asking people literally to eat his flesh and drink his blood; rather, he was asking people to understand the spiritual significance of this message.

As for the second part of the verse, many commentators take this to mean "the words are spiritual and life-giving"; however, other commentators (such as Beasley-Murray, Barrett, and Brown) agree with how the scribes of $\mathfrak{P}^{66}$ and $\mathfrak{P}^{75}$ treated this—namely, as a nomen sacrum. For example, Beasley-Murray said, "The words of Jesus in the discourse are Spirit and life for those who receive them in faith, since they who accept them and believe in the Son receive the Spirit and the life of which he speaks."[38] This means that the Spirit was transmitted through Jesus' words.

Now, let's turn our attention to Paul's Epistles—and specifically to the work of the copyist of $\mathfrak{P}^{46}$, who did some very interesting things with the word *pneuma* (Spirit) and its cognates, especially in 1 Corinthians. In 2:10–11, he wrote out in full (*plene*) the word *pneuma* (twice in the extant portion of 2:10, and then probably again in 2:11a, which is not extant). A translation of this is as follows: "For God has revealed them through the spirit, for the spirit searches all things, even the deep things of God. For what man knows the things of man except the spirit of man which is in him." While most commentators and translators would render the first *pneuma* as the divine Spirit ("God has revealed them through the Spirit"), the written text of $\mathfrak{P}^{46}$ indicates that this scribe considered this verse to be speaking of the human spirit: God reveals spiritual mysteries through the human spirit (2:10).

Another interesting verse for distinguishing the divine Spirit from the human spirit is found in 1 Corinthians 6:17, which reads, "But the one joining himself to the Lord is one spirit." This statement is generally understood to indicate spiritual union between the believer and Christ. As two bodies join to become one through sexual union, two spirits join to become one in spiritual union. It is a union of the divine Spirit with the human spirit; as such, "spirit" should not be capitalized, for it is not just the divine Spirit. The scribe of $\mathfrak{P}^{46}$ showed this interpretation by not writing *pneuma* as a nomen sacrum; rather, he wrote out the word *pneuma* (in *plene*).

Yet another significant verse in the Corinthian correspondences is 2 Corinthians 3:6, for here we see two different facets of the Spirit. In this verse, Paul contrasts the nature of the two covenants, saying that the new covenant is "not of the letter but of spirit" (*ou grammatos alla pneumatos*). The sense of this is appropriately captured by the NEB: "not in a written document, but in a spiritual bond." The next clause says, "For the letter kills but the Spirit gives life." This statement affirms that it is the divine Spirit that enlivens the new covenant, whereas the previous statement contrasts two kinds of covenants—one of letter and one of spirit. The distinction between the two uses of *pneuma* is found in the writing of the scribe of $\mathfrak{P}^{46}$, who wrote, "not of the letter but of spirit [*pneuma*—written in full], for the letter kills, but the [divine] Spirit [$\overline{\Pi N A}$] gives life."

The copyists of $\mathfrak{P}^{13}$ and $\mathfrak{P}^{46}$ realized that Hebrews 12:9 was speaking about the human spirit in the expression "the Father of spirits," so they wrote out in full (in *plene*) the word *pneuma*. Then, in Hebrews 12:23 the scribe of $\mathfrak{P}^{46}$ wrote out *pneuma* (in *plene*) because it clearly refers to "the spirits of men." The scribe of $\mathfrak{P}^{46}$ also wrote out *pneuma* (in *plene*) in 1 Corinthians 14:14 ("my spirit prays"); 14:32 ("spirits of prophets"); 2 Corinthians 7:13 ("his spirit was refreshed"); and Philippians 3:3 ("the ones serving in spirit").[39]

As noted before, the word *pneuma* in some verses is very difficult to decipher because it does not explicitly denote the divine Spirit or the human spirit or even the human spirit regenerated by the divine Spirit. Rather, it seems to refer to that which is characterstically "spirit," as often denoted by the anathrous expression in Greek. For example, the New Testament has expressions like "spirit/Spirit of slavery . . . spirit/Spirit of sonship" (Rom. 8:15), "spirit/Spirit of stupor" (Rom. 11:8), and "a different spirit/Spirit" (2 Cor. 11:14), "through the eternal spirit/Spirit" (Heb. 9:14). Significantly, the copyist of $\mathfrak{P}^{46}$ wrote out *pneuma* (in *plene*) in all of these instances. He may have simply been following his exemplar, or he may have been exercising some exegetical discernment.

Only four instances (all in $\mathfrak{P}^{46}$) among all the early papyrus manuscripts fail to fit the pattern: Romans 8:23 ("the firstfruits of the Spirit"); Romans 15:13 ("the power of the Holy Spirit"); Romans 15:16 ("sanctified by the Holy Spirit"); 2 Corinthians 13:14 ("the fellowship of the Holy Spirit"). In all of these instances, *pneuma* should have been written as a nomen sacrum because the divine Spirit is indicated. Other scholars would assert that the scribe missed several other verses that also appear to be speaking of the divine Spirit, even though I presented an argument for it not being the divine spirit. These other verses would be Romans 8:15b ("the Spirit of sonship"); 1 Corinthians 2:10–11 (see discussion above); Philippians 3:3 ("serving by the Spirit"); and Hebrews 9:14 ("the eternal Spirit"). Add these verses to those mentioned, and a case can be made that the scribe of $\mathfrak{P}^{46}$ failed to designate the divine Spirit in nearly ten places.

What accounts for this phenomenon? My best guess is that the scribe was using an examplar where *pneuma* was—more often than not—written in *plene*. It is also possible that his exemplar did not have the nomen sacrum at all; it may have been written out as *pneuma* throughout the entire exemplar. This situation would have prompted the scribe, who knew about the nomen sacrum for *pneuma,* to make interpretive decisions about each occurrence of *pneuma,* and thereby determine whether it should be written as a nomen sacrum. Somehow the scribe knew that it was his responsibility to do this, and often he succeeded in doing it, but not always.[40] This would account for the occurrences in which he left *pneuma* written in full (*plene*) when he should have turned it into a nomen sacrum. If such was the case, we can make a few assumptions: the exemplar for 𝔓⁴⁶ was quite early, for it probably showed the primary four nomina sacra (for "Lord," "Jesus," "Christ," and "God") but not yet the nomen sacrum for *pneuma* (or, at least, a fully developed system for *pneuma*). This would consequently mean that 𝔓⁴⁶ is also quite early—probably earlier than all the extant manuscripts that show *pneuma*, which is treated as a nomen sacrum where appropriate. This leads to another interesting observation: Codex Vaticanus never uses a nomen sacrum for *pneuma*; it displays only the primary four nomina sacra. This suggests that the exemplar for Codex Vaticanus did not have this as a nomen sacrum. If so, the exemplar for Vaticanus is also very early.

Before we conclude this section on "Spirit," it is worth noting that all early scribes of the New Testament considered Jesus' personal *pneuma* to be worthy of designation as a nomen sacrum. Contrary to modern exegetes and translators, who generally consider Jesus' *pneuma* to be the human spirit of Jesus or even the deep emotions of Jesus, the ancient scribes dignified Jesus' spirit by giving it nomina sacra status. A few examples illustrate this.

In Luke 1:80, the scribe of 𝔓⁴ indicated that Jesus "grew strong in Spirit" (*ekrataiouto* $\overline{\Pi N I}$). This means he was empowered by the Spirit's strength. Most English versions, however, indicate that Jesus grew strong in his human spirit.

John 11:33 can be understood in two ways: (1) "Jesus . . . was greatly angered in his spirit and was troubled in himself" or (2) "Jesus . . . was greatly angered in the Spirit and was troubled in himself." All modern exegetes and translators understand *pnuema* in this verse as referring to Jesus' human spirit or his "inner being"—equivalent to the expression, "he had deep anger within himself." They see the phrase *en pneumati* (in spirit) of 11:33 = *en eautō* (in himself) of 11:38. Barrett and Carson say it has no reference to the Holy Spirit, but is equivalent to "in himself." Brown says it a semitism for the inward emotions. Beasley-Murray provides a strong argument for indicating that this emotion was anger, not just agitation.[41] But the ancient scribes of 𝔓⁴⁵, 𝔓⁶⁶, and 𝔓⁷⁵ wrote it[42] as a nomen sacrum: *enebrimēsato tō* $\overline{\Pi N I}$, which means "he was troubled in [by] the Spirit."

If interpreters are so confident that the spirit here refers to the inward emotions, why would scribes note it as the divine spirit? I have three reasons: (1) Ancient scribes saw it as referring to the divine Spirit, inasmuch as Jesus' spirit was considered divine. (2) Ancient scribes saw the verse as referring to Jesus holding back the divine Spirit of anger. (Westcott allows for the rendering, "He sternly checked his Spirit" but prefers "he groaned in his spirit" (the verb is in the middle voice)—the subject acting with respect to itself.[43] (3) The variant reading in 𝔓⁶⁶ᶜ and 𝔓⁴⁵ allows for the interpretation "he was brought to anger by the Spirit" (instrumental) or "he was angry in the Spirit"—i.e., his anger was a divine anger and therefore justifiable.

A similar verse, John 13:23, can be interpreted in two ways: (1) "Jesus was troubled in his spirit and said, 'One of you will betray me'" or (2) "Jesus was troubled by the Spirit and said, 'One of you will betray me.'" As with John 11:33, all commentators say that *pneuma* here does not refer to the Holy Spirit, but to Jesus' inner emotions. But could it not mean that "Jesus was troubled by the Spirit" or "troubled in his Spirit, which was divine"? This is how the ancient scribe of 𝔓[66] understood it.

Another verse, John 19:38, can be interpreted in two ways: (1) "then he bowed his head and gave up the spirit" or (2) "then he bowed his head and gave up [over] the Spirit." Most modern exegetes see *pneuma* here as referring to Jesus' human spirit—not just his "breath" as in expiration. (This means they think the language here does not equal the expression in Mark 15:37, *exepneusen*.) Westcott calls it a voluntary act of death—not just expiring. F. F. Bruce says it is the giving up of his spirit, which is somewhat equivalent to Luke's expression, "Father, into your hands I commit my spirit."[44] However, the text does not specify to whom Jesus handed over the spirit. Thus, certain expositors have seen this as Jesus handing over the divine Spirit to the believers. In this light, Raymond Brown offers this interpretation:

> John seems to play upon the idea that Jesus handed over the Holy Spirit to
> those at the foot of the cross, in particular, to his mother who symbolizes the
> church or new people of God and to the beloved disciple who symbolizes the
> Christian. In 7:39 John affirmed that those who believed in Jesus were to
> receive the Spirit once Jesus had been glorified, and so it would not be inappropriate that at this climactic moment in the hour of glorification there would be a
> symbolic reference to the giving of the Spirit. If such an interpretation of "he
> handed over the spirit" has any plausibility, we would stress that this symbolic
> reference is evocative and proleptic . . . In Johannine thought, the actual giving
> of the Spirit does not come now but in 20:22 after the resurrection.[45]

Brown's interpretation concurs with the Johannine presentation that the Spirit is given as the result of Jesus' glorification, which involves both his death and resurrection, but is not culminated until the resurrection (John 20:22). The presence of the nomen sacrum in 𝔓[66] can allow for this interpretation.

Spiritual Ones, The Spirit-Ones

The final aspect we need to consider concerning the nomen sacrum of *pneuma* is another form of this word, *pneumatikos*, which was sometimes treated as a nomen sacrum by the earliest scribes. In most instances, the word is used to describe spiritual things, such as spiritual gifts, spiritual songs, spiritual words, etc. (Rom. 1:11; 7:14; 15:27; 1 Cor. 9:11; 10:3–4; 12:1; 14:1; 15:44, 46; Eph. 1:3; 5:19; 6:12; Col. 1:9; 3:16). But the word was also used, especially by Paul, to designate a "spiritual one" or "spiritual ones" (plural). This is the case in 1 Corinthians 2:15; 3:1; 14:37; Galatians 6:1. The adverbial form, *pneumatikōs* (spiritually) is found in 1 Corinthians 2:14 (also

Revelation 11:8). First Corinthians 2:13b (*pneumatikois pneumatika sugkrinontes*) is ambi-guous; it can mean "matching spiritual things with spiritual things/words" or "explaining spiritual things to spiritual people."

The scribe of $\mathfrak{P}^{46}$ decided in a few instances to designate *pneumatikōs* (the adverb, "spiritually") and *pneumatikos* (the noun, "spiritual one") as nomina sacra. We first see this in 1 Corinthians 2:13–3:1. In 2:13, the scribe uses the common nomen sacrum $\overline{\Pi N C}$ in the expression *didaktois pneumatos* (taught by the Spirit). Then the scribe wrote *pneumatikois pneumatika sugkrinontes*, which reveals his interpretation: "matching spiritual things with spiritual things/words." Had the scribe intended *pneumatikois* to convey "spiritual people," he could have written this as a nomen sacrum (which he does in 2:15 and 3:1), but his choice to write it in full (*plene*) indicates that he was probably not thinking of "spiritual ones."

Then, in 2:14 the scribe of $\mathfrak{P}^{46}$ wrote the nomen sacrum $\overline{\Pi N C}$ for the adverbial word *pneumatikōs* in the expression "they are spiritually discerned." It is possible that the scribe of $\mathfrak{P}^{46}$ was providing a variant reading—namely, "they are discerned by the Spirit." Or, it is just as likely that this was the scribe's way of indicating the divine activity of the Spirit. As such, it is unique among the nomina sacra.

In 2:15 and 3:1 the scribe of $\mathfrak{P}^{46}$ wrote the nomen sacrum $\overline{\Pi N C}$. This written form could denote two things: (1) It is a special nomen sacrum for "the one who is spiritual" and "the ones who are spiritual" (*pneumatikos* and *pneumatikois*). In the context of 2:15 and 3:1, it denotes "a person of [belonging to] the Spirit" and "persons of [belonging to] the Spirit." The decision to write these as nomina sacra was the scribe's way of dignifying the identity of spiritual people by virtue of their union with the Holy Spirit. In other words, "the spiritual man" is "a person of the Spirit." (2) The nomen sacrum $\overline{\Pi N C}$ in 2:15 could be a textual variant—namely, *pneumatos* (genitive)—"the one of the Spirit discerns all things." But this doesn't work for 3:1, where the grammatical form has to be dative and therefore the nomen sacrum must represent *pneumatikois* (spiritual ones). Thus, it stands to reason that in both 2:15 and 3:1, the scribe of $\mathfrak{P}^{46}$ used a nomen sacrum for "spiritual people."

One would expect this to continue throughout the manuscript of $\mathfrak{P}^{46}$, but it does not. This is first noticeable in 1 Corinthians 14:37, where the scribe of $\mathfrak{P}^{46}$ wrote out in full *pneumatikos* for "the spiritual one." Then, a curious phenomenon occurs in 1 Corinthians 15:44–47, concerning Paul's discussion of the resurrected spiritual body. In 15:44, the scribe writes out (in *plene*) *pneumatikon* (spiritual) twice. Then, in 15:46–47, he uses the nomen sacrum in three similar forms: $\overline{\Pi N K O N}$ and $\overline{\Pi N I K O N}$ (both as adjectives for "spiritual" body in 15:46) and $\overline{\Pi N K O C}$ (for "spiritual" man—a singular variant in 15:47). I can't help but ask—what caused the scribe to make the shift from 15:44 to nomen sacrum form in 15:46? My sense is that the scribe perceived 15:44 as a generic statement about the resurrected spiritual body, whereas he thought 15:46 (following 15:45, which calls Christ $\overline{\Pi N A}$ *zoōpoioun* = lifegiving

Spirit) was Christocentric and therefore worthy of a divine designation. This is reiforced by the singular textual variant in $\mathfrak{P}^{46}$ in the next verse (15:47)—*ho deuteros anthrōpos* $\overline{\Pi N K O C}$ *ex ouranou* (the second man, a spiritual One from heaven). Given the scribe's usage in 15:47, the expressions in 15:46, $\overline{\Pi N K O N}$ and $\overline{\Pi N I K O N}$, could also mean "the Spirit-One" (hence the rendering, "but the Spirit-one is not first; rather, the natural one, then the Spirit-one"). But it is more likely that the nomina sacra refer to the spiritual body and/or spiritual existence as exemplified in the resurrected Christ (hence the rendering, "but the spiritual is not first; rather, the natural, then the spiritual").

In no other instances did the scribe of $\mathfrak{P}^{46}$ write *pneumatikos* as a nomen sacrum, including Galatians 6:1, where one might be expected. The decision to use the nomen sacrum or not affirms what I noticed about this scribe before: he was experimenting on his own, not copying an exemplar. Furthermore, the diversity of written forms suggests that the scribe was creating forms afresh, as he went. In 1 Corinthians 2 he used one form, then in chapter 15 he used another (with its own variations). All of this further shows, in my opinion, the nomen sacrum for *pneuma* was in flux at this period of textual transmission and thereby serves to underscore that $\mathfrak{P}^{46}$ is indeed a second-century manuscript.

To conclude this section, it should be noted that the scribe of $\mathfrak{P}^{72}$ also designated the adjective "spiritual" in a unique way. In 1 Peter 2:5, he wrote the term as $\overline{\Pi N A T I K O C}$ for "spiritual [house]" and $\overline{\Pi N A T I K A C}$ for "spiritual [sacrifices]." These designations show that the Spirit is highlighted for its divine quality.

Father, Son, Son of God, Son of Man

There were four basic nomen sacrum in the earliest New Testament manuscripts: "Lord," "Jesus," "Christ," "God," soon followed by "Spirit" (if my analysis of $\mathfrak{P}^{46}$ is correct). Beyond these primary five, there were several others, but these others were definitely not part of the original group because we do not see them consistently written as nomina sacra in all the earliest manuscripts. In other words, only certain scribes in the second and third centuries decided to write the names "Father" and "Son" as a nomina sacra. Others chose not to do so at all. And still other scribes did so on some occasions and not on others. And even when the nomina sacra were used, there was diversity in written form.

This fluctuation in the second and third century manuscripts concerning the names "Father" and "Son" could reflect the theological developments of the time. In the second and third centuries of the church, Christian theologians were exploring the mysteries of the Triune God. During this period, the theologians described God as being one God in three Persons (or *personae*). These three persons were identified as God the Father, God the Son, and God the Spirit. In the previous section, we examined at length the early Christian concept of the Spirit. To their way of thinking, the

"Spirit" was the invisible presence of Jesus. But what did they think of the terms "Father" and "Son"? It seems they were considered in two ways: (1) as descriptive nouns for the Father-Son relationship presented in Scriptures, and (2) as solitary titles—"the Father" and "the Son." A verse that shows a descriptive use of "father" and "son" is Hebrews 1:5, which reads in the RSV as, "I will be to him a father, and he shall be to me a son" (note the lower case of "father" and "son," which is discussed later). A verse that shows the titluar use of both names is 2 John 9—"he who abides in the doctrine of Christ . . . has both the Father and the Son."

Father and Son

Some of the earliest New Testament manuscripts showed scribes' respect for the divine names, "Father" and "Son," by writing them as nomina sacra. The nomen sacrum for "Son" is found in $\mathfrak{P}^1$, $\mathfrak{P}^9$, $\mathfrak{P}^{40}$, $\mathfrak{P}^{45}$ (in part), $\mathfrak{P}^{46}$ (in part), $\mathfrak{P}^{66}$ (in part), $\mathfrak{P}^{75}$ (in part), and $\mathfrak{P}^{101}$. The nomen sacrum for "Father" is found in $\mathfrak{P}^5$, $\mathfrak{P}^{22}$, $\mathfrak{P}^{27}$, $\mathfrak{P}^{39}$, $\mathfrak{P}^{45}$ (in part), $\mathfrak{P}^{46}$ (in part), $\mathfrak{P}^{47}$, $\mathfrak{P}^{53}$, $\mathfrak{P}^{66}$ (in part), $\mathfrak{P}^{72}$, $\mathfrak{P}^{75}$ (in part), and $\mathfrak{P}^{91}$. The notation "in part" signifies that the manuscript displays the title both in *plene* form (fully written out) and nomen sacrum form. It should also be noted that where a manuscript displays a nomen sacrum for either "Son" or "Father" only, the other name is not extant, so I cannot determine if the scribe used only one or the other. The only exception to this is found in $\mathfrak{P}^{72}$, where the scribe consistently used a nomen sacrum for "Father," whereas "Son" in its one occurrence (2 Peter 1:17) is not written as a nomen sacrum.

The divine title "Father" was contracted by using the first letter and last letter of PATHP ($\overline{\text{ΠΡ}}$; the short form), or by using the first two letters and the last ($\overline{\text{ΠΗΡ}}$; the long form), ($\mathfrak{P}^{22}$ has the two forms.) For various declensions, the scribe would also write $\overline{\text{ΠΡΣ}}$ (ΠΑΤΡΟΣ), $\overline{\text{ΠΡΙ}}$ (ΠΑΤΡΙ), or $\overline{\text{ΠΡΑ}}$ (ΠΑΤΕΡΑ). Another early variation of the form is found in P. Chester Beatty VI (early second century), which has $\overline{\text{ΠΡΤΙ}}$ (along with $\overline{\text{ΠΡΙ}}$). And other forms appear in various manuscripts, thereby revealing that the form of this nomen sacrum was not fixed.

The term "Son" ($\overline{\text{ΥΙΟΣ}}$) was contracted as $\overline{\text{ΥΣ}}$. As was previously stated, these two divine names were not part of the original names to be written as nomina sacra. We know this because they do not appear in sacral form in some of the earliest manuscripts (such as $\mathfrak{P}^4$+$\mathfrak{P}^{64}$+$\mathfrak{P}^{67}$) and because in several other manuscripts of the second and third century ($\mathfrak{P}^{45}$, $\mathfrak{P}^{46}$, $\mathfrak{P}^{66}$, $\mathfrak{P}^{75}$) the scribes fluctuated between writing out the full name and writing it as a nomen sacrum, even when it was clear that it was a divine title. For example, the scribe of $\mathfrak{P}^{45}$ sometimes wrote out *Patēr* (Father/father) in full, and sometimes he wrote it as a nomen sacrum. In most instances, the scribe of $\mathfrak{P}^{75}$ wrote out the name in full as *Patēr*; in a few other places, however, he wrote it as a nomen sacrum. This fluctuation shows that the scribes were not yet comfortable with writing this name as nomen sacrum.

As would be expected, in various passages of Scripture, certain scribes exercised discernment in distinguishing the divine Father from a human father, and the divine Son from a human son, by writing or not writing the word as a nomen sacrum. Let us look at a few examples.

Throughout the New Testament, various people are named "fathers." Such a title is not worthy of being a nomen sacrum because these people were not divine. Accordingly, the name *Patēr* (father) in its ordinary use is not written as a nomen sacrum in several manuscripts. For example, a certain sick child's "father" is written out as *Patēr* in both $\mathfrak{P}^{66}$ and $\mathfrak{P}^{75}$ in John 4:53. The scribe of $\mathfrak{P}^{75}$ wrote out "father Jacob" in John 4:12. In John 6:42, the scribe of $\mathfrak{P}^{66}$ first wrote the title "father" for Jesus' earthly father Joseph as a nomen sacrum ($\overline{\Pi P A}$), then he corrected it to $\Pi A T H P A$.[46]

The term *father* can also be used generically to denote "the one who originates or institutes," as in the expression "the father of poetry." For example, James 1:17 has the expression "father of lights"; it describes God as the One who originated light. The scribe of $\mathfrak{P}^{22}$ wrote out the word *Patēr* in full so as to indicate that this is not a title. The term *father* also means "source." This is exemplified in John 8:44, which says that the devil is "the father of lies." This means that lies originate from the devil. The scribe of $\mathfrak{P}^{75}$ wrote out the word *Patēr* so as to indicate that this is not a title.

Son/Son of God

As with the word *Father,* so the word *son* is used in the New Testament in its normal sense. *Huιos* designates a "male child." As such, this word with this usage is not worthy of being written as a nomen sacrum. Thus, in both $\mathfrak{P}^{66}$ and $\mathfrak{P}^{75}$, Jacob's "son" Joseph (John 4:5) and the nobleman's sick "son" (John 4:46–50) are written out in full as *huios*. When Jesus was dying on the cross, he told his mother to look upon John the apostle as being her son. In $\mathfrak{P}^{66}$, *huios* is written out here (John 19:26).

As with the term *Father,* so the *Son* also has a generic use, meaning "the product of, the issue of." It appears in expressions like "the son of peace" (see Luke 10:6) and "the son of destruction" (John 17:12; 2 Thess. 2:3). In both of these instances, the word *huios* is written out in full (in $\mathfrak{P}^{75}$ and in $\mathfrak{P}^{49}+\mathfrak{P}^{65}$, respectively).

Jesus had status as human son and Son of God. As such, scribes had a choice of making his human sonship distinct from his divine Sonship by writing out the word ΥIOC or making it a nomen sacrum, written as $\overline{YC}$. Among the extant manuscripts, there is some diversity here. For example, in Mark 6:3, the scribe of $\mathfrak{P}^{45}$ wrote "Son" as a nomen sacrum in the expression "son of Mary." By contrast, the scribes of $\mathfrak{P}^{66}$ and $\mathfrak{P}^{75}$ wrote out "son" in the expression "the son of Joseph" (John 6:42).

At times, the term is ambiguous; it could refer to God's Son or to a human son or both. This is illustrated in the text of Matthew 2:15, where Matthew quoted Hosea 11:1, "out of Egypt I called my son," to show that Jesus' coming up out of Egypt fulfilled Scripture. This prophecy also pertains to Israel's coming up out of Egypt from their bondage. Thus, most modern English versions are reluctant to capitalize "son" in this quote (see, for example, RSV, NIV, NRSV). A few versions do capitalize it so as to demonstrate that the prophecy was fulfilled in the Son (see TEV, NLT). The scribe of 𝔓⁷⁰ must have been of the same opinion, for he made "Son" A nomen sacrum in this verse.

In John 8:35, there is some ambiguity as to whether the verse is talking about the "Son of God" or simply one who is a son. The statement is, "A slave does not belong to a family forever; a son [or "the Son," as in KJV] belongs to it forever." Most scholars think that verse 35 is an aphorism about the difference between a slave and a son. Not a member of the family, a slave has no permanent standing in his master's house; he can easily be sold to another. But a son always has a place in his father's house; once a son, always a son. But it cannot be denied that the reference to "the son" in this verse has double significance: (1) it refers to a son, as opposed to a slave, who has a permanent place in his father's house, and (2) it refers to the Son of God who has an eternal place in his Father's house. The definite article "the" before "Son" lends support to this view, and the next verse could be seen as affirming it: "If the Son makes you free, you are free indeed." The Son of God alone has the power and authority to liberate men from their bondage to sin. Interestingly, ancient scribes were divided as to how to write the two terms for *huios* in verses 35 and 36. The scribe of 𝔓⁶⁶ made them both nomina sacra; the scribe of 𝔓⁷⁵ wrote out the first word in *plene* (ΥΙΟC) and made the second a nomen sacrum (Υ̅C̅), thereby indicating his interpretation: verse 35 concerns "a son" generically speaking and verse 36 pertains to "the Son."

In the parable of the rented vineyard, the evil men killed the servants whom the owner sent and then they killed his only son. This, being a parable, does not explicitly name "the Son of God," though that is the intent. The scribe of 𝔓⁴⁵ decided to make it clear to his readers that this parable was explicitly about "the Son of God" by writing "my only Son" as a nomen sacrum.

In many other passages, there is absolutely no ambiguity about the expressions "the Son" or "his Son" being "the Son of God." As with the term "Father," so with the "Son," scribes in the second century vacillated between writing it out in full and writing it as a nomen sacrum. In the third and fourth centuries, scribes began to make *huios* a nomen sacrum more and more consistently.

Son of Man

When Jesus spoke of himself, he used the enigmatic title "the Son of Man." This was his way of saying that he was the Messiah without coming out directly and saying, "I am the Messiah." If he told the Jewish people directly, "I am the Messiah," they would have thought he was claiming to be the next "Maccabean" revolutionary leader and deliverer, come to set them free from Roman military rule.

So Jesus used a title borrowed from Ezekiel and Daniel. In the book of Ezekiel, the prophet was referred to as "Son of Man" ninety times. Often, God addressed

Ezekiel as "son of man"; in the same breath, God called him "son of dust." As such, it pointed to Ezekiel's humanity. It also pointed to Ezekiel's position as a servant. Thus, in adopting this term for himself, Jesus was adopting a term that emphasized that he had become a man to carry out service to God (see Phil. 2:5–11).

This is one side of the coin. The other side shows that "Son of Man" is a divine title, taken from Daniel 7:13–14. This passage describes a vision of one "like a son of man" who "comes with the clouds" into the presence of "the Ancient of Days," who gives him the universal and eternal kingdom of God. Jesus repeatedly quoted parts of this text in his teachings (Matt. 16:27; 19:28), especially about his second coming:

The sign of the coming of the Son of Man will appear in the heavens, and there will be deep mourning among all the nations of the earth. And they will see the Son of Man arrive on the clouds of heaven with power and great glory (Matt. 24:30 NLT).

Then again, Jesus quoted this passage in his trial before the Sanhedrin:

Then the high priest said to him, "I demand in the name of the living God that you tell us whether you are the Messiah, the Son of God."

Jesus replied, "Yes, it is as you say. And in the future you will see me, the Son of Man, sitting at God's right hand in the place of power and coming back on the clouds of heaven."

Then the high priest tore his clothing to show his horror, shouting, "Blasphemy! Why do we need other witnesses? You have all heard his blasphemy." (Matt. 26:63–65 NLT)

Clearly, Jesus understood the passage in Daniel about "the Son of Man" to be a title for the Christ, the Son of God. Evidently, the high priest also understood the passage in this way, for he considered it blasphemy for Jesus to have applied the passage to himself.

In the Gospels, the term "Son of Man" is used by Jesus about 80 times as a mysterious, indirect way of speaking about himself as the Messiah (Matthew, 32 times; Mark, 14 times; Luke, 26 times; John, 10 times). In all these texts, Jesus was always the speaker, and no one ever addressed him as "Son of Man." For several New Testament scribes, there was no question of interpreting this expression as a messianic title in the Gospels. Many of the early Gospel manuscripts exhibit the title as a nomen sacrum—namely, $\mathfrak{P}^{45}$, $\mathfrak{P}^{66}$, and $\mathfrak{P}^{75}$ (though not consistently). The scribe of $\mathfrak{P}^4 + \mathfrak{P}^{64} + \mathfrak{P}^{67}$ wrote out this title in full (see Luke 6:5). $\mathfrak{P}^1$ and $\mathfrak{P}^5$ have no extant portion that contains the title, "the Son of Man."

Beyond the Gospels, the term occurs only four other times in the New Testament.[47] In Acts 7:56, Stephen says, "Look, I see the heavens opened and the Son of Man standing in the place of honor at God's right hand." In Hebrews 2:6, the writer quotes the psalmist who wrote, "What is man that you are mindful of him? What is the son of man [or, Son of Man] that you visit him?" (Psalm 8:4). Revelation 1:13 and 14:14 record visions of someone "like a son of man" who is undoubtedly the glorified

246 \\ ENCOUNTERING THE MANUSCRIPTS

Jesus. In these texts, Jesus is described in his heavenly position as "the Son of Man," in accord with the vision in Daniel.

Interestingly, two scribes displayed their interpretations of two of the passages just mentioned—one by using a nomen sacrum, and the other by not. In Hebrews 2:6, the phrase "son of man" is ambivalent. It primarily refers to humanity in general, but it also looks forward to Jesus, the son of man (or Son of Man)—inasmuch as he partook of humanity to uplift the human race. Most modern translators do not capitalize "son of man" in this verse so as to exhibit the primary meaning. A few translations, however, do have it capitalized (see TLB, NLT mg.). The scribe of $\mathfrak{P}^{46}$ displayed his thoughts about the text by making it a divine title.

The scribe of $\mathfrak{P}^{47}$ exhibited his interpretation of Revelation 14:14 by not making the expression "son of man" a nomen sacrum. Consequently, his text reads, "There was one sitting who was like [a] son of man." This is the way it is rendered in many modern versions (NIV, NASB, RSV), while others made the title explicitly messianic: "the Son of Man" (NRSV, NLT).

"The Son of Man" was one of the earliest nomina sacra. However, it is doubtful that it was part of the original writings inasmuch as it does not show up consistently in the earliest papyrus manuscripts. In other words, some of the second-century scribes made it a nomen sacrum and some did not. The title is composed of two words that were written as nomen sacrum by themselves: *huios* (son—see above discussion) and *anthrōpos* (man). There is plenty of evidence among the literary papyri to show that *anthrōpos* was being abbreviated by the first century.

In Greek, the written title for "the Son of Man" appears in different ways in the extant manuscripts:

O ΥΙΟC ΤΟΥ $\overline{\text{ΑΝΟΥ}}$

$\overline{\text{ΥC}}$ ΤΟΥ ΑΝΘΡΩΠΟΥ

O $\overline{\text{ΥC}}$ ΤΟΥ $\overline{\text{ΑΝΟΥ}}$

Sometimes, just *huios* (Son) was contracted; other times, just *anthrōpou* (man); and other times, both words.[48]

The effect of writing "Son of Man" as a nomen sacrum is the same as when Jesus first used it: the identification could be made only by the initiates. Only those who knew who Jesus was understood what "Son of Man" meant. Only Christian scribes and readers (lectors) would recognize that O $\overline{\text{ΥC}}$ ΤΟΥ $\overline{\text{ΑΝΟΥ}}$ signified "the Son of Man." What better way to write it? The mystery inherent in the term is thereby sustained.

Cross and Crucify

People nowadays are fond of wearing crosses around their necks and putting crucifixes on their walls. If ancient Romans or Greeks saw us doing this, they would think we were crazy. To their way of thinking, we might as well be wearing a hangman's noose on our neck or hanging a replica of an electric chair on our wall! In ancient times, the cross was used to execute the worst criminals.

In the Greek language, the word "cross" (*stauros*) denoted a vertical stake with a crossbeam either across the top (T) or across the middle (+). Crucifixion was practiced first by the Medes and Persians and later by Alexander the Great (356–323 BC) and the Romans. Both Greeks and Romans restricted its use to slaves, considering it too barbaric for their citizens. This is best illustrated in the famous story of the slave uprising led by Spartacus in the first century BC. Captured in war and made a Roman gladiator, Spartacus eventually escaped with seventy other men. While in hiding on Mount Vesuvius, he gathered a large army of rebel slaves from Italy's farms. His army made some significant victories, gaining most of southern Italy. They would have been able to escape to freedom over the Alps had not Spartacus's troops urged him to attack Rome. They were defeated in this attempt, and Spartacus himself died in battle. All the other captured rebel slaves—and there were hundreds if not thousands of them— were crucified all along the Appian Way, as a warning to other slaves in Italy.

The Romans extended the use of crucifixion to foreigner criminals, but even so, it was used mainly for crimes against the government. This is why Barabbas, a revolutionary (Greek *lēstēs*) against Rome, was supposed to be crucified (John 18:40). In his place, Jesus was crucified. Jesus was also considered a revolutionary *(lēstēs)* by the authorities who arrested him (Matt. 26:55; Mark 14:48). Of course, the political charges against him were trumped up by the Jewish leaders. Even Pilate knew that Jesus had no aspirations to overthrow Rome. Nonetheless, he was crucified on the grounds that he claimed to be a king.

Crucifixion was universally recognized as the worst type of execution. The condemned criminal was brutally beaten and forced to carry the crossbeam to the spot where a stake had already been erected. A tablet stating the crime was often placed around the offender's neck and was fastened to the cross during the execution. The victim was tied or nailed to the crossbeam (with the nails through the wrists, since the bones in the hand could not take the weight). The beam was then raised and fixed to the upright pole. If the executioners planned a slow, agonizing death, they could drive blocks into the stake for a seat or a step to support the feet. Death came about through loss of blood circulation, followed by coronary collapse. Since that could take days, the executioners could break the victim's legs below the knees with a club, thereby eliminating any further possibility of easing the pressure on the wrists. Usually a body was left on the cross to rot, but in some instances was given to relatives or friends for burial.

Jesus' death on the cross was like any other crucifixion in that it was agonizingly painful and humiliating. What glory could there be in this kind of death? Yet Christians chose to glory in the cross of Jesus because they realized what his death meant. They knew that God sent his beloved Son into the world to die on the cross for their sins. The Son had paid the price for redemption.

The Bible says that Christ, as the Lamb of God, was foreordained to crucifixion (1 Pet. 1:19–20). His death on the cross was not an afterthought or merely a remedy; it was the fulfillment of the determined counsel and foreknowledge of God (Acts 2:23). Thus, the Scripture can speak of "the Lamb slain from the foundation of the world" (Rev. 13:8). Redemption could not have been accomplished if God had not partaken of flesh and blood—i.e., mortality. God cannot die because he is immortal; he had to partake of actual humanity in order to participate in mortality. The Son of God, out of love for his Father, willingly relinquished his equality with the Father to become subservient to him for the purpose of accomplishing redemption. He was sent by the Father to experience incarnation, human living, and crucifixion. This involved an "emptying-out" (in Greek called kenosis—"the process of emptying") of his divine prerogatives and equalities with the Father (see Phil. 2:5–11). The Son did it because he loved the Father.

But God's great act of sending his Son to die on the cross was done not only for the sake of accomplishing a legal redemption; it was done for the purpose of demonstrating God's ultimate love for humanity (see Rom. 5:8). God went all the way—to the extent that he sacrificed his own Son—to show how much he loved the world. Mysteriously, the cross of Christ became an attracting force, drawing peoples' hearts to God like a great magnet. Christ knew that when he was lifted up on the cross, he would draw all people to him. He declared this prior to his crucifixion (see John 12:32). Millions of people have been drawn to God by the constraining power manifested in Christ's cross. Paul, as if speaking for all who have known that love, exclaimed, "For the love of Christ constrains me. Because we thus judge, if one died for all, then all died. And he died for all, that those who live might no longer live for themselves but for him who for their sake died and was raised" (2 Cor. 5:14–15).

The earliest Christian writers decided to dignify the Greek word for "cross" (stauros) by making it a nomen sacrum; this was also done for the verb form, "crucify" (staurōmai). In fact, staurōmai is the only verb in the New Testament to have been treated as a nomen sacrum. The noun form was written in a very interesting manner. Scribes usually wrote the noun as follows:

$\overline{\text{CPΩC}}$; the rho was written as a staurogram—i.e., a P with a cross. The verb was usually written as $\overline{\text{CPΩMAI}}$—the rho was also written as a staurogram—i.e., a P with a cross.

The noun form, stauros, is treated as a nomen sacrum in every occurrence (except one) where it appears in extant manuscripts prior to AD 300. This is quite significant, for it tells us that the early Christians valued this term to the extent that they gave it sacred status in written form. This contrasts greatly with Roman sentiment about the word cross. Romans considered verbal references to the cross as being dirty, not fit for polite society, and generally either avoided them or else used circumlocutions such as "the extreme penalty."

For the portions of Matthew and Mark that have the word "cross," we have no extant text prior to AD 300. In Luke, the word appears in 9:23; 14:27; 23:26; it is written as a nomen sacrum in $\mathfrak{P}^{75}$ in all three verses and in 14:27 in $\mathfrak{P}^{45}$ (9:23 and 23:26 are not extant in $\mathfrak{P}^{45}$). The word "cross" appears in John 19:17, 19, 25, 31, where it appears as a nomen sacrum in $\mathfrak{P}^{66}$ in 19:19, 25, 31 (19:17 is not fully extant). In Paul's Epistles the word *cross* appears numerous times (1 Cor. 1:17, 18; Gal. 5:11; 6:12, 14; Eph. 2:16; Phil. 2:8; 3:18; Col. 1:20; 2:14), and in all of these occurrences $\mathfrak{P}^{46}$ has "cross" as nomen sacrum. This is also true for Hebrews 12:2. The only manuscript that writes out the word is $\mathfrak{P}^{13}$ in Hebrews 12:2.[49]

The verb form, *staurōmai* ("crucify") was also treated as nomen sacrum by many scribes—but not always. Some chose to write it out in full, some chose to make it sacral, and some did both. The scribe of $\mathfrak{P}^{77}$ wrote out the verb in Matthew 23:34. By contrast, the scribe of $\mathfrak{P}^{46}$ always made it a nomen sacrum, and it appears as such in 1 Corinthians 1:13, 23; 2:8; 2 Corinthians 13:4; Galatians 2:19; 5:24; 6:14; Hebrews 6:6. When a prefix appears with the verb *staurōmai*, such as *sun* (with) (see Gal. 2:19, "I am crucified with Christ") or *ana* (again) (see Heb. 6:6 "crucify again"), the scribe of $\mathfrak{P}^{46}$ abbreviated only the part of the verb (or participle) with *staurōmai* and placed an overbar over only that part. In the expression "where they crucified the Lord" (in Rev. 11:8), the scribe of $\mathfrak{P}^{47}$ wrote the verb as a nomen sacrum. The scribe of $\mathfrak{P}^{66}$ preferred to make the verb a nomen sacrum (as in John 19:6 [three times]; 19:15 [two times]; 19:18; 19:20). However, he occcasionally wrote it out (John 19:10, 23, 41). The scribe of $\mathfrak{P}^{75}$ made the verb a nomen sacrum on occasion (Luke 24:7); in the other verses, he wrote it out (Luke 23:21, 23, 33; 24:20). The Christian homily found in P. Oxyrhynchus 406 (ca. 200) also has the participle for "crucified" as a nomen sacrum in a discussion about the "Son of God, [the] crucified Christ."

The extant manuscript evidence strongly suggests that the noun form, "cross," was made a nomen sacrum early in the transmission of the text, and that this then influenced scribes to treat the verb form, "crucify," in similar fashion.

The early Christians gloried in the cross of Christ, as is evidenced by Paul's writings (see 1 Cor. 1:17–18; Gal. 6:12–14) and by the writings of the earliest martyrs, such as Polycarp (see *The Martyrdom of Polycarp*). They highly regarded Jesus' act of shedding his blood on the cross for the sins of the world. In Paul's epistles, the terms *blood* and *cross* were used synonymously to denote Jesus' sacrificial death (see Eph. 2:13; Col. 1:20, NLT). *Blood* and *cross* both stand for the death of Jesus in reconciling Jews and Gentiles to God. The writer of Hebrews argued that the whole Old Testament system of sacrifices found its ultimate fulfillment in the blood of Christ— that is, in his sacrificial death (Heb. 9:7–28; 13:11–12).

The scribe of a very early manuscript, $\mathfrak{P}^{46}$, on one occasion decided to make the Greek word for blood *(haima)* a nomen sacrum. He did this in Hebrews 9:14: "how much more will the blood of Christ . . . purify our consciences from dead works to serve the living God." In this verse the scribe made "blood of Christ" a nomen sacrum by writing it $\overline{\text{AIMA}}$ TOY $\overline{\text{XPY}}$.

Sacred Places: Israel, Jerusalem, Heaven

When we look at some of the earliest New Testament manuscripts, another group of names attracts our attention. These are names held in high regard by Jews and Christians. The Jews were named after Israel; hence, they were called Israelites. Jerusalem was their capital, the home of the temple of God. And heaven was considered to be home of God himself. Christians did not have the same regard for historical Israel as the Jews had; instead, they considered themselves the true, spiritual Israel (see Gal. 6:16). The earliest Christians held Jerusalem in high regard, both for historical reasons and because it was the birthplace of the church. They saw this Jerusalem, however, as typifying a heavenly one—the new Jerusalem they expected to be established on the new earth when Jesus Christ returned.

Early in the process of making copies of New Testament books, certain scribes decided to make "Israel" and "Jerusalem" nomina sacra. As was discussed previously, this could show that all the nomina sacra were first created in the Jerusalem church—and so it would have been quite natural for the Jewish Christians there to designate "Israel" and "Jerusalem" as sacred names. Some time later, a few scribes decided to make "heaven" a nomen sacrum.

Israel

In some of the earliest New Testament manuscripts ($\mathfrak{P}^{27\text{vid}}$, $\mathfrak{P}^{40\text{vid}}$, $\mathfrak{P}^{75}$, $\mathfrak{P}^{115}$, 0189), the name "Israel" is treated as a sacred name, written as $\overline{\text{IHΛ}}$. It is possible that these New Testament manuscripts had been affected by Jewish-Christian Greek Old Testament manuscripts, where the term *Israel* is frequently treated as a nomen sacrum. For example, the early second-century manuscript known as P. Chester Beatty VI (containing Numbers and Deuteronomy) has "Israel" as a nomen sacrum.

The dignifying of the term *Israel* shows that the early scribes considered the people of God to own God's name and to be a witness for God's name. In fact, the Old Testament consistently tells us that Israel was called upon to display God's Name (i.e., be a testimony) to the nations around them.

Jerusalem

Of all the places on earth, Jerusalem is the most sacred to Jews and to Christians. The city was considered holy because it was the habitation of God's holy temple. In fact, the name itself signifies that it was a holy city. "Jerusalem" translates the two Greek words *Ierousalem* and *Hierosoluma*. The former is the Greek transliteration of the Old Testament Aramaic form; the latter reflects the Greek word *hieros* (holy)—a hellenistic paranominen.

A few Christian scribes (apparently Jewish-Christian) treated the name as a nomen sacrum—namely the scribes of $\mathfrak{P}^{50}$, $\mathfrak{P}^{75}$, and 0189. The scribe of $\mathfrak{P}^{75}$ used a nomen sacrum for "Jerusalem" only in Luke, not in John. Furthermore, the nomen sacrum for "Jerusalem" in $\mathfrak{P}^{75}$ is used only for the Greek transliteration of the Aramaic form, never the hellenized form. This could indicate that the scribe was simulating an earlier Greek Old Testament scribal practice. The scribe of $\mathfrak{P}^{50}$ and the scribe of 0189 also used the nomen sacrum for the transliteration of the Aramaic form.

The city of Jerusalem was considered to be an earthly archetype of the eternal, heavenly city. In most Christian's thinking, the eternal Jerusalem is equivalent to heaven. This is not exactly scriptural. The New Jerusalem, according to the book of Revelation, is said "to come down out of heaven from God" and thereby become the eternal habitation of God with his redeemed people on the new earth (see Rev. 21:1–4).

There are five passages elsewhere in the New Testament that help to fill in the background to Revelation 21–22. In Galatians 4:26 Paul speaks of "Jerusalem above," the mother city of all who receive salvation by faith, as opposed to the old Jerusalem, where those belong who seek to please God by trying to obey the law (Gal. 4:25). In Ephesians 5:25–32 he speaks of the bride of Christ, by which he means the church; in John's vision the "bride" is the "city" (Rev. 21:9–10). In Philippians 3:20 we are told that the heavenly city is not simply the future home of believers, but also the place of their present "citizenship." Hebrews 12:22 makes the same point: those who believe have arrived already at the "heavenly Jerusalem." In other words, this Jerusalem is the home of all God's believing people, Jew and Gentile, from Old Testament and New Testament times, and it seems not only to be future, but also to exist already, in some sense, in the present. The fact remains, of course, that everything John records in the last two chapters of Revelation belongs to a world that will appear only after the first heaven and the first earth have passed away—a world which is (to us, at any rate) still future.

Taking into account all these Scriptures, we may come closest to understanding the New Jerusalem if we see it as the community of Christ and his people, which will appear in its perfection only when this age has come to an end. Yet in another sense, Christians belong to it already, and it gives them both an ideal to strive for in this world and a hope to anticipate in the next.

Heaven

In light of the discussion on Jerusalem above, it was only natural for certain scribes to consider "heaven" to also be dignified. But this term was not as readily and early recognized as a nomen sacrum by the majority of early Christian scribes.

The term was probably made a nomen sacrum because Jesus indicated that heaven is the dwelling place of God (Matt. 6:9) and because it is often seen as a synonym for

God himself. Indeed, the Jews had a habit of using "heaven" as a circumlocution for "God." In that way, they got around using the name of God. For example, in the book of Ecclesiastes, the writer used "heaven" as a circumlocution for "God" (see 1:13; 2:3; 3:1). This was carried over into New Testament times. Even Jesus used "heaven" as a synonym for "God" (see Matt. 5:34; 23:22). This is best illustrated in the story of the prodigal son, where the son comes to his senses and says to his father, "Father, I have sinned against heaven and you" (Luke 15:18, 21).

The scribe of 𝔓¹¹⁵ (ca. 300) wrote it as a nomen sacrum (Rev. 12:4, 8, 10; 13:7; 14:6 in the extant part of the text). This designation in the book of Revelation may signal the scribe's understanding that *ouranos* does not denote the "sky," but actually "heaven"—as the sphere in which the apocalypse is unveiled. The scribe of Codex Sinaiticus also made *ouranos* a nomen sacrum (more often when it is singular than plural—as in "heavens). No other early scribe wrote this term as a nomen sacrum.

Conclusions

What is amazing about the nomina sacra is that they appear in all the earliest New Testament manuscripts and Christian Old Testament manuscripts, no matter if the manuscripts were produced by professional scribes, documentary scribes, or those barely able to write in Greek. As was noted before, the handwriting of Christian biblical manuscripts falls into one of four categories: professional (those produced by full-time professional scribes), reformed documentary (those produced by scribes accustomed to making copies of documents and works of literature), documentary (those accustomed to making copies of documents only), and common (those who knew Greek as a second language or were just barely able to write Greek). There are extant manuscripts in all of these categories, and in all of them there are nomina sacra. This indicates that the practice was well-known to all Christians, not just professional scribes.

They appear in common men's copies of Revelation (𝔓¹⁸ and 𝔓²⁴); in a school boy's exercise of Romans (𝔓¹⁰); in an amulet or good luck charm of a third-century Egyptian (𝔓⁷⁸); in a Roman soldier's copy of Hebrews (𝔓¹³); and in copies produced by professionals (as in 𝔓⁴⁺⁶⁴⁺⁶⁷, 𝔓³⁹, 𝔓⁴⁶, 𝔓⁶⁶, 𝔓⁷⁵). All of these exhibit the same nomina sacra as found in the private copies. Professionals and nonprofessionals alike wrote the divine names as nomina sacra. This was a global phenomenon, not limited to Egypt. Though nearly all the early New Testament manuscripts were discovered in Egypt, this does not mean that they originated in Egypt. Furthermore, manuscript 0212 (containing a portion of a Gospel harmony) came from Dura-Europos, and it has a nomen sacrum for *staurōmai* (crucify). And nomina sacra appear in all the earliest copies of Latin and Coptic manuscripts. The point is clear: all throughout the Christian church in its early centuries New Testament texts displayed the nomina sacra. Special notice was given to "Lord," "Jesus," "Christ," "God," and "Spirit." In many of the earliest manuscripts "the cross" and the verb *crucify* were also written in a way to signal special notice. In due course, a host of other expressions were dignified and sanctified by being written as nomen sacrum: "Father," "Son," "Son of Man," "heaven," "Jerusalem," and "Israel." Scribes wrote these names with special regard, and readers (lectors) uttered these names with special attention in church meetings as they read the Scriptures aloud.

Chapter Five

Historical Overview of Textual Variation in the Greek New Testament

This chapter is pivotal for the student's understanding of New Testament textual criticism because we will herein consider the transmission of the New Testament text during the first three hundred years of the church—that is, we will be looking at the progressive reproduction of New Testament copies generation after generation from the late first century to the end of the fourth century. This is the time period in which most of the major textual changes occurred. As we attempt to reconstruct this transmission, we will look at the origin and development of textual variants. The key question is: Were some copies done with accuracy and fidelity to the originals, or were all copies altered in the process? Since we do not have any of the original manuscripts, this is an exceedingly important issue. The reconstruction of the original text depends upon fidelity in at least some copies.

The New Testament Text in the First Century

Let us first ask: What kind of changes might have happened to the text of the New Testament in the few decades after their initial publication? First, we must allow for the possibility that the author himself and/or an authorized cowriter may have edited (or redacted) the text prior to another publication of the same writing. For example, it is very likely that John added another chapter to his Gospel (chap. 21) in its second edition. It is also possible that Luke produced two editions of Acts. And many scholars think that an editor (such as Timothy) combined two of Paul's letters to the Corinthians to make the epistle now known as 2 Corinthians. None of these changes, however, were unauthorized.

Once the final, authorized publication was released and distributed to the churches, I think it unlikely that any substantive changes would have occurred during the lifetime of the apostles or second-generation coworkers. By "substantive," I mean a change that would alter Christian doctrine or falsify an apostolic account. The primary reason is that the writers (or their immediate successors) were alive at the time and therefore could challenge any significant, unauthorized alterations. As long as eyewitnesses such as John or Peter were alive, who would dare change any of the Gospel accounts in any significant manner? Any one among the Twelve could have testified against any falsification. And there was also a group of 72 other disciples (Luke 10:1) who could do the same. Furthermore, according to 1 Corinthians 15:6, Jesus had at least five hundred followers by the time he had finished his ministry, and these people witnessed Jesus in resurrection. Most of these people were still alive (Paul said) in AD 57/58 (the date of composition for 1 Corinthians); it stands to reason that several lived for the next few decades—until the turn of the century and even beyond.

Historical sources tell us that the apostle John lived until the end of the first century.[1] During the last years of his life on earth, as can be gathered from his epistles, John was defending apostolic, eyewitness truth against heresy. (This would have been in the 80s or even 90s.) Since aberrations from apostolic truth were noted and dealt with, any attempt at altering their writings (which were circulating in the churches) would have been spotted and stopped.

Furthermore, in their actual writings, the authors themselves affirmed the apostolic authority of their writings and gave warnings against anyone altering what they had written. Paul told the Galatians that God would curse anyone who altered their gospel (see Gal. 1:6–9). Paul and Silas commended the Thessalonians for accepting their message as "the word of the Lord, and not the word of men" (1 Thess. 2:13) and then went on to command them "in the name of the Lord to read this letter to all the Christians" (1 Thess. 5:27). In their second epistle to the Thessalonians, they warned them not to accept any forgeries (2:2), and then Paul personally signed the epistle to guarantee its authenticity (3:17). In his first epistle to the Corinthians (14:37), Paul specifically mentioned that his "writings" be recognized as coming from the Lord himself.

In his writings, John repeatedly affirms his eyewitness authority. In his Gospel, he affirms that he had seen Jesus' glory (1:14)[2] and that he had been an eyewitness of Jesus' trial (18:15ff.), crucifixion (19:35–36), and resurrection (20:8, 30; 21:24).[3] In his first epistle, John also claimed to be an eyewitness of the God-man, Jesus Christ, and because of this he claimed apostolic authority for his written message (see 1 John 1:1–4). In the book of Revelation, John gives an explicit warning against anyone altering his account—whether by adding to it or taking away from it (see Rev. 1:3; 22:18–19). As such, he was making a pronouncement on its sacred inviolability. The warning against changing his Apocalypse is well worth repeating here: "I warn everyone who hears the words of the prophecy of this book: if anyone adds to them, God will add to that person the plagues described in this book; if anyone takes away from the words of the book of this prophecy, God will take away that person's share in the tree of life and in the holy city, which are described in this book" (22:18–19 NRSV). Other writers in antiquity penned the same kind of warnings about their writings so as to guard them against textual corruption. For example, in Rufinus's translation of Origen's *Peri Archōn*, he pens this warning in the preface: "One request, however, I solemnly make of every one who shall either transcribe or read these books, in the sight of God the Father and the Son and the Holy Spirit . . . he shall neither add anything to this writing, nor take anything away, nor interpolate anything, nor change anything."[4]

Since writers in antiquity were well aware that their books could be changed by scribes in successive copies, they made these warnings. Undoubtedly, they knew that there would be unintentional mistakes, which come through the course of making manuscripts. What they were hoping to protect against was intentional alteration of the writing.

We have discussed Paul's attitude about his writings and John's; now let us turn to Peter. This apostle also affirmed that his writings were based on firsthand, eyewitness events. He explicitly said that he (and the other apostles) had not followed cleverly devised myths when they told others about the coming of the Lord Jesus Christ, for Peter had personally been with Jesus on the mount of transfiguration and had seen his excellent glory (see 2 Pet. 1:12–18). As such, Peter warned against the false teachers who would pervert the truth of the apostolic message. Peter also warned against those who were trying to twist Paul's writings, and in the process of making this warning he called those writings "Scriptures." In effect, Peter was affirming the scriptural status of Paul's writings when he wrote: "Regard the patience of our Lord as salvation. So also our beloved brother Paul wrote to you according to the wisdom given to him, speaking of this as he does in all his epistles. There are some things in them hard to understand, which the ignorant and unstable twist to their own destruction, as they do the other Scriptures." In this statement (2 Pet. 3:15–16), we discover that the author unequivocally indicates that Paul's letters are on the same par as "the other Scriptures." According to the Greek, the statement is even stronger, for he says *tas loipas graphas* (the rest of the Scriptures)—thereby indicating that Paul's epistles comprise a certain portion of the whole canon. What is also apparent in the Greek is that the author would have been a contemporary of Paul, because he intimates that Paul was presently speaking to the churches through his epistles. The present participle carries this force: "in all his epistles speaking [Greek *lalein*] in them concerning these things." The implication of this is that Paul's Epistles were already considered "Scriptures" by the early church; as such, they should not be altered.[5]

The New Testament Text in the Second Century

After the second century began, most of the living witnesses to Jesus' life and words would have died. Consequently, the New Testament writings could have been vulnerable to unauthorized alteration—unless, of course, the writings had already been considered sacred Scripture or the copyists were trained professionals whose task was to replicate documents with acumen—no matter what their attitude was about their content. Thus, in exploring the condition of the New Testament text in the second century we have to look at what were the prevailing scriptural attitudes about these writings and what was the "scriptoral acuity" in making copies. "Scriptural attitude" denotes the mind-set about the New Testament writings: Were they considered "Scripture" on a par with Old Testament Scriptures? If so, were they considered inviolable as to their every word, or was it just their message that was considered sacred? This leads to another important question: What kind of impact did different attitudes have on the copying of Scripture? This is the "scriptoral acuity" I am talking about. Did scribes making copies of various New Testament books see their task as (1) reproducing the text word by word, (2) re-presenting the message with allowance for some verbal variance, or (3) reshaping (redacting) the text for theological and/or ecclesiastical reasons?

The issue pertaining to the first two views focuses on whether the total message of the text or the exact wording was perceived as being inspired. In other words, did they consider every word to be sacred or was it just the message? We have the same dilemma in modern times: some believe in the inspiration of the message of Scripture, whereas others espouse verbal plenary inspiration. Are there indications that some Christian scribes held the latter view? Or, even if they didn't have this view, were there some Christian scribes who thought it was their task to copy every word accurately? In other words, their motivation for accuracy could have come from their respect for the sacredness of the text or from their regard for Alexandrian scribal acumen, or both. Any Christian scribe with Alexandrian scriptoral training—whether from Alexandria itself or elsewhere—should have been inclined to reproduce an accurate copy. It is primarily to their manuscripts that we look for preserving the original wording of the various writings of the published New Testament.

As for the work of several other scribes, we can ascertain that they probably did not share the sentiment that every single word of the New Testament writings was "God-inspired." Perhaps they believed that it was the message behind the words that was sacred. Therefore, to change the wording without changing authorial intention (as they perceived it), in the interest of making a better reading, was deemed acceptable. These scribes attempted to reproduce the text they were copying in the sense that they were re-presenting the message. They may have omitted a few words, transposed other words, or added a few words here and there as they produced a copy. In their minds, they probably considered that they had done a good job of transmitting a text—and maybe a better one at that. However, the final product is not a strictly faithful copy. Of course, it must also be said that various scribes were so unprofessional that they simply produced inaccurate copies, no matter what their attitude was about the text.

The third perspective (i.e., that of redacting the text) calls for an entirely different line of investigation. Redaction involves purposeful emendation, whatever the motivation. With time, many scribes emended the text with the intent of harmonizing various Gospel accounts and/or smoothing out difficulties in the text. From their perspective, they probably thought they were doing a good job. One such redactor was Lucian of Antioch (who is discussed below). Other men purposefully altered the text to make it conform to their doctrinal position. Marcion, a heretic, is a prime example of this kind of redactor (see discussion below). Still others, such as Tatian, wove together one Gospel narrative from four, thereby eliminating any discrepancies among the Gospel accounts.

Some scholars, such as Ehrman, view the early period of textual transmission as a time when the text was being redacted more by the orthodox than by heretics.[6] Ehrman's position is that certain orthodox Christians altered key Christological passages in an effort to make the text accord with what they considered true orthodox Christology. Although not all scholars will agree with Ehrman's conclusions on a text-by-text basis, most will agree with the basic premise that the New Testament text was corrupted by well-intended orthodox scribes. In fact, this is a major part of Metzger's thesis in his well-known volume *The Text of the New Testament: Its Transmission, Corruption, and Restoration*.[7] Those who study the text and the history of its transmission realize that most of the substantive changes were made in the interest of "improving" the text. Various scribes were motivated to make changes in the text for the sake of harmonizing Gospel accounts, eliminating difficult doctrinal statements, and/or adding accounts from oral tradition.

The "Scriptural" Attitude about the New Testament Writings and the Effect of Canonization on Textual Transmission

The primary question here is simple: When were the New Testament writings considered to be "canonized Scripture"? The second question follows: If they were considered Scriptures, did that mean that scribes considered every word sacred or just that the message was sacred? The answer to the first question varies considerably among various scholars, largely depending on one's view of when the canonization of the New Testament occurred and what effect that had on people's attitude toward the New Testament writings. The answer to the second question has to be addressed on a case-by-case basis—that is, each manuscript must be examined to determine the scribe's attitude about his or her copying.

A brief survey of the development of the New Testament canon should make it quite clear that there was no fixed point in history prior to the fourth century when all would agree that the twenty-seven books now in the New Testament canon were worthy of the title "Scripture." As was discussed in chapter 1, we know that the Gospels and certain epistles were "canonized" in the minds of many Christians as early as AD 90–100—that is, the four Gospels and Paul's Epistles were deemed Scripture worthy to be read in church. As was noted above, the apostles themselves made statements in their writings that affirmed that their words were to be taken as authoritative, for their message had come from the Lord Jesus. This, in and of itself, purports that the writing should be considered "canonical"—that is, an authoritative, sacred text worthy of use in the Christian church.

We also know that the church fathers of the second century had a high regard for the New Testament text. Indeed, a study of the writings of the first five outstanding church fathers (all writing before AD 150)—namely, Clement, Ignatius, Papias, Justin Martyr, and Polycarp—indicates that they used the New Testament writings with the same—or nearly the same—sacred regard they attributed to the Old Testament writings. Both were Scripture. During the second half of the second century, more apostolic fathers were affirming that the New Testament writings were Scripture. This is especially evident in the writings of Irenaeus. In short, the general sentiment throughout the second and third centuries was that these writings should be treated as sacred documents given by the Lord Jesus through his apostles to the church.[8]

To be fair, we should view the period of 100–300 as being variegated with respect to the status of the New Testament canon. We cannot paint it with broad strokes, presenting a picture of full canonical status or a picture on noncanonical status. Many scholars, however, paint this early period as being characteristically noncanonical— that is, the New Testament writings were not yet considered "Scripture" and therefore were categorically subject to all kinds of changes. For example, the Alands, with some sweeping statements, give this impression of the early period. In *The Text of the New Testament*, the Alands said that second-century Christian scribes felt they had a direct relationship with God and therefore "regarded themselves as possessing inspiration equal to that of the New Testament writings which they read in the church meetings."[9] The Alands affirm that the New Testament scribes felt free to make changes in the text, "improving it by their own standards of correctness, whether grammatically, stylistically, or more substantively." According to the Alands, this freedom was exhibited during "the early period, when the text had not yet attained canonical status, especially in the earliest period when Christians considered themselves filled with the Spirit."[10] Other scholars, such as Petzer and Colwell, have also characterized the transmission of the text in the early period as being "uncontrolled," "wild," and "unstable."[11]

What the Alands and others describe is only one part of the picture. True, there were many scribes who altered the text, but I don't think most of them considered themselves to have inspiration equal to that of the New Testament writers, unless they were Montanists. But we have no record of the Montanists ever changing the text. The Montanists believed in extracanonical inspiration—that is, God kept speaking after the time of the apostles and beyond what the apostles said. The fuller picture is that there were some scribes in the early period who must have recognized that they were copying authoritative, apostolic documents on a par with "Scripture." Even the Alands indirectly admit this when they categorize several of the early New Testament papyri as being "strict"—i.e., they were faithful (strict) copies of the New Testament text (see discussion below). Furthermore, I must state that I have personally examined every word of all the New Testament manuscripts dated before AD 300. In some of these manuscripts, I have seen the uncontrolled wildness described by others. In other manuscripts, I have observed control. And most of the other manuscripts fall in between these two extremes.[12]

As was discussed in chapter 1, the New Testament canon was more or less fixed in the third century and finalized in the fourth. In the beginning of the fourth century, Eusebius was the chief proponent of establishing the four Gospels, as well as other recognized books, as comprising the New Testament canon. In the middle of the fourth century the canon was established once and for all. In his *Festal Letter for Easter* (AD 367), Athanasius of Alexandria included information designed to eliminate once and for all the use of certain apocryphal books. This letter, with its admonition, "Let no one add to these; let nothing be taken away," provides the earliest extant document which specifies the twenty-seven books without qualification. At the close of the century, the Council of Carthage (AD 397) decreed that "aside from the canonical Scriptures nothing is to be read in church under the Name of Divine Scriptures." This also lists the twenty-seven books of the New Testament.

The common view espoused by many scholars is that final canonization of the New Testament writings basically put an end to textual alteration. But this is only true from one perspective—it put an end to heretical alterations and excluded unauthorized writings from the canon. Indeed, the whole purpose of the final canonization was to protect the New Testament text from heretical and/or unorthodox writings, which had been circulating in the church during its early centuries. Final canonization excluded nonapostolic writings and with it, any potential unorthodoxy or heresy. Thus, the New Testament canon declared itself to be the final say on orthodoxy. As such, no one thereafter could alter the text in this regard. However, did that mean that canonicity protected the New Testament text from other kinds of changes? Absolutely not. In fact, canonicity promoted a whole new view of this unified text that prompted full-scale harmonization of the Gospels and other interpolations supporting various church doctrines.

Ironically, as the text became more and more canonized, it was more vulnerable to these kinds of alterations. This is the position of Frederik Wisse, who counters the common assumption that "Christian scribes would have been reluctant to tamper with the text of a canonical writing, but would have felt free to introduce changes before a text was recognized as apostolic and authoritative." His argument is twofold: (1) It is only when a text is considered authoritative that its teachings become problematic if they no longer conform to current beliefs and practices. Hence, authoritative texts would be subject to textual change, whereas in the precanonical period scribes were less hesitant to take liberties with the text. (2) The number of textual interpolations increased rather than decreased after the second century. Wisse said, "Many of them, including the pericope adulterae [John 7:53–8:11], are not attested before the fourth century. It would appear that the frequency of copying was a much more important factor in the creation of interpolations than was the canonical status of a writing." Thus, Wisse concludes:

> These facts speak against the common assumption that by the early third century emerging orthodoxy brought an end to the period of considerable redactional freedom by deciding on a "standard" text and by suppressing all manuscripts that deviated. Long after the third century the church was in no position to establish and control the biblical text, let alone eliminate rival forms of the text. Though there may have been an attempt at establishing a standard text as early as the fourth century, only beginning with the twelfth century do we have evidence for a large-scale effort.[13]

In the end, we must see that canonization was a process, which lasted from the second to the fourth century. The Gospels, for example, were "canonized" in the minds of many Christians as early as AD 100; that is, the four Gospels were deemed Scripture worthy to be read in church. By the time we get to the fourth century, the four Gospels were canonized throughout all of Christendom. But this canonization did not necessarily protect the text against textual tampering. In fact, some scribes took the liberty to harmonize the Gospel accounts so that they would be more palpable to the church or less prone to attack from the critics of Christianity. Indeed, it appears that harmonizations and other textual alterations increased significantly in the fourth century and beyond. (More will be said on this in what follows.)

Overall, the more balanced view, in my opinion, is that the early period of textual transmission can be characterized as being both free and controlled, depending on which scribe (with what training) had produced the manuscript. And this leads us to the next discussion.

Scribal Influences on New Testament Scribes

The earliest Christian scribes would have had one of two influences when it came to preparing texts. They would have been influenced by Alexandrian scriptoral practices. This is not debated, because the influence of Alexandrian bookmaking spread over the entire Greco-Roman world. The other influence may have come from Jewish scriptoral practices and/or what could be called Septuagintal-copying influence.

Alexandrian Influences

Unquestionably, Alexandrian scriptoral practices had become influential throughout the entire hellenized world by the time the church first began. By the third century BC, the Alexandrian library had over 500,000 volumes and had become a center of learning—like a modern university. The eminent paleographer Kenyon elaborates: "Besides being a library, it was an Academy of Letters and Learning. Eminent men of letters and scholars, such as Callimachus, Apollonius Rhodius, and Aristarchus, were placed in succession at its head; students gathered around it; a corps of copyists was employed to multiply manuscripts; and Alexandria became the centre of the literary life of the Hellenistic world."[14]

The Alexandrians were concerned with preserving the original text of works of literature. Textual criticism was applied to Homer's *Iliad* and the *Odyssey* because these were ancient texts existing in many manuscripts. The Alexandrians would make text-critical decisions from among many different manuscripts concerning the original wording and then produce an archetype. The archetype was the manuscript produced officially and deposited in the library. From this were copied, and with it were collated, further manuscripts as required.[15]

Aristotle of Alexandria classified manuscripts as to their date and value. His work was continued on by men such as Zenodotus, Aristophanes of Byzantium, and Aristarchus of Samothrace—all librarians in the great library in Alexandria. Zenodotus initiated the first scientific attempt to get back to the original text of the Homeric poems. Aristophanes produced much-improved critical editions of Homer and other poets. Aristarchus is said to have been the founder of accurate literary scholarship. These learned men of Alexandria were the creators of scholarly philological criticism and textual criticism. Michael Grant said, "Their methods became canonical in determining the forms of book-production and literary analysis in all Hellenistic centres, and the earlier writings they had so carefully preserved and studied were handed down to the Romans, and thus to ourselves."[16]

As far as we know, there was no full-scale textual criticism of the New Testament text during the second and third centuries. The one who could have done it was Origen, but Origen did not engage in any full-scale textual criticism of the Greek New Testament because he was afraid to tamper with the Word of God. Instead, he applied his textual criticism to the Septuagint because he felt it was safer to work with what was only a translation of the sacred text (see his *Commentary of Matthew* 15.14). Consequently, he became entirely involved with his Hexpala project and made only a few comments about variant readings in the New Testament text.[17] Nonetheless, we know that Origen had various copies of New Testament books for his studies by the fact that he commented about the accuracy of some compared to the inaccuracy of others (for example, see his *Commentary of Matthew* 19.18).

What we do know, from the manuscript evidence, is that several of the earliest Christian scribes were well-trained scribes who applied their training to making reliable texts, both of the Old Testament and the New Testament. We know that they were conscientious to make a reliable text in the process of transcription (as can been seen in manuscripts like $\mathfrak{P}^{4+64+67}$ and $\mathfrak{P}^{75}$), and we know that others worked to rid the manuscript of textual corruption. This is nowhere better manifested than in $\mathfrak{P}^{66}$, where the scribe himself and the *diorthotes* (official corrector) made over 450 corrections to the text of John. As is explained in the next chapter, the *diorthotes* of $\mathfrak{P}^{66}$

probably consulted other exemplars (one whose text was much like that of $\mathfrak{P}^{75}$) in making his corrections. This shows a standard Alexandrian scriptoral practice at work in the reproduction of a New Testament manuscript.

Old Testament Scribal Influence

The scribes we read about in Jesus' day primarily had two functions: they made judgments for various Jewish sects about the application and meaning of the law, as well as made a living by copying Torah texts.[18] Modern readers of the Gospels tend to think of "the scribes" as a kind of religious sect, but, as Meier correctly indicates, "scribes" refers to a function—that of copying sacred texts, not to a particular party of Jews or merely to a role as adjudicator of the law.[19] In short, the scribes were just that—scribes, copiers of the sacred Old Testament text. Scribes did, however, belong to various religious parties. Some scribes were Essenes (as is evident from the Dead Sea Scroll discoveries), and some scribes were Pharisees (see Acts 23:9).

The book of Acts indicates that several Pharisees became Christians (Acts 15:5). Thus, by way of conjecture, it would stand to reason that some Pharisaic Jewish scribes became Christians. If so, the question must be asked: Would they have transferred their high regard and scribal acuity for copying the Old Testament Scriptures to the New? Unfortunately, there is no historical documentation about particular persons or groups to substantiate this query one way or the other.

What we have to go on comes from a few paleographic links between Jewish scribal practice and early Christian scribal practice. First, as was discussed in the previous chapter on the nomina sacra, it is quite likely that the special written formation of the Tetragrammaton YHWH gave rise to the nomen sacrum for *Kurios* (Lord). Second, some Christian Old Testament manuscripts and New Testament manuscripts display nomen sacrum for "Israel" and "Jerusalem" (namely, Chester Beatty VI [Num.–Deut.], $\mathfrak{P}^{66}$, $\mathfrak{P}^{75}$). This sacred regard for Israel and Jerusalem, Jewish in origin, was carried over into New Testament manuscripts. Third, as was pointed out in chapter 1, we see that the Greek Minor Prophet scrolls from Nahal Hever and Christian biblical manuscripts display the "enlarged letter, preceded by a small blank space, marking the beginning of a new phrase, while verses are marked off by larger spaces."[20] These paleographic features prompted two papyrologists, C. H. Roberts and Peter Parsons, to think that Jewish scriptoral practice had influenced Christian scriptoral practice.[21]

In the days of the early church, Christians made manuscript copies of both Greek Old Testament texts and New Testament texts. Unquestionably, Christians recognized that the Septuagint was "Scripture." And the extant Greek Old Testament manuscripts produced by Christians (see chap. 3 for discussions on second-century OT manuscripts) reveal that the Christians who produced these texts were concerned with their textual fidelity. In speaking of his evaluation of the early Old Testament manuscripts produced by Christians, C. H. Roberts wrote:

> In the second century, locally produced texts such as the scrap of *The Shepherd* [of Hermas] on the back of a document from the Fayum or the Baden Exodus-Deuteronomy might be carefully collated and corrected; the numerous duplications and omissions of the first hand of the Chester Beatty Numbers-Deuteronomy codex were put right by the corrector. This scrupulous reproduction of the text may be a legacy from Judaism and reminds us that no more in this period than in any other does quality of book production go hand in hand with quality of text.[22]

The question remains: Would the same kind of care given to Old Testament writings also be given to the New Testament writings? An entire collection of Christian manuscripts (purchased by Chester Beatty), both of Greek Old Testament and New Testament manuscripts, coming from the same source, could give us some insights. On November 17, 1931, *The London Times* announced the discovery of twelve manuscripts said to have been found in a Coptic graveyard, stowed away in jars—eight books of the Old Testament and three of the New Testament. This was a sensational discovery—one almost as monumental as the discovery of the Dead Sea Scrolls, which were found about twenty years later, in jars in the Qumran caves. The eight manuscripts containing portions of the Greek Old Testament are as follows: two manuscripts of Genesis (one from the third century, another from the fourth); one of Numbers and Deuteronomy (second century); one of Ezekiel and Esther (third century); one of Isaiah (third century); one of Jeremiah (late second century); one of Daniel (third century), and one of Ecclesiasticus (fourth century). The three Greek New Testament manuscripts said to be found in the Coptic graveyard were the earliest manuscripts to contain large portions of the New Testament text. The first manuscript, $\mathfrak{P}^{45}$ (late second/early third), is a codex of the four Gospels and Acts; the second, $\mathfrak{P}^{46}$ (second century), is a codex of the Pauline epistles; and the third, $\mathfrak{P}^{47}$ (third century) is a codex of Revelation.

The manuscripts, both of the Old Testament and the New Testament, were produced by Christians because all the manuscripts are codices (as opposed to rolls) and all display nomina sacra. This Christian library of Greek biblical texts was quite full: Genesis (two copies), Numbers, Deuteronomy, Isaiah, Jeremiah, Ezekiel, Daniel, Esther, Ecclesiasticus, Gospels and Acts, Pauline epistles, Revelation—plus Enoch, Melito, Apocryphal Ezekiel. Not one of the manuscripts was written in Coptic (although there are a few Old Fayyumic Coptic glosses written in the margin of the Isaiah manuscript).

Several scribes were responsible for producing the manuscripts, and there is no paleographic indication that one particular scribe worked on more than one manuscript. Some of the manuscripts are the work of professional scribes—namely, the

Numbers/Deuteronomy manuscript, $\mathfrak{P}^{46}$ (the Pauline epistles), the Isaiah manuscript, and the Jeremiah fragment. The Daniel manuscript and $\mathfrak{P}^{45}$ (Gospels and Acts) may have also been done by professionals—at least, they display the reformed documentary hand. The smaller Genesis manuscript was written in a documentary hand. The other manuscripts are not as well written, calligraphically speaking.[23]

The editor of all these manuscripts, Frederic Kenyon, made this observation about the textual fidelity of both the Old Testament and New Testament manuscripts in the collection:

> The first and foremost conclusion derived from the examination of them is the satisfactory one that they confirm the essential soundness of the existing texts. No striking or fundamental variation is shown in either the Old Testament or the New Testament. There are no important omissions or additions of passages, and variations that affect vital facts or doctrines. The variations of text affect minor matters, such as order of words or the precise words used. On these matters, which are of high interest rather than of fundamental importance, they offer evidence of great value to Biblical critics. But their essential importance is their confirmation, by evidence of an earlier date than was hitherto available, of the integrity of our existing texts.[24]

Scholars might disagree with his assessment of manuscripts like $\mathfrak{P}^{45}$, but in general Kenyon is right. Most of the early Christian scribes gave the same care to a New Testament manuscript as to an Old Testament manuscript.

This care is further manifested in the fact that Christian scribes generally resisted the temptation to alter Old Testament texts in the interest of heightening messianic passages. Robert Kraft did a study of Greek Old Testament manuscripts in which he looked for textual changes wherein Christian scribes may have altered the text—specifically, in three ways: (1) places where the title "Christ" appears in such a way as to betray Christian interests; (2) the use of specifically Christian terminology in the Greek Old Testament; (3) passages in the Old Testament that have been rephrased to agree with quotations of them in the New Testament or in the writings of the church fathers. Kraft came to the conclusion that while isolated examples may be found in the corpus of Septuagint manuscripts, overall, little evidence is found of distinctively Christian theology being imposed on the Greek text of the Old Testament as it was copied and preserved by Christians.[25] Jobes and Silva come to the same conclusion with respect to their investigation of the evidence—namely, Christian scribes, for the most part, did not alter the Septuagint in light of Christian theology.[26]

What these observations tell us is that most Christian scribes exercised control in their work as copyists. This applies to their task of making copies of the Old Testament, and this also applies—for several scribes—to their task of making New Testament copies, which leads us to our next discussion.

New Testament Textual Reliability in the Early Centuries

All those who have studied the New Testament manuscripts of the earliest centuries recognize they display a diversity of textual reliability. It is misleading to describe them all by the same adjectives—especially as being "uncontrolled" or "free." As noted above, the Alands speak of the early period in general terms (as being "uncontrolled") but then they apply specific categories to specific manuscripts of the early period that, for some manuscripts, contradict their general description of the early period. Thus, we need to overlook their sweeping statements and instead explore the viability of their specific categories for the early papyri. The Alands have given us the categories "strict," "at least normal," "normal," and "free" presumably to evaluate the textual fidelity of each manuscript. I say "presumably" because the Alands never told us exactly what they were measuring; thus, the terms are question-begging inasmuch as we do not know if they refer to a strict copy of the original or of an exemplar. I understand the terms to describe scribal control or the lack thereof in the copying process. Thus, "strict" refers to manuscripts produced by scribes who allowed for little variation in the copying process. "Normal" refers to those manuscripts that were produced by those who allowed a normal amount of variation. "At least normal" manuscripts display some liberties with a tendency toward strictness. And "free" manuscripts are those that exhibit disregard for faithful textual transmission. The Alands place nine papyri in what they call a "strict" category ($\mathfrak{P}^1$ $\mathfrak{P}^{23}$ $\mathfrak{P}^{27}$ $\mathfrak{P}^{35}$ $\mathfrak{P}^{36}$ $\mathfrak{P}^{64/67}$ $\mathfrak{P}^{65}$ $\mathfrak{P}^{70}$ $\mathfrak{P}^{75}$), and they categorized nine papyri ($\mathfrak{P}^9$ $\mathfrak{P}^{13}$ $\mathfrak{P}^{37}$ $\mathfrak{P}^{40}$ $\mathfrak{P}^{45}$ $\mathfrak{P}^{69}$ $\mathfrak{P}^{78}$) as being "free." This equal number shows that the early period was not overly "free" nor overly "strict." Indeed, the majority of early papyri are considered "normal" by the Alands—that is, a normal text is that "which transmitted the original text with the limited amount of variation characteristic of the New Testament textual tradition."[27]

These variations can be observed by analyzing a scribe's personal interaction with the text, which can be ascertained by a study of singular variants in each manuscript, because these leave telltale signs of the scribe's individualism. Colwell commenced this kind of study with the papyri $\mathfrak{P}^{45}$, $\mathfrak{P}^{66}$, and $\mathfrak{P}^{75}$.[28] Royse went further in his extensive study of the same manuscripts, plus $\mathfrak{P}^{46}$, $\mathfrak{P}^{47}$, and $\mathfrak{P}^{72}$.[29] I implemented some of the same procedures, with the addition of reader-reception theory, in a doctoral dissertation, to determine a scribe's interaction with the text as he read it and copied it.[30] My task was to determine what it was in the text that prompted the scribes of $\mathfrak{P}^{45}$, $\mathfrak{P}^{66}$, and $\mathfrak{P}^{75}$ to make individual readings. Since this process involves looking at singular variants, we are definitely looking at divergences from the normative text and can thereby determine particular scribal tendencies, as well as make determinations about textual reliability in the end product.

I suggest that textual critics could use the categories "reliable," "fairly reliable," and "unreliable" to describe the textual fidelity of any given manuscript. The chart below shows that many of the early papyri are "reliable," several "fairly reliable," and a few "unreliable." One of the ways of establishing reliability (or lack thereof) is to test a manuscript against one that is generally proven for its textual fidelity. For example, since many scholars have acclaimed the textual fidelity of $\mathfrak{P}^{75}$ (both for intrinsic and extrinsic reasons), it is fair to compare other manuscripts against it in order to determine their textual reliability. In essence, I have already done this when determining the members of the $\mathfrak{P}^{75}$ group (which is discussed in chap. 7).

The most reliable texts are $\mathfrak{P}^1$, $\mathfrak{P}^4+\mathfrak{P}^{64}+\mathfrak{P}^{67}$, $\mathfrak{P}^{23}$, $\mathfrak{P}^{27}$, $\mathfrak{P}^{30}$, $\mathfrak{P}^{32}$, $\mathfrak{P}^{35}$, $\mathfrak{P}^{39}$, $\mathfrak{P}^{49}+\mathfrak{P}^{65}$, $\mathfrak{P}^{70}$, $\mathfrak{P}^{75}$, $\mathfrak{P}^{86}$, $\mathfrak{P}^{87}$, $\mathfrak{P}^{90}$, $\mathfrak{P}^{91}$, $\mathfrak{P}^{100}$, $\mathfrak{P}^{101}$, $\mathfrak{P}^{106}$, $\mathfrak{P}^{108}$, $\mathfrak{P}^{111}$, $\mathfrak{P}^{114}$, and $\mathfrak{P}^{115}$. These manuscripts, produced with acumen, display a standard of excellence. Each scribe's motivation for accuracy could have come from their respect for the sacredness of the text or from their scriptoral training, or both. In any event, these scribes produced reliable copies that largely preserve the original wording of the authorized published texts. It is to these manuscripts that we look for the preservation of the original wording of the various writings of the published New Testament. This is not to say that these manuscripts are perfect. Many of these manuscripts contain singular readings and some "Alexandrian" polishing, which needs to be sifted out. Once this is done, I think we can be quite confident that we have the original wording of the published text.

Some may argue that we can only be confident that we have good manuscripts of an "early" form of the text but not necessarily of the originally published text. This hypothesis cannot be disproven. However, I think it is highly doubtful for four reasons: (1) The intervening time between the publication date of various New Testament books (from AD 60–90) and the date of several of our extant manuscripts (from AD 100–200) is narrow, thereby giving us manuscripts that are probably only three to five "manuscript generations" removed from the originally published texts. (2) We have no knowledge that any of these manuscripts go back to an early "form" that postdates the original publications. (3) We are certain that there was no major Alexandrian recension in the second century. (4) Text critics have been able to detect any other other second-century textual aberrations, such as the D-text, which was probably created near the end of the second century, not the beginning. Thus, it stands to reason that these "reliable" manuscripts are excellent copies of the authorized published texts.

Papyri (pre-AD 300)

$\mathfrak{P}^1$ (P. Oxy. 2) Matt. 1; early 3rd c. (earliest); ref. doc.; reliable

$\mathfrak{P}^4+\mathfrak{P}^{64}+\mathfrak{P}^{67}$ Matt. 3, 5, 26; Luke 1–6; mid-late 2nd c. (earliest); prof.; reliable

$\mathfrak{P}^5$ (P. Oxy. 208, 1781) John 1, 16, 20; early 3rd c.; doc.; fairly reliable

$\mathfrak{P}^9$ (P. Oxy. 402) 1 John 4; 3rd c. (earliest); common; unreliable

$\mathfrak{P}^{12}$ Heb. 1:1, late 3rd c., too small to determine

$\mathfrak{P}^{13}$ (P. Oxy. 657) Heb. 2–5, 10–12; early 3rd c.; doc; reliable with peculiarities

$\mathfrak{P}^{15}+\mathfrak{P}^{16}$ (P. Oxy. 1008, 1009—probably part of same codex) 1 Cor. 7–8, Phil. 3–4; late 3rd c.; doc.; fairly reliable

𝔓¹⁷ (P. Oxy. 1078) Heb. 9:12–19; late 3rd c.; doc.; too small to determine

𝔓¹⁸ (P. Oxy. 1079) Rev. 1:4–6; 3rd c. (earliest); common; fairly reliable

𝔓²⁰ (P. Oxy. 1171) James 2–3; 3rd c. (earliest); doc.; reliable

𝔓²² (P. Oxy. 1228) John 15–16; mid 3rd; doc.; fairly reliable

𝔓²² (P. Oxy. 1229) James 1; c. 200 (earliest); doc.; reliable

𝔓²⁴ (P. Oxy. 1230) Rev. 5–6; 3rd c.; common; too small to determine

𝔓²⁷ (P. Oxy. 1355) Rom. 8–9; 3rd c.; doc.; reliable

𝔓²⁹ (P. Oxy. 1596) John 6; late 3rd c.; doc.; reliable

𝔓²⁹ (P. Oxy. 1597) Acts 26; early 3rd c. (earliest); doc.; perhaps D-text but too small to be certain

𝔓³⁰ (P. Oxy. 1598) 1 Thess. 4–5; 2 Thess. 1; early 3rd (earliest extant for 2 Thess. 1, with 𝔓⁹²); ref. doc.; reliable

𝔓³² Titus 1–2; late 2nd c. (earliest); ref. doc.; reliable

𝔓³⁵ Matt. 25; c. 300; ref. doc.; reliable

𝔓³⁷ Matt. 26; late 3rd c., doc.; fairly reliable

𝔓³⁸ Acts 18–19; c. 300 (earliest); ref. doc.; related to D-text

𝔓³⁹ (P. Oxy. 1780) John 8; first half of 3rd c.; prof.; reliable

𝔓⁴⁰ Rom. 1–4, 6, 9; 3rd c. (earliest for 1–4); ref.doc.; fairly reliable

𝔓⁴⁵ Gospels and Acts; early 3rd c. (earliest for several portions); ref. doc.; fairly reliable in some portions, unreliable in others

𝔓⁴⁶ Paul's major epistles (less Pastorals); late 2nd c. (earliest for several portions); prof.; reliable in some portions, fairly reliable in others

𝔓⁴⁷ Rev. 9–17; 3rd c. (earliest for several portions); doc.; fairly reliable

𝔓⁴⁸ Acts 23; early to middle 3rd c. (earliest); doc.; D-text

𝔓⁴⁹+𝔓⁶⁵; Eph. 4–5; 1 Thess. 1–2; 3rd c.; doc.; reliable

𝔓⁵⁰ Acts 8, 10; c. 300; doc.; unreliable

𝔓⁵² John 18, c. 125 (earliest); ref. doc.; too small to determine

𝔓⁵³ Matt. 26, Acts 9–10; middle 3rd c.; doc.; fairly reliable

𝔓⁶⁶ John; late 2nd c. (earliest for several portions); prof.; reliable in 𝔓⁶⁶ᶜ

𝔓⁶⁹ (P. Oxy. 2383) Luke 22; mid 3rd c.; ref. doc.; unreliable

𝔓⁷⁰ (P. Oxy. 2384) Matt. 2–3, 11–12, 24; late 3rd c.; doc.; fairly reliable

𝔓⁷² 1–2 Peter, Jude; c. 300; doc.; reliable in 1 Peter; unreliable in 2 Peter and Jude

𝔓⁷⁵ Luke and John, c. 200 (earliest for several portions); prof.; reliable

𝔓⁷⁷ (P. Oxy. 2683 + 4405) + 𝔓¹⁰³ (P. Oxy. 4403—probably part of same codex) Matt. 13–14, 23; late 2nd c. (earliest); prof.; reliable

𝔓⁷⁸ (P. Oxy. 2684) Jude vv. 4–5, 7–8; c. 300; common; unreliable

𝔓⁸⁰ John 3:34; 3rd c.; doc.; too small to determine

𝔓⁸⁶ Matt. 5; c. 300 (earliest); doc.; reliable

𝔓⁸⁷ Philem. late 2nd c. (earliest); ref. doc.; reliable

𝔓^{90} (P. Oxy. 3523) John 18–19; late 2nd c. (earliest, with 𝔓^{66}); ref. doc.; fairly reliable

𝔓^{91} Acts 2–3; early 3rd c. (earliest); doc.; reliable

𝔓^{92} Eph. 1; 2 Thess. 1; c. 300 (earliest of 2 Thess. 1, with 𝔓^{30}); doc.; reliable

𝔓^{95} John 5; 3rd c.; ref. doc.; too small to determine

𝔓^{98} Rev. 1:13–20; late 2nd c. (earliest); common, fairly reliable

𝔓^{100} (P. Oxy. 4449) James 3–5; c. 300 (earliest); ref. doc.; reliable

𝔓^{101} (P. Oxy. 4401) Matt. 3–4; 3rd c. (earliest); doc.; fairly reliable

𝔓^{102} (P. Oxy. 4402) Matt. 4; c. 300; ref. doc.; too small to determine

𝔓^{104} (P. Oxy. 4404) Matt. 21; mid to late 2nd c. (earliest); prof.; reliable

𝔓^{106} (P. Oxy. 4445) John 1; 3rd c.; doc.; reliable

𝔓^{107} (P. Oxy. 4446) John 17; c. 200; doc.; reliable?

𝔓^{108} (P. Oxy. 4447) John 17; c. 200; ref. doc.; fairly reliable

𝔓^{109} (P. Oxy. 4448) John 21:18–20, 23–25; c. 200 (earliest); ref. doc.; too small to determine

𝔓^{110} (P. Oxy. 4494) Matt. 10; c. 300; ref. doc.; unreliable

𝔓^{111} (P. Oxy. 4495) Luke 17; 3rd c.; doc.; reliable

𝔓^{113} (P. Oxy. 4497) Rom. 2; 3rd c. (earliest); doc.; too small to determine

𝔓^{114} (P. Oxy. 4498) Heb. 1; 3rd c.; doc.; reliable

𝔓^{115} (P. Oxy. 4499) Rev. 2–3, 5–6, 8–15; 3rd c. (earliest for certain portions); ref. doc.; reliable

More specific information concerning the dates can be found in chapter 3. (The Oxyrhynchus Papyri are noted—P. Oxy.—simply to show the student that most of the earliest manuscripts have come from Oxyrhynchus.) The designation "earliest" means that this is the earliest extant manuscript for that portion of the New Testament. The classification of hands—professional (prof.), reformed documentary (ref. doc.), documentary (doc.), and common—are discussed in chapter 1. The designations "reliable," "fairly reliable," and "unreliable" are general descriptions of the manuscript's textual fidelity. According to my estimation, of the 61 early papyri noted above, 29 are reliable, 13 are fairly reliable, 5 are unreliable, and 9 are too small to determine. Three manuscripts (𝔓^{45}, 𝔓^{46}, 𝔓^{72}) are reliable in some portions but not in others (see above); and two manuscripts, 𝔓^{38} and 𝔓^{48}, display a D-text.

Textual Alterations of the Early New Testament Text

In the previous pages, we have been discussing textual fidelity and textual alteration in the early stages of the copying process. It should now be quite clear that manuscripts were produced with varying degrees of accuracy during the early period of textual transmission. The early third-century theologian, Origen, is often quoted as the one who noted this diversity when he said, "Nowadays, as is evident, there is a great diversity between the various manuscripts, either through the negligence of certain copyists, or the perverse audacity shown by some in correcting the text, or through the fault of those who, playing the part of correctors, lengthen or shorten it as they please" (*In Matthew 15.14*). What is important to note about Origen's observation is that he saw textual aberrations as emanating either from negligence (carelessness) or purposeful emendation (corrupting the text). In this regard, Origen was right. However, concerning the particular verse he was commenting about (Matthew 19:19), he was not right—in that he was blaming disharmony of wording between Matthew 19:19 and Mark 10:19; Luke 18:20 on textual corruption. Because Mark and Luke do not have the statement "love your neighbor as yourself," while Matthew does, Origen blamed it on scribal tampering. However, among all the extant manuscripts, there is no evidence of textual corruption in any of these passages. Origen, like many modern harmonists, was trying to blame scribal tampering for the lack of harmony among the Gospels. Nonetheless, Origen's comments, when corroborated with other statements he made, tell us that there was textual tampering in his era (i.e., late second century and early third)—especially in the Gospels.

Origen's observations are corroborated by Celsus, an infamous critic of Christianity. Celsus condemned Christians for harmonizing the Gospels to avoid criticism from secular writers. In AD 178, Celsus said, "Some of the believers . . . have changed the original text of the Gospels three or four times or even more, with the intention of thus being able to destroy the arguments of their critics" (see *Contra Celsum* 132.2.27; for other comments about Celsus's knowledge of the Gospels, see 1.34; 1.40; 1.58; 1.68; 2.24; 2.32; 2.34; 2.36; 2.55; 2.59; 5.52; 6.16; 7.18). This quote shows that some scribes were harmonizing the Gospels to make them free from the criticism that the four writings had contradictory accounts. Indeed, the date of this statement reveals that such changes were occurring in the second century. But note that Celsus says that only "some" scribes were doing this. Others were, in fact, faithfully copying the words of each Gospel text, as we know from our studies of some of the early Gospel papyri. As was mentioned before, extremely good copies of the Gospels can be found in manuscripts such as $\mathfrak{P}^1$, $\mathfrak{P}^{4+64+67}$, $\mathfrak{P}^{39}$, $\mathfrak{P}^{75}$, $\mathfrak{P}^{77+103}$, $\mathfrak{P}^{90}$, and $\mathfrak{P}^{104}$.

Discrepancies in the Gospels could be eliminated by harmonizing all the Gospels into one account. In the second century, Tatian (who died c. 180) produced a Gospel text by weaving together all four Gospels into one. It is called the Diatessaron (meaning "through the four"). This Gospel compilation eliminated all the discrepancies that exist between the four Gospels. For example, if one were to read the resurrection accounts in all four Gospels, the differences are readily apparent. How many and who were the women at the tomb? Was there one (Mark, Matthew) angel at the tomb, or were there two (Luke, John)? Did the women come to anoint Jesus' body (Mark, Luke) or to see the tomb (Matthew)? Did the women say nothing to anyone because of fear (Mark), or did they give a report to the disciples (Matthew)? What was the order of the appearances, and did they take place in Jerusalem (Luke, John 20), or in Galilee (Matthew, John 21), or in both places? Can the appearances be harmonized? Tatian, who considered himself to be a Christian apologist, sought to remove any such questions by composing his Diatessaron, with the hope that Christians would accept his work as a variant-free substitute for the Gospels.

The Diatessaron did have significant influence in Syria and in the East. Christians in Syria from the third to the fifth centuries generally read the Diatessaron as their Gospel text. As late as AD 423, Theodoret (a bishop in Syria) found that many copies of the Diatessaron were being used in his diocese. Because Tatian had become heretical later in life and because Theodoret believed his congregations were in danger of being corrupted by Tatian's work, he destroyed all the copies he could find (about two hundred of them) and replaced them with copies of the four separate Gospels (see Theodoret's *Treatise on Heresies* 1.20). As the result of Theodoret's zeal, and probably others like him, Tatian's Diatessaron was virtually eliminated. Only one small Greek fragment has been discovered from Dura-Europas—namely, codex 0212.

Harmonization of the Gospels was an increasing trend in the production of Gospel manuscripts, beginning in the second century and reaching its culmination in the fourth and fifth centuries. There are two causes for this. The first was just metioned with respect to Celsus. Christian scribes may have wanted to harmonize the Gospels for the sake of avoiding criticism from the enemies of Christianity. The second reason is that it was natural for scribes to harmonize the wording of the Gospels—almost unconsciously. They may have had all four Gospels nearly memorized, or they were greatly influenced by one Gospel over against another. In most cases, harmonization was influenced by Matthew, the leading Gospel.[31]

Other people of the second century had other reasons—besides harmonization— for making textual alterations to the New Testament text. The first was Marcion, the second and unnamed creator of what has come to be known as the D-text. Marcion, a native of the Roman province of Pontus, went to Rome about AD 138 and became the founder of a heretical sect called the Marcionites. The basic tenet of his heretical position was there exists a radical difference between the Old Testament and the New, between the law of the Old and the love and grace of the New, and between the creator god of the Old and the Christian God of the New. For him, the god of the Old Testament was the author of evil, which he associated with matter and the world in general, while the God of the New was our Father and the giver of everything good.

This being his belief, Marcion set out to establish for himself a canon of Scripture to support it. This canon included only one gospel, which was the Gospel according to Luke—which Marcion purified of anything connected with the Old Testament, the Jews, the creation of this sinful material world, and anything that related to a true humanity for our Lord. As Irenaeus wrote in *Against Heresies* (1.17.2), "He [Marcion] mutilates the Gospel which is according to Luke, removing all that is written respecting the generation of the Lord, and setting aside a great deal of the teaching of the Lord, in which the Lord is recorded as most clearly confessing that the Maker of this universe is His Father." Irenaeus then wrote, "In like manner, too, he heavily redacted the Epistles of Paul, removing all that is said by the apostle respecting that God who made the world, to the effect that He is the Father of our Lord Jesus Christ, and also those passages from the prophetical writings which the apostle quotes, in order to teach us that they announced beforehand the coming of the Lord." In summary, Marcion's canon consisted of his gospel, which was his redacted edition of Luke, and ten of the Pauline epistles (excluding the Pastoral Epistles).

Another unnamed scholar produced an edition of the Gospels and Acts that is now known as the D-text. This theologically minded redactor (editor), living in the late second century, created a text that had short-lived popularity—reaching its culmination with Codex Bezae (D). Three third-century papyri, $\mathfrak{P}^{29}$, $\mathfrak{P}^{38}$, $\mathfrak{P}^{48}$, each containing a small portion from the book of Acts, may be early copies of the D-type text in Acts. Another fifth-century papyri, $\mathfrak{P}^{112}$, also has a D-text. But there are other papyri containing portions of Acts that provide even earlier testimony to a purer form of Acts— namely, $\mathfrak{P}^{45}$ (early third) and $\mathfrak{P}^{91}$ (early third), thereby showing that the D-type text of Acts did not necessarily antedate the purer form.

The D-text editor primarily functioned as a reviser who enhanced the text with redactional fillers. This reviser must have been a well-informed scholar who had a penchant for adding historical, biographical, and geographical details. More than anything, he was intent on filling in gaps in the narrative by adding circumstantial details. Furthermore, he shaped the text of Acts to favor the Gentiles over the Jews, to promote Paul's apostolic mission, and to heighten the activity of the Holy Spirit in the work of the apostles. J. H. Ropes considered this text to be "a paraphrastic rewriting of the original," the "work of a single editor trying to improve the work on a large scale."[32] R. P. C. Hanson characterized this reviser as an interpolator who made large insertions into an Alexandrian type text. Hanson hypothesized "that these interpolations were made in Rome between AD 120 and 150, at a time when the book of Acts was not yet regarded as sacrosanct and inspired."[33] (More on the D-text is found in chapter 6 on the manuscripts for the book of Acts.)

Accumulative Alterations:
From the Second to the Fifth Centuries

Some scholars have argued that nearly all the changes that ever happened to the New Testament text were created in the earliest period (the first through third centuries). For example, Ehrman said that the "majority of textual variants that are preserved in the surviving documents, even the documents produced in a later age, originated during the first three Christian centuries."[34] But the extant documents do not prove this. The early manuscripts show some evidence of harmonization among the Gospels, assimilation among the Epistles, and conformation of New Testament wording to the Old, but harmonization does not become fully manifest until the fourth century. However, some will argue that the extant documents of the fourth and fifth centuries must have ancestors of an earlier date, which must have had the same textual variations. This is only hypothetically true and could therefore be said of all textual variants. We have no way of knowing if a particular variant reading originated in an earlier exemplar, unless an extant, earlier document displays the same reading.

As was discussed before, the most noteworthy change in the text of the New Testament involved Gospel harmonizations. These kinds of changes began to occur in the second century and were fully manifest in the fourth. In the early period of textual transmission, each Gospel was usually treated as an individual literary work. At the end of the second century and beginning of the third, the Gospels began to be put together in one codex volume. Beginning in the fourth century, the Gospels, together with the other books of the New Testament, were placed in volumes containing the entire Greek Bible (Old Testament and New Testament). This physical positioning affected the outlook of fourth-century and fifth-century scribes, who may have felt more and more compelled to harmonize Gospel accounts.

Generally speaking, the earlier the manuscript, the less harmonization there is to parallel passages in other Gospels (technically called "remote parallels"). According to Colwell, only ten harmonizations to remote parallels in other Gospels occur in the three major Gospel papyri of John—namely, $\mathfrak{P}^{45}$, $\mathfrak{P}^{66}$, and $\mathfrak{P}^{75}$:

> Although they are not frequent, harmonizations to remote parallels do occur. Ten occur in our [papyrus] manuscripts. Peter's confession in John (6:69, $\mathfrak{P}^{66}$) is enriched by adding "the Christ" from Matthew 16:16. In Luke (11:12, $\mathfrak{P}^{45}$) the hungry son asks for Matthew's bread, while Matthew's "birds of the air" (6:26) are added to Luke's ravens (12:24, $\mathfrak{P}^{45}$). In both $\mathfrak{P}^{66}$ and $\mathfrak{P}^{75}$ the Baptist's statement of his unworthiness in John uses the language of the Synoptic Gospels.[35]

To add to this, I could point out that the scribe of $\mathfrak{P}^{66}$ conformed John 21:6 to Luke 5:5. This makes a total of eleven harmonizations to remote parallels in the early papyri. Hypothetically, the number would be larger if all the three papyri ($\mathfrak{P}^{45}$, $\mathfrak{P}^{66}$, $\mathfrak{P}^{75}$) exhibited complete Gospel texts—perhaps as much as twenty-five to thirty. By comparison, three manuscripts appearing around AD 350–400 (namely א, A, and W), have a total of two hundred harmonizations among the Gospels. This is quite an increase! This dramatic change must be accounted for. I believe one of the primary reasons for the change was due to a tremendous shift in the horizon of expectations of fourth and fifth century scribes.

Several extant codices from the fourth and fifth centuries (א A B C) were at one time entire Bibles. (There is no extant New Testament volume by itself dating earlier than the eighth century.) The placement of the New Testament with the Old Testament in one volume, which was the result of the canonization process, put the New Testament on a par with sacred Scripture. Once the twenty-seven books of the New Testament (each of which had had an individual existence for three hundred years) were officially canonized as one sacred volume (together with the Old Testament), Christian scribes took a different view of the text. It was deemed necessary that the four Gospels should conform to one another—so there was a great deal of harmonization of the Gospels. Furthermore, the scribes began to think that the Old Testament quotes that appeared in the New Testament had to have verbal equivalence to the Old Testament—so there was a great deal of change in the wording of Old Testament quotations in the New Testament.

In addition to these changes, the New Testament Scriptures had to affirm various ecclesiastical practices; so, there were many insertions put into the text reflecting ecclesiastical practices such as fasting, public confession of faith according to standard formulas, and other rituals. And some considered that the canonized text as the official text of the church needed to include the oral traditions that had become part of the ecclesiastical oral tradition; thus, many additions from the oral tradition were added into the written text. All this worked together to produce an ecclesiastically standardized text.

Many scholars think a full-scale recension of the New Testament text was occurring in Antioch in the latter decades of the third century and early part of the fourth century, during a period in which the church was free from persecution—i.e., between the persecutions under Decius (AD 250) and Diocletian (AD 303–313). It has been thought by some that Lucius of Antioch in Syria completed this project before or during the Diocletian persecution, in which he suffered martyrdom (AD 312).[36] According to Jerome (in his introduction to his Latin translation of the Gospels: *Patrologia Latina* 29, col. 527), Lucian's text was a definite recension (i.e., a purposely created edition). Jerome complained of Lucian's bad recension, as opposed to the older, excellent manuscripts that he (Jerome) used. Lucian's text was the outgrowth and culmination of the popular text; it is characterized by smoothness of language, which is achieved by the removal of barbarisms, obscurities, and awkward grammatical constructions, and by the conflation of variant readings. Lucian (and/or his associates) must have used many different kinds of manuscripts of varying qualities to produce a harmonized, edited New Testament Greek text. The kind of editorial work that went into the Lucianic text is what we would call substantive editing.

While Lucian was forming his recension of the New Testament text, the Alexandrian text was taking on its final shape. The formation of the Alexandrian text involved minor textual criticism (i.e., selecting variant readings among various manuscripts) and minor copyediting (i.e., producing a readable text). There was far less tampering with the text in the Alexandrian text type than in the Lucian, and the underlying manuscripts for the Alexandrian text type were probably superior to those used by Lucian. Perhaps Hesychius (who also was martyred in the Diocletian persecution) was responsible for giving the Alexandrian text its final shape. (Jerome mentions Hesychius along with Lucian as being another editor of a different text, though less is known about Hesychius than Lucian—see op. cit.). Athanasius of Alexandria may have been the one who made Hesychius's text the archetypal text for Egypt.

Fourth-Century Christianity and the New Testament Text

The early fourth century was an extremely significant period in early Christian history, for it witnessed the last great Roman persecution against the church (the Diocletian persecution) and Constantine's endorsement of Christianity as a "legal religion." Diocletian believed that the old Roman religion would help to reinforce imperial unity. This policy prompted his persecution against the Christians. An edict issued at Nicodemia on February 23, 303, commanded the demolition of churches and the burning of Christian books. This was the first Roman persecution that was designed not only to destroy Christians but to eradicate their sacred text, the New Testament. The persecution lasted for nearly ten years.

Eusebius, the first church historian, witnessed the persecution and wrote of the many savage atrocities committed by the Romans against the Christians. He wrote, "All this [persecution] has been fulfilled in our day, when we saw with our own eyes, our houses of worship thrown down from their elevation, [and] the sacred Scriptures of inspiration committed to the flames in the midst of the markets" (*Ecclesiastical History* 8.2.1).

Those who were the most severely persecuted were the Christians living in Palestine, Egypt, and North Africa. Throughout the third century, Christians had secured permission from the government to purchase property and erect church buildings. These buildings were now demolished, and the property was confiscated. The church historian, W. H. C. Frend wrote: "No one in an official position in any part of the empire is recorded to have failed to carry out the emperor's orders. . . . All over the empire the authorities set about burning down Christian churches and collecting copies of Scriptures. In proconsular Africa, for which there is good documentation, the first thing people knew of the emperor's orders was the sight of churches going up in flames."[37]

Many Christians complied with the orders and handed over their copies of the Scriptures. However, there were those who kept their copies of the Scriptures from being destroyed. Some Christian leaders (such as Felix, bishop of Thibiuca) refused to hand over the Scriptures and suffered martyrdom as a consequence. Other Christian leaders fooled the authorities by handing over heretical works or medical books. Others hid their texts.

In Africa, Alexandria was hit first and hardest. Bishop Peter fled from Alexandria to Oxyrhynchus. But the persecution followed him into rural Egypt. By the end of the third century we know that there were at least two Christian churches in Oxyrhynchus, Egypt—one in the north and and one in the south. These churches were very likely destroyed in the persecution under Diocletian. Need it also be said that many copies of the New Testament perished in the flames? But not all. Several second-century and third-century New Testament manuscripts have been discovered in Oxyrhynchus, all of which survived this persecution. And entire (or nearly entire) Christian libraries escaped the Diocletian persecution. Two collections of biblical manuscripts known as the Beatty papyri and Bodmer papyri were preserved from the flames. These Beatty manuscripts were hidden somewhere in the Fayum, and the Bodmer near the Dishna Plain in Jabal Abu Mana. Hearing of the persecution in Alexandria and beyond, various Christians in rural Egypt would have done their best to get the New Testament manuscripts and other Christian writings out of their churches and hide them in their homes, in caves, or wherever else they could keep them from being confiscated by the authorities.

In the North African city, Cirta (capital of Numidia), the mayor attempted to confiscate all the Scriptures from Bishop Paul. After searching the home in which the Christians used to meet and finding only one copy of the Christian Scriptures, Paul was called upon to tell the mayor where he had hid other copies. Paul had been wise; the other copies had been taken to the homes of all the readers (or lectors—those who read the Scriptures in church meetings) in that church. The wife of one of the readers handed over the books, and the house was searched to make sure there were no others.

In Abitina (in North Africa) the bishop handed over the Scriptures on demand. But his congregation disowned his act and carried on the church meeting in the home of the reader, Emeritus. When the interrogators asked Emeritus to hand over his copies, he refused, saying he had "the Scriptures engraved on his heart." Others from Carthage shared the same sentiments. They all were imprisoned, but would never recant. Their attitude about the Bible (both testaments) was steadfast: to alter a single letter of Scripture was sacrilegious and an insult to their author, and it followed that to destroy the testaments and divine commands of Almighty God and the Lord Jesus Christ by handing them over to be burned merited lasting damnation in inextinguishable fire.

Furthermore, we very likely owe the preservation of many New Testament Scriptures to the churches in rural Egypt, more than to the church in Alexandria, which was probably devastated by the Diocletian persecution. Of course, all of Egypt—not to mention the entire Greco-Roman world—had been influenced by Alexandrian scriptoral practices. Though it is possible that some New Testament manuscripts in Alexandria survived the persecution, it is far more likely that rural Egyptain churches preserved far more copies. Copies of the text may have been taken by Bishop Peter to Oxyrhynchus when he fled from Alexandria. However, it is more likely that indigenous copies from Oxyrhynchus (i.e., copies made in Oxyrhynchus) and other rural towns in the Fayum or Upper Egypt were used by the Alexandrians after the persecution to provide archetypes for making new copies of the text. This hypothesis has backing in the fact that certain Alexandrian manuscripts (i.e., Codex Vaticanus and Codex Sinaiticus), made after the age of Constantine, are close copies of the kind of rural Egyptian manuscripts that survived the Diocletian persecution—manuscripts such as $\mathfrak{P}^4+\mathfrak{P}^{64}+\mathfrak{P}^{67}$ (from Coptos), $\mathfrak{P}^{13}$ (from Oxyrhynchus), $\mathfrak{P}^{46}$ (from the Fayum), $\mathfrak{P}^{66}$ (from the Dishna Plain), and $\mathfrak{P}^{75}$ (also from the Dishna Plain).[38]

Not long after this period of devastation, Constantine came to power and then recognized Christianity as a legal religion. There was, of course, a great need for copies of the New Testament to be made and distributed to churches throughout the Mediterrenan world. Around 330, Constantine commissioned Eusebius to make fifty copies of the Scriptures to be used by the churches he planned to build in Constantinople (*Life of Constantine* 4.36). Some scholars have conjectured that Codex Vaticanus and Codex Sinaiticus are survivors of these fifty copies. But this conjecture is unlikely, as is fully explained by F. F. Bruce:

> It has frequently been surmised that the Vatican and Sinaitic codices of the Greek scriptures (one of them, if not both) are survivors of this consignment. That is unlikely: apart from some indications that the Vatican Codex may have been produced in Egypt, they are our two chief witnesses to what is called the Alexandrian text type, and there is no indication that this text type was current in Constantinople and its neighborhood in the period following 330. . . . If a guess may be hazarded, it is more likely that the fifty copies exhibited the text of the recent edition of Lucian of Antioch (martyred in 312), the ancestor of the Byzantine or "majority" text. If they did, this would help to explain the popularity of this form of text in Constantinople and the whole area of Christendom under its influence from the late fourth century on, a popularity which led to its becoming in fact the majority text and to its being called by many students nowadays the majority text.[39]

As noted by Bruce, the text that was propagated and popularized was probably that produced and/or finalized by Lucian of Antioch. Lucian's text began to be propagated by bishops going out from the Antiochan school to churches throughout the east, taking the text with them. Lucian's text soon became the standard text of the Eastern church and formed the basis for the Byzantine text—and is thus the ultimate authority for the Textus Receptus.

The Text of the New Testament after the Fourth Century

In the third and fourth centuries, there were two primary centers of manuscript production: Alexandria and Antioch, producing two different kinds of texts. Eventually, Constantinople in the Byzantine Empire became a major center for manuscript production. The text multiplied there was essentially that which came from Lucian of Antioch. As the years went by, there were fewer and fewer Alexandrian manuscripts produced, and more and more Byzantine manuscripts manufactured. Very few Egyptians continued to read Greek; most read Coptic in one of its dialects, while the rest of the Mediterranean world turned to Latin. It was only those in the Greek-speaking churches in Greece and Byzantium that continued to make copies of the Greek text. For century after century—from the sixth to the fourteenth—the great majority of New Testament manuscripts were produced in Byzantium, all bearing the same kind of text. This text has come to be known as the Byzantine text and Majority Text.

When the first Greek New Testament was printed (ca. 1516), it was based on a Greek text that Erasmus had compiled, using a few late Byzantine manuscripts. Erasmus's text then went through a few more revisions by Robert Stephanaus and then Theodore Beza. Beza's text was then published by the Elzevir brothers in 1624, with a second edition in 1633. In this edition they announced that their edition contained "the text which is now received by all, in which we give nothing changed or corrupted." As such, the name Textus Receptus became a descriptor of this form of the Greek New Testament text. The irony of the Elzevir's statement is that the Textus Receptus is the culmination of textual corruption, as has been proved by the last four centuries of manuscript discoveries and textual criticism. (See chap. 2 for a discussion of the Textus Receptus and the Majority Text.)

The Origin of Textual Variants from the Perspective of Reader-Reception Analysis

In the previous discussion, we have been looking at the origin of textual variants from a historical perspective and what could be called a theological perspective. I would suggest that there is another way to look at the origin of textual variants—from the perspective of reader-reception analysis. By this, I mean that we can look at the origin of textual variants as having been created by various individual scribes as they interacted with the text in the process of reading it, not just copying it. In the centuries prior to the simultaneous-multiple production of copies via dictation (wherein many scribes in a scriptorium transcribed a text dictated to them by one reader), manuscript copies were made singly—each scribe producing a copy from an exemplar. Many of the differences in wording in the manuscripts came about as the result of transcriptional errors, but other variants were created during the process of reading, which is a clear indication that each scribe interpreted the text as he read it and did not merely copy it verbatim. Whether consciously or unconsciously, the scribe altered the text as he copied it and thereby left a written legacy of his individual reading.

As far as I know, no textual scholar has developed a theory for New Testament textual transmission that deals with the aspect of scribal reception. Perhaps it seems too obvious. The good scribe is expected not to have really processed the text but to have mechanically copied it word-by-word, even letter-by-letter. But no matter how meticulous or professional, a scribe would still become subjectively involved with the text and—whether consciously or unconsciously—would produce a transcription that differed from his exemplar. Scribes internalized the text in the process of reading it and transcribing it, especially since many of them were subjectively involved with a work of literature they deemed sacred and inspired. And the changes increased with time.

The observations of certain literary theorists, who focused on reader-reception theory, help us understand the dynamic interaction between the scribe (functioning as a true reader) and the text he or she was copying. Each scribe had his own "horizon of expectations" for the text as he read it and produced a copy. The theorist Gadamer posits that to every reader of a text written in a different milieu with a different history, there is a sense of strangeness, as well as a sense of familiarity. Gadamer said, "The place between strangeness and familiarity that a transmitted text has for us is that intermediate place between an historically intended separate object and being part of tradition. The true home of hermeneutics is in this intermediate area."[40] The lesser the gap (both in time and culture) between the historicity of the text and the historicity of the reader the greater the chance for the fusion of horizons. A text written by authors living in the Greco-Roman world in the first century is more likely to be understood by scribes living in the Greco-Roman world during the second to fourth centuries than by twentieth-century scholars living in the Western world.

Gadamer contends that we cannot escape our situation in history; we cannot suspend all of our prejudices in order to apprehend the text in all its purity. A consciousness that is defined by "actively effected history" (*Wirkungsgeschichte*) is part of the process of understanding, and a literary historicism that forgets its own historicality is naive. We always bring our present reality and present consciousness into our reading of a text. In other words, no one is able to entirely abandon his own horizon in order to adopt some absolute horizon with which to evaluate a text.

Yet in arguing for the reality of prejudices, Gadamer does not conclude that there can be no fusion of horizons. Rather, he believes that the prejudices can provide the reader with an entrance into the text because they provide the provisional knowledge a reader brings to an object. A reader comes to a text with prejudices that are eventually revised by interaction with the text. What a reader brings to the text both opens up and closes off possibilities of understanding. If a reader is open to the text's newness, the reader's inadequate and false prejudices can be shaped by the tradition and thus transformed into productive elements of understanding. Gadamer elaborates: "Anyone who wants to understand a text always performs an act of projection. He projects in advance a sense of the whole as soon as the initial sense appears. Likewise the initial sense appears only because one is already reading within certain expectations of a definite meaning. In working out such a fore-projection, which is of course continually revised, consists the understanding of what is there."[41] This constant revision of fore-projections Gadamer calls a "fusion of horizons." With the fusion comes the merging of two horizons, and communication is accomplished. Thus, the historicity of the interpreter is not an obstacle to understanding and interpretation, but a vital component that must be taken into account as part of the hermeneutic process undertaken by the reader.

Textual critics must take into account the historical situation of the scribes who produced the manuscripts we rely on for doing textual criticism. Textual critics must also realize that scribes were interactive readers. Indeed, as many literary critics in recent years have shifted their focus from the text itself to the readers of the text in an attempt to comprehend plurality of interpretation, so textual critics could analyze variant readings in the textual tradition as being the products of different, personalized "readings" of the text created by the scribes who produced them.

This is where the work of Wolfgang Iser is helpful. To be specific, Iser's work is useful for understanding how scribes read and processed a text as they transcribed it. Iser is concerned not just with the question of what a literary text makes its readers do but with how readers participate in creating meaning. In other words, the meaning of a text is not inherent in the text but must be actualized by the reader. A reader must act as cocreator of the text by supplying that portion of it which is not written but only implied. Each reader uses his or her imagination to fill in the unwritten portions of the text, its "gaps" or areas of "indeterminacy." In other words, as the reader adopts the perspectives thrust on him or her by the text, experiences it sequentially, has expectations frustrated or modified, relates one part of the text to the other, imagines and fills in all that the text leaves blank, its meaning is gradually actualized. The reader's reflection on the thwarting of his or her expectations, the negations of familiar values, the causes of their failure, and whatever potential solutions the text offers require the reader to take an active part in formulating the meaning of the narrative.

Whereas readers do this gap-filling in their imaginations only, scribes sometimes took the liberty to fill the unwritten gaps with written words. In other words, some scribes went beyond just imagining how the gaps should be filled and actually filled them. The historical evidence shows that each scribe who made a copy of a text created a new written text. Although there are many factors that could have contributed to the making of this new text, one major factor is that the text constantly demands the reader to fill in the gaps.

A literary work is not autonomous but is an intentional object that depends on the cognition of the reader. As an intentional object, a literary work cannot fill in all the details; the reader is required to do this. During the reading process, the reader must concretize the gaps by using his or her imagination to give substance to textual omission and/or indefiniteness. Since this substantiation is a subjective and creative act, the concretization will assume many variations for different readers. For example, the Gospel of Luke says that the crowds who had watched Jesus' crucifixion "returned home, beating their breasts." Although it would seem that most readers are given enough text to visualize this scene, the imagination of various scribes was sparked to consider how extensive their grief was or to recreate what they might have been saying to one another as they walked home. A few scribes, imagining a more intense reaction, added, "They returned home, beating their breasts *and foreheads*." Other scribes took the liberty to provide some dialogue by making this addition: "They returned home beating their breasts, *and saying 'woe to us for the sins we have committed this day, for the destruction of Jerusalem is imminent!'*"

Iser calls the textual gaps "blanks"; each blank is a nothing that propels communication because the blank requires an act of ideation in order to be filled. Iser wrote, "Blanks suspend connectibility of textual patterns, the resultant break in good continuation intensifies the acts of ideation on the reader's part, and in this respect the blank functions as an elementary function of communication."[42] According to Iser, the central factor in literary communication concerns the reader's filling in of these textual blanks. His theory of textual gaps is useful for understanding scribal reader-reception. Of course, his perception of gaps or blanks is far bigger and more demanding on the reader's imaginative powers than can usually be applied to New Testament scribes. Nonetheless, scribes were confronted with gaps or blanks that begged for imaginative filling. Many scribes, when confronted with such textual gaps, took the liberty to fill in those gaps by adding extra words or changing the wording for the sake of providing what they thought would be a more communicative text. Indeed, the entire history of New Testament textual transmission is one of the text getting bigger and bigger due to textual interpolations—i.e., the filling in of perceived gaps.

We must also bear in mind that, in ancient times, written texts were vocalized. A written document was first produced by an author who usually dictated the material to an amanuensis. The author would then read the text and make editorial adjustments. If the author wrote the document himself, it was also vocalized by the author himself. According to Achtemeier, the "oral environment was so pervasive that *no* writing occurred that was not vocalized. That is obvious in the case of dictation, but it was also true in the case of writing in one's own hand. Even in that endeavor, the words were simultaneously spoken as they were committed to writing, whether one wrote one's own words or copied those of another."[43] Thus, the original writers spoke as they wrote, as did those who made manuscript copies of the original work and/or successive exemplars.

Metzger articulated this vocalization process when he presented the four fundamental operations that take place in the act of making a manuscript copy: (1) the reading to oneself (in antiquity no doubt reading half-aloud) of a line or a clause of the text to be copied; (2) the retaining of this material in one's memory; (3) the dictating of this material to oneself (either silently or half-aloud); (4) the movement of the hand in executing the copy.[44] There are two important factors to note in this depiction of scribal transcription. First, it must be realized that scribes read in chunks (a line or a clause), even though they may not have copied in similar fashion. Thus, the semantic unit was not always duplicated with exact verbal equivalence because a scribe would sometimes copy the sense, not the words. Second, it is important to note that a scribe usually vocalized the text twice (if Achtemeier is correct, it was never done silently)— once in reading it and then when writing it.

Although these four steps would eventually become automatic with the scribe, there was enough opportunity for the mind of the scribe to interfere with the "automaticness" of the copying process because the entire process involves a dynamic (versus automatic) interaction between text and reader, reader and text.

Furthermore, the reading process normally calls for decoding in semantic chunks, not lexical; but the transcriptional process calls for transferring lexical units from one text to another. Explaining the reading process, Smith writes:

> In the reading process decoding proceeds in chunks rather than in units of single words and these chunks correspond to the syntactic units of a sentence. The syntactic units of sentences are residual chunks for perception within the literary text, although here they cannot be identified merely as perceptual objects, because the denotation of a given object is not the prime function of such sentences. The main interest here lies in the sentence correlate, for the world of the literary object is built up by these intentional correlates.[45]

A scribe would have a difficult time both reading and copying a text at the same time because his tendency would be to read ahead of himself (on a chunk-by-chunk basis), when his task called for word-by-word copying. This would often lead to faulty concretization that produced all kinds of transcriptional errors, the most common being haplography—the skipping over of entire semantic units. The scribe's eyes would shift to the same word he had just finished copying on one line to two or three lines later to the same word, where he would begin again. The resultant haplography would create a lacuna, often left unfixed if the scribe (or corrector) did not reread the portion.

Sometimes scribe's minds would wander or their previous "horizon," created by reading an earlier portion in the book, would be superimposed on their present reading, thereby leading to faulty copying. This happened to the scribe of $\mathfrak{P}^{66}$ when he was copying John 5:28. The passage reads, "An hour is coming when all who are in *the graves* will hear his voice." For a moment the scribe's mind wandered and he wrote "an hour is coming when all who are in *the wilderness* will hear his voice." Something in the phrase about "hearing his voice" must have made the scribe think of an earlier verse (John 1:23), where John the Baptist spoke of himself as "a voice crying in the wilderness." As such, the scribe projected his previous horizon on his present reading and then realized that he made a mistake in the transcription process. So he immediately corrected "the wilderness" to "the graves."

The dynamics of the reading process do not just produce faulty concretization; they also produce creative interaction between the reader and the text. This kind of dynamic interaction is similar to what Iser perceived in the reading act: "Textual structures and structured acts of comprehension are therefore the two poles in the act of communication, whose success will depend on the degree to which the text establishes itself as a correlative in the reader's consciousness. This 'transfer' of text to reader is often regarded as being brought about solely by the text. Any successful transfer however—though initiated by the text—depends on the extent to which this text can activate the individual reader's faculties of perceiving and processing. . . . Reading is not a direct 'internalization,' because it is not a one-way process, and our concern will be to find means of describing the reading process as a dynamic interaction between the text and reader."[46] Iser then explains that the linguistic signs and structures of the text instigate the comprehension but do not control it. "Indeed it is the very lack of control that forms the basis of the creative act of reading."[47]

A New Testament scribe (as with any scribe), ideally speaking, should have been completely controlled by the text in the reading process so that he or she could produce an exact copy of the exemplar. However, the evidence of the extant manuscripts shows that the scribes were engaged in the creative act of reading and were not completely controlled by the linguistic signs and structures of the text. Scribes became active, creative readers and interpreters of the text they were copying. This freedom, rather than being looked upon as reckless disregard for the integrity of the original text, should be viewed as normal processing.

As noted before, Kurt and Barbara Aland have noted four kinds of textual fidelity in the early New Testament manuscripts, which they call "normal," "free," "strict," and "at least normal."[48] Though I disagree with several of their specific identifications, I think the idea of classifying the manuscripts according to scribal fidelity is a good one. The Alands say the "normal" text is found in manuscripts in which the scribes transmitted the exemplar with a limited amount of variation characteristic of the New Testament textual tradition. The "normal" text is found in manuscripts like $\mathfrak{P}^{5}$, $\mathfrak{P}^{15+16}$, $\mathfrak{P}^{18}$, $\mathfrak{P}^{20}$, $\mathfrak{P}^{29}$, $\mathfrak{P}^{46}$, and $\mathfrak{P}^{66}$. The "strict" text is found in those manuscripts in which the scribes reproduced the text of an exemplar with greater fidelity than in the "normal" text—although still with certain characteristic liberties. In short, the "strict" text exhibits far less variation than the "normal" text. The "strict" text is found in manuscripts like $\mathfrak{P}^{1}$, $\mathfrak{P}^{4+64+67}$, $\mathfrak{P}^{23}$, $\mathfrak{P}^{27}$, $\mathfrak{P}^{35}$, $\mathfrak{P}^{39}$, $\mathfrak{P}^{65}$, $\mathfrak{P}^{70}$, and $\mathfrak{P}^{75}$. Other papyri, however, display a very "free" rendition of the text—that is, they are characterized as having a greater degree of variation than the "normal" text. The "free" text is found in manuscripts like $\mathfrak{P}^{9}$, $\mathfrak{P}^{37}$, $\mathfrak{P}^{45}$, $\mathfrak{P}^{69}$, and $\mathfrak{P}^{78}$. The fourth category, called "at least normal," includes those manuscripts that are "normal" but also display a distinct tendency toward a "strict" text. The "at least normal" papyri are manuscripts such as $\mathfrak{P}^{22}$, $\mathfrak{P}^{32}$, $\mathfrak{P}^{72}$, and $\mathfrak{P}^{77}$.

The "strict" text is the best copy in that the scribe who produced it allowed for little variation from his exemplar in the copying process. The "strict" manuscripts are those that were usually produced by professional scribes or those attuned to Alexandrian scriptoral practices. However, the "strict" is found only in one-fourth of the early manuscripts; the great majority are "normal" or "at least normal." Therefore, the impression one receives of the New Testament papyri made during the early centuries is that the "normal" situation was that most of the New Testament scribes respected the thought and meaning of the text to a high degree but not necessarily the exact wording. The message was sacred but not necessarily the exact wording. Most scribes did not attempt to alter *what* the text said but did take some liberties in changing *how* it was said. Often, they did this to make a better lectionary text—in the same way that modern translators provide nouns (for pronouns), conjunctions, and glosses to fill out the meaning of the text and/or to avoid ambiguity. If the scribe thought the text could be improved grammatically or stylistically or if the scribe thought there was an error in his exemplar that needed correction, he would make such improvements or emendations according to good Alexandrian scriptoral tradition.

Furthermore, the more a scribe subjectively interacted with a text, the greater the probability that the transcription would differ from the exemplar. The changes created therein could have happened for a number of reasons: (1) the scribe corrected a text he knew or thought was faulty, (2) he harmonized the text to an oral tradition, (3) he restructured and/or reworded a passage to make it more expressive of what he thought the original writer was trying to say, or (4) he changed the text for theological reasons. Most importantly, the scribe's reading of the text itself could have prompted some kind of gap-filling—even unconsciously. But if they were aware of their changes, most scribes would not have considered they were tampering with the text but "re-presenting" the text as an improved expression of the original work. These improvements then became accumulative throughout the centuries of textual transmission, each scribe improving on the work of the previous ones.

What we must realize is that it was nearly impossible for a scribe who became subjectively involved with the text to make an accurate word-for-word transcription because he would have processed the text in units of meaning—chunks of thought, rather than word by word. Therefore, the scribe-become-reader would tend to produce thought-for-thought equivalence, not lexical equivalence. This is normal processing for most readers in that readers concretize at the semantic level, not at the lexical level.[49]

Thought-for-thought copying is exemplified in the manuscript $\mathfrak{P}^{45}$ (a "free" text), because the scribe of this manuscript had a tendency to paraphrase the text, usually providing an abbreviated yet readable rendition of the *Vorlage*. For example, in $\mathfrak{P}^{45}$'s rendition of the multiplication of the loaves, he excludes the details about the five thousand sitting down "by hundreds and by fifties," as well as the details about how many loaves and fishes there were. In Mark 6:48 he does not bother to include that it is the "fourth watch of the night," since the previous verse mentions it was evening. In Acts 8:36, the Ethiopian eunuch does not say, "here is water," since the water had already been mentioned. In John 11:25, he abbreviates Jesus' statement "I am the resurrection and the life" to simply "I am the resurrection."[50]

Most other scribes added words to the text when they interacted with it. This is especially evident in the later manuscripts, but there are signs of it in the early papyri as well. The manuscript $\mathfrak{P}^{66}$ (a so-called "normal" text) provides several examples. In John 1:36, the scribe added "taking away the sin of the world" after John the Baptist's proclamation, "Behold, the Lamb of God!" This was a natural addition prompted by the same proclamation a verse earlier (1:29). In John 7:8, the scribe added "yet" to Jesus' statement, "I am not [yet] going to this feast," in order to avoid any misconception about Jesus' character. Given the context of John 7, in which Jesus makes this statement to his brothers and then later goes to the festival, it would make more sense if he said he was not *yet* going to the festival than he was simply not going to the festival.

The scribe of $\mathfrak{P}^{66}$ added the definite article "the" before "prophet" in John 7:52, thereby creating the reading, "Look and see that the prophet does not come from Galilee." This addition was probably prompted by the context, in which the Pharisees were doubting Jesus' claim to the messiahship because he came from Galilee. To speak of "the Prophet" is one and the same as speaking of "the Messiah." Without the article, the Pharisees' statement to Nicodemus is, "A prophet does not come from Galilee." Many modern exegetes had affirmed this sense even before the discovery of $\mathfrak{P}^{66}$. The fact that it reads "the Prophet" reveals that the scribe of $\mathfrak{P}^{66}$ was thinking the same thing. After the first sentence of John 21:6 ("He said to them, 'Throw the net to the right side of the ship and you will find fish'"), the scribe of $\mathfrak{P}^{66}$ added, "but they said, 'throughout the whole night we labored and caught nothing, but at your word we will cast the net.'" This story must have reminded the scribe about a similar story in Luke 5, from which he borrowed these words.

Many more examples will be given in the following chapter, but these should sufficiently show, for starters, that scribes became coproducers of a new text as they interacted with it dynamically. Of course, such creations were not consistent with accurate transmission. The most accurate copying was done by scribes who concentrated on the exemplar and then copied it word for word. This was done for the most part by the scribe of $\mathfrak{P}^{75}$. Checking the kind of subjective interaction found in $\mathfrak{P}^{45}$ and $\mathfrak{P}^{66}$, he produced a faithful copy of his exemplar, with limited corrections. But even a careful scribe like that of $\mathfrak{P}^{75}$ could not avoid using his imagination to fill in textual gaps. In the Gospel of Luke Jesus tells the story of the blind beggar, Lazarus, and the rich man who rejected him and then was sent to hades (see Luke 16:19–31). In all but one Greek manuscript the rich man is left unnamed—all but $\mathfrak{P}^{75}$. The scribe of $\mathfrak{P}^{75}$ provided him a name, "Nineveh." Later, Priscillian gave him the name Finees. Metzger said, "It was probably the *horror vacui* which led more than one reader to provide a name for the anonymous rich man."[51]

Other large portions of text were added to the Gospels because the text itself begged for fulfillment and closure. According to Iser's theory, the text itself codictated the need for this gap-filling. This is nowhere more apparent than in the conclusion to the Gospel of Mark. According to the earliest manuscripts (ℵ B), the Gospel abruptly ends with 16:8—"So they went out and fled from the tomb, seized with terror and amazement; and they said nothing to anyone, for they were afraid." Mark's Gospel may have purposely ended here or an original longer ending may have been lost. Either way, many ancient readers were baffled by this abrupt conclusion, probably because they, having read the other Gospels, had a different horizon of expectation for Mark. Why conclude with merely an announcement of Jesus' resurrection and a description of the women's fear and bewilderment? In the Gospel of Mark, a pattern is set in which every one of Jesus' predictions is actually fulfilled in narrative form. Thus, since Jesus announced that he would see his disciples in Galilee, the narrative should have depicted an actual appearance of the risen Christ to his disciples in Galilee. With this expectation, several ancient scribes created various extended endings for Mark's Gospel—and five different endings are extant (see the NRSV text and marginal notes for the different readings). Each of these endings is a product of different scribes being prompted by both the text and their horizon of expectation to provide a satisfying conclusion to the Gospel.

Finally, we need to consider one other aspect about early Christian scribes—namely, they were often church lectors, the readers of the text to their congregations. Thus, many of the early Christian scribes probably carried on a double function as they made copies: they read it for its own textual integrity (with all due consideration to the original writer and readers), and they read it for their congregation as the actual intended audience. The scribe, while doing his best to preserve the integrity of the original text, could not help but adjust it for the sake of reading it aloud to his congregation. The temptation to do the latter was increased by the fact that in the earliest centuries of the church the oral tradition was just as authoritative and alive as the written tradition. It was not until the third century that the oral apostolic teachings were superseded by the written apostolic teachings embodied in the various books of the New Testament. Many of the early Christian scribes had to contend with the two competing traditions when they (as lectors) provided an oral reading of the Scriptures to a congregation that probably had some oral catechism. The tendency, especially in the four Gospels, was for scribes to interpolate stories from an oral tradition into the written account because they themselves and their audience would have perceived the text as having a significant gap otherwise.

A few examples will illustrate the impact of the oral tradition upon the written. In Luke 22:39–46, the account of Jesus' agonizing prayer in the Garden of

Gethsemane prior to his crucifixion, several early manuscripts ($\mathfrak{P}^{69\text{vid}}$ $\mathfrak{P}^{75}$ $\aleph^1$ B N R T W) do not have the words traditionally printed as Luke 22:43–44 ("And an angel from heaven appeared to him, strengthening him. In his agony he prayed more earnestly, and his sweat became like drops of blood falling on the ground"). According to Marcion, Clement, and Origen these verses were not part of Luke's Gospel. But other early church fathers (Justin, Irenaeus, Hippolytus, Dionysius, Eusebius) acknowledged this portion as part of Luke's Gospel, and the passage appears in $\aleph*$,[2] D L 0171 Maj. The debate about the genuiness of this passage has focused on what view one takes concerning whether or not Jesus needed to have been strengthened by angels during his trial in the Garden of Gethsemane. Some have argued that the passage was excised because certain Christians thought "the account of Jesus overwhelmed with human weakness was incompatible with his sharing the divine omnipotence of the Father."[52] But it is more likely that the passage was an early (second-century) interpolation, added from an oral tradition concerning the life of Jesus.[53]

A prime example of another oral tradition making its way into the written Gospels is the insertion of the pericope of the adulteress into the Gospel of John (7:53–8:11). This passage is not found in any of the earliest manuscripts ($\mathfrak{P}^{39\text{vid}}$ $\mathfrak{P}^{66}$ $\mathfrak{P}^{75}$ $\aleph$ A^{vid} B C^{vid} L T W); its first appearance in a Greek manuscript is in D, but it is not contained in other Greek manuscripts until the ninth century. When this story is inserted in later manuscripts, it appears in different places: after John 7:52, after Luke 21:38, at the end of John; and when it does appear it is often marked off by asterisks or obeli to signal its probable spuriousness. Most scholars think the story is part of an oral tradition that was included in the Syriac Peshitta, circulated in the Western church, eventually finding its way into the Latin Vulgate, and from there into later Greek manuscripts, the likes of which were used in formulating the Textus Receptus.[54] Papias may have been speaking of this incident when he "expounded another story about a woman who was accused before the Lord of many sins, which the Gospel according to the Hebrews contains" (Eusebius, *Ecclesiastical History* 3.39.17). However, in the pericope of the adulteress there is no mention of many "sins," only one—that of adultery.[55]

These examples show how pieces of oral tradition were interjected into the written text. The scribes who resisted the temptation of adding these pieces were the ones who did the best job of preserving the integrity of the written text. On the whole, the Christian Egyptian scribes tended to do a better job of preserving the written text than scribes in the west—for it is in "Western" manuscripts where we see many more interpolations from the oral tradition than in those produced in Egypt.[56]

Chapter Six

Theories and Methods of New Testament Textual Criticism

As the title indicates, this chapter focuses on the theories and methods of New Testament textual criticism. It begins with a discussion of what it means to recover the original wording of the Greek New Testament, and then moves on to discuss the theories and methods textual critics have developed and used.

The Primary Task of Textual Criticism: Recovering the Original Wording

Because the New Testament is an ancient document—one that existed before the time of the printing press—it exists in many handwritten manuscripts. And since there is not complete agreement of wording among these manuscripts, textual critics must sort through these manuscripts and the variant readings therein in an effort to reconstruct the original wording of the Greek New Testament. This process is called textual criticism. As defined by the *Oxford Classical Dictionary*, it is "the technique and art of restoring a text to its original state, as far as possible, in the editing of Greek and Latin authors."[1]

The purpose of textual criticism, classically defined, is to recover the original wording of an ancient written text, no longer extant in its original form by means of examining the extant manuscript copies and then applying the canons of the discipline for determining the wording most likely original. This discipline pertains to all ancient manuscripts, whether Homer's *Iliad*, Virgil's *Aeneid*, or the Greek New Testament. In order to accomplish this task, textual critics need manuscripts—the more the better and the earlier the better. Textual critics working with nonbiblical literature have angst over the fact that so few manuscripts exist for certain works and/or that there is a large gap of time between the original composition and the extant copies. By contrast, New Testament textual critics dedicated to the task of textual criticism should be enthusiastic and optimistic about recovering the original wording of the Greek New Testament because we have so many early and reliable manuscripts. The time gap between the autographs and the extant copies is quite close—no more than one hundred years for most of the books of the New Testament. Thus, we are in a good position to recover most of the original wording of the Greek New Testament. This was the attitude of the well-known textual critics of the nineteenth century. For example, Samuel Tregelles said that his task was to restore and reconstruct the New Testament text "as nearly as can be done on existing evidence."[2] Westcott and Hort said it was their goal "to present exactly the original words of the New Testament, so far as they can now be determined from surviving documents."[3] In the twentieth century, two eminent textual critics, Bruce Metzger and Kurt Aland, affirm the same purpose. Metzger states that the purpose of textual criticism is "to ascertain from the divergent copies which form of the text should be regarded as most nearly conforming to the original."[4] In speaking of the Nestle-Aland text, Kurt Aland says, "The desired goal appears now to have been attained, to offer the writings of the New Testament in the form of the text that comes nearest to that which, from the hand of their authors or redactors, they set out on their journey in the church of the first and second centuries."[5] It should be noted that in each of these quotes the textual critics qualified their statements by saying that they think textual criticism can bring us close to recovering the original wording of the Greek New Testament.

Each of the people just mentioned—whether Tregelles, Tischendorf, Westcott and Hort, Metzger, or Aland—has provided histories of the transmission of the New Testament text and methodologies for recovering the original wording. Their views of textual criticism were derived from their actual experience of working with manuscripts and with the task of doing textual criticism in preparing critical editions of the Greek New Testament. Other New Testament textual critics, working with ever-increasing quantities of manuscripts (especially earlier ones) and refining their methodologies, have continued with the task of recovering the original wording of the Greek New Testament.

By contrast, a certain number of textual critics in recent years have abandoned the notion that the original wording of the Greek New Testament can ever be recovered. Let us take, for example, Bart Ehrman (who wrote *The Orthodox Corruption of Scripture*) and David Parker (who wrote *The Living Text of the Gospels*). Having analyzed their positions, J. K. Elliott says, "Both [men] emphasise the living and therefore changing text of the New Testament and the needlessness and inappropriateness of trying to establish one immutable original text. The changeable text in all its variety is what we textual critics should be displaying."[6] Elliott then speaks for himself on the matter: "Despite my own published work in trying to prove the originality of the text in selected areas of textual variation, . . . I agree that the task of trying to establish the original words of the original authors with 100% certainty is impossible. More dominant in text critics' thinking now is the need to plot the changes in the history of the text."[7]

Not one textual critic could or would ever say that any of the critical editions of the Greek New Testament replicates the original wording with 100 percent accuracy. But that has to be the goal of those who practice textual criticism, as classically defined. To veer from this is to veer from the essential task of textual criticism. It is an illuminating exercise "to plot the changes in the history of the text" (as Elliott puts it), but this assumes a starting point. And what can that starting point be if not the original text? In analyzing Ehrman's book, *The Orthodox Corruption of Scripture*, Silva notes this same reality. As Silva puts it: "Although this book is appealed to in support of blurring the notion of an original text, there is hardly a page in that book which does not in fact mention such a text or assume its accessibility . . . Ehrman's book is unimaginable unless he can identify an initial form of the text that can be differentiated from a later alteration."[8] In short, one cannot speak about the text being corrupted if there is not an original text to be corrupted.

I am not against the endeavor of textual critics examining textual variations so as to see the history of the text. In fact, I devoted many years to studying all the early Greek New Testament manuscripts (before AD 300) and then compiling a fresh transcription of them in *The Text of the Earliest New Testament Greek Manuscripts* (coedited with David Barrett). One result of this work is that it provides a representative sampling of New Testament books that were actually read by Christians in the earliest centuries of the church. By contrast, critical editions of the Greek New Testament, displaying the preferred reading on a case-by-case basis, never replicate in its entirety the wording of any one particular manuscript. But this does not mean that we abandon the goal of producing the best critical edition, one that most likely replicates the original wording of the Greek New Testament. Thus, I echo Silva's comments entirely, when he says: "I would like to affirm—not only with Hort, but with practically all students of ancient documents—that the recovery of the original text (i.e., the text in its initial form, prior to the alterations produced in the copying process) remains the primary task of textual criticism."[9]

I have tried to work through all the significant textual variants in the Greek New Testament and can say, with some degree of certainty, that the original text usually stands somewhere in the critical edition produced by Westcott and Hort and that produced by Nestle-Aland. I do not think each text got it all right in and of itself. I think that many of the papyri discoveries in the twentieth century affirmed readings in Westcott and Hort, but these readings were not always accepted by Aland and the UBS committee. And I think that several of the readings in the early papyri show that Westcott and Hort needed to be revised, and this was done in the Nestle-UBS text. And yet there are textual readings which, in my estimation, are likely original but were not adopted for either text. Finally, I must admit that there are several instances wherein one or more variant readings have equal qualifications to claim the right as being "the original wording." Many textual critics would say the same—though probably about different textual-variant units than the ones I consider. But this is, by no means, a large number of textual variants. And this should not cause us to abandon the task of recovering the original wording of the Greek New Testament. New insights have come and will keep coming, in the form of actual documents, new methodologies, and new understandings.

In the future, it would be good for critical editions to cite these viable alternatives so that the reader will know that these readings are considered to be "just as likely" original. This is essentially what Westcott and Hort did in their edition, when they printed a variant reading in the lower margin. A simpler and clearer way to handle this on the printed page would be to cite the alternative reading in the margin as an "Or" reading. For example, scholars are evenly divided on the reading in John 1:34—in that there is good manuscript support for two readings: *ho huios tou theou* (the Son of God) and *ho eklektos tou theou* (the chosen one of God), which are discussed in chaper 7. Depending on which reading the editors choose, the other could be listed in the margin with "Or."

Theories and Methodologies of Textual Criticism

Before we discuss the various theories and methodologies of New Testament textual criticism, it is important to recognize that nearly all textual critics first begin their task by identifying transcriptional errors. These are scribal errors caused by faulty copying. These are identified by the following names: dittography, haplography (or, scribal leap), homoioarchton (or homoeoarchton), homoioteleuton (or homoeoteleuton), and transposition. Definitions and examples of each will be given in the final section of this chapter.

Textual critics also recognize a few other variants as being telltale signs of purposeful scribal alteration. Two of the most common are "conflated readings" and "interpolations." A conflation is the scribal technique of resolving a discrepancy between two or more variant readings by including all of them. This phenomenon is more prevalent in later manuscripts because the scribe was confronted with a greater variation among the extant witnesses. Interpolations are scribal additions to the manuscript that attempt to clarify the meaning of the text. These account for a host of variants.

As for the rest of the textual variants, textual critics have developed theories and methodologies for selecting the reading that is most likely original. These theories and methodologies generally fall into two categories: (1) those that pertain to external evidence (with a focus on the classification of manuscripts or studies of the documents themselves) and (2) those that pertain to internal evidence (with a focus on discovering the one "original" reading from which all others deviated). Theories and methodologies concerning external evidence focus on establishing criteria to evaluate variant readings present in various manuscripts. Various New Testament textual critics have posited canons for determining the original wording on the basis of external evidence—the evidence of the documents themselves. This endeavor began in the early 1700s, when scholars became dissatisfied with the accuracy of the Textus Receptus. At first, scholars appended variant readings to the Textus Receptus; then they began to abandon the Textus Receptus. In 1707 John Mill of Oxford produced a critical edition of the Textus Receptus with an extensive critical apparatus and a thorough prolegomena that detailed several principles of textual criticism pertaining to genealogical method. Though he did not change the Textus Receptus, he laid the foundations for modern textual criticism. In the 1730s Bengel became the first man to categorize manuscripts according to their age and location, and to formulate the significant principle that textual witnesses must be weighed and not merely counted.

In 1751 J. J. Wettstein published a Greek text, *Novum Testamentum Graecum*, and from 1775 to 1807 J. J. Greisbach published three editions of the Greek New Testament. Both these men provided canons of external criticism that are still recognized as useful today. Karl Lachmann, a classical philologist, produced a fresh text (in 1831) that presented the Greek New Testament of the fourth century. Soon thereafter, Samuel Tregelles produced a text on nearly the same principles as did Lachmann, without knowing it. His text reflects the work of a man who rigidly followed the rule that the reading supported by the earliest manuscripts is preferable. Tischendorf also produced a text, but his work was too heavily influenced by Codex Sinaiticus.

Westcott and Hort then made known their theory (which was chiefly Hort's) that Codex Vaticanus and Codex Sinaiticus (along with a few other early manuscripts) represent a text that most closely replicates the original writing. Based on this theory, they developed a genealogical tree that traced back from extant witnesses (such as Vaticanus and Siniaticus) to the original autographs. According to their theory, Vaticanus was almost a perfectly transmitted text from the original. It was a "Neutral Text"—i.e., a text void of textual corruption. Their theory was revolutionary, and their text was responsible for overthrowing the Textus Receptus.

However, this was not the opinion of many textual critics, who became skeptical of recovering the original text through genealogical means. It was judged by several scholars that Westcott and Hort had made a subjective selection about the purity of Codex Vaticanus and then used that to determine the impurity of other manuscripts. Thus, Westcott and Hort's theory was no longer heartily endorsed. Left without a solid theory for making external judgments, textual critics turned more and more to internal evidence. They began to endorse the canon that the reading that is most likely original is the one that best explains the variants. This canon is a development of Bengel's maxim, *proclivi scriptoni praestat ardua* (the harder reading is to be preferred), a maxim he formulated in responding to his own question as to which variant reading is likely to have arisen out of the others.[10]

This overarching canon for internal criticism involves several criteria, which one scholar or another has posited and/or implemented during the past three hundred years of New Testament textual criticism. Having made a thorough historical survey of the development of canons for internal criticism, Eldon Epp summarized all the criteria as follows:

1. A variant's status as the shorter or shortest reading.

2. A variant's status as the harder or hardest reading.

3. A variant's fitness to account for the origin, development, or presence of all other readings.

4. A variant's conformity to the author's style and vocabulary.

5. A variant's conformity to the author's theology or ideology.

6. A variant's conformity to Koine (rather than Attic) Greek.

7. A variant's conformity to Semitic forms of expression.

8. A variant's lack of conformity to parallel passages or to extraneous items in its context generally.

9. A variant's lack of conformity to Old Testament passages.

10. A variant's lack of conformity to liturgical forms and usages.

11. A variant's lack of conformity to extrinsic doctrinal views.[11]

The primary canon that the shorter reading is usually to be preferred is borne out by the fact that the longer reading is often the result of scribal gap-filling and expansion. Though this is explained at length in a previous chapter, by way of review it can be said that scribes often encountered perceived gaps in the text (especially narratives), which prompted some kind of filling. This gap-filling was often done cognitively in the reading process. However, scribes also took the liberty to insert the gap-filler in writing, so as to make the text more lucid for their readers. Such insertions, whether one word or one sentence, account for the ever-expanding text of the New Testament throughout the course of its transmission. By way of example, gap-filling is nowhere more evident than in the interpolations that occur in the D-text of Acts. Thus, while it cannot be said that the longer reading is always suspect, it can be affirmed that any reading which looks like an attempt to fill in textual gaps is suspect as a scribal addition. This understanding adds new light to the canons number 1 through number 3, listed above. However, it must always be kept in mind that many manuscripts of the earliest centuries were produced by scribes who were inclined to brevity—often with a view to achieving better readability. Therefore, the "shorter reading" canon is not absolute.

Furthermore, it should be admitted that some of the other criteria are problematic when implemented. Two textual critics, using the same principle to examine the same variant unit, will not agree. For example, with respect to number 4, one critic will argue that one variant was produced by a copyist attempting to emulate the author's style; the other will claim the same variant has to be original because it accords with the author's style. And with respect to number 5, one will argue that one variant was produced by an orthodox scribe attempting to rid the text of a reading that could be used to promote heterodoxy or heresy; another will claim that the same variant has to be original because it is orthodox and accords with Christian doctrine (thus a heterodoxical or heretical scribe must have changed it). Thus, internal arguments—

in and of themselves—often lead to opposite decisions about textual variants because each textual critic has his or her own subjective biases.

As I argued in chapter 5, I think scribal gap-filling accounts for many textual variants (especially textual expansions and interpolations) in the New Testament—especially in the narrative books, the four Gospels, and Acts. (I will summarize here what I wrote in chap. 5.) Usually, textual critics examine textual variants as written deviations from the original text. However, there is another way to look at textual variants—namely, as individual "reader-receptions" of the text. By this, I mean that we can look at the origin of textual variants as having been created by various individual scribes as they interacted with the text in the process of reading it. In the centuries prior to the simultaneous-multiple production of copies via dictation (wherein many scribes in a scriptorium transcribed a text dictated to them by one reader), all manuscript copies were made singly—each scribe producing a copy from an exemplar. Many of the differences in the manuscripts came about as the result of transcriptional errors, but other variants were created during the process of reading, which is a clear indication that each scribe interpreted the text as he read it and did not merely copy it verbatim. Whether consciously or unconsciously, the scribe altered the text as he copied it and thereby left a written legacy of his individual readings.

As far as I know, no textual scholar has developed a theory for New Testament textual transmission that deals with this aspect of scribal reception. Perhaps it seems too obvious. The good scribe is expected not to have really processed the text but to have mechanically copied it word-by-word, even letter-by-letter. Jewish Masoretic scribes were trained to copy the Hebrew Scriptures in this manner. After every page, they would count the number of letters and compare them with the number of letters on the exemplar. If the copy differed, it was rejected. But even with this safeguard, some of these scribes became subjectively involved with the text and made changes as they copied. This phenomenon also applies to New Testament scribes. No matter how meticulous or professional, a scribe would still become subjectively involved with the text and—whether consciously or unconsciously—would produce a transcription that differed from his exemplar. Scribes internalized the text in the process of reading it and transcribing it, especially since many of them were emotionally involved with a work of literature that they deemed sacred and inspired.

The observations of certain literary theorists, who focused on reader-reception theory, help us understand the dynamic interaction between the scribe (functioning as a true reader) and the text he or she was copying. Textual critics must take into account the historical situation of the scribes who produced the manuscripts we rely on for doing textual criticism. Textual critics must also realize that scribes were interactive readers. Indeed, as many literary critics in recent years have shifted their focus from the text itself to the readers of the text in an attempt to comprehend plurality of interpretation, so textual critics could analyze variant readings in the textual tradition as being the products of different, personalized "readings" of the text created by the scribes who produced them.

This is where the work of Wolfgang Iser is helpful. To be specific, Iser's work is useful for understanding how scribes read and processed a text as they transcribed it. Iser is concerned not just with the question of what a literary text makes its readers do but with how readers participate in creating meaning. In other words, the meaning of a text is not inherent in the text but must be actualized by the reader. A reader must act as cocreator of the text by supplying that portion of it which is not written but only implied. Each reader uses his or her imagination to fill in the unwritten portions of the text, its "gaps" or areas of "indeterminacy." In other words, as the reader adopts the perspectives thrust on him or her by the text, experiences it sequentially, has expectations frustrated or modified, relates one part of the text to the other, imagines and fills in all that the text leaves blank, its meaning is gradually actualized. The reader's reflection on the thwarting of his or her expectations, the negations of familiar values, the causes of their failure, and whatever potential solutions the text offers require the reader to take an active part in formulating the meaning of the narrative.

Whereas readers do this gap-filling in their imaginations only, scribes sometimes took the liberty to fill the unwritten gaps with written words. In other words, some scribes went beyond just imagining how the gaps should be filled and actually filled them. The historical evidence shows that each scribe who made a text created a new written text. Although there are many factors that could have contributed to the making of this new text, one major factor is that the text constantly demands the reader to fill in the gaps. During the reading process, the reader must concretize the gaps by using his or her imagination to give substance to textual omission and/or indefiniteness. Since this substantiation is a subjective and creative act, the concretization will assume many variations for different readers. Iser calls the textual gaps "blanks"; each blank is a nothing that propels communication because the blank requires an act of ideation in order to be filled. Iser wrote, "Blanks suspend connectibility of textual patterns, the resultant break in good continuation intensifies the acts of ideation on the reader's part, and in this respect the blank functions as an elementary function of communication."[12] According to Iser, the central factor in literary communication concerns the reader's filling in of these textual blanks. His theory of textual gaps is useful for understanding scribal reader-reception. Of course, his perception of gaps or blanks is far bigger and more demanding on the reader's imaginative powers than can usually be applied to New Testament scribes. Nonetheless, scribes were confronted with gaps or blanks that begged for imaginative filling. Many scribes, when confronted with such textual gaps, took the liberty to fill in those gaps by adding extra words or changing the wording for the sake of providing what they thought would be a more communicative text. Indeed, the entire history of New Testament textual transmission is one of the text getting bigger and bigger due to textual interpolations—i.e., the filling in of perceived gaps. We especially see the work of gap-filling in the substantial number of expansions in the D-text of the Gospels and Acts. Whoever edited this text had a propensity for filling in textual gaps, as he perceived them. Such gap-filling is especially pronounced in the book of Acts.

Reasoned Eclecticism

Most modern textual critics recognize that textual criticism cannot be myopic; it must be practiced with two eyes—one on the documents (external evidence) and the other on scribal tendencies (internal evidence). This method has been called "reasoned eclecticism." According to Holmes, "Reasoned eclecticism applies a combination of internal and external considerations, evaluating the character of the variants in light of the manuscripts evidence and vice versa in order to obtain a balanced view of the matter and as a check upon purely subjective tendencies."[13] Holmes further expands on this method in an article entitled "The Case for Reasoned Eclecticism," wherein he makes a solid case for this method as being the most viable for the actual practice of New Testament textual criticism.[14] First, he urges that the critic must know and use the documents, citing the famous dictum of Hort, "Knowledge of documents should precede final judgment upon readings."[15] But he then explains that this can take us only so far—in two respects. First, he argues that "documentary evidence can take us back to the earliest recoverable (or surviving) stage of the textual tradition, but it cannot take us any further. That is, on the basis of external evidence alone we cannot determine whether the earliest recoverable stage of the textual transmission is the autograph or a copy of it."[16] Second, the extant documentary evidence often presents a situation where one cannot clearly determine which reading has the best documentary support. In the end, then, Holmes concurs with Zuntz who said that documentary evidence can "throw a very considerable weight into the scales of probability [but] will not by itself suffice to determine [a] choice between competing readings."[17]

Those who practice textual criticism know this all too well. The situation then becomes one of emphasis. Does one give more weight to documentary evidence or to internal consideration? Scholars such as Tregelles, Hort, and Colwell (see comments below) place more emphasis on the documents. I tend to follow their lead. Other scholars, such as Kilpatrick, Boismard, and Elliott, place more emphasis on internal criticism, such that they advocate "thoroughgoing eclecticism."[18] Other scholars practice reasoned eclecticism, as explained by Holmes. Among those are Aland and Metzger, though each has his own emphasis.

Aland's Local-Genealogical Method and Classification of Manuscripts

Kurt Aland favors a type of textual criticism that he calls the local-genealogical method. He defines it as follows:

It is impossible to proceed from the assumption of a manuscript stemma, and on the basis of a full review and analysis of the relationships obtaining among the variety of interrelated branches in the manuscript tradition, to undertake a recensio of the data as one would do with other Greek texts. Decisions must be made one by one, instance by instance. This method has been characterized as eclecticism, but wrongly so. After carefully establishing the variety of readings offered in a passage and the possibilities of their interpretation, it must always then be determined afresh on the basis of external and internal criteria which of these readings (and frequently they are quite numerous) is the original, from which the others may be regarded as derivative. From the perspective of our present knowledge, this local-genealogical method (if it must be given a name) is the only one that meets the requirements of the New Testament textual tradition.[19]

The "local-genealogical" method assumes that for any given variation unit, any manuscript (or manuscripts) may have preserved the original text. Applying this method produces an extremely uneven documentary presentation of the text. In fact, the modern critical text of the Greek New Testament—as printed in NA[27] or UBS[4]—was never read by any ancient reader.

The danger of doing textual criticism on the local-genealogical basis is that the editors must decide what the authors most likely wrote on a variant-unit by variant-unit basis, which leads to extensive atomistic eclecticism. The eclecticism is evident in the selection process that went into accepting and rejecting various variant readings even within the same verse. I would urge the student to look at the critical apparatus of NA[27] and/or UBS[4] and note the unevenness of documentary presentation. Look, for example, in Mark 6:51 at the two notes in UBS[4]. The first reading has the support of A f[13] Maj, while the reading of ℵ B (L) is rejected. In the second reading, in the very same verse, the text of ℵ B L is accepted, while A f[13] Maj is rejected.

This same kind of eclecticism can be seen in Matthew 16. The testimony of ℵ and B is accepted in Matthew 16:20 (for the reading "the Christ," versus other manuscripts that read "Jesus Christ") and then rejected in 16:21 (for the reading "Jesus Christ," versus other manuscripts that read "Jesus"). A documentary approach cautions against this. This approach looks to the external testimony first and then seeks to substantiate that testimony on internal grounds. If internal arguments are inadequate, then it is possible that the reading with inferior textual support could be original. But in most instances, internal evidence supports superior textual evidence. It does so here. In

Matthew 16:16, Peter calls Jesus "the Christ." Jesus then tells Peter and the other disciples (James and John) not to tell anyone he is "the Christ" (16:20). In 16:21, which marks a major turning point in the ministry of Jesus as he faces his destiny of suffering and death in Jerusalem, Matthew says "Jesus Christ began to explain to his disciples that he had to go to Jerusalem and suffer many things."

Another occurrence of eclecticism occurs in the NU text of John 9:4. In the first part of the verse, NU follows the testimony of $\mathfrak{P}^{66}$ $\mathfrak{P}^{75}$ $\aleph$* B D L W 0124. In the second part of the verse, NU follows $\aleph^c$ A B C D 0124, and rejects the testimony of $\mathfrak{P}^{66}$ $\mathfrak{P}^{75}$ $\aleph$* L W. In the first part of this verse, the testimony of $\mathfrak{P}^{66}$ $\mathfrak{P}^{75}$ $\aleph$ B L W is accepted, but in the next part of the very same clause, the testimony of the $\mathfrak{P}^{66}$ $\mathfrak{P}^{75}$ $\aleph$* L W was rejected. (See critical apparatus of UBS[4].)

A study of these examples and others will show that modern textual criticism tries to operate according to a syncretism of two conflicting theories: one that says the best readings are perserved in the best manuscripts and another that says the best readings are simply those that best fit the context, no matter what manuscripts they come from. As far as I am concerned, the best approach is to first establish which manuscripts (and/or groups of manuscripts) are the best authorities for each particular book or section (i.e., Paul's Epistles, General Epistles) of the New Testament. Once these are reckoned, the burden of proof for any textual variation is to show that these manuscripts do *not* have the original wording. In order to do this, the critic must first look for transcriptional causes of error or variation. If this approach doesn't give results, then the critic has to look for internal reasons. But one needs very strong and convincing arguments on internal grounds to overthrow strong documentary attestation.

Allow me to give an example that illustrates the tension between documentary evidence and internal evidence. An example occurs in Matthew 27:46, which in the NU text has the shorter reading, "Others said, 'Leave him alone, let us see if Elijah comes to save him.'" This has the support of A D W Q 090 f[1],[13] Maj it syr cop[sa],[bo] Diatessaron. However, other manuscripts ($\aleph$ B C L) add to this, "But another took his spear and pierced his side, and out came water and blood." According to internal criticism, it appears that the longer reading is an addition taken from John 19:34.[20] However, the variant cannot be easily dismissed, for the following reasons: (1) The manuscript evidence for its inclusion is strong; indeed, the testimony of $\aleph$ B C has far more often refuted that of A D W than vice versa in the NU text—why not here? The scribes of B (especially) and $\aleph$ usually refrained from being Gospel harmonists. (2) If it was taken from John 19:34, why wasn't it taken verbatim? As is, the order of the last words in Matthew is "water and blood," whereas in John it is "blood and water," and there are four other words used in Matthew that do not appear in John (*allos de labēn* and *exēlthen*. (3) The reason scribes would want to delete it from the text is because the spearing (according to John) happened *after* Jesus' death, whereas here it occurs just *before* his death (see 27:50). Thus, the deletion was made in the interest of avoiding a discrepancy among the Gospels. Such harmonization was done full-scale in manuscripts like A D W. (4) Another reason for scribes to delete it is that it appears to present a jarring contradiction to what was just described: while many of the bystanders were waiting to see if Elijah would come and save Jesus, a Roman soldier (in complete opposition to this sentiment) lances Jesus' side with his spear. Therefore, the longer text should not be easily dismissed because, in fact, it is the harder reading and has excellent documentary support.

Metzger's Judgment of Variants according to Text Types

Because there are so many individual manuscripts, textual critics are hard-pressed to know the individual characteristics of each manuscript. Consequently, many textual critics categorize the manuscripts into text types, which they then use in their evaluation of textual variants. One of the foremost textual critics of our era, Bruce Metzger, exhibits this kind of evaluation. He would place the extant manuscripts into one of four text types, usually called Alexandrian, Western, Caesarean, and Byzantine. Each of these requires some explanation here. (More detailed explanations can be found in Metzger's book, *The Text of the New Testament*, 211–19).

The Alexandrian text is found in manuscripts produced by scribes trained in Alexandrian scriptoral practices, the best of its kind in Greco-Roman times. Such scribes were schooled in producing well-crafted, accurate copies. Among the New Testament manuscripts, it can be seen that there are several early Alexandrian manuscripts (sometimes called proto-Alexandrian) and later Alexandrian manuscripts. The earlier manuscripts are usually purer than the later ones in that the earlier are less polished and closer to the ruggedness of the original writings. In short, these manuscripts display the work of scribes who had the least creative interaction with the text; they were produced by scribes who stayed with their task of making good copies. Quite significantly, several of the earlier or proto-Alexandrian manuscripts display a text that was transmitted quite faithfully, as demonstrated in later Alexandrian manuscripts that bear great resemblance to earlier manuscripts. This is exemplified in the high percentage of textual agreement between $\mathfrak{P}^{75}$ and B, thereby affirming Hort's theory that Codex Vaticanus must trace back to an early, pure text. This textual relationship and others are detailed in my book, *The Quest for the Original Text of the New Testament*.[21]

Metzger lists the following Alexandrian witnesses, in the categories "Proto-Alexandrian" and "Later Alexandrian."

Proto-Alexandrian:

$\mathfrak{P}^{45}$ (in Acts) $\mathfrak{P}^{46}$ $\mathfrak{P}^{66}$ $\mathfrak{P}^{75}$ ℵ B Coptic Sahidic (in part), Clement of Alexandria, Origen (in part), and most of the papyrus fragments with Pauline text

Later Alexandrian:

Gospels: (C) L T W (in Luke 1:1–8:12 and John) (X) Z Δ (= 039) (in Mark) Ξ (= 040) Ψ (= 044) (in Mark; partially in Luke and John) 33 579 892 1241

Coptic Boharic:

Acts: $\mathfrak{P}^{50}$ A (C) Y 33 81 104 326

Paul's Epistles: A (C) H^p I Ψ 33 81 104 326 1739

Catholic Epistles: $\mathfrak{P}^{20}$ $\mathfrak{P}^{23}$ A (C) Ψ 33 81 104 326 1739

Revelation: A (C) 1006 16 11 1854 2053 2344; less good $\mathfrak{P}^{47}$ ℵ

The so-called Western text is a loose category. Actually, it is probably best to call it a kind of "popular" text inasmuch as most of the manuscripts that get put in this text type share the common traits of scribal expansion, harmonization, and amelioration. Those who defend the cohesiveness of this text type indicate that it seems to have developed at one point in history (mid to late second century) and in a certain geographical region (Western Christendom). This form of the text, for the Gospels, Acts, and Paul's Epistles, circulated in North Africa, Italy, and Gaul (which are geographically Western), but so-called "Western" manuscripts have also come from Egypt and in the East. It is represented in the Old Latin manuscripts, Syriac manuscripts, and in the D-text (a special brand of the Western text—see discussion on textual groupings for Acts). The Western text also prevails in the writings of Marcion, Tatian, and Tertullian.

The Western witnesses listed by Metzger are as follows:

Gospels: D W (in Mark 1:1–5:30), 0171, Old Latin, syr^s, syr^c (in part), early Latin fathers, Tatian's Diatessaron

Acts: $\mathfrak{P}^{29}$ $\mathfrak{P}^{38}$ $\mathfrak{P}^{48}$ D syr^{hmg}, early Latin fathers

Paul's Epistles: The Greek-Latin diglots D^p E^p F^p G^p; Greek fathers to the end of the third century; the Old Latin and early Latin fathers; Syrian fathers to about AD 450

The Western text is not apparent in the General Epistles and Revelation. The recently published papyrus, $\mathfrak{P}^{112}$ (fifth century) is Western. And I would put a question mark next to $\mathfrak{P}^{29}$ because its text is too small to determine its textual affinities.

Another small group of manuscripts constitute a group known as the Caesarean text. Various scholars such as Streeter and Lake demonstrated that Origen brought a text with him from Egypt to Caeserea, which was then transported to Jerusalem. This text, showing a mixture of Alexandrian and Western readings, is apparent in the following manuscripts—only in the Gospels: $\mathfrak{P}^{45}$, W (in Mark 5:31–16:20), family 1 (f^1), family 13 (f^{13}), Θ (= 038), 565, 700.

The Byzantine text constitutes the largest group, which is the furthest removed from the original text in most sections of the New Testament. The one notable exception is the book of Revelation, where several Byzantine manuscripts preserve a purer form of the text.

The Byzantine manuscripts are as follows:

Gospels: A E F G H K P S V Ω (in Matthew and Luke 8:13–24:53) Π (= 041) Ψ (= 044) (in Luke and John) Ω (= 045) and most minuscules

Acts: H L P 049 and most minuscules

Epistles: L 049 and most minuscules

Revelation: 046 051 052 and many minuscules

In doing the work of textual criticism, Metzger argues that usually a variant reading "which is supported by a combination of Alexandrian and Western witnesses is superior to any other reading."[22] The observant reader will see that this kind of statement appears repeatedly throughout Metzger's textual commentary on the United Bible Societies' *Greek New Testament*, in support of the committee's decisions about certain readings. Metzger also made the following important observation:

> In the evaluation of readings which are supported by only one class of witnesses, the student will probably find that true readings survive frequently in the Alexandrian text alone, less frequently in the Western group alone, and very rarely only in Caesarean witnesses. As a rule of thumb, the beginner may ordinarily follow the Alexandrian text except in the case of readings contrary to the criteria that are responsible for its being given preference in general. Such a procedure, however, must not be allowed to degenerate into merely looking for the reading which is supported by B and ℵ (or even by B alone, as Hort was accused of doing); in every instance a full and careful evaluation is to be made of all the variant readings in the light of both transcriptional and intrinsic probabilities. The possibility must always be kept open that the original reading has been preserved alone in any one group of manuscripts, even, in extremely rare instances, in the Koine or Byzantine text.[23]

Metzger's observations are important, for they evolved from years of working with textual variants. But I would add one qualifier to the notion that a reading is likely original if it has support from several text types. I would stipulate that the documentary support must be *early* and diverse. Diverse testimony among many later manuscripts (i.e., not the earliest ones), in my mind, signals only that the reading had been copied frequently in various sectors of the church; it does not necessarily validate a reading's originality.

The Importance of the Documentary Approach

"Reasoned eclecticism" and/or the "local-genealogical" method in actual practice tend to give priority to internal evidence over external evidence. I think it has to be the other way around if we are going to recover the original text. This was Westcott and Hort's opinion. With respect to their compilation of *The New Testament in the Original Greek*, Hort wrote, "Documentary evidence has been in most cases allowed to confer the place of honour against internal evidence."[24] Colwell was of the same mind when he wrote "Hort Redivivus: A Plea and a Program." In this article, Colwell decried the "growing tendency to rely entirely on the internal evidence of readings, without serious consideration of documentary evidence."[25] Colwell called upon scholars to attempt a reconstruction of the history of the manuscript tradition. But very few scholars have followed Colwell's urgings because they believe (as Aland noted above) that it is impossible to reconstruct a manuscript stemma for the Greek New Testament. Perhaps they say this because they fear that some will attempt to make a stemma back to the original, and that such a reconstruction will involve a subjective determination of the best line of manuscripts. Westcott and Hort have been criticized for doing this when they created the "Neutral" text, leading from B back to the original. However, a reconstruction of the early manuscript tradition does not necessarily mandate a genealogical lineage back to the original text—although that is the ultimate purpose of making a stemma. The reconstruction can help us understand the relationships between various manuscripts and provide insights into origination and associations. In the process, it might also be discovered that, out of all the extant manuscripts, some of the earliest ones are, in fact, the closest replications of the original text.

One of the most compelling reasons for returning to a documentary approach is the evidence that $\mathfrak{P}^{75}$ provides. This is the Gospel manuscript (containing Luke and John) that has changed—or should have changed—nearly everyone's mind about abandoning a historical-documentary approach. It is a well-known fact that the text produced by the scribe of $\mathfrak{P}^{75}$ is a very accurate manuscript. It is also well known that $\mathfrak{P}^{75}$ was the kind of manuscript used in formulating Codex Vaticanus; the texts of $\mathfrak{P}^{75}$ and B are remarkably similar, demonstrating 83 percent agreement.[26]

Prior to the discovery of $\mathfrak{P}^{75}$ (which was published in 1961), many textual scholars were convinced that the second- and third-century papyri displayed a text in flux, a text characterized only by individual independence. The Chester Beatty Papyrus, $\mathfrak{P}^{45}$, and the Bodmer Papyri, $\mathfrak{P}^{66}$ (uncorrected) and $\mathfrak{P}^{72}$ (in 2 Peter and Jude), show this kind of independence. Scholars thought that scribes at Alexandria must have used several such manuscripts to produce a good recension—as is exhibited in Codex Vaticanus. Kenyon conjectured the following:

> During the second and third centuries, a great variety of readings came into existence throughout the Christian world. In some quarters, considerable license was shown in dealing with the sacred text; in others, more respect was shown to the tradition. In Egypt this variety of texts existed, as elsewhere; but Egypt (and especially Alexandria) was a country of strong scholarship and with a knowledge of textual criticism. Here, therefore, a relatively faithful tradition was preserved. About the beginning of the fourth century, a scholar may well have set himself to compare the best accessible representatives of this tradition, and so have produced a text of which B is an early descendant.[27]

Much of what Kenyon said is accurate, especially about Alexandria preserving a relatively pure tradition. But Kenyon was wrong in thinking that Codex Vaticanus was the result of a "scholarly recension," resulting from "editorial selection" across the various textual histories.[28] Kenyon can't be faulted for this opinion because $\mathfrak{P}^{75}$ had not yet been discovered when he made these judgments. The discovery of $\mathfrak{P}^{75}$ and Vaticanus's close textual relationship to it has caused textual critics to look at things differently, for it is now quite clear that Codex Vaticanus was simply a copy (with some modifications) of a manuscript much like $\mathfrak{P}^{75}$, not a fourth-century recension.

Zuntz held an opinion similar to Kenyon's about there being an Alexandrian recension. After studying $\mathfrak{P}^{46}$, Zuntz imagined that the Alexandrian scribes selected the best manuscripts and then gradually produced a text that reflected what they considered to be the original text. In other words, they functioned as the most ancient of the New Testament textual critics. Zuntz believed that, from at least the middle of the second century to the fourth century, the Alexandrian scribes worked to purify the text from textual corruption. Speaking of their efforts, Zuntz wrote:

> The Alexander correctors strove, in ever repeated efforts, to keep the text current in their sphere free from the many faults that had infected it in the previous period and which tended to crop up again even after they had been obelized [i.e., marked as spurious]. These labours must time and again have been checked by persecutions and the confiscation of Christian books, and counteracted by the continuing currency of manuscripts of the older type. Nonetheless they resulted in the emergence of a type of text (as distinct from a definite edition) which served as a norm for the correctors in provincial Egyptian scriptoria. The final result was the survival of a text far superior to that of the second century, even though the revisers, being fallible human beings, rejected some of its own correct readings and introduced some faults of their own.[29]

The point behind Zuntz's conjecture of a gradual Alexandrian recension was to prove that the Alexandrian text was the result of a process beginning in the second century and culminating in the fourth century with Codex Vaticanus. In this regard, Zuntz was incorrect. This, again, has been proven by the close textual affinity between $\mathfrak{P}^{75}$ and B. The "Alexandrian" text already existed in the late second century; it was not the culmination of a recension. In this regard, Haenchen wrote: "In $\mathfrak{P}^{75}$, which may have been written around 200 AD, the "neutral" readings are already practically all present, without any need for a long process of purification to bring them together *miro quodam modo* out of a multitude of manuscripts. . . . $\mathfrak{P}^{75}$ allows us rather to see the neutral text as already as good as finished, before that slow development could have started at all; it allows us the conclusion that such manuscripts as lay behind Vaticanus—even if not all New Testament books—already existed for centuries."[30]

Kurt Aland's thinking was also changed by $\mathfrak{P}^{75}$. He used to speak of the second- and third-century manuscripts as exhibiting a text in flux or even a "mixed" text, but not after the discovery of $\mathfrak{P}^{75}$. He wrote, "$\mathfrak{P}^{75}$ shows such a close affinity with the Codex Vaticanus that the supposition of a recension of the text at Alexandria, in the fourth century, can no longer be held."[31] Hort thought that Codex Vaticanus must trace back to a very early and accurate copy. Hort said that Codex Vaticanus preserves "not only a very ancient text, but a very pure line of a very ancient text."[32] $\mathfrak{P}^{75}$ shows that Hort was basically right. But some scholars may point out that this does not automatically mean that $\mathfrak{P}^{75}$ and B preserve the original text. What it does mean, they say, is that we have a second-century manuscript showing great affinity with a fourth-century manuscript whose quality has been highly esteemed. However, Gordon Fee has demonstrated that there was no Alexandrian recension before the time of $\mathfrak{P}^{75}$. In an article appropriately titled "$\mathfrak{P}^{75}$, $\mathfrak{P}^{66}$, and Origen: The Myth of Early Textual Recension in Alexandria," Fee posited that there was no Alexandrian recension before the time of $\mathfrak{P}^{75}$ (late second century) and Codex Vaticanus (early fourth) and that both these manuscripts "seem to represent a 'relatively pure' form of preservation of a 'relatively pure' line of descent from the original text."[33] In other words, the original text of Luke and John is virtually preserved in $\mathfrak{P}^{75}$. Of course, $\mathfrak{P}^{75}$ is not perfect, but it is more perfect than Codex Vaticanus because it is 125–150 years closer to the original text.

Some textual critics, however, are not convinced that the $\mathfrak{P}^{75}$/B type text is superior to another type of early text, which has been called the "Western" text. The "Western" form of the text was early in that it appears to have been used by Marcion, Irenaeus, Tertullian, and Cyprian—all of whom were alive in the second century. The name "Western" was given to this type of text because this text circulated primarily in western regions like North Africa, Gaul, and Italy, but it was also present in Syria and even in Egypt. Thus, most scholars recognize that this type of text is not really a text-type; rather, it is loose categorization of an early type of text that is not Alexandrian. Thus, "Western" is always put in quotations marks when this text type is mentioned. Some scholars see it as a complete misnomer. Colwell, for example, said, "The so-called Western text or Delta type text is the uncontrolled, popular edition of the second century. It has no unity and should not be referred to as the 'Western text.'"[34] The Alands also see it to be nothing more than a loose association of manuscripts, saying, "Wherever we look in the West, nowhere can we find a theological mind capable of developing and editing an independent 'Western text.'"[35]

These observations aside, some scholars are still skeptical that the $\mathfrak{P}^{75}$/B type of text is in any way superior to the Western text. They argue that the preference given to B and $\mathfrak{P}^{75}$ is based on a subjective appreciation of the kind of text they contain (as over against the "Western" text) rather than on any kind of theoretical reconstruction of the early transmission of the text.[36] It is argued that this same subjective estimation was at work when Westcott and Hort decided that B was intrinsically superior to D (see their Introduction 32–42). Some scholars, such as Epp, have argued that the high esteem accredited to $\mathfrak{P}^{75}$ and B comes only from a subjective assessment of their relative purity in comparison to other manuscripts. One of the points of criticism is that the Alexandrian text is perceived to be purer only because it is terser and shorter than the Western. However, textual critics who have worked with many actual manuscripts—both of the proto-Alexandrian type and the so-called Western type—in the task of compiling transcriptions and/or doing textual analysis and who have thereby seen firsthand the kind of errors, expansions, harmonizations, and interpolations that are far more present in Western manuscripts, are convinced that manuscripts like $\mathfrak{P}^{75}$ and B represent the best of textual purity.

Assessing Manuscripts through a Study of Singular Variants

In accord with Westcott and Hort's mandate that "knowledge of documents must precede all judgments of readings," Colwell devised a method wherein he could determine the peculiarities of each manuscript by studying the singular variants in that manuscript. Colwell believed that the singular readings of a manuscript were the textual creations of the scribe, and that an analysis of the patterns found within these singular readings would reveal the habits of the scribe.[37] James Royse did an extensive study of the major early papyri focusing on the singular readings which was based on the same rationale that Colwell proposed. In a lengthy, thorough dissertation, entitled "Scribal Habits in Early New Testament Papyri," Royse characterized the scribal habits exhibited in several early manuscripts ($\mathfrak{P}^{45}$, $\mathfrak{P}^{46}$, $\mathfrak{P}^{47}$, $\mathfrak{P}^{66}$, $\mathfrak{P}^{72}$, $\mathfrak{P}^{75}$) by studying each manuscript's singular readings (i.e., readings found in that manuscript only, independent of all other extant documents).[38] Students should make good use of the work of Colwell and Royse in their description of the papyrus manuscripts. They should also apply the reader-reception methodology explained in the previous chapter to ascertain the response of the scribe to the text as a reader, as opposed to a mere copier. In other words, students should attempt to explain the creation of certain singular variants as being the result of scribal interaction with the text.

Singular readings provide the best—and perhaps only—means of studying a scribe's reception of the text because they are individualized readings. Other variation units cannot be used for this study because it is always possible that the scribe was simply copying a reading from a previous exemplar. Since we are fairly certain that singular readings were not copied from other manuscripts, they must have been prompted by the text itself—or, should I say, by the scribe's interaction with the text as a real reader. This is where we see a confluence of Iser's theories and those of Jauss.

According to Iser, the implied reader is a textual prerequisite because it is regarded as a role of the reader that is written into the text. And it is a prerequisite for the production of meaning in that it is the composite of all the textual clues that are provided for the guidance of the actual reader in his interpretation of the text. The implied reader is therefore a sign-like, text-immanent to which actual readers could react in many different ways. The actual reader's reactions depend upon what horizon of expectations the reader brings to the text. This is Jauss's position.[39] When we combine these theories, it becomes clear that scribes who functioned as readers produced some very creative responses to the gaps (or lapses of meaning) they encountered in the text. These responses have been preserved for us in the form of singular variants.

Colwell and Tune defined a textual variation unit as that length of the text (1) where the Greek New Testament manuscripts present at least two variant forms and (2) where each variant form is supported by at least two Greek manuscripts.[40] When there is a variant reading supported by only one Greek New Testament manuscript, this is called a singular variant—as understood by many textual critics today.[41] It is important to note that the definition of a singular variant does not include any mention of versional or patristic support, only of Greek manuscripts. Versions (as translations) have their own history of textual appropriation and transformation, which may have coincidentally matched what occurred in a Greek textual alteration without having been directly influenced by that Greek manuscript. Patristic citations are also problematic and cannot be counted toward excluding a Greek reading from being a singular variant if they happen to line up with the singular variant.

My criteria for a singular variant accords with Royse's, who said that a singular reading is any variant reading which is found in only one of the continuous-text Greek manuscripts—that is, it is a reading found in one of the New Testament papyri, uncials, or minuscules.[42] This categorization excludes lectionaries, patristic sources, and ancient versions because of the well-known difficulties of studying the evidence of such witnesses. Exclusion of this material not only facilitates the task of constructing a list of singulars easier; it also helps to enhance the objectivity of the list. My criteria for a singular variant also includes Colwell's observation that there are such things as identical singular readings—that is, two scribes of two completely different eras and regions may have created the same reading coincidentally. Colwell said, "Since corruption was universal, identical singular readings with only minor scattered support elsewhere should be assumed to be coincidental in these agreements—unless other external evidence establishes relationship."[43]

Not all singular readings are significant. Some must be categorically eliminated from a study of scribal reception. These include obvious transcriptional errors, meaningless transpositions, itacisms, and nonsense readings. A few other kinds of singular readings may or may not be noteworthy; these are minor lexical substitutions and grammatical adjustments. Of course, both of these changes could have been prompted by some kind of perceived lack in the text, but not in the Iserian sense of a blank. A student needs to be judicial in dealing with such variants. Most of the other singular readings are worthy of analysis.

It is important to note that Colwell and Royse describe only the habits of particular scribes as copyists; they do not describe the receptions of scribes as readers. Thus,
Colwell and Royse primarily analyze the results of their copying and attempt to
explain all singular variants in the traditional terms of textual criticism. They both
speak of spelling errors and grammatical emendations or flaws. They both speak of
homoeoteleuton and homoeoarchton causing parablepsis or scribal leaps. They both
speak of harmonization to the immediate context and harmonization to remote parallels. However, neither of them focus on the activity of the scribe as a reader, who
brings his own horizon of expectations to the text and who is also impelled by various
textual constructs to produce individualized interpolations or ingenious modifications.
Such singular readings are not a display of aberrant copying as much as they are a
reflection of how the scribe became involved with the reading process. True, many singular variants can be identified as having been created by the immediate context,
which is a traditional canon in textual criticism. So, admittedly, there will be some
overlap between internal criticism based on immediate context and an analysis of
reader reception because both look to the context as providing the textual clues for
reader reception. However, Colwell and Royse did not analyze what structured act in
the text (in the Iserian sense) prompted the scribes as readers to make various changes.
Nor did Colwell and Royse consider the scribe's horizon of expectation as a motivat-
ing factor in stimulating some textual change. I think students analyzing singular variants should also attempt to see how the scribes, functioning as readers, reacted to the
network of response-inviting structures in the text and filled in various blanks by
drawing upon their repository of reading experience and life experience (*Lebenswelt*).

When Colwell asks the question, "why singular variants?" he furnishes the answer
from a textual transmission perspective,[44] not necessarily from a reader-text interaction perspective. Thus, his characterizations of individual scribes is based on his
observation of them as copyists, not as interactive readers. This is evident in the
following comment: "One scribe is liable to dittography; another to omission of lines
of text; one reads well; another remembers poorly."[45] In context, Colwell's definition
of "reading" describes nothing more than the act of rote reading for the sake of copy-
ing. In Royse's final analysis of the scribal tendencies of $\mathfrak{P}^{45}$, $\mathfrak{P}^{66}$, and $\mathfrak{P}^{75}$, he provides an illuminating profile of each of the scribes.[46] However, not one of these profiles
describes the scribes as individualized, interactive readers. I do not say these things to
criticize Colwell's methodology or Royse's analysis, for both scholars presented solid
results that were consistent with what they set out to do. And the student is encouraged to follow their guidelines. But I would also urge students to analyze what Colwell
and Royse did not analyze—namely, the interactive process of reading and how this
was responsible for the creation of several significant variant readings.[47]

Refining the Documentary Method

All textual critics—including those working with the classics—utilize both external criticism and internal criticism in the process of selecting the one variant reading that is most likely original. And all textual critics must do this on a variant-unit by variant-unit basis. Some give priority of place to internal criticism over external criticism; others do the opposite. The editors of the NU text demonstrate that they tried to do both; this can be seen in Metzger's discussions in *A Textual Commentary on the Greek New Testament* (TCGNT). However, it is my observation that the resultant eclectic text exhibits too much dependence on the "local" aspect of the "local-genealogical" method. This means that the decision-making, on a variant unit-by-unit basis, produced a text with an uneven documentary presentation. Furthermore, the committee setting, with committee voting on each significant textual variant, cannot help but produce a text with uneven documentation. In short, the NU Greek text, being eclectic, does not reconstruct a text that any ancient Christian actually read, even though it is probably a close replication of the original writings.

Those who adhere to the documentary approach should be aware of the best manuscripts for each book of the New Testament and/or section of the New Testament. Ideally, one should select the premier group of manuscripts as the primary witnesses for certain books and/or sections of the New Testament, not for the entire New Testament. Since each book of the New Testament was, in its earliest form, a separate publication, the manuscript selections need to be made on a book-by-book basis. Hort was too broad-reaching to have embraced Codex Vaticanus as the preeminent text for the entire New Testament, when we now know that there are superior witnesses for certain sections of the New Testament. The same can be said for Tischendorf, who was too enthusiastic about his prize find, Codex Sinaiticus. However, for several books of the New Testament, we can hardly do better than start with Codex Vaticanus and/or with Codex Sinaiticus—if only for the simple reason that they often contain more extant text than do the earlier papyri and that they usually provide witness to an early text.

Once the best manuscripts for each book and/or group of books in the New Testament are established, these manuscripts need to be pruned of obvious errors and singular variants. Then these will be the manuscripts used for determining the most likely original wording. The burden of proof on the praxis of textual criticism is to demonstrate that the best manuscripts, when challenged by the testimony of other witnesses, do *not* contain the original wording. The part of this process that corresponds to the Alands' "localness" is that the text must be determined on a variant-unit basis. However, my view of the "genealogical" aspect is that it must be pre-established for an entire book and not re-created verse by verse, which accounts for an eclectic presenting a very uneven documentary presentation. Of course, internal criticism will have to come into play when documentary evidence is evenly divided. And, on occasion, it must be admitted that two (or more) readings are equally good candidates for being deemed the original wording.

In my book *The Quest for the Original Text of the New Testament*, published in 1990, I described various groupings of the papyrus manuscripts exhibiting textual affinities, on a book-by-book basis. These groupings covered the early papyri from $\mathfrak{P}^{1}$ to $\mathfrak{P}^{92}$. In some significant articles written during the past few years, Eldon Epp has also explored grouping manuscripts into what he calls "textual clusters."[48] He sees the papyri as belonging to one of four clusters, which he calls the "A" group for later Alexandrian papyri; the "B" group for early papyri that have affinities with Vaticanus (B); the "C" group for the papyri that are linked with what could be called "Caesarean," and the "D" group for those papyri that have associations with Beza (D). My groupings are not as broad-based because I think groups need to be established for books or sections of the New Testament (such as the Gospels and Paul's Epistles), as compared to the entire New Testament per se. Nonetheless, there is a great deal of overlap between my groupings and Epp's. With the accession of more published papyri ($\mathfrak{P}^{100}$ to $\mathfrak{P}^{115}$ in 1998–1999), we can expand the population of each broad group and then establish tighter textual communities—that is, manuscripts showing a high degree of textual agreement. Admittedly, this is somewhat of a tenuous procedure because of the fragmentary condition of several of the papyri. Nonetheless, it is a fruitful exercise to compare the smaller manuscripts with the larger papyri in an effort to establish textual relationships. The purpose of these efforts is to establish the premier textual group for each section of the New Testament.

The selections I list below largely follow Metzger's identification of witnesses, but I would especially modify and expand Metzger's list of Proto-Alexandrian manuscripts in two ways: (1) I would add more manuscripts, especially the more recently published papyri; (2) I would specify the proto-Alexandrian manuscripts by New Testament book or section. Thus, the Proto-Alexandrian manuscripts are as follows:

Gospels: $\mathfrak{P}^{1}$, $\mathfrak{P}^{4/64/67}$, $\mathfrak{P}^{5}$, $\mathfrak{P}^{29}$, $\mathfrak{P}^{35}$, $\mathfrak{P}^{39}$, $\mathfrak{P}^{52}$?, $\mathfrak{P}^{66c}$, $\mathfrak{P}^{71}$, $\mathfrak{P}^{75}$, $\mathfrak{P}^{77}$, $\mathfrak{P}^{90}$, $\mathfrak{P}^{95}$, $\mathfrak{P}^{101}$, $\mathfrak{P}^{103}$, $\mathfrak{P}^{104}$, $\mathfrak{P}^{106}$, $\mathfrak{P}^{107}$, $\mathfrak{P}^{108}$

Acts: $\mathfrak{P}^{45}$, $\mathfrak{P}^{53}$, $\mathfrak{P}^{91}$, 0189

Paul's Epistles: $\mathfrak{P}^{13}$ (Hebrews), $\mathfrak{P}^{15/16}$, $\mathfrak{P}^{30}$, $\mathfrak{P}^{40}$, $\mathfrak{P}^{46}$, $\mathfrak{P}^{65}$, $\mathfrak{P}^{92}$, 0220

General Epistles: $\mathfrak{P}^{20}$, $\mathfrak{P}^{23}$, $\mathfrak{P}^{72}$ (in part), $\mathfrak{P}^{81}$, $\mathfrak{P}^{100}$

Revelation: $\mathfrak{P}^{18}$, $\mathfrak{P}^{24}$, $\mathfrak{P}^{47}$, $\mathfrak{P}^{98}$, $\mathfrak{P}^{115}$

In the main, I see the proto-Alexandrian manuscripts as being the best witnesses to the original text. Some may call this a subjective predetermination. But I honestly say that this favoritism has come from studying thousands of textual variants, as well as studying scribal tendencies, and usually coming to the conclusion that the proto-Alexandrian manuscripts have preserved the most primitive, if not the original, wording. Of course, these manuscripts are not perfect. $\mathfrak{P}^{75}$, one of the most pristine manuscripts, has flaws. Nonetheless, its fidelity and acuity far outweigh its imperfections.

Textual Groupings for the Gospels

Primary Manuscripts (with substantial extant text): $\mathfrak{P}^{4+64+67}$ $\mathfrak{P}^{75}$ $\mathfrak{P}^{66c}$ B $\aleph$ (but not in John 1–8)

Primary Manuscripts Dated Post-400: C (in part) L W (in Luke 1–8, John) Z Δ (= 039) (in Mark) Ξ (= 040) Ψ (= 044; in Mark) 33 (in part)

Secondary Manuscripts (with smaller portions of text): $\mathfrak{P}^1$ $\mathfrak{P}^7$ $\mathfrak{P}^{29}$ $\mathfrak{P}^{35}$ $\mathfrak{P}^{39}$ $\mathfrak{P}^{71}$ $\mathfrak{P}^{77}$ $\mathfrak{P}^{101}$ $\mathfrak{P}^{106}$ $\mathfrak{P}^{108}$ $\mathfrak{P}^{111}$

Unquestionably, $\mathfrak{P}^{75}$ and B constitute the best witnesses for the Gospels, specifically Luke and John (the Gospels extant in $\mathfrak{P}^{75}$). We can add several other manuscripts to the $\mathfrak{P}^{75}$-B group. One of the primary additions is $\mathfrak{P}^{4+64+67}$ (as one codex). Other members of the group are $\mathfrak{P}^1$, $\mathfrak{P}^{28}$, $\mathfrak{P}^{35}$, $\mathfrak{P}^{39}$, $\mathfrak{P}^{71}$, $\mathfrak{P}^{77}$, $\mathfrak{P}^{101}$, $\mathfrak{P}^{106}$, $\mathfrak{P}^{108}$, and $\mathfrak{P}^{111}$. I think $\mathfrak{P}^{66c}$ ($\mathfrak{P}^{66}$ corrected) also belongs in this group, though it is a bit more removed. A later yet extremely significant member of this group is Codex Vaticanus (B), as well as Sinaiticus, though it is not as prominent. (In John 1–8, it shows "Western" tendencies, as demonstrated by Fee.[49]) With the addition of $\mathfrak{P}^{4+64+67}$ to this group, as well as $\mathfrak{P}^{66c}$, it is apparent that this textual group existed before $\mathfrak{P}^{75}$—as early as 150–175 (the time period for $\mathfrak{P}^{4+64+67}$, and $\mathfrak{P}^{66}$), and it is also known that this text was maintained thereafter throughout the third and fourth centuries. Thus, we have evidence of a relatively pure form of the Gospel text from the mid-second century to the mid-fourth century.

The leading manuscripts of this group, $\mathfrak{P}^{4+64+67}$ and $\mathfrak{P}^{75}$, have overlapping text in Luke and therefore can be compared in this Gospel. In a paper given in November of 1998 at the Society of Biblical Literature convention, William Warren demonstrated that there is 93 percent agreement between $\mathfrak{P}^4$ and $\mathfrak{P}^{75}$ in Luke (as well as 93 percent between $\mathfrak{P}^4$ and B). In my own comparative study of $\mathfrak{P}^4$ and $\mathfrak{P}^{75}$, I observed that both $\mathfrak{P}^4$ and $\mathfrak{P}^{75}$ are identical in forty complete verses, with only five significant exceptions (Luke 3:22, 36; 5:39; 6:11, 14). The portion of concurrence in these two manuscripts is amazing. Out of approximately 400 words, they differ in fewer than 10 words. This is 97.5 percent agreement. The Matthean portion of $\mathfrak{P}^{64+67}$ cannot be compared with $\mathfrak{P}^{75}$ because there is no overlapping text. However, we can compare $\mathfrak{P}^{64+67}$ with B and $\aleph$, the natural extensions of a $\mathfrak{P}^{75}$-type of text. My studies show that $\mathfrak{P}^{64+67}$ agrees with B in 10 out of 13 variants, and with $\aleph$ in 12 out of 13.

Other Members of this Gospel Group

Certain early papyri can be compared with $\mathfrak{P}^{75}$ because they have overlapping text. However, other early papyri can be compared only with B and $\aleph$. The same kind of extension—from $\mathfrak{P}^{4+64+67}/\mathfrak{P}^{75}$ to B and $\aleph$—can be applied to these other papyri whose text does not overlap with $\mathfrak{P}^{4+64+67}$ or $\mathfrak{P}^{75}$. Consequently, several papyri show that they belong to this group. These manuscripts are $\mathfrak{P}^1$, $\mathfrak{P}^7$, $\mathfrak{P}^{28}$, $\mathfrak{P}^{35}$, $\mathfrak{P}^{39}$, $\mathfrak{P}^{71}$, $\mathfrak{P}^{77}$, $\mathfrak{P}^{101}$, $\mathfrak{P}^{106}$, $\mathfrak{P}^{108}$, $\mathfrak{P}^{111}$. The data is as follows:

$\mathfrak{P}^1$ concurs in 11 out of 12 variants with B.

$\mathfrak{P}^7$ (dated third/fourth century? by Aland) concurs completely with $\mathfrak{P}^4$ and $\mathfrak{P}^{75}$ in Luke 4:1–2, even with respect to making *pneumati* a nomen sacrum in 4:2.

$\mathfrak{P}^{28}$ agrees with $\mathfrak{P}^{75}$ in 7 out of 10 textual variant units.

$\mathfrak{P}^{35}$ concurs in 6 out of 6 variants with B.

$\mathfrak{P}^{39}$ agrees with $\mathfrak{P}^{75}$ (in its corrected form) verbatim—with the exception of two transposed words and one *de* found in $\mathfrak{P}^{75}$—thus, making $\mathfrak{P}^{39}$ agree with $\mathfrak{P}^{75}$ in 6 out of 7 variant units and with B in all 7 units.

$\mathfrak{P}^{71}$ agrees in 5 out of 5 variants with B.

$\mathfrak{P}^{77}$ concurs with $\aleph$ in 6 out of 6 variants, and with B in 4 out of 6. $\mathfrak{P}^{103}$, probably belonging to the same codex as $\mathfrak{P}^{77}$, shows the same tendencies.

$\mathfrak{P}^{101}$ concurs with $\aleph$ in 8 out of 10 variants, and with B in 7 out of 10.

$\mathfrak{P}^{106}$ shares 12 verses (John 1:29–35, 40–46) and about 100 words with $\mathfrak{P}^{75}$. Out of 10 variant units, $\mathfrak{P}^{106}$ concurs with $\mathfrak{P}^{75}$, 8 out of 10 times. $\mathfrak{P}^{106}$ shows strong alignment with other "B" group manuscripts: with B, 9 out of 10; with $\aleph$ 8 out of 10, and with $\mathfrak{P}^{66}$ 8 out of 10.

$\mathfrak{P}^{108}$ agrees in 7 out of 7 variants with $\aleph$.

$\mathfrak{P}^{111}$concurs with the text of $\mathfrak{P}^{75}$ completely, except in one variant in 17:22. Even though the mutual text is small (Luke 17:11–13, 22–23), the two manuscripts concur in 8 out of 9 textual variants.

$\mathfrak{P}^{66c}$ also belongs in this group, though marginally. The data is as follows: Fee's studies on $\mathfrak{P}^{66c}$ and $\mathfrak{P}^{75}$ in John 1–9 show that $\mathfrak{P}^{66c}$ demonstrates more agreement with $\mathfrak{P}^{75}$ than does $\mathfrak{P}^{66}*$.[50] This means that $\mathfrak{P}^{66}$ was often corrected in the direction of $\mathfrak{P}^{75}$ in John 1–9. When we add John 10–21 to the equation and track $\mathfrak{P}^{66}$-corrected's relationship to $\mathfrak{P}^{75}$ in John 10:1–15:8 and then to B in 15:9–21:22, where $\mathfrak{P}^{75}$ is not extant (presuming B to be the closest textual extension of $\mathfrak{P}^{75}$), then the percentage of agreement goes up significantly. Of the 450 corrections in $\mathfrak{P}^{66}$, about 50 are of nonsense readings. Of the remaining 400, 284 made the text of $\mathfrak{P}^{66}$ normative (i.e., in agreement with a text supported by all witnesses). Of the remaining 116 corrections, 88 brought the text into conformity with $\mathfrak{P}^{75}$ in John 1:1–13:10; 14:8–15:10, and with B in the remaining sections of John. This means that 75 percent of the substantive changes conformed $\mathfrak{P}^{66}$ to a $\mathfrak{P}^{75}$/B type text.

With respect to the premier Gospel group, it should be observed that many of these manuscripts are the work of professionals: $\mathfrak{P}^{4+64+67}$, $\mathfrak{P}^{39}$, $\mathfrak{P}^{66c}$, $\mathfrak{P}^{75}$, and $\mathfrak{P}^{77}$. Among all the copyists, professionals would be the ones most likely to produce the best copies. Second, this group has representation from the second century to the early fourth—from manuscripts like $\mathfrak{P}^{4+64+67}$, $\mathfrak{P}^{66c}$, and $\mathfrak{P}^{77}$ (of the second c.), to $\mathfrak{P}^{75}$ (ca. 175–200), to $\mathfrak{P}^{29}$, $\mathfrak{P}^{39}$, $\mathfrak{P}^{106}$, $\mathfrak{P}^{111}$ (of the third century), and on to B and $\aleph$ of the fourth century. The manuscripts in this group serve as the primary manuscripts for reconstructing the original text of the Gospels. For Matthew, it appears that most of the early papyri support the readings of ℵ over against B, when the two differ. In Luke and John, it is the other way around.

One final note is due concerning the Gospel of Mark. Ironically, the earliest Gospel has not been preserved in very many early manuscripts. And to add to the irony (and mystery), Mark is traditionally said to have taken his Gospel with him to Egypt—and yet there are hardly any early extant copies of Mark among the many discoveries of manuscripts in Egypt. The earliest copy of Mark is preserved in $\mathfrak{P}^{45}$, but it is not a very faithful copy. In the Gospel of Mark especially, the scribe of $\mathfrak{P}^{45}$ exerted many personal liberties in making a text that often replicated more the thought of his exemplar than the actual words. As is well known, $\mathfrak{P}^{45}$ has marked affinities with the fifth-century manuscript, W. The more "normal" text of Mark is preserved in one early fourth-century manuscript, $\mathfrak{P}^{88}$, and two fourth-century manuscripts, ℵ and B. Until there are more discoveries of early Markan texts, it is difficult to reconstruct the early history of the text.

A few witnesses have been identified as Caesarean in the Gospel of Mark. These manuscripts probably came from Origen's text, a text that he took with him from Alexandria to Caesarea and that bears a mixture of so-called Western and Alexandrian readings. These witnesses are Codex Koridethi ($\Theta = 038$) 28 565 700 f[1] f[13], the Armenian and Georgian versions, $\mathfrak{P}^{45}$ and W (in 1:1–5:30).

Textual Groupings for Acts

The Alexandrian Text

Primary Manuscripts (with substantial extant text): $\mathfrak{P}^{45}$ B ℵ

Primary Manuscripts Dated Post 400: $\mathfrak{P}^{74}$ A C (in part) Ψ ($= 044$) 33 81 104 326 1739

Secondary Manuscripts (with smaller portions of text): $\mathfrak{P}^{8}$ $\mathfrak{P}^{41}$ $\mathfrak{P}^{50}$ $\mathfrak{P}^{53}$ $\mathfrak{P}^{91}$ 0189

The Western Text and D-Text

Primary Manuscripts: D it[d]

Secondary Manuscripts: $\mathfrak{P}^{29}$(?), $\mathfrak{P}^{39}$, $\mathfrak{P}^{48}$, $\mathfrak{P}^{112}$; also African Old Latin manuscript it[h], marginal readings in the Harclean Syriac translation (noted as syr[hmg] or syr[h**]—when obeli appear with the text), as well as citations by Cyprian and Augustine

The book of Acts existed in two distinct forms in the early church—the Alexandrian and the Western. The Alexandrian text is found in manuscripts such as $\mathfrak{P}^{45}$ $\mathfrak{P}^{74}$ ℵ A B C Ψ ($= 044$) 0189 33. The Western text is found in a few third-century papyri ($\mathfrak{P}^{29}$ $\mathfrak{P}^{38}$ $\mathfrak{P}^{48}$), a fifth-century papyrus ($\mathfrak{P}^{112}$), the uncial 0171 (ca. 300), and Codex Beza (D, of the fifth century). The Western text is also attested to by the African Old Latin manuscripts, marginal readings in the Harclean Syriac translation (noted as syr[hmg] or syr[h**]—when obeli appear with the text), and the writings of Cyprian and Augustine. The Western text, which is nearly one-tenth longer than the Alexandrian, is more colorful and filled with added, circumstantial details. The Western text must be referred to loosely because it is a conglomerate of variant readings which are (1) generally non-Alexandrian, (2) found in early Western witnesses, and (3) found in D.

The leading witness of the Western text is Codex Bezae (D) of the fifth century. But this form of the Western text was not created by the scribe who produced Codex Bezae, even though he himself may have added his own enhancements. The creation of the text as later found in D could have happened prior to the third century. The Alands said, "When and how the Greek exemplar of D originated is unknown ($\mathfrak{P}^{29}$, $\mathfrak{P}^{38}$, $\mathfrak{P}^{48}$, and 0171 of the third and fourth centuries show earlier or related forms), but the additions, omissions, and alterations of the text (especially in Luke and Acts) betray the touch of a significant theologian. . . . . When D supports the early tradition the manuscript has a genuine significance, but it (as well as its precursors and followers) should be examined most carefully when it opposes the early tradition."[51] Metzger considered the early Western text to be the work of a reviser "who was obviously a meticulous and well-informed scholar, [who] eliminated seams and gaps and added historical, biographical, and geographical details. Apparently the reviser did his work at an early date, before the text of Acts had come to be generally regarded as a sacred text that must be preserved inviolate."[52]

Theories abound as to which form of the text is the original one—or even if Luke wrote both.[53] The major scholarly consensus is that the Alexandrian text is primary and the Western secondary. J. H. Ropes considered the Western text to be "a paraphrastic rewriting of the original," the "work of a single editor trying to improve the work on a large scale."[54] R. P. C. Hanson characterized this reviser as an interpolator who made large insertions into an Alexandrian type text. Hanson hypothesized "that these interpolations were made in Rome between AD 120 and 150, at a time when the book of Acts was not yet regarded as sacrosanct and inspired."[55]

More often than not, the editors of the UBS/NA text considered the Alexandrian text, as the shorter text, to have preserved the original wording in Acts. My view is that in nearly every instance where the D-text stands alone (against other witnesses—especially the Alexandrian), it is a case of the Western scribe functioning as a reviser who enhanced the text with redactional fillers. This reviser must have been a well-informed scholar, who had a penchant for adding historical, biographical, and geographical details (as noted by Metzger). More than anything, he was intent on filling in gaps in the narrative by adding circumstantial details. Furthermore, he shaped the text to favor the Gentiles over the Jews, to promote Paul's apostolic mission, and to heighten the activity of the Holy Spirit in the work of the apostles.

Textual Groupings for Paul's Epistles and Hebrews

Primary Manuscripts (with substantial extant text): $\mathfrak{P}^{13}$ (for Hebrews) $\mathfrak{P}^{46}$ ℵ B

Primary Manuscripts Dated Post-400: A C I H^P 33 81 104 326 1739

Secondary Manuscripts (with smaller portions of text): $\mathfrak{P}^{13}$ $\mathfrak{P}^{15+16}$ $\mathfrak{P}^{27}$ $\mathfrak{P}^{30}$ $\mathfrak{P}^{40}$ $\mathfrak{P}^{49+65}$ $\mathfrak{P}^{92}$

It is not as easy to determine the primary manuscripts for Paul's Epistles as it is for the Gospels. $\mathfrak{P}^{46}$ has to be considered as a primary manuscript because of its early date (second century) and coverage of text (Romans–2 Thessalonians, including Hebrews). Though its textual testimony is not as pure as that found in $\mathfrak{P}^{75}$ for the Gospels, $\mathfrak{P}^{46}$ has to figure significantly as a leading manuscript for reconstructing the original text of Paul's Epistles.

The three most comprehensive and significant studies of the textual character of $\mathfrak{P}^{46}$ were done by Kenyon, Sanders, and Zuntz. Both Kenyon and Sanders affirm the Alexandrian textual character of $\mathfrak{P}^{46}$, noting especially its affinities with B. According to Kenyon's tabulation, $\mathfrak{P}^{46}$ and B have the following percentages of agreement: Romans (66%), 1 Corinthians (75%), 2 Corinthians (77%), Galatians (73%), Ephesians (83%), Philippians (73%), Colossians (78%), and Hebrews (79%). $\mathfrak{P}^{46}$ also has an affinity with ℵ (but the percentages of agreement are about 5% lower for each book than for B).[56] Note the extremely high agreement in Ephesians and Hebrews, and lower agreement in Romans—this is because B is noted for its "Western" tendencies in Romans. $\mathfrak{P}^{46}$ also shows great affinity with other witnesses. Zuntz affirmed an early eastern group of manuscripts: $\mathfrak{P}^{46}$ B 1739 Coptic Sahidic, Coptic Boharic, Clement, and Origen for the Pauline corpus.[57] The relationship between $\mathfrak{P}^{46}$ and 1739 is noteworthy because 1739 is a tenth-century manuscript that was copied from a fourth-century manuscript of excellent quality. According to a colophon, the scribe of 1739 for the Pauline epistles followed a manuscript which came from Caesarea in the library of Pamphilus and which contained a Origenian text.[58] The three manuscripts, $\mathfrak{P}^{46}$ B and 1739, form a clear textual line: from $\mathfrak{P}^{46}$ (early second century) to B (early fourth century) to 1739 (tenth century based on fourth century).

The most thorough study on the text of $\mathfrak{P}^{46}$ was done by Gunther Zuntz, who wrote this:

> Within the wider affinities of the 'Alexandrian' tradition, the Vaticanus is now seen to stand out as a member of a group with $\mathfrak{P}^{46}$ and the pre-ancestor of 1739. The early date of the text-form that this group preserves is fixed by its oldest member and its high quality is borne out by many striking instances. B is in fact a witness for a text, not of c. AD 360, but of c. AD 200.[59]

Quick to point out the many scribal blunders found in $\mathfrak{P}^{46}$, Zuntz was just as eager to demonstrate that $\mathfrak{P}^{46}$ is a representative of "a text of the superior, early-Alexandrian type."[60] This quotation from Zuntz encapsulates his impression of the $\mathfrak{P}^{46}$'s text:

The excellent quality of the text represented by our oldest manuscript, $\mathfrak{P}^{46}$, stands out again. As so often before, we must here again be careful to distinguish between the very poor work of the scribe who penned it and the basic text that he so poorly rendered. $\mathfrak{P}^{46}$ abounds with scribal blunders, omissions, and also additions. In some of them the scribe anticipated the errors of later copyists; in some others he shares an older error; but the vast majority are his own uncontested property. Once they have been discarded, there remains a text of outstanding (though not absolute) purity.[61]

Thus, Zuntz made it clear that $\mathfrak{P}^{46}$ B and 1739 are primary manuscripts for Paul's major epistles and Hebrews (which was considered part of the Pauline corpus by people in the early church). The other primary manuscripts are ℵ, A and C (where extant). A textual comparison of these manuscripts with the secondary manuscripts listed above yields the following results:

$\mathfrak{P}^{13}$ agrees with $\mathfrak{P}^{46}$ in 40 out of 50 variants (80%), and it agrees with B in 13 out of 18 variants (B lacks much of Hebrews). No other textual affinities are clearly manifest, even with ℵ and 1739.

$\mathfrak{P}^{15}+\mathfrak{P}^{16}$ shows the greatest affinity with B (34 out of 43 variants = 79%); and ℵ (32 out of 43 = 74%). It demonstrates only 55 percent agreement with $\mathfrak{P}^{46}$. By way of comparison, $\mathfrak{P}^{15}+\mathfrak{P}^{16}$ shows significant divergence from D (agreeing only 15 out of 33 variants) and F G (11 out of 33).

$\mathfrak{P}^{27}$ demonstrates the greatest affinity with ℵ and B (both 10 out of 11 variants), as well as with A (9 out of 11 variants), and C (8 out of 11 variants). $\mathfrak{P}^{27}$'s agreement with $\mathfrak{P}^{46}$ is less: 7 out of 11. For comparison purposes, $\mathfrak{P}^{27}$ demonstrates significant divergence from D (agreeing only 5 out of 11 variants) and from F G (each 6 out of 11 variants).

$\mathfrak{P}^{30}$ displays the highest agreement with ℵ (11 out of 13 variants) and then with B (9 out of 13 variants). Its text cannot be compared to $\mathfrak{P}^{46}+\mathfrak{P}^{65}$ because there is no overlap of text among these manuscripts. For comparison purposes, $\mathfrak{P}^{30}$ demonstrates significant divergence from D (agreeing only 5 out of 13 variants).

$\mathfrak{P}^{40}$ exhibits the highest agreement with ℵ (13 out of 15 variants) and then with A and B (both 12 out of 13 variants). Its text does not overlap with $\mathfrak{P}^{46}$. By way of comparison, $\mathfrak{P}^{40}$ demonstrates significant divergence from D (agreeing only 6 out of 13 variants) and from F G (3 out of 13 variants).

$\mathfrak{P}^{49}+\mathfrak{P}^{65}$ demonstrates the greatest affinity with ℵ and B (both 14 out of 16 variants), as well as with A (12 out of 16 variants). It shows less agreement with $\mathfrak{P}^{46}$ (8 out of 14 variants). For comparison purposes, $\mathfrak{P}^{49}+\mathfrak{P}^{65}$ demonstrates significant divergence from D (agreeing only 7 out of 16 variants) and from F G (5 out of 16 variants).

$\mathfrak{P}^{92}$ exhibits the greatest affinity with ℵ (6 out of 7 variants) and B (5 out of 7). For comparison purposes, $\mathfrak{P}^{92}$ exhibits divergence from D F G (agreeing only 3 out of 7 variants for each manuscript).

The data clearly shows that ℵ and B had their precursors—namely, papyri from the third century—$\mathfrak{P}^{15+16}$, $\mathfrak{P}^{27}$, $\mathfrak{P}^{30}$, $\mathfrak{P}^{40}$, $\mathfrak{P}^{49+65}$, $\mathfrak{P}^{92}$. Significantly, none of these papyri exhibit a marked affinity with $\mathfrak{P}^{46}$ in the Pauline epistles. Only $\mathfrak{P}^{13}$, in Hebrews, has this textual closeness with $\mathfrak{P}^{46}$ (with 80 percent agreement). Thus, we must be wary of $\mathfrak{P}^{46}$'s independence, while also recognizing its witness to the original text. It should also be noted that the early papyri agree slightly more with ℵ than with B. This probably affirms the impression that B shows so-called Western tendencies in Paul's Epistles, while ℵ is more pure. The situation seems to be that any combination of the papyri with ℵ and with B (especially both) must be seriously considered as providing solid testimony for the original text. When the Western tendencies of B (noted by its alignment with D F G) are eliminated, its testimony with ℵ and the above noted papyri often represents the original text. Another strong witness is the manuscript 1739. Lightfoot was convinced that where ℵ B and 1739 concurred in supporting a Pauline reading, the original text was invariably reflected.[62] Add to this the testimony of $\mathfrak{P}^{46}$ and the other papyri, and the certainty becomes more certain.

Textual Groupings for the Pastoral Epistles

Primary Manuscripts (with substantial extant text): ℵ (B lacks the Pastorals) I 1739

Secondary Manuscripts (with smaller portions of text): $\mathfrak{P}^{32}$

The Pastoral Epistles have a different history than the other Pauline epistles because they were private letters to individuals that would not have been circulated among the churches in its early years. Gradually, the Pastoral Epistles gained recognition and acceptance into the Pauline canon. (The epistle to Philemon, although also a personal letter, gained immediate recognition because of its connection with Colossians.) There is only one early copy of one Pastoral Epistle, $\mathfrak{P}^{32}$, displaying part of Titus (chap. 2). This manuscript, dated around 175, was probably the work of a professional scribe; and this papyrus (which cannot be compared with B because Vaticanus lacks the Pastoral Epistles) shows affinity with ℵ and then with F G. Overall, the best witness for the Pastoral Epistles is ℵ.

Textual Groupings for the General Epistles

Primary Manuscripts (with substantial extant text): $\mathfrak{P}^{72}$ (for 1 Peter) ℵ B
Primary Manuscripts Dated Post-400: $\mathfrak{P}^{74}$ A C 33 81 104 326 1739
Secondary Manuscripts (with smaller portions of text): $\mathfrak{P}^{20}$ $\mathfrak{P}^{23}$ $\mathfrak{P}^{81}$ $\mathfrak{P}^{100}$ 0232

The General Epistles (also known as the Catholic Epistles) have had a textual and canonical history distinct and separate from the four Gospels and Paul's epistles. From as early as the second century, the four Gospels were being collected together into one volume, as were Paul's Epistles (minus the Pastorals). But this was not so for the other New Testament books. In fact, only a few other books were widely read in the Christian church—namely, 1 Peter and 1 John. The other General Epistles had a difficult time making it into the New Testament canon: James, because of its apparent opposition to Pauline soteriology; 2 Peter, because of its dissimilarity to 1 Peter; 2 John, 3 John, Jude, because of their obscurity. Interestingly, the book of Acts was often attached to the General Epistles, as is shown by the ordering in Codex Vaticanus (where the General Epistles follow Acts). Given their preference for Codex Vaticanus, Westcott and Hort's text follows this order. The seventh-century papyrus, $\mathfrak{P}^{74}$, has only Acts and the General Epistles in one codex. It is a good witness for both.

As canonical lists were made, indicating which books belonged in the New Testament, the inclusion of the Catholic Epistles was often disputed. The Muratorian Canon, a list expressing the views on canonicity of church leaders in Rome (about AD 180), included only 1 and 2 John and Jude. Origen concluded that 1 Peter and 1 John were the only undisputed writings of the seven, but he accepted all of them as canonical. All seven appeared in Codex Claromontanus (Egypt, sixth century AD), Codex Sinaiticus, and Codex Vaticanus (both fourth century), Athanasius's thirty-ninth Festal Letter (367), Jerome's writings (about 394), Codex Alexandrinus (fifth century), and Augustine's writings (fourth-fifth centuries). The textual situation for each book or section must be discussed separately.

James

James has been preserved in three third-century manuscripts, exhibiting the following affinities:

$\mathfrak{P}^{20}$ bearing resemblance to ℵ (in 10 out of 14 variants) and B (also in 10 out of 14 variants)

$\mathfrak{P}^{23}$ showing affinities with ℵ A C (in 7 of 8 variants)

$\mathfrak{P}^{100}$ agreeing most predominantly with B (in 22 out of 27 variants) and then with ℵ (18 of 27 variants).

The entire text of James is best preserved in the fourth-century manuscript B and the fifth century manuscripts A and C.

1 Peter

Peter's first epistle, accepted from the onset as authentic and apostolic, was well preserved in its early textual transmission. This textual fidelity is manifest in one late third-century manuscript, $\mathfrak{P}^{72}$ (Papyrus Bodmer VII-VIII), and another fourth-century manuscript, $\mathfrak{P}^{81}$. Excluding singular variants, $\mathfrak{P}^{72}$ displays a text that resembles B and yet is closer to the original than B, while $\mathfrak{P}^{81}$ has more affinity with ℵ than with B. $\mathfrak{P}^{74}$, of the seventh century, also has a fairly good text for 1 Peter.

2 Peter and Jude

The original text of 2 Peter and Jude was not as well preserved in the early period of textual transmission because these books were not readily acknowledged as apostolic, canonical texts by all the sectors of the early church. The manuscript evidence for these books is quite diverse, marked by independence. This is evident in the two papyri, $\mathfrak{P}^{72}$ (especially for Jude) and $\mathfrak{P}^{78}$. All in all, Codex Alexandrinus (A) is usually the best witness for these epistles. $\mathfrak{P}^{74}$ B and C are also good witnesses.

John's Epistles

The best manuscript for John's epistles is B, followed by ℵ. Codex Alexandrinus (A) tends to be expansive and erudite in these epistles. Several Western witnesses, especially in the Vulgate manuscripts, have extended interpolations (see notes on 2:17; 4:3; 5:6b, 7b–8a, 9, 10, 20). First John has one early, third-century witness, $\mathfrak{P}^9$, but it is scant and its textual character is unreliable. Second John also has a third-century witness, 0232; its testimony *is* reliable.

Textual Groupings for Revelation

Primary Manuscripts (with substantial extant text): $\mathfrak{P}^{47}$ $\mathfrak{P}^{115}$ ℵ A C

Primary Later Manuscripts: 2053 2062 2344

Secondary Manuscripts (with smaller portions of text): $\mathfrak{P}^{18}$ $\mathfrak{P}^{24}$ $\mathfrak{P}^{85}$ $\mathfrak{P}^{98}$

According to Joseph Schmid (who produced a magnum opus on the text of Revelation),[63] the best text was preserved in A and C, supported by a few select minuscules (2053 2062 2344). This text seems to have been antedated by three third-century manuscripts, $\mathfrak{P}^{18}$ (which has agreement with C in 10 out of 11 variants), $\mathfrak{P}^{24}$ (though the extant text is too small to be certain), and $\mathfrak{P}^{115}$. Concerning the last mentioned manuscript, $\mathfrak{P}^{115}$, the textual affinities are as follows:

$\mathfrak{P}^{115}$ agrees with $\mathfrak{P}^{47}$ in 52 out of 131 variants (40% agreement)

$\mathfrak{P}^{115}$ agrees with ℵ in 81 out of 165 variants (49% agreement)

$\mathfrak{P}^{115}$ agrees with A in 109 out of 165 variants (66% agreement)

$\mathfrak{P}^{115}$ agrees with C in 94 out of 137 variants (68% agreement)

Thus, $\mathfrak{P}^{115}$ belongs in the A C group, though marginally.

Schmid thinks the second best text is that found in ℵ and $\mathfrak{P}^{47}$. (This would also have to include $\mathfrak{P}^{85}$, which accords almost completely with $\mathfrak{P}^{47}$.) But I think this is too simplistic of a heirarchy. Often, when A and C stand against ℵ and $\mathfrak{P}^{47}$, one is hard-pressed to say which combination is superior. It is true that ℵ displays several omissions and some interpolations in Revelation, but Codex A is full of accidental omissions, especially in the first half of the book. The scribe of A seems to have been very fatigued and/or inattentive when copying the first half of Revelation. Thus, we should be hesitant to accept the general maxim that A has the best text of Revelation. Perhaps, it is better to say A and C (with $\mathfrak{P}^{115}$) preserve one of the purest forms of the original text, but not necessarily any more pristine than that found in the combined testimony of ℵ and 𝔓⁴⁷.

Two other important sources for the Apocalypse are a mass of manuscripts that follow Andreas of Caesarea's commentary on Revelation (marked as M^A) and a common group of other Koine manuscripts (marked as M^K). The siglum M indicates the agreement of M^A and M^K. The manuscript 046 usually agrees with M^K, and the manuscript P concurs with M^A.

Finally, it should be noted that Erasmus's edition of Revelation (which eventually became the Textus Receptus) was based on one twelfth-century manuscript, which lacked the last six verses. Furthermore, other parts of this manuscript were so conjoined with the Greek commentary on this manuscript that text and commentary became almost indistinguishable. For many of these parts, as well as the last six verses, Erasmus used the Latin Vulgate to re-create the Greek text. As one might expect, this procedure produced a Greek edition with readings that have never been found in any Greek manuscript but are still perpetuated in the Textus Receptus.[64]

Chapter Seven

The Praxis of New Testament
Textual Criticism

This chapter provides several examples of doing textual criticism, exposing the students to the various facets of textual problems. At the same time, this chapter incorporates some paleographical analysis. When the two are put together—a close study of actual manuscripts with a thorough study of textual criticism—the results can be quite satisfying. Students should learn to work with actual manuscripts (and/or transcriptions) in the process of doing textual criticism. For this purpose, I would encourage students to use a volume I prepared (with David Barrett) entitled *The Text of the Earliest New Testament Greek Manuscripts* because it contains an up-to-date transcription of all the Greek manuscripts dated before AD 300.[1] This volume is often referred to in this chapter in shortened form as *Text of Earliest MSS.* Transcriptions of early Greek manuscripts do not include accent marks (as in modern printed Greek editions) simply because the early manuscripts rarely had accent marks (only an occasional rough breathing mark). Thus, the Greek readings I cite in this chapter are unaccented (as is the case in the critical apparatus of the Nestle-Aland text) so as to approximate more closely the readings in actual manuscripts.

Another goal of this chapter is to show where the early papyri have made significant changes in the Nestle-Aland/UBS text (noted below as "NU text") and/or should make significant changes. The purpose of this study is to encourage students to see where the papyri have made significant contributions to the praxis of textual criticism, and where there is work yet to be done. I would encourage students to study the critical apparatus of the Nestle-Aland text (27th edition) and the United Bible Societies' text (4th edition) when making decisions about textual issues. Bruce Metzger, a member of the committee of the NU text, prepared a textual commentary that describes the decisions of the committee on many significant readings. Students should use this excellent volume, entitled *Textual Commentary on the Greek New Testament* (abbreviated in this chap. as TCGNT).

The Praxis of New Testament Textual Criticism

The purpose of this section is to provide students with examples of the kinds of textual problems they will encounter in the act of doing textual criticism. We begin with transcriptional errors and then move on to purposeful alterations.

Transcriptional Errors

*Mistaking One Letter for Another

A good example of this is found in Luke 9:39. The adverb μογις is found in 𝔓[75] אᵃ A C D L; other manuscripts (B W Q f¹) read μολις. Both words have the same meaning ("scarcely" or "with difficulty") and could have been easily confused by scribes because there is only a one-letter difference and the capital gamma (Γ) and lambda (Λ) look so similar in many ancient manuscripts: ΜΟΓΙΣ / ΜΟΛΙΣ.

*Dittography

A scribal error involving the repetition of a word, letter, or phrase, caused by the eye skipping backward in the copying process.

At the end of Mark 1:34, the scribe of D accidentally recopied a phrase appearing at the beginning of the verse: και εθεραπευσεν πολλους κακως εχοντας ποικιλαις νοσοις και δαιμονια πολλα εξεβαλεν (and he healed many having illness with various diseases and he cast out many demons).

*Haplography (or Scribal Leap, or Parablepsis)

A scribal error involving the omission of a word, letter, or phrase, caused by the eye skipping that portion in the copying process. Because the scribe moved forward in his copying, this error is sometimes called "a scribal leap" or "parablepsis."

In Luke 12:8–10, we see that all of 12:9 was omitted in 𝔓[45] it^e syr^s and one cop^bo manuscript. The omission was probably accidental, due to haplography—the eye of a scribe passing from the last four words of 12:8 (which are the same at the end of 12:9—των αγγελων του θεου [the angels of God] to the beginning of 12:10. In 2 Peter 3:8, a few manuscripts (𝔓[72] א 1241) omit και χιλια ετη, (and a thousand years) but the deletion must have been accidental—due to haplography (the eye of a scribe passing from ετη to ετη).

*Homoioarchton (or Homoeoarchton)

A scribal omission in which the eye of the copyist skips accidentally from one word to a similar word having a similar beginning.

The entire verse of 1 Corinthians 16:19 was omitted by A, due to homoeoarcton. The next verse begins with the same two words—ασπαζονται υμας (greets you). In Revelation 10:6, A and Maj^A omit και την γην και τα εν αυτη (and the earth and the things in it). The omission was probably accidental—due to homoeoarchton— the eye passing from the και before την γην to the και before την θαλασσαν.

*Homoioteleuton (or Homoeoteleuton)

A scribal omission in which the eye of the copyist slips accidentally from one word to a similar word having a similar ending.

Matthew 4:21–22 is not present in W and 33—most likely due to homoeoteleuton; both 4:20 and 4:22 end with ηκολουθησαν αυτω (they followed him). In Matthew 5:19, some important manuscripts (א* D W) omit the last clause of this verse: ος δ αν ποιηση και διδαξη, ουτος μεγας κληθησεται εν τη βασιλεια των ουρανων (but whoever does [them] and teaches [them], this one will be called great in the kingdom of the heavens)—most likely due to homoeoteleuton (the previous sentence ends with the same last six words). The scribe of D continued the omission to the end of 5:20, which ends with the same last three words. In Matthew 7:27, two scribes (ℵ* 33) accidentally omitted επνευσαν οι ανεμοι και (the winds blew and), due to homoeoteleuton (the previous clause ends with same last six letters: ποταμοι και).

There are several cases of homoeoteleuton in Revelation, especially in Codex A. For example, in Revelation 5:4 a few scribes (A 1854 2050 2329) omitted the entire verse accidentally—due to homoeoteleuton. The previous verse ends with exactly the same last six words as does 5:4 (ανοιξαι το βιβλιον ουτε βλεπειν αυτο). In Revelation 8:10, the scribe of A omitted the last phrase of this verse: και επι τας πηγας των υδατων (and upon the springs of waters). Again, the omission was probably accidental—due to homoeoteleuton. The previous phrase ends with a similar-looking word, ποταμων (rivers). In Revelation 22:11, a few manuscripts (A 2030 2050 2062^txt) omit και ο ρυπαρος ρυπανθητω ετι (and the one who is filthy let him be filthy still)—probably due to homoeoteleuton. The previous clause ends with the same word: ετι (still).

*Transposition

A scribal error in which two letters or two (or more) words are accidentally reversed.

By way of example, it can be said that Χριστους Ιησους (Christ Jesus) and Ιησους Χριστους (Jesus Christ) were often transposed. In 1 Corinthians 1:1, the reading is αποστολος Χριστου Ιησου (apostle of Christ Jesus) in 𝔓^46 B D F G 33. But the reading is αποστολος Ιησου Χριστου (apostle of Jesus Christ) in ℵ A Ψ Maj. In this case, the preferred word order is found in the first reading, supported by superior documentation and normative Pauline usage. Paul typically refers to "Christ Jesus" when speaking of his exalted state in glory, and to "Jesus Christ" when speaking of his earthly ministry or when speaking of "our Lord Jesus Christ."

Sometimes, scribes made purposeful transpositions, as in Mark 10:23–26. Against all other documents, D it^a,^b,^d have a transposition of verses 23 and 25, creating this order: 23, 25, 24, 26. This transposition is probably the editorial work of the scribe of Codex Bezae (or his predecessor), who wanted the aphorism in 10:25 (describing the impossibility of wealthy people entering the kingdom) to be juxtaposed with Jesus' statement in 10:23 about how difficult it is to enter the kingdom of God.

Purposeful Alterations

These kinds of textual changes cannot be blamed on scribal inadvertence or carelessness. They are conscious, purposeful changes made to the text.

*Conflated Reading

A conflation is the scribal technique of resolving a discrepancy between two or more variant readings by including all of them. This phenomenon is more prevalent in later manuscripts because the scribe was confronted with a greater variation among the extant witnesses.

A good example of this is found in Philemon 2. One textual variant has Απφια τη αδελφη (Apphia the sister), with excellent support: ℵ A D* F G I P 048 0278 33 1739 cop[bo]. Another variant is Απφια τη αγαπητη (Apphia the beloved), found in D[2] Ψ Maj syr[p]. A third variant conflates these two: Απφια τη αδελφη τη αγαπητη (Apphia the beloved sister), as in 629 it[a] syr[h].

*Interpolation

Interpolations are scribal additions to the manuscript that attempt to clarify the meaning of the text. These account for a host of variants.

An example of this can be found in Romans 11:6. The superior text simply reads ουκετι γινεται χαρις (it [grace] would no longer be grace), with the excellent support of 𝔓[46] ℵ * A C D F G 1739 cop. However, an interpolation appears in other manuscripts (B ℵ[2]Y 33[vid] Maj), expanding the reading to ουκετι γινεται χαρις. ει δε εξ εργων ουκετι εστι χαρις, επει το εργον ουκετι εστιν εργον (it [grace] would no longer be grace. But if it is of works, then it is no more grace; otherwise work is no longer work). The purpose of the gloss is to help elucidate the text, which plainly depicts the nature of grace as being a free gift, not a reward for doing work.

*Insertions from Oral and Extrabiblical Traditions

Some manuscripts display added text that was derived from oral traditions or extrabiblical traditions. One of the obvious signs that there are additions is that they appear in different places in the Gospel texts. Two of the most noteworthy ones are known as the "bloody sweat" passage and the pericope of the woman caught in adultery. Each of these is discussed in chapter 5.

*Insertions from Ecclesiastical Practices

Throughout the course of textual transmission, certain scribes were prone to expand the text by adding some wording that reflected church practice. This is apparent in the addition of the words "and fasting" to "prayer." It is also apparent in certain additions concerning Christian confession and baptism.

There are two clear examples in the New Testament where the words "and fasting" were appended to the simple prescription of prayer. In Mark 9:29, the original wording is most likely τουτο το γενος εν ουδενι δυναται εξελθειν ει μη εν προσευχη (this kind does not come out except by prayer), supported by ℵ B 0274 it[k]. The two words και νηστεια (and fasting) were appended to the end in ℵ[2] A C D L W 33 so TR). In 1 Corinthians 7:5, the best reading is σχολασητε τη προσευχη (you may devote yourselves to prayer) with the solid support of 𝔓[11vid] 𝔓[46] ℵ* A B C D F G 1739 cop. This was expanded in the TR to σχολασητε τη νηστεια και τη προσευχη (you may devote yourselves to fasting and to prayer)—so ℵ² Maj syr. The addition, which is late, reflects the ascetic tendencies of certain scribes influenced by the monastic movement.

There are another two examples where the practice of Christian confession and baptism have made an intrusion into the text—one in John and another in Acts. In John 9:38–39, several manuscripts (𝔓⁶⁶ A B C D Maj) have the wording ο δε εφης πιστευω, κυριε· και προσεκυνησεν αυτω. 39 Και ειπεν ο Ιησους (And he [the cured blind man] said, "I believe, Lord." And he worshipped him. And Jesus said.) However, these words are lacking in significant manuscripts: 𝔓⁷⁵ ℵ* W itᵇ copᵃᶜʰ² copˢᵃᴹˢˢ. Brown suggests that "the words were an addition stemming from the association of John 9 with the baptismal liturgy and catechesis."[2] Beasley-Murray notes that in early lectionary usage the lesson extended from 9:1 to 9:38, and that 9:38 constituted the confession made at baptism.[3]

A similiar interpolation found its way into Acts 8:37 (see 4ᵐᵍ E 1739 it syrʰ**), which is clearly a baptismal confession inserted into the text. Prior to his baptism, the Ethiopian eunuch says: "I believe that Jesus Christ is the Son of God"—after having been asked by Philip if he believed with all his heart. But these words are not found in any of the early manuscripts (𝔓⁴⁵ 𝔓⁷⁴ ℵ A B C syrᵖ copˢᵃ, ᵇ). This verse is a classic example of scribal gap-filling, in that it supplied the apparent gap left by the unanswered question of the previous verse ("The eunuch said, 'Look, here is water! What is to prevent me from being baptized?'"). The interpolation puts an answer on Philip's lips that is derived from ancient Christian baptismal practices. Before being baptized, the new believer had to make a confession of his or her faith in Jesus as the Son of God.

*Lectoral Expansions

Since the New Testament text was read in church meetings, it was natural for scribes to add certain words that enhanced oral reading. In this regard, the word (αμην) was often appended to the end of every book of the New Testament, concluding doxologies were often expanded, and/or doxologies were simply added.

As for the adding of the word αμην, it can be said that this was appended by later scribes to the end of every book of the New Testament (see critical apparatus of NA²⁷ for textual evidence concerning each variant). Only three epistles (Romans, Galatians, Jude) appear to have a genuine αμην for the last word.

The final greetings, the blessings of grace and peace, and concluding doxologies were expanded throughout the course of textual transmission. For example, one can look at the textual variants for verses such as Philippians 4:23; 2 Timothy 4:22; Titus 3:15; 1 Peter 5:14; 2 Peter 3:18; Jude 25 and clearly see the expansions.

Sometimes scribes added a concluding doxology to round out a prayer. This is no more evident than in the various additions to the Lord's Prayer (Matt. 6:9–13), which ends with "deliver us from evil" in the earliest witnesses (ℵ B D Z 0170). The various appended endings are as follows: (1) add αμην (amen) in 17 vgᶜˡ; (2) add *because yours* is the power and the glory forever. Amen in cop^sa,^fay (Didache omits *Amen*); (3) add *because yours is the kingdom and the glory forever. Amen* in syr^c; (4) add *because yours is the kingdom and the power and the glory forever* in it^k syr^p; (5) add οτι σου εστιν η βασιλεια και η δυναμις και η δοξα εις τους αιωνας. αμην (because yours is the kingdom and the power and the glory forever. Amen.) in L W Q 0233 f^13 33 Maj syr; (6) οτι σου εστιν η βασιλεια του πατρος και του υιου και του αγιου πνευματος εις τους αιωνας. αμην (because yours is the kingdom of the Father and the Son and the Holy Spirit. Amen) in 1253 Chrysostom. This shows the continual expansion of the addition—from the simple "amen" in variant 1 to the elaborate Trinitarian doxology in variant 6.

*Narrative Gap Fillings

These are additions inserted by scribes to fill perceived gaps in the narrative. Many examples were provided in chapter 5 and chapter 6. A few examples herein will suffice. In Matthew 22:7, certain scribes (C D W 0102 Maj) add that the king first has to hear what happened to his servants before he expresses his anger. The best text (א B L 085) skips this link in the narrative, calling upon the reader to fill in the gap. In Acts 15:24, the best manuscripts (𝔓^33 𝔓^45vid 𝔓^74 א A B D 33) present the wording in the Jerusalem Council's letter as simply saying that certain men were "unsettling your souls." This leaves a gap, which the reader can fill in, but which certain scribes (C E Maj) felt obligated to supply for the reader: "unsettling your souls by saying [it is necessary] to be circumcised and to keep the law." Other such gap-filling occurs in the narrative of Acts in 15:34; 24:6b–8a; 28:29 (see standard translations and commentaries). In these portions, certain scribes added verbiage to fill perceived narrative gaps. The scribe of D added a host of narrative gap-fillers in the book of Acts (see, for example, Acts 3:11; 4:18; 5:14–15, 18, 21–22a; 8:24, 37; 10:17, 21–29, 32; 12:17; 13:8, 43; 14:2–7, 19; 15:24, 41; 16:10, 29–30, 35–40; 17:5; 18:12–13, 19, 27; 19:14, 16, 28; 20:12; 21:25).

*Gospel Harmonizations

Scribes were prone to conform the wording of one Gospel to another. This is called Gospel harmonization. The entire phenomenon was discussed in detail in chapter 5. Some examples will help the student see specific instances of Gospel harmonization.

In Matthew 1:25, the purer text reads ετεκεν υιον (she gave birth to a son), per the testimony of א B Z^vid 071^vid f^1,^13 33. This was changed to ετεκεν υιον αυτης τον πρωτοτοκον (she gave birth to her firstborn son) in C D L W 087 Maj (TR) by way of harmonization to Luke 2:7 (a parallel passage). In Matthew 11:19, the wording is εδικαιωθη η σοφια απο των εργων αυτης (wisdom is justified by her works) according to excellent testimony: א B* W syr^h,^p cop^bo MSS^according to Jerome. This was changed to εδικαιωθη η σοφια απο των τεκνων αυτης (wisdom is justified by her children) in B^2 C D L Θ f^1 Maj syr^c,s (TR). The variant is the result of scribal conformity to Luke 7:35, a parallel passage. As for Matthew 23:14, the verse does not exist in ℵ B D L Z f¹ 33 itᵃ,ᵉ syrˢ copˢᵃ. It was added in W 0102 0107 Maj itᶠ syrʰ,ᴾ (before 23:13) and in f¹³ it syrᶜ (after 23:13—so TR). This verse, not present in the earliest manuscripts and several other witnesses, was taken from Mark 12:40 or Luke 20:47 and inserted in later manuscripts either before or after 23:13.

Many other such Gospel harmonizations can be seen in verses such as Matthew 27:35; Mark 6:11; 11:26; 15:28; Luke 4:4; 4:8; 5:38; 8:54; 9:35; 17:36; 22:64; 23:17; 23:38. (See standard commentaries; see Metzger's *Textual Commentary on the Greek New Testament*.)

*Harmonization of OT Passages Cited in the NT to the LXX

Scribes tended to harmonize Old Testament quotations, cited in the New Testament, to the wording of the Septuagint. Such alterations were common in the fourth century (and thereafter), when scribes tended to produce a standardized text.

A few examples help illustrate this. In Matthew 2:18, the better manuscripts read κλαυθμος και οδυρμος πολυς (weeping and great mourning)—so ℵ B Z 0250. This was expanded to θρηνος και κλαυθμος και οδυρμος πολυς (lamentation and weeping and great mourning) in C D L W 0233 Maj. Because Matthew's rendition of Jeremiah 31:15 (which is Jer. 38:35 in the LXX) differs significantly from the LXX, various scribes wanted to conform Matthew's rendition to the LXX. One way to do this was to add θρηνος και (weeping and). In Matthew 15:8, the reading is ο λαος ουτος τοις χειλεσιν με τιμα (this people honors me with the[ir] lips), according to ℵ B D L 084 f¹³ 33 syrᶜ,ˢ cop. This was expanded to εγγιζει μοι ο λαος ουτος τω στοματι αυτων και τοις χειλεσιν με τιμα (this people draws near to me with their mouth and honors me with the[ir] lips)—so C W 0106 Maj (TR). The expanded text is the result of scribal conformity of the Old Testament quotation to Isaiah 29:13 (LXX). Another example is in Luke 4:18, which reads κηρυξαι αιχ-μαλωτοις αφεσιν (to proclaim release to the captives), according to ℵ B D L W f¹³ 33 syrˢ cop. This was expanded to ιασασθαι τους συντετριμμενους την καρ-διαν, κηρυξαι αιχμαλωτοις αφεσιν (to heal the broken-hearted, to proclaim release to the captives) in A Θ Ψ 0102 f¹ Maj (so TR). The variant reading, which has poorer support, must be deemed a scribal interpolation that brings Luke's text into conformity with Isaiah 61:1–2 (LXX).

*Theological Alterations

Scribes changed the text for theological purposes. Some of these were discussed in chapter 5, with respect to the changes made by Marcion, a heretic, and those made by the D-reviser from his theological perspective. Other scribes made changes in the text, thinking they were guarding orthodoxy or simply adjusting the text for a better theological presentation.

A few examples help illustrate this. Let us first look at Matthew 24:36. According to good textual evidence (ℵ*,² B D Θ f¹³ it MSSᵃᶜᶜᵒʳᵈⁱⁿᵍ ᵗᵒ ᴶᵉʳᵒᵐᵉ), Jesus said that the angels and he (the Son) did not know the hour or day of the parousia; only the Father knows. Scribes found it difficult to conceive of Jesus not knowing something his Father knew—specifically, the time of the second coming. So they deleted reference to "the Son"—as in $\aleph^1$ L W f^1 Maj syr cop MSS$^{according\ to\ Jerome}$.

Other theological alterations occurred with respect to statements about the relationship between Jesus' parents and Jesus. In Luke 2:33, the best text reads ο πατηρ αυτου και η μητηρ (his father and the [= his] mother)—so $\aleph^2$ B D W f^1 cop^{sa,bo} Origen ($\aleph$* L syr^s add a final αυτου). This was changed to Ιωσηφ και η μητηρ αυτου (Joseph and his mother) in (A) Θ (Ψ) f^{13} Maj Old Latin syr (so TR). The natural description of Joseph and Mary as the father and mother of Jesus caused offense to various scribes and led to this alteration.[4] In Luke 2:41, 43, and 48, various scribes, trying to preserve the doctrine of the virgin birth, altered the text so that it would not say that Joseph and Mary were the parents of Jesus. In 2:41, the expression οι γονεις αυτου (his parents) were changed to "Joseph and Mary" in many Old Latin manuscripts. In 2:43, again, the expression οι γονεις αυτου (his parents), found in $\aleph$ B D L W Θ f^1 33, was changed in many later manuscripts (A C Ψ 0130 Maj—so TR) to Ιωσηφ και η μητηρ αυτου (Joseph and his [Jesus'] mother). In 2:48, the words ο πατηρ σου καγω (your father and I) were altered to "we" in it^{a,b,l} syr^s. Interestingly, these scribes allowed for Mary being called Jesus' "mother" in the first part of this verse, but would not let the text say that Joseph was Jesus' father.

*Christological Changes

Certain scribes changed the text in the interest of making readings which, according to their theological perspective, improved upon the text. However, the resultant text presents a different view than the original. Many such changes can be illustrated in significant passages where the NU text and TR differ.

In Luke 4:41, NU reads συ ει ο υιος του θεου (you are the Son of God), with the outstanding support of $\mathfrak{P}^{75vid}$ $\aleph$ B C D L R W 33 700 syr^s cop^{sa} Marcion Origen. The TR reads συ ει ο Χριστος, ο υιος του θεου (you are the Christ, the Son of God), with the support of A Q Θ 0102 f^1,^{13} Maj. Influenced by Matthew 16:16 and other passages, scribes could not resist adding "the Christ."

In Luke 9:35, NU reads ο υιος μου εκλελεγμενος (my Son, the chosen One) with excellent testimony: $\mathfrak{P}^{45}$ $\mathfrak{P}^{75}$ a B L syr^c cop. The TR reads ο υιος μου ο αγαπητος (my beloved Son), with inferior testimony: A C* W f^{13} Maj it Marcion Clement. The change is the result of scribal harmonization to Matthew 17:5 and Mark 9:7.

In John 1:18, NU reads μονογενης θεος (an only One, God), with the excellent support of $\mathfrak{P}^{66}$ $\mathfrak{P}^{75}$ $\aleph$* B C* L. The TR reads ο μονογενης υιος (the only-begotten Son), with the inferior support of A C^3 W^s Maj. The TR presents a reading which conforms to other places in John—explicitly John 3:16. The best text in 1:18 reveals that Christ is the unique God, thereby affirming his deity.

In John 6:69, the NU reads ο αγιος του θεου (the holy One of God), with the excellent support of $\mathfrak{P}^{75}$ $\aleph$ B C* D L W it^d. The TR reads ο Χριστος ο υιος του θεου ζωντος (the Christ, the Son of the living God), with the inferior support of Θ^c 0250 f¹³ syr^{p,h,pal} Maj. The TR is the result of scribal harmonization to Matthew 16:16.

In Acts 16:7, the NU text has the unique title το πνευμα Ιησου (the Spirit of Jesus), with the excellent support of 𝔓⁷⁴ ℵ A B C² D E 33 1739 syr cop^{bo}. The TR reads το πνευμα (the Spirit), found in Maj. The TR misses out on a unique title which unites Jesus and the Spirit: "the Spirit of Jesus."

In Colossians 2:2, the NU reads του μυστηριου του θεου, Χριστου (the mystery of God, [namely] Christ), with the support of the two earliest manuscripts: 𝔓⁴⁶ B. The TR expands this to του μυστηριου του θεου και πατρος και του Χριστου (the mystery of God and of the Father and of Christ), with the support of D² Maj syr^h**. The TR obscures the fact that Christ is God's mystery revealed.

There are far more examples than these, but these are enough to show some significant differences between the NU text and the TR with respect to Christology.

*Inclusion and Exclusion of New Testament Verses and Passages

The other primary difference between the TR and modern critical editions (such as NU) involves several passages that are considered spurious by most contemporary scholars. These additions in the TR are found in the following verses: Matthew 5:44; 6:13; 16:2b–3; 20:16; 20:22–23; 25:13; 27:35; Mark 9:49; 10:7, 21, 24; 14:68; Luke 4:4; 8:43; 9:54–56; 11:2–4, 11; 22:19–20, 43–44; 24:42; Acts 28:16; Romans 16:24, 25–27; 1 Corinthians 11:24. And then there are entire verses which are excluded in the NU text but are included in the TR: Matthew 17:21; 18:11; 23:14; Mark 7:16; 9:44, 46; 11:26; 15:28; Luke 17:36; 23:17; John 5:3b–4; Acts 8:37; 15:34; 24:6b–8a; 28:29. Two other longer passages are also considered spurious by many contemporary scholars: the longer ending to Mark (16:9–20) and the story of the woman caught in adultery (John 7:53–8:11). These are included in the TR and in the NU text but set off with double brackets to signal spuriousness. I have offered discussion on each of the longer passages in my volume, *Essential Guide to Bible Versions* (chap. 8). Kurt and Barbara Aland have provided explanations for both the longer and shorter omissions in the NU text in their volume, *The Text of the New Testament* (292–306). I would encourage students to read these so as to understand why these portions should not be included in the Greek New Testament.

The key theological issue pertaining to these passages concerns their right to be considered "Scripture." If they are clearly scribal additions, then they cannot be considered part of the original text and therefore must not be treated on the same par as divinely inspired Scripture. As such, we must beware of forming doctrines based on any of these passages.

Studies in the Praxis of New Testament Textual Criticism

In the remainder of the chapter we will look at some textual variants for the purpose of working through the process of doing textual criticism. The examples so selected often highlight the significance of the papyri in textual criticism.

Matthew 21:44

The NU text includes this verse ("And the one falling on this stone will be broken to pieces; and it will crush anyone on whom it falls"). This has the support of ℵ B C L W Z (Θ) 0102 f¹,¹³ Maj syr^{c,h,p} cop. However, several witnesses do not include the verse: $\mathfrak{P}^{104vid}$ D 33 it syr^s Origen Eusebius. Though $\mathfrak{P}^{104}$ is not cited in NA²⁷ or UBS⁴, the exclusion of the verse is certain because the text on the verso of $\mathfrak{P}^{104}$ can only be reconstruccted with the verse missing (see *Text of Earliest MSS,* 644).

Though this verse is included in the NU text, it is bracketed to signal the editors' doubts about it being a part of Matthew's original composition. The text has good documentary support, the kind that would usually affirm legitimacy for most textual variants. However, the reading of the text is challenged by the earliest manuscript, $\mathfrak{P}^{104}$ (second century), Origen, D, and other witnesses. The testimony of $\mathfrak{P}^{104}$ heightens the suspicion that this verse may be an interpolation taken from Luke 20:18. One caution against this view is that one would have expected that the interpolation would have been inserted (quite naturally) after Matthew 21:42 (in order to get the two OT citations together, as in Luke 20:17–18), not after 21:43.

The first quote, in Matthew 21:42, is taken from Psalm 118:22–23; it is quoted in all the Gospels to underscore the reality that Jesus, though rejected by the Jews, would become the cornerstone of the church. The next verse affirms this truth when it says, "The kingdom of God will be taken away from you [the Jews] and given to a people who will produce its fruit." Then follows 21:44: "he who falls on this stone will be broken to pieces, but he on whom it falls will be crushed" (taken from Isa. 8:14–15 and Dan. 2:34–35, 44–45). This prophecy depicts Christ as both the stone over which the Jews stumbled and were broken (cf. Rom. 9:30–33; 1 Cor. 1:23) and the stone that will smash all kingdoms in the process of establishing God's kingdom.

Mark 6:3

The NU text follows the reading ο τεκτων, ο υιος της Μαριας (the carpenter, the son of Mary) with the support of ℵ A B C D L W et al. A variant is cited on this: του τεκτονος υιος και της Μαριας (son of the carpenter and of Mary) with the support of f¹³ 33^{vid} (565) 700 cop^{bomss} Origen. $\mathfrak{P}^{45vid}$ is also cited, but I think $\mathfrak{P}^{45}$ reads υιος του τεκτονος, ο υιος της Μαριας (the carpenter's son, the son of Mary). The extant portion of $\mathfrak{P}^{45}$ shows τεκτον]ος ου[ς (see *Text of Earliest MSS,* 166). This reading could perhaps support the first variant if ο υιος is attached to του τεκτονος = "the son of the carpenter." However, since $\mathfrak{P}^{45}$ appears to show υιος as a nomen sacrum (there is an overbar showing over the first letter of υιος), it seems just as likely that the scribe wrote what is indicated in the second variant—inasmuch as Jesus' divine status was attached to his virgin birth through Mary.

Mark 7:4

The NU text follows the reading βαπτισμους ποτηριων και ξεστων και χαλκιων και κλινων (washing of cups and pitchers and bronze vessels and dining couches) supported by A D W Q f¹,¹³ Maj. The varaiant is βαπτισμους ποτηριων και ξεστων και χαλκιων (washing of cups and pitchers and bronze vessels), supported by 𝔓⁴⁵ᵛⁱᵈ ℵ B L D. If 𝔓⁴⁵ were the only early manuscript to contain the shorter reading, it could be dismissed as 𝔓⁴⁵'s typical trimming of the text; but the words και κλινων are also lacking in several other significant manuscripts, including ℵ and B. Perhaps the words were omitted accidentally due to homoeoteleuton (χαλκιων and κλινων end in the same two letters), or purposely excised because the scribes may have thought that κλινων meant "beds" and therefore deleted it as incongruous with the other items. But in context it has to mean "dining couches" because the passage speaks of the legalistic requirements pertaining to eating utensils. This word could not have been added under the influence of Leviticus 15, as Metzger suggests (TCGNT), because "the bed" in Leviticus 15 is the conjugal bed, which is never said to be washed. If it was added by scribes, it was done so as to include the largest of eating utensils—the dining couch.

Luke 1:78

The NU text follows the reading επισκεψεται ημας ανατολη (the dayspring will visit us), with support cited from ℵ* B L W Θ 0177. A variant on this is επεσκεψατο ημας ανατολη (the dayspring has visited us), supported by ℵ² A C D Ξ Ψ 0130 f¹,¹³ Maj. 𝔓⁴ᵛⁱᵈ is not listed in NA²⁷ or UBS⁴ probably because the manuscript is very difficult to read in this place. My examination of the actual manuscript shows that the word in 𝔓⁴ is επισκεψεται (will visit), not επεσκεψατο (has visited) because the letter before the lacuna is a broken iota, not a broken epsilon.

Luke 3:22a

Most manuscripts read το πνευμα το αγιον σωματικω (the Holy Spirit in bodily form [descended]). 𝔓⁷⁵ lacks the article before pneuma, and 𝔓⁴ reads το ΠΝΑ το αγιον ΠΝΙ. The editor of the *editio princeps* for 𝔓⁴, Merell, explained ΠΝΙ as a simple case of dittography.⁵ But if that had been so, why didn't the scribe write ΠΝΑ again? Rather, he seems to have intentionally changed to the dative, ΠΝΙ = πνευματι. As such, 𝔓⁴ has this interesting variation that can be rendered in at least two ways: (1) "the Holy Spirit descended in spiritual form," or (2) "the Holy Spirit descended as spirit." The first option was probably the scribe's intent and provides a creative alternative to the difficult idea of the Spirit descending in bodily form.

Luke 3:22b

The NU text follows the reading συ ει ο υιος μου ο αγαπητος, εν σοι ευδοκησα (you are my Son, the beloved, in whom I am well pleased) with the support of 𝔓⁴⁺⁶⁴⁺⁶⁷ ℵ A B L W 0124 33 MSSᵃᶜᶜᵒʳᵈⁱⁿᵍ ᵗᵒ ᴬᵘᵍᵘˢᵗⁱⁿᵉ. A variant is υιος μου ει συ, εγω σημερον γεγεννηκα σε (you are my Son; this day I have begotten you), in D it Justin (Clement) Hillary MSSᵃᶜᶜᵒʳᵈⁱⁿᵍ ᵗᵒ ᴬᵘᵍᵘˢᵗⁱⁿᵉ.

The reading of the NU text has the earliest and most diverse documentary support—supported especially by 𝔓⁴ of the late second century. The variant reading is later and more localized (in the West)—a true "Western" reading. Augustine knew of both readings, although he made it clear that the variant reading was "not found in the more ancient manuscripts" (*De Cons. Evang.* 2.14).

In spite of the documentary evidence, many scholars have defended the variant reading as being the more difficult reading and therefore more likely original. They argue that the reading was originally a full quotation of Psalm 2:7, which (in the words of the NJB translators) shows Jesus to be "the King-Messiah of the Ps. [2:7] enthroned at the Baptism to establish the rule of God in the world." This reading was then harmonized to the baptism accounts in Matthew 3:17 and Mark 1:11 by orthodox scribes trying to avoid having the text say that Jesus was "begotten" on the day of his baptism—an erroneous view held by the Adoptionists.[6]

However, it can be argued that the scribe of D (known for his creative editorialization) changed the text to replicate Psalm 2:7 or was himself influenced by Adoptionistic views. Indeed, the variant reading was included in the second-century Gospel of the Ebionites, who were chief among the adoptionists. "They regarded Jesus as the son of Joseph and Mary, but elected Son of God at his baptism when he was united with the eternal Christ."[7]

In any case, Psalm 2:7 appears to have been used exclusively by New Testament writers with reference to Jesus' resurrection from the dead (Acts 13:33; Heb. 1:5; 5:5). Since in Luke's book of Acts it is explicitly used to affirm the prophetic word about Jesus' resurrection, it would seem odd that he would use it to affirm Jesus' baptism. Given the reading of the text, it seems more likely that Luke was thinking of Psalm 2:7 for the first part of the statement ("this is my beloved Son") and Isaiah 42:1 for the second part ("in whom I am well-pleased"). The Isaiah passage is especially fitting given its connection with the Messiah's reception of the Spirit.

Luke 4:41

The NU text follows the reading συ ει ο υιος του θεου (You are the Son of God), citing in support, ℵ B C D L R W 33 700 syrˢ copˢᵃ Marcion Origen. A variant on this is συ ει ο Χριστος, ο υιος του θεου (You are the Christ, the Son of God), with the support of A Q Θ Ψ 0102 f¹,¹³ Maj. 𝔓⁷⁵ᵛⁱᵈ should be added to manuscripts supporting the text (see *Text of Earliest MSS*, 508).

Luke 5:39

The NU text retains this verse, as do all English versions, which render it something like: "And no one drinking the old desires the new, for he says, 'the old is better.'" The documentary evidence supporting the inclusion of this verse is impressive: 𝔓⁴⁺⁶⁴⁺⁶⁷ 𝔓⁷⁵ᵛⁱᵈ ℵ A B C W Maj. However, the verse is excluded in the following witnesses: D it Marcion Eusebius Irenaeus. Marcion may have deleted it because he thought it validated the authority of the Old Testament. It is also possible that it was deleted to conform the pericope to the parallel passages in Matthew and Mark, which have no such verse. Or it is possible that it was deleted by scribes who took offense at Jesus speaking about wine-drinking with such candor and knowledgeable detail.

Westcott and Hort bracketed this verse perhaps thinking it might be a "Western noninterpolation" (though they left no note on this). The documentation favoring the text (from the two papyri 𝔓⁴ and 𝔓⁷⁵) is so impressive that all doubt should be removed, as well as the brackets.

Luke 8:43

The NU text follows the reading ητις ιατροις προσαναλωνσασα ολον του βιον ουκ ισχυσεν απ ουδενος θεραπευθηναι (who spent all her living on physicians and was not able to be healed by anyone), with the support of ℵ A C L W Θ Ψ 33 Maj. A variant reading is ητις ουκ ισχυσεν απ ουδενος θεραπευθηναι (who was not able to be healed by anyone), supported by 𝔓⁷⁵ B (D) 0279 syrˢ copˢᵃ Origen.

Though the above noted clause is included in NU, it has been bracketed in the text to show the editors' doubts about its inclusion. On one hand, it looks as though it could be a true Lukan condensation of Mark 5:26; on the other hand, it is just as likely that the clause was borrowed by scribes from Mark 5:26 and 12:44. If it had been original, it is difficult to explain why the clause would have been dropped by the scribes of 𝔓⁷⁵ B D. Most modern English translators have thought the clause did not belong as part of Luke's Gospel, and the testimony of 𝔓⁷⁵ especially strengthens their position—as does 0279, a manuscript discovered at St. Catherine's Monastery in the 1970s.

Luke 10:21

The NU text follows the reading τω πνευματι τω αγιω (in the Holy Spirit), with the support of 𝔓⁷⁵ ℵ B C D L 33. A variant on this is τω πνευματι (in the spirit), found in 𝔓⁴⁵ᵛⁱᵈ A W Ψ 0115 f¹³ Maj. In fuller context, a rendering of the text would be: "he [Jesus] rejoiced in the Holy Spirit." Prior to NA²⁶, the Nestle text displayed the variant reading in the text; then the editors of NA²⁶ and UBS³ adopted the first reading. Metzger (TCGNT) provides the rationale for the change: "The strangeness of the expression 'exulted in the Holy Spirit' (for which there is no parallel in the Scriptures) may have led to the omission of τω αγιω from 𝔓⁴⁵ A W etc." Indeed, this is a strange expression. The Gospel writers did not use the term "Holy Spirit" when speaking of an action that Jesus himself performed εν τω πνευματι (in the spirit/Spirit) or of an emotion that emanated from his spirit. Jesus is said to have "perceived in his spirit" (Mark 2:8), "sighed deeply in his spirit" (Mark 8:12), "grown strong in spirit" (Luke 2:40 in some MSS), "groaned in the [or his] spirit" (John 11:33), and "was troubled in spirit" (John 13:21). (In grammatical terms, any mention of the word πνευμα in the dative case preceded by any verb in the active voice never appears elsewhere in the Gospels—with respect to Jesus—as "the Holy Spirit," with the exception of the statement about Jesus baptizing "with [or, in] the Holy Spirit"). Whenever the Gospel writers spoke about Jesus' mental or emotional activity related to the spirit/Spirit, they viewed it as an activity happening within his spirit. Thus, it would be unusual for Luke to say that Jesus "rejoiced in the Holy Spirit." But it is this unusualness, coupled with such good textual support, that seems to favor the reading of the text.

However, in defense of the variant reading, it can be said that τω αγιω (the Holy) was added because (1) scribes had a propensity to add αγιω to πνευματι and (2) some scribes may have felt that they wanted to clearly distinguish the "spirit" (πνευμα) mentioned in Luke 10:21 from the "spirits" (πνευματα) mentioned in the previous verse (Luke 10:20, which says, "Do not rejoice in this, that the spirits are subject to you, but rejoice that your names are recorded in heaven"—NASB). If the second reading is original, the text could be read as Jesus rejoicing in the divine Spirit or in his spirit—the Greek can be taken either way. But it should be noted that all the scribes of the early centuries wrote πνευμα as a nomen sacrum even when referring to what most exegetes would consider Jesus' human spirit. (See the lengthy discussion on this in chap. 4.) They could have written it in *plene*, but chose not to. As a point of fact, the scribe of 𝔓⁴⁵ wrote the nomen sacrum Π̅Ν̅Ι̅ in Luke 10:21. Thus, even though αγιω was not attached to this, it is clear in the manuscript 𝔓⁴⁵ that Jesus was rejoicing in the divine Spirit.

Luke 15:21

The NU text follows the reading ουκετι ειμι αξιος κληθηναι υιος σου (I am no longer worthy to be called your son) on the strength of 𝔓⁷⁵ with A L W Θ Ψ f¹,¹³ Maj syrᶜ,ˢ cop. This overthrows the longer reading ουκετι ειμι αξιος κληθηναι υιος σου. ποιησον με ως ενα των μισθιων σου (I am no longer worthy to be called your son; make me like one of your hired men), which has the support of a B D 33 syrʰ. There are two factors that favor the reading of the NU text: (1) it has earlier and more diverse testimony, and (2) the words in the variant were carried over from Luke 15:19 so that the son's actual speech would replicate the one he had planned. The WH text includes the words in brackets to show doubt about their authenticity. Indeed, in this case the testimony of ℵ and B (favored by WH) is over-ridden by $\mathfrak{P}^{75}$ and others.

Luke 24:3, 6, 12, 36, 40, 51, 52

Westcott and Hort (1882:71) thought Codex Bezae (D) contained the original wording of Luke's Gospel in 24:3, 6, 12, 36, 40, 51, and 52. (All these portions are double-bracketed in WH to show the editors' strong doubts about their inclusion in the text.) Calling the omissions in D "Western noninterpolations," they posited the theory that all the other manuscripts contain interpolations in these verses. This theory affected the Nestle text until its twenty-sixth edition, at which point this theory was abandoned—note the changes in Luke 24:3, 6, 12, 36, 40, 51, 52, where none of the portions are double-bracketed. This theory also affected several modern English versions—especially the RSV and NEB, which in nearly every one of these Luke 24 passages followed the testimony of D against all other early MSS. The NASB was also affected by this theory, but not as much as the RSV and NEB. After all three of these translations were published, $\mathfrak{P}^{75}$ was discovered. And in every instance, $\mathfrak{P}^{75}$ attests to the longer reading. $\mathfrak{P}^{75}$ impacted the Nestle text, which now in every verse noted above follows the testimony of $\mathfrak{P}^{75}$ et al. And $\mathfrak{P}^{75}$ influenced the most recent versions (NIV, NJB, NAB, NLT), which in every case followed its testimony to include those portions previously excluded by previous translations.

One wonders why Westcott and Hort were so taken with the evidence of D only in the latter part of Luke, when all throughout Luke D displays many omissions. In Luke, D displays at least 75 omissions that are 2 words or more—and frequently the excision is of a phrase, a clause, or an entire sentence. In chapter 24 alone, D has 13 such omissions. With respect to these omissions, D often stands alone among the witnesses, or has slim support from an Old Latin or Syriac manuscript. In nearly every case, the omission cannot be explained away as a transcriptional error; rather, the deletions are the careful work of an editor having a penchant for pruning (in the critical apparatus of NA[27] see Luke 1:26; 5:9, 12, 26, 30, 39; 6:12, 21, 34; 7:3, 7, 18, 27, 28, 30, 47; 8:5, 15, 24, 28a, 28b, 43, 44; 9:12, 15, 16, 23, 48; 10:19, 23, 24; 11:8, 31, 32, 46, 49; 12:19, 41; 13:25; 16:6, 18; 17:24; 18:9, 40; 19:4, 25, 31, 36, 43, 44; 20:31, 36; 21:10, 24, 37; 22:19–20, 22, 54, 61; 23:39, 45, 56; 24:9, 12, 19, 20, 22, 25, 30, 36, 40, 46, 49, 51, 52). The reviser usually displayed an opposite penchant in the book of Acts—that of expanding but not always (see D-text subtractions in the textual commentary on Acts). The main point to realize about the D-reviser is that he was a redactor who both excised and enhanced.

In this verse, the longer text accords with Luke's style (see Acts 1:21; 4:33; 8:16). The shorter text is a Western excision, perhaps influenced by 24:23. What is most surprising is that the NRSV followed the D-text here.

John 1:18

The discovery and publication of both $\mathfrak{P}^{66}$ and $\mathfrak{P}^{75}$ strengthen the case for the reading followed by NU: μονογενης θεος (an only One, God), which is found in $\mathfrak{P}^{66}$ ℵ* B C* L. $\mathfrak{P}^{75}$ ℵ[1] read ο μονογενης θεος (the only-One, God). These two readings stand against ο μονογενης υιος (the only-begotten Son), found in A C[3] W[s] Maj.

The two early papyri ($\mathfrak{P}^{66}$ and $\mathfrak{P}^{75}$), the earliest uncials (ℵ B C*), and some early versions (Coptic and Syriac) support the text, and many church fathers (Irenaeus, Clement, Origen, Eusebius, Serapion, Basil, Didymus, Gregory-Nyssa, and Epiphanium) knew of this reading. The variant with υιος (Son) was known by many early church fathers (Irenaeus, Clement, Hippolytus, Alexander, Eusebius, Eastathius, Serapion, Julian, Basil, and Gregory-Nazianzus) and translated in some early versions (Old Latin and Syriac). However, the discovery of two second-century papyri, $\mathfrak{P}^{66}$ and $\mathfrak{P}^{75}$, both of which read θεος (God), tipped the balance. It is now clear that μονογενης θεος is the earlier reading—and the preferred reading. This was changed, as early as the beginning of the third century—if not earlier, to the more ordinary reading, μονογενης υιος (the only begotten Son).

Even without the knowledge of the papyri (which were discovered in the 1950s and 1960s), Hort argued extensively and convincingly for the reading μονογενης θεος.[8] He argued that Gnostics (such as Valentinus, the first known writer to have used this phrase) did not invent this phrase; rather, they simply quoted it. And he argued that this phrase is very suitable for the closing verse of the prologue, in which Christ has been called "God" (θεος—in 1:1) and "an only One" (μονογενης—in 1:14), and finally, "an only One, God" (μονογενης θεος)—which combines the two titles into one. This is a masterful way of concluding the prologue, for 1:18 then mirrors 1:1. Both verses have the following three corresponding phrases: (1) Christ as God's expression (the "Word" and "he has explained him"), (2) Christ as God ("the Word was God" and "an only One, God"), and (3) as the one close to God ("the Word was face to face with God" [Williams translation] and "in the bosom of the Father").

John 1:34

This is a case of the papyri being divided on a significant textual variant. $\mathfrak{P}^{66}$ and $\mathfrak{P}^{75}$ (followed by the NU text) support the reading ο υιος του θεου (the Son of God), as do ℵ[2] A B C W D Θ Ψ 083. $\mathfrak{P}^{5vid}$ $\mathfrak{P}^{106vid}$ read ο εκλεκτος του θεου (the chosen One of God), as do ℵ* it[e] syr[c,s]. A conflated reading is *chosen Son of God*, as found in it[a] (*electus filius*) syr[pal] cop[sa].

Though both 𝔓⁵ and 𝔓¹⁰⁶ are listed as "vid," it is fairly certain that both MSS read εκλεκτος, not υιος. The transcription of 𝔓⁵ in *The New Testament in Greek IV, The Gospel According to St. John* (volume 1, The Papyri), showing υιος is incorrect. The spacing on the line calls for εκλεκτος, as judged by the original editors, Grenfell and Hunt.⁹

The NU text has excellent external support among the papyri and early uncials, but so does the variant. Indeed, it is supported by two early papyri (𝔓⁵ and 𝔓¹⁰⁶), an early uncial (ℵ*), and two of the most reliable early Western witnesses (itᵉ syrˢ). The presence of the conflated reading, "chosen Son of God," shows that both readings were present at an early stage of textual transmission. The second corrector of Codex Sinaiticus (sixth or seventh century) deleted εκλεκτος and wrote the nomen sacrum for υιος in the margin.

Several scholars have argued that it is more likely that the reading εκλεκτος (chosen One) was changed to υιος (Son) than vice versa. For example, Gordon Fee thinks an orthodox scribe of the second century might have sensed "the possibility that the designation 'Chosen One' might be used to support adoptionism and so altered the text for orthodox reasons."¹⁰ Or the change could have happened because scribes thought "Son" conformed with the Synoptic accounts of Jesus' baptism (where God calls Jesus "my Son") and/or suited John's Gospel better than "chosen One." Indeed, "Son of God" frequently occurs in John's Gospel, but not all who recognized Jesus' deity called him "the Son of God." For example, Peter called him "the holy one of God" (6:69). All these reasons strenghten the case for "chosen One" as the original reading.

John 4:1

The NU text follows the reading εγνω ο Ιησους οτι ηκουσαν οι Φαρισαιοι οτι Ιησους πλειονας μαθητας ποιει και βαπτιζει η Ιωαννης (Jesus realized that the Pharisees heard that Jesus was gaining and baptizing more disciples than John) with the support of 𝔓⁶⁶* ℵ D Θ 086 f¹. A variant reads εγνω ο κυριος οτι ηκουσαν οι Φαρισαιοι οτι Ιησους πλειονας μαθητας ποιει και βαπτιζει η Ιωαννης (when the Lord realized that the Pharisees heard that Jesus was gaining and baptizing more disciples than John), with the support of 𝔓⁶⁶ᶜ² 𝔓⁷⁵ A B C L Wˢ 083 f¹³ Maj.

Upon close examination of 𝔓⁶⁶ it appears that the manuscript originally read I̅C̅, (the nomen sacrum for Ιησους—Jesus) and was changed to K̅C̅ (the nomen sacrum for κυριος—Lord) by adding the < stroke to the I = I< (K). Since the resultant K does not look like other kappas written by the original scribe,¹¹ it is suspect as a correction made by the *diorthothes*, the second corrector (see *Text of Earliest MSS*, 398). Most likely Ιησους (Jesus) was changed to κυριος (Lord) by scribes (such as the corrector of 𝔓⁶⁶) because they wanted to alleviate the awkwardness of repeating Jesus' name twice.

John 5:44

The NU text follows the reading την δοξαν την παρα του μονου θεου (the glory from the only God), with the support of 𝔓[63vid] ℵ A D L 063 0210[vid] f[1,13] 33 it[e] syr Maj. However, the reading την δοξαν την παρα του μονου (the glory from the Only One) has the support of 𝔓[66] 𝔓[75] B W it[a,b] cop[sa,bo,ach]. This reading, supported by the earliest manuscripts (𝔓[66] 𝔓[75] B) and also by several early versions (Old Latin and Coptic), was rejected by the NU editors on the grounds that the word for "God" (θεου—contracted as $\overline{\Theta Y}$) probably dropped from the text due to homoeoteleuton: TOYMONOY$\overline{\Theta}$$\overline{Y}$ (TCGNT). But there are a few problems with this view. First, scribes would not have easily dropped a nomen sacrum, especially because of the obvious overbar over the nomen sacrum. Second, would this have occurred in so many manuscripts? Third, certain ancient translators must have recognized the expression μονου as functional by itself, not needing the addition of θεου. But various Greek scribes were not of the same opinion; they added θεου to fill in what would otherwise seem incomplete. Scribes aware of the Jewish *Shema* (Deut. 6:4) would have been inclined to add "God" to get the phrase, "the only God."

John 7:53–8:11 (the pericope of the adulterous woman)

This portion is included in the NU text, albeit in double brackets. It should be excluded outright and printed in the critical apparatus as a variant reading, or it could be placed as an appendix (as in WH). The manuscript evidence supporting the exclusion of this passage is overwhelming: 𝔓[39vid] 𝔓[66] 𝔓[75] ℵ A[vid] B C[vid] L N T W D Θ Ψ 0141 0211 33 it[a,f] syr[c,p,s] cop[sa,bo,ach] geo Diatessaron Origen Chrysostom Cyril. The papyri, 𝔓[66] and 𝔓[75], have all the more affirmed that this passage was not part of the original text of John. I think it can also be said that 𝔓[39] did not include this passage (see the extended excursus at the end of this chap.). Documentary testimony is against the inclusion of this passage, as well as a host of internal arguments, all of which are discussed in my textual commentary.[12]

John 8:57

The NU text follows the reading πεντηκοντα ετη ουπω εχεις και Αβρααμ εωρακας (you are not yet fifty years old, and you have seen Abraham?) This has the support of 𝔓[66] ℵ[c] A B C D L W f[1,13] it syr[h,p]. A variant reading is πεντακοντα ετη ουπω εχεις και Αβρααμ εωρακεν σε (you are not yet fifty years old, and Abraham has seen you?). This has the support of 𝔓[75] ℵ* 0124 syr[s] cop[sa,ach2].

Typically, commentators say that the variant reading appears to be an assimilation to the preceding verse in which Jesus indicated that Abraham rejoiced to see his day (TCGNT). It is argued that Jesus had not claimed to be a contemporary with Abraham or that he had seen Abraham; he had said that Abraham had seen his day. As such,

Abraham had prophetic foresight about the coming of the Messiah. (According to Rabbinic tradition, Abraham was supposed to have been given foresight into future events pertaining to the descendants would come from his loins.)

But Abraham is not the focus of the statement, Jesus is; and it is for this reason that the variant reading makes good sense. The question in the variant focuses on the longevity of Jesus, not Abraham's foresight. In the next verse, Jesus responds by affirming his eternal existence: "Before Abraham was, I am." Thus, the reading in $\mathfrak{P}^{75}$ (which is known for its accuracy) and $\aleph*$ (which is not Western beyond 8:38)[13] is entirely consistent with the tenor of the passage.

John 9:38–39a

The NU text reads ο δε εφη, πιστευω, κυριε. και προσεκυνησεν αυτω. Και ειπεν ο Ιησου (And he said, "I believe, Lord." And he worshipped him. And Jesus said). This has the support of $\mathfrak{P}^{66}$ A B C D Maj. These words are not found in $\mathfrak{P}^{75}$ $\aleph*$ W it^b cop^{ach2} cop^{samss}. The evidence for the omission of John 9:38–39a is impressive, inasmuch as the manuscripts that do not include it are early and geographically dispersed. The three early Greek manuscripts ($\mathfrak{P}^{75}$ $\aleph*$ W) are impressive enough, let alone the testimony of three early translations (Old Latin and two Coptic versions). The Coptic testimony comes from the papyrus codex of the Gospel of John in the sub-Achmimic dialect and from the Michigan Fayyumic Papyrus 3521.[14]

It is usually argued that the omission was the result of a transcriptional error, but nothing in the text suggests the usual kinds of error, such as homoeoteleuton or homoearchton. And even if it was an error, how could this have occurred in so many diverse manuscripts? Furthermore, εφη (I said) is rarely used in John (only at 1:23), the exact verbal form προσκυνεω (I believe) occurs nowhere else in John (except in the singular reading of $\mathfrak{P}^{66}$ in 11:27) and is not used in John with "Jesus" as the direct object. These factors point to a non-Johannine origin.

If John did not write these words, why were they added? Brown suggests that "the words were an addition stemming from the association of John 9 with the baptismal liturgy and catechesis." He then elaborates: "When the catechumens passed their examinations and were judged worthy of Baptism, lessons from the OT concerning cleansing water were read to them. Then came the solemn opening of the Gospel book and the reading of John 9, with the confession of the blind man, "I do believe, Lord" (38), serving as the climax. . . . After this the catechumens recited the creed."[15]

To affirm Brown, it could be pointed out that many Christian teachers in the early church (such as Irenaeus, Ambrose, and Augustine) taught that the blind man's action of "washing at the pool of Siloam" depicted baptism. Furthermore, Beasley-Murray notes that in early lectionary usage the lesson extended from 9:1 to 9:38, and that 9:38 constituted the confession made at baptism.[16]

Porter argues that a similiar interpolation found its way into Acts 8:37, which is clearly a baptismal confession inserted into the text.[17] Before his baptism, the Ethiopian eunuch says: "I believe that Jesus Christ is the Son of God." But these words are not found in any of the early manuscripts (see comments on Acts 8:37). The same kind of interpolation found its way into John 9, but at an early date, for it is present in $\mathfrak{P}^{66}$, a second-century manuscript. Interestingly, several second-century depictions in Roman catacombs about baptism include the blind man's washing at the pool of Siloam. Therefore, it is not unlikely that certain manuscripts of the Gospel of John were affected by this addition by the middle of the second century, if not earlier. Thus, this passage is a prime example of how the New Testament text was affected by ecclesiastical practices such as baptismal confession.

Without this portion, the text in John 9:35–39 reads as follows:

35 Jesus heard that they threw him out. He found him and said, "Do you believe in the Son of Man?"

36 The man replied, "And who is he, sir, that I might believe in him?"

37 Jesus answered, "You have seen him and he is the One speaking with you."

[[38–39a He said, "I believe, Lord. And he worshipped him."

And Jesus said,]]

39b "I came into the world to bring judgment—so that those who don't see could see and that those who see would become blind."

The text, without 9:38–39a, presents a continuous statement from Jesus' lips. However, it does not show how the blind man responded to Jesus' question. Of course, this is disappointing and could very likely be the prime factor that motivated scribes or redactors to insert the addition and thereby fill the gap. The reader wants to know if the blind man became a believer. Indeed, he did, but this is not readily apparent in the shorter text. Yet in saying that "those who don't see could see," Jesus was implying that the blind man had come to see that Jesus was the Messiah.

John 13:32

The NU text follows the reading which includes the phrase: ει ο θεος εδοξασθη εν αυτω (if God is glorified in him), with the suppport of $\aleph^2$ A C^2 Θ Ψ f^{13} Maj it syr^p cop^{sa} Origen. However, the phrase is omitted in $\mathfrak{P}^{66}$ $\aleph$* B C* D L W syr^{s,h} cop^{ach}. Thus, the phrase is not present in the earliest witnesses and in other diverse witnesses. However, many scholars think the phrase is an intrinsic part of John's original writing—and that it was omitted from many manuscripts because of homoeoteleuton or deliberate deletion of perceived redundancy (see 13:31). Indeed, its inclusion makes for a nice chiasm and/or step parallelism in 13:31–32 (see TCGNT). But it is difficult to explain how the omission could have occurred in so many early and diverse manuscripts. Besides, it could be argued that the words were added to create a protasis—note the late corrections in $\aleph$ and C. In this case, therefore, documentary evidence should be given preference over internal considerations. Barrett said, "It seems inevitable to follow the majority of the early authorities and accept the short text. The longer probably owes its popularity to Origen."[18] Thus, we see how the text was changed later in its transmission (after the end of the fourth century) due to the influence of an earlier expositor, Origen.

John 16:23

The NU text follows the reading αν τι αιτησητε τον πατερα εν τω ονοματι μου δωσει υμιν (whatever you ask the Father in my name he will give it to you), with the support of $\mathfrak{P}^{22vid}$ A C^{3vid} D W Θ Ψ f^{13}. A variant reading is αν τι αιτησητε τον πατερα δωσει υμιν εν τω ονοματυ μου (whatever you ask the Father he will give it to you in my name), found in $\mathfrak{P}^{5vid}$ ℵ B C* L D. Both readings have support from early manuscripts, including the papyri; however, the variant reading has the earliest collective testimony and is the harder reading. Because Jesus usually spoke of making petition to the Father in his own name (see 14:13, 14; 15:16; 16:24, 26), it would have been quite natural for scribes to conform this clause to the more usual order. Furthermore, it would be difficult to imagine why so many early scribes would have rearranged the syntax to the more difficult reading. But both Metzger (TCGNT) and Tasker argue that the text is more suitable to this context that deals with praying in the Lord's name.[19] Many ancient scribes must have thought so, too; so they made a change to produce a more readable text to an audience that had become accustomed to asking (or praying) in the name of Jesus.

John 21:18

The NU text follows the reading αλλος σε ζωσει και οισει (another will gird you and he will carry [you]) with the support of A Θ Ψ f^{13} Maj. A variant reading is αλλοι σε ζωσουσιν και αποισουσιν (others will gird you and they will carry [you] off), with the support of $\mathfrak{P}^{59vid}$ $\mathfrak{P}^{109vid}$ (ℵ^1 C^2) D W 33. $\mathfrak{P}^{109}$ shows αλλοι on one line and . . .]ουσιν σε on another line. Space in the lacuna on the next line makes the exact wording uncertain, but it does support a plural verb (see *Text of Earliest MSS*, 653).

The entire verse reads, "When you grow old, you will stretch out your hands, and another/others will gird you and carry you where you do not want to go." The image depicts Peter's death by crucifixion (see *1 Clement* 5.4). Tertullian (*Scorpiace* 15, written AD 211), referring to John 21:18, said that Peter was "girded by another" when his arms were stretched out and fastened to the cross. The reading of the text indicates that only "one" would be responsible for taking Peter to this death; and that "one" perhaps could be the Lord, who was in control of Peter's life and death (see 2 Peter 1:13–15). Or that "one" could simply be a vague reference to an executioner. However, the plural has better textual support, $\mathfrak{P}^{109}$ (ca. 200), and gives the earliest testimony to the reading with the plural subject and plural verbs. And a diversity of other manuscripts affirm the plural. This variant, relegated to the margin of NA[27], challenges the reading with the singular subject and verb.

Romans 8:20–21

The NU text follows the reading τον υποταξαντα, εφ ελπιδι οτι και αυτη η κτισις ελευθερωθησεται (the one subjecting [it], in hope that the creation itself will be freed), with the support of $\mathfrak{P}^{27\text{vid}}$ $\mathfrak{P}^{46}$ A B C D² Ψ Maj. This is over against the reading τον υποταξαντα εφ ελπιδι, διοτι και αυτη η κτισις ελευθερωθησεται (the one subjecting it in hope, because the creation itself will be freed), found in ℵ D* F G. ($\mathfrak{P}^{46}$ ℵ B* D* F G Ψ read εφ ελπιδι, whereas $\mathfrak{P}^{27}$ A B² C D² Maj read επ ελπιδι—with no change in meaning. The letter spacing of $\mathfrak{P}^{27}$ strongly suggests that it read οτι instead of διοτι—see *Text of Earliest MSS*, 120.)

This is a difficult variant-unit to sort out because the word οτι (in the reading of the text) and the word διοτι (in the variant) can both be translated "because." But only οτι can be rendered "that"—which permits the first rendering, a rendering that connects together the last two words of Romans 8:20 with the beginning of 8:21 ("for the creation was subjected to futility, not willingly, but because of the one subjecting it, in hope that the creation itself will be freed from the slavery of corruption"). This reading indicates that God subjected creation to futility, but only for a time; in the end he will release creation from its bondage at the same time he releases his children from mortality.

The testimony of $\mathfrak{P}^{46}$ with A B C caused the editors of NA[26] to adopt the first reading over the second—a change from previous editions of the Nestle text.

Romans 8:23

The NU text includes the word υιοθεσιαν (sonship), with the support of ℵ A B C 33 1739 Maj syr cop. A variant reading excludes υιοθεσιαν (sonship)—supported by $\mathfrak{P}^{27\text{vid?}}$ $\mathfrak{P}^{46\text{vid}}$ D F G. (Even though there is a lacuna in $\mathfrak{P}^{27}$ for this verse, the average line lengths for $\mathfrak{P}^{27}$ strongly suggest that this manuscript did not include υιοθεσιαν; see *Text of Earliest MSS*, 120). Even though $\mathfrak{P}^{46}$ is listed as *vid,* it is certain that it did not include υιοθεσιαν.

According to the NU text, followed by nearly all English versions, the verse reads, "We also groan in ourselves, eagerly expecting sonship [or, adoption], the redemption of our bodies." This reading has an appositive: "The redemption of our bodies" describes what the sonship or adoption is. The variant reading lacks the appositive: "We also groan in ourselves, eagerly expecting the redemption of our bodies." This variant has early support, especially if we add the testimony of $\mathfrak{P}^{27}$. However, the omission of "sonship" in the variant is usually explained as a scribal effort to eliminate a seeming contradiction between Paul's statement here about sonship and the statement he made in Rom. 8:15 ("you have received a spirit of sonship"). But in Romans 8:15 Paul spoke about the believers' initial reception of the Spirit of sonship; whereas in 8:23 he was speaking about the ultimate appropriation of each son's inheritance—i.e., the possession of a glorified body. Thus, there is not really a contradiction. However, it must be allowed that certain scribes may have thought there was, so they eliminated the word. However, it is possible that certain scribes borrowed the word from 8:15 to make clear that the ultimate redemption equals the consummation of υιοθεσιαν.

1 Corinthians 2:1

The NU text follows the reading το μυστηριον του θεου (the mystery of God), supported by $\mathfrak{P}^{46vid}$ ℵ* A C it^{a,r} syr^p cop^{bo}. UBS^3 cites $\mathfrak{P}^{46vid?}$ in support of the text. The question mark follows *vid* because the editors were not sure that $\mathfrak{P}^{46}$ contains the word μυστηριον (mystery). Having examined the actual papyrus, I can affirm that the reading is μυστηριον (mystery), not μαρτυριον (testimony), because the Greek letter eta, though partially broken, is visible before the final four letters—also visible (ριον). The one letter makes all the difference in determining the reading. UBS^4 (as well as the Nestle text) now list it as $\mathfrak{P}^{46vid}$. The variant reading is το μαρτυριον του θεου (the testimony of God), supported by ℵ^2 B D F G Ψ 33 1739 Maj it^b syr^h cop^{sa}.

The text has uncontestable support from the earliest extant document, $\mathfrak{P}^{46}$. Several other witnesses, both early and diverse, also support the text. But the same can be said for the variant reading. So how then do we solve the problem? Competent textual critics such as Zuntz[20] and Fee[21] have argued that μυστηριον is a scribal emendation influenced by 2:7. Other scholars, such as Raymond Brown[22] and Metzger (TCGNT), have argued that μαρτυριον is a scribal emendation influenced by 1:6. Actually, one can draw upon the context of 1 Corinthians 1–2 to support either word, because Paul's message in these chapters is that his mission was to testify only of Christ, who is the mystery of God. The immediate context, however, seems to support "mystery," because chapter 2 focuses on the need for believers to receive revelation from the Spirit of God to truly understand all the hidden, secret riches of God that are in Christ Jesus (see 2:7ff.).

2 Corinthians 4:14

The NU text follows the reading ο εγειρας τον κυριον Ιησουν (the one having raised the Lord Jesus), with the support of ℵ C D F G Ψ 075 0150 it^{a,b} syr cop^{bo}. However, a variant on this is ο εγειρας τον Ιησουν (the one having raised Jesus), with the support of $\mathfrak{P}^{46}$ B (0243 33 1739 omit τον) it^r cop^{sa}. Although it is possible that the variant is the result of scribal assimilation to Romans 8:11, it is far more likely that the reading of the text is an expansion because scribes had a habit of expanding the name "Jesus" to "Jesus Christ" or "Lord Jesus Christ." But Paul was purposely using

only Jesus' name in this chapter (4:5, 6, 10, 11, 14) to underscore Jesus' human identification with the sufferings of men. Disagreeing with the NU committee's majority
decision to accept the reading of the text, Metzger argued that the variant has more
diverse attestation, while the text was the work of a pious scribe expanding Jesus'
name (TCGNT). Here is a case where $\mathfrak{P}^{46}$, with B and others, most likely preserves
the original reading and NU should be changed.

2 Corinthians 5:3

The NU text follows the reading ει γε και εκδυσαμενοι ου γυμνοι ευρεθησομεθα (for if indeed having been unclothed we will not be found naked) with the
support of D*,c itᵃ Marcion Tertullian. The variant reading is ει γε και
ενδυσαμενοι ου γυμνοι ευρεθησομεθα (for if indeed having been clothed we
will not be found naked), with the support of $\mathfrak{P}^{46}$ ℵ B D² Ψ 0243 33 1739 1881 Maj
it syr cop Clement.

This statement must be understood in context. Paul was using a double metaphor
to describe the death of our bodies: it is a putting off of old clothes and a departure
from a temporary habitation (a tabernacle or tent). The permanent house and new
clothes represent our resurrected bodies, while the earthly tabernacle and old clothes
represent our present, earthly bodies. Christians long to be released from earthly bodies—not to become spirits without bodies but to have new bodies. Thus, speaking of
this future body Paul says, "having been clothed we shall not be found naked." Some
scribes must have thought this was tautological, so they changed it to "having been
unclothed we will not be found naked." But this is not a trite statement or tautological; it is a proleptic affirmation of a Christian's future state of being. Furthermore,
this statement sets the stage for the next verse where Paul affirms that his desire is *to
be clothed*. And since a great array of witnesses attest to this reading, the variant and the
reading of the text should be transposed, which happened to be the personal opinion
of Metzger, who disagreed with the decision of the committee (see TCGNT). Indeed,
the testimony of $\mathfrak{P}^{46}$ (the earliest witness), with a host of other excellent witnesses,
calls for a change in the NU text.

Galatians 1:6

The NU text follows the reading χαριτι Χριστου (grace of Christ), with the
support of $\mathfrak{P}^{51}$ ℵ A B Fᶜ Ψ 33 1739 1881 Maj syrᵖ copᵇᵒ. There are three variants on
this: (1) χαριτι (grace) in $\mathfrak{P}^{46vid}$ F* G Hᵛⁱᵈ itᵃ,ᵇ Tertullian Cyprian Pelagius; (2) χαριτι Ιησου Χριστου (grace of Jesus Christ) in D 326 syrʰ**; (3) χαριτι θεου (grace
of God) in 327.

If "Christ" or "Jesus Christ" or "God" had originally been in the text, why would
any scribe have deleted them? Thus, it is likely that the shorter reading, having early

(𝔓⁴⁶) and diverse support, is original and that scribes adorned χαριτι (grace) with one of these divine titles.

Galatians 2:12

The NU text follows the reading τινας απο Ιακωβου (certain ones [came] from James), with the support of ℵ A B C D F G H Maj. A variant reading on this is τινα απο Ιακωβου (a certain one [came] from James), found in 𝔓⁴⁶ it^{d,r} Irenaeus. It is possible that the scribe of 𝔓⁴⁶ was thinking of the one Judaizer (from Jerusalem) who was negatively influencing the believers in Antioch—and perhaps in Galatia, as well. This one individual is alluded to in 3:11; 5:7–10 (note the singular "who" and "he"); he may have been the leader of the Judaizers who visited Galatia (see 5:12, where the plural "they" is used).

In the next part of the verse, the NU text reads ηλθον (they came), with the support of A C D² H Ψ 1739 1881 Maj. A variant on this is ηλθεν (he came), found in 𝔓⁴⁶ ℵ B D* F G 33 it^{b,d,g} Irenaeus. Metzger thinks the variant is the result of scribal error (see his comments in TCGNT). But in so many diverse manuscripts? The singular, ηλθεν, in 𝔓⁴⁶ is no mistake, for the scribe was writing of a particular individual who, having come from James, caused problems in the church at Antioch. I am inclined to think that ηλθεν, in so many good witnesses, is not a mistake but rather points to an original τινα in 2:12a, as in 𝔓⁴⁶ (and it^{d,g} Irenaeus). If so, then Paul was speaking of a particular individual who disturbed the unity among Jewish and Gentile Christians in Galatia.

Ephesians 1:1

The NU text follows the reading τοις αγιοις τος ουσιν εν Εφεσω και πιστοις εν Χριστω Ιησου (to the saints in Ephesus and faithful in Christ Jesus) with the support of B² D F G Ψ 33 Maj syr cop^{sa}. There are two variants on this: (1) τοις αγιοις πασιν τοις ουσιν εν Εφεσω και πιστοις εν Χριστω Ιησου (to all the saints in Ephesus and faithful in Christ Jesus) in ℵ² A P it^b cop^{bo}; (2) τοις αγιοις τοις ουσιν και πιστοις εν Χριστω Ιησου (to the saints being [ ] and faithful in Christ Jesus) in 𝔓⁴⁶ ℵ* B* 1739 Marcion.

The insertion of πασιν (all) in the first variant is clearly a scribal attempt to harmonize this opening verse with several other opening verses in Paul's epistles, where Paul addresses "all" the saints in a particular locality (see Rom. 1:7; 1 Cor. 1:2; 2 Cor. 1:1). The second variant now has the support of the three earliest manuscripts (𝔓⁴⁶ ℵ B), which do not include the words εν Εφεσω (in Ephesus). Since there is no reason to explain why the words would have been deleted if they were originally in the text, it must be assumed that "in Ephesus" is a later addition. Recognizing the shorter text as being original, some translators have rendered the last part of the verse as "to the saints who are faithful in Christ Jesus" (see RSV and NJB). However, this rendering does not take into account ουσιν. Thus, it is far more likely that the original document left a blank space between τοις ουσιν (the ones being) and και πιστοις εν Χριστω Ιησου (and faithful ones in Christ Jesus). The blank would be filled in with the name of each local church ("in Ephesus," "in Laodicea," "in Colossae," etc.) as the epistle circulated from city to city. In 𝔓[46] ℵ B we are left with very ancient testimony to the original exemplar, which would not have had the city name filled in.

Paul probably intended this epistle to be a general encyclical sent to the churches in Asia, of which Ephesus was one of the leading churches. No doubt, the epistle would have gone to Ephesus (perhaps first) and then on to other churches. Each time the epistle went to another church, the name of the locality would be supplied after the expression "to the saints [in _____]." Zuntz indicated that this procedure also occurred with some multiple copies of royal letters during the hellenistic period; the master copy would have a blank for the addressee and would be filled in for each copy.[23] (Lacunae would not be left in extant copies because the name would have been filled in.) Zuntz considered the blank space in the address to the Ephesians as going back to the original. In the later textual tradition, certain scribes identifed this epistle with Ephesus and thereby inserted "in Ephesus." In his own New Testament canon, Marcion listed this letter as the epistle to the Laodiceans. But this designation was never inserted into any manuscript that we know of. However, Marcion's designation signals that the epistle had probably gone to Laodicea.

This epistle is probably one and the same as the letter Paul mentions in Colossians 4:16, where he tells the Colossians, "See to it that you also read the letter *from Laodicea*." This language indicates that a letter (presumably written by Paul) would be coming to the Colossians from Laodicea. Since it is fairly certain that Ephesians was written and sent at the same time as Colossians (Tychicus carried both epistles and was very likely Paul's amanuensis for both—see Eph. 6:21; Col. 4:7–9), it can be assumed that Paul would expect that the encyclical epistle known as Ephesians would eventually circulate from Colossae to Laodicea. Coming from Rome, Tychichus would have first arrived at Ephesus along the coast, then traveled north to Smyrna and Pergamum, then turned southeast to Thyatira, Sardis, Philadelphia, Laodicea—and then on to Colossae (as perhaps the last stop). We can surmise that this circulation route would have been similar to the one for the book of Revelation (1:11), which was also sent to the churches in Asia Minor. (The book of Revelation was circulated from Ephesus to Smyrna to Pergamum to Thyatira to Sardis to Philadelphia to Laodicea.) Just to the southeast of Laodicea was Colossae, thereby making it the next logical stop. Thus, Ephesians was an encyclical for the churches in Asia Minor.

Ephesians 1:15

The NU text follows the reading υμας πιστιν εν τω κυριω Ιησου και την αγαπην την εις παντας τους αγιους (your faith in the Lord Jesus and love to all the saints) with the support of $\aleph^2$ D^1 Ψ Maj syr^h cop^{sa} (D* F G omit second την). A variant reading is υμας πιστιν εν τω κυριω Ιησου και την εις παντας τους αγιους (your faith [trust] in the Lord Jesus and in all the saints), with the support of $\mathfrak{P}^{46}$ $\aleph$* A B 33 1739 1881 Jerome.

Metzger (TCGNT) reasoned that the variant was the result of a scribal error; the words were dropped due to homoeoarchton—the eye of the scribe passing from the την before αγαπην to the την before εις παντας. However, it is difficult to imagine that this error would have been present in so many diverse witnesses. Contrarily, the first variant has the best attestation and is the most difficult of the readings. If this was the original text, Paul was saying that he had heard of the believers' "faith in the Lord Jesus and in all the saints." The only passage close to this is Philemon 5, which says, "having heard of your love and faith in the Lord Jesus and in all the saints." But this statement is usually understood to be a chiasm; hence, it is translated: "your faith in the Lord Jesus and love for all the saints." The first variant is not chiastic and has to be understood to mean that the believers trusted in Christ and in the saints. Since Paul emphasizes the universal solidarity of the church in this epistle and encourages mutual edification, it is not out of the question for him to have declared that they trusted Jesus *and* all the saints. Thus, it could be argued that all the other variants are merely attempts to fix what seemed incomplete and/or to make Ephesians 1:15 conform to Colossians 1:4, a parallel passage. In any event, the shorter text has the best testimony—that of $\mathfrak{P}^{46}$ $\aleph$* A B.

Philippians 1:14

The NU text follows the reading τον λογον (the word) with the testimony of $\mathfrak{P}^{46}$ D^2 1739 Maj it^r. There are two variants on this: (1) τον λογον του θεου (the word of God), found in $\aleph$ A B (D*) P Ψ 33 syr^{p,h**}; (2) τον λογον του κυριου (the word of the Lord) in F G. These two variants appear to be scribal attempts to make clear just what "the word" ("the message") means. Of course, this word is the message about the Lord, and it is a message that came from God. But this didn't have to be said by Paul for his readers to understand. The editors of NA^{26} (and UBS^3) considered the variant readings to be expansions of the first. They, therefore, chose the reading supported by $\mathfrak{P}^{46}$, thereby causing a change in the Nestle text, which previously read τον λογον του θεου (the word of God).

Philippians 3:3

The NU text follows the reading οι πνευματι θεου λατρευοντες (the ones worshipping in [by] God's Spirit), with the support of $\aleph$* A B C D^2 F G 33 1739 Maj syr^{hmg} cop. There are two variants on this: (1) οι πνευματι θεω λατρευοντες (the ones worshipping God in spirit) in $\aleph^2$ D* P Ψ it syr; (2) οι πνευματι λατρευοντες (the ones worshipping in spirit) in $\mathfrak{P}^{46}$.

According to Greek grammar, the first reading can be rendered, "the ones worshipping by God's Spirit" or "the ones worshipping God's Spirit." In Greek, the verb λατρευω (worship) is normally followed by the dative (in this verse, πνευματι—"Spirit"); hence, the Spirit becomes the recipient of the worship.[24] Since the grammar allows a rendering that might be offensive to those who do not think the Spirit should be worshipped, some scribes added another object in the dative case, θεω (God)—the first variant noted above. But it should be noted that Lightfoot demonstrated that the verb λατρευοντες had acquired a technical sense referring to the worship of God,[25] and therefore one does not have to understand the phrase "God's Spirit" as the object of the worship. Thus, the text does not have to include an object to convey the message that God is being worshipped in spirit.

In this light, it is reasonable to imagine that the original reading has been preserved in 𝔓[46], for it has no object after the participle and yet it must mean "worship God in spirit" because "God" is always the object of worship. But scribes were uncomfortable with this bare expression, and therefore filled it out with either θεου or θεω. It is for this reason that 𝔓[46] explains the origin of the other variants. It is unlikely that the scribe of 𝔓[46] accidentally dropped one of these objects because both would have been written as a nomen sacrum—and these are hard to miss. Furthermore, it is obvious that the scribe put some thought into this verse because he wrote out the word *pneumati* instead of abbreviating it as a nomen sacrum, thereby possibly indicating his perception that this "spirit" referred to the human spirit, not the divine Spirit. This corresponds with John 4:23–24, which reveals that worshippers should worship God (who is Spirit) in spirit and in reality.

Philippians 3:13

The NU text follows the reading εγω εμαυτον ου λογιζομαι κατειληφεναι (I count myself not to have laid hold), with the support of 𝔓[46] B D[2] F G Ψ Maj syr[h]. A variant reading is εγω εμαυτον ουπω λογιζομια κατειληθεναι (I count myself not yet to have laid hold), with the support of 𝔓[16vid] 𝔓[61vid] ℵ A D* P 33 syr[h**]. Here is a case where the papyri and other early uncials (ℵ A B) are divided on this reading. Thus, textual critics are hard pressed to pick one reading against the other. Nevertheless, the first reading is a slightly better candidate because of the 𝔓[46] B D combination supporting that reading and because it is likely that scribes added ουπω (yet) in view of the fact that Paul later in his life claims to have finished the race and gained the prize (see 2 Tim. 4:7–8).

Philippians 4:3

The NU text reads και των λοιπων συνεργων μου (and the rest of my coworkers), with the support of 𝔓[46] ℵ[1] A B D I[vid]. A variant reading is και συνεργων μου και των λοιπων (and my coworkers and the rest) in 𝔓[16vid] ℵ*.

The two readings are significantly different. In context, the first reading yields this translation: "they [Euodia and Syntyche] have labored side by side with me in the gospel together with Clement and the rest of my coworkers, whose names are in the book of life." The second reading is as follows: "They [Euodia and Syntyche] have labored side by side with me in the gospel together with Clement and my coworkers and the rest, whose names are written in the book of life."

Some scholars (such as Metzger, see TCGNT) think the textual variant in $\mathfrak{P}^{16vid}$ and ℵ* should not be taken seriously because it is the result of scribal inadvertence. Other scholars (such as Silva)[26] urge that it should not be easily dismissed as scribal inadvertence because the evidence of $\mathfrak{P}^{16}$ shows that "it was an early competing variant." And this variant appears to reflect "a different understanding of Paul's words (i.e., that the women and Clement are not included under the category of 'coworkers')." If so, this variant could reflect an antifeminist tendency to exclude women from among those who were considered apostles and/or colaborers with the apostles.

In any event, it is possible to interpret *both* variants as indicating that *all* the ones mentioned have their names written in the book of life. To make this interpretation, one has to consider that the pronoun ων is generically inclusive; it is not restrictive to συνεργων or to λοιπων, but includes all those previously mentioned, including Euodia, Syntyche, Clement, the unnamed coworkers, and the rest.

Colossians 2:23

The NU text follows the reading ταπεινοφροσυνη και αφειδια σωματος (humility and severe treatment of the body), supported by ℵ A C D H Ψ 075 Maj syr. There are two variants on this: (1) ταπεινοφροσυνη του νοος και αφειδια σωματος (humility of the mind and severe treatment of the body) in F G it[d,f,g]; (2) ταπεινοφροσυνη, αφειδια σωματος (humility, severe treatment of the body) in $\mathfrak{P}^{46}$ B 1739 it[b]. It is quite likely that the original reading is found in this second variant (supported by the Alexandrian trio, $\mathfrak{P}^{46}$ B 1739), wherein the expression "severe treatment of the body" (as an instrumental dative) describes the prepositional phrase, "in self-imposed worship and false humility." This indicates that the self-imposed worship and resultant humility was carried out by means of the worshipper treating his body harshly (so the rendering in NJB: "a humility which takes no account of the body"). The reading of the text has an additional και (and) because some scribe considered that there were three objects of the preposition, εν (in). The first variant is a carryover from 2:18, in that it specifies that this was an "imagined" humility and therefore not real.

1 Thessalonians 2:7

The NU text follows the reading εγενηθημεν νηπιοι εν μεσω υμων (we were infants in your midst) with the support of $\mathfrak{P}^{65}$ ℵ* B C* D* F G I Ψ* it cop[bo].

The variant reading is εγενηθημεν ηπιοι εν μεσω υμων (we were gentle in your midst), found in ℵ[c] A C[2] D[2] 33 1739 Maj. There is a one-letter difference (nu) between the variants: νηπιοι (infants); ηπιοι (gentle). It is difficult to know which reading produced the other. With respect to transcriptional errors, the first word (νηπιοι) could have been created by dittography—the preceding word (εγενηθημεν) ends in nu; or the second word (ηπιοι) could have been created by haplography—also influenced by the preceding word. The variant reading seems to be the most natural in context—especially in connection with the following metaphor: "We were gentle in your midst, like a nursing mother caring for her children."

However, there are several arguments against this. First, several manuscripts (ℵ C D Ψ) originally had the first reading, but were later corrected. This strongly intimates that scribes and correctors had a problem with the meaning of the wording νηπιοι and then made an emendation. Second, the reading of the text has early and diverse attestation. Third, Westcott and Hort (1882:128) argue that the adjective ηπιοι (gentle) is not compatible with the expression εν μεσω υμων (in your midst). The appropriate word should be a noun, not an adjective.

But none of these arguments overcome the obstacle that the reading of the text seems to create a very contorted metaphor: "We were infants in your midst, like a nursing mother caring for her children." Yet it can be explained. Fowl notes that such mixing of metaphors is consistent with Pauline style.[27] And Morris notes that in this very same chapter Paul likens himself to a father (2:11) and then an orphan (2:17 απορφανισθεντες = "made orphans by separation").[28] Indeed, this word, a hapaxlegomenon in the New Testament, suggests that Paul and Silvanus were thinking of themselves (metaphorically) as being children who had been separated from their loved ones. Their brief time with the Thessalonians, cut short by persecution and subsequent forced departure, caused them to acutely sense their separation. Thus, they used an emotive image in which they pictured themselves as children who had been orphaned from their parents. In like manner, in 2:7–8 they pictured themselves as infants in their midst to show that they were guileless, innocent, and unpretentious (see 2:3–6). In other words, they had no intention to take advantage of them. As such, the image of a child works.

The majority of editors of UBS[3] and NA[26] decided to adopt the word νηπιοι because it has the earliest support (𝔓[65] providing the earliest witness) and because it is the more difficult reading. Consequently, the Nestle text was changed to read νηπιοι.

Hebrews 3:2

The NU text follows the reading εν ολω τω οικω αυτου (in all his house), with the support of ℵ A C D Y 0243 0278 33 1739 Maj syr. The variant reading is εν τω οικω αυτου (in his house), with the support of 𝔓[13] 𝔓[46vid] B cop. According to the

NU text, the writer to the Hebrews said that Jesus was "faithful to the One having appointed him as was Moses in all his house." The reading of the text follows Numbers 12:7 in the LXX exactly and accords with Hebrews 3:5. These two facts, however, can be used to defend the variant reading, for one can argue that some scribe(s) conformed the text to Numbers 12:7 LXX and/or to Hebrews 3:5. Added to this argument is that of documentation: the three earliest manuscripts ($\mathfrak{P}^{13}$ $\mathfrak{P}^{46}$ B) do not include ολω (all). The NU text should drop ολω.

1 Peter 3:18

The NU text follows the reading περι αμαρτιων επαθεν (for sins he suffered), with the support of B P Maj. There are several variants on this: (1) περι αμαρτιων υπερ υμων απεθανεν (for sins he died on your behalf) in $\mathfrak{P}^{72}$ A cop^{c,s}; (2) περι αμαρτιων υπερ ημων απεθανεν (for sins he died on our behalf) in ℵ(*) C^{2vid} L 33 1739 1881 cop^{bo}; (3) περι υμων υπερ αμαρτιων απεθανεν (for us he died on behalf of sins) in Ψ; (4) περι αμαρτιων ημων απεθανεν (for our sins he died) in C^{*vid} syr^p cop^{sa}. There are a few more variants than these listed above, but none of them presents anything significantly different. The essential difference is whether or not Christ "suffered" (επαθεν) for our sins or "died" (απεθανεν) for our sins. (The choice of pronoun—our/your—is minor, as is the insertion of υπερ.) As in 2:21, in which the context seems to favor the reading "suffered" instead of "died," it would *seem* natural for Peter (again speaking about suffering—see 3:14–18) to say that Christ "suffered for sins" rather than "died for sins." But it is possible that Peter spoke of Christ dying for sins in anticipation of speaking of Jesus' redemptive act (the righteous dying for the unrighteous) and his actual death on the cross. However, a scribe, carrying with him the message of previous verses (which is a message about suffering), would be tempted to change "died" to "suffered" if he saw "died" in his exemplar. Or it is likely that the scribes of B P Maj simply conformed this verse to 2:18, which has the reading "suffered" in these manuscripts. Thus, I am inclined to accept the evidence of $\mathfrak{P}^{72}$ ℵ A C et al. for απεθανεν (died) over against επαθεν (suffered).

Revelation 11:8

The NU text follows the reading ο κυριος αυτων εσταυρωθη (their Lord was crucified), supported by ℵ^c A C P syr. There are two variants on this: (1) ο κυριος ημων εσταυρωθη (our Lord was crucified) in 1 (so TR); (2) ο κυριος εσταυρωθη (the Lord was crucified) in $\mathfrak{P}^{47}$ ℵ*.

The three textual differences display three scribal perspectives. The first reading (the NU text) makes "the Lord" (who is the Lord Jesus) the Lord of the two witnesses or the Lord of those in Jerusalem (which is symbolized by the names "Sodom and Egypt"). Thus, "their Lord" could be the two witnesses' Lord or Jerusalem's Lord. This was changed to "our Lord" (variant 1) in minuscule 1 and incorporated by

Erasmus in his edition (so TR). This reading shows a scribal personalization of the text and/or an attempt to rectify what could have been perceived as a theological problem—that is, how could Jesus be the Lord of the city who crucified him? The third reading (variant 2) is neutral because it lacks a pronoun; it simply states where "the Lord" was crucified. It could be the original wording, which has the support of the two earliest manuscripts ($\mathfrak{P}^{47}$ $\aleph*$).

Revelation 13:18

The NU text follows the reading εξακοσιοι εξηκοντα εξ (= 666), with the support of $\mathfrak{P}^{47}$ ($\aleph$) A P Maj Irenaeus Hippolytus. Another variant is εξακοσιαι δεκα εξ (= 616), supported by $\mathfrak{P}^{115}$ C MSS[according to Irenaeus]. Still another variant is εξακοσια εξηκοντα πεντε (665) in 2344.

Writing in the late second century, Irenaeus (*Against Heresies* 5.30) was aware of the reading "616" but denounced it as "heretical and deceptive." He claimed that "666" was found in "all the good and ancient copies" and was "attested to by those who had seen John face to face." Three significant witnesses ($\mathfrak{P}^{47}$ $\aleph$ A) must have their roots in those "good and ancient copies" because they read "666." However, the recently published $\mathfrak{P}^{115}$ reads "616", as does Codex C. These are ancient manuscripts, and the number they contain, "616," is not heretical. Either "666" or "616" could be original inasmuch as both symbolize "Caesar Nero." The number "666" came from a Hebrew transliteration of "Neron Caesar" from Greek into Hebrew.

Revelation 14:4

The NU text follows the reading απαρχη, which translates as "firstfruits." This has the support of A C Maj etc. However, $\mathfrak{P}^{47}$ and $\aleph$ read απ αρχης (from [the] beginning). The *editio princeps* of $\mathfrak{P}^{47}$ mistakenly has απαρχη,[29] when it should be απ αρχης (see *Text of Earliest MSS*, 346). In context, a translation of A and C is, "They were purchased firstfruits to God and to the Lamb." In $\mathfrak{P}^{47}$ and $\aleph$, it is, "They were purchased from the beginning for God and the Lamb."

The textual attestation for these two variants is divided, as is the internal evidence. In the ancient Greek manuscripts, the word for "firstfruit" (απαρχη) could easily be confused for the expression "from the beginning" (απαρχης), or vice versa. In the early manuscripts no space was left between the words.

Both readings are defensible exegetically. The notion of being redeemed or purchased as firstfruits points to the inestimable worth of these virgins in the sight of God. Christ paid the price for their purity with his own blood (1:5). But it is also possible that the text is speaking of their eternal worth insofar as Christ chose them from the beginning to be his very own special witnesses.

Excursus on P39 Excluding John 7:53–8:11

This manuscript displays the work of a professional scribe who wrote in an early form of the Biblical Uncial script. The hand of $\mathfrak{P}^{39}$ lines up remarkably well with P. Rylands 16, dated quite confidently to the late second/early third century, and with P. Oxyrhynchus 25, dated early third. I would not hesitate to date $\mathfrak{P}^{39}$ as early third century. C. H. Roberts and T. C. Skeat assigned it to the first half of the third century. (See discussion on the dating of $\mathfrak{P}^{39}$ in chap. 3.)

$\mathfrak{P}^{39}$ preserves one leaf of John's Gospel, 8:14–18 on the verso; 8:19–22 on the recto. There are 25 lines per page, with pagination on the recto page, showing oδ (= 74) at the left top of the sheet. This suggests that the manuscript was paginated on alternate, even-numbered pages. This page number plus the large letters on each page indicates that the codex probably contained only the Gospel of John. Furthermore, this page number and the uniform lettering on both extant pages facilitates a basic reconstruction of the contents of the manuscript from the beginning of the Gospel up to the extant pages.

Since the first key to reconstructing the content of the Gospel is the pagination number, it is well worth quoting Grenfell and Hunt, editors of the *editio princeps*, on this matter:

> A pagination figure, 74, has been entered (by the original scribe, apparently) in the left-hand corner of the recto; a comparison of the capacity of this leaf with the amount of the preceding part of the Gospel shows that the number refers to the page, not the leaf, and it will follow either that the pages were numbered alternately in the series 2, 4, 6 &c., or that they were numbered consecutively at the top of the left corner.[30]

Whichever method the scribe chose (and we cannot determine this because the upper left of the verso is not extant), the fact remains that the verso is page 73 and the recto is page 74. The first page of this codex would have been written on the page where John 1:1 began. Thus, the task is to determine how many words there would have been between John 1:1 in this codex and John 8:13, and to figure whether the pages could have accommodated the Pericope of the Adulteress.

Fortunately, the lettering on each extant page enables us to reconstruct the text on those pages with great certainty.[31] Furthermore, the work of the scribe is such a fine piece of calligraphy that we can be fairly certain that he executed the same kind of design on each page of the codex. This was not a casual scribe who lengthened and shortened lines or even significantly added or shortened the number of lines per page. Each extant page has 25 lines. On page 73 there are 330 characters, and on page 74 there are 333 characters. This means that there is an average of 331 characters per page. I think we can count on this number as a good average for the first part of the manuscript.[32] But for the sake of the argument, I'll use the higher number (333 characters). This number indicates that the scribe would have written 24,624 characters by the end of page 74 (John 8:19–22), 24,309 characters by the end of page 73 (John 8:14–18), and 23,967 characters by the end of page 72. We then subtract 180 characters for John 8:12–13, which would have been on page 72, making the total 23,796 (rounded off to 23,800) characters by the end of either John 8:11 (assuming the inclusion of the Pericope of the Adulteress–John 7:52–8:11) or by the end of John 7:52 (assuming the exclusion of the Pericope of the Adulteress).

In order to figure out if the scribe included 7:53–8:11, I did my figuring as follows.

1. I calculated that Codex Vaticanus has 25,450 characters from John 1:1–7:52. This was based on a count of the transcription provided by Tischendorf.[33]

2. The second process in the calculation was to subtract from the Vaticanus text the number of letters that would be excluded through the use of the nomina sacra in $\mathfrak{P}^{39}$. The extant text of $\mathfrak{P}^{39}$ shows nomina sacra for Ιησους, πατηρ, ανθρωπον. Given this kind of presentation, it would seem that the scribe used the full repertoire of nomen sacrum for κυριος, θεος, Χριστος, πνευμα, υιος, as well. This contrasts with Vaticanus, which has nomen sacrum for only κυριος, θεος, Χριστος, Ιησους. In John 1:1–7:52 this accounts for the lessening of about another 215 characters.

3. The scribe of $\mathfrak{P}^{39}$ also used the raised line for the final nu on the end of a line. It is hard to judge how often this would have occurred, but $\mathfrak{P}^{66}$ and $\mathfrak{P}^{75}$ seem to have about two per page. The slimmer columns in $\mathfrak{P}^{39}$ could double the number. This subtracts another 300 characters.

In total, one could subtract 515 characters from 25,450 in the Vaticanus count, yielding 24,935, which differs from the 23,800 by 1,135 characters. In other words, we still have another 1,135 characters to account for—up until John 7:52. If we were to add John 7:53–8:11, we would have to account for the scribe fitting another 820 characters. According to the extant manuscript, the scribe accommodated about 333 characters per page. To fit another 1,135 characters, he needed 3.4 pages; to fit another 820 characters beyond that he would need almost 6 pages total. Thus, it is very unlikely that $\mathfrak{P}^{39}$ could have included the Pericope of the Adulteress.

The way the scribe could have fit the extra 1,135 characters was for the manuscript to have about one extra line per page than what is shown in the extant pages of $\mathfrak{P}^{39}$. The extant sheet shows the upper and lower portion of the page. One would expect uniform height of letters and space between lines on all the pages. Thus, to conceive of even one extra line per page is difficult. To include the extra 820 characters to accommodate John 7:53–8:11 means that the scribe would have had to add two extra lines per page.[34] Given the regular format of this manuscript, that seems absolutely impossible.

In the end, therefore, it is very likely that $\mathfrak{P}^{39}$ did not contain the Pericope of the Adulteress (John 7:53–8:11); it could be listed in support of its exclusion as $\mathfrak{P}^{39\text{vid}}$, just as are the listings for A[vid] and C[vid].

Notes

Chapter 1: The Manuscript Publications of the Greek New Testament

1. P. J. Parsons, "The Earliest Christian Letter?" in *Miscellanea Papyrologica* (Florence, 1980), 289.

2. See "Mark" in the *Tyndale Bible Dictionary*, 857–58.

3. See "Silas" in the *Tyndale Bible Dictionary*, 1201.

4. Each of these instances is discussed in Comfort, *New Testament Text and Translation Commentary*.

5. In Galatians 6:11, most manuscripts read "see what large *[pēlikois]* letters I wrote to you." But a few important manuscripts ($\mathfrak{P}^{46}$ B* 33) have the adjective *hēlikois*. The manuscripts 0278 and 642 have the adjective *poikilois*, which means "variegated" or simply "different." Whichever adjective Paul originally used, the point is they indicate an observable difference between Paul's handwriting and that of the amanuensis.

6. B. F. Wescott, *Gospel According to St. John*, 306.

7. See discussion on John 21 in Comfort and Hawley, *Opening the Gospel of John*, 327–28.

8. See my discussion on Mark 16:8 in *New Testament Text and Translation Commentary*.

9. See David Trobisch's *The First Edition of the New Testament*, chaps. 1–3.

10. E. G. Turner, *Greek Papyri*, 113.

11. David Aune, *The New Testament in Its Literary Environment*, 66–67.

12. J. A. T. Robinson, *The Priority of John*, 92.

13. Richard A. Burridge, *What Are the Gospels? A Comparison with Greco-Roman Biography* (Cambridge: Cambridge University Press, 1992).

14. H. Gamble, *Books and Readers*, 101.

15. A. Deissman, *Light from the Ancient Near East*, 227–45. See also Stanley Stowers, *Letter Writing in Greco-Roman Antiquity*, 17–20.

16. F. Kenyon, *Our Bible and the Ancient Manuscripts*, 157.

17. Kim Haines-Eitzen, *Guardians of Letters*, 22–32.

18. C. H. Roberts, *Manuscript, Society, and Belief in Early Christian Egypt*, 23.

19. Roberts and Skeat, *The Birth of the Codex*, 46.

20. See Gamble, *Books and Readers*, 145–47, where he provides an account of Christian books being seized by Roman authorities during the Diocletian persecution

of AD 303 (from Eusebius, *Ecclesiastical History* 8.2.4–5). In this record, one of the readers (lectors) is identified as a *grammaticus* (scribe).

21. A description and new transcription of all the early New Testament papyri (date pre-AD 300) are found in a volume I prepared with David Barrett: *The Text of the Earliest New Testament Greek Manuscripts* (Wheaton: Tyndale, 2001).

22. Gamble, *Books and Readers*, 120.

23. Roberts, *Manuscript, Society, and Belief in Early Christian Egypt*, 24.

24. Ibid., 21.

25. The Oxyrhynchus NT papyri dated post 300 AD are $\mathfrak{P}^{10}$, $\mathfrak{P}^{19}$, $\mathfrak{P}^{21}$, $\mathfrak{P}^{26}$, $\mathfrak{P}^{36}$, $\mathfrak{P}^{51}$, $\mathfrak{P}^{54}$, $\mathfrak{P}^{71}$, $\mathfrak{P}^{82}$, $\mathfrak{P}^{85}$, $\mathfrak{P}^{105}$, $\mathfrak{P}^{112}$. Oxyrhynchus has also yielded several NT uncial manuscripts: 069, 071, 0162, 0163, 0169, 0170, 0171, 0172, 0173, 0176.

26. Turner, "Scribes and Scholars of Oxyrhynchus," 141–46.

27. Kilpatrick, "The Bodmer and Mississippi Collection of Biblical and Christian Texts," 34.

28. Robinson, "The Discovering and Marketing of Coptic Manuscripts: The Nag Hammadi Codices and the Bodmer Papyri," 4–5.

29. Robinson, *The Pachomian Monastic Library at the Chester Beatty Library and Bibliotheque Bodmer*, 1–6.

30. Gamble came to this conclusion because he thought it was doubtful that there were any full-scale Christian scriptoria in the early centuries of the church—that is, "those that would be operating . . . in a specially designed and designated location; employing particular methods of transcription; producing certain types of manuscripts; or multiplying copies on a significant scale" (*Books and Readers*, 121).

31. Kim, "Paleographic Dating of $\mathfrak{P}^{46}$ to the Later First Century," 254–55.

32. See Peter Parson's "The Scripts and Their Date" (pp. 19–26) in Emmauel Tov, *The Greek Minor Prophets Scroll from Nahal Hever (8HevXIIgr)* (Oxford: Clarendon Press, 1990).

33. C. H. Roberts, *Manuscript, Society, and Belief in Early Christian Egypt*, 18.

34. See T. C. Skeat, "Irenaeus and the Four-Gospel Canon" in *Novum Testamentum* 34 (1992): 194–99; "The Earliest Gospel Codex?" and in *New Testament Studies* 43 (1997): 1–34; and see Graham Stanton, "The Fourfold Gospel" in *New Testament Studies* 43 (1997): 317–46.

35. Roberts and Skeat, *Birth of the Codex*, 15–23.

36. T. C. Skeat, "Especially the Parchments: A Note on 2 Timothy IV. 13," *Notes and Studies*, 173–77.

37. See Edward Maunde Thompson, *An Introduction to Greek and Latin Paleography*, (Oxford: Clarendon, 1912), 49–50. See also Alan Johnson, "Revelation" in *Expositor's Bible Commentary*, 12:465; Theodore Zahn, *Introduction to the New Testament* 3.405–6.

38. T. C. Skeat, *Zeitschrift für Papyrus und Epigraphic* 102 (1994): 263–68.

39. See Appendix I in *Novum Testamentum*, 27th ed.

40. P. Oxyrhynchus 405, Irenaeus's *Against Heresies* was listed by C. H. Roberts as a codex (see *Manuscript, Society, and Belief*, 14). However, Val Haelst lists it as a scroll, as does Gamble, *Books and Readers*, 80.

41. H. I. Bell, *The New Gospel Fragments*, 16–20.

42. See H. I. Bell, "Evidences of Christianity in Egypt During the Roman Period," *Harvard Theological Review* 37 (1944):202; and see C. H. Roberts, *Manuscript, Society and Belief in Early Christian Egypt*, 14.

43. The *editio principes* for this manuscript is found in an article by J. Rudhardt, "Un papyrus chrétien de la Bibliothèque et universitaire de Geneve" in *Littérature, Historie, Linguistique,* Lusanne, 1973.

44. H. I. Bell, "Evidences of Christianity in Egypt During the Roman Period," 202.

45. A full discussion on these manuscripts as portions of individual codices is found in Comfort and Barrett's *The Text of the Earliest New Testament Greek Manuscripts*; see introduction to each manuscript.

46. T. C. Skeat, "The Oldest Manuscript of the Four Gospels?" 31–33.

47. David Trobisch, *First Edition*, 61; also note his book, *Paul's Letter Collection: Tracing the Origins* (Minneapolis: Fortress, 1994).

48. Moule, *The Birth of the New Testament* (New York: Harper & Row 1964), 204.

49. Zuntz, *The Text of the Epistles*, 271–72.

50. H. Gamble, *Books and Readers*, 53–57, and *The New Testament Canon, Its Making and Meaning* (Philadelphia: Fortress Press, 1985), 36–41.

51. For a full discussion of this matter, see Jeremy Duff, "$\mathfrak{P}^{46}$ and the Pastorals: A Misleading Consensus?" *New Testament Studies* 44 (1998): 578–90.

52. See C. H. Roberts, *Antinoopolis Papyri*, no. 12, 25–26.

53. See Aland and Aland, *The Text of the New Testament*, 49–50.

54. This section was adapted from Comfort's *Essential Guide to Bible Versions*, 59–60.

55. There are many documents discovered in Egypt that describe this form of postal circulation around the Mediterranean world. As for the Egyptians themselves, most of whom lived somewhere along the Nile River, they used the river as an all-weather highway. One could float northward with the current and sail southward against the weak current (three mph) by means of the prevailing northerly winds. The Nile was the road of ancient Egypt. Land routes normally conducted traffic only to the river's edge. This allowed for constant traffic between Alexandria and other cities on the Nile.

56. F. F. Bruce, *The Acts of the Apostles*, 349.

57. Bowman, *Egypt after the Pharaohs* (Los Angeles: University of California Press, 1968), 158–60.

58. W. H. C. Frend, *The Rise of Christiainity*, 458.

59. John G. Winter, *Life and Letters in the Papyri*, 181.

60. C. H. Roberts, *Manuscript, Society and Belief in Early Christian Egypt*, 8.

61. Frend, 459, quoting *A New Eusebius*, J. Stevenson, 287–89.

62. Frend, 462.

63. This section was adapted from my book, *The Quest for the Original Text of the New Testament*, 13–16.

64. For $\mathfrak{P}^{32}$, see A. S. Hunt, *Catalogue of the Greek Papyri in the John Rylands Library* vol. 1, 10–11. For $\mathfrak{P}^{52}$, see C. H. Roberts, *Bulletin of the John Rylands Library* 20, 45–55. For $\mathfrak{P}^{82}$ and $\mathfrak{P}^{85}$ see J. Schwartz, "Fragment d'evangile sur papyrus," in *Zeitschrift für Papyrologie und Epigraphik* 3 (1968), 157–58, and "Papyrus et tradition manuscrite," in *Zeitschrift für Papyrologie und Epigraphik* 4 (1969), 178–82.

65. J. Duplacy, "Historie des manuscripts du texte du Nouveau Testament," *New Testament Studies* 12 (1965): 124–39. English translation from Vagany and Amphoux, *An Introduction to New Testament Textual Criticism*, 112.

66. Burtchaell, *From Synagogue to Church*, 272–338.

67. Vermes, "Bible and Midrash: Early Old Testament Exegesis," 201.

68. As an interesting aside, it is worth exploring if Jesus, who was a lector, could have been a scribe for his local synagogue in Nazareth. This means that he would been responsible for making new copies of Scriptures for his synagogue. The ease with which he found the exact text—Isaiah 61:1–2—in a very large scroll having no versification (as in modern Bibles) shows how comfortable he was with the written text. Furthermore, he made many allusions throughout his ministry to the effect that he was one who had studied the Scriptures intensely. How often do we hear Jesus ask his audience, "Have you never read?" (Matt. 12:3, 5; 19:4; 21:16, 42; 22:31; Mark 2:25; 12:10, 26; Luke 6:3; 10:26)—the clear implication being that he had read it and understood its intent. And how often did Jesus utter a radical interpretation of Scriptures in the presence of those who prided themselves in their knowledge of Scriptures?

69. Gamble, *Books and Readers*, 151–52.

70. See each papyrus manuscript in Comfort and Barrett, *Text of the Earliest New Testament Greek Manuscripts,* for a presentation of these features.

71. Turner, *The Typology of the Early Codex*, 84–87.

72. For a complete listing of all the books represented and specific passages, see "Manuscripts in Canonical Order" in *The Text of the Earliest New Testament Greek Manuscripts*, 6–10.

Chapter 2: Significant Manuscripts and Printed Editions of the Greek New Testament

1. Metzger, *Manuscripts of the Greek Bible,* 54.

2. Comfort, "Exploring the Common Identification of Three New Testament Manuscripts: $\mathfrak{P}^{4}$, $\mathfrak{P}^{64}$, $\mathfrak{P}^{67}$," *Tyndale Bulletin* 46 (1995): 43–54.

3. T. C. Skeat, "The Oldest Manuscript of the Four Gospels?" *New Testament Studies* 43 (1997): 1–34.

4. Ernest Colwell, "Method in Evaluating Scribal Habits: A Study of $\mathfrak{P}^{45}$, $\mathfrak{P}^{66}$, $\mathfrak{P}^{75}$," 106–24.

5. Ibid., 118–19.

6. James Royse, "Scribal Habits in Early Greek New Testament Papyri," 156.

7. Comfort, "The Scribe as Interpreter: A New Look at New Testament Textual Criticism according to Reader Response Theory," 103–51.

8. Comfort, "New Reconstructions and Identifications of New Testament Papyri," *Novum Testamentum* 41 (1999): 215–16.

9. G. Fee, *Papyrus Bodmer II ($\mathfrak{P}^{66}$): Its Textual Relationships and Scribal Characteristics*, 71–75.

10. Colwell, "Method in Evaluating Scribal Errors," 121.

11. Ibid.

12. Calvin Porter, "Papyrus Bodmer XV ($\mathfrak{P}^{75}$) and the Text of Codex Vaticanus," in *Journal of Biblical Literature* 81 (1962): 363–76.

13. C. H. Roberts, *Manuscript, Society, and Belief in Early Christian Egypt*, 23.

14. Milne and Skeat, *The Scribes and Correctors of the Codex Sinaiticus*, 89–90.

15. Metzger, *Manuscripts of the Greek Bible*, 77.

16. Westcott and Hort, *Introduction to the New Testament in the Original Greek*, 246–47.

17. Fee, "Codex Sinaiticus in the Gospel of John: A Contribution to Methodology in Establishing Textual Relationships," 23–44.

18. Kenyon, *The Codex Alexandrinus*, 9ff.

19. Milne and Skeat, *The Scribes and Correctors of the Codex Sinaiticus*, 91ff.

20. Westcott and Hort, *Introduction to the New Testament in the Original Greek*, 232–33.

21. Milne and Skeat, *The Scribes and Correctors of the Codex Sinaiticus*, 87ff.

22. Westcott and Hort, *Introduction to the New Testament in the Original Greek*, 237.

23. Metzger, *The Text of the New Testament* (3rd ed.), 49.

24. Aland and Aland, *The Text of the New Testament*, 108.

25. D. C. Parker, *Codex Bezae: An Early Christian Manuscript and Its Text*, 261–78.

26. Ibid., 279–86.

27. Aland and Aland, *The Text of the New Testament*, 108.

28. Metzger, *The Text of the New Testament* (3rd ed.), 51.

29. Ibid., 56.

30. Metzger, *Manuscripts of the Greek Bible*, 100.

31. Aland and Aland, *The Text of the New Testament*, 116.

32. Zuntz, *Manuscripts of the Greek Bible*, 83.

33. Metzger, *The Text of the New Testament* (3rd ed.), 84.

34. Ibid., 89–90.

35. Ibid., 92.

36. Because he was very poor, Tregelles had to ask sponsors to help him with the cost of publishing. The text came out in six volumes over a fifteen-year period—the last being completed just prior to his death. I consider myself fortunate to own a copy of Tregelles's *Greek New Testament* with his signature.

37. See Prolegomena to Tregelles's *Greek New Testament*.

38. A palimpsest is a manuscript in which the original writing has been erased and then written over. Through the use of chemicals and painstaking effort, a scholar can read the original writing underneath the overprinted text. Tischendorf did this with a manuscript called Codex Ephraemi Rescriptus, which had the sermons of Ephraem written over a New Testament text.

39. See Prolegomena to Alford's *Greek Testament*.

40. Kenyon, *Handbook to the Textual Criticism of the New Testament*.

41. According to private conversations with Eugene Nida (the well-known Bible translator) in 1990, Nida told me that he instigated the union of the two works so that Bible translators around the world would be working from the same text in making their translations.

42. Aland and Aland, *The Text of the New Testament*, 42.

43. K. Aland, "The Twentieth-Century Interlude in New Testament Textual Criticism in Text and Interpretation," 14.

44. See "The Greek Text of the Gospel of John Compiled from the Earliest Papyrus Manuscripts As Compared to the Greek Text of NA[26]" in *New Testament Studies* 1990.

45. When I wrote to Barbara Aland concerning these matters, she responded kindly with a letter of apology for the errors. Better yet, she responded by making several corrections in the critical apparatus of the Nestle-Aland text.

Chapter 3: The Earliest New Testament Manuscripts

1. Scanlin, *The Dead Sea Scrolls and Modern Translations of the Old Testament*, 12.

2. See my discussion in *The Text of the Earliest New Testament Greek Manuscripts*, 52–53.

3. See, for example, Bell and Skeats's discussion in *Fragments of An Unknown Gospel and Other Early Christian Literature*, 6–7, and Skeats's comments on 𝔓[90] (= P. Oxyrhynchus 3523). See also E. G. Turner, who said, "For long it was held as dogma that codices did not exist before the fourth century after Christ. . . . Grenfell and Hunt pioneered a relatively early dating of examples of codices, though they tended (under the influence of the dogma) to date the handwriting later than they would have if it had been on a roll" (*Greek Papyri*, 10).

4. E. G. Turner, *Greek Manuscripts of the Ancient World*, 22.

5. For a discussion concerning the papyri in the Apollonios Archive, see J. Rowlandson's *Women and Society in Greek and Roman Egypt* (Cambridge Univ. Press, 1998), 118–24. For a few photographs of some manuscripts in this archive, see "Fragment of a Petition to Haterius Nepos" by Peter Rodgers in ZPE (2000) 133:191–201.

6. F. G. Kenyon, *The Paleography of Greek Papyri*, 73.

7. See C. H. Roberts, *Greek Literary Hands*, 1–24.

8. See E. G. Turner, *Greek Manuscripts of the Ancient World* (2nd edition), 1–23.

9. Ibid., 13, 23. Turner cites W. Cronert, *Memoria graece Herculansis* (especially p. 18).

10. See A. Schmidt, "Zwei Anmerkungen zu P. Ryl. III 457," *Archiv für Papyrusforschung* (1989), 11–12.

11. Peter J. Parsons, *Discoveries in the Judean Desert* VIII, 22

12. F. Kenyon, *Chester Beatty Biblical Papyri*, Fasciculus III, ix.

13. E. M. Thompson, G. F. Warner, F. G. Kenyon, J. P. Gilson, *The New Paleographic Society*, series 1 (1903–1912) and series 2 (1913–1930), London.

14. C. H. Roberts, *Greek Literary Hands*, 12.

15. G. Cavallo, *Richerche sulla Maiuscola Biblica*, 13–43.

16. Ibid., 34.

17. A. S. Hunt, *Catalogue of the Greek Papyri in the John Rylands Library* I, P. Rylands 16, 25–26 (plate V).

18. See E. G. Turner, *Journal of Egyptian Archeology* XL (1954): 106 (note 3). (Turner also assigns P. Rylands 57, of the same collection, to the second century.)

19. Milne, *Catalogue of Literary Papyri in the British Museum*, 57.

20. Wilhelm Schubart, *Griechische Palaographie*, 112.

21. E. G. Turner, *Greek Manuscripts of the Ancient World*, 21.

22. Parsons, *Discoveries in Judean Desert* VIII (Greek Minor Prophet Scrolls), 22.

23. Parsons, ibid, 23. Welles (*Yale Papyri*, 4) points to the following examples: Roberts [GLH] plates 10b, 10c (AD 30–35, 66); Schubart's Berol. plates 14, 18, 19c [= P. Berol. 6485], 22b, 28 [Augustan to c. AD 150] and Schubart's *Greek Paleography*, 115–18.

24. Skeat, "The Oldest Manuscript of the Four Gospels?" *New Testament Studies* 43 (1997): 31.

25. Hunger, "Zur Datierung des Papyrus Bodmer II ($\mathfrak{P}^{66}$)." *Anzieger der osterreichischen Akademie der Wissenschaften*, phil.-hist. Kl., 1960, Nr. 4, 22.

26. I have cited manuscripts only where the nomina sacra for "Son" and/or "Father" actually appear and are not assumed in a reconstructed lacuna. See *Text of Earliest New Testament Greek Manuscripts* (Comfort and Barrett) for a transcription of each of these manuscripts.

27. Oates, Samuel, Welles, *Yale Papyri in the Beinecke Rare Book and Manuscript Library*, 4–5.

28. This is reported by S. Emmel in *Zeitschrift für Papyrologie und Epigraphik* 112 (1996), 290. Emmels indicates that Roberts reported to Welles his opinion, Turner's opinion, and Skeats's opinion in 1963 and 1964. See also Welles, *Bulletin of the American Society of Papyrologists* 1 (1963): 25–29.

29. C. H. Roberts, *Manuscript, Society, and Belief in Early Christian Egypt*, 13. Contra Roberts's opinion, I think Welles provided suitable documentation for his dating.

30. F. Bilabel, "Septuagintapapyrus" in *Veroffentilichungen aus den Badischen Papyrussammlungen* (P. Baden 56), IV (1924), 24–27. See also H. I. Bell, "Evidences of Christianity in Egypt," 200.

31. See F. G. Kenyon, *The Chester Beatty Biblical Papyri* (Fasciculus I, General Introduction), 14; and then see F. G. Kenyon, *The Chester Beatty Biblical Papyri* (Fasciculus V, Numbers and Deuteronomy), ix-x.

32. Ulrich Wilcken, *Archiv für Papyrusforschung* 11 (1935): 113.

33. Seider, *Palaographie der Griechischen Papyri II* (1970): 86.

34. Bell and Skeat, *Fragments of An Unknown Gospel* (1935): 3.

35. Montevecci, *La Papirologia*, no. 49.

36. Turner, *Typology*, 95, 99.

37. Roberts, *Manuscript, Society, and Belief*, 78–81.

38. Jean Scherer, *Papyrus de Philadelphie*, 1.

39. C. H. Roberts, *The Antinoopolis Papyri* Part 1 (no. 7), 1–2.

40. C. H. Roberts and T. C. Skeat, *Birth of the Codex*, 40. See also "The Codex" in the *Proceedings of the British Academy* 40 (Oxford 1954): 186, note 2.

41. Barns and Kilpatrick, *A New Psalms Fragment* (1964): 229–32.

42. Bell and Skeat, *Fragments of an Unknown Gospel*, 6–7. In these pages, they indicate that Schubart also agreed with the dating of P. Oxy. 656 to the first half of the second century, perhaps even earlier. See also H. I. Bell, "Evidences of Christianity in Egypt," 201.

43. W. Schubart, *Das Buch bei den Griechen und Romeron* (Berlin 1922), 185.

44. F. Kenyon, *The Chester Beatty Biblical Papyri* (Fasciculus VI, Jeremiah), ix–x.

45. Roberts, *Journal of Theological Studies* 50 (1949): 157, dated it "second century." Later, in *Manuscript, Society, and Belief*, he changed the date to "ca. 200."

46. H. I. Bell, "Evidences of Christianity in Egypt," 200–201.

47. Kenyon, *The Chester Beatty Biblical Papyri* (Fasciculus VII, Ezekiel, Daniel, Esther), x.

48. Wilcken, op. cit., 112–14.

49. Roberts, *Journal of Theological Studies* 50 (1949): 157, dated it "second century." Later, in *Manuscript, Society, and Belief*, he changed the date to "ca. 200."

50. Bell, op. cit.

51. M. Norsa, *Bulletin de la Societe Archeologique d'Alexandrie, Alexandrie* 1926:162–64. For photograph, see *New Paleographic Society* vol 2, plate 12 (or plate 182).

52. Bell, op. cit.

53. C. H. Roberts, *The Antinoopolis Papyri* Part 1 (no. 8), 2–3.

54. H. I. Bell and T. C. Skeat, *Fragments of an Unknown Gospel and Other Early Christian Literature*, 1–2.

55. Bell, op. cit. In *The Birth of the Codex* (p. 41), C. H. Roberts and T. C. Skeat assign the date of second century to the Egerton Gospel.

56. Gronewald, Kramer, Maresch, Parca, and Romer, *Kolner Papyri*, band 6, P. Koln 255 (Westdeutscher Verlag).

57. C. Bonner, "A New Fragment of the Shepherd of Hermas (Michigan Papyrus 44-H)," *Harvard Theological Review* 20 (1927): 105–9.

58. C. H. Roberts and T. C. Skeat, *The Birth of the Codex*, 41.

59. Bell, op. cit.

60. Roberts and Skeat, op. cit.

61. C. H. Roberts, *Manuscript, Society, and Belief*, 53.

62. J. Rudhardt, "Un papyrus chrétien de la Bibliothèque et universitaire de Geneve," in *Littérature, Historie, Linguistique*, Lusanne, 1973.

63. Bell, op. cit.

64. For discussions concerning the provenance of the manuscripts in Cave 7, see Norman Golb's "Who Hid the Dead Sea Scrolls?" *Biblical Archaeologist* 48/2 (1985): 68–82 and "The Dead Sea Scrolls: A New Perspective," *American Scholar* 58/2 (1989): 177–207. Golb has the perspective that the manuscripts were taken to Qumran from Jerusalem libraries, from different groups and sects.

65. See *Novum Testamentum Graece*, 27th edition (1993): 684–90.

66. Turner, *Typology of the Codex*, 37.

67. Comfort, "Exploring the Common Identification of Three New Testament Manuscripts: $\mathfrak{P}^4$, $\mathfrak{P}^{64}$, and $\mathfrak{P}^{67}$," *Tyndale Bulletin*, Spring (1995): 43–54. Note: In *Eyewitness to Jesus* (Doubleday, 1995, 58–61), Thiede gives the impression that I changed my mind on the matter of $\mathfrak{P}^4$, $\mathfrak{P}^{64}$, and $\mathfrak{P}^{67}$ not being part of the same codex. But I have consistently affirmed that they belong to the same codex. See the above mentioned article and *The Quest for the Original Text of the New Testament*, 81–83. Furthermore, for those who question how one manuscript can end up in three different storage locations, see examples cited by Turner in *Greek Papyri*, 64.

68. T. C. Skeat, "The Oldest Manuscript of the Four Gospels?" *New Testament Studies* 43 (1997): 1–34. Both Skeat and I were working on this issue at the same time with much correspondence back and forth. He and I came to the same conclusion independently: $\mathfrak{P}^4$ and $\mathfrak{P}^{64}$ and $\mathfrak{P}^{67}$ belong to the same codex.

69. Carsten Peter Thiede, "Papyrus Magdalen Greek 17 (Gregory-Aland $\mathfrak{P}^{64}$): A Reappraisal, *Zeitschrift für Papyrologie* 105 (1995): 4–7.

70. Carsten P. Thiede and Matthew D'Ancona, *Eyewitnesses to Jesus* (Doubleday, 1996), 125.

71. C. H. Roberts, "An Early Papyrus of the First Gospel," *Harvard Theological Review* 46 (1953): 233.

72. Ibid., 236–37. In *The Typology of the Early Codex*, Turner dates $\mathfrak{P}^{64+67}$ to the second century (see pp. 25, 99, 149).

73. P. Roca-Puig, "Nueva publicacion del papiro numero uno de Barcelona," *Helmantica* 37 (1961): 13–14.

74. The original editor, Merrill, said that the Gospel fragments had been used as stuffing or padding for the Philo Codex. Whatever he meant by this, I am fairly certain he did not mean that the fragments were placed in the leather binding to fill it out much like modern publishers pad a cover. When I examined the actual leather cover and Gospel fragments at the Biblioteque Nationale in Paris (in June of 1998), I saw that writing from these fragments had been pressed up against the back cover and had left imprints.

75. C. H. Roberts, *Manuscript, Society, and Belief*, 53.

76. The above discussion is, in part, a condensation of an article written by Philip Comfort, appearing in the *Tyndale Bulletin* 46 (1995): "Exploring the Common Identification of Three New Testament Manuscripts: $\mathfrak{P}^4$, $\mathfrak{P}^{64}$, $\mathfrak{P}^{67}$," 43–54.

77. T. C. Skeat, op. cit., 26–31.

78. The Oxyrhynchus portion of the manuscript was first dated in the third century and then redated to the "later second century" due to the influence of redating P. Oxy. 661, with which it has many similarities.

79. Of P. Oxyrhynchus 2750, the editor of the *editio princeps* said, "The hand is another example of the early Biblical uncial style similiar to [P. Oxy.] 661 . . . and may be dated around the later part of the second century AD."

80. P. Oxyrhynchus 2334 was compared by its editor to P. Oxyrhynchus 661 and P. Rylands 547, and the editor called it "a precursor of the so-called biblical uncial."

81. Peter Head, "The Date of the Magdalen Papyrus of Matthew (P. Magd. Gr. 17 = $\mathfrak{P}^{64}$): A Response to C. P. Thiede," in *Tyndale Bulletin* 46 (1995): 273.

82. A. S. Hunt, *Papyrus Rylands* 5, 10–11.

83. H. I. Bell and T. C. Skeat, *Fragments of an Unknown Gospel*, 6–7.

84. H. I. Bell, "Evidences of Christianity in Egypt," 201.

85. Roberts and Skeat, *Birth of the Codex*, 40–41.

86. Bell and Skeat, *Fragments of an Unknown Gospel*, 1–2.

87. Henry Sanders, *A Third-Century Papyrus Codex of the Epistles of Paul*, 12–15.

88. F. G. Kenyon, *The Chester Beatty Biblical Papyri: Descriptions and Texts of Twelve Manuscripts on Papyrus of the Greek Bible*, 14.

89. F. G. Kenyon, *The Chester Beatty Biblical Papyri III/1: Pauline Epistles, Text*, xiv–xv.

90. Ulrich Wilcken, *Archiv für Papyrusforschung* 11 (1935): 113.

91. See comments by Zuntz, *The Text of the Epistles*, 252–54.

92. Young-Kyu Kim, "Paleographic Dating of $\mathfrak{P}^{46}$ to the Later First Century," *Biblica* 69 (1988): 248–57.

93. See Jose O'Callaghan's "Verso le origini del Nuovo Testamento" in *La Civilta Cattolica* 4 (1988): 269–72 and "Papyri und Ostraka" in *Das Grobe Bibel Lexicon* Bd. 3 (1989), 1120–29.

94. See Metzger's comments in *The Text of the New Testament* (third edition, 1992), 265–66.

95. See Roberts and Skeat, *The Birth of the Codex*, 58–60.

96. Grenfell and Hunt, in the *editio princeps*, wrote: "The papyrus [POxy 211] was found together with a large number of documents dated in the reigns of Vespasian, Domitian, and Trajan [i.e., AD 69–117], e.g., P Oxy xlv, xcvii, clxxiv, ccclxxxiii; and this fact, combined with the strong resemblance of the handwriting of the papyrus to that of the many documents of that period, leaves no doubt that it dates from the end of the first or the early part of the second century of our era."

97. Zuntz, *The Text of the Epistles*, 252–60.

98. C. H. Roberts, *An Unpublished Fragment of the Fourth Gospel in the John Rylands Library.*

99. Deissmann, "Ein Evangelienblatt aus den Tragen Hadrians," *Deutsche allgemeine Zeitung* Nr. 564 (Dec. 3, 1935).

100. In *Forschungen and Fortschritte* 12 (1936): 89, Ulrich Wilcken made his observation about $\mathfrak{P}^{52}$ being paleographically contemporary with what he saw in the Bremer Papyri. His publication of the Bremer Papyri came out in the same year (1936): *Abhandlungen der Preussischen Akademie der Wissenschaften, Nr. 2, Die Bremer Papyri* (Berlin: De Gruyter, 1936).

101. Kurt Aland, "Neue neutestamentliche Papyri II," *New Testament Studies* 9 (1962–1963): 307.

102. My examination of P. London 2078 leads me to believe that it is earlier than $\mathfrak{P}^{52}$ in that P. London 2078 is not as decorated and the letters are squarer, as was common in the first century.

103. A. Schmidt, "Zwei Anmerkungen zu P. Ryl. III 457," *Archive für Papyrusforschung* (1989): 11–12.

104. This is Turner's apt description in *Greek Manuscripts of the Ancient World*, 108.

105. Victor Martin, *Papyrus Bodmer II: Evangile de Jean, 1–14* (Cologny/Geneva, 1956), especially p. 15; *Papyrus Bodmer II: Supplement, Evangile de Jean, 14–21* (Cologny/Geneva, 1958); Victor Martin and J. W. B. Barns, *Papyrus Bodmer II: Supplement, Evangile de Jean, 14–21* (Cologny/Geneva, 1962).

106. Herbert Hunger, "Zur Datierung des Papyrus Bodmer II ($\mathfrak{P}^{66}$)," *Anzieger der österreichischen Akademie der Wissenschaften*, phil.-hist. Kl., Nr. 4 (1960): 12–23.

107. For discussion of the second corrector's hand (designated "c3"), see Comfort and Barrett, *Text of the Earliest New Testament Greek Manuscripts*, 384–87.

108. R. Seider, *Palaographie der Griechischen Papyri*, 121.

109. Cavallo, *Ricerche sulla maiuscola biblica*, 23.

110. E. G. Turner, *Greek Manuscripts of the Ancient World* (2nd edition), 21, 108.

111. E. G. Turner, *Toward a Typology of a Codex*, 3–4.

112. Rudolf Kasser and Victor Martin, *Papyrus Bodmer XIV-XV*, I: *XIV: Luc chap 3–24*; II:*XV: Jean chap. 1–15* (Cologny/Geneva, 1961), 13. Metzger also noted that "the script is a clear and generally executed uncial" (*Expository Times* 73 [1961–1962]: 201–3).

113. See discussion on each of these papyri in the Oxyrhynchus volumes.

114. R Seider, *Palaographie der Griechischen Papyri*, 132. Note: the plate in Seider's book shows $\mathfrak{P}^{75}$ in its actual size, thereby revealing the true character of the lettering. By comparison, the plates in the *editio princeps* are smaller than the actual size.

115. See Thomas's discussion in *Oxyrhynchus Papyri*, LXIV (London, 1997), 4403, 5–6.

116. Roberts and Skeat, *Birth of the Codex*, 40–41.

117. For the *editio princeps* of $\mathfrak{P}^{77}$ see *Oxyrhynchus Papyri*, XXXIV, edited by Ingrams, Kingston, Parsons, Rea (London, 1968), no. 2683, 1–3. For the *editio princeps* of P. Oxy. 4403 and 4405 see *Oxyrhynchus Papyri*, LXIV (London: 1997), no. 4403, 5–6; no. 4405, 8–9, both edited by J. David Thomas.

118. See Comfort, "New Reconstructions and Identifications of New Testament Papyri," *Novum Testamentum* XLI (1999): 216–17.

119. Kramer, Romer, Hagedorn, *Kolner Papyri 4: Papyrologica Coloniensa* Vol. VII (1982): 28–31.

120. T. C. Skeat, *Oxyrhynchus Papyri* L (London, 1983), no. 3523, 3–8.

121. G. Wagner, "Cette liste d'objects divers ne fait peut-etre pas partie d'une lettre," P. IFAO II (1971), 31.

122. D. Hagedorn, "P. IFAO II 31: Johannesapokalypse 1,13–20," *Zeitschrift für Papyrologie und Epigraphik* 92 (1992): 243–47, pl. IX.

123. For full discussion, see J. David Thomas, *Oxyrhynchus Papyri*, LXIV (London: 1997), no. 4404, 7–8.

124. Kim, op. cit., 252.

125. The first portion was published by Grenfell and Hunt, *Oxyrhynchus Papyri* VII (1910), no. 1008, 4–8. Another, smaller portion of the same manuscript was published by Vittorio Bartoletti, *Pubblicazioni della Societa Italiana, Papiri Greci e Latini*, XIV (1957), 5–7.

126. Grenfell and Hunt, *Archaeological Report* (1902–1903): 6–8.

127. Cavallo, *Richerche sulla Maiuscola Biblica*, 6.

128. Cited by B. Aland in *Die Katholishcen Briefe*, 14.

129. Their opinion is cited by K. Aland, *Studien zur Uberlieferung des Neuen Testaments und sienes Textes*, 104, note 4; also Roberts is cited in "Neue Neutestamentliche Papyri II" in *New Testament Studies* 9, 307, note 5.

130. Kenyon, *The Chester Beatty Biblical Papyri*, fascilus 2.1, *Gospels and Acts, Text*, x.

131. H. I. Bell, *Recent Discoveries of Biblical Papyri*, 7.

132. Grenfell, Hunt, Goodspeed, *The Tebtunis Papyri* Part II, 9–10.

133. See Comfort and Barrett, *The Text of the Earliest New Testament Greek Manuscripts*, 358.

134. Oates, Samuel, Welles, *Yale Papyri in the Beinecke Rare Book and Manuscript Library*, 9–13.

135. Grenfell, Hunt, Goodspeed, *The Tebtunis Papyri* Part II, 1–2.

136. The editor of P. Oxy. 2539 dated it "second to third century" on the basis of its comparability to P. Tebtunis 340 dated AD 206.

137. Of P. Oxy. 2659 (a list of comic poets and their plays), the editor Rea wrote, "This list is written on the verso of [P. Oxy.] 2660 in a small fluent hand, which used cursive letter forms of the second century (cf. P. London Plate II, no 59)."

138. See comments by A. H. Salonius, "Die grichischen Handschriftenfragmente des Nueun Testaments in den Staatlichen Mussen zu Berline," *Zeitschrift für die neutes-tamentliche Wissenschaft* 26 (1927): 116–19.

139. His opinion is noted by Aland, *Studien zur Uberlieferung des Neuen Testaments und Sienes Textes*, 92. Aland dates 0189 as "II/III" in Appendix I to *Novum Testamentum Graece* (27th edition), 700.

140. Aland, *Neue Neutestamentliche Papyri II*, 306.

141. Ibid., 307. See also Aland's *Studien*, 105; Appendix I to *Novum Testamentum Graece* (27th edition), 684.

142. The opinion of Roberts and Skeat is cited by Aland, *Studien*, 105, note 5.

143. See Comfort and Barrett, *The Text of the Earliest New Testament Greek Manuscripts*, 150–54.

144. Aland, *Neue Neutestamentliche Papyri II*, 307.

145. See Appendix I to *Novum Testamentum Graece* (27th edition), 699.

146. Kurt Treu, "Neue Neutestamentliche Fragmente der Berliner Papyrussammlung," *Archiv für Papyrusforschung* 18 (1966): 25–28 (number P. 11863).

147. See Appendix I to *Novum Testamentum Graece* (27th edition), 701.

Chapter 4: The Nomina Sacra in Greek New Testament Manuscripts

1. The earliest translations of the New Testament in Coptic and Latin also have their own form of nomina sacra for "Lord," "Jesus," "God," and "Christ."

2. The inventor of the term *nomina sacra* was L. Traube, in *Nomina Sacra* (Munich, 1906). After his study on the nomina sacra, the most thorough study was done by A. H. R. E. Paap, *Nomina Sacra in the Greek Papyri of the First Five Centuries AD* (Leiden: E. J. Brill, 1959).

3. For a full explanation of these matters, see C. H. Roberts, *Manuscript, Society, and Belief in Early Christian Egypt*, chap. 2.

4. Among the earliest manuscripts we see all the nomina sacra used. In the $\mathfrak{P}^4+\mathfrak{P}^{64}+\mathfrak{P}^{67}$, the scribe used nomina sacra for "Lord," "Jesus," "God," and "Spirit." In $\mathfrak{P}^{32}$, "God" is contracted. In $\mathfrak{P}^{46}$ we see contractions for "Lord," "Jesus," "God," "Christ," and "Spirit." In $\mathfrak{P}^{66}$, we see contractions for "Jesus," "Lord," "Christ," "God," and "Spirit." In $\mathfrak{P}^{90}$, the nomen sacrum abbreviation for "Jesus" appears in John 19:5, and it fits the lacunae for John 18:37 and 19:2. In $\mathfrak{P}^{107}$, the lacuna has to be filled with nomina sacra for "Son" and "Father" due to the spacing. In $\mathfrak{P}^{77}$, $\mathfrak{P}^{87}$, $\mathfrak{P}^{98}$, $\mathfrak{P}^{103}$, and $\mathfrak{P}^{109}$ (all second-century manuscripts), there are no extant portions or even lacuna where nomina sacra occur. See *The Text of the Earliest New Testament Greek Manuscripts* (Comfort and Barrett) for a new transcription of each of these manuscripts.

5. See *The Text of the Earliest Greek New Testament Manuscripts* for a new transcription of each of these manuscripts.

6. Other second-century Old Testament manuscripts believed to be Christian (because they are codices and not scrolls) but lacking nomina sacra are as follows: P. Yale 1, Genesis; Bodleian Gr. Bib. g. 5, Psalms (note: I think the transcription should be reconstructed using a nomen sacrum for *theos*); P. Lips. inv. 170, Psalms. For a listing and bibliography of these second-century Christian Old Testament manuscripts (all codices), see C. H. Roberts, *Manuscript, Society, and Belief in Early Christian Egypt*, 13.

7. Kathleen McNamee, *Abbreviations in Greek Literary Papyric and Ostraca*, xi, xxx.

8. F. Brown, S. R. Driver, and C. A. Briggs, *A Hebrew and English Lexicon of the Old Testament*, 218.

9. The exact meaning of the name Yahweh is difficult to determine. Some have sought the root in the verb *hayah* ("to be") or in an ancient form of that same verb *hawah*. There is no agreement as to whether the *qal* or *hiphil* form of the verb should be considered as the root. Those who opt for the *hiphil* form understand Yahweh to mean "cause to be." Thus, Exodus 3:14 would read, "I will cause to be what has come to be." Others look to the *qal* form and then translate the name as "I Am" or "I Shall Be" (from *Tyndale Bible Dictionary*, Elwell and Comfort, 540–41).

Some time after the eighth century AD, Jewish scholars called Masoretes added vowel points to the Hebrew text in order to aid readers in pronunciation. They inserted the vowels for Adonai to YHWH as a reminder that no one should read the sacred name, YHWH. This became something like: YaHoWaH. In late medieval times this was mispronounced as "Jehova." Then, various Reformers put it into Protestant Bibles as "Jehovah." However, the name Jehovah does not exist in the original Hebrew text or language. The correct pronunciation of the name must have been something close to Yahweh. But all attempts to discover the original pronunciation are conjectural.

10. P. Oxyrhynchus 656 is a codex and therefore would normally be considered as being of Christian origin. However, the nonuse of a nomen sacrum for *kurios* prompted Roberts and Skeat to call it a Jewish codex—see *The Birth of the Codex*, 41.

11. See Gamble, *Books and Readers*, 77, who cites G. Howard, "The Tetragram and the NT" in *Journal of Biblical Literature* 96 (1977): 63–83.

12. C. H. Roberts, *Two Biblical Papyri*, 47–62.

13. P. Chester Beatty VI has the following words written as nomina sacra: *anthrōpos, theos, kurios, Iēsous* (contracted and combined form in P. Chester Beatty VI), *kurios, pneuma, Israēl, Patēr* (two forms in P. Chester Beatty VI, which shows that the written form of this nomen sacrum was in flux). $\mathfrak{P}^{66}$ also has all these, except "Israel." P. Chester Beatty VI more closely corresponds with $\mathfrak{P}^{75}$, which occasionally has "Israel" written as nomen sacrum.

14. It is possible, though not likely, that the use of the overbar for the divine name may have been influenced by the ensignia יהוה having a line stroked through it, as it so appeared in Jewish coins of the second century BC and in one extant Old Testament manuscript, P. Oxyrhynchus 1007. But in my thinking, documentary use of the overbar would have exerted the stronger influence because an overbar signaled to the reader that the word so designated had to be read in a special way.

15. C. H. Roberts, *Manuscript, Society, and Belief*, 45–46.

16. C. H. Roberts and T. C. Skeat, *Birth of the Codex*, 60–61.

17. C. H. Roberts, "Books in the Graeco-Roman World and in the New Testament" in *The Cambridge History of the Bible*; vol. 1, *From the Beginnings to Jerome*, 64.

18. C. H. Roberts, *Manuscript, Society, and Belief*, 37.

19. See P. Köln 255 in *Kolner Papyri*, Papyrologica Coloniensia Vol. 7, Band 6, 136–42.

20. Clement of Alexandria quoted from this document frequently and ascribed it to "Barnabas, who himself also preached with the apostle [Paul]." Jerome believed the same. But the writer does not claim to be Barnabas, and the earliest claims of authorship come only from Alexandrian church leaders. The literary and interpretive style is entirely Alexandrian, so it is assumed that the epistle was written in Alexandria.

The epistle mentions the destruction of Jerusalem, so it was not written before AD 70. There was a second devastation of Jerusalem in 132 that ended the revolt of Bar-Cochba. This defeat would have served the author's purposes so well that he would surely have referred to it if he were writing after the event. Many scholars suggest that the letter was composed between 120 and 130, since this was a period of strong Jewish nationalism. This nationalism would have pressured many Jewish Christians to return to Judaism, and so the author of the *Epistle of Barnabas* wrote to defend Christianity against Judaism.

21. Larry Hurtado argues that the nomen sacrum $\overline{\text{IH}}$ developed from this kind of Jewish gematria. (Gematria was one of the rabbinic hermeneutic systems for interpreting the Old Testament. It consisted of explaining a word or group of words according to the numerical value of the letters.) Hurtado reasons that some Jewish Christians thought the number 18 symbolized Jesus because the numerical significance of 18 in Hebrew is "life." Thus, Jewish Christians thought it significant to use $\overline{\text{IH}}$ for Jesus. He cites Barnabas and Clement of Alexandria as proof that even second-century Christians knew that $\overline{\text{IH}}$ = 18. But it seems to me that the author of Barnabas's Epistle and Clement of Alexandria were simply reading the text of Genesis 14 in Greek and saw the number 318 written as $\overline{\text{TIH}}$—abbreviated numerals were always noted by a horizontal bar. Having seen $\overline{\text{IH}}$ in so many other New Testament manuscripts prompted them to think of Jesus and then make this interpretation. It seems hard to imagine that the number 18 in and of itself meant anything to them. See Larry Hurtado, "The Origin of the *Nomina Sacra*: A Proposal," *Journal of Biblical Literature* (1998): 655–73.

22. According to the *editio princeps*, $\mathfrak{P}^{90}$ (late second century) would be included in the list of manuscripts having the contracted form $\overline{\text{IC}}$. However, a reexamination of the manuscript reveals that it has the combined form, $\overline{\text{IHC}}$—see *The Text of the Earliest New Testament Greek Manuscripts* (Comfort and Barrett), 619–21.

23. See C. H. Roberts's reconstruction in P. Rylands 457, 1–2.

24. See Martin's *editio princeps* on $\mathfrak{P}^{75}$, John 6:11. A new reconstruction of the lines can be seen in *The Text of the Earliest New Testament Greek Manuscripts* (Comfort and Barrett), 582.

25. The reading "Jesus Barabbas or Jesus called Christ" was the one adopted by the editors of UBS[3], followed by the NRSV. The rationale for choosing this reading is spelled out by Metzger in *A Textual Commentary on the Greek New Testament* (2nd edition), 56. It should also be noted that there is a marginal note on "Jesus Barabbas" in Codex S, which is believed to be traced to Origen.

26. I know of only one exception to this: the manuscript PSI XI 1200 (second century) has the nomen sacrum for *theos*. Since the nomina sacra is a Christian invention, it stands to reason that a Christian scribe prepared this text.

27. According to superior manuscript evidence, the text reads *monogenes theos*, which means "an only One, God" or "God, the only begotten." This is supported by $\mathfrak{P}^{66}$ $\aleph$* B C* L. A few other manuscripts ($\mathfrak{P}^{75}$ $\aleph^1$ 33) read *ho monogenes theos* (the only begotten God). All other manuscripts, most of which are quite late, read *ho monogenes huios* (the only begotten Son). The manuscript evidence for the first reading (basically supported by the second reading) is superior to the evidence for the third reading. The papyri ($\mathfrak{P}^{66}$ and $\mathfrak{P}^{75}$—which adds the article *ho*), the earliest uncials ($\aleph$ B C), and some early versions (Coptic and Syriac) support the first reading.

28. This verse reads, "And we know that the Son of God has come and has given us understanding so that we may know him who is true, and we are in him who is true, in

his Son, Jesus Christ. This one is the true God and eternal life." In Greek, the deictic pronoun "this one" (*houtos*) refers to the nearest noun, which in this case is "Jesus Christ." Thus, the grammar indicates that Jesus Christ is "the true God and eternal life."

29. The translations that support this rendering are NRSV, NIV, NLT.

30. In the Greek, there is one article governing the two titles "God" and "Savior Jesus Christ" joined by the conjunction καὶ ("and"). According to a Greek grammatical rule (called the "Granville Sharpe Rule"—see Dana and Mantey, *A Manual Grammar of the Greek New Testament*, 146–53), this structure indicates that the two nouns describe one person. In this case, Jesus Christ is both God and Savior (as is translated in most modern versions: NASB, RSV, NRSV, NIV, NASB, NLT).

31. The "Granville Sharpe Rule" also applies to the first two verses of 2 Peter.

32. Dana and Mantey, op. cit., 129–30.

33. William Milligan, *The Resurrection of Our Lord* (1884), 246.

34. Richard Gaffins, *The Centrality of the Resurrection* (1978), 87.

35. David Somerville, *St. Paul's Conception of Christ*, 117.

36. See B. F. Westcott, *The Gospel According to St. John* (1881), 51; D. A. Carson, *The Gospel According to John* (1991), 197–98; C. K. Barrett, *The Gospel According to St. John* (1978), 210–11.

37. See Westcott (op. cit.), 109–10.

38. See G. Beasley-Murray, *John* (1987), 96; Barrett (op. cit.), 304–5, and R. E. Brown, *The Gospel According to John* I-XII (1966), 296.

39. Some of the preceding paragraphs were adapted (and adjusted) from my article, "Light from the New Testament Papyri concerning the Translation of Pneuma" in *The Bible Translator* (1984): 130–33.

40. There are other indications throughout the manuscript of 𝔓⁴⁶ revealing the scribe's uneasiness with making nomina sacra. The first indication is that he vascilated with the nomen sacrum for "Christ" between the contracted form ($\overline{\text{XC}}$) and the combination form ($\overline{\text{XPC}}$). He also did this with the terms "Father" and "Son"—using contracted forms and combination forms for each. His forms for "cross" and "crucify" were nonuniform, and the scribe experimented with finding a form for the term "spiritual."

41. See Barrett (op. cit.), 398–400; Carson (op. cit.), 415–16; Brown (op. cit.), 425–26; Beasley-Murray (op. cit.), 192–93.

42. 𝔓⁴⁵ and 𝔓⁷⁵ are both "vid" readings, but fairly certain. See reconstructions in *The Text of the Earliest New Testament Greek Manuscripts* (Comfort and Barrett), 186, 600.

43. See Westcott (op. cit.), 170–71.

44. See Westcott (op. cit.), 278; F. F. Bruce, *The Gospel of John* (1983), 374.

45. See Brown, *The Gospel according to John* XIII-XXI (1970), 931.

46. See Comfort and Barrett, *Text of Earliest New Testament Greek Manuscripts*, 409.

47. It stands to reason that the title "Son of Man" passed out of use after the age of the Gospels because the term was used only by Jesus speaking of himself (except

when others were responding to a statement he made about "the Son of Man"—as in the question, "Who is this Son of Man?"). While Jesus was alive on earth, this was his veiled way of claiming to be the Christ. After his death, resurrection, and ascension, he was clearly manifested and vindicated as the Christ, the Son of God. Thereafter, there was no need for his believers to call him the "Son of Man," when they could forthrightly call him "the Christ." Thus, all the New Testament writers, when speaking of his life after resurrection, proclaimed Jesus to be "the Christ." At the same time, the Christian writers showed their reverence for the name Jesus used for himself by making "the Son of Man" a nomen sacrum.

48. For examples of the different ways of writing this title, see $\mathfrak{P}^{45}$ (Matt. 26:2, 24; Luke 9:58; 11:30; 12:10); $\mathfrak{P}^{66}$ (John 1:51; 9:35; 12:34); $\mathfrak{P}^{75}$ (Luke 6:5, 22; 9:22, 26; 11:30; John 6:27; 12:23).

49. According to a letter count, the nomina sacra for *stauromai* would have best fit in $\mathfrak{P}^{91}$'s broken text of Acts 2:36, and for *stauros* in $\mathfrak{P}^{16}$'s text of Philippians 3:18.

Chapter 5: Historical Overview of Textual Variation in the Greek New Testament

1. There is the "tradition reflected by Polycrates, bishop of Ephesus (ca. 190), that John died a natural death in Ephesus, and by Irenaeus (ca. 175–195) that John lingered on in Ephesus until the time of the emperor Trajan (ruled c. 97–117)—from "John, the Apostle" in the *Tyndale Bible Dictionary*, 720.

2. In the expression "we have seen his glory" in John 1:14, the first person plural pronoun refers to the writer (John) and the other eyewitnesses who saw the glory of God's Son as manifest throughout his ministry (which would have included all the apostles and the disciples), and (perhaps) also specially to James, John, and Peter, who saw the magnificent glory of Jesus on the Mount of Transfiguration.

3. I understand the "beloved disciple" in John's Gospel to be one and the same as "the other disciple"—namely John. For a full discussion of this, see my commentaries on John: *Opening the Gospel of John* and *I Am the Way* (specific verses mentioned).

4. English translation of the Latin provided by Kim Haines-Eitzen, *Guardians of Letters*, 107–8.

5. Many scholars take the position that 2 Peter was not authored by Peter, for the very reason that the styles of the two epistles differ greatly (see, for example, Metzger's *The New Testament: Its Background, Growth, and Content*, 258–59). This can be answered quite simply. Peter used the services of Silvanus (Silas) to write his first epistle (1 Pet. 5:12), and he used the services of another unknown amanuensis to write the second. While in both letters Peter was the "author," the writer was the amanuensis. Thus, 2 Peter could have been composed during Peter's lifetime, which would have meant that Peter was living at the same time as Paul when he authored 2 Peter.

6. See Ehrman, *The Orthodox Corruption of Scripture*.

7. Metzger, *The Text of the New Testament: Its Transmission, Corruption, and Restoration* (3rd, enlarged edition).

8. F. F. Bruce, *The Canon of Scripture*, 170–79.

9. Kurt and Barbara Aland, *The Text of the New Testament*, 290.

10. Ibid., 69.

11. See Jacobus H. Petzer, "The History of the New Testament—Its Reconstruction, Significance and Use in New Testament Textual Criticism," 30–32; and see Colwell, "Hort Redivivus," 150.

12. My work on the early manuscripts is reflected in a volume entitled *The Text of the Earliest New Testament Greek Manuscripts* (coeditor, D. Barrett; Tyndale House Publishers, 2001), which provides a fresh transcription of all the NT manuscripts dated before AD 300. The remarks of Kim Haines-Eitzen, *Guardians of the Text*, 106, on the issue of control are worth stating: "My thesis is that the scribes who copied Christian literature during the second and third centuries were not 'uncontroled' nor were the texts they (re)produced marked by 'wildness.' Rather, the (re)production of texts by early Christian scribes was bounded and constrained by the multifaceted and multilayered discursive practices of the second-and third-century church."

13. Frederik Wisse, "Redactional Changes in Early Christian Texts," 44–45.

14. Kenyon, *Books and Readers in Ancient Greece and Rome* (2nd edition), 27.

15. Birdsall, "The New Testament Text," 312.

16. Grant, *From Alexander to Cleopatra*, 259.

17. Metzger, "Explicit References in the Works of Origen to Variant Readings in New Testament Manuscripts" in *Biblical and Patristic Studies in Memory of Robert Pierce Casey* (Frieburg, 1963), 78–95.

18. H. Balz and G. Schneider, *Exegetical Dictionary of the New Testament*, vol. 1, 259–60.

19. John P. Meier, *A Marginal Jew: Rethinking the Historical Jesus*, Volume 3: Companions and Competitors in The Anchor Bible Reference Library (New York: Doubleday, 2001), 249–60.

20. C. H. Roberts, *Manuscript, Society, and Belief in Early Christian Egypt*, 18.

21. See Peter Parson's article "The Scripts and Their Date" in Emmauel Tov's *The Greek Minor Prophets Scroll from Nahal Hever (8HevXIIgr)*, 19–26.

22. C. H. Roberts, op. cit., 22.

23. See Comfort, *Quest for the Original Text of the New Testament*, 71–72; and see Frederic Kenyon, *The Chester Beatty Biblical Papyri: Descriptions and Texts of Twelve Manuscripts on Papyrus of the Greek Bible*, vol. 1, 13–14.

24. Kenyon, *The Chester Beatty Biblical Papyri*, vol. 1, 15.

25. Robert Kraft, "Christian Transmission of Greek Jewish Scriptures: A Methodological Probe," in *Paganisme, Judaisme, Christianisme: Influences et affrontements das le monde antique: Melanges offerts a Marcel Simon* (Paris: de Boccard 1978), 207–26. The

comments on Kraft's work come from Karen Jobes and Moises Silva, *Invitation to the Septuagint*, 290.

26. Karen Jobes and Moises Silva, *Invitation to the Septuagint*, 97.

27. Aland and Aland, *The Text of the New Testament*, 93–95.

28. Ernest Colwell, "Method in Evaluating Scribal Habits: A Study of $\mathfrak{P}^{45}$, $\mathfrak{P}^{66}$, $\mathfrak{P}^{75}$."

29. James Royse, "Scribal Habits in Early Greek New Testament Papyri."

30. Philip Comfort, "The Scribe as Interpreter: A New Look at New Testament Textual Criticism according to Reader Reception Theory," D. Litt. et Phil. dissertation, University of South Africa (1997).

31. Ibid., 260–61. D. Bock said, "Most of the church fathers of the first five centuries held the view that Matthew was the earliest Gospel, possibly because of its direct apostolic roots" (Introduction to Mark, NLT Commentary).

32. Ropes, *The Acts of the Apostles*; Part I in *The Beginnings of Christianity*, ccxxii.

33. Hanson, "The Provenance of the Interpolator in the `Western' Text of Acts and of Acts Itself" in *New Testament Studies* 12:213–22.

34. Ehrman, *The Orthodox Corruption of Scripture*, 28.

35. Ernest Colwell, "Method in Evaluating Scribal Habits: A Study of $\mathfrak{P}^{45}$, $\mathfrak{P}^{66}$, $\mathfrak{P}^{75}$," 113.

36. See Westcott and Hort, *The New Testament in the Original Greek: Introduction and Appendix*, 138–39, where it is said, "Of known names his [Lucian's] has any other than to be associated with the Syrian revision, [but] no critical results are affected by the presence or absence of his name."

37. W. H. C. Frend, *The Rise of Christianity*, 458.

38. This section (pp. 278–80) was adapted from my book, *The Quest for the Original Text of the New Testament*, chap. 1.

39. F. F. Bruce, *The Canon of Scripture*, 204.

40. Gadamer, *Truth and Method*, 262–63.

41 Ibid., 236.

42. Iser, *The Act of Reading*, 189.

43. Achtemeier, "*Omne verbum sonat*: The New Testament and the Oral Environment of Late Western Antiquity," *Journal of Biblical Literature* 109:3–27.

44. Metzger, *The Text of the New Testament*, 16.

45. Smith, *Understanding Reading: A Psycholinguistic Analysis of Reading and Learning to Read* (New York, 1971), 196.

46. Iser, op. cit., 107.

47. Ibid., 108.

48. Alands, *The Text of the New Testament*, 56–64.

49. R. Ingarden, *The Cognition of the Literary Work of Art* (Evanston, 1973), 24–27.

50. Colwell, op. cit., 119.

51. Metzger, op. cit., 42.

52. Ibid., 177.

53. Westcott and Hort, op. cit., 64–67.

54. Metzger, *A Textual Commentary on the Greek New Testament* (second edition), 187–89.

55. F. F. Bruce, *The Gospel of John* (Grand Rapids, 1983), 417–18.

56. Portions in pages 281 through 290 were adapted from my dissertation in 1997, which was reproduced in part in the *Neotestamenica* article of 2004 (see bibliography).

Chapter 6: Theories and Methods of New Testament Textual Criticism

1. Hammond and Scullard, *The Oxford Classical Dictionary* (2nd edition; Oxford, 1970), 1048.

2. Tregelles, *An Account of the Printed Text of the Greek New Testament*, 174.

3. Westcott and Hort, *Introduction to the New Testament in the Original Greek*, 1.

4. Metzger, *The Text of the New Testament*, v.

5. K. Aland, "The Twentieth-Century Interlude in New Testament Textual Criticism in Text and Interpretation," 14.

6. J. K. Elliott, "The International Greek New Testament Project's Volumes on the Gospel of Luke: Prehistory and Aftermath," NTTRU 7, 17.

7. Ibid., 18.

8. M. Silva, "Response," p. 149 in *Rethinking New Testament Textual Criticism* (editor, Black).

9. Ibid.

10. Bengel, *Gnomon Novi Testamenti*, xiii.

11. Epp, "The Eclectic Method in New Testament Textual Criticism: Solution or Symptom?" *Harvard Theological Review* 69 (1979): 243.

12. Iser, *The Act of Reading*, 189.

13. Holmes, "New Testament Textual Criticism," 55.

14. Holmes, "The Case for Reasoned Eclecticism," 77–100 in *Rethinking New Testament Textual Criticism* (editor, Black).

15. Westcott and Hort, op. cit., 31.

16 Holmes, "The Case for Reasoned Eclecticism," 83.

17. Zuntz, *The Text of the Epistles*, 283.

18. See a good article on this by Elliott, "The Case for Thoroughgoing Eclecticism," pp. 101–24 in *Rethinking New Testament Textual Criticism*. Grand Rapids: Baker.

19. Aland, op. cit., 43.

20. See Metzger's assessment in *Textual Commentary on the Greek New Testament* (second edition), 59.

21. Comfort, *The Quest for the Original Text of the New Testament*, 101–18.

22. Metzger, *The Text of the New Testament* (second edition), 218.

23. Ibid., 218–19.

24. Westcott and Hort, op. cit., 17.

25. Colwell, "Method in Evaluating Scribal Habits: A Study of $\mathfrak{P}^{45}$, $\mathfrak{P}^{66}$, $\mathfrak{P}^{75}$," 152.

26. C. Porter, "Papyrus Bodmer XV ($\mathfrak{P}^{75}$) and the Text of Codex Vaticanus," 363–76.

27. Kenyon, "Hesychius and the Text of the New Testament," 245–50 in *Memorial Lagrange,* Uppsala: Seminarium Neotestamentium Upsaliense.

28. Kenyon, *The Text of the Greek Bible* (revised edition), 240. Vaganay and Amphoux (*An Introduction to New Testament Textual Criticism*, 106–9) espouse the same theory of an Alexandrian recension (perhaps tied to Hesychius), though they place it as having been inspired by earlier recensions, as evident (they claim) in $\mathfrak{P}^{66}$ and $\mathfrak{P}^{75}$. I find this line of reasoning unlikely, as especially argued by Fee (cited below).

29. Zuntz, *The Text of the Epistles*, 271–72.

30. Haenchen, *The Acts of the Apostles* (1971), 59.

31. K. Aland, "The Significance of the Papyri for New Testament Research," 336.

32. Westcott and Hort, op. cit., 250–51.

33. Fee, "$\mathfrak{P}^{75}$, $\mathfrak{P}^{66}$, and Origen: The Myth of the Early Textual Recension in Alexandria," 19–43.

34. Colwell, op. cit., 53.

35. Aland and Aland, *The Text of the New Testament*, 54.

36. Epp, "The Twentieth Century Interlude in New Testament Textual Criticism," 390–94.

37. Colwell, op. cit., 106–24.

38. James Royse, "Scribal Habits in Early Greek New Testament Papyri."

39. Jauss, "Literary History as a Challenge to Literary Theory," 7–37.

40. Colwell and Tune, "Variant Readings: Classification and Use," 259–61.

41. Epp and Fee, *Studies in the Theory and Method of New Testament Textual Criticism*, 50–57.

42. Royse, "Scribal Habits in Early Greek New Testament Papyri," 45–46.

43. Colwell, *Studies in Methodology in Textual Criticism of the New Testament*,123.

44. Ibid., 108.

45. Ibid., 114.

46. Royse, op. cit., 156–57, 423, 560.

47. This was the goal of my dissertation, specifically for $\mathfrak{P}^{45}$, $\mathfrak{P}^{66}$, and $\mathfrak{P}^{75}$ (Gospel papyri). See Comfort, "The Scribe as Interpreter: A New Look at New Testament Textual Criticism according to Reader Response Theory" (1997).

48. Epp, "The Significance of the Papyri for Determining the Nature of the New Testament Text in the Second Century: A Dynamic View of Textual Transmission," 71–103.

49. Fee, "Codex Sinaiticus in the Gospel of John: A Contribution to Methodology in Establishing Textual Relationships," 221–43.

50. Fee's studies on $\mathfrak{P}^{66}$ include: (1) "The Corrections of Papyrus Bodmer II and Early Textual Transmission," *Novum Testamentum* 7 (1965): 247–57; (2) *Papyrus Bodmer II (P66): Its Textual Relationships and Scribal Characteristics in Studies and Documents 34* (Salt Lake City: University of Utah Press, 1968).

51. Alands, op. cit., 108.

52. Metzger, *Textual Commentary on the Greek New Testament* (second edition), 222–36.

53. See Metzger's excellent survey, ibid.

54. J. H. Ropes, *The Acts of the Apostles*; Part I in *The Beginnings of Christianity* (1926), ccxxii.

55. Hanson, "The Provenance of the Interpolator in the 'Western' Text of Acts and of Acts Itself" (1965), 215–24.

56. Kenyon, *The Chester Beatty Biblical Papyri* (Fasciculus III, Supplement; 1936), xv–xvi.

57. Zuntz, op. cit., 265.

58. Zuntz, op. cit., 71–78; Metzger, *Text of the New Testament* (2nd edition), 65.

59. Zuntz, ibid., 83.

60. Ibid., 247.

61. Ibid., 212–13.

62. Lightfoot, *Biblical Essays* (1893), 380.

63. Schmid, *Studien zur Geschichte des griechischen Apokalypse-Textes* (1952–1953).

64. Metzger, op. cit., 99–100.

Chapter 7: The Praxis of New Testament Textual Criticism

1. See the excellent review by Harold Greenlee in *Asbury Theological Journal*, vol. 57/58 (2002–2003): 219–20.

2. R. Brown, *The Gospel according to John* (1966), 380–81.

3. Beasley-Murray, *John* (1987), 151.

4. I. Howard Marshall, *Luke* (1978), 121.

5. Merrell, "Nouveaux fragments papyrus IV," *Revue Biblique* 47 (1938), 14.

6. For a full discussion of this issue, see Ehrman, *The Orthodox Corruption of Scripture*, 62–67.

7. "Adoptionism" in *New International Dictionary of the Christian Church*.

8. Hort, *Two Dissertations*, 1–26.

9. See the Oxyrhynchus volumes on $\mathfrak{P}^5$ and $\mathfrak{P}^{106}$, and see *Text of the Earliest New Testament Greek Manuscripts* (Comfort and Barrett), 75, 646.

10. Fee, "The Textual Criticism of the New Testament," 431–32.

11. Fee, *Papyrus Bodmer II (P66): Its Textual Relationships and Scribal Characteristics*, 87.

12. Philip Comfort, *New Testament Text and Translation Commentary*—forthcoming, Tyndale.

13. Fee, "Codex Sinaiticus in the Gospel of John: A Contribution to Methodology in Establishing Textual Relationships," *New Testament Studies* 15:23–44.

14. Metzger, *The Early Versions of the New Testament*, 138–39.

15. Brown, op. cit., 380–81.

16. Beasley-Murray, op. cit., 151.

17. Porter, "John IX. 38, 39a: A Liturgical Addition to the Text," *New Testament Studies* 13: 387–94.

18. Barrett, *The Gospel according to St. John*, 450.

19. Tasker, "Notes on Variant Readings," 428.

20. Zuntz, *The Text of the Epistles*, 101.

21. Fee, *The First Epistle to the Corinthians* (1987), 88.

22. Brown, *The Semitic Background of the Term "Mystery" in the New Testament*, 48–49.

23. Zuntz, op. cit., 228.

24. Hawthorne, *Philippians* (1983), 122.

25. Lightfoot, *St. Paul's Epistle to the Philippians* (1913), 145.

26. Silva, *Philippians* (1992), 223.

27. Fowl, "A Metaphor in Distress, A Reading of νηπιοι in 1 Thessalonians 2:7," *New Testament Studies* 36 (1990): 469–73.

28. Morris, *1 and 2 Thessalonians* (1984), 56–57.

29. Kenyon, *The Chester Beatty Biblical Papyri* (Fasciculus III), 28.

30. See *Oxyrhynchus Papyri*, no. 1780.

31. See the *editio princeps* (above) and see *Text of the Earliest New Testament Greek Manuscripts* (Comfort and Barrett), 147–49. The reconstruction not only aligns with B but with most manuscripts inasmuch as John 8:14–22 has little variation in the textual tradition.

32. Scribes were known to write either larger or smaller and/or to increase or decrease line lengths as they got closer to the end of the codex, so as to make a better fit. ($\mathfrak{P}^{75}$ is an example of this.) But this would not have been the case for the first part of a codex.

33. See Tischendorf's transcription in *Novum Testamentum Vaticanum*.

34. For example, $\mathfrak{P}^{66}$ usually had 20 lines per page, but also some pages with 19 lines and others with 21 lines—but these average out to 20 lines per page. Another example, $\mathfrak{P}^{4+64+67}$, nearly always has 36 lines per column, on two occasions 35 lines.

Glossary of Terms

The following is an annotated glossary of terms used for textual studies of the New Testament.

Amanuensis. A scribe or secretary. In ancient times a written document was first produced by an author who usually dictated the material to an amanuensis. The author would then read the text and make the final editorial adjustments before the document was sent or published. Paul used the writing services of Tertius to write the epistle to the Romans (Rom. 16:22), and Peter was assisted by Silvanus in writing his first Epistle (see 1 Pet. 5:12).

Amulet. Small object worn by an individual, usually around the neck, as a charm or means of protection against evil, witchcraft, disease, or other physical and spiritual threats. The word is probably derived from either a Latin or Arabic term meaning "to carry." Amulets have been made of various substances and in many forms. Pieces of metal or strips of parchment with portions of sacred writings, even herbs and animal preparations, have been used. Semiprecious gems were often inscribed with a magical formula.

Many amulets uncovered in Palestine have been Egyptian in style. They were in forms of Egyptian gods (e.g., Osiris and Isis), animals (cats and apes), fruits (lotus and pomegranates), human legs and arms, lunar discs, pierced shells, and signet rings. Amulets were often colored red because blood was vital to life, or they were blue to ward off the evil eye.

A few extant New Testament papyrus manuscripts were probably amulets or talismans (see below)—namely, $\mathfrak{P}^{50}$ and $\mathfrak{P}^{78}$.

Anacoluthon. Grammatically incomplete or inconsistent construction—often begging scribal alteration. For example, in Revelation 3:20 the text literally reads, "If anyone hears my voice and opens the door—and I will come to him." To fix this, some scribes (A 2053 Maj[A] it syr[h] cop) dropped the word *and* [Greek *kai*]: "If anyone hears my voice and opens the door, I will come to him."

Apograph. A manuscript copy, as opposed to the original—the autograph.

Archetype. The copy of a text in a scriptorium or library used to make other copies. The archetype may or may not be the autograph—depending on whether the autograph had been redacted.

Assimilation. The process whereby one text is made to read like another text. This has been done by scribes and translators alike under the influence of similar wording in the same context. For example, at the end of Mark 13:2, a few witnesses (D W it Cyprian) add, "And in three days another will be raised without hands."

This interpolation (drawing upon Mark 14:58 and John 2:19) was made by scribes who, knowing the accusation made against Jesus in 14:58 (we heard Jesus say, "I will destroy this temple made with human hands, and in three days I will build another not made with hands."), felt it was their editorial obligation to have Jesus actually say what he is later accused of, because there would otherwise be no record of this in the Gospel of Mark.

Atticism. The process of making grammar or wording in Koine Greek appear to be like classical (Attic) Greek.

Authorities. Global term used especially by Bible translators (see RSV and NRSV— "ancient authorities") for Bible manuscripts, ancient versions, and citations of church fathers. The term should not be misconstrued to signify "authoritative testimony."

Autograph. The authored manuscript, whether penned by the author, dictated by him, or endorsed by him. By comparison, the "original manuscript" is the archetypal exemplar from which other manuscripts were made for publication and distribution. This could be one-in-the-same with the autograph but not necessarily so, especially if editing occurred between the time of the author's composition and publication. None of the original manuscripts of any book of the Bible are extant.

Biblical Uncial. Large letters (from the Latin meaning "one-inch" tall) commonly used in biblical manuscripts. Another name for the Biblical Uncial is the "Biblical Majuscule," which refers to large uncial letters, each stroked separately so as not to connect with other letters (as occurs with a running hand producing cursives). This name does not mean that all manuscripts written with such lettering were biblical, but that a great number of biblical manuscripts display this type of lettering. The Biblical Uncial is noted for retaining a bilinear appearance—that is, there is a conscious effort to keep a line of text within an imaginary upper and lower line. In Biblical Uncial there is a deliberate alternation of thick vertical strokes and thin horizontal strokes with sloping strokes coming in between. In this style, rectangular strokes display right-angled shapes, and circular letters are truly circular, not oval. There are no ligatures (connecting letters) and no ornamentation at the end of strokes (such as serifs and blobs). This style of writing began sometime in the second century AD.

Book. A set of written sheets—whether composed of wood, parchment, papyrus, or paper—containing records or a literary composition. With respect to the Bible, each individual composition is called a "book" because that was what the document was before it became part of the biblical collection. As such, the Bible has sixty-six books—such as Genesis, Isaiah, Matthew, and Revelation.

Canon. Those sets of books in the Jewish and Christian Bible considered to be Scripture and therefore authoritative in matters of faith and doctrine. The term translates both a Greek and a Hebrew word that mean "a rule," or "measuring rod."

It is a "yardstick" by which other books are compared and by which they are measured. After the fourth century AD the Christian church found itself with only sixty-six books that constituted its Scripture; twenty-seven of these were the New Testament and thirty-nine were the Old Testament. Just as Plato, Aristotle, and Homer form a canon of Greek literature, so the New Testament books became the canon of Christian literature. The criteria for selecting the books in the Jewish canon (the Old Testament) are not known, but clearly had to do with their worth in the ongoing life and religion of the worshipping nation. The criteria for the selection of New Testament books revolved around their apostolicity, according to early church writers. Like those of the Old Testament, these books were collected and preserved by local churches in the continuing process of their worship and need for authoritative guidance for Christian living. The formation of the canon was a process (rather than an event) which took several hundred years to reach finality in all parts of the Roman empire. Local canons were the basis for comparison, and out of them eventually emerged the general canon which exists in Christendom today, though some of the Eastern churches have a New Testament that is slightly smaller than that accepted in the West. Judaism, as well as Christianity as a whole, believes that the Spirit of God was operative in some providential way in the production and preservation of his Word.

Codex. Earliest form of the book, consisting of sheets of papyrus or vellum folded and bound together and enclosed between two wooden leaves or tablets. This was a revolutionary development, not only because it eliminated the use of cumbersome scrolls but also because it enabled the writer to use both sides of a page. The codex is discussed in detail in chapter 1.

Collation. Comparison of one manuscript against a known printed text for the sake of producing a list of the differences.

Colophon. Scribe's comments at the end of a manuscript. One scribe's comments at the end of manuscript 461 indicate that the work was written in the year 835, making it the earliest manuscript to have an actual date.

Conflation. The joining together of two variant readings in the creation of a third. Take, for example, Colossians 1:12. Some manuscripts ($\mathfrak{P}^{46}$ $\mathfrak{P}^{61vid}$ $\aleph$ A C D^1 syr) read, "The one who *qualifies* you to participate in the inheritance of the saints." Other manuscripts (D* F G 33 it) read, "The one who *calls* you to participate in the inheritance of the saints." Codex Vaticanus conflates these two readings: "The one who *calls and qualifies* you to participate in the inheritance of the saints."

Conjectural emendations. Corrections made to the text on the basis of scholarly conjecture without having any actual manuscript support. For example, 1 Peter 3:18 reads, "He [Christ] was made alive in spirit—in which spirit he also went to make a proclamation to the spirits in prison." Because of the difficulty of interpreting "in which spirit," a few scholars have conjectured that the text read: "He

382 \\ *ENCOUNTERING THE MANUSCRIPTS*

was made alive in spirit—in Enoch he also went to make a proclamation to the spirits in prison" or (2) "he was made alive in spirit—by which spirit Enoch also went to make a proclamation to the spirits in prison." These are ingenious conjectures (which call for only a few minor adjustments in Greek) but could not be considered as reconstructions of the original. In fact, the present thought among New Testament scholars is that conjectural emendations should be eliminated from the textual apparatus of the Greek New Testament because they do not have any manuscript support.

Critical apparatus. A listing of variant readings, with accompanying manuscript support, printed in critical editions of the Greek New Testament.

The United Bible Societies prepared an edition of the Greek New Testament in which a full citation is given in the critical apparatus for select, significant variants. After the United Bible Societies had published two editions of the Greek New Testament, they decided to unite with the work being done on a new edition (the twenty-sixth) of the Nestle-Aland text—and so produce two volumes containing the same text. Thus, the United Bible Societies' third edition of the Greek New Testament and the Nestle-Aland twenty-sixth edition of *Novum Testamentum Graece* have the same text. Each, however, has different punctuation and a different critical apparatus. The United Bible Societies' text has a plenary listing of witnesses for select variation units; the Nestle-Aland text has a condensed listing of the manuscript evidence for almost all the variation units. Both editions have since gone into another edition (the fourth and twenty-seventh, respectively), manifesting changes to the critical apparatus but not to the wording of the text itself.

Critical edition or critical text. A printed edition of the Greek New Testament that has been produced by critical analysis of textual variants. Such editions will usually have a critical apparatus (see above).

Copy. A handwritten manuscript. The Bible is an ancient document—one that existed before the time of the printing press—it exists in many handwritten manuscripts or copies. Many of these copies have been preserved.

Copyist. Another term for a scribe, which focuses on his task of copying.

Corpus. A collection of individual books. In the New Testament age, Christians and churches collected three different corpuses: (1) the four Gospels; (2) Paul's Epistles; (3) Acts and the General Epistles. This is discussed in chapter 1.

Corrector and corrections. One who made corrections to a manuscript. Corrections were made by the scribe himself, by an official corrector in a scriptorium (called a *diothortes*—see below), or by the purchaser of the newly made copy. Corrections were often made by comparing the newly made copy against a different exemplar than was used for making the copy.

Cursive manuscripts. Manuscripts written with a running hand, as opposed to manuscripts written in separate capital letters. Nearly all Greek New Testament manuscripts after the eighth century are cursives.

Diglot. A text that contains two languages—either side by side or one beneath the other (an interlinear). Diglots are helpful for students learning a new language and useful for language populations who have primary knowledge in one language and limited understanding in another. As such, Greek-Latin diglots were very popular in the early centuries of the church, as were Greek-Coptic diglots. Codex Bezae is a good example of a Greek-Latin diglot, and $\mathfrak{P}^6$ of a Greek-Coptic diglot.

Diothortes. A corrector of manuscripts. This was an actual position in a scriptorium; those who had this task performed much like the copyeditor or proofreader working in modern publishing houses.

Dittography. A scribal mistake of repeating the same word or letters from the preceding word or line. (Examples are given in chap. 7.)

Documentary Evidence. Actual manuscript support for any particular variant reading. Fenton Hort emphasized this as being the primary source of evidence for making decisions about textual variants; hence, his famous line, "knowledge of documents must precede judgments on readings" (*Introduction to the New Testament in the Original Greek*, 17).

Eclecticism. The process of doing textual criticism by selecting what is best from a number of different criteria and/or what appears to be the best reading from a number of different manuscripts. Thus, eclecticism in textual studies is two-tiered: it refers to an amalgamation of methods and of manuscripts. Almost all textual critics perform their task by some sort of eclecticism, without giving undo favor to one method or manuscript over against another. This is called "reasoned eclecticism." (See discussion in chap. 6.)

Editio princeps. The first printed edition of a book. In textual studies, this is usually used with respect to the book containing the first-printed transcription of a Greek manuscript.

Emendation. A correction of what is perceived to be an error. Emendations are the work of scribes or editors making what they think are justifiable adjustments to the text. An emended text, therefore, is a redaction.

Exemplar. The authoritative manuscript from which copies are made. In a scriptorium this would be the archetype; in a church or an individual's home, this would be the master-copy.

Extant. A term that describes surviving manuscripts and/or surviving portions of manuscripts.

External criticism or external evidence. An expression used in textual criticism (of variant readings) to refer to the analysis of actual manuscripts, as opposed to the analysis of what factors in the text might have prompted the variant reading(s) (which is internal criticism). External criticism makes judgment on variant readings on the basis of which manuscripts support which variant reading. This is the external evidence textual critics use in making decisions on readings.

Folio. A leaf of a codex manuscript that, when folded in half, provided for four pages (front and back).

Fragments. Portions of once-complete manuscript pages. Many of the Dead Sea Scrolls (especially those from Cave 7) are nothing but fragments. So also for several New Testament papyrus manuscripts; only small fragments of one page (both sides) are extant in such noteworthy manuscripts as $\mathfrak{P}^{52}$, $\mathfrak{P}^{64}$, $\mathfrak{P}^{67}$, and $\mathfrak{P}^{77}$.

Gap-filling. The filling in of perceived gaps in the literary text. Each reader uses his or her imagination to fill in the unwritten portions of the text, its gaps or areas of indeterminacy. In other words, as the reader adopts the perspectives thrust on him or her by the text, experiences it sequentially, has expectations frustrated or modified, relates one part of the text to the other, imagines and fills in all that the text leaves blank, its meaning is gradually actualized. The reader's reflection on the thwarting of his or her expectations, the negations of familiar values, the causes of their failure, and whatever potential solutions the text offers require the reader to take an active part in formulating the meaning of the narrative. Whereas readers do this gap-filling in their imaginations only, scribes sometimes took the liberty to fill the unwritten gaps with written words. In other words, some scribes went beyond just imagining how the gaps should be filled and actually filled them.

Gloss. A brief explanation of a difficult word or expression in the text; these explanations were usually written in the margin or between the lines. On occasion, such glosses were incorporated into the text by the next copyist, who may have thought the marginal or interlinear comment belonged in the text. For example, in 2 Corinthians 8:4, a few late manuscripts (6 945—so TR) have the added gloss "that we would receive," which is a scribal attempt to improve the grammar and sense of the sentence, which literally reads "begging us earnestly [for] the favor and the contribution of the ministry to the saints." One scribe inserted the gloss on the justification that "it was thus found in many copies"—as was written in a marginal note. Another scribe carelessly copied this marginal note right into the text, as if it were part of Paul's epistle.

Handwriting. Writing done by hand, especially the particular form of writing done by an individual scribe.

Haplography. Skipping over entire semantic units. The scribe's eyes would shift to the same word he had just finished copying on one line to the same word one or two lines later, where he would begin again. (Examples are given in chap. 7.)

Harmonization. The editorial process of making one text like another, whether it be a sentence, paragraph, or entire chapter. Some of the most noteworthy changes in the text of the New Testament involved Gospel harmonization. This kind of change began to occur in the second century and was fully manifest in the fourth. In the early period of textual transmission, each Gospel was usually treated as an individual work. Beginning in the third century the Gospels were sometimes placed together in one volume by themselves (as in $\mathfrak{P}^{45}$). Beginning in the fourth century, the Gospels, together with the other books of the New Testament, were placed in volumes containing the entire Greek Bible (Old Testament and New Testament). This repositioning changed the horizon of expectations of fourth-century and fifth-century scribes, who felt more and more compelled to harmonize Gospel accounts.

Homoeoarchton. The skipping over of semantic units because of similar beginnings in two words or two lines. (Examples are given in chap. 7.)

Homoeoteleuton. The skipping over of semantic units because of similar endings in two words or two lines. (Examples are given in chap. 7.)

Horizon of expectations. The preceptions, experiences, and prejudices readers bring with them to a text; the vista of the text in its own historical setting. The goal of reading is for the two horizons to connect.

Ink. Usually a black carbon (charcoal) mixed with gum or oil for use on parchment or mixed with a metallic substance for papyrus (cf. 2 John 12). It was kept in an inkhorn as a dried substance on which the scribe would dip or rub his moistened pen. It could be erased by washing (Num. 5:23) or with a pen-knife. This knife was also used for sharpening pens and trimming or cutting scrolls (Jer. 36:23).

Inscription. See Superscription.

Interlinear. Translation of one language by another in between the lines.

Internal criticism or internal evidence. Judgment of variant readings on the basis of internal factors such as grammar, style, scribal habits, and immediate context, as opposed to judgment based on manuscript support (external criticism).

Interpolation. A inserted new word or words that results in changing the original text.

Intrinsic probability. What an author would most likely have written, as judged by internal criticism.

Itacism. Similar sounding Greek vowels, usually involving the Greek letter eta. This was responsible for many scribal errors in spelling.

Kakiagraphy. General term for transcriptional errors.

Lacuna(e). Gap(s), blank space(s), tear(s), or missing page(s) in a manuscript. Most ancient manuscripts have lacunae, which are filled in by editors when they publish the *editio princeps* of the document. The siglum *vid* attached to a manuscript (such as $\mathfrak{P}^{4vid}$) often indicates that the editor has filled in a lacunae with the most likely letters or words. Of course, not all scholars will agree on exactly how the lacunae should be filled in.

Leather, Parchment, and Vellum. Writing material made from animal skins. Leather (tanned skins), the forerunner of parchment, was in use about as long as papyrus, but it was rarely used because papyrus was so abundant. The ancient Hebrews probably used leather and papyrus for writing materials. The Dead Sea Scrolls were sheets of leather sewed together with linen thread. Metal scrolls 384 (copper) also existed. See also Parchment, Vellum.

Parchment, made in the beginning from sheep and goat skins, began to replace leather as early as the third century BC, though actual parchment codices date from the second century AD. To prepare parchment or refined leather, the hair was removed from the skins and the latter rubbed smooth. The most common form of book for Old Testament and New Testament documents was evidently a roll or scroll of papyrus, leather, or parchment. The average length of a scroll was about 30 feet, though the famous Harris Papyrus was 133 feet long. Scrolls were often stored in pottery jars (Jer. 32:14) and were frequently sealed (Rev. 5:1).

Vellum had a finer quality than parchment and was prepared from the skins of calves or lambs. In the fourth century AD and thereafter, most Christian codices were made of vellum or parchment.

Leaves. Sheets of a manuscript, whether papyrus or parchment. For a codex, one sheet (or folio) would have two leaves.

Lectio brevior. The shortest variant reading, generally regarded by textual critics (especially Westcott and Hort) to be more likely original than a longer reading. However, recent studies have shown that many of the earliest New Testament manuscripts display a tendency for scribes to purposely shorten a text. Therefore, a shorter reading cannot automatically be judged as being more likely original.

Lectio difficilior. A difficult variant reading, generally regarded by textual critics as being more likely original than an easier variant reading. This canon is a development of Bengel's maxim *proclivi scriptoni praestat ardua* (the harder reading is to be preferred), a maxim he formulated in responding to his own question as to which variant reading is likely to have arisen out of the others.

Lectionaries. A collection of Scripture readings for use in synagogues and in church meetings. The Jews designated readings from the Law and the Prophets for each sabbath. In like manner, Christians selected reading from the Gospels and the Epistles for reading on Sunday in church meetings. Lectionaries have been used to some extent in New Testament textual criticism.

Lector (reader). Reader of Scripture in a church gathering.

Liturgical influence. Variant readings affected by liturgical influences. This is manifest in the frequent addition of *amen* to the end of the epistles, the introduction of baptismal formulas into the text (as in Acts 8:37), and the appendage to the Lord's Prayer: "For yours is the kingdom, the power, and the glory, forever and ever. Amen" (Matt. 6:13). (Examples are given in chap. 7.)

Majuscule. Large uncial letters, each stroked separately, so as not to connect with other letters (as occurs with a running hand producing cursives). See Biblical Uncial.

Manuscript (MS), manuscripts (MSS). Handwritten copies of texts. Prior to the fifteenth century when Johannes Gutenberg invented movable type for the printing press, all copies of any work of literature were made by hand (hence, the name "manuscript"). In the centuries prior to the simultaneous multiple production of copies via dictation (wherein many scribes in a scriptorium transcribed a text dictated to them by one reader), all manuscript copies were made singly—each scribe producing a copy from an exemplar.

Marginal note. Note appearing in the margin of a manuscript or translation. In manuscripts, such notes usually pertain to corrections but sometimes display interpretations or glosses. On occasion, such marginal glosses have been inserted in the text of a manuscript copy. In translations, a marginal note gives information about textual variants, alternative renderings, and related Scripture references.

Metathesis. A scribal error involving the transposition of two letters, words, or phrases. See Transposition below.

Nomen sacrum, nomina sacra. Divine titles (such as *Jesus, Lord, Christ, God*) and sacred words (such as *cross*) written in contracted form in Christian biblical manuscripts. (For a full discussion, see chap. 4.)

Numerical notations. The system of using letters of the alphabet to signify numbers. Almost everyone is familiar with Roman numerals to indicate chapters, outlines, or (sometimes) clock numbers. In that system, I=1, V=5, X=10, L=50, C=100, D=500, and M=1000, etc. Both Greek and Hebrew alphabets were similarly used. The first 10 letters stood for the corresponding numerals, the 11th for 20, the 12th for 30, and so on. Some of the older letters of the Greek alphabet, which had dropped out before New Testament times, were still retained as numerals, such as *digamma, koppa, sampi,* and *stau.* (See chap. 7, note on Rev. 13:18, for an example.)

Obelius, obeli. Symbol used in manuscripts to designate a questionable or spurious passage. The symbol used was ***** or ÷. Such obeli can be seen in many manuscripts pertaining to the passage of the woman caught in adultery (John 7:53–8:11), a passage not written by John but inserted later. The modern equivalent of such markings is found in modern English versions setting off John 7:53–8:11 with a line above it and below it (see NIV and NLT for examples). (See chap. 7 for note on John 7:53–8:11.)

Octavo. A book printed on octavo pages, that is, the pages were cut eight from a sheet. Such books are usually small-size (as compared to the larger quarto).

Omission. Deletion of a word, words, or phrases in the process of a scribe copying a text, whether done intentionally or unintentionally. Intentional omission, for example, is seen in the work of the scribe of D, who omitted nearly every mention of the ascension of Christ in the books of Luke and Acts (see Luke 24:52; Acts 1:2, 9, 11; see discussion in chap. 7).

Opisthograph. Scroll with writing on both sides. Though it was far more common for scrolls to have writing only on the inside, some scrolls had writing on both sides. Opisthographs were usually private, nonsaleable documents, whereas scrolls with writing on the inside were more official and valuable.

Oral reading. The process of reading texts aloud—whether in public or in private. In ancient times almost all reading was done out loud. The oral/aural environment for reading was pervasive in ancient times.

Oral tradition. Traditions passed down from generation to generation by word of mouth, as opposed to being transmitted by writing. Some Christian oral traditions were added to the written text, even though they were not part of the original written documents of Scripture. Prime examples are the "bloody sweat" passage (Luke 22:44) and the story of the woman caught in adultery (John 7:53–8:11). (See discussion on these in chap. 7.)

Original(s). The original manuscript is the archetypal exemplar from which other manuscripts were made for publication and distribution. This could be one-and-the-same with the autograph but not necessarily so, especially if editing occurred between the time of original writing and publication. For some books of the New Testament, there is little difference between the autograph and the original text. But other books seem to have gone through two stages: the book was first written, edited, and then published; afterwards, the book was reedited (redacted) and published afresh.

Orthography. The correct way to write letters according to standard usage.

Paleography. The study of ancient writing. Paleographers aid textual critics by identifying biblical texts among thousands of manuscripts (sometimes nothing more than scraps), dating manuscripts, and producing transcriptions of manuscripts. Textual critics can then use these transcriptions to analyze the textual characteristics of a particular manuscript.

Palimpset. A manuscript in which the original writing has been erased and then written over. Through the use of chemicals and painstaking effort, a scholar can read the original writing underneath the overprinted text. Tischendorf did this with a manuscript called Codex Ephraemi Rescriptus (C), which had the sermons of Ephraem written over a New Testament text.

Paper. Paper, made from wood, rags, and certain grasses, began to replace vellum and parchment as early as the tenth century AD in the Western world, though it was used considerably earlier in China and Japan. By the fifteenth century, paper manuscripts were common.

Papyrus, papyri. Tall, aquatic reed, the pith of which is cut into strips, laid in a cross-work pattern, and glued together to make a page for writing. The papyrus rolls of Egypt have been used as a writing surface since the early third millennium BC. The Greeks adopted papyrus around 900 BC and later the Romans adopted its use. However, the oldest extant Greek rolls of papyrus date from the fourth century BC. The inner pith of the papyrus plant was called *byblos*. From this comes the Greek word *biblion* (book) and the English word *Bible*. The word *paper* is derived from *papyrus*.

Papyrus is perishable, requiring a dry climate for its preservation. That is why so many papyri have been discovered in the desert sands of Egypt. Some papyrus fragments have also been found in the caves near the Dead Sea, where the climate is likewise sufficiently dry.

Parablepsis. The skipping over of words in the transcription process. The scribe's eyes would shift to the same word he had just finished copying on one line to two or three lines later to the same word, where he would begin again. The resultant haplography would create an omission. (Examples are given in chap. 7.)

Paraphrase. The restatement of a written work in the same language—usually in expanded form—for the sake of providing clarity or commentary on the written work.

Parchment. Writing material made from the skins of sheep and goats. This material was far more expensive than papyrus. Parchment was used for many Hebrew scrolls and for Christian codices after the fourth century. The expense of such manuscripts suggests that they were prepared for use in the synagogue and/or in the church. See also Leather, Vellum.

Pericope. A passage, story, or small section of the Bible.

Pleonasm. Using more words than are necessary to convey a message. Alexandrian scribes often trimmed unnecessary words.

Polyglot. A book presenting a text in two or more languages. Two languages comprise a diglot; three languages a triglot; and so on.

Punctuation. The insertion of standardized marks or signs in written material to clarify meaning and/or separate structural units. A common misunderstanding is that ancient Greek manuscripts had no marks of punctuation. To the contrary, most New Testament manuscripts of the second and third centuries have punctuation marks, including the midstop (a high period) and a full stop (indicated by a noticeable space between words). With time, Greek writings accumulated more punctuation marks: a comma, a period, and a question mark.

Quarto. A book printed on quarto pages, i.e., pages cut four from a sheet. Such books are usually midsize (as compared to the smaller octavo).

Quire. Four sheets of paper (or papyrus or parchment) folded once and stitched at the fold. Scribes would use several quires to make up an entire codex. After the fifteenth century, a quire denoted a collection of 24 sheets of paper of the same size, constituting one 20th of a ream.

Recension. A critical, thoroughgoing revision of a text.

Recto. The side of a leaf in a manuscript that is to be read first and/or the side of a leaf with the best surface for writing. The recto in ancient documents does not always coincide with the modern definition of *recto,* which denotes the right hand page.

Redaction. The process of selecting and editing oral material for a written work, as well as the process of editing written material for a specific publishing purpose.

Revision. A book (or translation) that has been reviewed and then corrected.

Scholium, scholia. Marginal comments or annotations in a manuscript.

Scribal error. Any kind of accidental mistake made by a scribe during the process of making a copy of a text.

Scribal leap. Another term for parablepsis (see above).

Scribe(s). One who served as a copyist, amanuensis, or secretary. Scribes were employed in Palestine, Egypt, Mesopotamia, and the Greco-Roman empire.

Scriptio continua. The writing of words with no spatial break between the words. Greek manuscripts were written in this format. The reading process was unquestionably slower than it is for modern readers who have the advantage of reading individually printed words. Of course, ancient readers were accustomed to their format, so they could read it more quickly than moderns can.

Scriptorium. A place where scribes worked to produce copies of books.

Scroll. A roll of papyrus, parchment, or leather used for writing a document or literary work. The papyrus scroll of Egypt can be traced as far back as 2500 BC. One of the most famous literary productions of ancient Egypt is the Book of the Dead.

Jews used leather scrolls for writing the books of the Old Testament. Most of the scrolls discovered from the Dead Sea area were written on leather, though a few were written on papyrus. The first-generation Christians read the Old Testament from scrolls. Jesus read from "a scroll" (Luke 4:17), and Paul may have used "scrolls" to read the Old Testament (see 2 Tim. 2:13). It is possible that the earliest Christians used scrolls when producing the books of the New Testament. A few early manuscripts of the New Testament were written on scrolls ($\mathfrak{P}^{13}$ $\mathfrak{P}^{18}$ $\mathfrak{P}^{98}$), but all these papyri were written on the back of other existing writings. Thus, none of these works were originally composed in the scroll format. As far as we know, first-century Christians and those thereafter predominantly used the codex.

Sigla. Special signs used in critical editions of the Greek New Testament text (such as insertion signs and omission signs), accompanied by corresponding textual information in the critical apparatus at the foot of the page.

Significant reading. A variant that substantially changes the meaning of the text; this usually excludes variations of word order and spelling, grammatical aberrations, and variant readings supported only by a few and/or very late manuscripts. The United Bible Societies' *Greek New Testament* was especially designed to display a full critical apparatus for all significant variant readings. The Introduction to this volume says, "The variant readings cited in the textual apparatus are primarily those which are significant for translators or necessary for establishing the text" (xii). There are approximately 1,700 such variations cited.

Singular reading. A variant reading that is found in only one manuscript. As such, textual critics can be quite certain that the variant was the creation of the scribe who produced that manuscript.

Solecism. An ungrammatical combination of words in a sentence or some spelling of a word deviating from the normal (see John 5:36).

Subscription. Comments made at the end of a written work that are not part of the body of the work itself. Subscriptions, therefore, are the writings of scribes providing circumstantial information concerning author, place of writing, recipients, etc. Most epistles of the New Testament have subscriptions. For example, at the end of Romans there are four extant subscription forms—each expanding on the other: (1) to the Romans, (2) to the Romans written from Corinth, (3) to the Romans written from Corinth [sent] through Phoebe the servant, (4) to the Romans written from Corinth [sent] through Phoebe the servant of the church in Cenchrea.

Superscription. A title attached to the beginning of a written work. Superscriptions (or inscriptions) were not the work of the author of the work; rather, they were scribal creations. The four Gospels have these superscriptions (or inscriptions). For example, at the beginning of Matthew there are three extant forms among various manuscripts: (1) According to Matthew, (2) Gospel According to Matthew, and (3) The Holy Gospel according to Matthew. Some manuscripts, reflecting the original form, do not have titles. English versions (for the sake of identification) have traditionally added titles to the beginning of all the books of the New Testament.

Talisman. An object thought to bring good luck and to shun evil. Some talismans had Scripture verses written on them. See Amulet.

Text. The original words of a written text (usually referred to as "the original text"), or a copy of the original words (usually referred to as "the text" of a particular manuscript).

Text-type. A term describing a close textual relationship among certain manuscripts. Each such group is called a "family" (such as family 1 and family 13 in New Testament manuscripts) or "text-type" (such as Alexandrian, Caesarean, Western, and Byzantine).

Textual criticism. Examination of variant readings in various ancient manuscripts in the effort to reconstruct the original wording of a written text. This kind of study is needed for texts whose autographs are not extant, including all the books of the New Testament.

Textual variation unit. Any portion of an ancient text where there is textual variation supported by at least two Greek manuscripts. When there is a variant reading supported by only one Greek New Testament manuscript, this is called a "singular reading" (see above).

Transcription. A copy of a text produced by a scribe.

Transcriptional error. Mistakes that scribes made in the process of producing copies. The most common transcriptional error was haplography—the skipping over of entire semantic units. The scribe's eyes would shift to the same word he had just finished copying on one line to two or three lines later to the same word, where he would begin again.

Translation. Rendering one language into another. With respect to the Bible, the Hebrew language (Old Testament) and Greek language (New Testament) are translated into a receptor language—such as Syriac, Coptic, and Latin.

Transmission. The process by which a text has been copied and recopied throughout the ages. This is known as textual transmission.

Transposition. Another term for metathesis; a scribal error or adjustment of changing letter order or word order.

Variant readings. Different readings in the extant manuscripts for any given portion of a text.

Vellum. Fine-grained lambskin or calfskin prepared for a writing surface or for a bookbinder. See also Leather.

Version. A translation of the Bible in a particular language. There is only one Bible, but there are hundreds—if not thousands—of Bible versions.

Verso. In ancient books, the side of the leaf that is less smooth and that was usually written on second (after the recto). In modern books, the verso is the left hand page when a book is folded open.

Vid. An abbreviation for *videtur*, meaning "it seems so." It is used by textual critics and paleographers to signal probable readings where there are gaps (lacunae) in certain manuscripts.

Vorlage. A German term for the manuscript from which another copy or other copies are made.

Witness, witnesses. Any written documents that bear testimony to the wording of the original text. These include original language manuscripts (in Greek), ancient versions (such as Coptic, Syriac, Latin), or the writings of church fathers.

Wood tablets. Wooden tablets, covered with stucco or wax, used as a writing surface. Such a tablet is referred to in Luke 1:63. At some point, a few such wooden
tablets were bound together and became the precursor to the codex.

Writer. In biblical studies, this usually refers to the author of a book of the Bible. On
occasion, it is used to speak of an amanuensis (see above).

Writing utensils. Different kinds of writing implements were used, depending on
the writing surfaces in use at various periods of history. Metal chisels and gravers
were used for inscribing stone and metal. A stylus was used for writing cuneiform
(wedge-shaped characters) on clay tablets. For writing on ostraca (potsherds),
papyrus, and parchment, a reed was split or cut to act as a brush. In Egypt, rushes
were used to form a brush. Later, reeds were cut to a point and split like a quill
pen. Apparently, this was the type of pen or "calamus" used in New Testament times
(3 John 13).

Bibliography

Achtemeier, Paul J. 1990. *"Omne verbum sonat*: The New Testament and the Oral Environment of Late Western Antiquity." *Journal of Biblical Literature* 109:3–27.

Aland, Barbara. 1989. "Die Munstereraner Arbeit am Text des Neuen Testaments und ihr Beitrag für die fruhe Uberlieferung des 2. Jahrhunderts: Eine methodologische Betrachtung." Pp. 55–70 in *Gospel Traditions in the Second Century*. Edited by William J. Peterson. Notre Dame: University of Notre Dame Press.

———. 1986. *Das Neue Testament auf Papyrus*, vol. I (Catholic Epistles). Berlin: DeGruyter.

———. 1989. *Das Neue Testament auf Papyrus*, vol. II (Romans–2 Corinthians). Berlin: DeGruyter.

———. 1993. *Das Neue Testament auf Papyrus*, vol. III (Galatians–Hebrews). Berlin: DeGruyter.

Aland, Barbara, Kurt Aland, Johannes Karavidopoulos, Carol Martini, Bruce Metzger. 1993 *The Greek New Testament* (4th edition). Stuttgart: Deutsche Bibelstiftung.

Aland, Kurt. 1963. *Kurgefasste Liste der Griechischen Handschriften Des Neuen Testaments*. Berlin: DeGruyter.

———. 1965. "The Significance of the Papyri for New Testament Research." Pp. 325–46 in *The Bible in Modern Scholarship*. Editor, J. P. Hyatt. Nashville: Abingdon Press.

———. 1967. *Studien zur Uberlieferung des Neuen Testaments und Sienes Textes*. Berlin: DeGruyter.

———. 1969. "Bemerkungen zum Schluss des Markus-evangeliums." Pp. 157–80 in *Neotestamentica et Semitica*. Editors, E. Earle Ellis and Max Wilcox. Edinburg: T & T Clark.

———. 1975–1976. "Neue neutestamentliche Papyri III." *New Testament Studies* 22:375–96.

———. 1979. "The Twentieth-Century Interlude in New Testament Textual Criticism in Text and Interpretation." Pp. 1–14 in *Text and Interpretation: Studies in New Testament Presented to Matthew Black*. Editors, Ernest Best and Robert M. Wilson. Cambridge: Cambridge University Press.

———. 1986. "Der Text des Johannesevangeliums im 2. Jahrhundert." Pp. 1–10 in *Studien zum Text und zur Ethik des Neuen Testaments*. Editor, Wolfgang Schrage. Berlin: de Gruyter.

————. 1987. "The Text of the Church?" *Trinity Journal* 8:131–44.

Aland, Kurt, and Barbara Aland. 1988. *The Text of the New Testament*. Grand Rapids: Eerdmans.

Aland, Kurt, Matthew Black, Carlo Martini, Bruce Metzger, Allen Wikgren. 1994 *Novum Testamentum Graece* (27th edition). Stuttgart: Deutsche Bibelstiftung.

Aune, David. 1987. *The New Testament in Its Literary Environment*. Philadelphia: Westminster Press.

————. 1997. *Revelation*. Word Biblical Commentary. Dallas: Word.

Barns, J. W., and G. D. Kilpatrick. 1964. "A New Psalms Fragment" in *Proceedings of British Academy 43*.

Barrett, C. K. 1978. *The Gospel according to St. John*. Philadelphia: Westminster Press.

Beasley-Murray, George R. 1987. *John*. Word Biblical Commentary. Waco, Texas: Word.

Bell, Harold I. 1937. *Recent Discoveries of Biblical Papyri*. Oxford: Clarendon Press.

————. 1944. "Evidences of Christianity in Egypt During the Roman Period." *Harvard Theological Review* 37 (1944): 185–208.

————. 1948. *Egypt: From Alexander the Great to the Arab Conquest*. Oxford: Clarendon Press.

————. 1953. *Cults and Creeds in Graeco-Roman Egypt*. Liverpool: University Press.

————. 1955. *The New Gospel Fragments*. London: British Museum.

Bell, Harold I., and T. C. Skeat. 1935. *Fragments of an Unknown Gospel and Other Early Christian Papyri*. London.

Bengel, Johannes Albert. 1855. *Gnomon Novi Testamenti* (third edition). Editor, J. Steudel. Tübingen.

Birdsall, J. Neville. 1960. *The Bodmer Papyrus of the Gospel of John*. London: Tyndale Press.

————. 1970. "The New Testament Text." Pp. 308–77 in *The Cambridge History of the Bible*, vol. 1, *From the Beginnings to Jerome*. Editors, Pater R. Ackroyd and Christopher F. Evans. Cambridge: Cambridge University Press.

Black, David Alan (editor). 2002. *Rethinking New Testament Textual Criticism*. Grand Rapids: Baker.

Brown, Raymond. 1966. *The Gospel According to John I-XII*. Garden City, New York: Doubleday.

————. 1968. *The Semitic Background of the Term "Mystery" in the New Testament*. Philadelphia: Facet Books, Biblical Series.

————. 1970. *The Gospel According to John XIII–XXI*. Garden City, New York: Doubleday.

Bruce, F. F. 1951. *The Acts of the Apostles*. Grand Rapids: Eerdmans. (3rd edition, 1990).

————. 1988. *The Canon of Scripture*. Grand Rapids: Eerdmans.

Bultmann, Rudolf. 1971. *The Gospel of John: A Commentary*. Philadelphia: Westminster.

Burridge, Richard A. 1992. *What Are the Gospels? A Comparison with Greco-Roman Biography*. Cambridge: Cambridge University Press.

Burtchaell, James T. 1992. *From Synagogue to Church*. Cambridge: Cambridge University Press.

Cavallo, Guglielmo. 1967. *Richerche sulla maiuscola biblica* (2 vols.). Le Monnier, Firenze.

———. 1983. *Libri scritture scribi a Ercolano*. Editor, G. Macchiaroli. Cronache Ercolanesi 13.

Clark, Kenneth. 1937. *A Descriptive Catalogue of Greek New Testament Manuscripts in America*. Chicago: University of Chicago Press.

———. 1966. "The Theological Relevance of Textual Variation of the Greek New Testament." *Journal of Biblical Literature* 85:1–16.

Clark, W. P. 1931. "Ancient Reading." *Classical Journal* 26:698–700.

Colwell, Ernest. 1965, 1969. "Scribal Habits in Early Papyri: A Study in the Corruption of the Text." Pp. 370–89 in *The Bible in Modern Scholarship*. Editor, J. P. Hyatt. Nashville: Abingdon, 1965. Reprinted as "Method in Evaluating Scribal Habits: A Study of $\mathfrak{P}^{45}$, $\mathfrak{P}^{66}$, $\mathfrak{P}^{75}$." Pp. 106–24 in his *Studies in Methodology in Textual Criticism of the New Testament*. New Testament Tools and Studies 9. Leiden: E. J. Brill, 1969.

———. 1969. "Hort Redivivus: A Plea and a Program" Pp. 131–55 in *Transitions in Biblical Scholarship*. Editor, J. Coert Rylaarsdam. Chicago: University of Chicago Press. Reprinted on pp. 148–71 in his *Studies in Methodology in Textual Criticism of the New Testament*. New Testament Tools and Studies 9. Leiden: E. J. Brill, 1969. (Reprint pages cited.)

Colwell, Ernest and Ernst Tune. 1964. "Variant Readings: Classification and Use." *Journal of Biblical Literature* 83:253–61.

Comfort, Philip W. 1984. "Light from the New Testament Papyri Concerning the Translation of *pneuma*." *The Bible Translator* 35:130–33.

———. 1989. "The Pericope of the Adulteress (John 7:53–8:11)." *The Bible Translator* 40:145–47.

———. 1990. "The Greek Text of the Gospel of John According to the Early Papyri (As Compared to Nestle-Aland's *Novum Testamentum Graece*, 26th edition—NA26)." *New Testament Studies* 36:625–29.

———. 1990. *Early Manuscripts and Modern Translations of the New Testament*. Wheaton: Tyndale. (second edition, Baker, 1996).

———. 1992. *The Quest for the Original Text of the New Testament*. Grand Rapids: Baker.

———. 1994. *I Am the Way: A Spiritual Journey through the Gospel of John*. Grand Rapids: Baker. (Reprinted, Wipf and Stock, 2001).

―――. 1995. "Exploring the Common Identification of Three New Testament Manuscripts: $\mathfrak{P}^4$, $\mathfrak{P}^{64}$, $\mathfrak{P}^{67}$." *Tyndale Bulletin* 46:43–54.

―――. 1997. "New Testament Textual Criticism." Pp. 1171–75 in *Dictionary of the Later New Testament and Its Developments*. Editors, Ralph Martin and Peter Davids. Downers Grove, Illinois: InterVarsity Press.

―――. 1997. "The Scribe as Interpreter: A New Look at New Testament Textual Criticism according to Reader Response Theory." D. Litt. et. Phil dissertation. University of South Africa (1997).

―――. 1998. *The Essential Guide to Bible Versions*. Wheaton: Tyndale House Publishers.

―――. 1999. "New Reconstructions and Identifications of New Testament Papyri." *Novum Testamentum* 41:214–30.

―――. 2004. "Scribes As Readers: Looking at New Testament Variants according to Reader Reception Analysis." *Neotestamentica* 38(1):28–53.

Comfort, Philip and David Barrett. 2001. *The Text of the Earliest New Testament Greek Manuscripts*. Wheaton: Tyndale.

Comfort, Philip and Wendell Hawley. 1994. *Opening the Gospel of John*. Wheaton: Tyndale.

Cox, Patricia. 1983. *Biography in Late Antiquity*. Berkeley: University of California Press.

Deissman, Adolf. 1909. *Light from the Ancient Near East: The New Testament Illustrated by Recently Discovered Texts of the Greco-Roman World*. Translator, L. Strachan. London: Hodder and Stoughton.

Edwards, Sarah Alexander. 1974. "$\mathfrak{P}^{75}$ and B: A Study in the History of the Text." Ph.D. dissertation, Hartford Seminary.

Ehrman, Bart. 1988. "Jesus and the Adulteress." *New Testament Studies* 34:24–44.

―――. 1993. *The Orthodox Corruption of Scripture*. Oxford: Oxford University Press.

Elliott, W. J. and D. C. Parker. 1995. *The New Testament in Greek IV: The Gospel According to St. John* (vol.1, The Papyri). Leiden: E. J. Brill. (In this volume acknowledged contributions were made by P. W. Comfort.)

Elwell, Walter and Philip Comfort. 2001. *Tyndale Bible Dictionary*. Wheaton: Tyndale.

Epp, Eldon J. 1973. "The Twentieth Century Interlude in New Testament Textual Criticism." *Journal of Biblical Literature* 93:386–414.

―――. 1981. *New Testament Textual Criticism: Its Significance for Exegesis*. Oxford: Clarendon Press.

―――. 1989. "The Significance of the Papyri for Determining the Nature of the New Testament Text in the Second Century: A Dynamic View of Textual Transmission." Pp. 71–103 in *Gospel Traditions in the Second Century*. Editor, William J. Peterson. Notre Dame: University of Notre Dame Press.

Epp, Eldon and Gordon Fee. 1993. *Studies in the Theory and Method of New Testament Textual Criticism*. Grand Rapids: Eerdmans.

Farstad, Arthur and Zane Hodges. 1982. *The Greek New Testament According to the Majority Text*. Nashville: Nelson.

Fee, Gordon. 1965. "The Corrections of Papyrus Bodmer II and Early Textual Transmission." *Novum Testamentum* 7:247–57.

———. 1968. *Papyrus Bodmer II ($\mathfrak{P}^{66}$): Its Textual Relationships and Scribal Characteristics*. Studies and Documents 34. Salt Lake City: University of Utah Press.

———. 1968. "Codex Sinaiticus in the Gospel of John: A Contribution to Methodology in Establishing Textual Relationships." *New Testament Studies* 15:23–44.

———. 1974. "$\mathfrak{P}^{75}$, $\mathfrak{P}^{66}$, and Origen: The Myth of the Early Textual Recension in Alexandria." Pp. 19–45 in *New Dimensions in New Testament Study*. Editors, Richard N. Longenecker and Merril C. Tenney. Grand Rapids: Zondervan.

———. 1979. "The Textual Criticism of the New Testament." Pp. 419–33 in *The Expositor's Bible Commentary*, vol. 1: *Introductory Articles*. Grand Rapids: Zondervan.

Finegan, Jack. 1974. *Encountering New Testament Manuscripts*. Grand Rapids: Eerdmans.

Fitzmyer, J. A. 1985. *The Gospel according to Luke* (2 vols.). New York: Doubleday.

Frend, William H. C. 1984. *The Rise of Christianity*. Philadelphia: Fortress Press.

Gadamer, Hans-Georg. 1975. *Truth and Method*. Translators and editors, Garrett Barden and John Cumming. New York: Crossroad-Continuum.

———. 1976. *Philosophical Hermeneutics*. Translator and editor, David E. Linge. Berkeley: University of California Press.

Gamble, Harry. 1995. *Books and Readers in the Early Church*. New Haven: Yale University Press.

Guelich, R. A. 1989. *Mark 1–8:26*. Word Biblical Commentary. Dallas: Word.

Grant, Michael. 1982. *From Alexander to Cleopatra*. New York: Charles Scribner's Sons.

Grenfell, Bernard P. 1897. "Oxyrhynchus and Its Papyri." Pp. 1–12 in *Egypt Exploration Fund: Archaeological Report 1896–1897*. London: Egypt Exploration Fund.

Grenfell, Bernard P., and Arthur S. Hunt. 1898. *The Oxyrhynchus Papyri* (70 volumes to date). London: Egypt Exploration Fund (later, Egypt Exploration Society)— with other editors continuing the work: Ingram, Parsons, Rea, Turner, Coles.

———. 1900. *Fayum Towns and Their Papyri*. London: Hogarth.

———. 1902–1903. "Excavations at Hibeth, Cynopolis and Oxyrhynchus." Pp. 1–9 in *Egypt Exploration Fund: Archaeological Report 1902–1903*.

———. 1902–1938. *The Tebtunis Papyri*, 3 vols. London.

———. 1906. "Excavations at Oxyrhynchus." Pp. 8–16 in *Egypt Exploration Fund: Archaeological Report 1905–1906*. London.

Greisbach, J. J. 1976. *Novum Testamentum Graece*. London.

Grobel, K. 1964. "Whose Name Was Neves." *New Testament Studies* 10:373–82.

Haines-Eitzen, Kim. 2000. *Guardians of Letters*. Oxford: Oxford University Press.

Hatch, William H. P. 1939. *The Principal Uncial Manuscripts of the New Testament*. Chicago: University of Chicago Press.

Head, Peter. 1990. "Observations on Early Papyri of the Synoptic Gospels." *Biblica* 7:240–47.

———. 1995. "The Date of the Magdalen Papyrus of Matthew (P. Magd. Gr. 17 = $\mathfrak{P}^{64}$): A Response to C. P. Thiede." *Tyndale Bulletin* 46:251–85.

Heinrici, C. F. G. 1903. *Die Leipziger Papyrusfragmente der Psalmen*. (Beitrage zur Geschichte und Erklarung des Neuen Testaments 4). Leipzig.

Holmes, Michael. 1989. "New Testament Textual Criticism." Pp. 53–74 in *Introducing New Testament Interpretation*. Editor, Scot McKnight. Grand Rapids: Baker.

———. 2002. "The Case for Reasoned Eclecticism." Pp. 77–100 in *Rethinking New Testament Textual Criticism*. Editor, D. Black. Grand Rapids: Baker.

Hort, Fenton. 1876. *Two Dissertations*. Cambridge: Macmillan.

Hunger, Herbert. 1960. "Zur Datierung des Papyrus Bodmer II ($\mathfrak{P}^{66}$)." *Anzieger der österreichischen Akademie der Wissenschaften*, philologisch-historischen Klasse 4: 12–23.

Hunt, Arthur S., and J. de M. Johnson, V. Martin, C. H. Roberts, E. G. Turner. 1911–1952. *Catalogue of the Greek Papyri in the John Rylands Library Manchester*, 4 vols. Manchester: Manchester University Press.

Iser, Wolfgang. 1971. "Indeterminacy and the Reader's Response in Prose Fiction." Pp. 1–45 in *Aspects of Narrative*. Editor, J. Hillis Miller. New York: Columbia University Press.

———. 1974. *The Implied Reader*. Baltimore: Johns Hopkins University Press.

———. 1978. *The Act of Reading*. Baltimore: Johns Hopkins University Press.

———. 1980. "Interaction Between Text and Reader." Pp. 106–119 in *The Reader in the Text*. Editors, Suleiman and Crosman. Princeton: Princeton University Press.

———. 1980. "The Reading Process: A Phenomenological Approach." Pp. 50–69 in *Reader-Response Criticism*. Editor, Jane P. Tompkins. Baltimore: Johns Hopkins University Press.

Jauss, Hans Robert. 1970. "Literary History as a Challenge to Literary Theory." Pp. 7–37 in *New Literary History* 2. Minneapolis: University of Minnesota Press.

Jobes, Karen and Moises Silva. 2000. *Invitation to the Septuagint*. Grand Rapids: Baker. 290.

Kenyon, Frederic G. 1897. *The Paleography of Greek Papyri*. Oxford.

———. 1901. *Handbook to the Textual Criticism of the New Testament*. London: Macmillan.

————. 1909. *The Codex Alexandrinus.* London: Longmans.

————. 1933a. *The Chester Beatty Biblical Papyri: Descriptions and Texts of Twelve Manuscripts on Papyrus of the Greek Bible,* Fasciculus I. London: Emery Walker Ltd.

————. 1933b. *The Chester Beatty Biblical Papyri: Descriptions and Texts of Twelve Manuscripts on Papyrus of the Greek Bible,* Fasciculus II: The Gospels and Acts. London: Emery Walker Ltd.

————. 1937. *The Chester Beatty Biblical Papyri* (Fasciculus III, Supplement). London: Emery Walker Ltd.

————. 1940. "Hesychius and the Text of the New Testament." Pp. 245–50 in *Memorial Lagrange.* Uppsala: Seminarium Neotestamentium Upsaliense.

————. 1949. *The Text of the Greek Bible* (rev ed.) London: Duckworth.

————. 1951. *Books and Readers in Ancient Greece and Rome.* Oxford: Clarendon Press.

————. 1958. *Our Bible and the Ancient Manuscripts.* New York: Harper and Row.

Kilpatrick, George D. 1963. "The Bodmer and Mississippi Collection of Biblical and Christian Texts." *Greek, Roman, and Byzantine Studies* 4:33–47.

Kim, Young-Kyu. 1988. "Paleographic Dating of $\mathfrak{P}^{46}$ to the Later First Century." *Biblica* 69:248–57.

Kubo, Sakae. 1965. $\mathfrak{P}^{72}$ *and the Codex Vaticanus* in Studies and Documents 27. Salt Lake City: University of Utah Press.

Leaney, Robert. 1954. "Jesus and the Symbol of the Child (Luke ix. 46–48)." *The Expository Times* 66:91–92.

Liddell, Henry G. and Robert Scott. 1968. *Greek English Lexicon* (originally printed in 1843; revised, with supplement by Henry Jones and Roderick McKenzie in 1968). Oxford: Clarendon Press.

Mann, Jacob. 1971. *The Bible as Read and Preached in the Old Synagogue,* vol. 1. New York: Ktav Publishing House.

Martin, Victor and Rudolf Kasser. 1956. *Papyrus Bodmer II: Evangile de Jean, 1–14.* Cologny/Geneva: Bibliotheca Bodmeriana.

————. 1958. *Papyrus Bodmer II: Supplement, Evangile de Jean, 14–21.* Cologny/Geneva: Bibliotheca Bodmeriana.

————. 1961. *Papyrus Bodmer XIV-XV, I: XIV: Luc chap. 3–24; II: XV: Jean chap. 1–15.* Cologny/Geneva: Bibliotheca Bodmeriana.

Marshall, I. Howard. 1978. *The Gospel of Luke.* Grand Rapids: Eerdmans.

Metzger, Bruce. 1963. "Explicit References in the Works of Origen to Variant Readings in New Testament Manuscripts." Pp. 78–95 in *Biblical and Patristic Studies in Memory of Robert Pierce Casey.* Editors, J. N. Birdsall and R. W. Thompson. Frieburg: Herder.

————. 1968, 1992. *The Text of the New Testament.* Oxford: Oxford University Press (3rd edition, 1992).

———. 1975, 1994. *A Textual Commentary on the Greek New Testament*. New York: United Bible Societies (revised edition, 1994).

———. 1977. *The Early Versions of the New Testament*. Oxford: Clarendon Press.

———. 1981. *Manuscripts of the Greek Bible*. Oxford: Oxford University Press.

———. 1983. *The New Testament: Its Background, Growth, and Content* (2nd edition). Nashville: Abingdon.

Mill, John. 1723. *Novum Testamentum Graecum* (second edition). Leipzig.

Milligan, George. 1922. *Here and There Among the Papyri*. London: Hodder and Stoughton Ltd.

Milne, H. J. M. 1927. *Catalogue of the Literary Papyri in the British Museum*. London.

Milne, H. J. M. and T. C. Skeat. 1938. *Scribes and Correctors of Codex Sinaiticus*. Oxford: Oxford University Press.

Montevecci, Orsolina. 1988. *La Papirologia* (2nd edition). Milan.

Nestle, Eberhard. 1901. *Introduction to the Textual Criticism of the Greek New Testament*. Translator, William Edie. London: Williams and Norgate.

Nolland, John, 1993. *Luke*. Word Biblical Commentary. Waco, Texas: Word.

Oates, John, Alan Samuel, C. B. Welles. 1957. *Yale Papyri*. New Haven: American Society of Papyrologists.

O'Callaghan, Jose. 1974. *Los Papiros Griegos de la Cueva 7 de Qumran*. Madrid.

———. 1995. *Los primeros testimonios del Nuevo Testamento: Papirologia neotestamentaria*. Madrid.

Osborne, Grant. 1992. *The Hermeneutical Spiral*. Downers Grove, Illinois: InterVarsity Press.

Pearson, Birger A. 1986. "Earliest Christianity in Egypt: Some Observations." Pp. 132–60 in *The Roots of Egyptian Christianity*. Editors, Birger A. Pearson and James E. Goehring. Philadelphia: Fortress Press.

Petzer, Jacobus H. 1994. "The History of the New Testament Text—Its Reconstruction, Significance and Use in New Testament Textual Criticism." Pp. 11–36 in *New Testament Textual Criticism, Exegesis, and Early Church History*. Kampen: Kok Dharos Publishing House.

Porter, Calvin. 1962. "Papyrus Bodmer XV (P75) and the Text of Codex Vaticanus." *Journal of Biblical Literature* 81:363–76.

———. 1967. "John IX. 38, 39a A Liturgical Addition to the Text." *New Testament Studies* 13: 387–94.

Rhodes, Erroll. 1968. "The Corrections of Papyrus Bodmer II." *New Testament Studies* 14:271–81.

Roberts, Colin H. 1935. *An Unpublished Fragment of the Fourth Gospel in the John Rylands Library*. Manchester: Manchester University Press.

———. 1936. *Two Biblical Papyri in the John Rylands Library*. Manchester.

————. 1953. "An Early Papyrus of the First Gospel." *Harvard Theological Review* 46:233–47.

————. 1963. *Buried Books in Antiquity*. Letchworth: Garden City Press.

————. 1970. "Books in the Graeco-Roman World and in the New Testament." Pp. 48–66 in *The Cambridge History of the Bible*, vol. 1, *From the Beginnings to Jerome*. Editors, Pater R. Ackroyd and Christopher F. Evans. Cambridge: Cambridge University Press.

————. 1979. *Manuscript, Society, and Belief in Early Christian Egypt*. London: Oxford University Press.

Roberts, Colin H. and Theodore C. Skeat. 1987. *The Birth of the Codex*. London: Oxford University Press.

Robinson, James M. 1986. "The Discovering and Marketing of Coptic Manuscripts: The Nag Hammadi Codices and the Bodmer Papyri." Pp. 2–25 in *The Roots of Egyptian Christianity*. Editors, Birger A. Pearson and James E. Goehring. Philadelphia: Fortress.

————. 1990. *The Pachomian Monastic Library at the Chester Beatty Library and Bibliotheque Bodmer*. Occasional Papers 19. Claremont, California: Institute for Antiquity and Christianity.

Robinson, John A. T. 1976. *Redating the New Testament*. SCM Press.

————. 1985. *The Priority of John*. Oak Brook, Illinois: Meyer Stone Books.

Ropes, J. H. 1926. *The Acts of the Apostles*; Part I in *The Beginnings of Christianity*. Editors, F. J. Foakes Jackson and K. Lake. London: Macmillan.

Rowlandson, J. 1998. *Women and Society in Greek and Roman Egypt*. Cambridge.

Royse, James Ronald. 1981. "Scribal Habits in Early Greek New Testament Papyri." Ph.D. dissertation, Graduate Theological Union.

————. 1983. "The Treatment of Scribal Leaps in Metzger's Textual Commentary." *New Testament Studies* 29:539–51.

Sanders, Henry A. 1912. *The New Testament Manuscripts in the Freer Collection*. New York: Macmillan.

————. 1955. *A Third Century Papyrus Codex of the Epistles of Paul*. Ann Arbor: University of Michigan Press.

Scherer, J. 1947. *Papyrus grecs de Philadelphie*. (Published de la Societe Fouad I de Papyrologie, Textes et Documents). Cairo.

Schleiermacher, F. D. E. 1977. *Hermeneutics: The Handwritten Manuscripts*. Editor, Heinz Kimmerle; translators, James Duke and Jack Forstman. Missoula, Montana: Scholars Press.

Schmid, Josef. 1955–1956. *Studien zur Geschichte des griechischen Apokalypse-Textes*. 2 volumes in 3. Munich: Zink.

Schmidt, A. 1989. "Zwei Anmerkungen zu P. Ryl. III 457." *Archiv für Papyrusforschung* 35:11–12.

Schmidt, Carl. 1931. "Die neuesten Bibelfunde aus Agypten." *Zeitschrift für die Neutestamentliche Wissenschaft* 35:285–93.

———. 1933. "Die Evangelienhandschrift des Chester Beatty—Sammlung." *Zeitschrift für die Neutestamentliche Wissenschaft* 32: 225–32.

Schofield, Ellwood M. 1936. "The Papyrus Fragments of the Greek New Testament." Ph.D. dissertation, Southern Baptist Theological Seminary.

Schubart, Wilhelm. 1922. *Das Buch bei den Griechen und Romeron*. Berlin.

———. 1925. *Griechische Palaographie*. Munich.

Seider, Richard. 1967. *Palaographie der Griechischen Papyri*. Stuttgart: Hiersemann.

Skeat, Theodore C. 1997. "The Oldest Manuscript of the Four Gospels?" *New Testament Studies* 43:1–34.

Skeat, Theodore C. and B. C. McGing. 1991. "Notes on Chester Beatty Papyrus I (Gospels and Acts)." *Hermathena* 150:21–25.

Stevenson, James. 1957. *A New Eusebius: Documents Illustrative of the History of the Church to AD 337*. New York: Macmillan.

Stowers, Stanley. 1986. *Letter Writing in Greco-Roman Antiquity*. Philadelphia: Westminster.

Talmon, Shemaryahu. 1970. "The Old Testament Text." Pp. 159–99 in *The Cambridge History of the Bible*, vol. 1, *From the Beginnings to Jerome*. Editor, Pater R. Ackroyd and Christopher F. Evans. Cambridge: Cambridge University Press.

Tasker, R. V. G. 1964. "Notes on Variant Readings." Pp. 411–45 in *The Greek New Testament* (being the Text Translated in the New English Bible, 1961). London: Oxford University Press.

Taylor, Isaac. 1859. *History of the Transmission of Ancient Books to Modern Times*. London: Jackson and Walford.

Testuz, Michael. 1959. *Papyrus Bodmer VII-IX: L'Epitre de Jude, Les deux Epitres de Pierre, Les Psaumes 33 et 34*. Cologny/Geneva: Bibliotheca Bodmeriana.

Thiede, Carsten. 1992. *The Earliest Gospel Manuscript?* London: Paternoster Press.

Thompson, E. M., and G. F. Warner, F. G. Kenyon, J. P. Gilson. 1903–1930. *The New Paleographic Society*, series 1 (1903–1912) and series 2 (1913–1930). London.

Tischendorf, Constantine. 1867. *Novum Testamentum Vaticanum*. Lipsiae: Giesecke and Devrient.

Tov, Emanuel. 1990. *The Greek Minor Prophets Scroll from Nahal Hever (8HevXIIgr)*. Oxford: Clarendon Press.

———. 1992. *Textual Criticism of the Hebrew Bible*. Minneapolis: Fortress Press.

Tregelles, Samuel P. 1854. *An Account of the Printed Text of the Greek New Testament*. London: Samuel Bagster and Sons.

———. 1857–1879. *The Greek New Testament*, 6 vols. London: Samuel Bagster and Sons.

Turner, Eric G. 1956. "Scribes and Scholars of Oxyrhynchus." Pp. 141–46 in *Akten des VIII, Internationalen Kongreses für Papyrologie: Wien 1955*. Mitteilungen aus der Papyrussammlung der Osterreichischen Nationalbibliothek (Papyrus Erzherzog Rainer) 5. Vienna: Rohrer.

———. 1968. *Greek Papyri: An Introduction*. Princeton: Princeton University Press.

———. 1977. *The Typology of the Early Codex*. Philadelphia: University of Pennsylvania Press.

———. 1980. *Greek Papyri: An Introduction*. Oxford: Clarendon.

———. 1987. *Greek Manuscripts of the Ancient World* (2nd edition). Oxford: Oxford University Press.

Vaganay, Leon and Christian-Bernard Amphoux. 1991. *An Introduction to New Testament Textual Criticism*. Cambridge: Cambridge University Press.

Van Haelst, Joseph. 1976. *Catalogue des Papyrus Litteraire Juifs et Chretien*. Paris: Sorbonne.

Vermes, G. 1970. "Bible and Midrash: Early Old Testament Exegesis." Pp. 199–231 in *The Cambridge History of the Bible*, vol. 1, *From the Beginnings to Jerome*. Editor, Pater R. Ackroyd and Christopher F. Evans. Cambridge: Cambridge University Press.

Westcott, Brooke F. 1881. *Gospel According to St. John*. London: Macmillan.

Westcott, B. F. and Fenton Hort. 1882. *Introduction to the New Testament in the Original Greek* (with "Notes on Select Readings"). New York: Harper and Brothers.

———. 1885. *The New Testament in the Original Greek*. London: Macmillan.

Williams, C. S. C. 1951. *Alterations to the Text of the Synoptic Gospels and Acts*. Oxford: Basil Blackwell.

Wimsatt, W. K. and Monroe C. Beardsley. 1976. "The Intentional Fallacy." Pp. 1–13 in *On Literary Intention*. Editor, Newton-deMolina. Edinburgh: University Press.

Wisse, Frederik. 1989. "Redactional Changes in Early Christian Texts." Pp. 39–54 in *Gospel Traditions in the Second Century*. Editor, William J. Peterson. Notre Dame: University of Notre Dame Press.

Wurthwein, Ernest. 1979. *The Text of the Old Testament*. Grand Rapids: Eerdmans.

Zuntz, Gunther. 1953. *The Text of the Epistles*. London: Oxford.

Index of Photographs

Index of New Testament Papyri

Index of Uncials

Index of Christian Old Testament
Greek Manuscripts

Index of Scripture References